Wiltshire Record Society

(formerly the Records Branch of the Wiltshire Archaeological and Natural History Society)

VOLUME 78

S^r. RICHARD HOLFORD of Lincolns Inn.
late one of the Masters in Chancery.
1714 Ætat. 81.

THE HOLFORD PAPERS AVEBURY 1695–1798

edited by

STUART A. RAYMOND

CHIPPENHAM

2025

Published on behalf of the Wiltshire Record Society
by The Hobnob Press,
8 Lock Warehouse, Severn Road,
Gloucester GL1 2GA
www.hobnobpress.co.uk

c/o Wiltshire and Swindon History Centre,
Cocklebury Road, Chippenham SN15 3QN

www.wiltshirerecordsociety.org.uk

ISBN 978–0–901333–55–1

Typeset by John Chandler

CONTENTS

ABBREVIATIONS

AWS	Raymond, Stuart A. *Avebury without the Stones: a social history 1550-1800.* Hobnob Press, 2024.
GA	Gloucestershire Archives
TNA	The National Archives
VCH	*Victoria County History*
WAM	*Wilshire Archaeological & Natural History Magazine*
WSHC	Wiltshire & Swindon History Centre

INTRODUCTION

Sir Richard Holford and his descendants were lords of the manor of Avebury from 1695 until 1767, when Stayner Holford bequeathed it to his half-brother, Arthur Jones. On Jones's death in 1789, he bequeathed the manor to his niece, Ann Williamson, whose husband, Adam Williamson, subsequently became the governor of Jamaica.

The Holford papers, held in both Wiltshire & Swindon History Centre,[1] and in Gloucestershire Archives,[2] cover this entire period, and provide a great deal of information on the history of both manor and parish. They cover an extraordinarily wide range of topic. Agricultural matters such as farm management, tenants, livestock, arable produce, and marketing, get much attention. Many letters and memoranda are devoted to tithe disputes between vicars and parishioners, the bankruptcy of John Rose, Stayner Holford's farmer, and the process of enclosure. Building work at Avebury manor, parish affairs (including both dissent, and the failure of the vicar to bury the dead), the morals of vicars and parishioners, turnpikes and the state of the roads, and leisure pursuits, are all covered. There is even advice on how to keep the Holford family's archives![3] Some comments are also devoted to non-Avebury matters such as the construction of the Kennet and Avon Canal, national politics, Richard Holford's departure to serve the East India Company, and the letting of Sir Adam Williamson's property at Hungerford and Bath.

These papers, and especially Sir Richard Holford's correspondence and journals between 1695 and 1718, and the letters of Richard Hickley to Ann Williamson in the 1790s, almost constitute a history of Avebury in their own right. The project to transcribe them grew out of my attempt to write the history of the parish in the early modern period. That history, *Avebury Without the Stones: a History of the Parish 1550-1800* (Hobnob Press, 2024) (*AWS* hereafter) has now been published, and provides, in part, an extensive introduction to these papers. A detailed introduction here would therefore be superfluous; readers should refer to *AWS*. I have, however, provided overviews of the specific types of documents, together with notes on editorial methodology. I have also attempted to provide brief biographical notes on all the correspondents, so that each letter can be understood in its context.

INTRODUCTION TO SIR RICHARD HOLFORD'S JOURNAL

The main portion of Sir Richard Holford's journal (described here as the bound journal) is now held at Gloucestershire Archives, together with the papers of the

1 WSHC 184 & 271.

2 GA D1956.

3 Memorandum, 4th November 1756.

Westonbirt branch of the Holford family.[1] Another portion (the sheet journal) is held by Wiltshire & Swindon History Centre with the papers of the Avebury branch of the family.[2] The journal is in part a diary, but it also includes many notes on estate matters intended for future reference. The two documents between them cover September and October 1700, and from 1709 until 1717. A note on the front cover of the bound journal indicates that it was 'perused' on 6th November 1767, presumably in connection with some issue that arose at that date.

Notes on the Bound Journal

The volume now held by Gloucester Archives consists of 15 paper leaves, folded and bound in a wrapper made from a re-cycled deed. The deed was made 8th September 1693 between Sir Robert Chantry, a master in Chancery (with his wife Mary), and Richard Holford (as he was before he was knighted), also a master in Chancery. The volume consists of Sir Richard Holford's journal from 1710 until 1717, together with the accounts of his widow, Lady Susanna Holford, 1718-21. Most of the journal has been paginated in pencil, in a modern hand, although four pages precede page 1. Page 25 is the last numbered page, and is also the last page of the journal. Lady Holford's accounts occupy a further 6 pages. 25 further pages are left blank.

The first four un-numbered pages (apart from the second page, which is blank) comprise notes on William Skeat's tenancy made in 1710 and 1711, but end with a brief note made in 1712. The 'journal' proper begins on the second numbered page (that is, page 1). Entries were made irregularly, commencing on 31st March 1711.[3] They are not all in chronological order, and it may be that some of the text was written subsequent to the dates given. The second page has entries for 3rd, 4th, 6th, 7th 13th and 14th April 1711; the entries on page 3 cover 1st, 2nd, 4th, and 15th April 1711. On p.7, the entry for 12th October is followed by one for 5th October, and then 11th October 1711. On p.18, the entry for 18th October is followed by 16th August, and then by 15th October.

After 1712, most entries were made in the summer months between June and October, presumably when Sir Richard was visiting Avebury. There are two exceptions to this rule. The memoranda dated March 8th 1715/16 on p.19 was clearly written some time after that date, and perhaps not in Avebury. The entry made on or after 4th November 1717 (p.24) was written in London a few months before Sir Richard's death; it records what may have been his last outing to Hyde Park in London whilst the problem he had with his foot (and from which he probably died) was being treated by Mr. Geekie.

Bound Journal Dates

Leaf 1. 1710 & October 1717
Leaf 1 verso. Blank

1 GA D1956/E2/8.
2 WSHC 184/8.
3 A table of dates is given below.

Leaf 2. April 1711
p.0. September 1710 & 1712
p.1. 31st March & 1st-2nd April, 1711
p.2. 3rd, 4th, 6th, 7th, 13th & 14th April 1711
p.3. 1st, 2nd, 4th & 15th April 1711
p.4. 1710
p.5. 30th July, & 3rd, 4th, 5th & 6th August 1711
p.6. 14th & 28th August, 7th September, & 1st, 6th-12th October 1711
p.7. 12th, 5th, & 11th October 1711
p.8. June, & 2nd July 1712
p.9. 12th & 15th August 1712
p.10. 20th September 1712
p.11. 26th September & 7th & 10th October 1712
p.12. 10th & 21st October 1713
p.13. Ditto
p.14. 11th October 1714
p.15. Ditto
p.16. 1714
p.17. 16th October 1714
p.18. 18th October, 16th August, 17th October 1715
p.19. 17th October 1715
p.20. 8th March, 1715/16; 19th October 1716
p.21. 15th & 19th October 1716
p.22. October 1716
p.23. 5th & 7th August 1717
p.24. 17th October & 4th November 1717

Notes on the Sheet Journal

The portion of the journal now held by Wiltshire and Swindon History Centre is written on five loose sheets of folded paper. These are not numbered in the original manuscripts, but sheet numbers, in square brackets, have been assigned in this transcript. On the verso of each sheet is a brief description of its contents; these descriptions have been transcribed as headings. Page numbers have been inserted to indicate page breaks.

The first sheet covers September and October 1700, much earlier than the bound journal. Later sheets cover the years 1709, 1710, 1711 and 1714, and overlap with the main journal. Indeed a few dates in the bound journal are also entered in these sheets, although their content differs. For some entries the actual dates are not stated, but only the days of the week. However, their dates can be inferred from the position of these entries in the manuscripts. The dates covered are:

Sheet 1. 9th-15th September; 1st October 1700
Sheet 2. 29th October; 5th & 7th November 1709
Sheet 3. 12th & 27th January; 3rd, 10th, 12th & 13th February1709/10; 25th, 26th, 28th & 31st March 1710
Sheet 4. 31st July; 3rd, 7th, 9th-14th August; 1st, 3rd, 4th, 7th, 11th, 13th,

16th, 20th October; 1st November 1711.
Sheet 5. 9th–13th, 15th–29th, & 31st August; 6th–13th, 17th, 18th, 20th–28th September; 8th, 10th, 12th October 1714.

INTRODUCTION TO THE LETTERS

The Holfords and their successors as lords of the manor of Avebury conducted an extensive correspondence. The only lords who actually lived for any length of time in Avebury itself (between c.1753 and 1786) were Stayner Holford and Arthur Jones. Stayner himself was probably resident at Portsea before 1753. His predecessors were residents in London; Arthur Jones' successors in Jamaica. They needed to be kept informed of the state of affairs on their manor and in the parish. It is likely that the letters which have survived are a small proportion of those which were written.

The 213 letters transcribed here are drawn from a number of collections. The most important of these are the Holford papers held at Wiltshire & Swindon History Centre, reference 184. These are found in several separate files. 184/1, consisting of two separate folders,[1] contains most of the correspondence of Sir Richard Holford, his widow Susanna, his son Samuel, and his grandsons Richard and Stayner. They maintained a regular correspondence with their tenants, William Skeat, John Rose, and Peter Griffin, with the vicars of Avebury, John White and the Mayos, and with a number of other local people. Occasionally, they also kept the correspondence of others which had been passed on to them. That included Richard Smith's letter to William Skeat, 27th June 1696, attempting to arbitrate on a tithe dispute, and James Mayo's condemnatory letter, 10th July 1753, to William Fowler, which Fowler presumably passed on to his landlord seeking his support. It was Sir Richard's practise to make copies of the letters he sent, which means that we can sometimes read both sides of his correspondence. There are 125 letters in this file.

Another file, 184/2, relates to the tithe dispute between Stayner Holford and the Rev. James Mayo, c.1756. This file contains 13 letters. A third file, 184/6, contains the letters and related correspondence of the bailiff, Richard Hickley, to the Williamsons in Jamaica, 62 letters in total. A variety of estate papers, including one letter, are found in 184/4

The archives of the Williamson family (271/16) include many letters, two of which relate to Avebury. Lord Ailesbury's correspondence (9/35/178) includes a letter from Arthur Jones of Avebury.

A number of letters relevant to Avebury are found amongst the archives of the Westonbirt branch of the family, held at Gloucestershire Archives, D1956/L1. These are between Stayner Holford and his Westonbirt cousin, Peter Holford. Peter, like his grandfather Sir Richard, was a Master in Chancery; his letters primarily offer legal advice regarding the bankruptcy of Stayner's tenant, John Rose.

1 There is no obvious rationale for the separation into two separate files, except that the letters would not fit into one.

The transcribed letters here are arranged chronologically, rather than by source.

INTRODUCTION TO THE MEMORANDA

The Holford papers include a wide variety of deeds, land tax assessments, parish records, invoices, and assorted memoranda. Space precludes publication of most of these documents. The memoranda selected for transcription here are only a small proportion of the documents preserved; they are mostly closely related to the letters and journals. They are drawn from a number of different files held by the Wiltshire and Swindon History Centre; full references are given with each transcript[1].

INTRODUCTION TO RICHARD HICKLEY'S ACCOUNTS

Richard Hickley, as noted above, sent his employer a monthly statement of accounts. Some of these statements have been lost, but 39 survive.[2] These are dated between 1791 and 1797, and are transcribed here.

Each month's accounts are written on a large folded sheet of paper. Income is written on the left hand side, expenditure on the right. The income side is headed by a statement of the accounting period, which frequently runs into the preceding and/or the succeeding month. The verso is left blank, except for a brief indication of the period covered. At the foot of the income statement, Hickley calculated the amount due to him or to the Williamsons at the end of each accounting period.

This file of accounts also includes a number of bills and receipts, together with a farmhouse account, for September 1793 to March 1794, a list of poultry sold, hatched and dead for 1794, and a summary of the accounts for April to September 1794.[3] None of these have been transcribed.

EDITORIAL METHODOLOGY

Original spelling, including the ampersand, has been retained in all documents. However, modern punctuation has been inserted, and abbreviations have been extended (especially for forenames) except where there is uncertainty. Signatures, however, have been transcribed without extending abbreviations. Where signatories made their mark rather than writing, this is indicated with an 'X' between forename and surname.

Place-names have been transcribed as in the manuscript, with modern spellings footnoted where necessary. Uncertain readings due to partial illegibility or damage to the manuscript are enclosed in square brackets with a question mark. Illegible words are noted in the form [*illegible*]. Superscript notation is ignored. Where the manuscript is torn, damaged or obscured, conjectural readings have been inserted where possible.

1 They are principally found in WSHC 184 & 271, but also in GA D1956.
2 WSHC 184/7.
3 This summary adds nothing to the accounts transcribed above.

Sums of money are frequently written as 10l 5s 4d, but have been transcribed by the editor as £10 5s 4d. Where the symbols £, s, and d have been omitted, they have been silently inserted. Amounts in columns have been standardised so that the columns can be easily added up. Roman numerals have been silently replaced by Arabic ones. Where prices are given in pounds only, zeros for shillings and pence are not transcribed. Amounts written in columns have been transcribed in the style £5-05-06 (rather than 5-5-6) so that the columns line up and can be easily checked. Where this has been done, the abbreviations 's' and 'd' have been ignored, and the £ sign has been inserted selectively.

In his journal, Sir Richard used planetary symbols to indicate the days of the week.[1] For these, see illustration 1. In this transcript these are noted in brackets, with an asterisk, thus: [*Monday]. In the journal, he frequently made marginal notes indicating the nature of the information in the main text. These are printed here as headings in bold and italic.

Letters are printed chronologically. Each of the letters is given a heading noting the names of correspondents. Standardised dates in the form 1 January 1738/9 (giving dates according to both Julian and Gregorian calendars before 1752) have been inserted at the beginning of all letters, in square brackets where they are not already in that position; where dates are in that position their original form is ignored. Elsewhere, abbreviations for the year have been silently extended. Dates and other notes on the verso are given at the end of each letter (dates in their original form). Addresses written on the verso are entered separately. Deletions and interlineations are ignored, except where they alter the sense of the passage, or provide additional information. Some letters run to several pages, but page breaks have been ignored, except in a few cases where the text requires them to be footnoted.

Memoranda are printed in date order. The headings used are editorial additions, unless otherwise foot noted. Page breaks have been ignored, except where they have been paginated.

Accounts are headed by statements of the dates covered, printed in bold. These are editorial additions, but are followed by the actual wording used in the manuscripts (although where the year has been repeated within a particular account this has been ignored). The details written on the verso are not transcribed, except where they provide additional information. Hickley's calculation of the amounts due to him or to the Williamson's is printed at the end of each account, except in those cases where Hickley merged it with the income statement. Additions have been checked, and discrepancies footnoted. The abbreviation 'do' has not been expanded to 'ditto'.

Note that this methodology reveals the eccentricities of the writers of these documents. For example, for Richard Hickley wages were always 'waigers', and expenses always 'expences'. The abbreviation 'exp' has been expanded in accordance with the latter spelling.

1 These are listed at **https://en.wikipedia.org/wiki/Planet_symbols**

THE CORRESPONDENTS: BIOGRAPHICAL NOTES

These notes are intended to set the letters edited here in their context, and are not full biographies. More detailed information on Avebury residents will be found in *Avebury without the Stones*.

John Adams

John Adams was a London lawyer who played some role in Sir Richard Holford's purchase of Avebury Manor. Holford wrote to him on 6th May 1695 requesting his assistance in expediting the purchase. No more is known of him.

Thomas Alexander

Thomas Alexander was baptised in Avebury 8th August 1704; his son, also Thomas, was baptised 25th December 1731. If this identification is correct, Thomas the elder was only sixteen when he wrote to Lady Holford on 12th December 1720. His letter offered advice on the value of a property in Beckhampton, and implies that he had been acting on her behalf in collecting rents (which he wanted to borrow) at Clyffe Pypard. In 1733, he surveyed Avebury Great Farm for Richard Holford.[1] He is also mentioned in John Caswell's letter, 16th November 1725. In 1734, this correspondent was probably a tenant of a Beckhampton cottage rented from Robert Holford.[2] He subsequently served as a tithingman in 1740 and 1741.[3]

Richard Bailey

Richard Bailey was born 12th February 1708/9, the son of a leading dissenter, and had probably been baptised in Avebury's dissenting chapel. As an adult, he continued his support for the dissenting cause, and was named in 1749 by Caleb Bailey as one of the trustees of his charity for dissenting ministers.[4] When Richard himself made his will in 1780, he bequeathed an annuity of two guineas to 'the present minister of the meeting house in Avebury and his successors'.[5]

Bailey was a maltster in 1775,[6] and possibly much earlier. Between 1747 and 1775, he was regularly named as a freeholder eligible to vote at Parliamentary elections, and to serve as a juror at Quarter Sessions.[7] He served as high constable in 1755.[8] He was a copyholder in Ogbourne St George, and held a freehold estate in Avebury. [9] He also tenanted the estate of Mr Nalder, another prominent dissenter.[10]

1 WSHC 1553/71H.
2 WSHC 371/1, pt.5. Lease, Robert Holford to Frances Truslow, 6th March 1734/5.
3 WSHC 9/23/1.
4 TNA PROB 11/782/93.
5 WSHC P3/B/1679.
6 WSHC 118/88.
7 WSHC A1/265/16-21 & 23; A1/110, Michaelmas sessions 1747-71, 1774,1777, & 1779.
8 WSHC A1/110, 1755M.
9 WSHC P3/B/1679.
10 WSHC A1/265/16-21 & 23; A1/110, Michaelmas sessions 1747-71, 1774,1777, & 1779.

His letter dated 30th April 1743 refers to a bill for £50 sent by Peter Griffin to Stayner Holford which mis-carried, and implicitly defends Peter Griffin, another leading dissenter (and his cousin), against Holford's charge that he had only pretended to send it.

John Brinsden

John Brinsden served as vicar of neighbouring Winterbourne Monkton from 1664 until 1719.[1] He occasionally stood in for John White, vicar of Avebury, especially during his final illness. Indeed, it may be that White employed him as a curate. Sir Richard Holford recorded in his journal that Brinsden 'preached a very good sermon' on 12th August 1711. Holford was not, however, pleased at Brinsden's reaction when he asked the clergyman to mediate in his dispute with John White concerning tithes. Brinsden's answer (13th November 1711) must have startled him, since he denounced Holford's actions in no uncertain terms. Several further letters followed, in one of which (21st May 1712) Holford referred obliquely to the 'private wayes and bye paths you frequented 45 yeares agoe', evidently referring to Brinsden's disreputable past. That was a marker, indicating that Holford knew more about Brinsden's past than Brinsden might feel comfortable with. In 1672-3, soon after he arrived in Winterbourne Monkton, Brinsden had been prosecuted in the ecclesiastical court for fathering a bastard child.[2]

Thomas Brudenell-Bruce (Lord Bruce), Earl of Ailesbury

Lord Bruce of Tottenham was one of the wealthiest landowners in late 17th century Wiltshire, and served as Vice-Chamberlain of the Bedchamber to George III,. He was created Earl of Ailesbury in 1776, three years after Arthur Jones thanked him for a gift of venison.[3] He carried on an extensive correspondence with his father-in-law, Henry Hoare of Stourhead; a fuller biography is included in Wiltshire Record Society's edition of Hoare's letters.[4]

Caswell, John

John Caswell owned a freehold estate in Bishops Cannings, where seven children were baptised between 1692 and 1704.[5] He had a brother, Robert, living in Cherhill, and a nephew, Richard, who was the lessee of a farm at Beckhampton owned by Sir Richard Holford. When John's nephew decided that he needed to be closer to his aged parents at Cherhill, he urged Holford to grant a new lease to his uncle. Holford had his mis-givings, recorded in his journal. John was too old, his sons were supposedly in poor health, and (contradictorily) Holford thought that John would not employ poor labourers because his sons could do

1 **https://theclergydatabase.org.uk/**
2 WSHC D1/42/61, f.46-55.
3 WSHC 9/35/178.Letter, Arthur Jones to Lord Bruce, 12th August 1773.
4 Dodd, Dudley, ed. *The Letters of Henry Hoare, 1760-1781.* Wiltshire Record Society, 71. 2018, p.245-8.
5 Parry, Joseph Henry., ed. *The Registers of Bishops Cannings, Wiltshire.* Devizes: Gazette Printing Works, 1906.

the work.[1] He also objected when he thought Richard Caswell was pressurising him to take his uncle as tenant. In the end, however, he granted the lease to John in 1713; it was regularly renewed on the same terms for almost two decades. In 1720, Thomas Alexander, in his letter to Lady Holford (Sir Richard's successor), evidently thought that his rent should be higher, and that he had too good a bargain.[2]

John served as churchwarden in 1720/21, and again for three years from 1730.[3] In that year, William Caswell, one of his sons, was said to be in possession of the Beckhampton property, although technically John was still lessee. [4] By then, John was elderly, unwell, and probably unable to work. When he 'attorned' the premises to Samuel Holford, Sir Richard's heir, in 1731, he was unable to sign the deed because he had 'broke his right hand wrist & hurt his left sholder'.[5] John died in 1735, and made his widow, Elizabeth, his executrix; she was given his freehold estate at Bishops Cannings as her dower. All his surviving children were also mentioned in his will.[6]

Richard Chandler

Sir Richard Holford's letters show that he negotiated with Mr Richard Chandler of Woodborough to take a lease of Avebury Great Farm in 1709, when William Skeat gave notice. However, the negotiations came to nothing, possibly because Chandler leased a farm in Woodborough instead (and subsequently, in 1731, purchased the freehold). If this identification is correct, his wife was the sister of John Franklin, the original owner of the property he purchased.[7]

John Cures

This correspondent has not been identified, but the content of his letter dated 5th May 1739 suggests that he was acting as an agent (steward?) for Richard Holford when Peter Griffin was tenant of Avebury Great Farm.

Fowler, William

William Fowler came from a family of innkeepers.[8] A relative, Richard Fowler, originally leased the Bear (subsequently the Hare and Hounds) at Beckhampton in 1685. He was succeeded by John Fowler, who had previously kept the White Hart at West Kennett. In 1745, he was succeeded by his son William, then aged

1 Journal, 2nd April 1711.
2 Letter, Thomas Alexander to Lady Holford, 12th December 1720.
3 WSHC D3/15/11; D1/50/13, f.35.
4 WSHC 371/1, pt.5. Conveyance, Samuel Holford to William Hunt, 17th December 1730.
5 WSHC 371/1, pt.5.
6 Elizabeth Caswell was cited to prove his will on 11th January 1731/2; cf. WSHC D3/8/2.
7 *VCH* 10, 1975. **www.british-history.ac.uk/vch/wilts/vol10/pp214-224**
8 Raymond, Stuart A. 'The Inns of Avebury, c.1600-1800', *WAM*, 117, 2024, P.162-3.

32.[1] That, coincidentally, was the year in which the Beckhampton Turnpike opened, and William was able to act as toll collector as well.

William's inn catered primarily for the lower class droving trade. The coaching trade, which catered for travelling gentry, patronised the neighbouring Catherine Wheel. The Hare and Hounds attracted drovers from as far away (probably) as Cornwall and West Wales. It also attracted the poor of Avebury - and the ire of the vicar, James Mayo, who wrote to him on 10th July 1753. He viewed Fowler's establishment as a den of iniquity, and thought Fowler was close to a 'state of damnation' His letter threatened Fowler's livelihood. The innkeeper obviously sought the protection of his landlord, Stayner Holford: that must be why Mayo's letter is now found amongst the Holford papers, and is transcribed below. Nothing is known of the repercussions of this letter.

Whether Mayo's opinions had anything to do with the fact that, many years later, Edward Popham, J.P., questioned the propriety of an innkeeper also being a tollgate keeper is not clear. Popham refused to renew Fowler's licence. Fowler offered to give up his turnpike duties, and wrote to his landlord, still Stayner Holford, on 6th April 1765, asking him to intervene. Whether he successfully contacted Popham is not clear: Fowler died in the following September, and Holford had to find a new lessee.

John Gardiner

Sir Richard Holford hoped that John Gardiner would take on the tenancy of Avebury Great Farm when William Skeat was threatening to give up his lease. He wrote to him on 9th August 1701, 21st August 1701, and 16th July 1703, inviting him to become the new lessee. In the event, however, Skeat remained as tenant for the rest of the decade. Nothing more is known of John Gardiner, except that he lived at Edington.

Peter Griffin

The Griffins were a prolific family in seventeenth and eighteenth century Avebury. Peter, the son of another Peter, and one of three brothers, was baptised 15th December 1676. For many years, he worked as a labourer for John Rose, the tenant of Avebury Great Farm. In 1719, a legacy of £80 from his father provided him with some capital.[2] He probably also inherited the common for 'one rother beast' which he sold c.1723.[3] When John Rose died in 1720, it seems probable that Peter Griffin managed Lady Holford's farm whilst she sought a new tenant. Eventually, in 1722, he leased the farm himself.

T.H. (Mr Hall?) severely criticised Griffin in his letter dated 26th August 1723 for his 'unruly servants'. Despite that, his lease was renewed in 1729[4] and again in 1732.[5] He probably regularly corresponded with his landlords – first,

1 Letter, James Mayo to Richard Holford, 19th September 1745.
2 WSHC P3/G/465.
3 WSHC 488/1. Abstract of John Nalder's title.
4 WSHC 435/24/1/7.
5 WSHC 184/4/1. Abstract of lease made 1739.

Lady Holford, then Samuel, then Richard, and finally Stayner. If so, most of these letters are lost. All but one of the letters printed here are between him and Stayner Holford. The only exception is his letter to Samuel Holford dated 22 November 1725, in which he reported, amongst other things, the flooding of the manor house. All of the other letters date from 1743, and whilst other topics are dealt with (for example, the implications of the proposed turnpike for Holford's estate), most of them concern Holford's insistent demands for payment of rent, which Griffin could not always meet immediately. In the end, Holford refused to renew the lease. In his letter dated 26th June 1743, Griffin told his landlord that 'to be turned out so suddenly it grieves me very much'.[1] He did, however, own the lease of another Avebury farm, which he had inherited in 1728.[2] Following his eviction, he probably went to live there. He was buried 22nd June 1762.

Mr Hall (T.H.?)

Humfry Wall wrote to 'Mr Hall' on 11 January 1721/2, and 'T.H.' wrote to Samuel Holford on 26 August 1723. It is likely that these two correspondents are identical. Mr Hall has not been identified, although the letters imply that he was acting in some capacity – perhaps as bailiff – for the Holfords.

Richard Hickley

Richard Hickley served as bailiff of Avebury Great Farm from at least as early as 1781.[3] Arthur Jones recommended Hickley to his niece, Ann Williamson, who inherited the property in 1789; he was 'a sober, honest, sensible, diligent man, and well acquainted with the property & every circumstance of the country',[4] although his wife was 'unfit for the management of the farm business'.[5] In his 1798 will, Sir Adam Williamson, Ann's husband, expressed the desire that Hickley 'shall be continued and employed as bailiff of my said farm lands and estates at Avebury during his life or for so long as he shall be able to carry on and manage the business of the said farm'.[6]

Hickley's management of the farm was complicated by the fact that Sir Adam Williamson served as governor of Jamaica from 1791 until 1798. After Mrs Williamson joined her husband in Jamaica, she received a letter from her bailiff every month, together with a statement of his accounts (see below, pt.4). Surviving letters cover most months between 1791 and 1794; a few earlier and later letters between Hickley and Sir Adam Williamson also survive.

These letters tell us much about the management of the farm, and about life in Avebury. Hickley regularly reported to his mistress on the state of the weather, the growth of crops, the prospects for sheep, and other agricultural matters. He frequently travelled to various markets, sent goods to the Williamsons via Bristol,

1 WSHC 184/1, pt.2. Peter Griffin to Stayner Holford, 26th June 1743.
2 WSHC P3/G/517.
3 WSHC 184/5. Receipt for a well bucket, 13th January 1781.
4 Memoranda, 14th June 1757. Arthur Jones's discourse with James Mayo.
5 WSHC 271/3.
6 TNA PROB 11/1315/187.

and looked after Sir Adam's property in Bath and Hungerford. Hickley expressed his opinions on a diversity of topics, such as the Avebury enclosure process, the care of the poor, and national politics. His comments were informed by the fact that he served as churchwarden (and in other parish offices) for much longer than the period covered by his letters. His career has not been researched later than 1800, but he died at the ripe old age of 87, and was buried 17th April 1833.

Peter Holford

Peter Holford was the son of Robert, and grandson of Sir Richard and his second wife, Elizabeth (nee Vandeput). He followed in his father's and grandfather's footsteps, becoming a master in Chancery, and holding various offices in Lincolns Inn. [1] Sir Richard left the manor of Westonbirt to Robert, and Peter inherited it (perhaps by dubious means) when his elder brother Robert died in India in 1763.[2] He also inherited the property at Beckhampton which his father had purchased from his nephew Richard in 1731. [3]

When John Rose, Stayner Holford's tenant at Avebury Great Farm, went bankrupt in 1756, Stayner sought the legal advice of his cousin Peter. He also sought advice on his tithe dispute with the vicar, James Mayo (in which Peter was also a concerned party), and on means of avoiding being 'pricked' as sheriff. When Peter's brother Robert died in India, he wrote to Stayner concerning the disposition of his estate. Sadly, only the wrapper of this letter survives. Most of the letters between the two cousins survived at Westonbirt, and are now held at Gloucestershire Archives.

Sir Richard Holford

Sir Richard was a successful London lawyer who served as a master in Chancery for many years. He married three wealthy heiresses in succession. Sarah Crewe (married 1664) brought him the Gloucestershire manor of Westonbirt. Elizabeth Stayner brought with her a portion of the fortune seized by Vice-Admiral Stayner from the Spanish Plate fleet in 1656 (some of which had been invested in the Catherine Wheel in Bishopsgate). Susanna Trotman's dowry was almost sufficient to purchase the manor of Avebury in 1695. These wives all bore children, although several died before their father. Sarah died giving birth, and her daughter died within a few weeks. Sir Richard had four sons by Elizabeth. Only Robert survived him; Richard died leaving two sons, Richard and Stayner, to be provided for by their grandfather. Susanna bore three children, but only Samuel survived his father. Samuel's two nephews followed him successively as lords of the manor of Avebury. Several of Sir Richard's family followed his profession: between 1693 and 1788, seven descendants were admitted to Lincoln's Inn.[4] Sir Richard died

1 *The Records of the Honourable Society of Lincolns Inn: The Black books, vol.3. from A.D. 1660 to A.D. 1775*. Lincolns Inn, 1899, passim.

2 For his journey to India, see Robert Holford's letters to Stayner Holford, 2 March 1742/3 & 3rd March 1742/3.

3 See entry for Robert Holford.

4 *The Records of the Honorable Society of Lincolns Inn vol.1. Admissions from A.D. 1420 to*

in 1718, leaving Westonbirt to Robert, and Avebury to Samuel (after the death of Susanna).[1]

Sir Richard was an indefatigable correspondent. He not only kept the letters he received, but also made copies of those he sent. Therefore, in several instances we can read both sides of his correspondence. He lived in the Rolls, just off Chancery Lane, and relied on his correspondents to keep him in touch with affairs in Avebury.[2] He also kept journals, which record his regular summer visits to Avebury and Westonbirt, together with a considerable amount of information concerning estate and parish affairs in Avebury. His letters and journals together reveal a skilled professional lawyer, who was determined to obtain value for money from tradesmen and tenants. He took a patriarchal attitude towards his tenants and neighbours, and wished to support the Church of England despite his scorn for the vicar. That scorn perhaps derived in part from his own sense of entitlement: John Brinsden certainly thought so[3]. Sir Richard was not afraid to tell his 'inferiors' what he thought of them in no uncertain terms. He expected deference, but did not necessarily get it.

As noted above, Sir Richard's papers cover an extraordinarily wide range of topics, and almost constitute a history of Avebury, 1695-1718 in their own right. Some of the topics covered are discussed in the entries here for his correspondents.

Richard Holford

Richard Holford was the grandson of Sir Richard by his son Richard. His father had married Anna Read without Sir Richard's consent in 1697; there were two surviving sons, Richard and Stayner, when their father died in 1703 without making any provision for them.[4] Their grandfather therefore accepted that responsibility, apprenticing Richard to an attorney in 1715, and giving him the Catherine Wheel pub in Bishopsgate in his will. [5] When Sir Richard's son Samuel died in 1739, his nephew Richard inherited the manor of Avebury, where, according to his Uncle Robert's letter dated 24th September 1737, he was 'reading law'. The only other letter to him in this collection was written by John Cures (5 May 1739), concerning the hatches in the water meadows. Richard died in 1742.

Robert Holford

Robert Holford was the son of Sir Richard and his second wife, Elizabeth, and was baptised at St Dunstans in the West on 6th June 1686. Like his father, he was a lawyer, and became a Master in Chancery. He inherited the manor of Westonbirt when his father died in 1718. In 1731, his nephew Richard sold him the property

A.D.1799. Lincolns Inn, 1896, passim.

1 TNA PROB 11/564/146.

2 His Westonbirt correspondence has not been preserved, as far as is known, although a few letters of his grandson Peter have been, and are printed below.

3 See his letters, 13th November 1711, 1st January 1712, and 24th January 1712.

4 See the entry for Stayner Holford for his mother's re-marriage, and for his step-father.

5 TNA PROB 11/564/122.

at Beckhampton which Sir Richard had purchased in 1710.[1] Hence the Holford name survived in Avebury after its manor passed to Arthur Jones in 1763. Most of Robert's letters in this collection were directed to Stayner Holford, offering him legal advice.

Samuel Holford

Samuel, Sir Richard's son by his third wife, Susanna, inherited the manor of Avebury when his mother died in 1723. Like his father, he was a lawyer, and resided in London. There are four letters to him in this collection, all of them from his agent or his tenants. When he died in 1728, the manor was inherited by his nephew Richard.

Stayner Holford

Stayner was the grandson of Sir Richard Holford, and was given his grandmother Elizabeth's maiden name. As noted above (in the entry for his brother Richard), his father (also Richard) died in 1703. His mother re-married, and had further children; his step-father, Rev. Evan Jones, became rector of Portsea in 1717.[2] Stayner received £1000 in the will of his grand-father.[3] He was still living in Portsea when he inherited the manor of Avebury from his brother Richard in 1742. He did not, however, gain immediate possession of the manor house, since his brother's will[4] granted that for life to his widow, Anne (nee Metcalfe). She died soon after, but not before a law-suit between Stayner and his sister in law (and her mother) concerning Stayner's inheritance had caused a serious family rift.[5] The law suit may explain Stayner's persistent need for cash, which resulted in the eviction of his tenant, Peter Griffin, presumably for non-payment of rent.[6] The eviction resulted in more trouble for Stayner than he bargained for; over a decade later, in 1755, the new tenant, John Rose, went bankrupt, and forced Stayner to take his farm in hand. He was, however, already resident there in October 1753.[7] The 26 letters he wrote, and the 30 he received, are primarily concerned with estate affairs, and especially with his demands on Peter Griffin, the bankruptcy of John Rose, and a tithe dispute with the rector, James Mayo.

Lady Susanna Holford

Susanna Trotman married Sir Richard Holford in 1689, becoming his third wife. He frequently referred to her as his 'Frogg'. The manor of Avebury was purchased with her dower. Her accounts are written at the end of her deceased

1 WSHC 371/1, pt.5. Lease & release, 24th February 1731/2. See also *VCH Wilts* 12, p.95, & Long, William. *Abury illustrated*. 1862, p.59.
2 Clergy of the Church of England Database **www.theclergydatabase.org.uk**
3 TNA PROB 11/564/146.
4 TNA PROB 11/721/329.
5 TNA C 11/818/16. See Stayner Holford's letter to Robert Holford, 9 March 1742/3.
6 Letter, Peter Griffin to Stayner Holford, 26 June 1743.
7 WSHC 184/3. Opinion on Stayner Holford's Land Tax Assessment, 12th October 1753.

husband's bound journal. The only letter addressed to her in this collection, dated 12th December 1720, was from Thomas Alexander, who was acting on her behalf in some capacity. At that time, she was still living in Lincolns Inn Fields, but it may be that she was resident in Avebury when she died in 1723, as she was buried there. The manor descended to her son Samuel. In her will, she left £200 to be used to establish a charity school in Avebury.[1] The school is mentioned in Robert Holford's letter to his nephew Richard, dated 24th September 1737.

Mrs A. Jenny

Mrs Jenny was the tenant of a house at 4, Miles Court, Bath, owned by Arthur Jones,[2] and then by Sir Adam Williamson. Richard Hickley had the task of collecting her rent, and frequently mentioned her in his letters to Mrs Williamson; in his letter dated 30 March 1794 he described her as 'a quear old quist as ever I met with'. Her letter to Hickley dated 18 July 1793 is concerned with her possible purchase of her house.

John Jerome

John Jerome was a poor cottager, and claimed to have lived in Avebury for almost twenty years when he wrote to Sir Richard Holford on 18th April 1707; however, no other information concerning him has been traced. The occasion of his letter (which he wrote with Christopher Page) was the fact that John White, the vicar, had purchased a portion of the manor of Avebury Truslow from John Griffin,[3] and was demanding that he take a lease, and pay an entry fine of £10. Sir Richard seems to have been happy to take up the cudgels on behalf of poor Avebury parishioners, but the outcome of this letter is not known.

Arthur Jones

Arthur Jones was Stayner Holford's step-brother. He was a lawyer, and was called to the bar in 1738.[4] In 1762, he was described as being 'of Avebury', and was perhaps residing with his brother during legal vacations. When Stayner died in 1763, Arthur inherited the manor of Avebury. He died in 1789, bequeathing the manor to his niece Ann, the wife of Adam Williamson.[5] His letter to her dated 8 December 1786 concerns family matters and his illness.

Samuel Martyn

Samuel Martyn was an attorney, who inherited the manor of West Kennett in 1750/51 from his father in law, Thomas Smith.[6] He represented James Mayo in a dispute over tithes with Stayner Holford. His letter to Stayner Holford dated 31st

1 TNA PROB 11/590/280.
2 WSHC 271/3.
3 *VCH Wilts.*, 12, p.93.
4 *The Records of the Honourable Society of Lincolns Inn: The Black books, vol.3. from A.D. 1660 to A.D. 1775*. Lincolns Inn, 1899, p.315.
5 TNA PROB 11/1181/174
6 TNA PROB 11/786/436.

December 1758, which Holford answered on the same day, concerns Holford's dispute with James Mayo, the vicar. Holford recorded Martyn's 'opinion' in a memoranda dated 3rd January 1760. At his death in 1775, Martyn was greatly in debt, probably to his clients; his debts included £221 4s 3d that he was holding on behalf of the trustees of Lady Holford's charity school.[1]

James Mayo

James Mayo was the son of John Mayo, and succeeded his father as vicar of Avebury when the latter retired in 1747. He wrote nine letters to Stayner Holford, one to his successor, Arthur Jones, two to their bailiff, John Scane, and one to William Fowler, the innkeeper at the Hare and Hounds. His earliest letters were written because John Rose, Stayner Holford's tenant, was illiterate, and employed the vicar as his amanuensis. On 11th February 1756 he had occasion to complain to John Scane concerning cattle going through the churchyard. Perhaps that dispute led to him, in his letter dated 19th August 1756, raising again the tithe issue which had afflicted the relationship between John White and Sir Richard Holford half a century earlier. His letter dated 5th January 1757 to Arthur Jones, Stayner's half-brother, seems to be aimed at re-establishing friendly relationships. For Mayo's letter to William Fowler, see above.

John Mayo

John Mayo became vicar of Avebury in 1712, after the death of John White.[2] He came from a Devizes family. Mayo's letter dated 16 June 1715 includes an account of money he had dispensed on behalf of Sir Richard Holford to village children to reward them for learning their catechism. Holford evidently did not clash with Mayo in quite the way he had with White.

John Norris

John Norris wrote to Stayner Holford from Chippenham on 24 May 1749, urging the cause of enclosure. He was a member of the Norris family of Nonsuch, Bromham, who owned the Avebury farms then known as Brunsdens and Pophams for most of the eighteenth century.

William Norris

William Norris was the son of John Norris, and inherited his Avebury properties. When Stayner Holford was endeavouring to avoid serving as sheriff (see his letter to Peter Holford, 19th December 1758) he noted that Norris had been nominated to serve in 1759. That nomination did in fact take effect[3]. Holford wrote to him on 14th June 1761 discussing the land tax assessment. He in turn wrote to Holford on 2nd March 1762 concerning a dispute with the vicar, James Mayo.

1 WSHC 118/88.
2 Clergy of the Church of England database **https://theclergydatabase.org.uk**
3 Jackson, J.E. 'Sheriffs of Wiltshire', *WAM* 3(8), 1857, p.230.

John Overton
Sir Richard Holford's journals frequently mention the tradesmen who worked on his house and his estate, but the only surviving letter to a tradesman is the one he wrote to John Overton on 4th November, 1707. Overton was a Devizes tyler and surveyor.

Christopher Page
Christopher Page married Elizabeth Pontin 22nd May 1676. He was described by John White, the vicar, as a yeoman in 1697, when he was one of nine Avebury men sued for small tithes in the Court of Exchequer.[1] White probably exaggerated his status; Sir Richard Holford thought he was a mere cottager. When White purchased the freehold of the cottage he lived in, and threatened to require him to take out a lease and pay an entry fine, he (and his fellow cottager John Jerome) appealed to Holford for advice. See their letter dated 18th April, 1707. Page was buried 8th January 1728/9, a few weeks after his wife's burial. Nothing more is known of him.

Philip
Philip was one of Sir Richard Holford's servants; his surname is not known. He travelled with his master to Avebury in 1698, together with a number of other servants. In his letter dated 26th November 1698, William Skeat had occasion to complain about the behaviour of Holford's servants. One of them saw Skeat's letter, and wrote a searing rebuttal of Skeat's allegations (undated letter, c.December 1698). Skeat,in his letter to Sir Richard dated 19th December 1698, said that he thought the letter's author was Philip, who he had not intended to blame.

Edward Popham
Edward Popham of Littlecote, Chilton Foliat, was a substantial Wiltshire landowner, who represented Wiltshire in the House of Commons on several occasions in the mid-seventeenth century.[2] He was also a Justice of the Peace. As such, in 1765 he refused to renew William Fowler's licence to run the Hare and Hounds at Beckhampton, on the grounds that a tollgate keeper should not also be a publican. See the entry for William Fowler above.

Mary Powditch
Mary Powditch was the postmistress at Hungerford in 1790.[3] Her letter to Sir Adam Williamson dated 3rd December 1792 shows that she owed him £10, and was unable to pay it.

1 WSHC 1569/5.
2 **www.historyofparliamentonline.org/volume/1754-1790/member/popham-edward-1711-72**
3 Recorded in the *Universal British Directory* at Hungerford in 1790; see **www.hungerfordvirtualmuseum.co.uk**.

John Rose

Confusingly, the Holford family had two tenants of this name. The first John Rose tenanted Avebury Great Farm from 1710 until 1720; a number of his letters are included here. He was illiterate; Sir Richard suggested he should use his 'Uncle Smith' as his amanuensis, [1] and it is likely that the letter dated 23 February 1711/12 described as being from Rose was in fact penned by Smith.

Rose was the brother in law of William Skeat, the former tenant.[2] Before he came to Avebury Great Farm, he had tenanted Higdens, another Avebury farm,[3] and had been sued by John White for 'riotous assembly' when he stopped White from seizing his tithes in 1699.[4] Curiously, he subsequently rented White's tithes[5], and served as churchwarden on a number of occasions between 1705 and his death.

When Sir Richard Holford purchased Higdens, Rose provided him with useful information on the property. [6] That placed him in a good position to become Sir Richard's tenant. His tenancy continued until his death in 1720.

The second John Rose, the nephew of the first, became tenant in 1733. He replaced Peter Griffin, who had been ousted by Stayner Holford. He, like his relative, was illiterate, and wrote no letters himself. However, he probably paid James Mayo, the vicar, to be his amanuensis.[7]

Rose became bankrupt c.1755, forcing Holford to take Avebury Great Farm in hand. His bankruptcy was the principal topic in most of the letters between Stayner Holford and his cousin Peter Holford.[8]

John Scane

John Scane became bailiff to Stayner Holford, probably immediately after John Rose's bankruptcy. His 1756 correspondence with James Mayo, the vicar, concerns his servants' use of the churchyard as a drove way for cattle. Scane served as churchwarden on eight occasions between 1757 and 1772.[9] He probably remained as bailiff until c.1780, when Richard Hickley became bailiff.

William Skeat

William Skeat was baptised in Wootton Bassett in 1654, but was living at Rockley before he became Lord Stawell's tenant of Avebury Great Farm in 1689. After Sir Richard Holford purchased the property in 1695, he exchanged many letters with his tenant, who he expected to keep him informed about Avebury affairs.

1 Letter, Sir Richard Holford to John Rose, 7th June, 1710.
2 Letter, William Skeat to Sir Richard Holford, 19th February, 1699/1700.
3 Letter, John Rose to Sir Richard Holford, 23rd February, 1711/12.
4 WSHC A1/110, 1699M, f.113; Letter, William Skeat to Sir Richard Holford, 19th February 1699/1700.
5 WSHC 188/8.
6 Letter, John Rose to Sir Richard Holford, 23rd February 1711/12.
7 See, for example, letter James Mayo to Sir Richard Holford, 31st March 1744.
8 These commence with Stayner Holford's letter dated 5th February 1756.
9 WSHC D3/15/15-18.

Hence their correspondence provides an invaluable source for Avebury's history in the late 1690s and 1700s.

Holford thought that Skeat was 'of no very obliging temper',[1] and was deeply embarrassed when Skeat treated the hunting son of his neighbour, Charles Tooker, disrespectfully.[2] He was however, a good tenant,[3] and therefore his 'temper' had to be put up with.

Skeat's 'temper' did not help his relationship with John White, the vicar. Despite the fact that he served two terms as churchwarden from 1690,[4] he was a leading dissenter. White accused him of setting up 'a hellish, factious, scandalous, & schismatical conventicle', although he probably exaggerated Skeat's role in Avebury's dissenting cause. [5] Their enmity played an important role in fomenting the long-running dispute over tithes between Skeat's landlord and the vicar – a dispute which, many years later, was resurrected by James Mayo and Stayner Holford.[6]

Skeat was seriously injured in 1698/9, when the limb of a tree fell on him, and it is possible that he never fully recovered.[7] Nevertheless, it was not until 1710 that he gave up his farm: 'hee pretends that hee is groweing old & is infirme, and his wife very crazy, and not fit for soe much troble'.[8] He seems to have retired to Rowden, near Chippenham, where Holford called on him on 13th April 1711.[9]

Richard Smith

Richard Smith was lord of the manor of West Kennett, and father in law of the vicar, John White. His letters to Sir Richard Holford (7th February 1695/6) and to William Skeat (27 June 1696), are attempts to mediate in their dispute over tithes with the vicar.

Thomas Smith

Thomas Smith was Richard Smith's son and heir, and inherited the manor of West Kennett when his father died in 1734. According to Stukeley[10] he trained as a lawyer, and lived in London for many years before his father died. He wrote to Stayner Holford on 29th May 1743 concerning estate matters. It seems likely that

1 Letter, Cornelius Yeate to Sir Richard Holford, c.9th March 1698.
2 Letter, Sir Richard Holford to Charles Tooker, 4th January 1697/8.
3 Letter, Sir Richard Holford to John Gardiner, 21st August 1701.
4 WSHC D3/15/3; D3/12/5.
5 Letter, John White to Sir Richard Holford, undated; c.25th January 1695.
6 See James Mayo's letter to Stayner Holford, 7th October 1756, and succeeding correspondence.
7 Letter, William Skeat to Sir Richard Holford, 30th January 1698/9.
8 Letter, Sir Richard Holford to Richard Chandler, 2nd June 1709.
9 Sheet journal. Skeat's letter to Holford, 20th June 1705 was written at Rowden; presumably he had family connections there.
10 Gillings, Mark, Peterson, Rick, & Pollard, Joshua. 'The destruction of the Avebury monuments', in Cleal, Rosemary, & Pollard, Joshua, eds. *Monuments and material culture: Papers in honour of an Avebury Archaeologist: Isobel Smith*. Hobnob Press, 2004, p.153.

he and Holford were acquainted with each other in London.

William Smith

William Smith of Calston was probably related to the Smiths of West Kennett, but that relationship has not been traced. We do, however, know that William Skeat was one of his kinsmen. His correspondence in 1700 and 1701 show that Smith was deeply involved in the tithe dispute between Sir Richard Holford and John White, which also involved both Skeat and Richard Smith, as noted above.

Charles Tooker

Charles Tooker purchased the manor of East Kennett in 1676, and was active in the land market; Sir Richard Holford purchased property at Beckhampton from him in 1710.[1]

His letter to Sir Richard Holford, dated c.29th December 1697, and Sir Richard's reply, 4th January 1697/8, concern hunting rights over Avebury manor. Hunting could be destructive to agriculture, and tenants therefore tried to prevent it. Gentlemen, however, had the right to hunt wherever they wished, and Holford expressed himself as being deeply embarrassed at the way in which his tenant, William Skeat, tried to prevent Tooker's son from indulging in this sport. Holford was probably mindful of the fact that Tooker was a Justice of the Peace.

A decade later, Tooker was called upon, as a Justice of the Peace, to resolve the 1711 dispute between the poor women of Calne and Avebury over gleaning rights in the Avebury open fields.[2]

Humfry Wall

Humfry Wall was a Marlborough attorney, who is mentioned on several occasions in these papers. His letter dated 11th January 1721/2 shows him acting as Sir Richard Holford's local agent in his tithe dispute with the vicar, John White. Holford subsequently employed him in his failed 1702 negotiations to buy property from John Truslow.[3] The property was in fact sold to Charles Tooker, who sold it to Holford eight years later, in 1710.[4] Wall's letter to Mr Hall dated 11 January 1721/2 shows that he was acting as agent for Lady Holford in her quest for a new tenant following the death of John Rose.

John Ward

A Marlborough lawyer, banker, and sometime mayor, Ward acted as agent for Adam Williamson during the enclosure process; most of his letters to Williamson concern this business, although Richard Hickley suspected that he only attended

1 *VCH Wilts* 12, p.95; WSHC 371/2, pt.2. Bargain & Sale, 13/14th June 1676; 371/1, pt.4. Lease & release, Charles Tooker to Sir Richard Holford, 31st November/1st December 1710. See also bound journal, and the entry for Humfry Wall below.

2 Bound journal.

3 Letter, Humfry Wall to Sir Richard Holford, 18th October 1702.

4 See note 1 above.

enclosure commissioners meetings to draw his fee.[1] Lord Ailesbury was another of his clients, whom he served as steward. In the 1780s, Ward acted vigorously but unsuccessfully on Lord Ailesbury's behalf in prosecuting poachers. In the process he was described as a 'worthless scoundrel'![2] He also served as principal clerk of the Company that was building the Kennet and Avon Canal:[3] hence his comment in his letter to Sir Adam Williamson dated 20th September 1793 that he would 'take care to insert a clause in the act for the purpose of securing you against any loss' in relation to Williamson's property in Hungerford.

John White

John White served as vicar of Avebury from 1671 until his death in October 1712. His wife, Mary, was the daughter of Richard Smith of Beckhampton; White's letters frequently refer to him as 'Father Smith'.[4] His ministry was not a happy one, as far as we can judge from the many letters between himself, Sir Richard Holford, and others. White found it difficult to control his temper. Even the Archdeacon, Cornelius Yeates, thought that he was 'passionate & apt to flye out in reproachfull language'.[5] Holford's letters frequently criticise his 'stubborne & peevish proud spirit',[6] although one suspects that constituted White's defence against Holford's condescending manner and sense of entitlement. Holford recorded one occasion when, after he had reviled White's behaviour, White 'told mee I gave him a good dinner, but run the spitt into his gutts'![7] William Skeat even warned Holford that he might be physically attacked by the vicar.[8] White did, however, have his defenders. John Brinsden, vicar of neighbouring Winterbourne Monkton, accused Holford of 'palpable injustice' in his tithe case against White.[9]

The major source of dispute between Holford and White concerned tithes. Most of the great tithes of the parish were in private hands, but the vicar still retained the tithes of a field close to the church, owned by Holford. He also claimed small tithes from his parishioners. Both of these were the subjects of dispute, and White was a party to several cases in the courts of Chancery and Exchequer, and at the Assizes.[10]

Disputes over tithe did not help White's relationships with his parishioners – and especially his relationships with dissenters. White regarded Avebury's dissenting congregation – which was flourishing - with abhorrence. On that, he

1 Letter, Richard Hickley to Mrs Williamson, 4th September 1792.
2 Jones, Eric L. *Landed Estates and Rural Inequality in English History: from the mid-seventeenth century to the present.* Palgrave Macmillan, 2018, p.84-8.
3 Berry, Warren. *The Kennet and Avon Navigation: a History.* Phillimore, 2009, p.18.
4 Letter, John White to Sir Richard Holford, c.25 January 1695/6.
5 Letter, Cornelius Yeate to Sir Richard Holford, 28th February 1697/8.
6 Letter, Sir Richard Holford to Richard Smith, 9th November 1697.
7 Bound journal , 10th August 1711.
8 Letter, William Skeat to Sir Richard Holford, 16th February 1698/9.
9 Letter, John Brinsden to Sir Richard Holford, 1st January 1711/12
10 For more details, see AWS. Many letters are concerned with these disputes.

was almost on the same page as Holford. The latter shared White's annoyance at the possibility that stones from his property might be used to build the dissenter's meeting house.[1] But he did not see it as his role to ensure that his tenants were good churchmen – although he did avoid leasing his property to a Quaker who might have made a good tenant.[2]

White had a particularly difficult relationship with William Skeat, whom he regarded as 'my profest enemy', and a leading figure in the dissenting cause.[3] He refused even to bury dissenters, despite the fact that they, as parishioners, had a right to burial in the churchyard. His refusal to bury the popular John Pope, in April 1711, may have been the trigger which led to White's prosecution in the Consistory Court. He was also accused of refusing to baptise babies, not catechising, and 'not saying publique prayers in the church according to the cannons of the church'. [4] The Diocesan Chancellor, Mr Loggin, found against him, but White was still unwilling to admit that he was in the wrong.[5]

Adam Williamson

Adam Williamson was a senior army officer, who was posted to Jamaica as Lieutenant Governor in 1791, subsequently becoming its governor, being made a Knight of the Bath, and unsuccessfully attempting to make St Domingue (now Haiti) a British colony.[6] He married Anne Jones, who inherited Avebury Manor in 1789. He also owned houses in Hungerford, and in Bath, which are mentioned in some of the correspondence between himself, Hickley, and John Ward. His correspondence with John Ward, his attorney, primarily concerns the enclosure business at Avebury. He also corresponded with his bailiff, Richard Hickley, before his wife arrived in the colony, and after her death. Williamson himself died from a fall at Avebury after he had returned from Jamaica; he was buried 30th October 1798.

Ann Williamson

When Arthur Jones died in 1789, he left the manor of Avebury to his niece Ann Williamson, and her husband Adam.[7] She was to be his executrix 'apart from every countroul by her husband'.[8] That explains why she, rather than her husband, administered the Avebury estate. After she joined her husband

1 Letter, Sir Richard Holford to John White, 6th March 1706/7. The Meeting House was licenced on 11th April 1707; see Chandler, John, ed. *Wiltshire Dissenters' Meeting House Certificates and Registrations, 1689-1852.* Wiltshire Record Society 40. 1985, p.14.
2 Letter, Sir Richard Holford to John Chandler, 2nd June 1709.
3 Letter, John White to Sir Richard Holford, undated; c.25th January 1695.
4 Sheet journal, 9th August 1711.
5 Sheet journal, 10th August 1711.
6 For a detailed account of his governorship, see Geggus, David Patrick. *Slavery, War, and Revolution: the British Occupation of Saint Domingue, 1793-1798.* Clarendon Press, 1982
7 TNA PROB 11/1181/174.
8 See below, p.333. Arthur Jones's Memorandum.

in Jamaica in 1791, she maintained a regular correspondence with her bailiff, Richard Hickley, until she died of yellow fever, 19th September 1794.[1] Her letters do not survive, although Hickley frequently mentioned them in his.

Cornelius Yeate

Cornelius Yeate was the Archdeacon of Wiltshire from 1696 until 1720, and was based in Marlborough, where he served as vicar of St Mary's until 1708.[2] For his attempt to arbitrate in the dispute between Sir Richard Holford and John White, see his 1698 letters.

1 Jamaican Family Search **www.jamaicanfamilysearch.com/Members/Barche03.htm** ; Knowles, Francis, Sir. 'Avebury Manor', *WAM* 56, 1955, p.368.

2 Clergy of the Church of England database **https://theclergydatabase.org.uk**

1
THE JOURNAL OF SIR RICHARD HOLFORD

A. The Sheet Journal, 1700-1714[1]

[Sheet 1]

Memorandums at Avebury 1700
September 1700

[*Monday] 9 September
I came out of London with my owne paire of horses, a hyred calesh,[2] my coachman Pillip & footman Thomas. Baited at Stow, lay at the Bere in Reading.

[*Tuesday]. Baited at the Bere at Spinhamland[3] & to Avebury to bed.

[*Wednesday]. Mr. White made a long visit which I promised to return.

[*Thursday]. Att home looking about the house &c.

[*Friday]. Mr. Chivers & Mr. Norris[4] dined with mee. Mr. Chivers gave mee a bushell of good old [?brandy]. Wee all went to visit Mr. White. Hee was a little unruely & forced them to fly.

Mr. William Crook the mason came to me about pitching the stable, but could not come to worke till ult° September, but promised then not to faile, and I promised to bee here againe by that time & to expect him.

[*Saturday]. I went to Marleborough, & in my way home visited Mr. Perceval[5] & his wife, and Mrs. Herring, Mr. Tucker[6] and Mr. Smith.

[*Sunday]. I staied at home.

1 WSHC 184/8.
2 A carriage with low wheels.
3 Speenhamland, Berkshire.
4 Probably William Norris of Nonsuch House, Bromham, another bencher of Lincolns Inn.
5 Edmund Percival became lord of the manor of Clatford, a few miles east of Avebury, when he married Ann Fitzjames in 1699; cf. *VCH Wilts.*, 12, p.173.
6 Charles Tooker, J.P., of East Kennett.

[*Monday]. I went by Nonsuch,[1] visited at Chipenham and to Weston[2] to bed, thence to Siston, Bath, Steple Ashton, Imber,[3] and on ult° September to Avebury.

[*Tuesday] October 1st I staied at home. The mason did not come as promised, but desired to bee excused for fornight longer, being hard at worke for Mr. Nurs at Woodlands.[4]

[*Wednesday]. I kept two courts[5] by Mr. Norris, steward, one at Mr. White's[6] & the other at Mr. Baskervilles.[7] Mr. White and Mr. Norris dined with mee in the little parlour. Farmer Skeate invited all the jury, & they brought as many more. There was victuall enough for them, and all of them very cherefull, but lamentable troblesome. The jury & homage made their presentments but very imperfectly, though I had labored to instruct and informe them.

Mr. White, though requested to the contrary, would breake into the differences between him & mee, which made us somewhat uneasy, & reflecting on our last conference at his house on 13 September where I readily submitted to Mr. Archdeacon Yates[8] to determine who was the agressor, & promised not to say a word, but to lay my letters & Mr. White's there before him, but bye & bye Mr. White in his passion declared that hee knew the Archdeacon would not give it against him. I thereupon withdrew my consent & refused to leave it him, being pre engaged, but I am perswaded that Mr. Yates is a gentleman of great integrity. Wee now refresht each other's memories, hee raileing at mee for putting him to troble & charge, & I complaineing that I was the [p.2.] sufferer, for that I was compelled in my own defence to have his answer, & desired it might bee faire and friendly, but hee had not graunted my request but had put in a short malitious & untrue answer, & was compelled after an appeal to the Court to put in a second answer, & had put mee to a great deale of unnescessary troble & expense, &c.

[*Thursday]. Thursday night Farmer Skeat & I made a visit to Mr. White & hee & his wife and Mr Brunsden[9]came with us home & supped & were very merry, & John Griffin was with us. That day Mr. Sloper[10] and Mr. Stokes of Calne dined with mee.

1 See p.1, n.4 above.
2 Westonbirt.
3 Imber was the home of Hannah Wadman, Sir Richard Holford's sister in law; cf. Sanders, John. 'John Sanders, his book, 1712: the account of my travils with my Mistress', *Records of Buckinghamshire*, 3, 1870, p.94.
4 Probably Mr Nourse of Woodlands, Ditteridge.
5 Probably for the manors of Avebury and Beckhampton.
6 Presumably he means the vicar, although quite why Holford would hold the manor court in his house is not clear.
7 The Baskervilles were lords of the manor of Winterbourne Basset; cf. *VCH Wilts* 12, p.187.
8 Cornelius Yeate.
9 John Brinsden, vicar of Winterbourne Monkton.
10 An attorney of Winterbourne Monkton; cf. *Avebury without the Stones*, p.326.

[*Friday]. In the morn Farmer Skeate & I had a great deal of talke about renewing the bargaine, but his demands were &c.

I now accompted with Richard Fowler[1] and outset for his rent for five yeares due at Our Lady day last xx shill., & gave him an acquittance, & charged him to kepe it by him.

I dined with Madam Percival[2] and her husband at Clatford, called on Mr. Fowl[3] at Lockeridge, and on Madam Tooker[4] in my way home. The farmer was my guide.

Mr. Smith of Calston and Isaac Humfries came hither, with them Mr. Michell.[5] They staied till I came home but went away that night.

[*Saturday] 5. I went to Marlborough, put up my horses at Farmer Nalder's,[6] & dined at the Angell.

[*Sunday] 6. Dined at home. Yesterday and this day Farmer Skeat & I had a great deale of discours about renewing his lease, which will determine at Our Lady 1702. He was stiffe in not offering more than £320 (16 score pounds he called it) & would take it but for 4 yeares from 1702. I put him in mind of £22 or £23 that I have layd out for the plancking the upper barne, of the many allowances I have made, that the garden between the house & the stable, the Shere Barton and the Cherry Court are not in his lease, yet injoyed by him, together with all the house & the new stables & coach house, without any increase of rent, that hee hath kept £200 in his hands without interest, & expects soe to doe, which I never agreed to, all which signified noething to him, he still persisting on £320, & affirmed the farm never yielded more till the last time hee took it, and that twas then made £350 by my Lord Stawell's request, because it was upon sale, but pretended never to [p.3.] to take any more than £320, & if hee sold it then to deliver up the lease, nay that my Lord promised out of that to give him £100, but died before hee performed it. After a multitude of words I made him a proposition, because I must be gone towards London tomorrow morn, that if hee would renew for 4 yeares or 8 yeares upon the same termes as his former articles containe, that I would give him a note under my hand to allow him £20 per annum out of the £350 rent for that 4 yeares, and permitt him to kepe £200 in his hands till Laday[7] 1702, & then to pay it, but I prefaced my proposition with this, that if twere not now presently accepted, I would never bee oblidged by the proposition, but

1 Tenant of the Bear (now the Waggon and Horses) at Beckhampton.

2 Lady of the manor of Clatford, per *VCH Wilts* 12, p.173.

3 Thomas Fowle, lord of the manor of Lockeridge per *VCH Wilts* 11. www.british-history.ac.uk/vch/wilts/vol11/pp181-203.

4 The wife of Charles Tooker of East Kennett, J.P.

5 Perhaps John Mitchell, lord of the manor of Beversbrook, Hilmarton (which included property in Calne); cf. *VCH Wilts*, v.17, p.128.

6 The Nalder family were subsequently prominent yeomen in Avebury; cf. *AWS*, p.104-9.

7 Lady Day.

would absolutely disowne it, & gave him the reason why.

Hee thereupon desired to speak with his wife about it, & did soe, and returned to mee as if shee was not willing. I staied there [*Sunday] all day & night, and hee never made any further mention of it.

A little after 6 I came from thence and hee brought mee up the Hill & cross the Gray Weathers, & then returned being to draw sheepe for the Vize[1] Green faire tomorrow, hee left me.

I baited at the Beare at Spinham Land[2] and thence to Reading to the Bere.

[Sheet 2]

November 1709. Avebury. John Rose

October 29

I writ a long and plaine letter to Mr. Wm Smith of Blacklands in answer to a letter written by him for John Rose to mee concerning John Rose's becoming my tennant at Avebury . I prayed him to consider with Farmer Skeate & John Rose upon what tearmes John Rose may come in, & if I must lend him money how it may bee secured, whether Farmer Skeate & his son will offer to bee bound for him for repayment of what I shall lend &c., & other matters in the letter, whereof I kept a coppy.

I prayed them speedily to answer it, but I received no answer.

5 November

John Rose came to London, but I did not see him till [*Sunday] the 6th, & then Mr. Skeate, the [?Bales] & hee came to my house after dinner (he brought my perriwig, I had given him the hatt and Mary Skeaet tooke the hatt band) wee had then noe discours about the farme, but I bid him come to mee tomorrow morn, Sunday, not being [?proper], &c.

[*Monday] 7 November

John Rose came to mee early and went with me to Symons Inn & their staid with mee till noone, & went home with mee to dinner, & intends tomorrow to returne home.

We discoursed about Mr. Tooker's[3] estate at Beckhampton; hee thinks tis let for £210 per annum to [ ][4] Caswell, & that the tennant payes the church & poore, but Truslows was never estimated at more than £55 per annum .

We alsoe talked about my farme. He tells mee that his stock is worth £600, & that if we agree I must lend him £400 at £5 per cent, that hee cannot get any sureties to bee bound with him for it, but that hee wilbee punctual in his dealings, and pay honestly, upon the whole matter, and not knowing what to doe

1 Devizes.

2 Speenhamland, Berkshire. For inns there, see Philips, Daphne. *The Bath Road.* Countryside Books, 1983, p.110.

3 Charles Tooker, J.P.

4 Blank; Richard Caswell was the then tenant.

because of Farmer Skeat's humor which hath been very prejudicial to mee, and [?haveing] read to him Farmer Skeate's lease from my Lord Stawell for 12 yeares, & fully informed him of everything, & of my agreement with Farmer Skeate that by reason of the very low price of wheat, the best yielding but 2s or the best 3 the bushell, & other grain proportionably, and the very low price of wooll &c. I had agreed to abate him £30 per annum out of the rent of £350 per annum. And when wee had fully discoursed the matter, and depending on his integrity, I bid him goe on, & that Farmer Skeate & hee may settle the matter as to the £400 stock or money [p.2.] and settle it as soon as possible, & let mee heare from them speedily in order to make a full & faire accompt with Farmer Skeate, & to place Rose quietly in the farme, his eight children & what more may come, give but a small addition to the invitation of takeing him to bee my tenant, & yet if hee proves, as I hope hee will, an industrious, diligent, honest man, I shall bee contented.

I positively denyed plowing the [?Prisfeild], not plowed these 3 or 4 yeares, and also the close called Rough Leaze, formerly sowed to French grass.

Heareing noething from them, I writ to Mr. Smith & alsoe to Farmer Skeate to the same effect.

See the next sheet

[Sheet 3]

John Rose

1709

Note

I writ severall letters by the post to Mr. Smith of Blacklands[1] and to Farmer Skeate relateing to John Rose, and to pray their resolutons on behalf of John Rose, who can neither write nor read written hand, hath 8 smal children & like to have more, must bee assisted with £400 at £5 per cent which are great discouragements, but neither of them gave mee any answer .

Farmer Skeate and his son Emanuel being in London with oxen against Christmas, I discoursed with them about it, & how I might bee secured, & I expected they would have been bound with him for the £400, but they severally refused it. But I pressed them to consider it when they came home, & consult Mr. Smith & John Rose, & to write fully to mee to prevent doubts and mistakes. They told mee they would but did not.

At Christmas, by Mr. Norris, I writ to Farmer Skeat to the same effect & prayed an answer by Mr. Norris, but received none, though my letter was delivered.

12 January

I writ a long letter to Mr. Smith and layd everything before him, & prayed him

1 Perhaps Matthew Smith, brother to the (lunatic) lord of the manor of Blacklands; cf. *VCH Wilts* 17, p.20.

to tell mee what he would doe in the like case, & prayed his speedy thoughts &c but received noe answer.

[*Friday] 27 January
John Rose came to my house when we were at dinner between one and two. Hee told mee that hee came from Beckhampton yesterday morn, that noe body knew of his comeing, & upon discours hee declared that hee thought I had agreed to let him the farme with the same abatement I had made to Farmer Skeate, but I told him it was a gross mistake, for I told him & his Brother[1] Skeate the Sunday night before I came away, that he should have it upon the same termes the Farmer had it from my Lord Stawell, & I did expect security for the money to bee sent, & I thought the Farmer & his son would have offered to bee bound, but they when here with mee had directly refused. John Rose produced to mee the letter I sent to Mr. Smith 12 January, which is full & plaine £350 per annum for 4 yeares (from Our Lady day 1700). Wee had a great deale of discours. I told him, as I had written, that his honesty & industry was all the encouragement I had. Yet at length, at the [?Pales] in Lyncolns Inn, when I was goeing to Councell, I told him that £350 per annum for 4 yeares out of which £10 per annum for wood, & to expect my assisting him with £400 at v per cent, notwithstanding all the discouragements. Hee went from me very cheerful, & on the morn, [*Saturday], 28th January tooke his journey homeward & intended to bee at home Sunday by noone, & not to let any body know where hee had been, wherefore I prayed him to get his unckle to write to mee forthwith an answer to mine of the 12 January, which promised to indeavour.

I refused to consent to his plowing the close where Skeat has liberty to plow, laying it downe with French grass 3 yeares before his terme expired, but did not. [p.2.]

3rd February 1709
I received a letter dated 29 January written by Mr. Smith & subscribed John Rose that hee is content to hold the farme at £350 per annum, with a proviso for mee to lend him £400 gratis for the 4 yeares & to abate £10 per annum besydes £10 per annum.

I took this letter very unkindly & writ to Mr. Smith a letter 4th of February, see the coppy.

[*Wednesday]10, [*Friday] 12, [*Saturday] 13 February
Farmer Skeate coming up with fatt cattle came to mee on Fryday, but was in haste, hee came and dined with mee on Sunday & after dinner I talked with him & put him againe in mind of his monstrous abuse relateing to the abatement of £XXX per annum contrary to his hand & seale, & by the best excuse he could make (if it were true) hee made himself a [ ][2] by consenting to cheate an honest

1 Rose was William Skeat's brother in law; cf. letter 19th February 1699.
2 Blank in mss.

purchaser. Monday hee came to me again, & I told him that hee and I must come to a further accompt & not part without further satisfaction. I prayed him to tell mee how hee intends to supply Farmer Rose with £400. Hee now told me twill take [£]1200[1] or £1400 to stock the farm as stock now is, but that Rose hath already about 800 sheepe. He told mee of Mr. John Griffen's purpose fully to stock &c., which would famish the sheep & cowes.

I prayd him to bee kind & assisting to John Rose. I read to him the coppies of my letters to him & to Mr. Smith, & Mr. Smith's letters to mee, & repeated to him my full purpose of £350 per annum and £10, wood, and noe plowing the Rough Lease.

I prayed him to take care of the repaires, & to leave everything as it ought to bee, and to take noething away but what belongs to him, & to leave everything that belongs to mee, without &c. I prayed him, as I often had, to let mee see his accompts with my Lord Stawell, which hee told me hee had, but that they were at Chipenham .

I told him that I was very desirous to give John Rose all the encouragement I could, & spoke to him to doe soe, and as soone as hee came home to speak with Mr. Smith & John Rose, and to write to mee everything they think material as soone as possible.

Hee told me that his wife hath bottled 5 douz of the old hogshead, & that it is very good, & proved for mee by filling my three vessells. I desired him to plant good store of beans, that if my wife & I can bee there the next sumer, that wee may not lack conveniences. Hee tells me that when we are there the brewhouse must serve John Rose and his wife & children, which wilbe much better than where they are. I doe expect to hear from them speedily.

[p.3.] I writ severall letters to Farmer Skeat & Mr. Smith relateing to John Rose, & still received little satisfaction from them as to security for the £400 & interest at £20, nor to the rent, but that the £400 should bee but gratis.

Note. I received many letters and visits from Mrs. Eliz Nash that her brother Thomas Nash[2] was very desirous to bee my tennant & was very importunate with mee, & at last caused her brother to come up to London as they said on purpose to treat with mee about it. I had very little time being very busy, & they agreed to come to mee at 7 that evening but did not, soe I had noe discours with him. She afterwards continued very importunate & that her brother did not scruple the rent and was an upright honest man & would bee a good tennant, but I was still unwilling to disapoint Rose & writ to Mr. Skeate and Mr Smith to let mee know what John Rose was damnified in case hee should not have the farme, to which they gave mee noe answer.

[*Saturday] 25 March

I came to Avebury. The farmer was gone to Marlebrough & John Rose to Chipenham. I spoke with neither of them till Sunday.

1 £ sign omitted in mss.

2 Perhaps the Thomas Nash who was baptised at Bishops Cannings 15th January 1670.

[*Sunday] 26
Both of them told me that Tho Nash had declared that I had sent for him, and that hee had been with mee at London, & had taken the farm, & that I had given him a [?guynia], at which John Rose was uneasy & indeavourd again to continue his old bargaine. I told them the truth & that Mrs. Nash had sollicited mee on behalfe of her brother, & that twas shee sent for her brother and against my directions.

[*Tuesday] 28
Farmer Skeate and I were in the fields viewing the bounds, & a man came to mee with a letter from Mr. Nash from Cannens,[1] that Farmer Skeate had been[2] her brother the day before & told him that his sister had been a [?base] & had tyred mee out with visites, & a great deal such stuffe. I read the letter to Skeate, & then hee confessed that hee had been with Tho Nash & had told some thing, though I had prayed him not to say anything of it, but that hee had gotten £10 upon account more than hee thought hee should have had. I was truely angry with him for telling what I desired him not to mention but twas all one to him. John Rose was very busy [*Tuesday], [*Wednesday], & [*Thursday], the weather being very bad & the waters out, & had sheepe below hill & must be brought away.

[*Wednesday] 31 March
We had full discourse & then agreed £350 per annum for eight yeares, & leave to breake up Row Leaze for 4 crops, & then fill it with good French grass & to preserve it for the last 3 yeares, & soe to leave it. And I to lend him upon his owne bond & judgement £400 at £5 per cent.

Hee afterwards complained of the dearnes of stock, & prayed mee to let it bee £500. I was too farr engaged to goe back and agreed to it.

Famer Skeate & I accompted & rested due to mee at Our Lady Day last [£]803 4[s] 2[d],[3] and hee desired to keepe £160 thereof till midsomer upon his bond.

I directed him to pay John Rose £500 and I allowed him the £500 & the £160 upon his accompt then rested [£]143 4[s] 6[d],[4] which he paid mee in guyneas.

[Sheet 4]
1711. Notes taken 1711 relateing to Mr White, Caswel, Pontin, et al.
[*Wednesday]. 31 July
This morning before 8 I came in from Marleborough hither.

Mr White & Caswell.

In the afternoon Mr. White came to see mee, seemed not to bee very well,

1 Probably Bishops Cannings; see p.xxx, n.xxx.
2 Perhaps 'seen' is meant.
3 £sd omitted in mss.
4 £sd omitted in mss.

but full of complaints against Councellor Pontin, Richard Caswell and others. I could not answer for either of their actions not being concerned otherwaies than as a friend & neighbour, & willing to doe good between them if I could. Mr. White and I talked over all the old matters but hee is the same man, and as possitive as ever, though in the wrong, especially as to christenings & buryeing the dead.

And as to the squabbles between him and mee &c.
He pressed mee to direct what to bee done between him & Caswell relateing to tythes. I told him I thought him very unkind in not telling Caswell before the event that hee would not abide by the composition of £3, but would have his 2 ell ridges, nor to mention it till 2 months after the corne removed, & then to insist on £5. He justified it by saying hee ought not to give any such notice, but twas Caswell's duty to have come to him to know his pleasure.

I refused to give him any directions otherwise than to put him in mind what his answer was to mee when I intreated him to tell mee what was the vicar's dues yearly out of my farme. His answer then was that I was not concerned, but my tennant, & therefore refused to tell mee. Which compelled mee to gett his answer in Chancery.

I now desired him to tell mee the viccar's right to two ell ridges in Beckhampton, whether out of the peice of wheate lying next the church yearly, or out of what peice of wheat hee pleased. After some pause hee told mee out of any piece of wheate. I told him twas otherwaies at Avebury, by his answer to my bill, & desired him to consider & to informe mee how the custome came to differ & when, to which hee would give mee noe answer, but I told him that I would expect his full answer. Farmer Rose being present intreated mee to mediate between Mr. White & Caswell. I told him I would if they desired mee soe to doe, but not otherwise.

[*Wednesday][1] 3 August
Farmer Caswell came to mee & told mee that John Rose had informed him that Mr. White had sent to let him know that hee would accept the £3 ancient composition. I told him I think hee ought to pay it, though that peice lying this year next the church hath received damage, but I bid him take a receipt or a witnes, & to declare twas for the ell rydge in that peice lying next the church, for that, as I think, was the truth, & John Rose now told mee, that he rented Mr White's tythes heretofore, & that Mr. White told him it was arising out of that peice lying yearly next the church, and tells me that if called thereto hee must sweare it.

[p.2.] [*Tuesday] 7 August [2]
Mr. Loggin, Chancellor, Mr. Frend, the Registrar of this Diocese, & Mr. Frome, Procter, came to Avebury to examine wittnesses for Councellor Pontin &

1 This should be Saturday. The scribe has used the wrong symbol.
2 In margin: the Chancellor, Registal.

Richard Caswell against Mr. White for not burying the dead, not catechizeing the children, not christening, & not visiteing the sick. [*Wednesday]. They examined severall wittnesses, and in the doeing they came downe to mee, Mr. White & Mr. Brinsdon being with mee, & staied 2 howers.

[*Thursday] 9
Pontin and Caswell came early to mee to request mee to goe up to the Wheele[1] to join with the Chancellor to reconcile all matters between them. I went up, but before I came the Chancellor had heard both parties & adjusted the matter. I expected that it might bee put in writeing,[2] & it was soe by the Chancellor's clerk, & both parties signed it & Caswell paid downe to the viccar the money awarded. I think twas £3 10s & 3d, & about a bushell, for all Mr. White's demands, & both sydes to beare their own charges. Then the Chancellor after long wrangling between Mr. White & Pontin & [?blamed][3] Mr. White for not performing his duty in burying the dead, not christening, not [?catechising],[4] and not saying publique prayers in the church according to the cannons of the church, & declareing that if complaint thereof made to him hee would compell him thereto. At length hee awarded Pontin his costs, & for this Commission (which I think came to £14 odd money) hee awarded £xi, & to bee paid in a month, or to that effect, & for the actions at law, I think hee left it to them to agree or to proceed as &c.

This evening John Rose told mee that Farmer Skeate could not come to mee tomorrow morn being to goe to a faire.

[*Wednesday][5] 10
Mr White dined with mee, & I indeavoured to persuade him that the Chancellor had dealt wonderfully kind towards him & his adversaries in reconciling them, but hee would not agree thereto, but spoke very disrespectfully, upon which I undertook the Chancellor's part, and put severall questions to him, particularly how hee presumed to omit the exhortation before the prayers morn and afternoon, whereupon hee fell into a passion and caught up his cane & hatt & told mee I gave him a good dinner, but run the spitt into his gutts, & such like nonsensical revileing stuffe, & went away in a seeming passion.

[*Saturday] 11
I received letters from London of the death of Dr Knipe, & of poore Poll's death.

[*Sunday] 12
Mr. Brinsden preached to us at Avebury a very good sermon. Mrs Smith of

1 Presumably the Catherine Wheel.
2 In margin: Pontin & Caswell
3 Torn.
4 Torn.
5 This should be Friday. The scribe has used the wrong symbol.

Kennet dined with us. After dinner Mr. Smith came to us, as alsoe Mrs. Percival[1] & Mrs. Tooker and one of Mr. Wall's daughters . Mr. White said prayers and wee all attended him.

[*Tuesday] August 14.
We went from Avebury to Weston Burt by Highway, Christian Malford, Sutton Draycot, &c., John Rose our guide. Tis somewhat nearer & at summer a better way than by Calne & Chipenham. Wee came to Weston about 3 after a long ramble [?put] per almanack.

[*Monday] October 1st
Wee came again to Avebury after haveing been a fortnight at Weston But, at Siston & Wells 3 weekes, at Bath 20 daies, at Imber 4 daies.

[*Wednesday] 3.
Mr. White said prayers. I invited him to dine with us, but hee put a rude answer.

[*Thursday] 4th
I writ a long & plaine letter to Mr. White, & because of my short stay desired an answer in writing in 3 or 4 daies, but hee neglected it.

[*Sunday] 7.
Mr. Jackson[2] preacht, & the morrow went to take his leave of Mr. White & had full discourse with him, & earnestly pressed [?him] to give an answer to my letter. He declared that hee would accept the composition dureing his life, but did not know how to answer my letter, [p.3.] and that if I trobled him hee would resign his Vicaridge.

[*Thursday] 11
Mr Smith of Cason[3] went to him, & discoursed fully with him particularly about the terrier. Mr. White declared hee had made & registered a new one about six yeares agoe, & hoped it was right, but said hee had noe coppy, nor could tell who signed it, but declared to Mr. Smith that hee would accept the old compostion from my tennants but did not know to answer my letter.

[*Saturday] 13
I went to take my leave of Mr. White, & wondred hee would not give mee any answer to my letter, & then I shewed him a supra, but hee prayed mee for God [?sake] not to serve him or give him any troble, & complained of his infirmities. [?I][4] told him I would forbeare because he prayed for God sake, but

1 See p.1, n.5 above.
2 William Jackson, the rector of Aldbourne.
3 Calston
4 Torn.

expected [?his answer].[1] Hee told me that hee had exhibited a terrier 5 or 6 yeares since & hoped it was right. I asked him why hee never told mee of it, but concealed it as if it would not indure the light, to which hee made idle and frivilous excuses, but declared hee would accept the old composition (as if it were a great condiscension). I asked him whether his terrier mentions the ell ridges in the peice of [?wheate] lying yearely next the church, or as hee hath pretended in any peice of wheate, whereto hee gave me noe answer, but I told him I would not now serve the supra, but must & would expect an answer whether twas out of the peice lyeing yearly next the church or not, & if doth not speedily produce the terrier & make it as it ought to bee, I would compell him to set it forth upon his oath.

John Rose tells mee it may be 30 or 40 shillings per annum.

16 October
At my comeing from Avebury I told the whole story to John Rose, who hath been before informed of most of all these transactions, & of my full purpose to have a right terrier or else &c. I directed him to inform Mr. White (as from himselfe, of my purpose & that if I don't speedily heare from Mr. White, hee shall here from mee.

20 October 1711
After our comeing to London hee writ a letter to my wife complaining of his great indisposition. She by my directions answered it the 20 day of October. See her draught .

1 November
I writ a long letter to Mr. Brinsdon, & desired him to speak with Mr. White and if possible to bring him to reason.

[Sheet 5]

Journal from 9 August 1714
1714
9 August 1714
[*Monday] 9.
We came out of London in my coach & 4 fine horses, my wife & I & her maid, Samuel[2] on horseback, my man Thomas behind the coach, the cook's maid by the carrier with some goods, on Thursday last for Avebury. Wee came to Uxbridge about 12. Wee staid till 2, & to Amersham by 5, found my sister Hicks very well and chereful, Mr. Hannds there with [?her], & Mr.Hickes, a cheesmonger in Thames Street.

1 These words are almost completely lost in a tear, as is another line of text
2 Sam in mss. Sir Richard's son.

[*Tuesday] 10
Tuesday wee broke fast with Mrs. Bent,[1] conversed freely with her daughter in law.

[*Wednesday] 11
Wee all went to church.

[*Thursday] 12
Hired a guide for 3s 6d to bring us to Maidenhead 9 miles by [ ][2] & Taploe,[3] baited at the Bere at Reading, & to the Bere at Spinham Land[4] to bed.

[*Fridday] 13
Staied near an hower at Ramsbury & before 3 came to Avebury, Samuel[5] on horsback.

[*Sunday] 15
Mr Mayo dined with us, & Farmer Rose & his wife.

[*Monday] 16.
We were about. Mr. Charles Hall[6] came came [sic] to mee & told mee hee was mistaken in the particular hee had given mee, & which [*illegible*][7] received.

[*Tuesday] 17.
Mr. Mayo & his wife dined with us. Shee went out with my wife upon the Downes. John Rose [*illegible*][8]

[*Wednesday] 18
Farmer Rose and I went to Hedington & talked there with Mr. Brooke[9] the tennant to the farme, & discoursed with him. Hee thinks the particular pretty true, only Mr. Hall[10] said hee had omitted some small parcells, and that the timber is too highly vallued, & ought not to bee vallued, if the liveings are valed at 7, 9 & 11, for that the coppyholders will oppose a sale of any timber.

The farme house is not inhabited nor habitable, but underpropt & in great

1 Perhaps Mrs Bennett?
2 Blank.
3 Taplow.
4 Speenhamland.
5 Sam in mss.
6 Perhaps he was acting as agent for the sale of land in Heddington. If so, his negotiations with Holford came to nothing; see below.
7 Indecipherable.
8 Possibly this sentence deleted in mss.
9 Conceivable Anthony Brooke, who purchased a portion of the manor of Heddington Cauntelo in 1719; see *VCH Wilts.*, 17, p.165.
10 Perhaps he was acting as agent for the sale of land in Heddington. If so, his negotiations with Holford came to nothing; see below.

decay. The tennant dwells in his coppy hold adjoyning to the farme. Sir Fr. Child[1] held it for lives Sir Francis was borne there. Tis a pretty dwelling.

[*Thursday] 19
My wife & I and Samuel[2] dined with Mr. Norris at Nonesuch.[3] Great plenty & great decency.

[*Friday] 20
Dined at home, Mr. Mayo & his wife with us.

[*Saturday] 21
I received letters from London in post in the evening. A nonsensical message from Mr. Wadman. James Andrews came to mee from Weston Birt.

[*Sunday] 22
Mr Mayo & his wife & Mr Baskerville's son[4] dined with, as did the Farmer[5] & his wife & James Andrews. Between 5 & 6 Mr. John Wadman on horseback & his wife, child, & maid, in a chaise & 2 horses & a man on horseback. Wee made the best shift wee could to receive and entertaine them, & did it pretty well, their 2 men lay at the Kath Wheele.[6]

[*Monday] 23.
My Frog[7] & I were oblieged to dine at Clatford with Madam Percival, & excused it to Mr Wadman, & left my son Samuel[8] to beare them company. Dame Andrews went home.

[*Tuesday] 24.
Bartholomews Day. Prayers in the church. My wife and I spoke fully with Mr. Wadman relateing to his letters & the £100 & £19 shee had mentioned in her letter to my wife. I showed him all the papers left with mee by my governor, & my Frog's letter to Mrs. Churchey, but did not show him Mr. Churchey's letter, for that there are some things which hee might take ill.

He would not stay to goe to church but posted away by 10, expressing great satisfaction, & pretending great haste. My Frog and I visited Mr. Mayo & his wife, & saw his improvement in his house and garden.

1 The London banker and lord mayor; cf. *ODNB*.
2 Sam in mss.
3 William Norris of Nonsuch, Bromham.
4 See p.2, n.8.
5 John Rose is presumably meant.
6 Catherine Wheel, then in the village.
7 Lady Susanna Holford.
8 Sam in mss.

[*Wednesday] 25.
Richard Caswell came to me but said noething more than that Mr. Tooker had promised him to speake to mee, & to prevent &c. Hee proposed noething, but that hee would have mee leave it to two [?mediators]. I told him that I was very desirous to prevent troble and indeavourd it in October last, & hee refused &c. I bid him to propose what hee thought fit but to doe it in writing, else &c.

He came to mee againe on Wednesday morn, & being or pretending to bee ignorant I layd before him the bill I had from Humfry Robinson in October last amounting to 3 or 4 & thyrty pounds besydes the mason & smith bills and bid him [?ex][1] of it and carefully to consider it and see what hee was cherefully willing to allow, & give it mee in writeing. Hee spent some time upon it & gave mee some particulars, to about £6 10s 0d. I bid him againe to consider of it, and that I would write to Mr. Sadler to forbere him till further order, & bid him attend Mr. Sadler tomorrow, & to come to mee again on [*Wednesday] morn, but that hee must enlarge his allowance and make it 10 guynias at the least, & that I should then bee at least £XXX Xs the looser.

Hee tells mee hee hath paid Mr. Sadler above £4 for law charges.

[p.2.] [*Thursday] 26 August 1714
Richard Caswell came to me, and wee again discoursed over the whole matter, and I againe spoke to him to peruse Humfrie's bill, now above £38, & again to consider &c. John Rose & Humfry Robinson being present, & Richard Caswell seeming trobled & very desirous to have an end of this affaire, they overruled mee to accept £10, for which hee gave his note to pay it to mee or my order by or before Michaelmas. I delivered the note to Humfry for him to receive the £10 in part of what due from mee.

[*Friday] 27.
My wife & I and Mrs. Mayo in the coach & Sam on horseback went to West Downe & Oldbury Castle.

[*Saturday] 28.
Wee went to see the Mount at Marleborough, & received great respect & civilities from Farmer Nalder[2] and his wife. Wee did not goe into the towne.

[*Sunday] 29.
Mr. Mayo & his wife and Mr. Baskerville's son, & Farmer Rose and his wife dined with us. In the afternoone I made a visite to Mr Tooker, but he was gone from home soe did not see him.

1 Perhaps 'examine'.
2 See p.3, n.6.

[*Tuesday] 31. [1]
We went to Weston Burt by Christian Malford, by Cleeve,[2] Bushton, Gretnam[3] farme. Wee staid at Weston till Fryday 13th September & thence by Dauntzey, Little Somerford to Malmesbury.[4] John Rose was our guide. Saw my Lord Wharton's little household, the Abby, King Athelstan's monument, & what else was to bee seen in the porch &c. Gott something to eate. Mr. Goodenough, John Rose, Dame Andrews with us. John Rose staid but one night and on [*Sunday] morn returned home, promising to come or to send for our cook maide on Wednesday next come 7 night.

[*Monday] 6.
Madam Gore the middle widdow came in her coach & 4 dined with us.

[*Tuesday] 7
We dined with my couzin Deacon & tooke Dame Andrews with us & were plentifully entertained. Whilst wee were there Mr. Na Stephens brought his wife to see my Frog.

[*Wednesday] 8.
Mr. Jackson's mother sent my wife a [?chint] & and 2 live turkyes.

[*Thursday] 9.
Wee dined with Dr. Goodenough. The Middle Widdow Gore dined with us. Her son & daughter Hedges were that day sent for to Compton to meet Mr Northey,[5] the late member for Calne.

[*Friday]
Wee made a visit at Alderton.

[*Saturday]
Was a very wett day we staid at home.

[*Sunday]
Mr. Robt Gore, Dr. Goodenough, Fr Gooden, Farmer Walter Watts, Wm Hiller, dined with us. In the afternoon, Mr Deacon jun & his eldest sister came to visit us.

---

1 In margin: Westonbirt.
2 Clyffe Pypard
3 Presumably Grittenham.
4 These lines are very jumbled with interlineations, and not easy to transcribe; nevertheless, a glance at the map suggests that Holford mis-recorded his route.
5 William Northey, M.P. for Calne in 1713; cf. **www.historyofparliamentonline.org/volume/1715-1754/member/northey-william-1690-1738**

[*Monday] 13.
We dined and were very genteely entertained by Mr. Nath Stevens at Chevenage.[1] I discussed with Nath Power about altering my long table in the hall[2] to take it off at the ioynt & to make 2 tables. Hee liked it & will doe it. Hee viewed the tree in the Long Meade, t'is a maiden fine tree, will make good boards & bee two lengths & about six C, which hee will get well squared and sawd & percht & then place them in the coach house for nescessary uses.

Hee will fit up the great tester bedsteed taken out of the brewhouse chamber and place it over the stable, & will make a good halfe headed bedsteed ready to bee put into the new chamber. That old bedsteed is now taken to pieces & placed in the garret. Dame Andrews, George, & John and I agreed to make & take a new lease of the farme for six years from Our Lady day next. At the same rent &c., But I promised to allow for cleaneing the 3 Stockwell closes, & to allow what fitt for making a pool in the downes, per our agreement in writing and endorsed on the last lease.

[p.3.] [*Friday] 17 September
Wee went from Weston Birt to Bath, baited ¼ of an hower at Toghill House, put up our horses at the Queens Head stables, & lodged at Mr. Hickes in the Market Place.

[*Saturday] 18.
My brother Trotman[3] and Lady Drake came to Bath from London. [*Sunday]. Wee dined and suppt with them at the Tunns.

[*Monday] 20.
They went to Siston. Wee brought them over Lands Downe[4] & afterwards tooke severall turnes on the Downes, & returned presently after 4. Wee herd the news this morn that the King and Prince came safe to Greenwich on Saturday last .

[*Tuesday]
This afternoone my Frog carried the mayor's wife and daughter[5] & our landlady Mrs. Hickes to Landsdowne.

[*Wednesday] 22
We staid at home and drank the waters.

1 Lord of the manor of Chavenage; cf. *VCH Gloucestershire,* v.11.
2 Presumably at Westonbirt.
3 Presumably Samuel Trotman, lord of the manor of Siston, and brother of Lady Susannah Holford.
4 Lansdown, the site of a Civil War battle.
5 The mayor was Richard Ford.

[*Thursday] 23
Wee went to Wells, stoped at the Red Lyon in the parish of Eaton Stoney,[1] came to the George in Wells before 3 & went to church.

[*Friday] 24.[2]
I reckoned with as many of my tennants as came to mee.[3] In the afternoone we received the Bishopp & his lady and Mrs. Prous. I went to Coll Cowards, but hee was not at home. Sent a compliment to the Recorder & his wife. Mr. Shereston an attorney there very civile to mee, is brother to Mrs. Ford the present mayor of Bath's wife, and to Mr. Bushell at the Tunns in Bath.

[*Saturday] 25.
We came from Wells to Bath.

[*Sunday] 26.
Mr. Wicherley dined with us.

[*Monday] 27.
My governor & Coll Codrington[4] came to Bath to dine with the mayor elect,[5] & returned to Siston. My son Samuel went home with him.

[*Tuesday] 28.
Dr. Bramston, Dr. Layton, Arch Deacon Hunt[6] & his wife and my landlayday dined with us.

[*Thursday] 8th October
Wee returned from Bath to Avebury. Baited at the Bere at Sandy Lane.

[*Sunday][7] 10.
My poore tennants at Beckhampton, & Fowler & his wife, dined with us.

12. Farmer Green & Farmer John Caswell & wife, Mr. Mayo and his wife, dined with us. Wee talked of the meadow at Silbury which Mr. Green hath set out into lotts & imployed John Overton to draw it. Hee hath done and given mee a coppy of it. I think tis well done, & for the benefit of everyone that is concerned. John Overton demands 40 shill for his paines. I think hee is very reasonable therein.

1 Stone Easton, Somerset.
2 In margin; Avebury returned the morrow.
3 Holford owned the manor of St Etheldred's chapel, in St Cuthbert's, Wells (also known as Southover); cf. TNA PROB 11/564/122, & Potter, Angela. *Weston Birt House and the Holfords, 1665-2017*. 4th ed. Holfords of Westonbirt Trust, 2017, p.9.
4 Probably John Codrington of Codrington (Glos.), M.P. for Bath.
5 Presumably Richard Bigges.
6 William Hunt, Archdeacon of Bath & Wells.
7 This should be Saturday. The scribe has used the wrong symbol.

My part is two shares, 20 shill. I submit to pay half, though no benefit to mee, & John Caswell to pay the other halfe, 20sh.

John Caswell and I evened our accompt for Our Lady Day last.

B. ***The Bound Journal, 1710-17***[1]

[Cover]
Wiltes Avebury and Beckhampton 1710
Perused November 6th 1767

[1st leaf].[2]

Avebury 1710
Farmer William Skeate's terme being expired, and hee refusing to continue unles &c., I agreed with John Rose to bee my tennant from Lady Day 1710, according to the course of husbandry for 8 yeares at £350 per annum.

The tenements at Backhampton purchased by mee of Charles Tooker esq – see the articles – with the personage. Truslows, and Goddards. £205 per annum & soe lett.

~~Richard~~ Edith Pointing widdow worth £1 10s 0d per annum. 2 lives, rent reserved	10-00
Mary Rose widdow £1 10s 0d per annum, 2 lives, rent reserved.	2-06
Walter Pope £1 10s 0d per annum, 2 lives, rent reserved	3-06
John Bradfield £1 per annum, 2 lives, rent reserved	3-04
	19-10

1717 October. John Bradfield is dead. Frances his daughter affirmes hath a lease for her life.

October 1717. John Caswell tells mee that there is demanded as due to the Crowne a pention of [ ][3] shillings per annum out of Backhampton Chappell.

[2nd leaf].[4]

Notes taken April 1711 out of my last yeares papers.
At my being at Avebury in April 1711, I tooke these notes relateing to Farmer Skeate & the bounds, gates & fences. Upon former discours between us & John

1 GA D1956/E2/8.
2 The first leaf is un-numbered, and its verso is blank. Page numbers follow.
3 Blank.
4 This page is also un-numbered.

Rose, they agreed to referr it to Richard Fowler[1] & Samuel Morris.[2]
Upon Farmer William Skeate's leaving my farme at Avebury, which hee had injoyed under a lease from my Lord Stawell for 12 yeares at £350 per annum, whereof about 5 yeares were expired when I bought the farme, and after I had bought & paid for it £7500, and had layd out a great deale of money in repaires, hee informed mee that though his rent was £350, yet that my Lord had promised to abate him £30 per annum, but that being willing to sell it would have £350 reserved by the lease in order to sell it, & though I bought at that rate, & although Mr Bennet, my Lord Stawell's steward, had upon my purchase offered to procure a tennant that should give £380 per annum (which I could not accept because Skeate's lease was not expired), and though everybody told mee I had a great pennyworth, yet Farmer Skeate by continuall complaints of hard times prevailed with mee to leave about £200 in his hands without interest as often as wee accompted, & compelled me to allow his pretences of repaires, especially mason's & carpenter's work, which for quietnes sake I submitted to, and when his lease expired hee cunningly staved off & discouraged other tennants, & thereby made mee promise to abate £30 per annum besydes the (£10) for half an acre of wood[3] yearely allowed by his lease, and at that rate hee continued 4 yeares, & then 4 yeares, in all 8 yeares, whereupon I being weary of his continuall complaints & exactions was willing to part with him, & to get a new tennant, in which hee practised many country tricks, telling that hee was not to goe, or that it was lett, or &c., often intimating that his brother[4] John Rose if able to compass it, would make the most of it, but must borrow at least £400 to enable him to stock it, as it ought to bee stockt.

All others being beate off, & I at a great distance could not prevent being abused, but being at Avebubury [sic] at Michaelmas 1709, and Farmer Rose his terme at Beckhampton expireing at Our Lady 1710, and I haveing heard a very good character of John Rose, his industry, dilligence and integrity, & quiet disposition, I inclined to take him my tennant to the farme at £350 per annum, & hee to beare and pay all rates & duties except the land tax by act of Parliament. In order to settle all matters, upon discours with Farmer Skeat & John Rose, I produced a counterpart of Skeate's lease from my Lord Stawell, whereby it appeared that every little thing was taken particular notice of, & not one word relateing to any abatement or allowance out of the rent. I repeated to him, as I had often before, how wretchedly hee had imposed upon mee, & made me allow £30 per annum for 8 yeares, but it was chiefly in respect that wheate was at 2s 6d or 3s the bushell, & all other grains in proportion, & that money was very scarce in the country, & not in respect of his pretences to my Lord's promise to abate

1 Innkeeper at the Hare and Hounds.

2 His house was licenced for dissenting worship in 1707, and he signed another meeting house certificate in 1723; cf. Chandler, J.H., ed. *Wiltshire Dissenting Meeting House Certificates and Registrations, 1680-1852.* Wiltshire Record Society, 40. 1985, p.14 & 20.

3 Note in left margin: 'q what is ½ an acre of wood worth'.

4 Actually brother in law.

or allow £30 per annum, it being expressly contrary to the lease, & noe note in writeing nor any witness to make out the least intimation of any such agreement. Mr Cox, a servant to my Lord,[1] & Mr Richard Smith of Kennet,[2] who Farmer Skeate named as his witnesses, expressly denying their knowledge or beleife of any such thing, but their knowledge & reasons to affirme the contrary, and yet Skeate insisted on this pretence, & affirmed, but most untruely, that hee had told mee of it before I purchased, & by his owne affirmations made himselfe a naughty man, to enter into covenant to pay £350, purposely to deceive a purchaser

[p.o.][3] But the chiefe matter now is to settle matters between John Rose & him him (sic) about the bounds & fences.

By William Skeate's lease it seemes to appeare that at his entry on the premises the bounds & fences were in great decay (John Baskerville, my Lord's former tennant, having been a very bad husband and ill tennant) wherefore Farmer Skeate then insisted to bee allowed £30 in order to set all the gates, railes, and fences in compleate repaire, and had £30 then allowed him for doeing thereof, and in his lease covenants at the end or determination of his terme to have the sum of £30. Upon reading this covenant to him he was outragious, & charged mee with cruelty that I should expect £30 & yet the bounds in good repaire.

But I presently eased him therein, that I did not expect it, but that I did expect hee should leave all the gates, railes, stiles & bounds in sufficient repaire or else repay the £30. And because hee now affirmed that the bounds is very well, & John Rose declareing the contrary, they named Richard Fowler and Samuel Morris, two experienced workmen to view all the bounds, & to see what is defective, & Farmer Skeate forthwith to amend the same or allow to John Rose the vallue thereof. All this for quietnes sake. I earnestly prest to prevent hardship or clamor on either syde, & for my owne satisfaction put it into writeing, that it might not bee forgotten.[4]

1710

I was at Avebury in September 1710, and perceived that there remained great difference between Farmer Skeate & John Rose about the bounds. I repeated to both of them the substance of what is above, & blamed John Rose for his not fully informing mee in relation to what Fowler and Morris had done.

I this sumer was overuled to remove the old woodhouse & conny house and made a very convenient building for convenience of the tennant & his family whilst wee are here. It cost mee at the least £47 (insteed of an estimate of £10). I alsoe made a pump in the brewhouse instead of the buckett well, & the brew house to be new paved, & the dairy to bee the greatest part of it new paved, & a pitched or paved path from the kitchin to the brewhouse. Cost me at least £47.

1 Presumably Lord Stawell is meant.
2 Lord of the manor of West Kennett.
3 This is the verso of the second leaf, on which o is written in pencil.
4 In margin: '£10 per annum for half an acre of wood is ¾ too much, but Farmer Skeat untruely pretended it had been [?allowed] by my lord'.

This sumer the dwelling house was new [?rippt], all save towards the garden, & all the leaden gutters repaired & put in order cost at least [ ].[1]

1712
Note. I could never prevaile with Farmer Skeate to produce his lease from my Lord Stawell, nor any of his accompts with my Lord or his agents relateing to the rent or yearely allowances or any paper relateing thereto, hee always makeing some frivilous excuse on purpose as I perceived to impose upon me as he did.

[p.1.] [*Saturday] Ultimo March 1711
[*Saturday] March 31
I came by seven this morn in the Bath coach to Avebury, found all there pretty well. My governor's man left there by the Bristoll carrier on [*Wednesday] last, was taken home on [*Tuesday] 3 April by his man who brought my guelding.

The chest of drawers where in Dame Rose had put the lynnen, which I now had occasion for, being swelled, I could not open them nor get out any lynnen, but in the afternoone Dame Rose came home from London & shee assisted mee with sheets, table cloth, & napkins for my use.

1711
I looked round upon everything. The house & every thing within dores was very nicely clean at my comeing.

[*Sunday] April 1
Mr. White preacht but did not dine with mee because of the sacrament.[2]

John Pope
In the afternoone Humfry Robinson's son in law, John Pope, was buried. I was invited, & about 3 went up. All the neighbors round were invited & a very greate many of them were there, cakes, wine & good drink. Mr. White the minister not there. A great number of the neighbors, at least 60, attended the corps to the grave, but noe minister, Mr. White haveing expressly refused to bury him because a dissenter.[3] All doe agree hee was a very quiet, honest, laborious, industrious man, & a very inoffensive neighbor, & often frequented the parish church.

Farmer Caswell & I and Farmer Rose went to view South Mead, the willows & the hatches[4] &c., and thence wee went to Beckhampton & viewed the buildings, miserable out of repaire, thence to Fowlers.[5] I bid Caswell consider &

1 Blank.
2 Holy Communion was frequently tacked on to the end of matins at Sunday services, and many worshippers departed before it was said. Holford probably left the service at this point, leaving White to carry on.
3 His burial is recorded in the parish register, 1st April 1711. For White's refusal to bury dissenters, see *AWS*, p.411 & 426-7.
4 For controlling the flow of water in the water meadows.
5 The Folly (originally the Bear).

to let mee know tomorow whether he will leave Beckhampton or not.

[*Monday] 2 April
Mr. John Griffin came to mee by 7. Farmer Rose made him a toast &c. Hee of his own accord offered his assistance for an inclossure of the barren land near to Fowler's,[1] for which I thanked him, & will accept his assistance when I can.

William Pitt[2]
William Pitt came to me from Potterne, & brought me a gamon of bacon & some apples, & I found that he & his mother & all the children are in a pretty good condition.

Mr Smith
Counsellor Pontin came to mee to speak with me about Captain Scoles' wife's estate,[3] but I refused to give any kind of directions, but left him to doe or say what hee thinks fitt to them without nameing or concerning mee in the matter. Farmer Richard Caswell promised last night to call on mee this forenoone but did not. After dinner John Rose & Humfry Robinson went with mee to Beckhampton. We first looked upon the house, late Goddards, & they went into it & viewed it, & considered the charge of makeing it into two tenements & to make the two chymneys usefull & the dores, thatch, & everything as it ought to bee, for all which Humfry demanded & will undertake to finish all the worke, & to find all matterialls, for five pounds to make it two compleat tenements.

[p.2.] Wee then looked over all the bounds, & the defects of the Parsonage house, barnes & stables. All in a miserable condition as to repaires. I could but find fault with Richard Caswell, that hee tooke a lease without haveing had the usuall repaires, as Mr Tooker had covenanted in his lease. Mr. White and Mr. John Griffin dined with mee, a good leg of veale, bacon & coleworts,[4] with a surloyne of rost biefe, very good.

3 April
Farmer Skeate came to me, & brought his book, and the receipts for money paid, but did not bring the notes I drew on him & directed him to pay for my use, which displeased mee because I had pressed him for them, & in January last, when hee was in London, he had promised to get them into his hands & to let mee have them. Hee dined with me but presently after dinner went away, because it was their day for passing their parish accompts.

Hee left his book of accompts with me tille my coming back hither out of

1 Richard Fowler, innkeeper at the Folly. One wonders whether this land was being used by drovers who stayed at the Folly to rest their beasts overnight.

2 WSHC catalogue entries suggest that the Pitt family were prominent in 18th c Potterne.

3 Jasper Scoles married Joan, the widow of Thomas Smith, lord of the manor of West Kennett, and is mentioned in the common recovery by which the Smith family settlement was broken in 13th May 1712; see WSHC 568/5.

4 A type of cabbage, common in the 18th century, but now rarely grown.

Gloucester[1] I told him that I hoped to bee here by or before [*Thursday] 12th of April.

4. I spoke fully with Richard Caswell; see my notes thereof. The same day John Lad came to mee & expected to receive some money, but I was plaine with him, see my notes taken thereof, & how basely hee had dealt with mee in the floore of the parlor chamber.

6. Went from Avebury towards Weston Birt. By the unkind weather forct to lye at Chipenham. The morrow I called on Mr Goodenough,[2] who was home the last night from London.

7. I came to Weston Birt. See my notes of what done there. I staid there till the 13th.

13. I came to Avebury called & staid ½ an hower at Rowden with William Skeate.

14. I spent all my time Saturday in viewing what done & what to bee done by John Rose, and I walked about the grounds to view the repaires &c.

I spoke fully with Richard Caswell. Hee & Fowler & Rose went with mee to see the trespass & way cross the corne feilds at Beckhampton. They promised to speake with the ancient inhabitants & people that can best informe themselves & mee relateing to this way, & how to remedie it, & to give mee their testimony in writeing, whereon I might depend, & might indeavour to remedy the abuse. I am of opinion that there is an ancient pack & padway from Devizes to Malbrough, but not a cartway. They now used it as a common wagon & cartway, nay, they pass that way & cross West Downe to Calne with their heavy carriages, which is very injurious, & fit to be remedied therefore &c.

[p.3.] Richard Caswell
Avebury April 1711
Memorandum. Farmer Richard Caswell haveing by severall letters told me of his desire to leave Beckhampton, because hee hath taken or was about takeing another farme more convenient, & neare to his father and mother, who are antient, & desire hee should bee close to them at Cherrill[3], I answered his letters that I could not resolve what to doe, till I should bee there, & that I could not till then answer his propositions of accepting his uncle John Caswell of All Cannings[4] to be my tennant in his rome.

[*Sunday] 1 April
I now spoke fully with him thereabouts, & spoke to him to declare plainely

1 i.e. from Westonbirt.
2 Of Sherston; he received £10 in Sir Richard Holford's will, TNA PROB11/564/122.
3 Cherhill.
4 Probably Bishops Cannings was intended; cf. *AWS*, p.61

whether hee did intend to remove or not, & if hee resolved to remove I should bee easily prevailed on to consent thereto, soe as hee left the bounds & fences in good repaire, and the thatch of the houses which are now very much out of repaire by the late tempestuous wind, but that I would not promise to take his uncle to bee my tennant until further considered of it.

[*Monday] 2 April
I being at Beckhampton, John Caswell was there. I told them to the same effect as above, & bid Richard Caswell give mee his plaine & positive answer the morrow, which hee promised to do, & that I would then quickly resolve.

I had then a tennant proposed to me (Thomas Nash of Cannings[1]) who I liked much better than either of the Caswells, hee being a sensible faishionable man & reputed a very honest man & a good husband, and about £60 per annum of his owne estate in Cannings, & a more desirable tennant, and John Caswell being antient, & haveing 5 or six sonns at home with him, several of them very much impaired in their health, & not likely to imploy the poor labouring neighbors. I did not readily accept him, till I had Richard Caswell's positive answer.

[*Wednesday] 4.
Richard haveing some intimation that Nash was like to bee my tennant & not haveing declared &c., I rid up to him & took John Rose & him to Fowlers,[2] and hee then and there declared that hee did not incline to remove, unless his uncle might come thither, which I expressly refused, for that I would not have a tennant forct upon mee, & thereupon wee parted, but I desired him not to neglect the hatch[3] & the bounds, but forthwith to doe all that requires &c.

Nash waited the meane while at my house to know &c., & John Rose told him what had passed, wherewith he seemed well satisfied.

April 15
Richard Caswell
At my returne out of Gloucestershire Richard Caswell came to mee on Sunday 15 April, but said noething in relation to his leaeveing Beckhampton, but told mee of Mr White's persecuting of him with great severity, &c., and prayed mee to reconcile them. I told him that I was & should bee ready & willing to doe all good offices, & if they signified their desire would willingly heare both sydes & give them my best advice and directions, but that without their consent I was not willing to concern myself.

[p.4.][4] 1710
Expences at Avebury in necessary repaires when John Rose came thyther and in

1 Probably Bishops Cannings.
2 Probably a reference to the White Hart at West Kennett, run by the Fowler family.
3 For the water meadow. It had to be opened and closed at regular intervals.
4 The verso of this page is blank and un-numbered.

order to make all things convient.

The house now repairet and all the leads, gutters, tyle, &c substantially done, except the tyle towards the garden for which I paid Overton[1] the tyler of the Devizes, and for masons, carpenters' work, bricks, tyles, lyme, smith's work &c., for removeing the woodhouse & conny house &c., and seting the same where it now is, to fence in the [?Peark] Court, and for a dore to that Court and makeing in that new building a convenient rome for a kitchen & another conveniet rome & a little chamber over the kitchin, which, with the brewhouse & dry larder within it, may bee fully sufficient for the use of the tennant's family &c., whilst wee are there. It cost mee at the least	£47-00-00
The same	
Other work since done by Humfry Robinson, the glazier, and others	£3-18-00
The Well	
Turneing the buckett well in the brewhouse, & making an excellent pump there, cost at the least	£5-00-00
The Brewhouse & dairy	
New paving the dairy, and new paving the brewehouse, wherein but little of the old stone would serve, at least	£5-00-00
New building, little house	£9-10-00
New tiling the romes over the dairy at best 10m of new tyles, carriage, & turnepike 4s 10d.,[2] [illegible] lyme, pinns &c., at the least all the bills amount to £51 10s	£51-10-06
Paveing the porch in the backyard, & a path to the kitchin and new pitching there at the least (tis part of the £9 6s)	

1 John Overton, who is mentioned several times below.
2 Or perhaps £4 10s is meant.

6-00

Planting a double hedge to part the garden from Barr Close, wood plant & labor &c., about £6.

£6-00-00

Besydes the new piping the house all save towards the garden the mending all the leaden pipes, all the rowe cast &c., cost me at least £30.

£30-00-00

John Rose desires a wall from the end of the old stable to the Syccomore trees on the Wall Ditch, & to turne it off to the end of the new barne, which will take up nine lug of wall, & to have it eight foot high, 12 shillings per lug makeing, and will require [ ][1] lode of stone at 3 shillings per lode, [ ][2] quarters of cours lyme at [ ][3] per quarter, 37 lodes of gravell or earth at 1s 6d per lode, timber & thatch at least, and the mason's work at least 12 shillings per lug.

Hee likewise desires there may bee a penthouse or leanetoo there for sheltering his cattle & rayles & gates from the stable & hows & the charge [ ][4]

A Shedd

John Rose affirms that it will save half the fodder & soyle, & bee a great comfort to his cattell, & very beneficial, & the Syccamore ground & the ditch of great advantage when soe separated, at least 40 shillings per annum.

A gate to the Cherry Court

£6-00-00

Making a gate to the Cherry Court: Humfry Robinson for the wood worke £4; to Thomas Jordan for iron work 40 shillings.

[p.5.] 1711 July 30
Journey to Avebury 1711 & what done there
I came out of London with my wife and her maid [?Chenell] in my coach & 4

1 Blank.
2 Blank.
3 Blank.
4 Blank.

horses, Richard Bradney my coachman, John Hutchins[1] my footman, Mary the cooke maid being sent before or by the carrier with some goods.

Wee had the company of my Lady Drake, Madam Trotman,[2] Mr Thrup & Rachell in her coach & six, Mr Warren, the Batts & John Penny, a footman on horseback, & Austen a footman behind the coach. Wee baited at Stow, lay at the Bere at Reading.

31 Baited at the Bere at Spinhamland, lay at the Angell in Marlebrough. John Rose met us at Marlbrough in the morn by 6.

[*Wednesday] 1 August
Before 8 wee came to Avebury, stopt a little at the Kath Wheele & my Lady Drake pursued her journey, but sent 5 shillings to the ringers.

At my coming I was displeased to find the pavement in the garden not begun nor any of the Busleton stone brought, though it was to have been finisht in June.

The gate to the Cherry Court set up & painted this morning but noe [?iregeere][3] on it, though undertaken and promised to be finisht in June.

The grate in the kitchen not set up till this morning, noe racks nor fender, but a paire of borrowed racks, noe jack but the little one Jordan lent us the last yeare. Hee pretended he could not get a better though sent often to get one.
I that day talked fuly with Mr. White, & went over as many particulars as I could call to mind of his great unkindness. He [?continues] in his most absurd humors. See the notes I took in a single paper.

Humfry Robinson worked to finish the new little kitchin for the farmer's use.

Orchard

William Thomas, a gardener who dwells at Broad Towne came to speak with me about planting the orchard. Hee viewed the ground & liked it very well, & that it will take neare 100 trees. Some of those there may stand. Hee will if imployed undertake to doe it well & as cheape as any man, & take care of theire good fruite of every sorte, & will undertake to preserve them & to supply any decay or defect. Hee will come again to mee before Michaelmas.

A great riot by Calne people

A very grievous complaint was made to mee by severall of the inhabitants of Avebury, that's at least 25 of Calne people came yesterday & this day to gleane & lease corne in Avebury field, & beate some of the men & weomen of Avebury & threatened to kill them. Particularly … a woman of Calne cut off her haire

1 Holford uses the spelling Hitchins elsewhere in this manuscript.

2 Lady Drake was the wife of Samuel Trotman, Sir Richard's brother in law; cf. Phillimore, W.P.W. *Collections relating to the Family of Trotman*. Privately published, 1892, p.65. Madam Trotman must have been one of his relatives.

3 Iron ware.

yesterday & threatened to beat, & did beat severall, & flourisht her knife &c.

Upon their complaint I sent my coachman Richard Bradney to indeavor to preserve the peace. He did soe, but brought me a very melancholly account of the bad behaviour of the Calne women.

August
[*Wednesday][1] 3.
The Calne weomen fetcht a warrant from Mr Tooker against … Fowler[2] & other inhabitants of Avebury who attended him, but I think hee did noething therein.

[*Saturday] 4.
I received 2 letters, one from my son Robert, which mentions a basket sent by Mr. Green by the coach (but I received none). The other from my son Samuel to his mother.

[*Sunday] 5.
Mr. White, the farmer & his wife, his Mother Rose, & Mother Skeat[3]e, and my tennants at Beckhampton, the Widdow Rose, Widdow Pontin & Frances Bradfield dined with us.

[*Monday] 6.
The poor women came againe to mee & complained that the Calne women to the number of 50 are again come into the corne field to plunder & threaten the Avebury weomen to take away their lives if resisted.

[p.6.] The fighting woman of Calne [ ][4] not prevailing to have her will then went to Mr Tooker's at Kennet[5] to sweare the peace against Richard Fowler's son & 2 more of Avebury, but Mr Tooker refused to grant a warrant. Shee afterwards obtained a warrant from Mr Montague & Mr Thomas Long & the men & some of the neighbors, John Rose and Mr Griffen[6] with them. Mr Montague put an end to the wrangle, but I think made the men pay this 5 & different woman.

The new gates set up, but not finished, the paved walk nothing done.

[*Tuesday] 14 August
I went from Avebury to Weston Burt, & my wife & 2 maids in the coach, John on horseback, John Rose our guide, by Highway, Christian Malford, Sutton, Draycot &c., to Weston Birt, thence the 28 to Siston, the 4 September wee went into Wells by Keinsham.

1 Actually Friday; Holford used the wrong symbol if the symbols for the following days are accurate.
2 Richard Fowler's son (see below).
3 Presumably Elizabeth Skeat, William's wife.
4 Blank space.
5 East Kennett.
6 Presumably John Griffin.

[*Tuesday] 28 August
John … my governor's gamekeeper, brought us to Marsbury,[1] thence by High Sutton & Chewton to Wells. Lay at the George.

[*Thursday] 7 September
Returned the same way to Siston, & from thence [*Monday] 17th to Bath, lay at Mr Cornishe's at the Abby Gate, our coach & horses at the Lamb. Thence [*Thursday] 27 to Imber by Steple Ashton, Tinhead & up that hollow way, very good.

[?Monday] 1 October.
Wee came from Imber by the Lyde Way[2] to Avebury.

Avebury [*Monday] 1 October
Nothing done to the paveing which vext mee. On Wednesday Mr Nicholls sent one man to work, & on Friday another, but very unskillfull &c.

The Chancellor & Registrar of Salisbury were brought to Avebury by Pontin & Caswell to examine witnesses against Mr. White, the last [?mostly] indeavord, & the Chancellor Mr Loggin made them friends.

When I went last from here, Mr. White dined with us the day before. I then spoke freely to him & put him in mind of his rough temper & his not burieing the dead & omitting other duties expressly injoyned by the litturgie &c. He tooke it very ill, and told me I feasted him, but run the spitt in his gutts.

I tooke a note in a single sheet relateing to Mr White
Now at my comeing I expected hee would visite us, but hee did not, & meeting him on [*Wednesday] at church, I sent my man to invite him to dine with us, but hee returnd a rude answer, wherefore on the 4 of October I writt him a long & plaine letter offerring friendship, & prayd him to let mee have an answer in writeing in 3 or 4 daies, because of my short stay here.

[*Saturday] 6 October
Mr Jackson[3] came hither & preacht on Sunday, woe to the world because of offence; offences will come, but woe to them by whome they come.

[*Monday] 8.
Mr. White came, & thanked him for Mr Jackson's very good sermon. Mr Jackson made a visit to Clatford

9 Hee visited Mr. White.

1 Presumably Marksbury (Somerset) is meant.
2 Probably through Urchfont.
3 William Jackson, vicar of Aldbourne.

10. We dined at Nonsuch[1] and returned at night.

11-12 ***The bills & [?receipts] left in my berrow.***

I paid several workmen's bills:	
Humfry Robinson's bill of £24 6s 7d, & £10 3s 7d. Paid him	£34-10-00
John Overton the tyler £21 17s 10d. Paid him £20 15s & gold 2s 6d.	. £20-17-06
Thomas Sadler the glazier's bill £4 9s 8d paid him	£4-06-00
Thomas Jordan the smith's bill £3 18s 8d. Paid him	£3-13-06
Abated 5s for lad.[2]	
William Crooke the mason's bill £4 04s 04d. Paid	£4-00-00
	£67-07-00

[p.7.] 1711
October 12
I ordered John Rose to pay Mr Nichols £9-10s-0d in full of that bil now delivered by him to mee as due for the brewhouse, dairy &c., which is farr more than was at 1st proposed. £9-10-00.

Mr Nichols hath very much abused mee in not laying the pavement in the garden till now, in the wet & frost, which certainly will doe it noe good. It is not now layd above halfe way, & with small stones, good for little.

A gardener
When I was here in August William Thomas, a gardener who dwells at Broad Towne offered his services to plant an orchard. I shewed him the orchard; hee guessed that it will take 80 or 100 trees. John Rose advised to make an orchard of the Sheir Barton. I bid Thomas come to mee about Michaelmas, when I purpose to againe at Avebury.

October 5th
Hee came to mee. I directed him to make a nursery between the orchard & the new hedge, as some of the stones are taken away, which J Rose will speedily remove, but not to plant any fruit trees in the orchard or Shere Barton till further order. Hee brought & gave mee a little lyme tree, & planted it at the dore going out of the Shere Barton to the church yard.

[*Tuesday] 11 October
Caswell
Richard Caswell brought his paper of disbursments, & made up his account till our Lady last, and I, alloweing what disbursed & what paid, received then

1 The home of William Norris at Bromham.
2 It is not elear whether this refers to the previous or the subsequent entry.

due £29 10s 00d. See his accompt. Hee promiseth to pay this £29 10s-00d on Saturday next. See my note relateing to Caswell & Backhampton.[1]

Dairy

John Overton estimates the tyling of the dairy between 5 & 6 perch, 5 loads of tyle, or 5 M[2] will cost 16s per M at the quar[3] neare Corsham; carriage from the quar to the Devizes 13s; from thence hither 8s per M; six sacks of lyme at 1s 8d – 10s; six hundred of hard laths at 1s 6d per C.[4] Workmanship, nailes &c., 40 shillings, & that twill come to about £13.

John Rose thinks to fetch the tyle from Weston Burt, the price there being 10 shillings per M, & the carriage somewhat cheaper than from Corsham.

John Rose againe proposed and prayed mee to build a skelling at the uper end of the barton, that it will save fodder, save the soyle or dung, shelter his cattell, & bee of wonderfull comfort & benefit to him & the Syccomore Close & ditch very beneficial.

Shed or skelling

William Crook & John Rose measured it from the end of the new barne to the Syccomore tree on the banck, 9 lug, & to make a wall 8 foot high will take up 27 loads of stones, & that the stones at the great wallnut tree will doe it[5]
Estimate for a skelling

the stones at 3s per load	£4-01-00
The masons' worke 12s per lug	5-08-00
4 wagon loads of cours lyme at 2s 6d	10-00
3 loades of gravel to every lug of wall at 1s 4d	2-14-00
4 posts to support the shedd	6-00
Six peices of timber & work about the shedd or skelling	2-08-00
Humfry Robinson estimates the timber work, rafters, and to make a very substantiall gate, good posts & rayles, & a little gate from the corner of that wall to the old stable will cost above £20, besydes iregear[6] say	21-00-00
	£36-05-00[7]

Nothing concluded on but I proposed to beare halfe the charge & straw for thatch &c.

1 This paragraph is followed in the mss by a wide blank space.
2 The Roman numeral for 1,000.
3 Quarry.
4 The Roman numeral for 100.
5 Is this a reference to the megaliths?
6 Iron ware.
7 The actual total is £36-07-00.

[p.8.] Avebury June 1712

Whitsontyde 1712

Tuesday 10 Junii 1712. I came to Avebury in the Bath flying coach by ten, my footman John Hicthins[1] with me.

A dry spring

A dry spring. After dinner John Rose, Humfry Robinson, & I walked around the Briefe Field.A very dry season, the grass very short, & not one spoonefull of water in the brook.

[*Wednesday].

I sent to desire Jonathan Nichols the mason to come to mee, but he was not at home.

Paveing

Some of our bottle drink musty & mothery, by reason of bad corks, or the bottles not dry. Farmer Rose went to Chipenham & brought home a quarter of lamb & leg & shoulder of mutton at 3¼d per pound. Hee saw a nag which Emanuel Skeate[2] recommended, but I did not like the price, nor the trot, nor pace, & full 7 yeares old.

[*Thursday].

Nichols came to mee. I showd him the great defects of the pavement, as far as it was layd. The frost had torne & shattered it soe that it is scandalousous &c. Hee acknowledged it to bee very bad, & beggd mee to excuse it, & promised to make amends & to doe it better, & with better stone, & should last forever, & to finish it by the end of this month, nay within a fortnight. Wee again spoke fully about a garden dore, whether to have it of freestone or timber, & at length agreed to have it, as the mason called it, a pellament freestone dore case, & will make it very substantiall and creditable.

Garden dore

Humfry Robinson hath a dore which hee made for this place above 12 months last past, & will put it up as soone as the mason's work is done. I charged them to let their worke bee well done, & in time. Nichols now undertaks perimptorily to finish the whole by this day month, or 2 or 3 daies after, without any excuse or further delay, & that noe man shall find fault with it, and that the pavement shalbee as good as any at Compton House.[3]

A new dore to the stable

I then talked with Humfry Robinson & Crook about a dore to bee made out

1 Hitchins is meant; see below.
2 The son of Holford's former tenant, William Skeat.
3 Probably a reference to Compton Park House, the home of the Penruddock family.

of the garden into the stable, & to have 2 stout peices for lantornes[1] & good substantiall dore posts, & a good substantial double oke door. They agreed to doe it forthwith.

Uping stock

Note the quoin stones to bee now taken out of the garden dore wilbee of noe use in that place, but will make very good steps for an upping stock,[2] which I would have made against the end of the stable. John Rose will provide a capstone. I think that window may bee walled up, & the uping stock placed there. Mr Crook will doe it well, as I charged him.

The penthous, shedd, or skilling

Farmer Rose now againe renewed the discours about the shed or skelling, & the great benefit to bee thereby to the farme. I proposed to beare halfe the charge. They are sure the stones already provided will bee enough for the wall (which stands mee in 3 shillings per loade) & the 2 trees in the Shere Barton cannot bee less worth than £6. The posts, rayless, gates, and iregeere,[3] ought to bee very substantiall. Humfry Robinson often measured & took an exact account of all the timber worke & will undertake to doe all the posts, rafters &c., for the skelling. The posts, rayles, great gate or yate & a lesser gate for common use for £23. Noething agreed on save for that to remove the stones out of the Close, & the mason to goe to work as soone as hee will. Humfry demands too much for the tymber work.

2 July

I received a letter from John Eatwal of Moncton[4] (an absolute stranger to mee) that he had seen & measured the whole timber worke, & proposed to doe it perfectly well, with good & seasond timber, for £21. John Rose told mee that Humfry would undertake it, & doe it as well as any man & as cheape.

[p.9.] My Journey from London 1712
August 1712
[*Tuesday] August 12

Avebury

We came out of London (my wife and her maid [?Clench], my sister Hickes and myselfe in my owne coach & 4 horses, the leaders bought last weeke of Mr. Robinson in Wedge Lane cost mee £45, my coachman William Jones, my footman John Hitchins upon my new nag bought by John Rose & sent to mee by Ruben Horsell, my sister Hickes boy Jack behind the coach. Baited at the Crowne at Stow, lay at the Bere at Reading Wednesday baited at the Bear at Spinhamland, lay at the Angell at Marelbrough, & God be thanked, came safe

1 Lanterns.
2 A mounting block.
3 Iron ware.
4 Winterbourne Monkton

hither [*Thursday] by 9.

Mr Nichols the mason had finished the pavement in the garden, but not till Saturday last. Tis not well done, & the freestone gate is very slight. The stable dore there is pretty well don. Is not double, but not soe well as intended. I intend at that end of the stable to make a saddle house.

The garden dore &c

When I came Humfry Robinson was puting up the timber worke for tyleing the wall there, but I stopt it inclyneing rather to have it coped with freestone. The free masons have agreed with John Rose to doe it with excellent freestone, near 3 foot wydd & 7 inches thick, for 16d per foot, whereto I the rather inclined for that as the dore case is now set up, the tyles would bee almost as high as the dore case. But the copeing with freestone will not bee soe high by about a foot, whereby the dore case will gaine soe much, & alsoe the view of the Barton or backside will bee now open to the parlour chamber windows, and because the timber frame is now already prepared for that wall, I intend to make use of it for tyleing that part of the wall which is now thatcht between that garden & the Shere Barton, & to bee at the charge to carry it on to that part of that wall which is already tyled, & this is to bee done forthwith.

Humfrey Robinson hath put up some [?boades][1] between the stable & the coach house and made it pretty fine.

[*Wednesday] 15

Pavement

Mr Nichols the mason came to mee. I shewd him the great defects of the paveing & the dore case, & was displeased with him for not doeing it as well as hee undertook & promised, & told him I would not pay him till I could see how the wynter shall agree with the paveing, the rather alsoe for that he hath made me waite for the doeing of it above 15 months.

Dairy

The dayry is now very well tyled, and is hansome & safe, but very deare.

Stable dore

The new dore to the stable is placed where I ordered it, but I ordered a double dore & tis only a single dore.

I now put on a new parltoo catch. John Rose bought it at Chipenham for 16d. Humfry Robinson put on a lock, but the dore was not what I orderd.

A saddle house

I now ordered Humfry to make a saddle house at the end of the stable ,& to put up two rowes of strong pinns, the dore to open into the stable will take up more than one [?state], and I ordered William Crooke, the rough mason, to wall up the

1 Perhaps Holford missed out an 'r', and meant 'boardes'

window, & to make an uping stock, which hee did where the window is walled up.

William Crooke now worked upon the wall intended for the skelling at the upper end of the Barton, & will finish it forthwith, thinks there are stones enough at the end of the orchard[1] to finish the wall, that Humfry Robinson may bee ready with the timber work, & put it up as soone as the mason hath done, & take care to cover it well with good straw.

The Garden Wall Coping

The garden dore & dore case is too slight & too low, & Humfry in order to have the wall tiled hath put up the timberwork. When the tyle is on it will make the dore look low & little, & John Rose telling mee that a mason of Corsham, haveing seen and measured it, will undertake for [ ][2] per foot to cope it with an excellent hard freestone ariseinge in a quar about Corsham Ridge that shalbee about [ ][3] inches wyde & about [ ][4] inches thick in the middle. I thereupon orderd Humfry not to proceed further thereon, but that the timber work may bee used on the syde of the garden towards the Shere Barton, which I now purposed to be coped with tyle, & directed John Rose to set the mason to worke.

[*Wednesday] 27 August
We went from Avebury to Weston Birt

[p.10.] 1712
[*Saturday] 20 September
I left my wife at Siston and came to Avebury, where I staied till the 27th & then returned to Siston.[5] William Crook had finished the wall for the skelling, & I think done it very well, & Humfry is preparing the timber work.

The copeing of freestone is put up & I think pretty well by a mason imployed by John Rose, but not soe thick nor soe wide as I expected.

John Overton came to worke on that wall between the garden & the Shere Barton, & worked up all the tyle hee had, & hee & John Rose will contrive to have more forthwith, & to finish that wall to that part which is already tyled, next the house.

1 Is this a reference to the megaliths?
2 Blank.
3 Blank.
4 Blank.
5 Obscured.

Trotman's wedding October 7[1]

24. John Overton patcht up some holes in my wife's closet or dressing rome. I staid at Siston from 27 September till 7 of October, & then return to Avebury leaving my wife & sister Hicks there to assist at the wedding to bee solemnized Thursday the 16th.

Lyme burner

The lyme burner William Wallis brought mee his bill for lyme delivered in 1710, 1711, 1712. John Rose affirmes him to bee a very honest man. I orderd John Rose to pay him £6 in full & to take his receipt.

Jonathan Nichols £12

Jonath Nichols brought mee his bill for the pavement in the garden, & with the pavement before the new dore to the stable makes it 1008 foot, which at 5d per foot comes to £21, and for the freestone dore case £3, & for other worke 13s, in all £24-13s-0d. I ordered Farmer Rose to pay him £12, but noe more, for that hee hath made mee waite a yeare & halfe, & made use of very unfit stone, and the winter tore it in peeces, & when he saw it hee complained that hee had been abused & beggd pardon, & prayed to amend it and to make it faire & good, but whether it bee soe or not is very doubtful, therefore not pay more till wee see how twill agree with the winter weather. Query[2] sand & lyme

John Overton £3 16s 0d

John Overton brought mee his bill for worke about the dairy house &c. Comes to £3 10s 10d, besides 5s 8d for 1 stone, 17li & ½ of lead. I ordered John Rose to pay him £3-16s 0d in full & take his receipt.

Note the worke done at the garden wall is not yet reckoned.

William Crooke £10

William Crook the mason's bill is £10 4s 5d, whereof £5 17s 0d for the wall at the skelling or shed, the rest for the stable, new dore, wall, the garden dore wall, the uping-stook & walling up the window there & other jobbs. I ordered John Rose to pay him £10 in full & to take his receipt.

Thomas Jordan £3 14s 0d

Thomas Jordans bill is £3 14s for smith's work, whereof the racks, fender for the kitchen chyney, & new barr for the kitchen grate, comes to £1 16s 6d, the rest is for the iron worke for the stable new dore, garden new dore, & other jobbs. I ordered John Rose to pay Thomas Jordan £3 14s 0d in full & take his receipt.

1 This was the marriage of Dorothea Trotman, daughter of Samuel TrotmanHolford's brother in law, to Samuel Trotman of Bucknell, at Siston; cf. Phillimore, W.P.W. *Collections relating to the Family of Trotman*. Privately published, 1892, p.23. The proceedings were described in Sanders, John. 'John Sanders, his book, 1712: the account of my travils with my Mistress', *Records of Buckinghamshire*, 3, 1870, p.96-8.

2 Q in text.

Hee must make good the [?cheekes] in the kitchen grate.

Humfry Robinson brought mee his bill 28 September tot £22 12s 11d, but in it hee hath charged forty shillings for work done in Farmer Skeate's time in repaires. Hee was by covenant to keepe & to leave every thing in good repaire, but left all the bounds, fences &c in great disorder & defective, & though by his covenant hee was to leave all in good repaire, & to repay £30 which hee received in money at his comeing on, yet hee hath done neither. I have refused, & doe refuse, to pay his 40 shillings.

A great many of the other items are for repaires which the tennant is bound to, but at John Rose his comeing on I have taken care that every thing within dore & without should bee & is put into suche repaire.

The worke done at Backhampton I am not willing to allow, for that the tennant don't deale well with mee.

[p.11.] 1712
26 September 1712
Humfry Robinson
John Rose. Pray pay Humfry Robinson the sum of £18, & take his receipt for it. His bill is above £22, but £2 there are not to bee paid by mee, & some ther doubts thereupon, therefore not now to pay more than £18. His bill for the new skilly, not yet brought in, nor his work done thereabout.

I went from hence 27th to Siston, & there staied till Tuesday the 7th October, & came thence hyther in order to goe to London.

7 October
I left my Frog & my sister Hickes & Jack there to attend the great ceremoney designed for [*Thursday] the 16 of October, for which wonderfull preparations are made, & will without doubt bee cherefully accomplisht to the satisfaction of all concerned. My Lady Read and her eldest daughter there, & Mr Dashwood with … heres … & … servants.

9th
Glazier £1 13s 0d. Tis £55 3s 0d n.b.[1]
Thomas Sadler the glazier brought mee his bill £1 13s 6d,[2] but hee reckons too much in almost every article, especially 2s too much for colloring the stable & garden dores, not well done. I under his bill ordered John Rose to pay him £1 13s, & take his receipt in full.

John Rose hath already payd to the free mason for copeing the garden wall, by the garden gate £3 4s 6d, & will place it to his next account. See John Rose his accompt in my other book

1 The meaning of the last clause is not clear.
2 This does not agree with the note in the margin.

[*Sunday] 12 October
I went to Avebury in my owne coach, & tomorrow to London in the Newberry[1] coach.

[*Wednesday] 27 October
I returned by the Bath coach to Avebury. John Rose hath paid Mr. Smith of Tockenham £30 & taken his acquitance for the £30 paid to Mr Wall, & for the £35, & now gave mee Mr Smith's acquittance taken for £60 for two yeares interest £600 due at Michaelmas last by mortgage.

31 October 1712
Richard Fowler brought mee a bill for 5 trees planted on Silbry Hill, & for fencing them, & for other worke, in all £2. Hee owed mee for his rent due at Michaelmas last 4s per annum xiis and I ordered Farmer Rose to pay him £1 8s in full of his bill. Fowler promiseth hee will take care to preserve those trees. Farmer Rose & Richard Fowler now planted twelve apple trees on the banck between the two new hedges, between the orchard & Barr Close. I tooke the name of the apples.

12 Apple trees
2 Kentish pippins, 2 golden pippins, 2 Kenton pippins, & 2 golden russetes, as the gardener had marked them. I left the numbers in a note in the kitchen chamber closet.

John Caswell
I that day agreed with Farmer John Caswell to let the estate at Backhampton to him for 4 yeares at the same rent & under the same covenants as in Mr Tooker's lease to Richard Caswell, which will expire at Lady Day next, but hee not to plow more than 150 acres any one yeare, the rest to lye still, & at the end of that fower years for fower yeares more, unless either party shall one full yeare before the end of the first 4 yeares, give notice in writeing to the contrary.

Richard Caswell's covenant in his lease is to leave the premises in good repaire. It is now very much out of repair. By his own neglect, Mr Tooker haveing in the lease covenanted to put it in good tennantable repair by the 2d of June 1709, but did not. Richard Caswell will endeaver to give mee full satisfaction.

[p.12.] Avebury 10 October 1713
Farmer John Caswell on behalf of himselfe & Richard Caswell new tenant accompts with mee, from said last last accompt 9 October 1712, there then rested due to me at Lady 1712, £79 14s 00d.

Where off Emanuel Skeate paid me for him to mee	£69-14-00
Hee paid for mee to John Rose	£10-00-00
	£79-14-00

1 Newbury.

See the accompt evend to Our Lady Day 1712.

Note hee hath also paid for mee to John Rose three pounds for two yeares rent of Goddard's Tenement, which he received of Mrs Truslow due at Michaelmas 1712, for which John Rose is to accompt to mee.

21 October 1713
John Caswell tells me he hath received another load, 800 of bricks from Worton. I prayd him to take care they are not imbezeled nor misused.

Note
Richard Caswell haveing left the bounds & fences, & the barnes, gates, rayles, stables, &c., in great decay, & utterly out of repaires, and plowed more than, I resented it, & having his covenant in his lease to Mr Tooker to leave everything in tennantable &c., John Caswell makeing grivious complaint, I prayd Humfry Robinson to see it, & to tell mee what is fit to be done, & the charge, & prayed John Caswell to assist him therein, and send my request to Richard Caswell.

A partition in the Cellar
John Caswell's wife complained for lack of a partition in the cellar to keepe a little good drink & that twould cost but 20 shillings. I promised it should bee done.

Dairy
She shewed mee her dairy & complained that it was too little & very inconvenient, & shewed mee how it might bee made much better for a small charge. I talked thereof to Humfry, & to Mr Crook the mason, and directed them to doe it, & to mend the [?drook] at the well, because I would make them as easy as I could.

House of office
Shee also complained that there was noe house of office, & that at 20 shillings with the old matterials would make one as good as shee desired. I told her if shee did get it well done, I would at the end of their terme allow what was fit, if left in good repair. But I prayed her to let it well done.

Richard Caswell
I sent severall times by John Rose and John Caswell &c to desire Richard Caswell to look out his covenant, & to propose to me what hee thought fit to allow. Hee refused to come to mee, but sent rude answer, & said that Mr Tooker ought to doe it, or to that effect, & never came neare mee, though I staid till 28 October, wherefore in Hillary terme I directed Mr Sadler of the Devizes to bring an action in the name of Mr Tooker for breach of covenant in plowing more than 2 thyrds, & leaveing the bounds &c in soe ruinous a condition, and prayd him to be as favourable to the man as hee could. Afterwards delivered him the counterpart of the lease to draw a declaration.

Hee afterwards sent mee word, he had bayle, and afterwards that hee had judgment for want of a plea.

[p.13.] Avebury 10 October 1713
John Caswell

Farmer John Caswell and I then accompted for the yeare's rent due at Our Lady Day last, when Richard Caswell's lease expired		£210-00-00
Whereout allowed as paid		
to Mrs Truslow 4 quarters of her annuity of £20 per annum ended at Our Lady last	20-00-00..	
Alsoe to Mr Thomas Goddard for his annuity of £20 per annum for 4 quarters ended at at [sic] Our Lady Day last	20-00-00..	
Paid for one yeare's taxes for 4 shillings per £ ended at our Lady last.		
For the Parsonage 13-07-05		
For Goddards 8-03-06½		
For Truslowes 7-04-06¼		
28-15-5¾	28-15-05¾	
Paid to my Lord Aylesbury's agent one yeres rent – high rent due at our Lady last	10-6¼	
Rent due at Our Lady Day last	69-06-00	69-06-00
		140-14-00
		210-00-00[1]

Note. John Caswell now demands 10sh for thatch at Goddards tenement since ye accompt in October 1712 and 10sh for 800 of bricks from Worton, but I bid him respite these 2 yeares till Humfry Robinson & Mr Crooke have finisht the repaires they are now upon there.

October 21 1713
John Caswell paid in part £40-14s-0d, & remains then due at Our Lady Day last £100, which £100 hee promiseth to [?return] & pay by or before Christmas next.

1713 – January	
Received by a bill on Mr Burchal by order of John Caswell	£60-00-00
1714 April 20th received by a bill on Mr Burchal by order of John Caswell	40-00-00
	£100-00-00

All rent evened & paid till Our Lady Day 1713.
See my note on the other syde relating to Richard Caswell [2]
Note. I am informed that John Caswell hath plowed more acres than hee ought.

1 This calculation is checked in the right margin of the mss.
2 See p.14 below.

[p.14.] 1714
11 October 1714
At Avebury: John Caswell
John Caswell now showed me my receipts or letters menconing the payment of £100 being the ballance of due to me on our accompt made up in October last 1713 for the yeare ended at Our Lady Day 1713, & then we proceeded to take his accompt for the yeare ended at Our Lady Day 1714.

Note. Richard Caswell haveing dealt very unkindly by mee and though often intreated refused to come to mee the last year, & sent mee rude and surly articles by his cousin & by John Rose, wherefore I resolved to bring an action against him in the name of Mr Tooker upon his covenant not to plow more than two thyrds, & to leave the bounds in good repaire &c. But John Caswell & John Rose intreated mee to forbeare for a month, dureing which time they would indeavor to make him sensible &c. Accordingly forbore, but to noe purpose.

I alsoe sent a letter thereof to Mr Toocker, & that I must make use of his name. Hee requested mee to forbeare one month, which I did 2 or 3 months. I then gave directions to Mr [?Sadler] of the Devizes to prosecute him, but as gently as possible.

Mr Sadler got bayle & declared, & for want of a plea entered up judgment.

Note Now the beginning of September Richard Caswell came to me with great submission, & complained that hee had paid 4 or £5 to Mr Sadler, & prayed mee to bee kind. I referred it to John Rose & Humfry Robinson, who againe pressed mee to favor him. At length hee submitting to pay £10 they intreated mee to accept it. I submitted soe to doe in compassion, but £50 will not make mee satisfaction.

Richard Caswell paid the £10 to Humfry Robinson in part of his bill, for what done by him at Backhampton

[p.15.] 1714
At Avebury, 11 October 1714
Account with John Caswell
Then accompted with John Caswell for his rent due at Our Lady Day last, £210, towards payment whereof hee now gave mee a note of his disbursements as followeth

For straw and helme for thatch at Goddards in the yeare 1713, & for serveing the thatcher	10-00
For carriage of 16 C of bricks from Worton being two loadd	9-00-00
Paid for that 16 C of bricks at Worton	1-12-00
For thatch for the new skelling at Goddards in 1714	10-00
For three loads of earth then	3-00
for a tun of hay sold to John Rose in September 1714 for his landlord	2-10-00
And carriage of it	2-06
For 5 C paveing bricks & tyles bought at Marlebrough at 3 shillings per C	17-06
For carriage of these 500 tyles & bricks	5-00
Paid Lords rent or court silver to the Earl of Aylesbary due at Michaelmas last 1714	10-06½
Allowed now for a barrel of drink given the tennants in 1713	10-00
	£8-10-06½
Paid Mr Goddard's annuity of £20 per annum, four quarters £5 per quarter, ended at Our Lady Day 1714	20-00-00
Paid Mrs Truslow's annuity of £20 per annum 4 quarters, £5 per quarter, ended at Our Lady Day 1714	20-00-00
Now allowed to him for the tax at 2s per £[1]	
for the Parsonage 6-13-08½	
for Goddards 4-01-09½	
for Truslowes 3-12-03½	14-07-09½
	-
	62-18-04

11 October

Now this 11 October 1714 John Caswell paid me	£76-10-00	
And by a bill dated 27 September 1714 drawne by Nath Hillier on Mr Wm Barnard in Croacked Fryars payable to Robert Sloper or order a month after the date endorsed by Robert Sloper to bee allowed if paid	£14-00-00	
Tot		90-10-00
Which £153-08-04 being deducted out of the £210 rent there remains due at Our Lady Day last 1714 the sum off		153-08-04
		56-11-08
		£210-00-00

Pray Farmer Caswell pay to William Crooke £3 15s[2] upon his bill for mason's

1 Land tax.
2 This and the following amounts are added in the left margin, totalling £25-02-00.

work done at Beckhampton, taking his receipt for it on his bill
Pray pay to Humfry Robinson for work done at Goddards £1 7s 0d.
Pray pay Humfry Robinson upon his bill for work done at Beckhampton £20
John Rose, let it be paid by J.Caswell.

[p.16.] 1714 Beckhampton
Note
The meadows at Silbury Hill belonging to the 4 farmes at Backhampton, being great part of it, excellent meadow ground. The owners or their tennants heretofore by not joyning friendly in the mowing and cleareing thereof have prejudiced each other and Mr. ... Green,[1] Mr Grubb's tennant at Kenet), [2] haveing purchased one of the said farmes late Mr Smith's, and observing great inconveniency in the former methodicall takeing like profitts, proposed to have it cast into lotts, that everyone may know his share upon drawing the lotts yearely.

Mr. Green imployed John Overton of the Devizes to survey it very carefully & divide it into 4 lotts.[3] John Overton did soe, and hee & Mr. Green shewed it to mee, & methoughts it was well contrived & the lotts pretty equall & beneficiall, & an improvement. John Overton expects 40 shillings for his paines &c., and though John Caswell hath a terme of 4 yeares in my two farmes, & I shall have noe profit by this improvement, yet I submitted to allow halfe for my two farmes, which is 10 shillings, & will allow it to John Caswell, who consents to allow the other 10 shillings.

N.B. Repairs &c above £50
Being at the Parsonage House at Backhampton, John Caswell shewed mee what had been done towards puting it into good repaire. The cellars, the dairy, the well &c, & a good many of the last 800 bricks, which I prayed them to take care of & preserve.

The woman complained for lack of a woodhouse, but I shewed them that I had already layd out there above £50, & find them still craveing & therefore gave noe order.

John Caswell shewed me that a new wall would be absolutely nescessary at the lower end of the rick barton. I told him, if well done, I would allow halfe the reall charge; they estimated it at 15 shillings, & I to allow halfe.

Hee complained for lack of a stone wall where there is now a dry hedge from the Close gate to the end of the barne, that it would bee very beneficial &c., and offered to bring stones to the place sufficient to build a wall six foot high, if I would bee at the charge of making the wall. William Crooke & Humfry Robinson being there with us, I prayed them to give mee a true estimate what the workmanship would cost, stones being brought to the place. William Crooke soon after brought mee a note that it would cost mee 16 shillings per lugg, & that

1 Probably Mr Richard Green; see *AWS*, p.241.
2 Walter Grubb of Potterne; see *AWS*, p.219-20.
3 For Overton's survey, see WSHC 184/4/1.

tis [ ][1] lug. I thought it too much by halfe, the stone being provided & brought to the place by the tennant, who will by a wall save 40 shillings every other yeare in a drye hedge, soe I gave no direction, nor for removeing the gate to the barton, though I doe believe if removed as Caswell proposed, it wilbee more convenient.

There is two yeares rent due from Mrs Truslows, which John Caswell promised to stop out of the annuity.

[p.17.] Beckhampton
1714
John Caswell complained of the passage between his hall & parlor at the comeing into the house, & that hee can get it paved and well done for 3d per foot with good Compton stone, which wilbee very hansome & very lasting, and I am of the same opinion. But if hee would he might make the floor very well with a little earth & lyme well prepared, & yet I am inclined to gratifie him therein, if well done, but gave noe direction. I do hope he will prove a good tenant & thrive. If soe I shalbee willing to encourage him as I have hitherto.

Plowing
Mr. Green, who is a good neighbour, & a man of good understanding in husbandry, now found great fault not only with plowing more than ⅔ yearly, but with plowing in an irregular manner & contrary to the old custome of plowing there, & is very prejudicial, & may lessen the vallue & profit of my farmes there if not remedied, as hee & John Rose now exposed and agreed, in the presence of John Caswell. I recomened to them & by all means to plow as formerly & to preserve good neighborhood, & hee promised to bee very just therein, & not doe any wrong nor give any cause of complaint, but will plow regularly & bee a good neighbour.

I drew a bill upon John Caswell to pay £20 to Humfry Robinson for worke done at Beckhampton.

Note 16 October 1714
The dry well
Farmer John Caswell came to take his leave of mee & my wife. I then told him I would not agree to what hee had proposed of makeing a wall from the gate by his well to the corner of his barne, where there is now a drye hedge, unless it may bee done at a reasonable rate, William Crooke haveing asked double what it was worth to make it substantiall & six foot high.

Farmer Caswell had expected to bring the stones & earth at his owne charge & I to bee only at the charge of mason's worke (hee will save the charge of a drye hedge). I promised to consider it at my next comeing hither.

Allowed 7s 6d
John Caswell the last weeke shewed me the wall between his reeke barton & the

1 Blank.

outward barton, & prayed my help therein, & that it would cost 15s to have it well done, and I bid him let it bee well done, and if soe I will allow halfe.

I gave noe direction for altering his lower gate, but thought it fit to bee done, but not at my charge.

The survey taken of Beckhampton common meadow by John Overton by order of Mr. Green & Caswell &c., comes to 40 shillings, which is 10 shillings to each farme. John Overton demanded halfe of mee for my two farmes, but it being let to John Caswell hee to have the benefit thereof. However Mr. Green et al affirming that Overton's allotment by his survey is very benefical, I agreed to allow halfe the twenty shillings & John Caswell was content to allow the other 10 shillings.

[p.18.]

18 October 1715. Remained due upon our last accompt made up 11 October 1714	56-11-08
John Caswell hath paid to William Crooke as ordered	3-15-00
Paid to Humfry Robinson as ordered	20-00-00
Paid more to him	1-07-00
Returne to London as hee affirmes his bill drawne by Mr Clement Burchall, on Mr Robert Burchall, factor in Bread Street, London. I doe believe tis paid, though my receipt is not produced.	32-00-00
Which £57 2s 0d being allowed, the £56-11s-8d is overpaid 10s 4d, which is allowed in our next accompt.	57-02-00

1715
August 16
I being at Avebury, Mr [ ][1] Goddard of Marlebrough ... & his son, who is a clerk to the Common Serjeant in London, came to mee and offered to sell mee the £400 secured to bee paid by Mr Tooker out of the farm called Goddards at Beckhampton, for which I am to pay £20 per annum to [ ][2] Goddard, gent during his life. Hee now affirmes that his brother is 72 yeares old, & that upon his brother's death the £400 wilbee due to him, & came now to offer to sell it to mee, subject to the payment of £20 per annum dureing his brother's life, and demands £300 for it. I told him that 7 yeares purchase for a life is £140. Wee agreed on nothing. I made them welcome, & they staied and dined with us, & promised to come againe, when I shall return hither.

1 Blank. Actually Edmund; see WSHC 371/1, pt.4. Lease & release, Charles Tooker to Sir Richard Holford, 31st November/1st December, 1710.

2 Blank. Actually Thomas; see ditto.

17 October
Mr [ ][1] Goddard came againe to mee, and repeated what hee had before proposed. Wee did not agree, I being very [?basyd]. Hee promised to send his son to mee at London with a reasonable price. I mentioned £250 as enough, his brother being a lusty healthy man as I am told. Hee spends most of his time at Richard Fowler's.[2]

1715 17 October
I went to Backhampton, John Rose with mee, and speakeing with John Caswell about the wall we had formerly talked of from the end of the barne to the gate by the well, about 7 lug, for which John Caswell [?is] to bring the stones & earth to the place, if I would pay the mason.

William Crook's demand to make a wall 7 foot high, 10s 6d per lug, or 1s 6d per perch, and 21 lods of earth & 40 loads of stones, and 14 horse loads of lyme. I now offered to pay the mason's work £3 15s 0d, & to pay for the lyme to have it done forthwith, if hee will bring the stones & earth to the place, but hee said hee had considered better of it, and that hee did not think he could raise so many stones about the closes,[3] & therefore was not willing to bee at the charge, but would continue it with a dry hedge as now it is.

The stables and barnes &c are well repaired.

[p.19.] 1715

~~October 18~~[4]	
~~My tenant John Caswell and I then accompted~~	
~~resting due upon our last accompt this time twelve months~~	
~~after all [?deductions] & allowance~~	
~~Paid since to William Crook the mason & order for work done~~	£56-11-08
~~Paid Humfry Robinson by order for work done at Godards~~	3-15-00
~~Paid more to Humfry Robinson by order for work done at Beckhampton.~~	1-07-00
~~£32. I am content to allow the £32 which he againe affirmes was paid by a bill drawne by Mr Burchall~~	20-00-00
~~whereby the £56 11s 8d is overpaid 10s 4d which is allowed in our accompt underwritten~~	32-00-00
	£57-02-00

1 Blank. Actually Edmund.
2 Innkeeper at the Folly.
3 A reference to the sarsen stones known as 'grey wethers', which lay naturally in the fields around Avebury.
4 See previous page in the manuscript for the account which replaced this one.

John Caswell's rent for Lady Day 1715

Due for rent for the yeare ended at Our Lady Day 1715	210-00-00
A yeare's rent then due for Goddards from Mrs Truslow	1-10-00
	211-10-00

His disbursements

Paid to the land tax of 2s in the pound for the yeare ended at Our Lady Day last 1715, viz't	
For the Parsonage 6-13-8½	
For Godards 4-01-9½	
For Truslowes 3-12-03½	14-07-9½
Paid the Lord's rent & court money	10-06
Paid 116 foot of Swindon stone at 2½d per foot ~~& laying it~~ £1 4s and carriage of it 10 shillings	1-14-00
For straw for thatch, and spikes & worke done at Goddards	1-10-00
Paid Mr Goddard for 4 quarters £5 per quarter, for his annuity of £20 per annum ended at Our Lady Day 1715.	20-00-00
Paid the like to Mrs Trusloe for one yeare ended at Our Lady Day 1715	20-00-00
	58-02-03½
11 October 1715 received of John Caswell in money at Avebury £83	83-00-00
	141-02-03½
Overpaid upon the last accompt per ut	10-00
	141-12-03½
which £14 12s 3½d being deducted out of the £211 10s 0d, there remaines due at Our Lady Day 1715	69-17-8½[1]

A copy of this delivered to Farmer Caswell 17 October 1715.

On 18 October this accompt made up Farmer Carswell paid mee £5 17s 6d. Then remained due £64, which Farmer Caswell will pay as I shall order, or returne it by bill by or before Christmas next.

[p.20.] Resting due from Farmer Caswell at Our Lady Day 1715, as on the other syde £64 10s 0d.

1715/6
Rent £50

Memorandum

March 8th. Farmer Caswell haveing promised to pay this £64 (remaining due at Our Lady Day 1715) at Christmas last, but faileing, writ mee a letter of his disapointment, & that I should have it at Candlemas, but heareing nothing from him, and William Skeate being now in towne, & haveing money which hee would willingly returne,

1 This amount is also calculated in the left margin.

offered to pay mee what I should desire.

I not haveing heard from John Caswell, took up £50 of William Skeate, & he accepted a bill for it on Farmer Caswell. I writ then of to him by William Skeate & thought it would bee a great case to Caswell. Hee will have my letter the 10 instant.

I shortly after received a short letter from John Caswell dated 16 March 1715, that hee had paid to William Skeate of Rowden the £50, and also £14, in all £64, & hath his receipt for it.

Soe that when William Skeate shall pay the £14 Farmer Caswell's rent of £210 for the yeare ended at Our Lady Day 1715 wilbee cleared.

William Skeate paid the £14 to John Rose for mee, soe John Caswell's rent cleered to Our Lady Day 1715. John Rose paid me the £14.

19 October 1716
Farmer Caswell hath cleared his accompt for rent due at Our Lady Day 1715, as also Mrs Truslow's rent.

[p.21.] 15 October 1716
Farmer John Caswell's accompt for what due at Our Lady Day 1716

His rent due at Our Lady 1716	210-00-00
Mrs Trusloe's rent for the year ended at Our Lady Day 1716	01-10-00
Paid for the kings tax[1] at 2s per £	201-10-00
For the Parsonage 6-13-04½	
For Goddards 4-01-09½	
For Trusloes 3-12-3½	14-07-09 1½
Paid the Lords rent and court money	0-10-06
Paid Mrs Trusloe's annuity for the year ended at Our Lady day 1716	20-00-00
Paid Mr Goddard's annuity for the year then ended	20-00-00
John Caswell this day paid in part of his rent	79-05-09
Paid as above	134-04-00 ½
Which £134 4s 0½d being deducted out of the £211 10s there remains due at Our Lady Day last	77-06-00 ½
19th October 1716	
John Caswell then paid in further part of his rent for the yeare above mentioned.	26-10-00
And left with mee a bill of exchange dated 18 October 1716 drawne by Thomas Collins on Mr Thomas Webb at the Woollpack in Aldermanbury payable at 16 January sight, to bee allowed when received	30-00-00
Which £56 10s being deducted out the £77 6s 0d there	56-10-00
remains due at Our Lady Day 1716	20-16-00
Farmer Caswell hath a copy of ths under my hand.	

1 The land tax.

Farmer Caswell will pay this £20 16s 0d within a month.
Note. I delivered Collins his note for £30[1] to Mr Nicholls the goldsmith, whose servant tendered it to Mr Thomas Webb, but hee refused to accept it, or to pay the money, whereof I writ to John Caswell the 3d of November, & bid him take speedy care thereof. Twas afterwards paid. John Rose afterwards returned by his dealer £20 upon the next fo

.

Memorandum [p.22.] October 1716
Memorandum. Upon my being at Avebury in September & October 1716, Farmer John Caswell showed mee our agreement in writeing whereby hee was to hold my farm in Backhampton, which I bought of Mr Tooker, for 4 yeares from the expiration of 4 yeares by lease made by Mr Tooker to Richard Caswell, and a note under that agreement that 12 months notice should bee given in writeing before the end of the 4 yeares, or else 4 yeares more from the expiration of this 4 yeares to be added.

Neither he nor I have given such notice, & now the terme will expire within six months, therefore now too late to give such notice. Upon discourse thereof, and hee haveing neglected to prepare a lease as by the said agreement hee ought to have done, and now declareing his earnest desire & request to have a further terme for 4 yeares, upon the same rent termes &c., as before, I consented thereto, but not abate any of the rent, not to let him have Goddard's house as hee desired. I endorsed the second agreement upon the back of the former agreement, and hee forthwith to procure it to bee put into a lease on parchment, duely stampt, & to give bond as by the former agreement. Mr Mayo, the vicar of Avebury, John Rose, & my man William Harris are witnesses to both the endorsements under our hands & seales, each of us haveing one.

24 December 1716. John Rose, his dealer Mr Herne, paid for mee £50 at Mr Nichols, I think hee said twas £30, upon Rose his accompt and £20 upon John Caswell's accompt. I writ to John Rose to write to mee thereof, that I may place it accordingly

1717 15 August
John Rose now declared the £30 to bee on his owne accompt & £20 for John Caswell's accompt. I accordingly placed it.

John Caswell's rent &c rest at Lady Day 1716 16s 0d.

[p.23.] 1717
5 August 1717
My wife & I & her maid in my coach & 4 excellent horses, my man Joseph [?Reaves] upon my nag, & my son Samuel on one of his brother's gueldings, came from my house about 12, lay at the Crowne at Stow, where wee were

1 A calculation in the left margin totals this with the previous payment, making a total of £50 16s 0d.

presently after 4. Samuel returned Tuesday morn. Wee stopt at John Millard's at Twiford, as also at the Falcon at Theale, and came to the Bere at Spinhamland by ½ an hower after.

[*Sunday] we stopped at Froxfield, & came safe & well to Avebury by two, by Malbrough without staying because the smal pox is very busye there.

[*Wednesday] 7 August 1717
When we came to Avebury wee found wheate harvest begun, and all hands very busy. John Rose got old Harry Curry to help my coachman.

Wheate barn's floore £15
The wheat barne floore was new made last Michaelmas with excellent new well seasond oke planks an inch & quarter thick, & full length, & good oken sylls. Cost mee in all £15.

This barne was new layed or tyled on both sydes & both ends, & finished this very forenoone by John Overton. Q. The charge & the lyme burner's bill. The crabtrees in Shere Barton, tis now the best garden, grafted with excellent good codlynes & severall other choice apples, & thrives wonderfully. Mr Nicholas Norris the garden hath planted fruite trees against the stable wall, & alsoe to the [?noth] wall towards Barr Close (& some apple trees there) which if not carefully weeded & preserved will come to noething.

Nicholl Norris hath plashed that syde of the new hedge to the Barr Close, & preserved standing crab trees in it, & twilbee an excellent fence by the time the dry hedge now there is decayed, and as hee declares hath grafted at the least [ ][1] crab stocks in the inner hedge towards the orchard with choice apples of the best sorts, & will take care in a proper time to remove as many of them as may encourage the rest & make a very fruitefull plantation.

John Rose hath now made a kitchin garden there, but planted it with beanes, and not levelled the ground as it ought to bee.

Norris hath there alsoe planted apple trees, but very improperly for a kitchin garden, & hath foolishly planted a rowe of wallnut trees on the insyde of that hedge, & soe neare to it that if they thrive, that fruitefull hedge wilbee spoiled in a few yeares. Norris hath filled the Wallditch or New Plantation there with ashes and siccamore, as hee says above 100, besydes those removed out of Barr Close, but many of them on the sydes of the banck, especially towards Mr Bromham's, that it can't bee expected they should live or prosper for lack of nourishment.

The new orchard or garden heretofore called the Shere Barton is fully planted with peare trees, apple trees, cherry trees, & plum trees, goosberrys & currants, & seemes to thrive very well, but if not carefully weeded & preserved will come to little. The ground is now full of leeks & onions & kidney beans, but too full of weeds, & the fruite trees planted against the wall in the best garden choked up with weeds. My man Joseph now cleared them as well as he could. Q

1 Blank.

the numbers & names of the fruit trees there.

During our stay here I had little ease, & could not stir much abroad by reason of a sore toe, which pained mee very much whilst here but very grievously afterwards at Weston Burt, Bath, Wells, and after our return from Wells to Bath. I was under the hands and care of Monsieur Ranjot, an eminent French surgeon, & constrained to come from Bath in a horse litter, for which I paid £3.

When at Avebury [p.24.] When at Avebury my wife and Mr Mayo dressed it carefully every day with Mons Ranjot's plaister, one according to his order, but Mrs Seymour's playster, very famous hereabouts for such a wound, and Mr Mayo haveing a great opinion of it, (especially for the benefit Mr Chivers of Quemberford[1] received thereby after hee had lost 2 or 3 of his toes, and foot condemned to bee cut off, and his leg in great danger, but preserved by this playster, and knowing of many other almost wonderfull cures merely by the application of this playster) my wife submitted to use it. And Mrs Mayo finding something very hard in the wound did with lynt keepe the orifice open, and on [*Thursday] 17 October tooke out a hard substance & a splinter of the bone, & afterwards kept it open with lent, & dressed it twice a day, whereby it drew out [?coruption].

When wee came to London my wife constantly dressed it once or 2 daies, and often shewed it to Mr Geekie, who liked it very well, but the plaister constantly drawd some matter from it, & therefore required to bee opened as before. [*Tuesday] 4 November being a fine morning, I wrapt myself very warme & went with wife to Hyde Park, & returned by one, without any hurt.

I now took a note of the tennement at Backhampton as leased out for lives or yeares determinable on lives when I purchased Mr Tooker's estate at Backhampton, & these tennements, (vizt)[2]

[p.25.] 1717
Accompted with John Caswell for his rent due at Our Lady Day 5 November 1717.

Left unpaid for his rent due at Our Lady Day 1716	16-00
His yeare's rent due at Our Lady Day 1717	210-00-00
Received one yeare's rent of Mrs Trusloe	1-10-00
Due at Our Lady Day 1717	212-06-00

Note Thomas Alexander's rent £1 10s 0d from Our Lady Day 1717. I ordered him to pay it to John Caswell, farmer .

1 Probably Henry Chivers, the owner of mills at Quemerford, and of an estate at Stock; cf. *VCH Wilts* 17, p.69, 71 & 88-9.

2 The rest of this page is blank.

John Caswell's disbursements for the year ended at Our Lady Day 1717, (vizt)	
Tax at 4s per £ for the Parsonage	£13-07-05
For Goddards	8-03-06
For Trusloe's	7-04-07
Paid Lord Ailesbury's chiefe rent of ten shillings per annum and for his steward's fee six pence at Our Lady Day last	10-06
Poore Alexander[1]	
Paid for 300 bricks used in a chimney for Thomas Alexander at Goddard's House	5-00
For six sacks of lyme for the same	6-00
for fetching the 300 bricks from the Devizes	3-00
Paid for his share of the vagrant and bridge money for the Parsonage & farmes	12-06
Paid fower quarters annuity to Mrs Trusloe due at Our Lady Day last	20-00-00
Paid 4 quarters annuity to Mr Thomas Goddard due at Our Lady Day last	20-00-00
	70-12-06
25 October 1717 Farmer Caswell paid to mee	70-17-06
5 November 1717 paid to mee	10-16-00
then remains £40	
19 November	
Farmer John Rose haveing bills on his chapman, Mr Joseph Herne, he paid £40 to Mr Nicholas Nicholls & brought his note	40-00-00
	212-06-00
Balance & evened 21 November 1717. I writ a full accompt to John Rose that Mr Hearn had paid his bills	
[1] Written in left margin, heading the next three entries.	

Note Humfry Robinson in his bill for work done for mee since October 1716 hath charged to my account for mending the barne floore, barne doores, racks, mangers in the stables, rayles, &c., which Caswell ought to pay by his covenants. (I submitted to pay for the new doore to the well, because it seems to bee well done & convenient). I found great fault with Humfries charging the rest to me, & forewarned him.

John Caswell lacks a granary. I am told twill cost £60 if well done. I am willing to doe it if a rent bee increased accordingly, if not &c.[1]

1 Sir Richard Holford died a few months after this was written; he was buried in the chapel of Lincolns Inn, 16th May 1718.

2
LETTERS

1	184/1, pt.2	1695-05-08	Holford, Richard, Sir	Adams, John
2	184/1, pt.2	1695-05-17	Skeat, William	Holford, Richard, Sir
3	184/1, pt.2	1696-01-04	Skeat, William	Holford, Richard, Sir
4	184/1, pt.2	1696-01-11	Holford, Richard, Sir	White, John
5	184/1, pt.1.	1696-01-25	White, John	Holford, Richard, Sir
6	184/1, pt.1.	1696-01-30	Holford, Richard, Sir	White, John
7	184/1, pt.1.	1696-02-07	Smith, Richard	Holford, Richard, Sir
8	184/1, pt.1.	1696-02-22	Holford, Richard, Sir	Smith, Mr
9	184/1, pt.1.	1696-04-04	White, John	Holford, Richard, Sir
10	184/4, pt.2.	1696-06-27	Smith, Richard	Skeate, William
11	184/1, pt.1.	1696-09-30	Holford, Richard, Sir	White, John
12	184/1, pt.1.	1696-09-30	White, John	Holford, Richard, Sir
13	184/1, pt.1.	1696-10-10	White, John	Holford, Richard, Sir
14	184/1, pt.1.	1697-01-29	White, John	Holford, Richard, Sir
15	184/1, pt.1.	1697-02-04	White, John	Holford, Richard, Sir
16	184/1, pt.2	1697-04-29	Holford, Richard, Sir	White, John
17	184/1, pt.2	1697-11-09	Holford, Richard, Sir	Smith, Richard
18	184/1, pt.2	1697-12-29	Tooker, Charles	Holford, Richard, Sir
19	184/1, pt.2	1698-01-04	Holford, Richard, Sir	Tooker, Charles
20	184/1, pt.2	1698-02-26	Skeat, William	Holford, Richard, Sir
21	184/1, pt.2	1698-02-28	Yeate, Cornelius	Holford, Richard, Sir
22	184/1, pt.2	1698-03-08	Holford, Richard, Sir	Yeate, Cornelius
23	184/1, pt.2	1698-03-09	Yeate, Cornelius	Holford, Richard, Sir
24	184/1, pt.2	1698-04-26	Yeate, Cornelius	Holford, Richard, Sir

25	184/1, pt.2	1698-05-05	Holford, Richard, Sir	Yeate, Cornelius
26	184/1, pt.2	1698-06-05	Wall, Humfry	Holford, Richard, Sir
27	184/1, pt.1.	1698-07-14	Skeat, William	Holford, Richard, Sir
28	184/1, pt.1.	1698-07-14	Holford, Richard, Sir	Yeate, Cornelius
29	184/1, pt.1.	1698-07-20	Skeat, William	Holford, Richard, Sir
30	184/1, pt.1.	1698-11-23	Skeat, William	Holford, Richard, Sir
31	184/1, pt.1.	1698-11-26	Holford, Richard, Sir	Skeat, William
32	184/1, pt.1.	1698-12-??	Philip, servant	Skeat, William
33	184/1, pt.1.	1698-12-09	Skeat, William	Holford, Richard, Sir
34	184/1, pt.1.	1698-12-19	Skeat, William	Holford, Richard, Sir
35	184/1, pt.1.	1698-12-21	Skeat, William	Holford, Richard, Sir
36	184/1, pt.1.	1699-01-30	Skeat, William	Holford, Richard, Sir
37	184/1, pt.1.	1699-02-16	Skeat, William	Holford, Richard, Sir
38	184/1, pt.1.	1699-02-23	Skeat, William	Holford, Richard, Sir
39	184/1, pt.1.	1699-05-12	Skeat, William	Holford, Richard, Sir
40	184/1, pt.1.	1700-01-29	Skeat, William	Holford, Richard, Sir
41	184/1, pt.1.	1700-02-19	Skeat, William	Holford, Richard, Sir
42	184/1, pt.1.	1700-07-06	Smith, William	Holford, Richard, Sir
43	184/1, pt.1.	1700-07-06	Skeat, William	Holford, Richard, Sir
44	184/1, pt.1.	1700-11-20	Smith, William	Holford, Richard, Sir
45	184/1, pt.1.	1701-01-11	Smith, William	Holford, Richard, Sir
46	184/1, pt.1.	1701-01-28	Smith, William	Holford, Richard, Sir
47	184/1, pt.1.	1701-02-11	Smith, William	Holford, Richard, Sir
48	184/1, pt.1.	1701-02-22	Holford, Richard, Sir	Smith, William
49	184/1, pt.1.	1701-08-09	Holford, Richard, Sir	Gardiner, John
50	184/1, pt.1.	1701-08-21	Holford, Richard, Sir	Gardiner, John
51	184/1, pt.1.	1702-10-18	Wall, Humfry	Holford, Richard, Sir
52	184/1, pt.1.	1702-12-23	Holford, Richard, Sir	White, John

53	184/1, pt.1.	1703-01-07	White, John	Holford, Richard, Sir
54	184/1, pt.1.	1703-07-16	Holford, Richard, Sir	Gardiner, John
55	184/1, pt.1.	1704-11-09	Holford, Richard, Sir	White, John
56	184/1, pt.1.	1704-11-25	White, John	Holford, Richard, Sir
57	184/1, pt.1.	1705-06-20	Holford, Richard, Sir	Skeat, William
58	184/1, pt.1.	1707-03-06	Holford, Richard, Sir	White, John
59	184/1, pt.1.	1707-04-18	Page, Christopher, & Jerome, John	Holford, Richard, Sir
60	184/1, pt.1.	1707-11-04	Holford, Richard, Sir	Overton, John
61	184/1, pt.2	1708-07-22	Holford, Richard, Sir	White, John
62	184/1, pt.2	1708-10-20	White, John	Holford, Richard, Sir
63	184/1, pt.2.	1708-10-30	Holford, Richard, Sir	White, John
64	184/1, pt.2	1709-06-02	Holford, Richard, Sir	Chandler, Richard
65	184/1, pt.2	1709-06-15	Holford, Richard, Sir	Chandler, Richard
66	184/1, pt.2	1709-07-21	Holford, Richard, Sir	Chandler, Richard
67	184/1, pt.2	1710-02-23	Holford, Richard, Sir	Skeat, William
68	184/1, pt.2	1710-04-02	Holford, Richard, Sir	White, John
69	184/1, pt.2	1710-06-07	Holford, Richard, Sir	Rose, John
70	184/1, pt.2	1710-11-23	Holford, Richard, Sir	Rose, John
71	184/1, pt.2	1711-10-04	Holford, Richard, Sir	White, John
72	184/1, pt.2	1711-11-01	Holford, Richard, Sir	Brinsden, John
73	184/1, pt.2	1711-11-13	Brinsden, John	Holford, Richard, Sir
74	184/1, pt.2	1711-11-22	Holford, Richard, Sir	Brinsden, John
75	184/1, pt.2	1712-01-01	Brinsden, John	Holford, Richard, Sir
76	184/1, pt.2	1712-01-24	Brinsden, John	Holford, Richard, Sir
77	184/1, pt.2	1712-02-23	Rose, John	Holford, Richard, Sir
78	184/1, pt.2	1712-05-21	Holford, Richard, Sir	Brinsden, John
79	184/1, pt.2	1715-06-16	Mayo, John	Holford, Richard, Sir

80	184/1, pt.2	1720-12-12	Alexander, Thomas	Holford, Lady
81	184/1, pt.2	1722-01-11	Wall, Humfry	Hall, Mr
82	184/1, pt.2	1723-08-26	H., T.	Holford, Samuel
83	184/1, pt.2	1725-10-29	Caswell, John	Holford, Samuel
84	184/1, pt.2	1725-11-16	Caswell, John	Holford, Samuel
85	184/1, pt.2	1725-11-22	Griffin, Peter	Holford, Samuel
86	184/1, pt.2	1737-09-24	Holford, Robert	Holford, Richard
87	184/1, pt.2	1739-05-05	Cures, John	Holford, Richard
88	184/1, pt.2	1742-02-03	Holford, Stayner	Griffin, Peter
89	184/1, pt.2	1743-01-21	Holford, Stayner	Griffin, Peter
90	184/1, pt.2	1743-01-29	Griffin, Peter	Holford, Stayner
91	184/1, pt.2	1743-02-10	Holford, Robert	Holford, Stayner
92	184/1, pt.2	1743-02-20	Griffin, Peter	Holford, Stayner
93	184/1, pt.2	1743-02-21	Holford, Stayner	Griffin, Peter
94	184/1, pt.2	1743-02-24	Holford, Stayner	Griffin, Peter
95	184/1, pt.2	1743-03-02	Holford, Robert	Holford, Stayner
96	184/1, pt.2	1743-03-03	Holford, Robert	Holford, Stayner
97	184/1, pt.2	1743-03-06	Griffin, Peter	Holford, Stayner
98	184/1, pt.2	1743-03-09	Holford, Stayner	Holford, Robert
99	184/1, pt.2	1743-03-11	Holford, Stayner	Griffin, Peter
100	184/1, pt.2	1743-03-15	Holford, Stayner	Holford, Robert
101	184/1, pt.2	1743-03-22	Holford, Robert	Holford, Stayner
102	184/1, pt.2	1743-03-23	Griffin, Peter	Holford, Stayner
103	184/1, pt.2	1743-04-09	Holford, Robert	Holford, Stayner
104	184/1, pt.2	1743-04-23	Griffin, Peter	Holford, Stayner
105	184/1, pt.2	1743-04-30	Bailey, Richard	Holford, Stayner
106	184/1, pt.2	1743-05-01	Griffin, Peter	Holford, Stayner
107	184/1, pt.2	1743-05-29	Smith, Thomas	Holford, Stayner

108	184/1, pt.2	1743-06-26	Griffin, Peter	Holford, Stayner
109	184/1, pt.2	1743-10-18	Holford, Stayner	Griffin, Peter
110	184/1, pt.2	1743-10-28	Griffin, Peter	Holford, Stayner
111	184/1, pt.2	1744-03-31	Mayo, James	Holford, Stayner
112	184/1, pt.2	1745-09-19	Mayo, James	Holford, Stayner
113	184/1, pt.2	1746-04-27	Mayo, James	Holford, Stayner
114	184/1, PT.2	1746-07-02	Mayo, James	Holford, Stayner
115	184/1, PT.2	1749-05-24	Norris, John	Holford, Stayner
116	184/1, pt.1.	1750-05-29	Holford, Stayner	Unknown
117	184/1, pt.1.	1753-07-10	Mayo, James	Fowler, William
118	184/1, pt.1.	1754-03-21	Howson, Henry	Holford, Stayner
119	G.A. D1956/L1	1756-02-05	Holford, Stayner	Holford, Peter
120	184/1, pt.1.	1756-02-11	Mayo, James	Scane, John
121	184/1, pt.1.	1756-02-12	Scane, John	Mayo, James
122	G.A. D1956/L1	1756-06-10	Holford, Stayner	Holford, Peter
123	G.A. D1956/L1	1756-06-20	Holford, Stayner	Holford, Peter
124	G.A. D1956/L1	1756-06-22	Holford, Stayner	Holford, Peter
125	G.A. D1956/L1	1756-07-22	Holford, Stayner	Holford, Peter
126	G.A. D1956/L1	1756-08-01	Holford, Stayner	Holford, Peter
127	184/2	1756-08-19	Mayo, James	Holford, Stayner
128	184/2	1756-08-19	Holford, Stayner	Mayo, James
129	184/2	1756-08-20	Mayo, James	Holford, Stayner
130	184/2	1756-08-20	Holford, Stayner	Mayo, James
131	184/2	1756-08-20	Mayo, James	Holford, Stayner

132	184/2	1756-08-20	Mayo, James	Holford, Stayner
133	184/2	1756-08-20	Holford, Stayner	Mayo, James
134	184/2	1756-10-07	Mayo, James	Holford, Peter
135	184/1, pt.1.	1756-12-02	Holford, Stayner	Holford, Peter
136	184/2	1756-12-11	Holford, Peter	Holford, Stayner
137	184/2	1756-12-21	Holford, Stayner	Holford, Peter
138	184/2	1757-01-05	Mayo, James	Jones, Arthur
139	G.A. D1956/L1	1757-03-03	Holford, Stayner	Holford, Peter
140	G.A. D1956/L1	1758-04-30	Holford, Stayner	Holford, Peter
141	G.A. D1956/L1	1758-12-19	Holford, Stayner	Holford, Peter
142	184/2	1758-12-31	Martyn, Samuel	Holford, Stayner
143	184/2	1758-12-31	Holford, Stayner	Martyn, Samuel
144	184/1, pt.1.	1761-06-14	Holford, Stayner	Norris, William
145	184/1, pt.1.	1762-03-02	Norris, William	Holford, Stayner
146	184/1, pt.1.	1763-12-15	Holford, Peter	Holford, Stayner
147	184/1, pt.1.	1765-04-06	Fowler, William	Holford, Stayner
148	184/1, pt.1.	1766-01-04	Holford, Stayner	Popham, Edward
149	271/14	1766-10-15	Peter Holford	Stayner Holford
150	9/35/178	1773-08-12	Jones, Arthur	Lord Bruce
151	271/2	1784-04-23	Jones, Arthur	Williamson, Mrs
152	271/16	1786-12-08	Jones, Arthur	Williamson, Mrs
153	184/6	1791------	Ward, John	Williamson, Adam
154	184/6	1791-05-03	Ward, John	Williamson, Adam
155	184/6	1791-05-03	Williamson, Adam	Ward, John
156	184/6	1791-06-28	Hickley, Richard	Williamson, Mrs
157	184/6	1791-07-29	Hickley, Richard	Williamson, Mrs

158	184/6	1791-08-03	Hickley, Richard	Williamson, Mrs
159	184/6	1791-08-22	Hickley, Richard	Williamson, Mrs
160	184/6	1791-10-04	Hickley, Richard	Williamson, Adam
161	184/6	1791-10-05	John Ward	Belford, Mary, Mrs
162	184/6	1791-10-05	Ward, John	Durnell, Richard
163	184/6	1791-10-31	Hickley, Richard	Williamson, Adam
164	184/6	1791-12-05	Hickley, Richard	Williamson, Adam
165	184/6	1792-01-02	Hickley, Richard	Williamson, Adam
166	184/6	1792-01-30	Hickley, Richard	Williamson, Adam
167	184/6	1792-03-06	Hickley, Richard	Williamson, Mrs
168	184/6	1792-03-22	Ward, John	Williamson, Adam
169	184/6	1792-04-03	Hickley, Richard	Williamson, Mrs
170	184/6	1792-04-30	Hickley, Richard	Williamson, Mrs
171	184/6	1792-06-05	Hickley, Richard	Williamson, Mrs
172	184/6	1792-07-09	Hickley, Richard	Williamson, Mrs
173	184/6	1792-07-31	Hickley, Richard	Williamson, Mrs
174	184/6	1792-09-04	Hickley, Richard	Williamson, Mrs
175	184/6	1792-10-01	Ward, John	Williamson, Adam
176	184/6	1792-10-02	Hickley, Richard	Williamson, Mrs
177	184/6	1792-11-06	Hickley, Richard	Williamson, Mrs
178	184/6	1792-12-03	Powdich, Mary	Williamson, Adam
179	184/6	1792-12-04	Richardson, William	Williamson, Mrs
180	184/6	1792-12-04	Hickley, Richard	Williamson, Mrs
181	184/6	1792-12-31	Hickley, Richard	Williamson, Mrs
182	184/6	1793-01-01	Ward, John	Williamson, Adam
183	184/6	1793-02-04	Hickley, Richard	Williamson, Mrs
184	184/6	1793-03-02	Hickley, Richard	Williamson, Mrs
185	184/6	1793-03-31	Hickley, Richard	Williamson, Mrs

186	184/6	1793-04	Ward, John	Williamson, Adam
187	184/6	1793-04-30	Hickley, Richard	Williamson, Mrs
188	184/6	1793-06-04	Hickley, Richard	Williamson, Mrs
189	184/6	1793-07-02	Hickley, Richard	Williamson, Mrs
190	184/6	1793-07-18	Jenny, Mrs A	Hickley, Richard
191	184/6	1793-08-05	Hickley, Richard	Williamson, Mrs
192	184/6	1793-09-09	Hickley, Richard	Williamson, Mrs
193	184/6	1793-09-20	Ward, John	Williamson, Adam
194	184/6	1793-09-27	Ward, John	Williamson, Adam
195	184/6	1793-10-01	Hickley, Richard	Williamson, Mrs
196	184/6	1793-11-08	Hickley, Richard	Williamson, Mrs
197	184/6	1793-11-30	Hickley, Richard	Williamson, Mrs
198	184/6	1793-12-31	Hickley, Richard	Williamson, Mrs
199	184/6	1794-02-01	Hickley, Richard	Williamson, Mrs
200	184/6	1794-02-02	Hickley, Richard	Williamson, Mrs
201	184/6	1794-03-20	Hickley, Richard	Williamson, Mrs
202	184/6	1794-03-30	Hickley, Richard	Williamson, Mrs
203	184/6	1794-05-02	Hickley, Richard	Williamson, Mrs
204	184/6	1794-06-02	Hickley, Richard	Williamson, Mrs
205	184/6	1794-06-xx	Hickley, Richard	Williamson, Mrs
206	184/6	1794-07-30	Hickley, Richard	Williamson, Mrs
207	271/16	1794-08-05	Richardson, William	Williamson, Mrs
208	184/6	1794-08-31	Hickley, Richard	Williamson, Mrs
209	184/6	1794-09-27	Hickley, Richard	Williamson, Mrs
210	184/6	1794-11-02	Hickley, Richard	Williamson, Mrs
211	184/6	1794-11-30	Hickley, Richard	Williamson, Mrs
212	184/6	1794-12-01	Richardson, William	Williamson, Mrs
213	184/6	1795-02-02	Hickley, Richard	Williamson, Adam

214	184/6	1798------	Williamson, Adam	Hickley, Richard
215	184/6	1798-02-28	Hickley, Richard	Williamson, Adam

1. Sir Richard Holford to John Adams WSHC 184/1, pt.2.

[8 May 1695]

Mr Adams,

I am the worst in the world to find fault or bee troublesome, for that I have alwaies studdied to bee quiet, yet I cannot but complaine of the delay I have met with in the matter of Awbry.[1] Pray consider how long it is since you offered £7500, which is in truth a great deal more than tis worth or will yield, & when I would have blamed you for your soe doeing I remember you told mee I should have it and that I should pay for it, & that you would bid but once, and that the title being good I could not buy it too deare, or to that effect, whereupon I submitted, after which my name was carried to market as if proclamation was made after who would give more, I haveing bid soe much. I don't blame you, nor the gentleman of the Temple (who seemes to bee a faire man in the matter) nor any of the trustees,[2] who I am informed are all persons of honor & integrity, but I am sure some body hath been too blame, since the trustees have all consented, it would not have been this long delayed. And tis not for that only but in truth the mansion house is soe very much out of repaire that in severall places of the tyleing and [*illegible*], as in the hall & parlour downe, a truss [*illegible*] & take it up through the breaches & the foundation & walls of the house and alsoe of the best stables are grievously in decay & must bee speedily amended else it may prove [?incurable] & indeed all the out housing are in great decay.

Pray therefore hasten the draughts of the deeds, also send them with the title deeds to Mr Sargeant Hallatt. And though I cant bee soe kind to you as I must have been if I had been kindly used in the price, and shall ever owne your integrity & your justice to your clients, though I am saddled by it, & soe as I may not bee longer delayed, will give it under my hand that I am

Your friend & servant[3]

Chancery Lane, 8 May 1695

I writ a note to Mr Adams & inclosed this, that seeing hee had sent my other letters to the trustees I would have him to send this.

Verso Note: Copy of letter to Mr John Adams, May 28 1695[4]

1 The purchase of the manor.
2 The trustees for the sale of Lord Stawell's estate, which included the manor of Avebury.
3 The letter is not signed – although it is admittedly a copy.
4 Recto gives 8th.

2. William Skeat to Sir Richard Holford WSHC 184/1, pt.2.

17 May 1695
Aubury[1]

Sir,
When you come to speake with the trustees my Lord Stawell, pray put them in mind that my Lord Stawell agreed & faithfuly promised to allow mee £100 out of my rent in consideraton of the bad times & my loses, which my Lord tooke notice of, & in the presence of Mr Sherrwood. Pray pres them earnestly therein, for this is true & Mr Smith[2] & Mr Tucker[3] can attest my Lordship's promises that I should not bee a loser, which I have lost £300 by it & except I ham a loud I cannot hould it.

The hous is very much out of repair & the ould baren[4]; which if not spedy cours tooke they'll drop down.
My hand,
Will Skeat

Verso Note: Mr William Skeat. Letter, to speake to the trustees on his behalf

3. William Skeat to Sir Richard Holford WSHC 184/1, pt.2.

4 January 1695/6

Sur,
I never reseued yours tell this morning, and for Mrs Bromham her fites be as bad as ever. But Mr Bromham[5] thinkes of coming to London him self, & then hee will call upon your Worship. Mr Smith ordered mee to paye to Mr White 4 pound for his dues & accordingly I sent him 4 pound & hee refues to take it, & soue I have tendred the mony to him before witness, but hee resovels to sue mee. Soe I would bag your Worship to rite to Mr Whit what you know of the bargan, & how much mony I must pay him, for hee will be trobelsum to all his naibors. Hee have [?sard][6] John Mills with a rite & senc promised to send to his layer to know the charg & to take his mony, but never let him know nothing bat sent forfwith [?warrants][7] against hee & his bayl &c. This wee be like to love with a milichises[8] passon. Thar is a grete dole of the wall in the chirrie cort fill doun. I have set 2 okes & elm & aishes according to your order. For the mony wee can't take none that is good nor yet paye non if be good, & so wee don't gooe to market, & what wee shall doe I don't well know. I & my wife presents our umbell

1 Date and address written on left hand side of letter.
2 Richard Smith.
3 Charles Tooker, JP.
4 Barn.
5 Probably John Phelps als Bromham (a clothier and dissenter) and his wife Mary (nee Dyke).
6 Served.
7 Text torn.
8 Malicious.

saruice to your Worship & our good lanlady & mis & letel master. This is all at present from your saruant & tenent,
Will Skeate
Avebury

My man desiers your Worship to know what thar is don in his bisnes.

Verso Note: Farmer Skeat, January 4 1695. Answered the 11 January. Writ to him againe 30 January 1695
Verso Address: Thes for Sir Richard Holford in Chancri Lane nere the Rowls, London

4. Sir Richard Holford to John White WSHC 184/1, pt.2.
[11 January 1695/6]

Sir,
Since I came last from Awbery, I have often had it in my thoughts to write to you as methinks I ought to doe frequently, being become as it were your parishioner, but doubting you might rather desire to bee excused from such a correspondence, & you not haveing hitherto signify anything to the contrary, made me forbeare. Upon my word nothing made me more uneasy there than the impertinent differences betweene you & some of the neighbours, which as soone as I observed I endeavoured to reconcile by pressing you to the practice of true Christian charity, & to give them who are in great want thereof a good example, as well as wholesome precepts & doctrines, & to persuade them to pay to you the respect due to your quallity & function, as also all their dues with cherefullness & by the best arguments I could use I indeavourd to create a mutuall neighborly & friendly conversation, & did hope I had in a good measure prevailed, the rather for that I knew twas for both your interests. But I was troubled when I found that my indeavours & good wishes had not obtained the desired effects, &, much more, when I saw the heats increased & blowne into a flame, & a mutuall inclination to unneighborly squabbles, & each party inclined to listen to (it may bee false) reports & whispers, & which is worst of all a seperation in the publick worship of God, & participation of the holy & blessed communion of our Lords Supper. I could not but mention this to mine & your good friend, Mr Smith[1], as a matter of very dangerous consequence, & requested his friendly assistance to prevent the growing mischiefe of such a separation, & also prayed his determination of the matter between you & Farmer Skeate about his tithes, & after some discourse thereabout Mr Smith assured mee that that breach should never more bee opened on your part. But I am now informed that you are againe indeavouring to dispute that matter, & sueing him & others for more than of right belongs to you, which, if true, methinks is very unkind, not to say worse. And I doe pray you to informe mee by 3 or 4 lines the plaine truth of the matter

1 Richard Smith, White's father in law.

without prejudice, that I may if you please indeavour to prevent further trouble & expence therein, & pray believe that I will gladly interpose betweene you & any of your neighbours in order to make & preserve peace & good neighbourhood.

My good Lord Bishopp[1] hath severall times mentioned his dislike as well of the rude & unmannerly behaviour towards you, as of your haughty & passionate behaviour towards them, & of your bad example directly opposite to the doctrine & example of our blessed saviour, & seemed trobled that his visitacon & pastorall care & advice had no better effecte.

My wife & I doe remember our true love & service to you to to your good wife & children, & pray as you have opportunity present our humble service to Mr Tucker[2] & his lady, & to Madam Fitzjames, & her good mother,[3] with our thanks for all their favours to us, & that wee shalbe glad to heare of all theirs & your good healths & welfare, & pray don't think that I have any other end or designe in what I have said or done, but to discharge the duty of a good neighbour & to shew my selfe as I am
Your true friend & servant
R.H.
Chancery Lane
Janry 11 1695

Verso Note: Copy of a letter to Mr White at Avebury, 11 January 1695. I shewed the originall to my Lord Bishop of Sarum, & hee approved it.

5. John White to Sir Richard Holford WSHC 184/1, pt.1.[4]
[c.25 January 1695/6][5]

Sir,
I return you many thanks for your great kindnesse so largely exprest in your late letter, & for giving your selfe the trouble of using many arguments with my neighbours when you was in the country to reduce them from their foolryes, but I knew they were prepossest with such a strong prejudice & leavend with <u>so much malice</u> that there would be no working upon them. You cast pearl before swine who trampled upon them. I find Farmer Skeate, who is my profest enemy, as appeares sufficiently by his setting up a <u>hellish, factious, scandalous, & schismatical conventicle</u> in opposition to me, & by his exposinge me in all company where he comes, thinking therby to take away my good nam, for the mobb is very apt to beleeve any reports that are raisd upon ministers, hath preferd a bill against me to you, & by <u>his lies</u> endeavours to make you out of conceit with me, but you are wiser then to give credit <u>to his lies</u>, though I beleeve him

1 Bishop Burnet.
2 Charles Tooker, J.P., of East Kennett.
3 Ann Fitzjames, widow, was the lady of the manor of Clatford at this date; cf. *VCH Wilts* 12, p.173.
4 There is a copy of this letter at WSHC 184/4, pt.2.
5 Undated; conjectural date based on date received.

to be the greatest & most impudent liar in the county, wherefore I thinke my selfe obliged to justify my dealing with him. My father Smith[1] hath often told me that by the bargain which he & Farmer Skeate made at the Folly[2] for my tithes Farmer Skeate was to pay me £4 & offerings for your farm, & he was to pay for Mr Norris[3] his farm as much as the last tenant ever gave which I know was above £10. The farmer not paying this mony, I demanded it of him, who pleaded ignorance & pretended that he did not know the bargain it being made by you & Mr Norris & Mr Smith, but he told me that he should shortly see you, & then he would know what the bargain was, though my father Smith had told him what it was, but one would thinke there should be no need to tell him of it because he made it, but not goinge to London he told me he would write to you about the businesse, & accordingly he did write, & by Mr Smith's letter I find he told you this notorious lie, that I had sued him. I have not done any such thing but I did threaten to sue him & will certainly do it if he doth not pay me shortly, for which reason have I forbear him, unlesse by his hectoring, rude, abusive, insolent, imperious behaviour lately at my house, he thinkes he hath obliged me to be kind to him, but this is not the way to deal with me. I know he designs to wrangle me out of £10, but his skill may fayl, & if I can I will prevent him from cheating me any more. If he shuffles with you as he hath often with me he will prove no very good tenant. In time you will detect him & find him as well as I & others have done. As to what I have done to John Mills, who is the only man that I have sued since you was at Avebury, I have this to say for my selfe, he owed me £20 upon bond, & being not very well satisfyed with his condition, I cald upon him for it, & allowd him 20 weekes to pay it in, but he not paying it I sued him, for I had no mind to lose it, & I hope it is no crime to sue for mony, especially when it is in danger of being lost. I suppose the farmer hath given you a false account of all matters relating to me, & therefore I thought fit to give you a right state of the case, that you might be no longer under a mistake concerning me, for I assure you I am no such man as the Farmer represents me. But not to trouble you any more at present, I begge leave to subscribe my selfe what really I am
Your humble servant
John White

I pray Sir, give my humble service to your Lady. My wife gives her humble service to you both.
Because I am unwilling to disoblige you I desire to know of you what course you would have me take with the farmer, whether you would have me lose my mony, or whether you will give me leave to sue him, for he is such a crosse fellow, & hath so great an antipathy against the clergy that I beleeve he will not pay it till he is forct. If you please to be so kind to write to me again, I desire you to direct your letter to be left at Mr William Baylyes shop, silkman in Marlbrough.

1 John White's father in law, Richard Smith.
2 One of the inns at Beckhampton; see *AWS*, p.320, for its various name changes.
3 Probably William Norris of Bromham and Lincolns Inn, who owned Pophams in Avebury, and who served as steward to Sir Richard in 1700; cf. WSHC 184/8.

Verso Note 1: Mr John White of Avebury, received 27 January 1695. Answered the 30th & directed to Mr Baylys.
Verso Note 2: [1] Mr Rousell of Cadnam[2] a scholemaster is the preacher at the meetings.
Verso Address: For the Right Worshipfull Sir Richard Holford, Knight, at his house in Chancery Lane, London

6. Sir Richard Holford to John White WSHC 184/1, pt.1.
[30 January 1695/6]

Master White
I have yours (not dated) & am perswaded you had not mine before you or did not mind it when you wrote yours, else you would have told me whether Farmer Skeate had tendred or offered to pay you £4 for his last yeares dues for the farme, which I particularly inquired after (& if I remember right) twas the chiefe ingredient of mine, for that his letter to me was that hee had sent it to you, & you had refused it, & that hee afterwards tendred it to you & you not onely refused it, but threatned to sue him for it, to prevent which hee requested mee, to write to you about it, which was the whole of his letter to mee about that matter, tho your fancy suggests much more, else you would not have termed it a Bill drawne to mee against you, & by his lyes make mee out of conceite with you, as your words. In answer to his I promised & thought myselfe obliged to write to you as I soone after did, & did expect if any a much more Christianlike answer. Mr White, I doe think myself obliged plainely to tell you, that you indulge your passion to the prejudice of your prudence, & that such revileing language (though deserved) would better become a man of a lower & meaner education & of any other profession. I wish wee could duely observe the doctrine of St Paule in his epistle to the Corinthians 1 Cor 13[3] & would intreate you againe to read over the most excellent booke of the wise son of Syrach[4] & more particularly observe ch. 28 ver 8, 9, 10 &c.,[5] & Chap 38 ver 25, 26[6] & certainely twill put you in a better temper. Good God! How unwilling should wee bee to bee snatchd out of the world with such thoughts in our hearts or such words in our mouths, & how unfitting would such conversation bee to the company wee hope for after this life. Pray don't I think that I doe hereby or ever did or will diswade you from any lawfull meanes for recovery of your just dues, if in a neighborly manner they may not otherwise bee had. But you must excuse me if I don't applaud or approve of your boysterous haughty & uncharitable words & actions exposing your selfe thereby more than the malice of the ignorant & unruley men you complaine of can doe. Methinks I doe guess by the speritt of your lines why my worthy good

1 Note in a different hand.
2 Cadenham, in the parish of Bremhill, is probably meant.
3 Concerning love.
4 The apocryphal book of Ecclesiasticus.
5 Concerning arguments.
6 On gaining knowledge.

friends Mr Smith[1] hath not afforded mee 3 or 4 lines as I desired. Pray doe me the favour to put him in mind of my request that hee will tell mee the agreement wee made at the Folly. As I remember twas £4 in full of all dues for the farme, & I doe protest I don't remember that there was any word mentond of offerings. Pray advise with him & good men, & don't hearken to whisperers nor backbiters, nor give any just provocations to anye, even the worst of your neighbors.

I would gladly heare from you againe at your leisure & in a milder temper, & doe pray you in the meanetime to give mine & my Frogg's service to Mrs White, &, when you have any opportunity, to Mr Smith & Mrs Smith, & to Mr Tucker & his lady, & to Madam Fitzjames & her mother, & that you will excuse the plaine dealinge of,

Sir,
Your friend & Servant
R.H.
Chancery Lane 30 January 1695

Your postscript haveing a much milder ayre than your epistle though introduced with a complement of your being unwilling to disoblige mee, I doe wish & would advise that before you conduct any action against the farmer or any body else, that, you will first demand & bee ready to receive what is due. And I hope hee hath not such an antipathy against the clergy as you mention, but will rather cheerfully pay what is his due than to bee at a great deale of trouble & expence, & afterwards pay it with costs. I have by this post writt to him to pay the £4 if hee hath so much money that you will receive, for I doubt tis almost as great a [?rakitie] at Avebury as elsewhere. If you desire it I believe hee will shew you my letter, & to prevent mistakes I think you may show him this postscript. And when I shall find him answer your character of him I shall not bee fond of his further acquaintance. In the meane time, I will expect & hope the best, but must take care that my inheritance bee not clogged with more than justly due.

Verso Note: Coppy letter to Mr John White at Avebury, 30 January 1695, directed to bee left at Mr Baylyes, a mercer in Marlebrough.

I write to Farmer Skeat at the same time, directed to the Folly, & wished him to tender the £4, & shew my letter if desired.

7. Richard Smith to Sir Richard Holford WSHC 184/1, pt.1.

Kennett
7 February 1695/6[2]

Most Honored Sir,
After mine & my wifes harty & humbl servis to you & your good Lady presented,

1 His name is inserted on the side of the letter.
2 1695 is actually written; see verso note 1.

this is to acquiante you that I received yours and therein I find that Farmer Scate has misinforemed you in what he writ, which was that Mr White had renewed his unkindnes in suing severall of his neighbors for what he mought have had without trouble or charge, particularly Farmer Scate, which is a great untruthe & denyed by the farmer that ever he wret you any such thing, but to convince him I shewed him yours but he still denied it. Tis true he did [?sheue] Farmer Mills but it was for moneyes uppon bond. How he could be blamed for that I know not, haveing given him warning to prouid it long before, but as to the agreement we made at the Folle, Mr Whit did never bogel, which was 4 pound for your farm, & as much for Mr Nores[1] farem. Euen Farmer Garraway payed, which will be sufeciently proveed, but if the farmer denies that he will insist uppon the former bargaine, which was five pound for that year being a uery great coren yeare, & 4 pounds ten for the last year which will be as well proved. I am sorry you should be troubled so much about such triuall business, the farmer being in all the false, not standing to his agreements, but indeuering still as I thinke to make the breach wider, which [?conclueds] from him that shall ever faithfuly & honestly serve you in any thing capabel of,
Rich Smith

Verso Address: For his Honored Frend Sir Ritchard Holford in Chancere Lane, London, these are.
Verso Note 1: Mr Smith 7 February 1696; answered 20 February 1695[2]
Verso Note 2:: Holford & White. Perused 26th October 1756. Proper to be at hand on the present dispute.[3]

8. **Sir Richard Holford to Mr Smith** WSHC 184/1, pt.1.
[22 February 1695/6]

My worthy good friend!
I doe thank you for yours of the 7th instant, and am glad of your & Mr Smiths good health. A little before the receipt of yours, I received a letter from Mr White, which intimated to bee an answer to mine, but in truth 'twas not, for hee hath not told mee whether Farmer Skeat had or had not tenderd or offered to pay £4 for his dues for the farme, but was pleased to fill his letter with passionate & (hee must forgive mee if I say) imprudent expressions, noe words tending to peace or good neighourhood. I by the next post returned my answer to it, and did (as I think becomes a true friend) deale very plainely with him & repeated my request to shew a good example. I hope hee hath shewed it you, & if hee had thought fit to have said anything in answer, it might have eased you of the troble & expense of this. I beleive in mine to you I might mistake, if I said Mr White had sued the Farmer, but fhe Farmer writ mee word that hee had tendered & offered to pay

1 Probably Mr Norris.
2 That is, 1695/6.
3 This letter was obviously consulted when Staynor Holford was in dispute with John Mayo; see their letters of 1756 below.

£4, & Mr White refused it, and threatened to sue him, and therefore prayed my directions, & I might well think Mr White would not threaten in vaine, & in his to mee hee sayth, I have threatened to sue him, and I will certainely doe it if hee don't shortly pay mee, soe that it was a bare mistake grounded upon probability. I [*illegible*] the agreement at the Folly was, as you say £4 for the farme, and I should bee very angry with Skeate if hee neglected or refused to pay it, but I canot bee angy with him for not paying it, if hee who was to receive it refused it.

I am not easie when I doe [?busye] you or my selfe with such impertinent, idle, wilfull, squabbles between men, who will sacrifice their discretions to indulge their humors. But mee thinks I ought to doe my utmost, to make & preserve peace and good neighbourhood, & I doe assure you that is the utmost of my aime in this & what I have formerly said or done upon this subject. But I must bee very plaine with Mr White, & doe pray you to let him know that if hee shall insist to have 2d more out of the farme than what is justly due I must (though unwillingly) undertake the controversy, else my inheritance may bee burthened, and tennants are too apt to bee terrified, or at least will pretend to bee soe if what they are to pay bee not reduced to a certainty. And I can't tell how soone I may want a good tennant if the one half of Mr White's predictions prove true. And I shalbee heartily thankfull to him & you or any other that can & will helpe mee to a better than the present tennant. Mr Smith, since I have trobled you, with this tedious stuff, pray give mee leave to bee a little more trob[1] troblesome. The Act for 4 shillings in the pound[2] for this yeare will require a speedy-execution. And though I must not think what is given by Parliament too much, yet I am not fond, nor doth it suite very well with my inclinacons to pay more than my proportion, and though tis scarce possible a tax can bee layd equally on all, yet I am sure it may bee layd much more equally than that I shall pay 4 shillings in the pound according to the letter of the law, & others in the same county & hundred not much above halfe soe much. I do know you are very knowing in all these affaires, and doe therefore beg your assistance as a neighbour and friend to take a little care and paines therein with your neighbour Commissioners to make the rates as equall as you can, for that, if I have harder measure than others, I must complaine in the Exchequer, which I shalbee heartily unwilling to doe because I know the inconvenience. I had it in my thoughts to have trobled Mr Tucker with a few lynes in this matter, but would therein willingly bee directed by you. And now pray excuse this troble. Present mine & my Froggs service to Mrs Smith, & to Mr Tucker & his Lady & Madam Fizjames and her mother, & let mee continue
Your faithfull friend & servant
Richd Holford
22 February 1695

Farmer Skeat hath been here, but staied too short a time, & that soe taken up with his other affaires that I had noe opportunity to talke much with him, but hee

1 Page break.
2 Land Tax.

protested hee had respectfully tendred & offerred to pay & was ready & willing to pay Mr White the £4 when ever hee will appoint to recieve it. Upon my word, hee never did nor shall receive any encouragement from mee, to deny or detaine from Mr White or any body else, what is justly due, nor to disrespect him or any body else.

If Mr White thinks fit to receive the £4, let him give a receipt in writeing, & express that it is in full for one yeares dues from the farme for the year ended at … .

Verso Note: Copy of a letter to Mr Smith, 22 Februar 1695.

9. John White to Sir Richard Holford WSHC 184/1, pt.1.[1]

Sir,

[4 April 1696]

By my long silence you may conclude that either I cannot or am afraid to answer your last letter, wherin you alter your style, make grosse reflections, & fall upon me with hard words, but I know great men take a liberty to say anything of their inferiors. You tell me that I indulge my passion to the prejudice of my prudence, but if you please to consider with what sort of man I have to do, & how I have been & still am abused, affronted & injured by them, you would excuse me for being passionate, & be more moderate in your censures, I assure you what ever you thinke of me I will allwayes prove honest, & make it appear that I have been misrepresented to you. You caution me against hearkeninge to backbiters, but I doubt you have an ear open to such, for how else could you have an ill opinion of me, who never did you nor any of the schismatical crew here any wrong, though you intimate that I have been injurious to some of my factious neighbours by suinge them before I demanded what was due to me, & in a letter that you sent to my father Smith you charged me particularly with suinge Farmer Skeate. This you must have from the farmer or from such a malicious fellow as he is, who misinformd you, for then I had not sued him, neither shall I sue any man before I have made a demand, but if the brethren of the separation will not pay me what they owe me, I thinke without the breath of charity I may make use of what meanes the law directs for the recovery of my just dues, & that if I sue any of them after they refuse to pay me I shall not incur the crime of being litigious. Whereas you say you must take care that your inheritance be not cloggd with more than justly due, you are in no danger of any such thing, & if any man should offer at it he must be a fool or a madman, but as you will secure your estate so you have no reason to be angry with me for endeavouringe to assert the rights of my small vicaridge. In any such thing my Lord Bishop hath promised his assistance to the inferior clergy that want it, but I hope there will be no need of it, for it is not probable that a worthy Gentleman who writes & speakes Divinity should be guilty of sacriledge. I desire nothing but what is my due from my neighbours, & if they will pay that without

1 There is a copy of this letter at WSHC 184/4, pt.2.

trouble I will give them none. Since you thinke I was partial in relating the bargain between Farmer Skeat & me, I suppose my father Smith before this time hath given you an account of that affair, & because the farmer will not stand to that bargain which was made at the Folly, I will force him to stand to a former bargain that he made for the last yeares tithes, which will be proved as well as that, I should be glad if I am under a mistake concerning your tenant, & that he will not answer the character which I gave him. But if Theophrastus[1] were alive he could not give him a full character. Whereas you do not remember that there was any mention made of offerings at the Folly, that is not material, for tithes & offerings are distinct things, & if nothing was said of them then the farmer did not take them & consequently he must pay them. I wish all differences & quarrels between your tenant and me were at an end, but as long as he playes the knave with me & endeavours to cheat me there will be no good correspondence between us. If I were to pay mony to him I do not question but he would remember the bargain exactly, but because I am receive mony of him this alters the case. He is good at a rake. I intend for the future to take the tithes that are due to me upon your farm in kind, because Skeate falsifyes his word & will not perform any bargain that he makes with me. Begging your pardon for giving you this trouble, I rest,
Your most humble servan,
John White
Avebury, April 4, 1696

I pray, Sir, give mine and my wive's service to your Lady.

Verso Note: Mr White of Avebury Apr 4 1696.
Verso Address: For the Right Worshipfull Sir Richard Holford, Knight at his house in Chancery Lane, London.
Received per post 13 Apr 96, answered 16th. [2]

10. Richard Smith to Farmer Skeate WSHC 184/4, pt.2.

27 June 1696

Farmer Skeate,
Upon considering the matter betweene Mr White and you, my opinion is that you ought to pay him presently four pounds for his dues out of Sir Richard Holford's farme, and six shillings and eight pence for his dues out of Mr Norris farme for the last yeare, and that the four pounds per annum be paid yearely for three yeares, and that you ought quietly to permitt Mr White's cows to goe and feed on Hackpin Downe as usuall, he paying his proportion of wages to the

1 A noted Greek philosopher who had a 'divine style of expression', according to Aristotle.

2 A copy of an answer to this letter is written on its inside page. However, much of it is in shorthand, and it has not been deciphered. At its foot is the following note: 'for Mr White at his house in Avebury, Wiltes. To be left with Wm Bayly, silkman, in Marlbrough, Wiltes'.

hayward.
I am
Your loving friend
Rich Smith
27th June 1696

A copy of this given to Mr White the 29 day of September 1698. I coppied it, & sent it by my man Rich [?Hemin].
R.H.

Verso Note: Mr Richard Smith's award, 27 Junii 1696, beetween Mr White & Farmer Skeate. See Mr White's answer, fo.[1]

11. Sir Richard Holford to John White WSHC 184/1, pt.1.
[30 September 1696]

Sir,
Seeing you affect to bee soe great a stranger & doe avoid being spoken with, therefore as much as in mee lyes to prevent mistakes & to preserve peace if possible, I doe take leave to put you in mynde, that when I was here at Whitsontide last, ~~and gave you the trouble of 2 or 3 visits~~ I did request you (if you thought fit) to give mee in writeing a particular of your dues or demands (out of my farme) as Vicar of Avebury. I then told you why I desired it, & for the same reason (upon a little more experience of your dispositon) I doe now repeate my request, but if you shall rather incline to indulge your singular humor I am unwilling now to disturbe you farther, than to let you know, that I have been willing and desireing to show myself
Sir, your friend & servant
Ultimo September 1696

I have a copy of this & will expect your answer in 3 or 4 daies
I sent it to Mr White by my servant Richard the day of the date who told mee that hee deliverd it to Mr White's owne hand.
Ultimo September 1696

Verso Note: A copy: of a letter or note to Mr White, 30 September 1696.

12. John White to Sir Richard Holford WSHC 184/1, pt.1.[2]
[30 September 1696]

Sir,
You may easily guesse at the reason of my being so great a stranger. I have been

1 This presumably relates to Holford's filing system, but no folio number is given.
2 There is a copy of this letter in WSHC 184/4, pt.2.

seldom in your company, but you were pleased to take an occasion to quarrel with me,[1] the first time you sent for me to your house you gave me such a rough salutation that some who were present wondred to see me take it so patiently, & therefore I am unwilling to give you an oportunity to renew your former kindnesses, wheras you say I avoid the being spoken with, I am not yet forct to hide my head, & I hope never shall, unlesse might overcome right. If you or any other men have any businesse to me, you know where I dwell & tis an easy matter to speake with me. I am glad to hear that you pretend to have an inclination to preserve peace.[2] I hope your intentions & words go together, I assure you I have no desire to have an engagement with you for I know you you (sic)will overmatch me.[3] I thinke there is no need yet to do what you propose, for the businesse about tithes upon your farm was by your cousent referred to my father Smith, who hath determined it & orderd Farmer Skeate to pay a certain sume of mony to me for some yeares, & when that term is expired, if I am concernd in the Vicaridge here I shall endeavour to gratify you in what you require. In the meantime, I must desire you to give me leave to make further enquiry into this matter for I suppose my vicaridge is better endowed than I yet am sensible of, & as I would not have more then my due, so for want of a litle care I would not lose my right. I hope you will perswade your good tenant to pay me the mony that he owes me for this year, for he hath received all the profits & I thinke he hath not obliged me to tarry for mony when it is due. What you have shewed your selfe to me I am not ignorant, but notwithstanding all your threatnings & blustringe expressions about last Whitsontide, I shall continue unlesse I see great cause to the contrary, Sir
Your most humble servant
John White
Sept 30 96

Verso Note: Mr White 30th 7r 96. Mentoning that Mr Smith had determined the matter of tythes.
Verso Address: For Sir Richard Hollford, Knight.

13. John White to Sir Richard Holford WSHC 184/1, pt.1.[4]
[c.10 October 1696][5]

Sir,
I have been lately informd that you intend to sue me, but I am sure you have no just cause of action against me for I owe you nothing, & if I have done you any

1 In margin: 'Q. who?', in Sir Richard Holford's hand.
2 In margin: 'My former letters to Mr White are all to that purpose', in Sir Richard Holford's hand.
3 In margin: 'Why won't hee then gratifie meee in my request', in Sir Richard Holford's hand.
4 There is a copy of this letter in 184/4, pt.2.
5 The date is not given in the actual letter, but in the recipient's note on the verso.

wrong (as I cannot remember that I have) I shall be ready to make you satisfaction, & if you sue me without cause it will not be much for your reputation, & you will act contrary to your religious letters that pretend Christianity, which I beleeve allowes no such thing. As to what you require of me, I cannot do it yet, because I know not how much land the ell ridges (about which the great dispute arose between Skeate & me) contain, & I hope you will not be so unreasonable as to put me upon impossibilities, but if you please to peruse your own writings, there I suppose you may be satisfyed. I hear you are angry with me because I did not preach before you when you was last in the country, but if you was not at home whan I preacht (for your Lady knowes that I preacht several times while she was at Avebury.[1] That was no fault of mine, and when I was not at home I procured other ministers to your great content, & therefore this was so far from being a crime that I thought I had obliged you by it. I am no salamander neither do I love to live in the fire of contention. I have children enough to bestow what I have upon without feeding lawyers. I make it my request therfore to you not to give me the trouble & charge of a lawsuit, & I shall looke upon it as a kindnesse to,
Sir
Your most humble servant
John White
Avebury

Verso Address: For Sr Richard Hollford, Knight, in Chancery Lane, London
Verso Note: Mr White, Clerk, not dated, received 12 October 1696 at 4°

14. John White to Sir Richard Holford WSHC 184/1, pt.1.[2]
[29 January 1696/7]

Sir,
The reason that you give me why you exhibite a bill in Chancery[3] against me to force me to set forth my dues upon your farm is, because if your tenant should go of it would be a hard matter to get another tenant unlesse my dues are ascertaind. But you need not feare your tenants goinge of, for he never got anything by renting till he came to your farm, & therefore I beleeve he undersands his interest so well that he will never leave it as long as he can hold it. I know who gave £500 per annum for it, & he got well by it, though he had not the priviledge to plow up the grounds as Farmer Skeate doth, out of which he raiseth great part of his rent. I doubt you hearken too much to a pack of cunning fellowes who hold all together, & are not willing to let you know the worth of your farm that they may the better make a market upon you. However, to please you, if possible, & to prevent future charge & trouble, for I assure you I desire neither, I shall present you with the following account of dues upon your farm. Imprimis, I may choose

1 Note on left side: 'but once & then sent to know &c'.
2 This letter is copied in 184/4, pt.2.
3 TNA C5/166/23.

two ell ridges of wheat when it is ripe, containinge by estimation one acre, & cut carry them away. Item the tithe of agistment cattle, & of grazing cattle, the tithe of the orchard, garden, & of all fruit trees, of pigeons, turkyes, geese, ducks, eggs, piggs, & four pence for the fall of a calfe, and three pence for the milke of every cow that is kept upon the farm belongs to me. If you exhibit a thousand bills against me, & put me to my oath as many times, I can give you no other account, & therefore I hope you will rest satisfied with it, & not prosecute me at law when there is no pretence. Wishing the recovery of your good Lady to whom I pray give my humble service, I rest,
Your humble servant
John White
Avebury
Jan 29 96

I suppose my children have committed no crime against you, but you will punish them if you make me spend the portion which they should have, & by your proceedings against me that proverb, the fathers have eaten soure grapes, and the children's teeth are set on edge, which God would not have used among his people, will be verified.

Verso Note: Mr John White letter 29 Janurii 96
Verso Address: For Sir Richard Holford, knight, at his house in Chancery Lane, London.

15. Sir Richard Holford to John White[1]

Chanc Lane
4 February 1696/7

Sir,
I have your favour of the 29 of January, & (because I cant help it) I am not much displeased that you are pleased to continue your mistake of all that I offer, & because I ~~am unwilling~~ [?won't imitate your way of writing] to widen the breach you have soe fondly made, I doe write this to tell you that I doe expect your full & plaine answer to my bill, whereof I hope you have ere this time a coppie. You might have saved yourselfe & mee the troble if you had thought fit, and it may bee in time you may bee as willing to afford entire your friendship as I have hitherto been to shew my selfe
Sir
Your friend & servant
R.H.

My poore wife continues very ill, shee & I doe present our love & service to Mrs White & your children.

1 This letter was copied on the inside page of the previous letter.

16. Sir Richard Holford to John White WSHC 184/1, pt.2.
29 April 1697
Mr White,
I think it becomes me as a neighbour & a Christian to condole with you upon the death of your son, & therefore I doe troble you with this on that errand (I heard not of it till last night, else I would sooner have taken notice of it) to tell you that my wife & I are sensible of your great loss, but God who governs the world knows best what is fit for us, & wee must submit to his will. And lett me take this opportunity to ask why you are pleased to delay your answer to the Bill you constrained me to exhibite. The clerks & solicitors wilbe pressing for costs, but I had rather you would prevent them. The loss of your friendship & your very unkind rayleing at mee with base & scandalous reflections shall not provoke me to doe anything unbecoming, but it hath in great measure interrupted & prevented mine & my wife's paying our respects to Mrs White, & our love & service to my good friend Mr Smith[1] & his wife. Which I doe now pray you to present with our best wishes for all their healths. If the charge of this (2d by the post) bee more than you are willing to beare, pray charge it on me & I'le cheerfully make it good, for that I never did designe any waies to burthen you, & should have been very well pleased if you would have imbraced the friendshipp of (hee that never wilbe otherwise than)
Your true friend
R H

Verso Note: Copy letter to Mr White 29 April 1697

17. Sir Richard Holford to Richard Smith WSHC 184/1, pt.2.

London
9 November 1697

Master Smith,
Though I canot think this can bee very welcome to you, because I have observed your dislike of some things I shall menton, yet I am sure I ought & doe give my hearty thanks to Mr Tucker and you, for your friendly indeavors to set matters between Mr White & mee in a true light, and to have quieted that stubborne & peevish proud spirit which creates & carries on unnessesary and needles squabbles at Avebury. Because though Mr Tucker might bee a stranger to the indeavors I had used to invite & incourage a friendship between Mr White & mee, I was willing to informe him of the severall steps I had made, & was trobled that I had that very morning sent away with the rest of my things Mr White's owne letters, & the coppies of mine to him, which was all the evidence I need use to shew his most unkind carriges, & though I perceived hee had all my letters to him, & coppies of his to mee, yet hee would not produce above one or two. I did often importune him, both by word of mouth & letters, to let mee know what his demands were, as Vicar, out of my farme, and often told him the reasons why

1 White's father in law.

I desired it, & assured him I would rather increase than any way deminish it, and was very glad that you had somewhat interposed & put an end to the then difference between him & Famer Skeate, but hee set mee at defiance & with very unbecomeing (because untrue reflections) of supporting fanatiqs & [*illegible*] & pretending to religion, &c., & ~~puting me to defiance~~ &c. Wherefore I was constrained for quietnes sake to exhibit a bill against him, yet doubting that his passion might prejudice his prudence. I even then writ to him & desired him duly to consider & to give in a ful & plaine answer, & thereby prevent unnessary troble & expence to himselfe & mee, but hee not thinking fit to putt in his answer I repeated my request & told him that the clerks & solicitors are great sharpers, & will insist on costs, or to that effect (hee hath my letters), and when hee did put in that which hee calls a full answer, it was soe evasive & unjust, as if hee had designed noething more than troble & expence, wherefore I was constrained to take exceptions, and hee ought by the rules of the Court to have answered them in eight daies, or else I might referr them ~~to a Master &c~~, but I hoped by giving him a long vaccation to consider of it that hee would have been willing to have given a just & plaine answer, but tis soe much [?time] lost, as desired. I must now pursue the usual method. He was pleased amongst the rest of his unkind & unjust reflections to say that I designed to undoe his wife & children, which was not ~~not only unkind but very untrue, for~~ whereas I never had the least thought that way, and his & my letters must judge betweene us, & am trobled that hee is of soe rough a temper, and soe reguardles of his words.

This part is not a true copy, but tis to the same sense.[1]

I think I should not have trobled myselfe or you about this matter at this time, but that there is now before mee, a complaint by or on behalfe of the poore shopkeeper Hayward that Mr White hath served him with a subpena in the Exchequer [?for] the matter, his defence that I am told not above the value of 12d. And it had been worth his troble to bee informed himself [?but includes this very Parliament], to prevent vexation, & for the more easy recovery of smal tythes, have made a law impowering two of the neighbor Justices of the Peace to heare and determine the same,[2] which meethinks gave him a much more easy & friendly remedie than by a chargeable & Exchequer suite. And I am afraid tis vexation puts him upon such designes. I doe therefore give you this intimation, & probablie you may shew it to Mr Tucker, & both of you being friends to peace, may (it may bee) have an opertunity of discoursing Mr White, & bring him to a more neighborly temper, & then I should think thy troble well recompenced, & therefore doe hope you will take it in good part, being well intended by
Your Sincere friend & servant
Rich Holford

God bee thanked my poor wife is much better since her returne, than whilst in the country. Shee and I doe remember our service to Mr Tucker & his good lady,

1 This sentence is written in the left-hand margin.
2 7 & 8 William III, c.6, c.34.

& to you and Mrs Smith, & pray when you goe to Clatford to present our service to Madam Fitzjames & her mother &c.
Wee are every moment expecting the good news of the King's being safely landed, and all hands at worke in prepareing for a welcome reception.

Verso Note: The substance of a letter written to Mr Smith of Kinnet, 9 November 1697.
Verso Address: 'for my good friend Mr Richard Smith at Kennet, neare to Marlebrough, Wiltes.

18. Charles Tooker to Sir Richard Holford WSHC 184/1, pt.2.
[c.29 December 1697][1]

Honoured Sir,
My son I have latly taken home from Oxford.[2] He is much inclined to cuntry sportes, especialy hunting, & has now some houndes. Your farmer William Skeate has often thretnd that if he came uppon your manner he would shute his doggs. Without any provocation, he has not onely exprest this to one or two, but to severall. Yesterday being Munday he was a hunting with Mr Richard Smith of Kennett & 3 of his sons. They did not finde the hare they ware hunting in your manner, but she running into it, he watchd for her & with a grayhound or a brace that he now keepeth, he kild her before theire houndes, crossing up & downe the grounds till he could meete her. I came to the gentmen about halfe an houre after. Had I bin there present I would have causd his doggs to be hangd presently. Sir, my request to you is that you would favour me with a line or 2 by the next post, to lett me know whether he does this by your order. I am unwilling to grant a warrant to take away his doggs & gunns, till I had acquainted you with it. You know by a late Act of Parlament made for the preservation of the game noe lord of a manor can authorise any gamekeeper[3] to keepe dogs & gunns to destroy the game, or to use them but in the company of his master. Whether you have made him yours I know not, but as I am infomd he has kild a brace of hares in a day with his grayhounds.

Sir, I am very well satisfid you are more a gentleman than to countenance such a high shewd cuntry clowne to doe such an ungenteele action, who presumes to say on this & all other unwarrantable actions his landlord will bare him out. I have a little manor at Kennett. If any gentleman that is qualified is pleasd to course or hunt there I doe waight on him & assist him what I can, & soe I will the same to you, & if I can divert you when you come into these parts with such recreations as wee use, I shall thinck myselfe happy. In hopes to injoy more of yours & your good ladye's company in these parts shall allwayes be my study to

1 Letter undated.
2 Charles Tooker, baptised at East Kennett 29th November 1677. He cannot be identified in *Alumni Oxoniensis* **www.british-history.ac.uk/alumni-oxon/1500-1714**.
3 Skeat was Holford's gamekeeper; see Holford's letter to John Rose, below, 7th June 1710, (no. 69) withdrawing his warrant.

oblidge & sarve you who am
Your most faithfull friend humble servant
Chas Tooker

My wife & son presents theire humble sarvis to you & your good lady, & to all the rest of your fire side, as well as my selfe.

Verso Note: Mr Tooker, not dated, received 31 December 97. Answered 4 January 1697.
Verso Address: To Sir Richard Holford on of the masters in Chancery at his house in Chancery Lane, London, these.

19. Sir Richard Holford to Charles Tooker WSHC 184/1, pt.2.

Chancery Lane,
4 January 1697/8

Sir,
Haveing spent 2 or 3 days with a friend 3 or 4 miles out of towne to begin the new yeare, at my returne last night I found yours (without any date but by the post marke it came last Fryday). It seemes to be written with a more than ordinary warmth but concludes very friendly, and soe I doe take it, and because I don't love to mistake, nor to be mistaken, your words are "Farmer Skeate has often threatened that if my son came to hunt in your manour he would shoote his doggs, without any provocaton, and has not only expressed this to one or two, but to severall, & yesterday he was hunting with Mr Smith & his sons, and the hare running into your manor (not put up there) Skeate watcht for her and crossing the grounds with one or a brace of greyhounds killed the hare before their hounds. I comeing to the gentlemen about halfe an houre after, had I beene there present I would have caused his doggs to be hanged presently. Pray by the next let me know whether he doth this by your order. I am unwilling to graunt a warrant to take away his doggs & guns till I had acquainted you with it. You know by a late act of Parliament noe lord of a mannor can authorize any gamekeeper to keepe doggs & guns to destroy the game, or use them but in the company of his master. I am informed he hath killed a brace of hares in a day with his greyhounds, and says that in this & all other his unwarrantable actions that his landlord will beare hime out &c".

Sir, I never did nor ever will incourage him or any one, nor indeavour to beare him or any other out in any unwarrantable actions. But when at Avebury for three or four days, and walkeing or rideing about the grounds, I have often wisht for a greyhound (tho but a sollatery companion, & yet more suitable to my short stay than hounds, which I doe alsoe love very well), and the Farmer's last letter told me that Mr Sloper[1] had given him one & that he would keepe it for

1 Walter Sloper of Winterbourne Monkton was the attorney who, in 1684, acquainted John Aubrey with the fact that the great stone at the Avebury end of West Kennett

me (he did not mention a brace). As to his gunns I ordered him to keepe a good one, well fixed, to defend his house & preserve his goods (I have alsoe some there of which I doe expect his care) and I cannot, will not blame him if he does soe, nor will I interpret this an authority to destroy the game, though the late act were as you mention, but therein I am sure you will give me leave to be of another opinion, because the words will not beare your interpretacon, yet am farr from encourageing him or any one else, though of better quality, to destroy game, and doe assure you that, had I beene there, I would not have taken up the hare before your son's doggs, but rather cherefully assisted him in his sport, and I thinke Mr Smith can doe me right in this matter, who I dare say will not complaine for want of his share in that game. I thanke God I never found my selfe of a very timerous nature, unlesse of doeing wrong, & can suffer a pretty deale rather than find fault, and in all things am willing & desirous to doe as I would be done to. My farme at Avebury is not fitt to shift tenants often, & therefore I must beare with the present tenant till I can meete with a better, but I am trobled when I doe heare of any rude or indecent behaviour towards his superiours, the rather for that it is contrary to his repeated promises to me, which I believe I signified in a letter to you on his behalfe. I doe intend to send him the substance of your letter, with my thoughts relateing to his rude language and disrespect, and doe expect in his next the usuall plea of not guilty, however doe hope he will not for the future give you any just cause of offence, & doe hope you will be as kind as you can to soe rough a temper. I doe heartily thanke you for your proposed kindnesse, & should be glad to have frequent oportunityes of mutuall civilityes for preservacon of friendshipp. My poore wife is, God be thanked, much better than at summer, but is weake and very tender. Shee & I doe present our service to you, & to Madam Tucker, and pray remember our service to Mr Smith and his good wife. I did in a letter to him in November last thanke you & him for your friendly visit & bringing Mr White with you, which I wisht might have answeard your purpose. Pray Sir, be pleased to present my service to your son, & tell him I will be the last that shall discourage his country sports, but shall be allwayes ready to imbrace your & his friendshipp, as becomes
Sir,
Your faythfull friend & servant,
Rich Holford

Directed to Charles Tooker esq at Kennet neare to Marlbrough, Wiltes

Verso Note: Copy letter to Charles Tooker, esq, 4 January 97.

Avenue had fallen; cf. Aubrey, John. *John Aubrey: my own life*, [ed.] Ruth Scurr. Chatto Windus, 2015, p.339.

20. William Skeat to Sir Richard Holford WSHC 184/1, pt.2.

Avebury
26 February 1697/8

Sir,
This morning Hillier wife com throo the backside & as my men & I was lodding the waggon for Malbro marcut & I asked her what twas that shee had [?sore][1] against me att Mr Toker's, & shee ansard me & sed nothing. If I did aske Mr Toker he would tell shee had soore nothing against me but shee had against Hayerd, & so hafter I had don my marcut I went to Mr Yates & spock to hee about itt, & Mr Yates did tell me that shee did speak in relaishein to that which you rite to me, that I should preswaid her to fetch a warrant of the pece against Mr White. But Mr Yates did tell me that Mr Toker took her to the tother side of the rome & he did beleve that in Mr Tooker's giving her the othe shee did mince it as concerning me, but for Hayard's he is sartain tis truth. But my wife & a kinswoman & one of our maids herd every word as Hayeard sed, & they herd not one word of what is aleged against him, & so to thayr sarten nolledg tis all false. The 28 day of this instant I went to Mr Tookers, & desiered him to let me have a coppy of her oath, & hee refused to let mee have one. His ansar was twas not a yousfell[2] thing to unclose the King's secrets, but do say thar is nothing soore against mee, & Mr Yates & Mr Tooker have prommiesed me that they will satisfie your Worship that thar is nothing against mee. Mr Tooker nowes this woman to be a great thife, for shee stole clothes of the hidge as shee went throo his cinnet, which his men [?troker][3] her & had her in before thayr master, & hee would have whept her but that shee was bige with childe, & severall more such things as this, but tis to long to relate it at present. Sir, Mr White do behave himself as hee did ever since I newe hime, for wee have had a naibor which have lost his wife ye 14 day of this instant Febary, & went to ye parson to bery her, & hee refuesed to doe it, & would not let her have Christen burrell, nor would not let ye bell ring for her, & threatens as long as your Worship kipes him in law hee will plage & torment his naibors. Hee do give out speches that hee will ruin Hayeard. Sir, if you find mee gilty of anny such crime, I don't desire your frindshipe in anny such thing which is unjust, but if not gilty of anny such thing I hope your friendship will continu. I & my wife presents our umbell sarvice & duty to your selfe & my Lady & mis & littel master. All from your tenent to sarve you,
Will Skeate

Mr Hayerd presents his sarvis & duty to yourself & lady & children, with many thankes for his last kines.[4]

Verso Note: Farmer Skeate 26 Febuary 1697, relateing to Hilliar's wife.
Verso Address: For Sir Richard Holford in Chancry Lane near the Rowlls, London.

1 Sworn?
2 Useful.
3 Took?
4 Kindness?

21. Cornelius Yeate to Sir Richard HolfordWSHC 184/1, pt.2.

Marlburrough
28 February 1697/8

Honoured Sir,

I heartily thank you for the favour of your letter. What I writt to my Lord Bishop of Sarum was, no other than what I my self (and several others) heard Hellier's wife relate when she came before Justice Tooker, though I since find that when the depositions came to be pennd she hath minced the matter with respect to Farmer Skeate, but not with respect to Hayward, her written deposition against whom is in all respects as full as what I have reported to my Lord. I did at that very time enquire the character of the woman, being as unwilling to believe on the one hand that the malice of Skeate or Hayward could stirr them up to so great a wickedness, as upon the other hand that Hellier should offer her self to be perjured gratis. But upon the whole the character given of her was very faire, & till Farmer Skeate came to me Saturday last I never heard anything ill concerning her, & then onely from his mouth referring me to Justice Tooker himself, of whom I will make farther inquiry when I see him next, which I believe will be to morrow, & of what he shall saye in this matter I will give you an impartial account. It is certain that there is a great piece of villany either on the one side or the other, which deserves to be searchd out, & on which side soever it be found it ought to be severely punishd. I showd your letter to Mr White Saturday last, and he still avowes that he hath in his answers fully sett forth whatever he knows to be demandable, so farr as hath as yet come to his knowledg. I know he is passionate & apt to flye out in reproachfull language, for which I & all his friends have blamed him, but whether he hath mixd his pashion with his ink is what I doe not know, it being more than half a yeere since I saw his letters with your answers (all but the first which he says is lost or mislayd) so that I neither can nor does ot become me to give my judgment in this matter. All that I humbly begg is that what is past may be forgotten, & that if possible there may be an amicable reconciliation for the future (and so a stop may may [sic] be putt to those (otherways) still growing mischiefs at Avebury). And since you are pleased in a most Xn[1] maner to make some advances that way, my humble request to you is that you would please in your next to inform me what it is that you desire farther of Mr White, & if thereupon he refuse to give a full answer to your reasonable demands, I will represent his obstinacy to my Lord Bishop of Sarum.[2] But I doe hope & am verily persuaded that he will give me no such occasion. I have represented to him my utter dislike of his Exchequer prosecution when a late act of Parliament hath provided an easyer & shorter meanes for the recovery of his dues. But he sayes that his demands are of longer standing than what that act hath provided for. If you please therefore to propose any terms of accommadation in that matter I will use my utmost endeavours that[3] that they may be effectual as

1 Christian.
2 Bishop Burnet.
3 Page break.

haveing no other design but to approve my self a hearty friend of peace &,
Honoured Sir
Your most obliged and most humble servant
Cor Yeats

My most humble service to my Lady Halford of whose health I should be heartily glad to hear.

Verso Note: Dr Yeate 28 February 1697.
Verso Address: for Sir Richard Holford at his house in Chancery Lane, London.

22. Sir Richard Holford to Cornelius Yeate WSHC 184/1, pt.2.

8 March 1697/8

Sir,
Your favor of the last of February made mee expect another as soone as you had spoken with Mr Tooker, else I would not have soe long delayed my thanks for it. In truth, it was truely welcome, & the more welcome for that my good Lord Bishop told mee you had written to him to the same effect. I was glad that Farmer Skeate had waited on you, and though I cannot take his part in many things, especially in his unmannerley behaviour to his betters, yet I did verily think that hee was injured in this, it being a villany which I dare say hee from his hart abhores. In his letter to mee, he tells mee (as I believe hee did you) that the woman hath some very bad quallities, & if this bee one, I pray God forgive her. I am apt enough to believe (if his character of her bee true), that shee might observe the unkindness between Mr White & Hayward, which might incline her to indeaver to widen the breach, & to ingratiate her selfe with Mr White, but I cannot think Mr White would give an easye eare thereto.

Since I received yours, I have borrowed & looked over his bill in the Exchequer against Hayward & a great many more of the poore inhaibitants, & Hayward's [?answer] therto, & if Mr White will send them to you, & you will spare the time & give your selfe the troble to doe soe, I doe think, considering the nature & vallue of the demand, & the circumstances of the persons, you will think that there is little justice & less charity in the prosecution. I am sure Mr White hath been too liberal in his language as to mee, and though I never thought it worth my while to heare or give credit to tales and tale bearers, and I wish hee had not, yet I must take notice that in his letters written by himself to mee, hee hath, as I think, given a very unbecomeing liberty to his passion, & therefore I doe insist to have his answer upon his oath to those letters. I have not nor ever had the least prejudice to Mr White, but was alwaies desireous to pay him all due respect, & never designed to deprive him of one penny of his dues, & would have rather added to than taken from him anything, which hee could rightfully demand, and to have submitted therein to any man of integrity. Butt when hee had often & in a very disdainefull & haughty manner refused to let mee know his dues, I was constrained for quietnes sake & to bee at a certainty (the mother of peace) to exhibite my bill, to bee sealed from those terrible threats, which might frighten a new tennant or a stranger, yet then I by letter requested him to make it as easy as possible hee could, & to let mee have a full & faire answer, without mixing too much of his passion. But hee was pleased to put in, I think, a very imperfect answer, & when I had put in my exceptions & waited in expectation, that hee would have perfected his answer without troble, hee forced mee to referr[1] referr it, & to obtain a report, to which report (as if it were in sport) hee hath put in exceptions & appealed to the Court. And because you are soe very kind, to bee trobled with it, I will mention some of my exceptions to his answer.

Hee doth not confess or deny, whether hee did or did not declare to mee, that hee had in his custody or power the terriers, rolles, or bookes particularly shewing when & how the farme became exempted from paying tythes in kind,[2] and whether hee did or did not afterwards declare that hee was mistaken in his information given mee, & that hee would not bee content with less, than his tythes in kind, & that I should not scape for £4 nor for 4 times £4 per annum, & that I or my tennant should pay it, or not live there. Nor whether by letter to mee, mentoned in my bill, & left with the clerk in court for him to peruse, are of his writing or not. He hath the bill, answer, & exceptions & can tell whether I doe abuse your patience, or not.

And since you have given mee this liberty which else I could not have presumed to take, give mee leave to shew you wherein hee hath mixt his passion with his inck, viz., in his long letter of 27 January 1695:

That I have favord the setting up a hellish, factious, scandalous, & schismaticall conventicle.

In his of April 4 1696, I never did you or any of the scismatical crew any wrong &c.

In his of 12 October 1696, you will therein act contrary to your religious letters that pretend Christianity.

In his of the 30 April 1696: I am glad to heare that you pretend to have an inclination to peace, what you have shewed your selfe to mee I am not ignorant, but not withstanding all your blustering &c., & other letters have the same in other or worse words.

I have alwaies pittied his passion & was trobled & very much disapointed that I could not have a friendly correspondence, whereby I hoped all the unneighborly squabbles at Avebry might have been moderated & in a little time quieted & a neighborly friendship establisht, but &c. He hath mine & coppies of his owne letters.

And now, Sir, I have given you this troble, & set the matter in a true light, in hopes it may have the good effect you doe most charitablie propose. I will ad this, that if you wilbee pleased to take the troble & Mr White requests it, that I will leave my selv to your determinaton as of any person of integrity you shall

1 Page break.

2 These books were probably destroyed in 1643, when the vicarage was sacked by Royalist soldiers; cf. TNA C2/Chas1/A9/39.

name of [*illegible*], whereto I will submit as becomes,
Sir,
Your most humble servant
Rich Holford

When your leasure will best permit, I shallbee glad to heare that you have received this & pardond the troble.

Verso Note: The substance of a letter to Dr Yeate, 8 March 1697/8
Verso Address: These for the Reverend Dr Yeate at his house in Marlebrough, Wiltes

23. Cornelius Yeate to Sir Richard Holford WSHC 184/1, pt.2.

[c.9 March 1697/8][1]

Honoured Sir,
The onely reason of my so long deferring to give you Justice Tooker's answer is because I have not yet had an oportunity of speaking with him my self, his business calling him elsewhere the day I went to meet him. But I left my business with Mr. Cross,[2] who brought me this answer by word of mouth, viz., that Mr. Tooker knows nothing of that story which Farmer Skeate suggested to me concerning Hellier's wife, her attempting to steal clothes from his (or any other neighbour's) hedge. Nor does he at present remember any information or complaint that was ever brought to him against her in any matter of that nature. I should easily conclude, as you do, that had that story been true, as William Skeate informed me, she might have other bad qualityes as well as that, but finding from all indifferent unconcernd persons a fair report concerning her, I dare not think so hardly of her that she should attempt by a most solemn dreadfull perjury to ingratiate herself with him who is thought by all to be of no very obligeing temper. I heartily thank you for the favour of your second letter, the contents of which I will take the first oportunity to impart to Mr. White, & shall ever acknowledg myself,
Honoured Sir,
Your most obliged and most humble servant,
Cor Yeate

Verso Note: Dr Yeats (not dated), received 11 March 1697/8.
Verso Address: For Sir Richard Holford in Chancery Lane, London.

1 The letter is undated; this date is inferred from the recipient's note.
2 Latimer Cross at this date was curate of East Kennett (Tooker's residence); cf. The Clergy of the Church of England database **https://theclergydatabase.org.uk**.

24. Cornelius Yeate to Sir Richard Holford WSHC 184/1, pt.2.

[26 April 1698]

Honoured Sir,

That you may not think me unmindfull of what I have undertaken, this comes to acquaint you that Mr White hath committed to my hands the copies of the bills & his answer, together with your & his letters (all but the first of his which he says is lost or mislaid). But I have not yet had time to peruse them fully, nor an oportunity of speaking with Mr White since I read the exceptions to his answer. When I see him, I will take his particular answer to each exception, & desire him to give it in such a maner as he shall be able (if required) to confirm upon oath. When this is done I will faithfully represent the whole to you, which I can the more cherefully doe since Mr White hath promised that he will complye with what ever shall be judgd reasonable by

Honored sir

Your very humble & most faithfull servant

Cor Yeats

Marlburrough, April 26 1698

Verso Note: Dr Yates, 26 April 1698. Answered 5 May 1698.

Verso Address: for Sir Richard Holford in Chancery Lane, London.

25. Sir Richard Holford to Cornelius Yeate WSHC 184/1, pt.2.

Chancery Lane

5 May 1698

Sir,

Haveing spent 8 or 10 daies a little way out of towne for the benefit of the aire (which I wish had been more seasonable), at my returne last night I found your favor of the 26 of April, & doe choose rather to bee thus troublesome, than to neglect my thanks for it. And since it hath [?pleased] Mr White to put the bill, answer, exceptions and letters into your hands, and promised to bee governed by your directions, I will not offer any one word to incline your thoughts, & am sure you will blame mee, if I did not use my utmost indeavor to preserve peace and a neighborly friendship betweene Mr White and mee, imitateing the good old rule, cited by an excellent author treateing of peace & warr, to whome I think the translator hath done noe wrong in this distick:

> All meanes unarmed, wise men should first assay,
> who knows, if asked, but he'le unforced obey[1]

But when I had done all I could, and could obteine noe satisfaction, I was constrained fo quietnes sake, and to prevent future troble & mistakes, to take a more unpleaseing method, yet then prayed him to let mee have a full & plaine answer without any unnescesary troble or expence, & without reflections, but &c.

1 Quoted from Hugo Grotius, *The Rights of Peace & War.*

I must insist now to have his answer upon oath, & then shalbee intirely governed by your determination, unles hee shall think to take the opinion of the Court upon his appeale [?from] the Master's report. Sir, your kindness hath drawne this troble upon you, & therefore doe hope you will excuse it, and give mee leave to add my request that you will, when you see Mr ~~Justice~~ Tooker, thank him for standing up soe heartily & effectually for setting the tax in the most equall method for the service of the King and country. And pray when you see your good neighbor Madam Fitzjames & her mother, to present mine & my wife's service to them, and beleive mee,
Sir,
Your humble servant
Rich Holford

Verso Note: Copy letter to Dr Yeats 5 May 1698
Verso Address: These for the Reverend Dr Yeats, at his house in Marlebrough, Wiltes.

26. Humfry Wall to Sir Richard Holford WSHC 184/1, pt.2.

[5 June 1698]

Sir,
I have seen your exceptions to Mr White's answer. I perceave your designe & drift is to fix & settle your parson's dues. The parson gave Mr Archdeacon the inclosed, which the parson is ready to say & insist on by his oath, if you are there with intent, & will acquaint him how you would have it done. What service I can doe you in this or any thing else you may comand, I did not promise as I remember to returne this note, but least I should & be called on for it pray lett it be forth comeing. I hope you received the ~~rent~~ roll I sent you. I am,
Sir,
Your obliged humble servant,
H. Wall
Marlborough, 5° Junii 1698

Verso Note: Mr Humfry Wall, 5 Junii 1698. Answered 9 Junii 1698.
Verso Address: To Sir Richard Holford, one of the masters in Chancery, att his howse in Chancery Lane, present, London.

[Account of Tithes etc][1]

An accompt of dues & tythes belonging to the vicar of Avebury upon Sir Richard Holford's farme there.

Inprimis the vicar may choos 2 ell ridges of wheat in the peice of wheate that is sowne next to the church.

Item the tenth shilling that is made of agistment cattle & of grazeing cattle,

1 This account was written by Sir Richard Holford on Wall's letter; see note at foot.

the tyth of the orchard, garden, & of all fruit trees, of pidgions, turkeys, geese, ducks, eggs, piggs, rape, hemp, honey wax, & one shilling for the fall of colt, & 4 pence for every calfe, & 3 pence for the milke of every cowe that is kept upon the farm, belongs to the vicar.

The tythe alsoe of a peice of meadow called the Little Hooke at the upper end of Southmead belongs to the vicar.
This is the utmost of what I know.
John White

This a true coppie of what is mentoned in Mr Wall's letter. The original under Mr White's hand I delivered to Mr Wall at his house, 1 October 1698, & Mr White being then there Mr Wall delivered the same unto Mr White.

27. William Skeat to Sir Richard Holford WSHC 184/1, pt.1.

Avebury
14 July 1698

Sir,
My Lady red your letter to me concerning the trustees & I doe desier to send them a hundred & fifty pound next wicke if I can gete return for it. Mr Child have partly promised me to pay it to your worship, & I would bag your worship to let them nouit as soun as you can, & as sone as harvist is over I will waite uppon them where thay shall appoint me & make even the acount & pay them the resedue of the mony bating the hundred pound. As sone as I ham shure of the return I will send a letter in closed to your worship for them with all the arguments I can think of as far as truth & honesty is. My lady & child are pretty well thankes be to God, & all the rest of the family. I & my wife presents our duty & sarvis to your worship, hoping you are in good helth – all at present from your oumbell sarvant to sarve you
Will Skeate

Verso Address: This for Sir Richard Holford In Chanc Lane, neare the Rowlles, London.
Verso Note: Farmer Skeate July 14 1698 to Sir R. Holford

28. Sir Richard Holford to Cornelius Yeate WSHC 184/1, pt.1.

14 July 1698

Sir
I am sure I should not bee troblesome & am trobled when I am soe, and that your intended charitable inclinations have not not taken the desired effect. I was a night or two in the Whitson weeke at Avebury, and accidentally seeing Mr White, & speakeing to him of something relateing to my tennant there (which I intended for both their benefit), Mr White without the least occasion or provocaton, fell into a furious passion, & let fly such imprudent stuffe &

in such a haughty manner, that I could not forbeare laughing at the humor, though I pittied his passion, inter al hee told mee that I had prevaricated with Mr Yates, but would not tell mee how or wherein, at which I could have been pretty warme, but resolved my tongue should not offend. I perceived by him that hee intended noe other fruite of your offerrd mediation, but to gaine time & a pretence to boast (as I am told hee hath done to many) that I had acknowledged I had injured him, and submitted &c. Sir, not heareing from you and having an oportunity by Mr Wall to put this into your hands, I doe give you my hearty thanks for your friendly & neighborly favors, and am pretty sure you will not take it ill, if I doe now, for soe long an [?expectation], call for Mr Whites further answer, according to the usuall methods of the Court, & that you will permit mee to continue,
Sir,
Your humble servant,
Rich Holford

Verso Note: Draft of a letter to Mr Yates, 14 July 1698, by Mr Wall.
Verso Address: These for the Reverend Mr Yates, Archdeacon of Wiltes, at his house in Marlelbrough, Wiltes, by Mr. Wall

29. William Skeat to Sir Richard Holford WSHC 184/1, pt.1.
[20 July 1698]

Sir,
I have sent a leter in closed for the trustes & have sent 2 bills of a one hundred & 50 pound which I would bag your worship to derect it to the trustees, & to let me have one word in my Lady letter on how your worship ples wher the bill be excepted. My wife & I presents our duty & sarvice to your worship, hoping you are in gad helth, as we are all at present thankes be to God. All from your sarvant to sarve you, Will Skeate.
July the 20 1698
Avebury

Sir,
If your worship don't thinke fit to deliver the letter that I will leve to to[sic] your worship.

Verso Address: Thes for Sir Richard Holford in Chancry Lane, neare The Rowlls, London.
Verso Note: Farmer Skeate, 20 July 1698.

30. William Skeat to Sir Richard Holford WSHC 184/1, pt.1.

[c.23 November 1698][1]

Sir,

I have reseved yours & should have rite to you soner, but I have not ben very will, but God be thanked I am now sumthinke beter. As to the getting of trese & cutting the heges tis not yet done – but wee will now do it. Sir, in your letter you was pleasd to say that it was not the least of my Lady troble that shee was thought troublesome the last somer, but I nor my wife did not thinke my Lady or yourselfe or children troblsome. But the sarvants I thinke was very troblsome. I can giue your worship a beter account of thayr passages then I could when you went from Avebury, for I have heard & sene a gret dole more then every I nue before. Your man Richard, after hee have had your worship and my Lady to church, have come home and had my men in to the seller and thare they have drinked what thay had a mind to, and then fild a great woodden botel and card[2] out in to the hay and thar to make merry and severell other explaits. Sunday in the afternon our hous was more licke a nalhous then a privit house and all thorowe your sarvants occasion. Your maid Bety I have bene att severell times to goe to bed and shee have tould mee shee would not goe tell she had a mind to goe and so shee have led up tell 2 or 3 a clock in the morning and whether shee have hald my men, [?yes], or no – I cant well tell, or whether shee did a pointed them to rise out of thayr beds and com in and thare mad [?gonteth] & corrousd – and when my wife carried the cay[3] of the seller to bed with her they had a contrifince to puluy a bord over the seller and fettch out what drinke they plesd, and this is the life that wee have had with saruants and this is truth, and sumthincke else which I shall rite in the other side.

Your maid Bety that shee cold not leve the hous nastie [?ann] but shee [?surruerence] in her chamber chimly and carked it up, in the [?apson]. My wife takes it a little unkindly of your worship that you shold love such a carricter of her when you went from Avebury. Your man Richard tould that you should call my wife hollow harted, desaitfull, damd bich, & Mrs Baskifilld have reported it about the contry, and tis our contry nues that I am to be torned out of the farme att or Ladyday next but I hope if be anny such thing your worship will giue mee notis for I shall never desier – to be your hindrence. My wife would fain know how litel masters nose is & how his esshu[4] is & how you all doe. I have sent a bill of fourscore pound to be paid to Mr Norris in closd in this letter.

I and my wife umbell sarvis & duty to yourselfe and Lady & mis & littel master. All from your sarvant to sarve you,

Will Skeate

Sir, pray give my umbell sarvis to Doctor Goold[5] and I give him many thankes for

1 Undated; conjectural date based on date received by Holford.

2 Carried?

3 Key.

4 'issue'?

5 Presumably a London medic.

his aduise. My wife promised to send him som piging[1] but we have tooke none never senc – but wee shant for get to send him sum. [2]

Sir,
After I concluded the last, my wife tould mee that the morning that your worship went from Avebury my Lady spock to Mall to gooe in to the parllor. Thare was some pigen pie if shee would ete sum. Your man Richard com in presently oppon her & thretend her if shee tocht it hee would stricke of her fingers, & cald her plagy damd bich what had her to doe with it, but he cold call in John Baskifild[3] & Rubin Horsell[4] & Thomas Gordon[5] to ete it, but my children was not worthy of one bit. Sir, before I was tooke hil I did take notis of the fittels after thay had all supt wee good baken & bife & poding. I went in to the pantry & their was a lofe of bred which was but one cut ofe the lofe & the next morning I was up the furst in the hous, & thar was halfe the lofe gone & all most halfe a ches & a bout 2 pound of backen. I never tacke anny notes of the fitels [?before] or since & this is true to my sartain nollidg. But who had it I don't know, for the dors was left open all nite severell times thorrow Betys neglect. I have lost the gret gack nife, which I belefe Bety have carried a way with her, as well as the paty pan, for I beleve they went all one way. If her hant them I beleve I shall find them somewhere else. Pore John Cue[6] was found ded uppon the douns with the extremety of this could wether.

Verso Note: Farmer Skeate. Received 25 November 98.
Verso Address: For Sir Richard Holford in Chancry Lane near the Rowlles – London.

31. Sir Richard Holford to William Skeat WSHC 184/1, pt.1.
26 November 1698

Farmer Skeate,
~~Yesterday your Chapman at Taplow came to mee, & told mee that hee had lately seen you, and that you were pretty well, which I was very glad to heare, and last night the post brought mee a letter (not dated) with a bill in it for Mr Norris, which I delivered to him. You therein tell me that you had received one from mee whereby I doe perceive that another wich I writ to you is miscarried. I was afraid that you had not been soe well recovered as I doe hope you are, and Mrs Fitzjames when shee came to towne told us that shee heard you was very ill. If you don't take a great deale of care of yourselfe you may relaps & fall back,~~

1 Pigeons.
2 Page break.
3 Perhaps John Baskerville, Skeat's predecessor as tenant of Avebury Great Farm.
4 Reuben Horsell, subsequently the parish clerk; see *AWS*, p.414.
5 He has not been identified in Avebury.
6 He was buried 21st November 1698.

~~therefore dureing the winter bee sure to take care.~~[1]

I writ to you the 30th November last & told you I would write again by Mr Norris.

I doe wonder you should think soe meanely of mee that I should advise with or open my mind to Mr Baskerville[2] in any thing unles to what relates to setting dog. I am sure I never did after your geing from or staying. I doe know how to convers with sucn men, without intrusting them with my thoughts or concernes, therefor if any lyes are raised, keep them amongst your selves and not father any of them upon mee, nor mention my name in your wrangleing conversation. But I doe now admire that all the complaints you speake of should bee concealed & not mentioned whilst wee were with you. Tis pretty hard for mee to think halfe what you mention to bee true, the rather for that my man Richard denyes that hee ever mentiond any such base words as you say hee repeated, as if spoken by mee of your wife. I am sure I never used any such words of her, nor ever said an ill word of her to him or anybody else. I can't think the fellow would dare to say hee heard mee say any such words. I am apt enough beleve that Betty is a slutt and a foole, & behaved her self soe at Avebury, and that shee & the rest of my servants might misbehave themselves there where they had full bellies & little business. But my wife, at her first comeing downe last summer, ~~prayed~~ you were to take notice of fomer miscarriages, & prayed you to let her know if any of her servants should misbehave themselves, to the end shee might endeavor to prevent it. And though shee was full of troble, by the indisposition of her poore boy, and the negligence of her servants, yet if shee had been informed of her servants lyeing up, at night, and of their abuseing the Lords day, as you now mention, shee would have taken such courses with them, that would have prevented their making use of their time to such evill purposes soe very contrary to her inclinacon & her repeated request to them. But as to their devouring eight hogsheads of drink of twelve bushells to the hogshead, of the best malt, you must give mee leave to say tis not possible to bee true. I have been a housekeeper above thyrty yeares, & never let my servants want what was fit, nor ever had soe many complaints of drink in my life, as whillst I was at Avebury, & I am sure there was not a drop of drink, that I tasted all the time I was there the last sumer, but I could make better & more wholsome with a sixth part of the malt you mentioned, nay the said drink was [?roped], sower & unwholsome, therefore I drank very little being better pleased with whay, milk & water & the like, & I am sure my wife and children did not drink much. I doe know what eight hogsheads of drink of 46 shillings the hogshead will doe, and won't believe any gentleman within seaven miles of Avebury spent soe mych of such drink the 4 months of June, July, August, & September, of which I was thereabout 3 weeks. I would not have you think mee a coxcombe to bee soe imposed upon.

Pray don't mistake mee. I don't nor won't excuse the fault my servants might

1 This paragraph deleted in mss.

2 He had been the tenant of Avebury Great Farm before Skeat, and was perhaps the son of Thomas Baskerville, lord of the manor of Winterbourne Bassett. See *VCH Wilts* 12, p.187-8, & the will of Thomas's widow Mary, WSHC P3/B/1234.

bee guilty of there, nor did I any waies intend to bee burthensome or troublesome to you, but to make honest and reasonable satisfaction for what wee had. And I am sure my wife was very unwilling to bee troublesome or unthankfull, and if her servants' faults were concealed from her, by those who knew them & ought to have spoken of them, I am sure neither shee nor I could help it. I say don't mistake mee, nor give trust to lyes & reports. I have not made mention of these things or any of them to any of your lying, idle, tale beareing neighbors. I doe understand my selfe & them, better than to take counsell of them or advise with them in such matter, and what I have here mentiond is in [?secret] to yourself, that you may know that I doe know when I am well used, and when not, & if you doe think the contrary it will make our correspondence more uneasy & difficult than I could wish, or than I ever expected, or intended.

I was very much displeased at the freedome Mr Baskervill & Rubin[1] used the morn wee came from thence, & chid Richard for encouraging it, but my wife & I had many other things to mind, & could not doe as wee would, but Richard protests hee never gave your daughter an ill word. If hee did twas against my will, & neither my wife or I could help it, but if it had been then spoken of, I would have made him aske forgiveness or broken his head, for I doe abhor such language especially against a poore girl that seemed to us to bee very quiet & good disposition. And I don't remember that I said any hard word of or to any of your family, unles to the woman that helpt wash &c., who had displeased my wife, yet shee paid her full wages.

Note at top of letter: I intended to have sent this by the coach, but doubting it might miscarry I writ to him 30 November, that it will answer his letter by Mr Norris.

Verso Note: Letter to Farmer Skeate, sent by Mr Harding, Mr Norris his clerk.

32. Philip, servant of Sir Richard Holford,[2] to William Skeat

WSHC 184/1, pt.1.

[December 1698?][3]

Honest Mr Skeate,

I thanke you and your wife for the kind letter which you sent to my master in my behalf, though I thinke you have done me but little diskindnesse in it. You had better have sayd what you had a mind to against mee before wee came away. Then I would have spoke to you face to face and vindicated myselfe, but I thought your Presbiterian principles had taught you not to back bite mee or anyone else, but I hope you are disappointed in your expectation, for I believe my Master and Lady are soe good not to give credit to your pittifull letters which

1 Reuben Horsell.

2 The name of the correspondent, is not given in the letter, but is suggested in Skeat's letter dated c.23 November 1698.

3 The date is conjectural.

[?seem] no otherwise than a silly curs standing at a distan[ce][1] and barkeing at one when at the same time it dares not come neare one for feare of being beaten for his simplicity or impertinency. I thought you might have bestowed your time better than to have concerned your selfe with me or my relations. If you looke at home, you may see your selves. If not, your neighbours can tell you if they dare what you are, but I believe you can see a mote in any other's eye and cannot see the beame in your owne. If both of you doe seriously consider of this you wilL thinke me not much mistaken, and therefore I would advise you to learne better things and minde your owne businesses better, which you neglect when you are contriveing or writeing silly stuffe to my Master and Lady, for while you are doeing that, the maggotts have time, as they did when wee was there, to grow to a great biggnesse in the salted beefe, and not long before that in the bacon to. A little more salt and a little more care taken instead of the time you loose when you are contriveing and writeing lyes would prevent that and keepe the vessells sweete and then the beare that comes out of them would not stinke nor be soapy. It is pitty that time should have beene lost in writing this letter to you, but I hope you will take warneing by it and never more mis spend your time soe idly and foolishly as you have already done, and soe I leave you to consider of it seriously together, and I wish that it may bee for both your goods and soe I rest

Verso Address: For Mr Willam Sceate at Abury near Mallbury, present

33. William Skeat to Sir Richard Holford WSHC 184/1, pt.1.
[9 December 1698]

Sir,
I have reseved yours this morning & Sattarday last I reseved a letter from Mr Bennet[2] that the Trustees had ordred hee to sue me for the mony which is behind. I don't know well what is behind, but I would desier your worship to pay them the 150 pound which you have & I will return them 50 pound more in a wick or fornites time, & as sone as they have a noportunity to let me [*illegible*] with them I shall be glad to make a nend of the acount. I would bage your worship to let Mr Bennet know it as sone as possebell, & to be me frind what you can. I & my wife presents our duty & sarvis to your selfe & Lady & mis & littel master, & are sory to here that my Lady has ben elle, but God be thanked you say shee is sum thing beter. All from your sarvant to sarve you,
Will Skeate
Avebury December the 9, 1698

Verso Note: Farmer Skeate 9 December 98 to Sir R. Holford.
Verso Address: For Sir Richard Holford in Chancry Lane, neare the Rouls, London.

1 Torn.
2 Lawyer for the trustees for the sale of Lord Stawell's estate.

34. William Skeat to Sir Richard Holford WSHC 184/1, pt.1.

[19 December 1698]

Sir,

I sent a letter about nine days agoe to desier your worship to pay Mr Benet the 150 pound which your woship have & heare I have sent a bill in closd of 50 pound more which I would bag your woship to pay them, & I should be glad of an opertunity to make even the account. Sir, I would bag you to rite to Mr Chipman Sharp at Tapla[1] to pay your worship 28 pound & 10 shiling which will make up the half years rent & senc you went from Avebury I have payd in bills and taxes ennof to make evin the last years rent. Sir, I have reseved a letter from sum of your sarvants, but which I can't tell. But what I rite in my letter is true of Richard & Bety but I beleeve twas Philip which rite this letter, which I beleue had but littell resson to rite any such thing of my wife as to have stenking bife & baken & that the barrels should stenk, but I have sent the letter hear in closd, which I hope your worship & my Lady will considder where wee are a buesed or not, for I never knew so much trobell with sarvants before in my life as I have this last year, for my own sarvants be groud to that pas that I harly darse to speck to them. I and my wife presents our sarvice & duty to your selfe & Lady & mis & littell master, hoping you are all in good helth. All from your sarvint to sarve you, December the 19 – 98

Will Skeate

Avebury

My wife thinkes of sending a torky & chine of backon after Chrismas which I hope will prove [?swet].

Note at foot: A bill for £50 dated 13 December 1698 by Jos Smal drawne on Mr James Smat at the Black Eagle in Fryday Street, payable on six daies sight to Mr Edw Hancock or order endorsed by Edw Hancock accepted this 29th December. Received the £50, 10 January 1698, by my man Phillip.

Verso Address: These for Sir Richard Hollford in Chancry Lane, near the Rowlls, London.

35. William Skeat to Sir Richard Holford WSHC 184/1, pt.1.

[21 December 1698]

Sir,

I have reseued yours & to the complaint about the bridge the water hant ben bayd up never one day nor one nite nor one ouere[2] senc May last & the gate have stod open all thess his [?watey] & hant reseved one farding of mony of noobody

1 Taplow?

2 Hour.

except the coches & waggons & thay pay twel pence a time & well thay doe desarve it, thay have spoild of much whet & land & meddow ground which I shall lost 10 pound by this yeare, & so I would bag your worship that you will give consent to the puellen of him up, for I have nothing consedirebull tovard what I am damnifide & thretened to have my brains bote out att every tuern. Wee dooe intend to gete tres in the Chrismas wicke, the hegges be cut, thar is a pash of chery root wall fil doune. I & my wife presents our sarvis & duty to your worship & my Lady & mis & littell master. All from your sarvant to sarve you,
Will Skeate
December the 21.
Avebury

Sir, as to your man Richard, what have bene sed of him will be justified to his face. I have not time to answer your last letter att present but att sume other time.
Verso Address: For Sir Richard Holford, in Chancry Lane near the Rowlles, London

Verso Note: Farmer Skeate 21 December 98, concerning the bridge & gate at Southmead.

36. William Skeat to Sir Richard Holford WSHC 184/1, pt.1.
30 January 1698/9

Sir,
I have not reseved one word from your worship senc the 16 day of Desember I rite one letter with a bill in closed of 50 pound, & I will bag your worship to lett mee know when you have reseved the bill for I have payd the bill here & wheare you reseved of Mr Chipman at Tapla[1] the 147 pound & 10 shilling, & 28 pound 10 shilling, & senc I have sent a letter about pulling up of Southmede Bridg which I hant heard one word from your worship. Sir, I would desier you to be my frind concerning the Trustess. Mr Smith[2] is now gone to London, & I dout hee will tell the Trusttess of the bond of 20 pound, but if your worship & Mr Norris can make a nend of it if you do giue Mr Benet or who you shall thinke fite 20 pound to save the 100 pound, I shall think my silfe gretly obleged to you as long as I leve.

About fortnite a gooe I went to priming[3] the sommers trese and let a lem[4] fall oppon my lag & brust it so that I have ben under the surgents hands ever senc, & when I will be well God noues. Sir, John Griffin in the forst place [?serv] the peace against mee & then in dite mee for asalt & batry, and now have preswaided his man to swar to a nother salt & batry which now I am forced to send for a rite for him, for driveing over my grass, which I hope your worship will own the action if you pay none of the cost for thay bost myttyly, that you will not stand

1 Taplow?
2 Probably Richard Smith, lord of the manor of West Kennett.
3 Pruning?
4 A limb.

by me in anny thing & soe thay now think to do any thing, and all will be well in thayer side. I am not gilty of ither of thes inditments, & have very good witnes to proue itt, but wee have a gret many setters one.

My wife & I presents our duty & sarvis to your worship & my Lady & mis & littell master, all from your sarvant to sarue you.
Will Skeate
Avebury

Verso Note: Farmer Skeat 30 January. Answered at large 2 February & directed it bee left Farmer Nalders.[1]
Verso Address: Thes for Sir Richard Holford In Chancry Lane, near The Rowlles, London.

37. William Skeat to Sir Richard Holford WSHC 184/1, pt.1.
[16 February 1698/9]

Sir,
I have reseved yours the 2 of this instant Februry & if you send yours by the post & derect them to Farmer Nallders[2] with the figer of 2 under the superscripsshon thay com safe. I have bought Mr Bromam[3] estate but I cannot have it except Mr Tooker & both the wimin will consent to yet. Thay doo seme to be all willing of it, but did desier time to scout for an estate to put it all in one thing, but I left it purposly for your worship & for disparigeing of your farme tis no such thing. I thinke Mr Smith & Mr Baskifild[4] have disparidged Abuery farem more then I, for thay never paid a grete dele of rent, & I think they rent it as long as twas convenient if I don't mistake, for Water Strach[5] & I have had to or 3 words but not so much deference as popel doe make of it for wee be very good frinds as ever I think. I beleve Mr Smith had bisness a nouf of his own att London, & not to conserned his self about mee, but hee is now as ever hee was to mee, & so tis no nue thing to mee. Sir, you rite in your last letter that you would not have mee or my wife harbour any ill opinions of you or your Lady which wee be not a littell trobled about it bine wee had never any such thotes. I did never grogd to sarve you or my Lady in anything in my life & for my wife doe profest the same, & I hope you will believe us. About 3 weeks agon your frind, Mr White, cominge from Malbrow[6] with a naighbroe of mine did exclaim very much against you & did declare you to be one of the gretest villains in the kingdom, & that never any man was soo plagued in law with a knave as hee, but said neverthelesse he did not care a fart for you, & was resolued to have such a tryall with you as that it should

1 Thomas Nalder; see *AWS*, p.104.
2 Nalder.
3 Mr Bromham.
4 Both had been tenants of Avebury Great Farm; see *AWS*, p.231.
5 Walter Stretch, innkeeper at the Catherine Wheel, which was then in the centre of the village; see *AWS*, p.320.
6 Marlborough.

be said that you did once meet with your match in a clergyman. He in great passion did say he would have such a tryall with you as he never had yett, but said he would not say what sort of tryall it should be, but did in sume jest make it out to be by fighting, & was resolved not to give you of this he would sue you rott & damd first. The party to whom these words were spoken was willing to have you made aquainted with it, not knowing but he may doe you some deadly mischief if oportunity serves. The naighbree which hird this will justifie it if you doe desiere it & have a copy of the same. The eind of the nue stabell is coming doun, but wee have trast[1] it up for the present, but must be troock doun as sone as it tis fine wether, or else it will all fall. Wee have had so much hie winds & rainny wether that it have bete into the house, which I beleve will be gret damig. I & my wife presents our duty & sarvis to your selfe & Lady & mis & littel master. All from your sarvant to sarve you
Will Skeate
February the 16 1698
Avebury

I have rite to or thre lines one the other side.[2]

Sir,
I heare my Lord Rennells[3] wants a gray gilden for his coach, & if your worship do think it fite to specke to him about mine, & if my Lord think it fite, I will send him up to my Lord. He is about 15 hans & halfe hie, or hard thare about, & will mach with Flanders gelding or Englesh. If thay think fite I wil send him about or Lady day.

My wife will send you a chine of bacon & torky by Calne wagner to be att the White Swan in Hoborn next Thursday. Wee should have send it soner bu we was disapointed in cilling our piges. My dafter presents her sarvis to mis & littell master, & have sent in the hamper a litell bascat of apels for them.

Verso Note: Farmer Skeate, 16 February 1698
Verso Address: This for Sir Richard Holford, in Chancry Lane, neare the Rowlles, London.

38. William Skeat to Sir Richard Holford WSHC 184/1, pt.1.
23 February 1698/9

Sir,
I have reseved yours of the 16 of this instant February, & itt fill out so that I was not a tome[4] or els I should have ben in London before this time. I went to

1 'trussed'.
2 Page break.
3 He has not been identified.
4 'at home'.

Wessonburt[1] last Satterday morning & did not return till Wansday, & so that I nue nothing of the letter tell then, & you rite in your letter that Mr Newcoart & Mr Benet would not be in toune above 10 days, & I was fearfull in coming up for fear thay should be gone out of toune, but if thay be not gone out of toune, if your worship thinke it fite for me to come up the latter end of next wicke, I will come. But I have noe proofe for the a batement but my self, except Mr Sherwood, but God nous where to find him. But I thinke it tis profe a nof for me to give 350 pound a year for the farme, which was never above 320 pound before, but a pone my Lord's siling of the farme preswald me to sele[2] a lese for 12 years att 350 pound a yeare, & now to make me pay 150 pound for 5 yeare more then the ould rent I think twill be very hard upon a pore tenant but if it will not be a bated I murst leve it to your worship to doe for me what you can. I hope thay wont desier that I should alost 6 yeres agine. I rite a letter to your worship the 16 of this month that you should send your man to the White Swan in Hoborn to the Calne waggoner for a hamper, but while I was att Wesson[3] thay send it by Malbro [4]wagoner which if it be not send up I dout it will be spoild. Sir, Mr White will take his tith in cind. Of what to pay him I can't tell. I must bag your worship advise what to pay him as I may be quiet in paying if possebull. As for Mr Smith informacion about the farme, tis all stuf, & when your worship comes down into the contry & if you are willing wee will speake face to face & then you will see what Mr Smith can say. I & my wife presents our duty & sarvice to your selfe & my Lady & lettell master. All from your sarvant to sarve you. [5]
Will Skeate

Verso Note: Farmer Skeate 23 February 1698.
Verso Address: For Sir Richard Holford, in Chancry Lane, neare the Rowls, London.

39. William Skeat to Sir Richard Holford WSHC 184/1, pt.1.

12 May 1699

Sir,
I have reseved yours yesterday, & for a workman to doe the stable. I cannot tell who can doe it better than John Lad, & if you thinke it fite in your next letter for mee to apoint him to mite you att Avebury in the whitson wicke I will doe it. I shall be very glad to see your worship att Avebury, but you must be sartain to bring a good soarde with you for the parson is in a greate rage against you, & doe bolsh out gret words against, you which you shall know when you dooe com doun. I hope my Lady will not be afraid of your comming douen to Avebuty conserning the parsons grete words, for I beleve you wil find more frinds att

1 Westonbirt, Gloucestershire.
2 'seal'.
3 Westonbirt.
4 Marlborough.
5 This paragraph is written on the side.

Avebury then hee. If you ples to let mee understand when you come I will mite your worship upon the douns, & gard you safe in to Avebury. I should have rite a gret del more, but I shall leve it tell your worship doe com doun. The walls be done up, but I won't send for the tilers tell you com doun. My wife have send my Lady 2 dussen of pigins & 2 dussen to Doctor Goold, & her would bage one of your sarvantes to derict them to the doctor. Wee have now don souing but att a very hard rate. Wee have had a wordell of trobell with our horses, but I have lost none. But John Broun have lost 5, & I thinke will lost all the rest. I & my wife doe present our duty & sarvice to your selfe & my Lady & mis & littell master. All from your sarvant to sarve you,
Will Skeate
Avebury

Verso Address: These for Sir Richard Holford, in Chancry Lane, near the Rowles ,London.
Verso Note: Farmer Skeat, 12 May 1699. Mr White severe threats.

40. William Skeat to Sir Richard Holford[1] WSHC 184/1, pt.1.
[29 January 1699/1700]

Honored Landlord,
After my humble service presented unto you & my landlady & all the rest of your family, hopeing you are in good health but for my selfe & some of my famyly are at present much out of health. Sir, I have sent you these to acquaint you that wee received your kinde toacken you sent unto us for which we yeeld you many thanks. It was 6^{li} of raisons, 4^{li} of currents, 8^{li} of suger & spice, and wee sent unto your worshipp a chine of bacon & a turkey & a goose, and a letter alsoe with the same, but haveing noe answer wee are in fear whether you received it or not, for which cause wee should be gladd to hear from you. Mr White have sued John Rose of Backhampton for his ell ridge of wheat, because hee would not suffer him to take it where hee pleasd at harvist last, but sett it forth by good evidence according to the coustom in a peece of wheat nearest the church. Afterwards there it stood soe long that the poore people cutt & fetcht it all away. The sute goeth in Wm White's name, one of Mr White's sons, the reason wee know not. It is to be tryed this Assizes.

There is a letter passed to one Mr Foarde of London about this sute, hee being one of the trustees for esq Popham,[2] being heir to this estate at Backhampton now in law. Wee suppose that the said Mr Foard will shew you the above said letter shortly, in hopes that you will be soe kinde as to put your conveniant assisting hand unto the said matter. Wee suppose that if Mr White gets any to swere for him at the Assizes it will be John Poop of Backhampton & Joseph Griffen the

1 This letter is in the hand of William Smith; see the footnote to Skeat's letter to Holford, 19 February 1699/1700.
2 Alexander Popham; see p.185, note 2.

elder of Avebury, soe that if Mr Foard can thinke of any way before the time to send sum check unto their foolish forwardings it may dooe much good.

There is alsoe another letter passd to esq Popham of Wanborrow, the other trustee with Mr Foard ,with the same methhoodd, in hopes hee will putt his helping hand. Wee doe suppose that if either of the said trustees will send Mr White but a crusty letter, that hee would throw down the cudgels, for hee is very willing of agreement if it might be most to his minde. But being soe much adicted unto covetiousness that hee have lost al his power of honesty. But above all the said John Rose humbly intreateth your assisting advice in this matter, & concerning Mr White's setting forth unto your worship in Chancery Court upon his oath there, that hee ought to take his ell rudge or rudges in all such peece or peeces of wheat nearest the church. Now wee should much admier if the same coustom should not hold att Backhampton, being one & the same parish. Wee in our opinion thinketh that Mr White's bringing the said action in his sonne's name, is to gett himselfe to be an evedence for his sone. I rest
Your Very Humble Servant & Tennant
Will Skeat
Avebury the 29th of January 99

Verso Address: To Sir Richard Holford in Chancery Lane near the Roles, these with care, London.
Verso Note: Farmer Skeate 29 Janry 99.

41. William Skeat to Sir Richard Holford WSHC 184/1, pt.1.
[19 February 1699/1700]

Sir,
I received yours dated the 12th of February. These are to acquaint you that there are nowe reddy broke 60 loads of sason stone upon Waden. If you think fitt to have them, or any part of them, you may have them at 1s the load. The said stones wase broken out of Mr Smith's Down by two workmen, & by them to be sold as above said[1]. Sir I have made bold to trouble your worshipp once more with the reading of these few following lines. Concerning Mr White's sute of law against my brother in law John Rose, hee hath caled the sute in his sone's name being but a youth. Wee cannot tell the reason, except it be in a way to become an evidence in his own case. Wee understand that hee very much dependeth upon a whome-made terrier,[2] & soe contrived that it was signed upon a cupp of ale

1 This letter was partially transcribed in Goddard, K.H. 'Sarsens at Avebury broken up 1799', *WAM* 40, 1919, p.354. Goddard's date is, however, a misprint; it should be 1699. The wording of this letter implies that the stones were not from the monument, despite Goddard's comment that they may have been from the Kennet Avenue.

2 Presumably the one made in 1682, printed by Hobbs, Steven, ed. *Wiltshire Glebe Terriers, 1588-1827*. Wiltshire Record Society, 56. 2003, p.17-18.

by Mr Trusler[1] & one or two more[2] at the same place & same time some years past, but by all report, the said Mr Trusler & the others didd presently after did much repent their soe doeing, upon which I humbly entreat your worshipp in my friends behalf, iff it may stand with your content, to send uss a coppie of Mr White's confession of the anciant terrier & coustom of the ell ridges of wheat, soe due unto him, togeather with any other convenient kindeness, that your worshipp shall be pleased to think fitt, to assist us with in this said matter, for if hee winn this sute, hee will grow so corrageous that hee will almost think himselfe the next man unto a king, that unless it bee as it were in prison & slavery none can live by him, unless it doe please Almighty God to cause his great reformation. Wee shall be very privett, & allsoe very thainkful for all such assistance, that your worshipp shall think fitt to bestow upon us. With our very humble service unto you & my Lady, & the children, hoiping you are all in good health, I rest
Your very humble servant & tenant Will Skeat
Avebury February the 19th, 99.
Sir

I being not very well, my uncle Smith wrought this & the last letler for mee, which I hope will not cause your displeasure.

Verso Note[3]: Farmer Skeate, Febry 19, 99. By Mr Smith of Casons.[4]
Verso Address: To Sir Richard Holford in Chancery Lane, near the Roles, with care, London.

42. William Smith to Sir Richard Holford WSHC 184/1, pt.1.

Calstone
6 July 1700

Honoured Sir,
I received yours dated the 29th June last, to which I confess my erors in hopes upon amendment I may be excused. But I delayed the more in hopes to have returned your Honour some privett lines about sumthing near Westonburt, which you mentioned to your tennants there, some time agoe.[5] The gentleman being of my old acquaintance & dealer, I gave him a visit, to state some by questions about the matter, but I found nothing to be done not yeet. Moreover, I well hoped that the commission would have been kept at Avebury some time since, that I might by the favourable admission seen you in person, & glad soe to doe, to the intent to have hadd the truth made manyfest betwixt Mr White & the neighbourhood

1 Richard Truslow.
2 If it was the 1682 terrier, it was actually signed by Richard Smith and John Mills, the then churchwardens.
3 The verso also has some scribbled calculations which do not seem to relate to the letter, and which are not transcribed here.
4 Calstone.
5 Holford was lord of the manor of Westonbirt, Gloucestershire.

about many of his transactions. I heard that hee was advised by some of his friends to come to your honour & humble himselfe, lest you should shame him to much. Wheather it be effected or not, I wish well to your courage; otherwise hee would runn over town & countery, but thainks be to God that some lambs can trample on lyons without damage. Hee now giveth out that hee will goe to tryall with John Rose this Assizes, although hee refused soe to doe the last Assizes. Hee didd not appear at the last Quarter Sessions against John Rose about his false putt for a riott. The [?stoap] wast John Rose & his reapers wase reaping in a peece of good wheat, not nearest the church, yeet notwithstanding Mr White came there with his reapers & sett them to work in the said wheat, upon which John Rose resisted them, upon which Mr White caused Mr Tucker forthwith to binde them over &c., notwithstanding Mr White & his reapers very evilly intreated the said John Rose. Wee cannot tell but hee may doe the like this harvist. If hee doth I think hee much more deserveth to be soe served himselfe, for he giveth the ocation. Thanks be to God wee have plenty of new hay & grass, & alsoe a very lykely cropp of corne in all our countery. Wooll doe something fall. But wheat doe hold at about 5s the better sort, but malt & barly hath fell much since Lady Day. Cheese at about 15s the hundred. Our commissioners have satt about the land tax, & have caused the countery to bring in two thirds of last years pay of 3s per pound, & have alsoe satte about the births, burialls, etc., and are sumthing strict. The report is that Sir Francis Child & the High Sherife, Mr Meryweather, puts in to bee burgess for the Devizes. I hear nothing to the contrary, but the tennants at Weston are all in good health. With mine & my sone's very humble service unto your honour, & all your honourable family unknown, with our humble thancks unto you for mindeing of uss in our absence & distance, & to our loveing landlord Mr Foard, when you see him. And for boath your former kindness unto us in being on our part, when wee wase last in trouble by Mr White, your names but being mentioned to be our just friends, silenced the tongues of many, wherefore when it layeth in our mean power to doe any service for you or either of yours, wee will endevour to perform itt. Alsoe hopeing you are all in good health, as wee all wase at the writting hereof, thanks be to God for the same, I rest
Yours to commaunde
Will Smith

I have not wrought every thing distincly for fear of miscarriage.
Avebury

Verso Address: To the Right Honourable Sir Richard Holford at his house in Litle Lincolns Infields, these with care, London.
Verso Note: Mr Wm Smith of Calston, 6 July 1700. I writ to him 16 July

43. William Skeat to Sir Richard Holford[1] WSHC 184/1, pt.1.

Avebury
6 July 1700

Honoured Landlord,

These are to acquaint you that the tyling & roughcast is all done. Mr Tucker is very ill, not lykely to live long. I lately received a letter from Mr Newcourt, in which hee saith except I speeddely pay the money due upon the old account, hee will put mee to trouble, which I think I doe not deserve, because I have been twice att London in order to pay it, but didd not pay itt by reason I could not have that faithfull promise which wase formerly promised unto mee made good, for the abatement of £100, but at any time upon totice to mee given when him or them that have any lawfull authority to receive the just some soe due unto them, let them be pleased to take the paines to call upon mee at Avebury. It shall be honestly paid, & this I pray you to acquaint them of. Alsoe I pray you to examine whether you have the acquitance for the £200 you paid them last. An acquaintance of mine have bought a little piece of land at Bushton of Mr Broadwrist of Westonburt, & being informed that your honour have a judgment upon the same, whereupon if your honour think fit, the party would be gladd to know. I lately sold a paire of good sound horses unto esq Popham of Littlecutt,[2] & lately hee being from whome some of his servants must needs undertake to drench them, to make them better then well, upon which the best of them is dead, which makes mee sorrow to hear the newes. Thainks be to God wee have a prospect of plenty of althings, according to our countrey, with mine & my wife's duty unto you all hopeing you are all in good health I rest

Your very humble servant & tennant

Will Skeat

44. William Smith to Sir Richard Holford WSHC 184/1, pt.1.

Calston
20 November 1700

Honoured Sir,

I received yours dated the 14th of this instant, and I have spoak with my kinsman Skeat about the farme, & hee saith that if it bee soe that hee & you doe part hee will soe endevour that you shall not want a good tenant for your farme. Hee hath received two letters from you since you went away & noe more, but neither speak of keyes but only screwes, & they were sent you in the baskett with the quinces, & for the keye you speak of they cannot give any account of itt. Your last saieth allsoe

1 This letter was written on the same sheet and in the same hand as William Smith's letter of the same date. Smith probably wrote the letter on Skeat's behalf because Skeat was ill. He had done so earlier; see the note at the foot of Skeat's letter 19th February 1699/1700.

2 Alexander Popham, lord of the manor of Littlecote, and of several other manors; MP for Bath 1698-1705; for his biograpy, see **www.historyofparliamentonline.org/volume/1690-1715**.

that you sent some papers with a letter to Mr Broomham desireing his answer, but he never received any such thing. But never the less hee have drawn up such lines that I hope will sute with your purpose. I humbly thank your Honour that you spoake with Sargeant Keen. Mr White is served with the subpoena, & therewith much displeased, & saith hee will sett aside the incme of Avebury on purpose to ruine John Rose & some others the inferiors. He demanded of John Rose before the said subpena £3 12s for his ell ridge, which hee refused to take last year 1699. Soe for fear they promised the money, but now since hee refuseth to take it to the intent to bring him to another tryall for the said ell ridge, because he declared for the last tryall but for battery, although it was all one in effect. Now wheather this Chancery bill wil stopp his action or not wee cannot tell, because of a promise of the money, or whether it is best to tender the money or not wee cannot tell, only to prevent his action if it may be don. I humbly pray your honours advice, if it may not bee to much trouble, to send it the next return. John Rose his mother did promise the money soe now & then hee threatins to sue her for it, but now as above said refuseth it at all hands. Some of our company are afraid that it will cost more than six pounds to bring him to his answer, because it cost you soe much to doe itt, whereupon they humly prayeth unto your honour to acquaint them in this said matter, & whether at length there will be any charges recovered from Mr White, touching the premisses. Some tells them one thing & some another, that they beginn to be afraid that the remeddy will be worse than the disease. If I have here omitted anything it is for want of memory, wherefore I pray you excuse, with my very humble thainkes unto your Honour for all favours, & my prayers to God for your good health, togeather with the rest of your good family, I am
Your much oblieged servant
Will Smith

Farmer Skeat & his wife alsoe presents their duty unto you & your Lady, & love to all the rest of your family, hopeing you are all in good health.

Verso Note 1: Mr William Smith, 20 November 1700. It did not come to mee till 27 November. Relates to Mr White. Answered 30 November 1700 relating to Backhampton.
Verso Note 2:[1] Oxon Ja [?Chamberlain]. Wiltes Mr Rich Jones; Glouc Rich Hames, esq; Berks Jo Breedon; Dorset Will Fite; Essex John Luther; Somerset William Hillier.
Verso Address: To the Right hounourable Sir Richard Holford, at his house in Litle Lincolne Infields, these with care, London.

1 This note appears to have nothing to do with the text of this letter. Perhaps it is a list of persons nominated to be sheriffs?

45. William Smith to Sir Richard Holford WSHC 184/1, pt.1.

[11 January 1700/01]

Honoured Sir,

I understand by your late letter to my kinsman Skeat, that you heard that Mr White have put in his answer to our bill, for which I give you my humble thanks for your kinde love & care towards us, especialy in that matter to let us hear of it. I have sent to Mr Stoakes to pray him not to faile in his speciall care tuching the said matter, but since that my kinsman Skeate spok with Mr White, & amongst other discurse hee told Wm Skeat hee intended to goe for London next Tuesday, to put in his answer, if hee speaketh truth. But hee is now very willing for agreement & pretendeth that hee is sorry about the late tryall with us at the Assizes. I doe belive that his evidence did swear that which they didd not well know. Hee doe alsoe proffer to goe back to the old composition for the ell ridges. His wife pretends her complyance in paying your honour your charges. I hope my kinsman Skeat & you will further agree for his continnuance, for my opinnion gives mee that it may be best at all hands. Mr White of [?Grittleton][1] & my Lord Peterbarrow stands burgess for Chippenham, Mr Long of Wraxall & Sir George Hungerford's sone for Calne, Sir Francis Child & Mr Meryweather the late shrieff for the Devizes. The smale pox is very busye in the countrey. Horse stealing & breaking of horses doe increase. When I know anything worthy your acquaintance I will doe itt, desireing the excuse in my troubling your honour soe often with my paper & ink, with my prayers to God for you, togeather with my humble service, hopeing you are in good health, togeather with the rest of your good family, I rest,

Your thankfull servant

Will Smith

Calston, January the 11th 1700

Verso Note: Mr Smith of Calston, 11 January 1700. Answered by the next post.
Verso Address: To the Right Honourable Sir Richard Holford, at his house in Litle Lincolns In Fields, these. London.

46. William Smith to Sir Richard Holford WSHC 184/1, pt.1.

[28 January 1700/1]

Honoured Sir,

I wish all unnessessary orations were ceased that I might not be soe troublesom unto you with my ink & paper soe often as I doe, but your favour being found soe great unto mee that I continue my boldness, which I hope you alsoe will now excuse as formerly. Sir, these are to acquant you that Mr White & us have had two meetings for a peace, but have not yet perfected. I suppose the last meeting it hade been don if Mr Brunson of Monkton[2] had not been there, with his bundle

1 Perhaps Walter White of Grittleton; see WSHC 212B/3124.

2 John Brinsden, vicar of Winterbourne Monkton.

of obstructions, but now it is referrd unto Fryday next for off or on. Wee cannot tell wheather hee delayeth the matter for any designe. I have been & acquainted our attorney with the matter, butt he seemeth not well pleased. I know not whoe in the countrey that I may safely confide in, wherefore if it may not be to much trouble unto you that you will be soe kinde to desire Sargeant[1] Keene, or him that you know best in such affayers, to make some speciall endevours against Mr White's takeing any advantage upon us touching the delayes abovesaid. Our attorney didd tell us some little while since that hee could stopp Mr White's depending action of travers against John Rose by vertue of an injunction, & alsoe that that [sic] if Mr White did faile of giveing his answer to our bill this terme that hee could take forth an attachment against Mr White, in way of a benefitt to us. Mr White is contented to make a new terrier betwixt this & Easter,[2] according to the right coustom of the place, with the approbation of the majoryty of the parish, & will give bond soe to doe, by entering the contents in an article, but Mr Brunson he entered into this cavitt to know who should be the absolute judge, in sort of a battering way, to which I gave this answer, that when the new terrier was made, that if in case that Mr White should insist upon any thing that the majoryty should oppose, that then & in that case, for expedition & confirmation of the same, Mr White should goe before a magistrate, if to goe as hee would say, & there to attest the same upon oath, soe that if wee cannot make it all goe well as wee would, wee would make it as well as wee can. We alsoe thinke fit to have Mr White first to release all concerned parties, & soe make his bond as abovesaid to be younger than the release, & this is the length & breadth of our cappassities touching the premises. If wee are to weake in the matter wee humbly pray your assistance, for without it wee cannot pretend to be safe. If wee know any thing worth your acquaintance, wee should be gladd to doe itt. With my prayers to God for you, hopeing you are in good health togeather with the rest of your good family I rest,
Your very humble servant to my power
Will Smith
Calston January the 28th 1700.

Mr White much desireth a peace wih your honou[r][3].

Verso Note: Mr Smith of Calston, 28 January 1700. Answered 1 February 1700 by Calne post; inquired of him whether hee had read my long letter written about this day 14 night because there is noe mention of it in this.
Verso Address: To the Right Honourable Sir Richard Holford, at his house in Litle Lincolns Infields, these with care, London.

1 Written as an abbreviation,'Sa^{t}', but expanded.
2 No new terrier was ever made, although Staynor Holford thought one might have been made in 1705; see WSHC 184/2, 'More Necessary remarks'. If it was made, it was never deposited in the Bishops' Registry; cf. Hobbs, Steven, ed. *Wiltshire glebe terriers 1588-1827*. Wiltshire Record Society 56. 2003.
3 Torn.

47. William Smith to Sir Richard Holford WSHC 184/1, pt.1.
[11 February 1700/01]

Honoured Sir,
I received yours of the first of February which speaketh of another letter write to mee about fortnight before, to which I cannot give any account of it. If I hadd received itt I should have been very gladd to have made return accordingly & will at any time if it cometh to my hand, for I acknowledge your kindness to be a sufficiant inducement for mee soe to doe, & what layeth in my mean power to serve your Honour, I shall at all times be reddy to doe itt according to my best skill. You have in your last wrought about a gelding, to which I return you this my opinnion, that if the case wase mine I would espye out a good coulered & well marked young gelding out of a countery mans hand, that hath not been tampered with & if hee handleth his leggs well. I could have him soon perfected for any gentillmans use by an exellent horserider liveing now at Calne, which of late hath shewn his skill in many horses to the admiration of many. He will doe it for 10s & this will be much the cheapest way to have a good sounde gelding, for to medle with the horse corsers it is but a lottery & deere to boote, & for any countery gentleman that hath a good perfect gelding it is hard to court him out of him unless for great advantage. I will make it my business to seeke at home & abroad to fitt your hand if it may be done according to your approbation, & I doe not question but that less than £15 wil doe it notwithstanding hee be more than 14 hands, for I feare 14 hands wil be to smale for you.[1] Unless you are for noe more, I submitt to your honours pleasure. If I prevaile in my endevors I will soone send you such word. If my endevours change to be with any acquaintance paradventure then I may make a conditional contract to stand if when I have sent the contents of it unto you that you approbate the matter, if otherwise then to be voyd. But if I should at a faire deal with a stranger, then it must be otherwise. Mr White & all of us concerned in the bill are agreed. Wee made an article with the contents of each man's dues, what itt is, & what to pay & when, and hath covenanted for all the ell ridges at Backhampton at the old rate dureing Mr White's continuance of being vicar of Avebury, & further wee have caused him to seal unto us a bond of £100 to performe as above said, & gave releases upon each side, the bond & article bearing even date, but the releases 4 dayes older, & for the sake of the peace each side is to stand to his own charges. Further Mr White hath much desired mee, to pray your honour in his behalfe, that you would accept of a refferance betwix you & him, for hee pretendeth much reformation touching peace, & further saith that hee will never goe to law with noe more of his neighbours. If your commission doe come against him the neighbourhood doe continue to appear for you in all things toaching the antiant coustom & misdemeniors. The smale pox doe much increase in the countery & very mortall. If I knew any thing worth your acquaintance I should be gladd to doe it, with my

1 The largest horses in the seventeenth century were between fifteen and sixteen hands, and were usually described as 'coach horses'; cf. Gerhold, Dorian. *Carriers & Coachmen: Trade and travel before the turnpikes.* Phillimore, 2005, p.48.

prayers to God for you, & my very humble thanks unto you for all your favours unto mee, hopeing you are in good health togeather with the rest of your good family, I rest
Your ever thainkfull servant
Will Smith
Calston February the 11th 1700.

Verso Address: To the Right Honourable Sir Richard Holford at his house in Litle Lincolns In Fields, these with care. London
Verso Note: Mr Smith of Calston 11 February 1700, answered in a long letter 22 February 1700.

48. Sir Richard Holford to William Smith WSHC 184/1, pt.1.
22 February 1700/01

Mr Smith,
I have yours of the 11th of February, and first as to the care you tell mee you will take about a guelding for mee, I am very well pleased with what you propose; 14 hands & halfe or 15 hands is the size I best like, well shaped, good eyes, good limbs & good goeings are to be wisht, & should be well pleased to have him disciplined by your neighbour at Calne, & doe leave it wholely to your care & kindnesse, & am not in hast, 3 moneths or more will suite well enough with my occasions

I am not troubled that my long letter did not come to your hands, & for that you earnestly requested my friendly advice, I did take the liberty to give you my full thoughts in relacon to your differences with Mr White with as much integrity as if I had been to determine it, & haveing found his temper to be proud & haughty & without charity, I told you that hee must be used as you usually doe to your unrulely cattle, to headline him, and I knew noe way how to doe it but holding him close to his oath, in answer to your bill in Chancery, where he must confesse or deny the facts charged. If he confessed he would condemne himselfe, if hee denyed you could easily prove, as much as would not only condemne him, but make him pay costs. I should not be troubled, if my letter came to his hands, & cannot but say he hath dealt prudently in complying with what is reasonable, & thereby covering those faults which must have exposed him, & I am glad your bill hath produced an agreement which I hope will be lasting, & that hee may live neighbourly & friendly with his parishoners, which will afford him more ease in his mind than all his blustering & exacting follies have hitherto brought. I cannot say that Avebury is peopled with many, nay I thinke I may say with few, whose conversasion is very desirable, but I am perswaded his bad example hath been of very bad consequence.

As to what Mr White desires, that you would desire mee to accept of a reference, in answer whereto I must tell you, as you may him, that all his base language, unmanly & unmannerly & I am sure unchristianlike revileings which he hath been pleased in all places & to all sorts of people, & upon all occasions to belch out against mee, & the affronting & abusive expressions in his letters owned upon his oath, nay the undertakeing to sweare in his answer to things notoriously untrue, as to the terrier made by himselfe, & to the submission made to Mr Smith & his award & severall other matters which when proved to his face may stick closer than his lawyer Watkins was aware of, I say all these things, & his usage of Mills, Hayward & others of his poor neighbours made me endeavour not to lye at his mercy, nor subject myselfe to his humor, but it never did nor shall provoke mee to doe him any wrong, nor to countenance or encourage any one else to doe so, but as I would rather pay more, than lesse, than what is due, soe I have advised the rest of his neighbours, & am perswaded that they would for quietnesse sake have done soe. But as to my interest I doe thinke I have prevented his doeing mee the wrong hee endeavoured, & when I come to make proofe by examineing my witnesses as I intend, I thinke I shall convince him that it hath been by himselfe & not by mee, that hee hath been at any expence. Noe I did allwayes pitty his wife & children, and was troubled that his insolent & ungovernable temper did soe expose him that there was noe making friendshipp with him. And yet I never refused to referr the matters in difference betweene him and mee, to any honest Gentleman, nay notwithstanding the trouble hee had formerly given therein to Mr Archdeacon Yates of Marlebrough, which occasioned severall letters between the Archdeacon & mee, which produced noe better effect than to leave it as he found it. Yet in September last, when Mr White againe proposed a reference to the same person, I cheerfully & readily submitted thereto, & because the Archdeacon is a person of great integrity & understanding, & a lover of peace & good neighbourhood, I told Mr White in his owne parlour that I would not only leave it to Mr Yates, but would not speake one word to him, but lay Mr White's owne letters & papers before him, & would abide by his determination, whereupon hee called his wife & told her of it, & poor woeman shee seemed well pleased, but before wee had made an end of the bottle of his drinke then before us, hee asked me whether I thought Mr Yates would Judge against him, whereto I answered that I did believe hee would judge according to his conscience, whereto Mr White sharply replyed, Noe, hee will sooner have his hand cutt off than judge that hee (Mr White) had done mee any wrong, whereto I sayd, nay then Mr White you must excuse mee, if I doe recall my submission, as I doe, for I will not referr anything to one that is soe engaged on one side. Not but that I did then & doe still thinke Mr Yates to be a very honest good man. This I am willing you should know least possibly you may thinke you have not soe good a share in my esteeme as to prevaile with mee to such a reference as you should thinke proper. And if you doe shew this my answer to your request to Mr White, I don't thinke but hee will confesse it to be true, & tell you why I did not confirme my submission to Mr Archdeacon Yates.

I have not heard one word from Farmer Skeate a great while, pray tell him soe. I am sure my last letter could not miscarry, because directed to his friend at Marlbrough. Pray remember mee to your son, & to Farmer Skeate & his wife. And to Mr White when you see him, & tell him that I am not to be frightened, nor wheedled, but shall be gladd of his friendshipp, if it may be had upon faire

termes. You must excuse this long tedious letter, for that you seemed to expect it from
Your loveing friend
Rich Holford

Pray keepe this letter, &, as soone as you can spare time, tell me that you have it, and your thoughts of it, cause tis written in haste I hant time to revise it.

Verso Note: Copy of a letter to Mr Smith of Calston, 22 Febry 1700.
Not received any letter from him, I writ to him againe the 17 Apr 1701.

49. Sir Richard Holford to John Gardiner WSHC 184/1, pt.1.

9 August 1701

My good friend,
You cannot guess how well pleased I was when, accidentally meeting you in Chancery Lane, you told mee that you knew my farme at Avebury and seeming inclined to become my tenant made mee hope to receive a letter from you. Farmer Skeate my present tenant hath rented it for a great many yeares at £350 per annum, and had about 6 or 7 years to come in his lease when I bought it of my Lord Stawell's trustees. And their agent then proposed to bring mee a substantiall tenant who should give £380 per annum, and I am perswaded tis well worth it. It hath been lett at £400 per annum, and was settled at that value in jointure to my late Lord Stawell's mother, with a covenant that it should soe continue, & tis very improveable with a small expense. But I could not thinke of parting with Farmer Skeate, and had rather hee should continue, than to let it to another at a greater rent, there being often great inconveniency in changing of tenants, and hee having increased his substance very well there, I was very well pleased that hee should continue. But now his terme being very near expired and hee being rich, & takeing advantage of the great distance I am at, hee hath declared that hee will not continue unlesse I wil abate him £30 per annum, which I am sure is very unreasonable. If your circumstances & inclinations be to become tenant to that farme, I will assure you that I shall be very well pleased therewith, and shall be glad to shew you all the kindnesse in my power. Pray let mee heare from you as soon as you can by post directed to mee at my house in Lincolns Inn Fields, and in two days it will be in the hands of
Your truely loving friend
Rich Holford

To my good friend Mr John Gardiner at Edington in Wilts., by Marlebrough Bag thence to the Devizes, Wiltes

Verso Note: 9 August 1701. A copy of a letter to Mr John Gardiner at Edington.

50. Sir Richard Holford to John Gardiner WSHC 184/1, pt.1.

21 August 1701

My good friend,

I have yours & doe thinke my last told you that the neighbours about Avebury doe all seeme to agree, that Farmer Skeate is growne rich, & is able & willing to live at ease, & therefore inclines to leave Avebury unlesse I will abate him £30 per annum, which I thinke is very unreasonable as I intimated to you in my last, & am sure that his rent of £350 per annum is very moderate, even now when the price of corne is soe very low, & was certainly very beneficiall when corne bore a greater price. The pasture as well as arable & meadow are constant steady ground, & I don't think that in the late great rott among sheepe that hee lost two out of both his flocks (Hackpin being as sound ground as any in England). The farme is tythe free, paying only about £4 per annum to the vicar, the house is a very good one, & fitt for an estate of four times the value of the farme, with all manner of conveniencies, court yards, gardens, orchard, 2 or 3 very good stables, besides the best stables, two barnes better than I ever saw upon one farme, an excellent pidgeon house, good granary, oxehouse, carthouse & a very large backside or barton, with an excellent horse pool in the middle, walled round, & very good water. In trueth there cannot bee more conveniencies belonging to an estate of double the value, fence wood excepted, for which the tenant is allowed. The late Lord Stawell was borne there, & hee & his father lived there, & twas his mothers joynture house. Farmer Skeate's lease for 12 years at £350 per annum expires at our Lady Day next, but is to hold the land sowed as is usuall in the course of husbandry. I can't say but that Farmer Skeate hath been a good tenant & preserved every thing as well as I could expect, & am of opinion that hee will speake as well of mee, for there or anywhere else in my small estate I never prest a tenant to pay his rent, but when he could with his best convenience, & never to sell any thing to losse to rayse rent. And I hope I shall be allwayes willing to encourage and reward an industrious tenant, & I cannot but thinke you are very well qualified & will deserve to be well used, & that if it be our fortune to come together & be soe related as landlord & tenant that wee may have a mutuall friendship for our lives. I doe thinke you have some knowledge of the farme, & I dare say the more you doe indeavour to informe yourselfe the better you will like it, & pray lett mee heare from you as soone & as effectual as you can. I shall be here till this day fortnight & doe designe soon after to be in Wiltshire, & shall gladly meet you anywhere. I shall have little time, for I must be in Gloucestershire, Somersetshire & elsewhere, which will consume the greatest part of my time, but will not neglect you, soe as you let mee receive your full thoughts before my goeing home, where I must be againe within a moneth. I have been the more particular because I would have you fully informed & if you doubt any thing, shall by the next after receipt of yours indeavour to assure you that I am

Your true friend

Rich Holford

For Mr John Gardiner at Edington in Wiltes, to be sent by Marlebrough to the

Devizes thence as directed.
Marlbrough Wiltes

Verso Note: Copy of a letter to Mr John Gardiner, 21 August 1701.
Not receiving any answer to this letter writ to him againe 6 September telling him that I shall bee in the flying coach at Marlebr on Tuesday by 9 & glad heare from him on Tuesday or to see him on Wednesday, & that I shall stay there till Saturday & then goe into Gloucestershire & elsewhere.

I spoke with Mr Gardiner at Avebury where hee came upon other business, and afterwards at Bath & after at Imber. He seemed [*illegible*][1] objected [*illegible*][2] over Mr Skeate's head though I told him that Skeat refused to stay unless I abated £30 per annum.

51. Humfry Wall to Sir Richard Holford WSHC 184/1, pt.1.

[18 October 1702]

Honored Sir,
I have yours, & wish I could serve you as I would. But on the Saterday after you went home one Farmer Browne went to Truslow & bidd him £1330 for his estate but noe price under 1350. On Munday I went abroad, did not returne untill Wednesday night, on Tuesday Mr Tooker agreed with Truslow to give him £1310, Truslow to enjoy all untill Lady Day , then to sow the summer cropp & to reape cutt & enjoy both winter & summer cropp next harvest & to enjoy the barnes & backside untill midsomer next 12 months. This I account to be worth neare £50. Mr Tooker deteyns £400 in his hands to discharge the annuity with the intrest & after the mothers death to pay £200 to Truslowe's sisters their father gave them. This price had I bin at home I durst not have given, soe there is an end of that. As to Griffen, I am satisfied noe man will soe readily purchass that, therefore I am not soe hasty in that, thinckeing it better to let him come to me then to send hastily after him. Yet I sent to him yesterday that when he comes to towne I would speake with him. My humble thancks for your care in delivering my matters to Natt Nobb's agent, & for all other favours, with my humble service to your selfe & Lady I remayne
Sir, Your obliged humble servant
H Wall
March 18 Oct 1702

Verso Note: Mr Humfry Wall, 18 October 1702, that Mr Tooker hath bought Truslow's estate for 1310[li].
Verso Address: To my honored friend Sir Richard Holford att his howse in Lincolns Inn Feilds neare Clare Markett, present, London

1 Written in cypher.
2 Ditto.

52. Sir Richard Holford to John White WSHC 184/1, pt.1.
23 December 1702

Master White!

Not having received any letter from you since I came from Avebury, I am unwilling to let Mr Norris come without one to you, for that by him, the postage wilbee saved, and I doe hope this will find you and your family in good health, & all the neighborhood in perfect peace and friendship, for the preservation whereof I would gladly contribute anything in my power. Wee are likely to have our taxes continued, which is of absolute nescessity for carrying on the warr against France and Spaine, and God bee thanked wee have glorious success this last summer, & with God's blessing may hope for the like the next summer, in order whereto wee must submit to pay our taxes cherefully. But the inequality of [*illegible*][1] the taxes makes it more grivious than the tax itselfe. I doe remember that the last yeare before the Act past, I writ a letter to you to request that you would use your interest to get the rate upon Avebury set as equally as might bee, to prevent any just complaint of inequality there, & yet the assessors, though upon their oaths, thought fit to bee very unequall, rateing mee much higher than others in proportion, though I told you and them of the great abatement of rents I have been forced to make, of which I canot but take notice, and doe think to exhibite an information against them in the Crowne Office for a willfull breach of their oaths the rather for that I don't find they have rated their owne heads, & those of their families, of which they can never pretend ignorance, and have omitted others which they doe know as well as their owne familes, & yet I observed they rated some servants. Tis pitty but those who vallue oaths noe better should smart for the wilfull breach, & learne thereby & teach others the danger of breakeing an oath, and I hope better care willbee taken for the future, or else the Act of Parliament requireing the assessors to bee upon their oaths thereby to obleidge them to an impartiall assessment according to the best of their knowledge.

Verso Notes: Copy letter to Mr White of Avebury, 23 December 1702, relateing to taxes praysed by assesors.
£xii xs received of Mr Jodrill 8 December 1702

53. John White to Sir Richard Holford WSHC 184/1, pt.1.
[7 January 1702/3]

Sir,

Your tenant Skeate beinge possesd with a turbulent, fanatick spirit (which I hope will in time be rasd out of the nation), & havinge grosly abusd me many yeares, but especially lately so that I cannot bear it any longer, I begge leave of you to vindicate my reputation by makinge him an example to all purse proud clownes who care not what they say or do, for though some good lawes are repealed which kept such rude abusive fellowes in order, yet I thinke there is still law enough in

1 Interlineation.

force to punish them that let their tongues run at what rate they please to wound their neighbours' reputation. Your farm is so good a bargain (& it would have been worth £50 per annum more if he had not been in it & might yet if he were out of it) that it hath puft him up, and made him so high & imperious that there is no livinge by him, wherefore it is high time to take him down a little, & to make him know himselfe, for I believe he hath forgot what he was when he came first to Avebury. I know, Sir, you have a particular kindnesse for him, & therefore I was willing to acquaint you with my design before I commenced a suit against him, but I hope you will not take his part in any thing that is unjust, nor patronize him any farther then right is on his side, and that the difference between your tenant and me will not create the least misunderstanding, disaffection, or distance between us, for I covet the continuance of your favour, and friendship, and should be glad of an oportunity to serve you. I suppose your tenant hath already, or will shortly, present you with a bundle of lies against me, but I believe you will take litle notice of them considering what he is. Wishing you and your Lady a merry & happy new year, I subscribe myself,
Your humble servant,
John White

I and my wife give our humble service to your Lady / Avebury January 7, 702.[1]

Verso Note: Mr John White of Avebury, Januarii 7 1702; answered the 13 January 1702. Complaineing of Farmer Skeate.
Perused 5th October 1756; of no use to the dispute now depending with Vicar.
Verso Address: For Sir Richard Holford, knight, at his house in Lincolns Inn Fields, London.

54. Sir Richard Holford to John Gardiner WSHC 184/1, pt.1.

16 July 1703

My very good friend Mr. John Gardiner,
I cannot forgett what passed betweene you & mee about 2 years ago relateing to Avebury farm, Farmer Skeate then threatening to leave it at the expiracon of his term (our Lady day 1702) unlesse I would abate him £30 per annum which I was very unwilling to doe because I knew it to be more worth than £350 at which hee had held it for 12 years, & it was formerly lett at £400 per annum and when I bought it (I gave neare £8000 for it) I was offered a very substantiall tenant at £380 per annum, but I was very unwilling to part with Farmer Skeate, who was a good husband and had a close stock upon it, and haveing thrived very well there, I was willing to thinke hee would not remove, & by that perswasion I did not looke out for another tenant & neglected it too long. But when I spoke with you I was incouraged to thinke you had an inclination to take it, but after your other affaires hindered your further proceedings, & I was faine to comply

1 Written in left margin.

with Farmer Skeate's proposall for four yeares (whereof one year expired at our Lady day last), since which farmers have been under pretty hard circumstances, but they must not be discouraged, and I think I must looke out for a new tenant, & shall not be troubled if I meet with one as rich & as knowing as Farmer Skeate, so as hee be not soe proud & stubbornly wilfull. I don't know any body whose quallifications would suite better with my inclinacons as my friend Mr. John Gardiner, and therefore doe give you this timely intimation that if you have any inclinacon to it you may have time enough to contrive your other affairs. And if God permitt I doe intend to be thereabouts within a moneth, & if you encourage mee I will endeavour to meet you to discourse the matter. But pray whatever your inclinacon be, lett me have a letter from you by the post to tell me that you have this. I doubt I shall be but little at home after the first of August, and therefore shall expect before that time to heare that you & your family are well, and that you doe you think I am
your very loveing friend
Rich Holford

Direct to mee at my house in Lincolns Inn Fields, London.
I never mentioned anything of yours & my discourse in this matter to anybody, and therefore &c.

Verso Note: Copy letter to Mr John Gardiner of Edington, 16 July 1703. The letter was inclosed to Mr Wadman.

55. Sir Richard Holford to John White WSHC 184/1, pt.1.

9 November 1704

Master White,
I received your kind letter of the 20th of October, & fully intended to have answered it last Thursday, but was kept longer at the Lords' house[1] that day than I expected & was thereby disappointed, & thinkeing that you are usually at Marlborough on Saturdays letters may come by Thursday's post easier than any other day, I delayed writeing till now. And doe now thanke you for your neighbourly & friendly intimacon in relation to Mr Spackman, of whom you have given mee a very satisfactory character. I am sure the farme is a very good bargaine at £350 per annum, at which rate Farmer Skeate tooke a lease for 12 yeares of my Lord Stawell, & when I bought it I was offered a tenant that would have given £30 per annum more, but then there was 5 or 6 yeares to come of that lease. You knew his condicon & circumstances when hee came thither, & can guess at them now. I should take a pride to see a tenant thrive, & be willing to assist a dilligent man, & I thinke I have not been backward therein to Farmer Skeate, but all my kindnes produced noe better effect than, when his lease was out, hee refused to renew it unlesse I would abate him more than I ever intended or than could be reasonably expected, yett by reason of my liveing at a distance, &

1 Holford was (probably) a doorkeeper in the House of Lords; see *AWS*, p.91.

my time otherwise imployed, I was forct to comply, & now haveing a little time to thinke of another tenant I take your friendly assistance therein very kindly, & doe hope you will give Mr Spackman all the information hee desires, & all the just encouragement you can. I hope his wife & her child are ere this time past the danger hee feared, & that hee may spare time to treate in this affaire. I told him the rent, & am not desirous to putt harder terms on him than Farmer Skeate putt upon himselfe with my Lord Stawell, who consented to allow halfe an acre of coppice wood yearly for the bounds. As soone as you have spoken with Mr Spackman I hope you will lett me know the result of your discourse, & when I may expect to see him, & lett us, if you thinke fit, establish a friendshipp and neighbourly correspondence which may be usefull to us both, & as you intimate may be soe to the parishoners, which will be very agreeable to
Your friend & servant
Rich Holford

To Mr John White at Avebury in Wiltes., to bee left with Mr Bayly, a mercer or silkman in Marlbrough, Wiltes.

56. John White to Sir Richard Holford WSHC 184/1, pt.1.
25 November 1704

Sir,
Yours I received, but not till last Saturday, which I shewd to Mr Spackman who intends to wait on you next weeke or the weeke after. I doubt not but he well deserves the character that I gave him, as you will find in time if he be your tenant, and what kindnesse you shew to him I am confident will produce a far better effect in him then it did in Farmer Skeate. Here is great complaint upon the malt taxe among the farmers, who looke upon it as a grievance, and if the Parliament doth not take some speedy course to redresse it many of them that rent estates which consist most of barly will breake and run away, for good barly here will not yield 13s a quarter. The Queen, if this taxe be not taken of, may have souldiers enough without pressing. You may do well to make use of your interest in the Parliament men that you are acquainted with to part with this taxe, for if they continue it, it will certainly be of ill consequence to themselves as well as to others for they must turn farmers, & take their estates into their own hands. With my humble service to you and your good Lady I rest
Yours at command
John White
Avebury Nov 25 1704[1]

Verso Note: Mr White [?28] November 1704. Writ to him 7.10^{ber} 1704 per sub coppie.
Verso Address: for Sir Richard Holford at his house in Lincolns Inn Fields

1 Written on left-hand side of text at right angles.

57. Sir Richard Holford to William Skeat WSHC 184/1, pt.1.

20 June 1705

Farmer Skeate,

I have yours of the 28th of this moneth dated from Rowdon, & therefore I doe direct this thither. Mr Selfe hath not payd mee any money, though I depended upon it as money in my hand, because hee is reported to be a very wary & punctuall dealer & in very good creditt. You seeme to resolve to leave Avebury, & whether I will be pleased that you shall helpe mee to a tenant you thinke you can doe it, & that you lately spoke with one who is able & honest & willing to be my tenant, truely I will take it as a very great kindnesse if you will assist mee therein, & noebody can informe a tenant of the value & condicon of that farme soe well as you can, if you will be friendly to mee therein. You have not named the man, & therefore I cannot like, or dislike, but I shall be gladd of an honest able man, such as you mention. Pray therefore lose noe time to discourse closely with him, & lett mee heare from you as soone and as fully as you can. The farme cost mee £7500 & I have layd out upon it a good deale of money. It was formerly lett at £400 & at that value setled on the marriage of Collonell Stawell, & a covenant that it should continue at that value, but the warrs came on, & yett I doe thinke & hope the ground &c is in better heart & creditt than it hath formerly been. It will be troublesome and chargeable changing a tenant especially to mee, who am at such a distance, therefore you must give mee your assistance therein. One Mr Spackman hath been proposed to mee, & I am informed that many reports have been raised thereupon, without my privity or consent. I shall be gladd of an honest & able man, & such a man shall never have any cause to blame mee in any thing. I have not sayd anything, nor can say anything to what you doe propose relateing to Isaac Humfryes. I hope hee will not give mee further cause to blame my kindnesse to him. As to the horse pray direct Fowler to take care of him for mee. I don't, I can't, think my Lord Aylesburye's agent will pretend to any such thing in Avebury. If they should I must dispute it. My Frogg is inclined to spend some time att Avebury, but will not thinke of it till I can bring her thither, & that cannot be yett. Shee & I doe remember our kind love to you your wife & children,

I am your loveing friend
Rich Holford

For Farmer Wm Skeate at Rowdon Farme, neare to Chippenham, Wiltes

Verso Note: Coppy of a letter to Farmer Skeate, 28 Junii 1705.

58. Sir Richard Holford to John White WSHC 184/1, pt.1.

6 March 1706/7

Sir,

Yours of the 1st of this moneth was the more wellcome because it intimates that money is plenty at Avebury. I am sure I can gett but little thereat, & if never soe plenty I cannot consent that it should be expended to superstitious or schismaticall uses. But I cannot thinke that you doe believe my writeing or speakeing will signifie much to these people, who slight or neglect your good example & pastorall care for their good, & will wilfully separate from the religious exercises by law establisht in our church government, & follow after their owne vaine imaginations.

However because you doe desire it, & that 'twill be a kindnesse to you, I will by this post write to Farmer Skeate, & use my endeavour to effect what you doe desire, the rather for that you apprehend my stones may be employed to the building of a conventicle house for hippocrits, which I must & will oppose.

You say you doe heare that I am buying John Griffin's Parsonage & I doe thanke you for the friendly caution you give mee relateing thereto, & shall be the better able to give him my answer, when hee shall thinke fitt to propose the sale, whereof I have heard noething save by your letter.

But it brings to my mind that when Mr Griffen offered to sell his manor to mee, I not having time to treat with him about it, left my instructions with an attorney at Marlborough to treat with him, & was soone after told they had agreed, & articles were sent hither for my approbacon & I submitted thereto soe as a good title might be made, & then you did mee the like friendly favour as now, & intimated that his demands were extravagant, & that hee proposed to sell more than was ever his, & what his father never bought, as by the terrier (by which his father purchased) then in your hands. I thanked you for your caution, & not likeing the title I desisted, & afterwards heard that it proved a mighty pennyworth and possibly this may prove as good a bargaine.

I have not been soe vigorous as I might be in presenteing the pound breakers, in hopes the actors might be sensible of their follies & make some reasonable satisfaction, without being exposed, which if they will yett doe (for some of their sakes) I am willing to be very easy in the matter; otherwise I must putt them into the Crowne Office and expect the event, not being willing to repaire a publick pound as often as folly or malice shall damnifie or destroy it. I am not unmindfull[1] unmindfull that the pound is wanting and the more for that I think some of your neighbours are perverse & troublesome enough. You don't mencon any thing to the contrary but that your wife & children are well, & my wife & I doe remember our respects to you all. I doe answer yours by the first post, being willing if you thinke fit of a frequent correspondence by letters at your leisure & am
Your friend & servant
Rich Holford

These for Mr White at Avebury Wilts, to be left with Mr Bayly, a mercer in Marlborough, Wiltes.

Copy letter to Mr White, 6 March in answer to his of the 5th March 1706/7 relateing to Mr Griffens Parsonage.

1 Page break.

59. Christopher Page and John Jerome to Sir Richard Holford
WSHC 184/1, pt.1.
[18 April 1707]

Sir,
We have made bolde to give you notis if the trouble as we are like to come into by the cruelty of Mr John White, which he doth thretten us with. We have each of us a house which have bing in our possions nere twenty years. But it stands opon the common, & now he have bought the mannor of John Griffin's[1] (which you doth alredy we sapose know), & now he doth command us to take leasses of our houses, which we woud give him for quietness sake, but that will not content hem but he will have tenn pounds a peice of us & we are poore men & not able to pay it. Now we would desier your worship to give us your advice in it, whether he can compell us to take a leese & give hem a fine, or no. Sir, we would desire your worship to send us your advice in it as soone as you can, for he doth require answer of us in a littell time, or else he will take out a injectment upon us, & take our houses from us. So we rest with our sarvis to you, youre humble sarvants to command,
Christopher Page & John Jorem
Avebury
Aprill the 18th, 1707

Verso Note: Christopher Page and John Jerome, cottagers at Avebury, 18 April 1707, being alsoe informed by others of Mr White's insulting the poore cottagers, I writ to him there about the 8th May 1707, per the copy.[2]
Verso Address: This for Sir Richard Holford liveing in Lincoln Inn Feilds in London, this.

60. Sir Richard Holford to John Overton WSHC 184/1, pt.1.
Lincolns Inn Fields
4 November 1707

Mr John Overton,
I have yours of the 29th of October wherein you tell mee your purpose of setting about surveying of Avebury the 10th of this moneth, and intimate as if I had soe ordered it, but I doe not remember that I gave any order or directions thereabouts, nor doe I ever undertake or direct such a worke until I have estimated the charge of doeing it, & could not resolve to sett about it till I had further considered whether all or what part should be comprehended in a particular mapp, & what it would cost. But I doe particularly remember that I did discourse with you thereabouts, and the charge, & declared that I was willing it should be done as soone as I could be satisfyed therein, & directed you to write to mee thereabouts, & I doe thanke you for your letter, but I would not have you sett about the worke

1 That is, a portion of the manor of Avebury Truslow; see *VCH Wilts.,* 12, p.93.
2 The 'copy' has not been found in this collection.

till further order, for I am not fond of spending money unlesse to good purpose or to give some satisfaction, especially since money is soe hard & difficult to be raised.

You told me how ill I had been used by the workemen who last tiled the new stable, and I have good reason to be displeased when abused by knavish workemen, but I doe love and am very willing to pay honest workemen, as I am told you are. And I doe expect when you goe about it in March or Aprill that you will cause it to be well done, the tyles to be well pinned, and good lime & laths, that there may be noe cause of complaint, & you shall have noe cause to complain for lack of your pay. I am
Your friend
Rich Holford

Address: For Mr John Overton, a tyler, at his house in the Devizes, by Marlborough bagg, Wiltes.

Verso Note: Copy of a letter to Mr John Overton, tyler at the Devizes 4 Nouember, 1707.

61. Sir Richard Holford to John White WSHC 184/1, pt.2.

Lincolns Inn Fields
22 July 1708

Master White,
I have often told you (& haveing this opportunity by Mr Norris & his wife by whome I am sure twill safely come to Avebury), & doe now repeate it, that I should be very well pleased with a neighbourly correspondence at your best leazure, and doe now take the liberty to tell you that your unkind silence hath often made mee reflect on my owne actions & behaviour towards you, & other neighbours at Avebury, & on yours & theirs towards me, & though I may clame myselfe as too subject to human frailties, yet I have allwayes & allwayes shall endeavour to doe to others as I would they should to mee, & can justifie all my actions towards you & them, & can cherefully passe by and forgett & forgive any thing that hath been done to mee, yett I don't finde any ready inclinaton in you or them to invite friendship. When I was first concerned at Avebury I waited on you in expectacon of what I mett with, your faire & friendly reception and encouragement of what I was about, and I liked all soe well that I was inclined to have layd out more money, if anything there or thereabouts was to be sold, a pennyworth for a penny, intending to have made it a comfortable dwelling, and to have been a good neighbour, but before I could looke well about mee, I found that you and my tenant farmer Skeate had great strifes & contentions, which as I thought was more out of humour and passion than any substantiall cause, yet foreseeing the mischiefes that might arise, & the consequences usually attending such brangles, and in hopes to prevent what I feared, I applyed myself to you, as a gentleman of breeding, & from whose qualifications & circumstances I might have

expected a neigbourly recepton, but my endeavours proveing fruitlesse, I againe personally as well as by letters requested you to informe mee what your dues were yearly out of my farme (which seemed to be the subject matter of your squabbles) for that any uncertainty therein might be very prejudiciall to mee, especially upon the change of a tenant, & assured you that whatever was justly due should be duely payd, but instead of complying with my request you positively refused to lett mee know what was your due, & was pleased to answer mee roughly & told mee that you demanded noething of mee, but of my tenant dureing his lease, & when that should be determined I should know your pleasure, or to that very effect, & soone after in a very unfriendly manner & without any just cause accused mee of countenanceing faction & fanatiqs, with other unexpected and reproachfull language as your letters now before mee doe evidently show. I was then constrained to exhibit my bill in Chancery[1] to discover the vicar's dues, & prayed you to give a full & faire answer & not to mix gaul with your inke, yett when you thought fit to putt in what you called an answer, it contained a great deale of what ought not to have been there, and wanted what was requisite, & the Court, notwithstanding your stubborne contention, compelled you to putt in a further answer, upon perusal whereof I found great slipps & oversights, of which in a friendly manner I informed you, & shewed you the Attorney Generall's opinion thereon (hee is now Lord Chiefe Justice of the Common Pleas) for which you found noe better excuse, than that your attorney or solicitor had drawne it & told you that you must sweare it, & boasted what a cunning man hee was and that he could headline &c., but the poore creature being dead, all that hee did amiss may sleepe with him in his grave. I replyed to your answer & intended to examine my witnesses, but then & not till then you seemed to desire to putt an end to that suite, & to be friends, & employed an honest neighbour to come to mee on your behalf with your offer to pay mee my costs, & to be a good neighbour from that time foreward, whereto I readily inclined (in case your friend thought you in good earnest), upon which you came to mee, & repeated what your friend had sayd to mee, & brought some money (but not halfe what I might fairely expect) & prayed mee to accept it & your future friendshipp, whereupon I submitted to be a great looser & accepted what you offered, & you haveing prepared mutuall releases, the same were executed, & you know how I distributed great part of the money. And then I thought I had purchased & ensured your friendshipp & have been allways willing to demonstrate mine. I am an enemy to whisperers & backbiters, and never inclined to favour such creatures (& doe wish you would not). And to prevent as much as in mee lyes all misunderstanding, I doe give you the trouble of this, & doe request you in a few lines & a friendly manner to tell me whether you have any reall cause of complaint, or wherein you thinke I have done you any wrong, & if your complaint be just I will recompence you seven fold. You know I bought and payd deare for the royalty whereof some small cottages inhabited by poore people are part, & I beleive you thought soe when Mr Griffen offered to sell them to mee, as your kind letter upon that occasion

1 TNA C5/166/23.

admonished mee, & told mee that they were none of his, & that you had the particular by which his father bought. I am told that the pound is sett up, the charge whereof I believe will be considerable, & because I would prevent the like [*illegible*], as of late I have consented to sett itt in a more publick place for the convenience of the neighbours. I cannot tell what new heats have happened betweene you & Farmer Skeate, but doe sensibly feele the effects of the former. And though I don't care to remember, yet tis difficult to forgett the law suite & tryall for the tythes at Backhampton, & the Exchequer suites (which swallowed all the money poore Hayward had in the world) & the like, which it may be you will tell mee, did not concerne mee, yett I am sure I ought to take warning by other men's harms, & endeavour to prevent all occasions of strife & ill will. I will depend upon receiveing a letter from you in answer to this before I goe out of towne, which I doe purpose with Gods permission the very beginning of August, and will bid it as welcome as you shall intend it, and am with due respects
Your friend and servant
Rich Holford

Verso Note: Copy of a letter of peace to Mr John White of Avebury, sent by Mr Norris, 22 July 1708.

62. John White to Sir Richard Holford WSHC 184/1, pt.2.
20 October 1708

Sir,
I have often found by your discourse that you are not so fond of Farmer Skeate, but you can (& I hope will) exchange him for a better tenant. Since you went to London I heard of a substantial man that is willing to be your tenant,[1] and will advance the rent. He is able to stock your farm without any help, which Farmer Skeate cannot do, & therefore he lets good part of it to others to ye great detriment thereof, for they carry the corn to their own houses, and what dung they make of the straw they lay upon their own land, by which meanes your farm hath been very much impoverished, & will in time be quite beggard if it be not speedily prevented. Farmer Skeate proves to me all as he ever did, & designes to cheat me of my dues as he hath done formerly. Wherefore I begge leave of you to make use of the remedy which the law prescribes in such cases, beinge unwilling to be cheated of my just rights by any man, but especially by him who hath been the worst enemy that I ever had in the world, having been the occasion of my spending a great deal of mony which would have been better bestowed upon my family.[2] With due regards to you & your good Lady, I am, Sir
Your most humble servant
John White
Avebury, Oct 20 1708

1 Note at side in Holford's hand: 'a good tenant'.
2 Note at side in Holford's hand: 'twas Mr White's owne pervers & stubborne humor'.

Verso Note: Mr White, 20 October 1708. Answered 10 November 1708. Hath a good tenant; the farme ill used & hee defrauded, therefore [*illegible*] have to take his legal remedye.
Verso Address: for Sir Richard Holford, knight, at his house in Lincolns Inn Fields, London.

63. Sir Richard Holford to John White WSHC 184/1, pt.2.

London
30 October 1708

Master White,
I received yours of the 20th of this moneth & doe thanke you for it, & cannot but approve the character you give of your proposed tenant. But I should have been glad if you had named him, not that I would mention his name any ways to his disadvantage.

I have formerly had severall proposed, but inquireing into their circumstances & reflecting on the great trouble &c., of changeing, & not dispairing of a better under standing betweene you & Farmer Skeate, I did not close with any other. Your acquaintance Mr Spackman (& you assured mee that hee was) an able industrious man, & a quiet neighbour, inclined me to have been very kind to him, but upon treating with him you know, hee refused to comply with the rent, at which Farmer Skeate had held it by a lease from my Lord Stawell for 12 years. I am sure you did then know the value of it as well as any body, & I am sure you have often told mee that hee had a good bargaine & had profitted considerably thereby. I have good evidence to shew that it was 50 yeares agoe covenanted to be £400 per annum & soe to continue, & when I purchased it, Mr Bennett, who had been my Lord Stawell's agent, offered mee a substantiall tenant (as hee affirmed) who should give mee £300 per annum. But Farmer Skeate's lease was then in being, & severall yeares to come, & I am very willing to beleive that tis now as good as then, & with good usage I did expect it would have been much better, but you have observed that which I did not know, that there are undertenants, & thereby likely to be impaired, which I am desirous to prevent & your assistance therein may be of great use & friendly.

You doe mention in yours as if I should obstruct your legall rememdy for recovery of your just dues. Truely Mr White I never did anyways obstruct any legall remedy, but ever was and am willing, if I can to prevent any suites at law about matters that may be otherwise adjusted, & to that very purpose was willing to heare what the matters in difference seemed to be, which was about the composicon or that you should take your tythes in kinde, & I thinke hee offered you your choice, & truely I thinke the difference was very little, & that you had this yeare made choice to take it in kinde, & did take the ell ridges, & I thinke the backside was the worst that I ever knew, but the law is an Englishman's birthright, & must putt an end to all controversies. I have been a very great sufferer by the squabbles already had, & did hope I had seen an end of them, & tis not difficult by compareing events with their causes, to place the injuries I have received upon

a right foot. And ever did & should be gladd whenever I have been & shall be concerned, that true Christian charity such as the Apostle heartily recomended to the Corinthians might be effectually practised & submitted to. I doe hope you will favour mee with your further thoughts & assistance upon the subject matter of your last, & am very heartily willing upon any encouragement to shew myself,
Your true friend & servant
Rich Holford

Mr White, this was written when dated, but an acquaintance of mine who intended to pass through Avebury, & to deliver it with his owne hand, failed to call for it, as hee made believe hee would, whereby I was disappointed till now this 10 November 1708

Address: These for Mr John White at Avebury, Wiltes; to be left with Mr Bayly, mercer, in Marleborough, Wiltes.

Verso Note: Copy letter to Mr White, 10 November 1708.[1]

64. Sir Richard Holford to Richard Chandler WSHC 184/1, pt.2.

Lyncolns Inn Fields
2 June 1709

Mr Richard Chandler,
It is a pretty many daies since I received your letter of the 21st May, & doe pray you to excuse mee for not answering it sooner, for in truth I have been out of order, & indisposed for some dais, but for a month past I have been afflicted by the great indispositon of my wife, who hath been extreame ill, but is I hope now some what better, yet very weake, else I had not delayd my answer soe long.
I am well pleased that you have carefully viewd the farme, & seen the farmer's lease for 12 yeares from my Lord Stawell, wherein I believe is such liberty for plowing as you mention, but I can tell you (as the farmer might have done) that when hee took the farme one Mr John Baskeville had been my Lord's tenant there, and had very much abused both the land and landlord, and that the land was then much wors for a tenant than it is now (by Mr Baskerville's ill husbandry) or else it would have brought a better rent. As to the acres, whether by estimation or by lug I cannot certainly affirme, but I can & doe affirme that by the particular, upon which I purchased, the number of acres were as I have briefly mentiond on the back syde of this[2], & when I compared it with Farmer Skeate & other knowing neighbors, they agreed it to bee a just & true perticular. I paid for it £7500 besydes a great deale of troble & charge, & then the dwelling house was very much out of repaire, & cost mee a great deal of money, in all at lease £500, and yet an honest gentleman not tenn miles from it, offered to give mee

1 This was the date the letter was actually sent.
2 See below.

1000li for my bargaine. And Mr Francis Bennet, who had been steward & agent for my Lord Stawell, then offered mee an able tenant at £380 per annum, but the farmer's lease was not then expired, and before it did expire, corne & wooll sunck to low rates, to the discouragement of tennants, yet that farme kept up its reputation, but too big for ordinary tennants. The farmer might have shewd you one peice of land in the common field, that hee hath often told mee is well worth 40 shilling per acre. And I don't know that the farmer hath been an ill husband upon it, unles in the bounds. And I doe dare say hee han't mett with any hardship or discouragement from mee, but the contrary (whatever hardship he hath mett with elsewhere). And now hee pretends that hee is groweing old & is infirme, and his wife very crazy, and not fit for soe much troble.

I cannot abate any thing of the rent of £350 per annum, but did hope to have raised it, had not the times discouraged tennants, but now God bee thanked wee have a faire expect of a speedy peace, the French king & his country being reduced to that extremity that hee must graunt all that is proposed.[1]

I am well assured that railes, gates & plow boote &c were duely considred at the makeing that lease, and to bee at the tennant's charge, there being a lack of timber upon the farme, but allowed halfe an acre of wood for the fences yearly.

I have been disquieted & trobled at the unneighborly & unfriendly squables between Mr White & the farmer, about trifles, to gratifie their humors without any profit or advantage to either of them, but to my great damage, & to my discomfort when there, but I hope if you come thither wee shall bring the neighbors to a more friendly temper, and for[2] and for that very purpose I the last Michaelmas refused a very able and very fit & well qaullified tennant, & a good neighbor, only hee was a Quaker (and a teacher) which I was sure would have given distate to Mr White, & given him a handle to bee troblesome. I am a great lover of peace & good neighborhood, and would not wrong Mr White of a 1d if it was in my power, but I beleive hee now thinks I won't bee imposed upon.

The troble of changing a tenant in such a farme wilbee a great troble, & the more by reason of my distance from it, but your being soe neare & soe well acquainted with the country will very much ease that troble. The farmer told mee hee will part with his stock upon it at easy & reasonable rates. And upon my word I wil use my best indeavor to make every thing as equal and as easy as I can, & will alwaies bee governed by reason, & shew myselfe,

Your true friend
Rich Holford

Pray let mee heare from you shortly

[Particular of Avebury Farm][3]

1 It took several more years before the War of the Spanish Succession was ended by the Peace of Utrecht in 1713.

2 Page break.

3 Heading inserted by editor.

Upon Hackpin in severall pieces 20/12/14/3/30/12/7[1]	98
Weedon Feild in severall pieces 20/40/12/3/8/7/5	95
West Feild in severall pieces 10/8/20/3/10/9/6/	65
Thornhill Feild 14/6/8/5/12/8/6/	59
Acres	317
Meadow 12/18½ /21/30/20½/18/14/7/	141
	448

Besydes the Wall ditch

The farmer & neighbors doe call every piece & parcell by a knowne name.

The note you mention to have seen in Farmer Skeate's hand of the number of acres, I tooke from his mouth the morning I saw you are Avebary

Verso Note: Letters written by mee to Mr Chandler, & because wee did not agree I desired my letters, & hee accordingly brought them to mee.
Verso Address: for my good friend Mr Richard Chandler at Woodborrow, Wiltes. Leave this at the Halfe Moone in Marleborough, Wiltes.

65. Sir Richard Holford to Richard Chandler WSHC 184/1, pt.2.

Lyncolns Inn Field
15 June 1709

Mr Richard Chandler,
On Monday last I received your answer to mine, wherein I intended & thought I had fully answered yours, & doe refer you to it. I would not have you doubtfull, nor uneasye in anything, you may depend upon it, that the rent is £350 per annum, & is a very moderate rent for that farme. Tis true tis too bigg for an ordinary tennant, &, if devided & made two farmes, it would yield a great increase of rent, (as hath often been proposed to mee), but I did not think fitt to devide it, being well assured that an industrious tennant who hath a full stock may make it more profitable than by devideing, and without a good stock and a wary tennant rent will not easily rise. And for lack of a good stock or by neglect or ill husbandry the tennant don't thrive, then the farme beares the blame. I was too well pleased with that little conversation I had with you, and the account I have received of your ability & of your knowledge, how to stock & manage it to the best advantage, and of your industry & integrity, that I am well assured you will live well upon it, more to my satisfaction than my honest Quaker, who hath been a good while recommended & is very able and willing, against whome my only objection is & hath been, that hee is a Quaker (and a teacher), and Mr White's haughty (I had almost sayd uncharitable) disposition, makes mee much rather incline to you, for the sake of peace and good neighborhood. Farmer Skeate was here the close of the last weeke with cattell, but I had very little of his company. Hee promised to stay a day or two, and that I should have spent time

1 These are presumably acreages.

with him, but hee afterwards came to mee in haste & told mee that a kinsman of his was very ill, & requested his company out of towne, soe that I could have but little discours with him, but hee spoke very well of you, in all ye circumstances, as every way well quallified to live well upon, & to bee a credit to the farme. I told him that I had received a letter from you, and had written fully to you, and expected your answer. Hee promised to speake with you as soone as hee could, and would write to mee. I can't think that hee will speake anything to the prejudice of the farme, or say that I have been in anything unkind to him, but hath good reason to say the contrary, for I have ever been, and doe hope I ever shalbee, willing to doe to others as I would have others doe to mee. Tis true I have chid him for grumbleing and complaineing. I doe know that of late money hath been very scarce in the country, and by the lowe price of cattell, corne, & wooll, tennants have been discouraged, espetially those who had the fortune to have had hard or nescessitous landlords, who would not, or could not, stay for their rent till convenient marketts. But wee ought in all things to submitt to God's providence without murmerring, more espetially in time of publique callamities, wherein landlord & tennant ought to share in the disapointment, in hopes of better times, and God bee thanked wee have now a blessed prospect.

Let your next tell mee that you are resolved to enter upon the farme at the same rent, as in Farmer Skeate's lease for 12 yeares (graunted by my Lord[1] my Lord Stawell (indeed I had hopes to have raised the rent, had not the times frowned upon tennants and consequently upon landlords). And that you will not grumble nor complaine without just cause. And then if I can mak you easy you may expect any thing reasonable. I doe think an honest industrious tennant ought to live comfortablie, & to enjoy the benefit as well of his stock as of his labor & industry, towards which I shalbee willing to give my helping hand. Especially I shall indeavor to make the scales even between Mr White and you. I am sure, that by the frequent squabbles between him & Farmer Skeat about trifles, & by their rough ungovernable passions, I have been deprived of the satisfaction I expected, and been greatly damnified, and neither of them one penny the better. But I doe know how to prevent or remedie it for the future, if occasion, but doe hope you will live neighborly and friendly, as becomes Christians, withough any willfull wrongeing or being wronged by each other, and I shalbee willing to shew myselfe,

Your true friend
Richd Holford

Let mee heare from you as soone as you can because I must write to my honest Quaker.

Upon reading over this long letter I han't mentoned in it the terme of yeares, & therefore would have you, in your next, to mention what terme you doe propose.

My letter is the longer because wee han't an opportunity to speak together

1 Page break.

Verso Address: for Mr Richard Chandler at Woodborough neare to Marlebrough, Wiltes. To bee left for him at the Halfe Moone in Marlebrough, Wiltes.

66. Sir Richard Holford to Richard Chandler WSHC 184/1, pt.2.

21 July 1709

Mr Chaundler,

To yours of the 24 of June I gave you a full & I intended it for a satisfactory & incourageing answer the 30th, & I hope you received it, and alsoe hope that you would have told mee soe before this time, & thereby have prevented this, which comes purely on the same errand, & to know, if I could, who was soe unkind to discourage you, for that though I have very few acquaintance thereabouts yet I cannot think anybody, except it bee Mr White the vicar of Avebury, soe very officious. I am very sure that I am a good deal the wors, for his & Farmer Skeate's groundles & unneighborly annimosities. At the time I writ last to you, I likewise writ to Farmer Skeate, but han't since heard from him. I directed his to Chipenham because of his farme neare it. I can't remember whether I directed yours to bee left at the Post House at Marlebrough or at the Halfe Moone there, but I hope you have it, & that I shall speedily heare from you, and that you are willing to think mee, as I am,

Your loveing friend

Rich Holford

If you have a good wife, as I think you told mee, pray let mee see her the later end of the next month at Avebury, where I doe hope bee with my wife, if it shall please God to enable her.

Verso Address: for Richard Chaundler at Woodborough, near to Marlebrough. To bee left for him at the Halfe Moon in Marlebrough, Wiltes.

67. Sir Richard Holford to William Skeat WSHC 184/1, pt.2.

23 February 1709/10

Farmer Skeate,

Last night I received yours dated the 19th, & if sent when dated it might have been with mee on Monday. I doe now find in part the inconvenience I feared by John Rose's not being able to write. You have often heard mee declare my very good opinion of John Rose's honesty & industry, and that notwithstanding other objections I was willing to take him for my tenant, & when you proposed that I should lend him £400 to help stock it you also proposed it at £5 per cent. But I expected I should have had some security besides his owne. Yet when I found that you & your son did refuse to be bound for him, & that it would be difficult for him to gett security, I told him I would depend upon his owne or to that effect. But now when our Lady Day is at hand, & you thinke I must accept of anything you tell mee I must have noe interest for the £400, whereto I told you that I would never submitt thereto. And when you seemed to say that John Rose would be a looser by being at an uncertainty, I tould you that it was your owne fault, by not putting into writeing what hee & you resolved on, & letting mee know it, & to prevent any misunderstanding I writ fully & plainely to you & to Mr Smith, & never till now lately heard of £400 to be lent gratis. When you went last from mee, I prayd you as soone as you should come home, to speake with John Rose, & to know what damage or losse hee may receive if hee can't goe on, & to write thereof to mee, for that I resolved John Rose or any other should not suffer by mee, & now you don't mention one word thereof. Time will stay for noe body. Therefore pray by the very next post, tell me what you thinke John Rose may suffer, by not takeing the farme.

I have been too much imposed upon and did not expect such usage. I will expect your answer by the post that comes by the Folly[1] on Sunday morning about 7, & will be here on Monday. I am troubled to thincke of a journey to Avebury this vacation, & had rather give £20 out of my pocket than undertake it, & did hope by your friendshipp & assistance to have prevented it. I doe hope your wife hath taken care for some good drinke. Pray putt her in minde to sett beanes, & to sett some parsley & sage, and cabbage or coleworts or other garden stuff at my charge. When you doe remove, I would have you take care to carry of only[2] what belongs to you. I tooke as particular a note as I could of what belongs to mee, & had a note from you of what was left when you came thither. You refused to shew mee your note, saying it was at Chippenham. My Frogg & I doe remember our love to your wife & children. I am your loving friend,
R.H.

Verso Note: Copy letter [to Farmer][3] Skeate, 23 February 1709, relateing to John Rose and himselfe.

68. Sir Richard Holford to John White WSHC 184/1, pt.2.

Avebury
2 April 1710

Master White and I hope good friend!
I have been here 9 or 10 days, and trobled for your indispositon, the more for that it hindred mee of your conversation, and sent every day to enquire & was willing to have made you a visit if it might have been convenient, but your wife whether her owne humor & thinks there may bee snares in a friendly conversation, did not think fit to signifie any inclination to such a visit, and as I never did, soe am willing never to give her any just cause of offence, and therefore doe take the liberty to express in writeing, what I purposed by word of mouth. First to wish you a firme establisht health, and then to intreat your friendship to John Rose,

1 One of the inns at Beckhampton, now the Waggon & Horses.
2 Text from this point is written at right angles on the left hand side of the letter. Space ran out at the bottom.
3 Torn.

now my tennant in the farme. And for that you & Farmer Skeate have not had such a quiet & neighborly friendship as I wisht (and therefore can the more easily part with him as you have often declared your desire I should) yet I hope you will mutually forget and forgive what is past, & part cherefully & friendly, and that you will not deale roughly with his successor, but beare and forbear, when tis not to your prejudice, and to alwaies let reason judge between you in case of any involuntary trespass, unforeseen accident or mistake. I have discoursed fully with him, and instructed him to that purpose, and am perswaded that hee will observe my directions therein, and that he will shew due respect to you & your family, and duely & honestly pay all your dues and doe all neighborly services to obteine & preserve your friendship. And whether it bee most convenient for you to receive your tythes in kind, or the usual composition, you can best judge, but I doe request that for peace sake you will make & declare your choice in reasonable time, and thereby prevent all future squabbleings about it, for lack of certainty , & methinks the composition is most certaine and most easy on both sydes, and I am encouragd to think, too, by [*illegible*] answer ~~to my bill~~, & for ought I know most equal.
Sir
Your true friend and servant
Rich Holford

Verso:[1] And I think it incumbent upon mee as well for my owne as for yours as my tennants sake to & for peace & quietnes sake to tell you that I have noe inclinacon to bee imposed upon nor to comply with any arbitrary or new demand, or other or more than due & formerly paid, but I think my tennant ought as privite respect to present you with now & then halfe a douzen or douzen of pidgions. I have directed him not to stop, or delay or deny, but justly & cherefully to pay all your dues & rather more than less, and I doe hope that you and hee and your families will live in mutuall love & charity as good neighbours, and if I can at any time contribute thereunto I shalbe ready & glad to doe it, & to shew my selfe as I doe desire to bee
Sir, your true friend & servant
R. H.

I read this to Mr Smith & to Farmer Rose & his wife, & Caswell & his wife, &c. Sent to Mr White by Mr Brinsdon, who preacht to us a very good sermon this afternoon, and before I sealed it I read it him, & he afterwards told mee that hee had deliverd to Mr White.

Verso Note: Draught of a letter to Mr White, 2 April 1710, sent the letter by Mr Brinsdon.

1 A first version of this paragraph is written on the recto, but deleted.

69. Sir Richard Holford to John Rose WSHC 184/1, pt.2.

Lincolns Inn Fields
7 June 1710

Farmer John Rose,
I am well pleased with your & your wive's & family's dilligence & care, & doe promise myselfe more satisfacton than ever I had at Avebury. Pray advise as often as you can with your Uncle Smith,[1] & gett him to write for you. You told mee that you can read my letters. If you cannot pray lett Richard Morris assist you. I doe thinke him an industrious young man, & fitt to be encouraged, & the neighbours testifyeing for him that hee is fit to live amongst them, & is an honest man. I will take the best care I can to support him in all things that are just & faire, & pray lett him assist you in keeping your accounts, & to write for you to mee, when ever there is reason, & if hee hath any trouble putt upon him for doeing anything that is lawfull & honest, pray lett him tell mee of it.

I have now written long & particular letters to John Ladd & to John Overton intreating to finish their worke before they leave it, and I doe hope they will doe soe, & be as little troublesome to you & your family as possibly they can. Pray as you passe to and fro put them in minde of it, & if either of them doe delay to finish their worke, lett Richard Morris know it, & write mee word thereof.

I did mention to the glazier to paint the wainscott in the parlour chamber, but I doe thinke not to doe it yett, & I have written to John Ladd to tell him, & pray doe you tell him, that I would not have him doe any thing to it till further order, but lett him & pray doe you call on the smith to make & fit up the casement for that chamber as soone as may be, for I know harvest is usually a busy time, and must be attended.

Remember my love to Farmer Skeate & his family, & desire him as I have often done to deale friendly & fairely with mee & you, and all future trouble be prevented. Pray remember mee to your wife & to Mr White when you see him, & enquire after Mr Sloaper's health, & lett mee know how hee is. Remember my love to all the neighbours, & let mee heare from you either by Mr Smith or Richard Morris or both as often as occasion, & you may expect to heare from mee as often, & doe thinke twill be best to direct mine to be left with Mr Kimber, a grocer at Marleborough for Richard Moris as hee desired. Pray speake to Farmer Skeate to send to mee, or give to you my warrant whereby I made him my game keeper, it not being proper for him now.

I am willing to be
Your loveing friend
Rich Holford

Pray keepe this & all other my letters by you, that I may see them if occasion.

Address: For Farmer John Rose at Avebury in Wiltes.

1 He has not been identified.

Verso Note: Copy letter to John Rose, 7 Junii 1710, sent by John Ladd's son.

70. Sir Richard Holford to John Rose WSHC 184/1, pt.2.

23 November 1710

John Rose,

Last Thursday I writt to you, & doe hope you received it, & doe refer you to it for the most part of what is contained in your letter of ye 15th, which came from you before mine could come to you.

As to Mr Smith's purpose to sell his estate, if his sister in law will joyne with him, I cannot tell what to say, unlesse hee had directed you to propose it to mee. If hee desires you as his friend to offer it, you may tell him that you doe believe I will expect a particular thereof & the price demanded, and if hee cannot gett his sister to joyne, then what he demands for his right without her joyneing, but this must not be by my directions or knowledge, but as you are his friend & mine. You may alsoe as from your selfe aske him, whether the shopp keep[1] hath made any further application to him.

As to Mr White's geat kindness, I would have you not regard his threats but to take the soyle[2] in the street as you have occasion, and whenever hee hath a mind to be troublesome, hee may doe as hee shall be advised. Hee knows I have bought & payd for the royalty, & that the mannor of Avebury & Truslows Avebury are mine at a full value, & I am very unwilling to part with any part of what I have bought & payd for, & therefore doe despise his threats, but if hee had at any time in a friendly manner desired to see my title, I would have shewed it to him or his councell, but hee never mentoned any such thing to mee. Hee wrongfully broke & carryed away a great stone, which I would not have parted with for £5 in the place where hee broke it. I told him of it, & now hee hath recovered his health I shall putt him againe in minde of it, & of some other things, but I would willingly have peace with him & every body else if possible. Pray remember my love & service to him & tell him that I have directed you to take & use the soyle as you shall thinke fitt upon my estate, & will defend you therein & justifie my inheritance. Lett me heare as soone as you can that the little new building is finisht, & what Fowler[3] & you thinke proper to be done about the orchard, hedge, & the wallnutt tree, & when. Remember mee kindly to everybody, & to lett your penman quickly answer my last & this. I am

Your loveing friend

Rich Holford

Address: For Farmer John Rose at Avebury, Wiltes., to be left with Mr Kimber, a grocer in Marlborough, Wiltes.

1 It is not possible to identify this shop keeper, but one wonders whether Joseph Hayward is meant; see *AWS*, p.85-6.

2 Probably a reference to dung.

3 A local tradesman; perhaps a forebear of the Fowler family of carpenters; see *AWS*, p.304.

Verso Note: Copy letter to John Rose, 23 of November 1710.

71. Sir Richard Holford to John White WSHC 184/1, pt.2.

Avebury
4 October 1711

Master White!
Upon my return hither, on Monday last after a long ramble, I did hope to have received your friendly visit in a better temper than when I last saw you, and haveing your assistance yesterday at prayers, I sent to invite you to take a short commons, to which you gave as I was told an unkind anser, but in order to prevent al misunderstanding I doe take this liberty (& give myselfe the troble) to put you in minde that I have alwaies declared & shewd my willingness to bee yours, & done what I could to encourage you to bee my friend.

You doe know that the haughty & uncharitable behaviour and bad example of those whose office & duty it is to instruct others in the knowledge & practice of their duty to God & their neighbors, hath too often a greater prevalency on their parishioners & others especially on their inferiors, than their wholesome doctrine & precepts. I wish twere not soe at Avebury. I am not without many faults (few have none) yet I never did nor will endeavore to support any, and alwaies took the admonitions & reproofes of a friend with thankfulnes. And I can with a good conscience justifie all my actions towards you, nay when I was highly provoked by your bitter language, & by nescessity compelled to call you into a Court of Conscience to discover what was your reall dues as vicar of Avebury out of my farme there, which you had expressly refused to tell mee, though often requested; yet it was without bitterness or passion, and purposely to prevent the like uncharitable, rude and needles squabbles as had been betwixt you and my then tennant Farmer Skeate, too likely to continue if not prevented. And you cannot forget (I never can) how unkind (not to say wors) you was to yourselfe and mee in your unwary answer upon your oath, & the meane, pittifull excuses you afterwards made to mee, for such your oversights ~~saying 'twas as your sollicitor drew and advised~~. For when I, a friend, demonstrated to you the errors you had thereby run into ~~upon your oath, and my declared resolution for peace sake to examine witnesses in order to establish your right~~ you then seemed sensible thereof, but layed on your sollicitor who drew it & advised you therein, & declared your desire of a friendly accomodation. And that I would forbeare any further prosecution & to [?involving thereto] you & proposed what you thought reasonable & signified the same to mee by your friend & plenipotentiary therein Mr William Smith, and confirmed afterwards by yourself your repeated offers & promises of a firme future friendship, & giveing credit thereto, I cherefully complied with your propositions, and submitted to sit downe a gret looser. Ever since I have acted as a true friend & expected the like from you and by your repeated advice I parted with that tenant who had, as you said, occasioned all the disturbance. And when occasion offerd, I took the freedome to speak freely to you my thoughts, of your rough disposition towards some, and your causeles severity against others to their utter undeoing, and put you in mind of not visiteing the sick, not burieing the dead, and your omitting other duties expressly required by the cannons & most excellent litturgie of our church, and did often, very often, by word of mouth, & by writing, request you to bee more circumspect & not permit your passion to governe your prudence, and to indeavor if possible to live peaceablie with all men, but instead of a friendly returne, you was pleased to throw out most uncomon, ungratefull & very unbecomeing expressions, indeavoring to justifie yourselfe in all, and have to mee & others untruely declared that I drew you into the accomadation above mentoned, which it may bee I should not have [*illegible*], but that your friend Mr Wm Smith being now here, affirmd that hee acted by your importunity & express directions, & now tells mee that your good wife was privy thereto, and approved thereof, and promised to give him a rump of beife and a barrell of good ale, if hee should prevaile. Nay as an evidence of your sincere friendship you have most untruely reported that I have defrauded the poore widows at Froxfield Hospital of one hundred pounds per annum,[1] and when I questiond you for such a scandalous untruth, you pretended that you had been told soe, but refused though earnestly intreated to tell mee by whom you was soe told. Therefore twas you owne ~~& notoriously untrue.~~ And when I lately put you mind of laying your selfe too open to some (it may bee not the best) of your neighbors & given them opportunities contrary to their duties to disrespect their pastor, you alsoe therein indeavored to justifie yourselfe. And I cant for [?better excusing] your unkindnes to mee, by demanding and insting to bee paid much more than was your due out of my estate lately purchased in Backhampton, though you know or was sufficiently informed that I had advised & directed my tennant to pay you all that could bee rightfully demanded without troble or expence, and hee hath since told mee, (I think in your presence) that hee had tendred & offerrd to pay it, and that you yet [*illegible*] had frightened him from his farme & out of the parish. Notwithstanding all which & a good deale more, which I am willing to forget if you valued it, & to place it on human frailties. I doe once more, Mr White, ask & request your true friendship & a neighborly correspondence suitable to our relation, & that wee may mutualy indeavor to doe each other all the good wee can, & give a good example to others. And because of my short stay here, I doe pray you to let mee have a few lynes from you in answer hereto within 3 or 4 daies, which if you shall refuse or neglect, it will not bee very grivous to mee, nor any greater disapointment than formerly, being prepared (though unwillingly) to expect the worst, yet I shall ever bee to my power

Your true friend

Rich Holford

I have not here taken notice of (as I think) your unjust pretences to the cottages,

1 This is probably a reference to the fact that Holford was involved, as one of the Masters in Chancery, in various court proceedings concerning Froxfield Hospital between 1696 and 1711; see Crowley, Douglas, ed. *The Minute Books of Froxfield Almshouse, 1714-1866.* Wiltshire Record Society 66. 2013, p.5-6, 8-9, 125-8 & 130-33.

the soyle in the river, pooles & highwaies, & the great stones within my royalty.

Mr Truslow's son.

Mr Phelps child & churching.

Many of the inhabitants put into the earth without &c.

Poore Hayward ruined.

A coppy the original sent to Mr White 5 October 1711 & delivered to him by my man John.

Verso Note: Copy of letter to Mr John White of Avebury, 4 October 1711. See my former letters to him particularly 22 July 1708, 2 April 1710, & many others.
Verso Address: These for Mr John White, vicar of Avebury, Wiltes.

72. Sir Richard Holford to John Brinsden WSHC 184/1, pt.2.

1 November 1711

My Worthy Friend!
I should have been glad to have seen you at my last being at Avebury, it being in my thoughts to have trobled you, as I have formerly, with the repeated unkindness of Mr White, & to have prayed your assistance for prevention of further troble, but considering that your time is filled with your owne affaires, I forbore to give you troble, & resolved againe to trye him by intreaties, and for that hee did not come to mee, though invited, I writ a long letter, the particulars are too tedious here to recite, and requested him to give mee a plaine answer thereto in 3 or 4 daies. But hee neglecting to give any and being resolved if I could to bee at a certainty, I had prepared a bill in Chancery, & a subpena ready to serve him, to answer, & being unwilling to make a nois, or troble anybody to serve him, I waited on him myself, and indeavoryd to obtaine his friendly answer, but not prevaileing, I then produced the subpena under seale. Upon sight thereof hee made most grivious complaints of his indisposition and prayed for Godsake & for Christsake that I would then forbeare to serve him with it. Whereupon in charitable compassion, I told him I would then forbeare, if hee for his owne & for my sake, and for peace sake, would give a plaine & true answer to my requests, & alsoe make and exhibite a true terrier. But then, & never till then, hee told mee that hee had made a terrier and fild it ~~put it into the Bishopps registers~~ five or six years since. I pray him to let mee see a coppy of it, which hee refused, saying hee had not coppy, nor anything relateing thereto, but scatterd & loose scrapps of paper, which hee knew not where to find. I then desired him to tell mee who made or assisted at the makeing thereof, & whether the ell ridge or ell ridges were explained & expressed to bee in that peice of wheat lyeing yearely next the church, & why hee had soe long concealed it, expecially from mee, who had very often & for severall yeares, requested that a true terrier might bee made & preserved according to the cannons of the church. I then againe took the liberty to put him in mind of burying the dead, visiteing the sick, & other duties expressly required, to all which hee made mee noe other answer but that hee was not well & not likely to recover. I then told him of the ill consequences of an

untrue terrier, whereby his successor might without blame, by his [*illegible*] bee informed & insist on what might bee rightfully due, & told him I would waite 2 or 3 daies longer for his answer, & that twas in his power to prevent troble, & a good deale to that effect, & left him as I thought in a pretty good humor, but I have not received any effects thereof.

Now Sir, I have trobled you with these matters I do declare that what I doe aime at is a charytable, neghborly right understanding for the preservation of peace, & I doe sincerely pitty the poore man, unhappy, pervers, stubborne & uncharitable temper, & am very unwilling to thwart or troble him, if by any friendly waies & meanes hee will doe what is fitt. And for that I know you have shewed him great friendship, I doe earnestly intreat you to give your selfe the troble to call upon him, & discours a little with him of these matters, & if you find it convenient, you may show him this & request him to show you my letters, & alsoe a letter which my wife hath written to him in answer to one shee lately received from him relateing to these matters, and pray if you can prevaile on him to bee ruled by you. And if you will please to tell mee in 3 or 4 lynes the effect of your visit and shall incourage mee to expect any benefit thereof, I will lay aside my thoughts of a suite in Chancery. But if you shall apprehend any ill consequence by concerning your selfe in this matter, I will not desire you to undertake it, the rather for that I doe know my way how to obteine peace, & shall alwaies esteeme your friendship & continue,

Sir

Your true friend & servant

Tis a lesson taught me by the learned Hugo Groting in his most excellent book of the *Rights of Peace & War*:

All meanes unarmed wise men should first assay,
How knowst, if asked, but hee'll unforced obey.

My wife joynes with mee in our due respects to you & to honest Mr Walter Sloper.

Verso Note: Draft of a letter to Mr Brinsden of Moncton[1] relateing to Mr White, I November 1711.

73. John Brinsden to Sir Richard Holford WSHC 184/1, pt.2.

13 November 1711

Honoured Sir,

Mr White being very ill at ease, and not able to performe his duty himselfe, I have been at Avebury November 4 & 10 to officiate for him. After service the first of those dayes as soon as I came out of the Church, your tenant John Rose gave me your letter, which I immediately communicated to Mr White. He apprehending that the main scope thereof was that a true terrier should be exhibited into my

1 Vicar of Winterbourne Monkton.

Lord Bishop's registry, he saith that a true terrier has already been exhibited with the usuall fees about six years since[1] by honest men of the parish viz, Farmer Richard Green and Humphry Robins, the then churchwardens,[2] with whome he the said Mr White did signe, as the 87 canon doth direct, and hopes that this doth give no just cause of offence, when the diocesan required it at their hands, and said further that he is ready to joyne in exhibiting another whensoever his diocesan shall require it. Indeed, I did not find him as accomplished a courtier as the famous Cecill in Queen Elizabeth & King James her heir, who being demanded how he kept so long in favour, returned answer, that it was by receiving injuries and giveing of thanks. For your first suit in court, which crampt him and his successors of the priviledge to take the ell ridges upon Avebury Farme (which about 40 years ago were esteemed a acre) where he pleased out of the whole crop, hath left some sournesse and uneasiness upon Mr White which will not easeily wear off;[3] unless you could convince him that he had no right so to doe, when yet his predecessor Mr Nath Power enjoyed in the time of Ralph Stawell, esq., afterward Lord Stawell, without the least grudge (and many favours heaped upon him dayly) but *tempora mutantur, et nos mutanture in illis.*[4] I was intimately acquainted with Mr Power, and know that he took up his ell rigdes &c., but did not know his [?heirs] never, but here in evidence in Avebury yet live that can testify that he took them and know the names of the pieces (not next to the Church). If you please to hearken without prejudice, which it may be difficult to do, especially where interest lyeth at stake, for the wise man tells us Prov 20:25, it is a snare to devour that which is holy and afterward to enquire of the vow. A man is ensnared and entangled now by his own art, for that he is not so free, nor fit now to judge aright of it, because his great life has forstalled his judgment, and (as it may fall out) corrupted and perverted it, ready therefore as one partiall in his owne cause, to passe no sincerer and indifferent sentence. Mr White saith that he hath no rough draught of the terrier you desire, and if he had he is not in a condition to look after it, or to answer your long letter, it being as much as he can do to go from his bed to the fire and back againe. But if your Worship would have a copy of that terrier, if you please to order me, I will send to the Register and procure it, and you having a copy of the former terrier exhibited in Bishop Ward's time[5], if upon comparing the old one and new one together any difficulty did arise, or any thing seem to be unduly inserted in either, then to examine some of the most ancient people of the parish who had most reason to be acquainted with the customs and usages hereof would be the readiest, the most neighbourly and charitably way to procure peace and a good understanding

1 Note in margin: Q what is it & who consentd six yeares.

2 Richard Green and Humphry Robinson were churchwardens in 1704-5; cf. WSHC D1/50/6, f.9V, & D3/12/13.

3 Note in margin: See Mr White's answer upon oath.

4 Times change, and we change with it.

5 Seth Ward, Bishop of Salisbury 1667-89. This terrier seems to have disappeared; it is not mentioned in Hobbs, Steven, ed. *Wiltshire Glebe Terriers 1588-1827*. Wiltshire Record Society 56. 2003.

between your selfe, Mr White, and all the rest, without some jury course as [?this] (in the judgment of four of my neighboring gentry and clergy to whome I have imparted the contents of your letter). All talk of good correspondence, charity, and peace &c., but like the modern policy of the great disturber[1] of Europe, quiet to amuse the world with treatyes of peace whilst he has war in his heart, and maketh himselfe ready to battell. It is altogether incomprehensible to us hereabout, that you should chose jury batterie against the terrier as yet unknown of such a poor[2] poor feeble vicarage as that of Avebury. And yea to sue in court to have it more infeebled in such a case as we know no paralell to it, unlesse it be that mentioned by the Roman Prater in his oration *Pro Sexto Rossio Amerino*[3] of Caius Fimbria who indicted Q Scavola for that he would not suffer himself to be slaine outright by him. *Diem Scavola dixit quod non totum telum corpore recepisset.*[4] If Mr White had been the aggressor[5] I could the better have told what to say to him, but as the matter stands, I can onely pray[6] with our Church, O God, who art the author of peace and lover of concord, who alone canst order the unruly wills and affections of sinfull people, and dost make men to be of one mind in an house and killest the outrage of a violent and unruly people, We most humbly beseech thee to grant us by grace that we may henceforth walk in obedience to thy holy commandments and lead a quiet and peaceable life in all Godliness and honesty, through Jesus Christ our Lord Amen.

Thus, Sir Richard, my most hearty prayers for your good lady, you selfe, and all that belong to you, I rest
Yours humbly to serve you in what I can
Jo Brinsden

Verso Note: Mr John Brinsden, 13 November 1711.
Verso Address: For Sir Richard Holford, at his house in Lincolns Inn Fields, these, London.

74. Sir Richard Holford to John Brinsden WSHC 184/1, pt.2.
22 November 1711

Master Brinsden!
I have received & doe thank you for yours of the 13 of this month, & for your friendly imparting the contents of mine to our friend, Mr White, but I don't perceive that you shewed him my letter, or that hee shewed you my last to him, in both which I intended & I think I did fully & plainely express my desire to prevent needless troble & expence, & to establish peace & good neighborhood (as I had often by word of mouth as alsoe in writeing) and did hope by your

1 The reference is probably to Louis XVIII, King of France.
2 Page break.
3 Cicero's speech in defence of Sextus Roscius.
4 On that day Scavola said that he did not recover the entire weapon from the body.
5 The letter's recipient wrote 'aggressor' in the margin.
6 In margin: 'I joyn with this prayer', in Sir Richard Holford's hand.

interposition to have prevaled and prayed your advice, what I might or what you would doe more in the like case.

But you are pleased only to answer that you don't find him a courtier soe quallified as the Secretary Cecil (the greatest statesman in his time). However, I am very well pleased that I gave you the troble, & Mr White an oppertunity of speakeing his mind freely, and should have been glad to have knowne whether hee did soe or not. You say if Mr White had been the aggressor you could the better have told what to say to him. Now to manifest that hee was, pray, Sir, give mee leave to tell you (I don't love to rub old sores) that before I bought Avebury Farme, I waited on Mr White to know the viccar's dues thereout, and showd him the perticular given mee by my Lord Stawell's agents, mentioning that it was tyth free saveing two ell ridges of wheat in that peice of wheat lyeing next the church yearely, upon reading whereof he declared that it was true, and that they had dealt faithfully with mee therein, & gave mee good encouragement to proceed, yet afterwards Mr White & my tennant Farmer Skeate [?disdiring] about trifles, Mr White declared & threatened & sent mee word that hee would have his tythes in kind, & not bee bound by any modus or compositon, at which being somewhat allarmed, I made further inquiry thereinto, & often, very often, by word of mouth & by letters, requested Mr White as a friend & neighbour to tell mee what was his due, but hee absolutely refused soe to doe, & slighted my repeated requests, wherefor for peace sake I was constrained to expect his answere thereto in Chancery, & hoped hee would have done himself & mee right therein, but hee was pleased to stuffe his answer with reflection & impertincies, being (as hee afterwards told mee) advised & guided therein by his [?favoute] & skilfull artist Mr Wilkens,[1] wherefore I was forct to get his further answer, and therein hee admits my applicaton to him & in plaine words sets forth that his right was two ell ridges in that peice of wheate lyeing next the church yearely, & that hee had alwaies received it or £3 per annum in money in lieu thereof, and xx shillings per annum for his other dues, which agreeing with my particular I inquired therein and cannot guess what argument hee now used to you that hee was not the aggressor. I have his & he hath my letters relateing thereto, & hath set forthe coppies of them upon his oath. His second answer, which doe demonstrate the truth hereof and inclined the Court to blame him as a stubborne wilfull man, yet now upon my purchase of another estate there hee seemes wiling to bee againe troblesome in that very matter, and complaines (as you intimate) that his answer hath crampt him, & left a sowernes upon his mind which will not easily were off, unles I can convince him that hee had noe right soe to doe. In truth I doe not understand what hee meanes thereby or what conviction hee expects to make the sowerenes of his mind easily weare off.

Sir, I don't conceive the great tyrant's amusement as you soe aptly menton can bee any waies applied to mee, for I had & have peace in my heart & in my intentons, & have used all honest waies & meanes in my power to obteine a faire,

1 White's 'lawyer'; see letter, Sir Richard Holford to John Brinsden, 24 January 1711/12 (no. 76).

friendly, & lasting peace, & doe abhor such amusements, tricks, & deceits as hee delights to countenance & encourage, but if I can't prevail shalbe compelled to defend myselfe. I must use the easiest & safest methods I can to prevent arbitrary & unjust exactions.

Sir, I doe thank you for your kind offer to peruse a coppy of the pretended new terrier, but I don't think I ought to put that troble upon you, but methinks an authentic coppy signed by the parties thereto or by by [sic] the register ought to remaine in the church chest for the information & satisfaction of those concerned, & not bee concealed for soe many yeares.

Sir, you say that you have imparted the substance of my letter to some neighbor gentry & clergy, & that it seems altogether incomprehensible to them that I should raise such batteries against the terrier as yet unknown of such a poore feeble vicaridge as Avebury, & then to sue in Chancery to have it more infeebled in such a case as wee know noe paralel to it, unles it bee in the case of the Roman orators Sexto Rosio, &c.

I know you have a worthy & judicious gentry & clergie, & doe think I might cherefully order by their determination in anything they will undertake, but I have not yet raised what you called batteries against a terrier I never saw nor heard of till very lately.[1]

Truly, sir, this [*illegible*], which, if it bee true, will suffice itself & those who made & exhibited it, & if not true expose them, & pray give me leave to affirme, as I doe with great sincerity, that I never indevered any waies to lessen the viccar's dues, but alwaies declared & advised the payment thereof to the full without, troble, expence, or grumbleing, but these are arrows out of his Mr White's ill bent weak bow & fitt to bee disposed.

Now Sir, having given you this tedious troble, give mee leave to add that the weak condicon you menton Mr White to bee in, and the Christian compascion I have for him, hath prevailed on mee not at present to pursue him but to deferr the batteries you mention til the next terme, in hopes hee may yet set matters in a true light & prevent further troble & in this & other matters & [*illegible*] him & mee. If not, & it shall please God that he shall live that then hee may expect & depend that I will put him in mind of these & other matters already knowne to him, and hope that you will forgive the troble of this, & permit mee to joyne heartily with you in the prayer of our Church, which concludes your letter as it shall this, with this, that it may bee a further conference with our friend may produce better effects than hitherto, which your [?leasure] wilbee very welcome to

Sir

Your obleidged friend & humble servant

Address: For my very worthy friend Mr John Brinsden at Moncton Wiltes., which sent in a letter to Mr Farmer [*illegible*].

1 This and the succeeding paragraph are interlined amongst extensive deletions, and much of it is uncertain reading.

Verso[1]: Draft of a letter to Mr John Brinsden 22 November[2] in answer to his of the 13th November[3] 1711.

75. John Brinsden to Sir Richard Holford WSHC 184/1, pt.2.

1 January 1711/12

Honoured Sir,

Yours of the 22 of November I received sometime since, but because some things seemed difficult to be understood and I was not willing to lean to my own understanding (your having given leave to answer at my leasure). I showed the same to severall gentlemen and clergymen with whome I sometime converse. But with all their assistance, after so much time spent, I cannot comprehend the depth of that distinction how Mr White, upon the sight of my Lord Stawells particular, did declare that the vicarage dues out of Avebury Farme were two ell ridges of wheat,[4] and yet would not tell what the dues were. Or how your Worship was constrained to make Mr White (at the expens of two years revenue of the Vicarage) sett forth in his answer in Court that his dues were two ell ridges, when he had declared the same befour. Or how Mr White was the aggressor[5] when your Worship sued him. Or how you bringing a Bill of Complaint in Cance[6] (*de lana caprina*)[7] can be said to defend yourself against unjust exactions, &c., when Mr White and your tenant were in composition for years to come. We may indeed be mistaken in the terms of law (defendant and aggressor)[8] as well as in the military (raising batteries), instead of bringing down your artillery against a supposed untrue terrier as yet unknown. But his much ink is as plaine as the grammaticall forme of the words can make it, viz, that Mr White did at first declare, and afterwards being tired out with a vexatious and chargeable suit in Canc[9] did in his answer set forth that the vicar's dues were two ell ridges of wheat &c, and that your Worship did acquiesce therein. Now hinc illae lacrimæ,[10] here is the grievance and the cause of all the unkindnesse you complaine of, and of all the murmuring, sowerness, and discontent. That the vicar's dues were two ell ridges of wheat, but now they are not. Your bill in court having pared away about a fourth part of them, and reduced them to a scantling of 120 perches, which cometh short of two ridges, as not onely other mens, but my eyes can testify, being desired to measure out that quantity instead of the two ell ridges,

1 There are also some calculations on the verso, which have not been transcribed here.
2 9[ber] in text.
3 Ditto.
4 In margin :'in that peice lying next the church', in Sir Richard Holford's hand.
5 In margin: 'but not telling the whole truth the 2 ell ridges in that piece next the church', in Sir Richard Holford's hand.
6 The Court of Chancery.
7 A futile argument.
8 Annotated in margin in Holford's hand: 'Agressor & raiseing batteries are his own words in his letter 13th 9ber'.
9 Chancery.
10 Therefore these tears.

lying near heretofore paid without measureing and were esteemed a acre, be it more or lesse. Now this, Honoured Sir, to me and those I converse with seemeth such a palpable injustice, that it is self evident two ridges are acknowledged to be due, and two are not paid. And although you sincerely affirm that you never did endeavour to lessen the vicar's dews, yet tis plaine enough that they are lessened, and in that particular may concerneth your estate onely. Indeed, Counsellor Ponting is endeavouring (no doubt but moved by your example) to lessen the trifling dues for pasturing of the cattell upon the Cowe Down, and to reduce it to a peny a cow, but that is not yet accomplished! Now, Honoured Sir, monstrato quid fit morbi, curatio restat.[1] The cure seemeth to be obvious, and in your own power, viz, to make restitution of the two entire ell ridges as they were formerly paid, before the estate was yours, and to make allowance for what the scantling of 120 perches hath come short of two ell ridges every year, since ye Bill has proved them, and to restore the charge of law that your Worship put Mr White to in order to make him set forth in his answer in court what he had answered at first. And to take off his answer from the file and to cancell it and all the proceedings thereabout, that they may not rise up against his successsors. By doing this, Honoured Sir, you will give the world a better evidence of your sincere desire of love, peace, good neighbourhood, charity, &c., than by all the thundrings out of involvings of law suits, than by all the suspitions of untrue terriers exhibited by honest neighbours with the minister's concurrence, than by all confusers of consealing those terriers when they are laid up in the proper repository (the Bishop's Registry) under the custody of a sworne officer, as all the terriers in the Diocese are, for anyone to see at his pleasure, but chiefly that the Diocesan may see from time to time whether any of the gleeb lands or other dues by embezelled. And by this restitution all the unkindnesse that you complain of, and all the discontent, sowernesse, uneasinesse, and murmuring will weare of from Mr White's mind, and I doubt not but he will resume his former blithe and perfect temper, and will converse as cheerfully and as obliegingly with your Worship as his predecessor and himself for many years did with that honourable person who was the former owner of the estate. But without restitution I cannot see how you can be easy in your own breast if you have any care of posterity or regard the old verse, *nomale quo filis vix gaudet tertium heeres*,[2] or give any credit to the known saying of St Augustine, *non remittetur postulum, nisi restitantur ablatum*.[3] I had almost forgotten to take notice that you say you were alarmed by Mr White's declaring that he would take his dues in kind, which is no more than is done at some time or other in most parishes in the Kingdom by clergy and impropriators, and is done in the parish of Avebury by the impropriators, and yet no man thereby alarmed. And surely his letting his ell ridges sometimes for £3 cannot give any alarm, for I have seen in Farmer Skeat's time, 43 tything of large [*illegible*] of wheat upon two ridges, every tything likely to yield a bushel, and wheat at 7s or upwards per bushel, so that I computed them to be

1 Pointing to what causes the disease, it remains to be cured.
2 'the name of which the third heir hardly enjoys'.
3 'If the demand is not conceded, neither will the purification be restored'.

worth, at that time, £15. And whereas you say Mr White seemeth willing to be troublesome to you upon your purchasing Beckhampton estate. If you would give him no trouble, there is no probability of such a weak man's giving you any, unless you suppose he may summon your soul (as Robert Grosshead[1] sometime Bishop of Lincolne, is said, at his death, to have summoned the then Pope who was to potent for him) to answer before the tribunall of Christ, which, some think you are not any approbation of. I perused both letters you sent me to Mr White, but have not seen those written to him, Mr White having gotten them into his hands, but they both say that the contents of them are much to the same effect with those to me, viz to get matters in a clear light, to do what is fit, to preserve peace, to prevent trouble, to promote harty good neighbourhood, and many other good morrows, with a sting in the taile a threatning of a bill, &c. But what you mean by that which is fit to be done in order to those good ends is not easily to be learned. What honest country men both worthy and reverend think fit to be done I have expressed plainly above, namely to make restitution. But if your Worship think fit that the ell ridges at Beckhampton should be curtalled and brought to the scantling of those at Avebury, as it is conjectured, your aim is, I beg your Worship excuse if I do not intermedle herein, lest I should lend my hand to trust Fimbria's dagger[2] (mentioned in my first) up to the hilt, not onely into the bowells of the present vicar but also into the bowells of his successors and their children which are yet unborne. I should be accessory to the wronging her Majesty and successors by lopping off a limb of that small living in the guift of the Crown, and should be afraid to pull down the vengeance of Almighty God who taketh such injuries as done to himselfe, Malachi 3, 8-9.[3] Now, Honoured Sir, after all this tedious scribble, which could not well be shorter considering your long winded epistles, give me leave to close up all in a short collect of our church with a small interpolation here. O God, who hast taught us that all our doings without charity are nothing worth, send thine Holy Ghost, and pour into our hearts that most excellent guift of charity which thinketh no evill, suffereth long, and is kind, and is not the firebrand of contention and all mischief, but is the bond of peace and of all vertues, without which whosoever liveth is counted dead before thee. Grant this o Father, for thy son's sake Jesus Christ our Lord. Thus with my most humble service to your good lady and all yours, I remaine
Your daily orator
Jo Brinsden

Verso Note: Mr John Brinsden, 1 January 1711 in answer to mine of the 22 of November 1711. I writ to him a long letter the 24 of January & inclosed it in a letter to Mr John Rose the 28 January franckt ST.
Verso Address: For the Worshipfull Sir Richard Holford at his house in Lincolns Inns Fields, these, London.

1 Presumably Bishop Grosseteste is meant.
2 A combination of a sickle and a dagger.
3 'Will a man rob God? Yet ye have robbed me. But ye say, wherein have we robbed thee? In tithes and offerings. Ye are cursed with a curse, for ye have robbed me'.

76. Sir Richard Holford to John Brinsden WSHC 184/1, pt.2.

24 January 1711/12

Master Brinsden,

Your favour of the 1st of this month came not to mee till the 11th, but was welcome, the rather for that by your silence I thought I had given you too much troble, but you don't seeme to say soe, only that the time was spent in takeing the opinion of some of your worthy & reverend acquaintance, in some doubtfull expressions in mine of the 22 of November.

Upon my word, Sir, I did intend, & doe hope I did express my meaning in plaine words (which made it, as you say, long winded) in order to cleere your doubt whether Mr White was the aggressor, by compelling mee, in my owne defence, to indeavore a discovery of the truth upon his oath, all other meanes of such discovery haveing proved ineffectual, hee haveing upon my purchase declared that his dues were two ell ridges out of that peice of wheat lyeing next the church yearely or £3 in money by composition, whereto I gave intire credit, till some few yeares after hee expressly denyed any such custome or composition, & positively refused to bee bound thereby, but declared & threatened to mee & others, that hee would take his tythes in kind upon the whole farme, which (as you in your letter seeeme to compute) might bee above £40 per annum difference, which was my gravamen. For releife I was compelled in my owne defence to bring my bill in Chancery, not, as you say *delana capricia*,[1] but (£40 per annum more than rightfully due, out of a farme for which I paid above 21 yeares purchase at a rack rent) tyth free save ell ridges as above, which suite upon heareing Councell on both sydes was by the Court adjudged to bee just & nescesary, & afterwards which Mr White & my good friends Mr Tooker & Mr Smith (now dead) upon peruseing my letters to him and his to mee, and his first & second answer to my bill, were of the same opinion with the Court, & not long after Mr White himself confessed it , but layd the blame upon the ill advice of his lawyer (as hee called Mr Wilkins) and earnestly importuned and prevailed on mee for charity & peace sake to accept of part of my costs & to acquiesce, upon and made repeated faire promises of a firme future friendship, and you canot but know the fruites those promises have produced, & if what I said in that letter did not cleere your doubts, I prayed you to looke over those letters & answers in Mr White's hands. And doe beg your pardon for this long winded and to mee not pleasant repetiton & that you will permit mee to think the worthy & reverend you advysed withall was only Mr White & his wife, & that they prevailed with you to take the wrong end of the perspective, & to set up a man of straw with two et ceteras, declareing two ell ridges &c., & setting forth two ell ridges &c., & then learnedly beating it downe, without saying one word of the two ell ridges, that peice of wheat lyeing next the church yearly [*illegible*].

Mr Brinsden! I never did intend or indeavor any waies to lessen, or, as you say, to pare off any part of the viccar's dues, as I have often told him & you, nor by my example or other waies incouraged his late friend & councellor Mr Pontin, or

1 For capricious reasons.

any body else, to lessen or pare off any part there of the viccar's dues, as you doe unkindly intimate, & therefore am not guilty of your accusation of selfe evident palpable injustice.

In truth your prescription for sweetening the uneasiness, murmurings, & sowernes of Mr White's mind, and restoreing him to his former blithe & pleasant temper, & to a cherefull and obleidging conversation, is I think only in his owne power. I surely not an experiment fit for mee further to attempt, especially by the method you [*illegible*], but I will never give up my sincere indeavor in matters soe desireable by his friends & as I think benefitial to himselfe, & have often taken the friendly liberty to tell him soe, as well by word of mouth as by writeing, shewing the disease & as I think the only cure.

~~I am perswaded you can't think I shall ever bee a Pope, and doe tell you that I never was Popeishly affected, and am not under any apprehension of such a summons, as Dr Goostheade (as I think you call him), Bishopp of Lyncolne prepared for the Pope.~~

I am fully perswaded, as you are, or as Mr White can bee, that, *de malis [?quasity] vix gaudet tertius hares*,[1] is an admirable caution against wrong, oppression & exaction, and unjust gaine, and doe thank God that all I have in the world hath been fairely & honestly obtained, and I doe hope with God's blessing it will continue without any dreadfull apprehension of the summons you say Dr Gooshead (as I think you call him), Bishop of Lyncoln, prepared for his holy father the Pope, but that at another time [*illegible*] proper occasion.

Sir, the words aggressor, raiseing batteries, bringing downe arillary[2] against a supposed unknowne terrier, Mr White's many other good morrows with a sting in the taile &c., are your owne words, used in your own letters, and I believe very well understood, or else would not have been there.

Notwithstanding your many partial mistakes, harsh, sharpe, & in some places I think uncharitable reflections, &c., I doe kindly thank you for your long & I think well intended letter. And doe assure you that noething in it shall incline or influence mee to show any indecente, unbecomeing, or unkind usuage towards Mr White, whose rough unpollishd temper I have often pittied, yet I must say it hath not abated my inclination & purpose to have a true terrier thereby if I can, to preserve peace and good neighbourhood, & prevent needles troble & expence to mee & mine & the other &[sic] parishioners & the present viccar & his successors, & though Mr White hath often unkindly denyed mee the sight of what hee calls his new terrier, yet I doe hope ere it bee long to know it, & when, how, & by whome made, and when exhibited &c. I hope Mr White hath not omitted (in that peice of wheat lyeing next the church yearely) if hee hath tis expressly contrary to his answer upon oath, or, in his own words, it may prove a nest egg or a sting in tayle &c.

I shalbee glad to receive your further favors when your leasure will permit, and for that I am told Mr White is pretty well & hopeing hee may recover his

1 That which is sauce for the goose is sauce for the gander.
2 Artillery.

perfect health & may yet in a friendly manner ascertaine the viccar's dues. I doe not intend to call on him this cold winter terme, otherwaies than by your remembering my best respects to him, as I hope you will in such manner as you shall think fitt.

I doe heartily approve & joyne with you in that excellent collect of our church (and don't object against your warme addition of firebrand &c) wherewith you close your letter. And shalbee alwaies ready & willing to repeat it & to shew myselfe
Sir!
Your sincere true friend & servant
Rich Holford

My poore wife is & hath been indisposed these six weeks past, & is now confined to her chamber. Shee presents her service to you & pray remember us both to your neighbour Mr Sloper.[1]

This hath waited from the date on purpose to bee inclosed this 31st of January to John Rose, to bee with him on Saturday & soone after with you.

Address: For the Reverend Mr John Brinsden at Moncton in Wiltes.

Verso Note: The rough draught of a letter to Mr Brinsden, 24 January, inclosed in one to John Rose, 3 January 1711.[2]

77. John Rose to Sir Richard Holford[3] WSHC 184/1, pt.2.

Avebury
23 February 1711/12

Sir,
I received your 2 letters, and the letter inclosed I delivered to Mr Brinsden. I have spoke with Mr John White, and I am sattisfied. Just before Mr Smith came to London Mr Goodanough came up to enter a morgage, and because hee came to our house Mr Smith (as I was told by his tennan) thinks that your Worship sent him, and the tennant told mee that there was one about it, and hee had the money ready att London to lay down for it, but who the man is I cannot yett here. As to a pad nag, if your Worship will venture my skill I will do the best I can to please you, and if hee prove not according to expectation not to bee blamed afterward. I have talkt with Richard Caswell, and they are plowing land for seed that ought not to bee sown. I told him of it & hee answered if hee did sow more [?thent] usiel this year hee would sow the less the next, but I think that not convenient. As to your new purchase in hand my advice is to do it att once (but

1 See p.xxx, n.xxx.
2 A note in similar terms is written on another verso of the letter.
3 This letter was probably written by an amanuensis, perhaps Rose's 'Uncle Smith'; see Sir Richard Holford's letter, 7th June 1710

you will ask what there is for the money perhaps). I answer as to Backhamton Farm it is now lett for £62 per annum. In Silberry Mead there is 5 acres of tithe free, and one part in four besides the little ground by Silberry Mead called the New Inclosier is 4 year Mr Smith's & 4 years your Worship's, a little ground by the barn about an acre and 1 half, a little ground cald by the name of Bell Close is your Worship's. As the new inclosier is ten cow leases upon the Down, four horse commons, two hundred & fifty sheep leases. There is 84 acres and a yard of earable land in the fild, so much if not any more that I cannt call to mind att present. Higdins is let for £40 per annum & Chestermans 16. I gave so much, & suppose the present tennant gives the same. I would have given the particulars of Backhamton land but had not now time, but if your Worship would bye it I will do it when you please. I am very sorry to hear your good lady is so ill. I and my family gives our humble services to your Worship & good lady, and rest att present your Worship's humble tenant to command.
John Rose

Mr White is [?not] able to preach. I desire your Worship, if you think fitt, to write a line [?or two to] him to desire him to gett a supply. Ye shepherd is willing to have his [?rest] but cares not if ye flock go astray.[1]

Verso:
There is 5 acres of land more belonging to Backhamton which I forgot. The tennant pays church and poor. The quit rent is 3s & sixpence paid to the Earl of Amsbury, 30 shillings a year, or the ell ridge paid to the Vicar of Avebury.

Verso Note: John Rose 23 February 1711. The account of the lands in Backhamton.
Verso Address: For Sir Richard Holford, living in Lincolns In Fields, London.

78. Sir Richard Holford to John Brinsden WSHC 184/1, pt.2.

Kensington
21 May 1712

Sir!
Haveing spent some time here with my wife for the benefit of the aire (after a confinement of 16 weeks to her chamber, & the conversation of doctors, apothecaries, & nurses), finding her somewhat releived,[2] I took a ramble about some smal affaires of my owne, & at my returne found yours of the 22th (but by the post marke the last of April). At the first reading I thought you would not expect any answer thereto but upon the second thought it might become mee not to neglect but [*illegible*] & long a favor rather for that think it as well worth the reading of the *Observator*, *Examiner*, *Medley*, *Review*, and other our weekly witty

1 This paragraph is written in the margin.
2 She was still 'in aweful condicion' on August 1st, according to her sister's footman, although she travelled to Avebury on 12th August; cf. Sanders, John. 'The Account of my Travels with my Mistress', *Records of Buckinghamshire* 3, 1870, p.93.

malitious pamphlets, interlairded as yours with grave and wise sentences in Greeke and Latine of great & cellebrated authors, now & then alsoe making bold with & misusing God's word, applying all to their present purposes & exercising their witt and cunning in frameing subtile arguments & prevarications to please those for whome they write, or that are pleased with their labors, without any regaurd to truth. I canot tell whether your business will permit you to spend any time on those [*illegible*] moderne authors, yet must observe, that great witts often jump, and your sharpe, unjust, & often repeated censorioius reflections would incline any one indifferent to think you therein highly approved, or had a good deale of their humor, else why should you (contrary to common charity & civility) take everything I say, by the wrong handle, & apply it accordingly by fictitious & imaginary whymseys, raiseing what you call batteryes on purpose to beat them downe. But I doe take all you say in good part, & in the best sense, thinking the greatest part thereof as joke & banter, & written for your divertion. Sir, as you are, soe am I, a great admirer & tender lover of all wee have of King Solomon's works, and when 'twas my misfortune to heare, see, & read Mr White's resolution to take the full tythes of my farme, without reguard to custome or antient usuage, & heareing Farmer Skeate's grumbleing complaints thereof, I used my utmost dilligence to obteine a right understanding thereabout (not offering to affront the Omnipotent searcher of the heart, as you unkindly reflect) but as advised in the 17th chapter of Proverbs (the beginning of strife is like the breakeing out of water, therefore leave off contention before it bee medled with) and what could I doe more to that purpose, than (by word of mouth when present, & by friendly letters when absent) supplicate Mr White to bee content with the two ell ridges of that peice of wheat lyeing next the church yearely, & his other dues, or the usual composition, as mentiond in the perticular given mee, and by mee shewed to him, and by him approved as true, before my purchase or fairely to let mee know what was his due, to which I received, I would say, rude, but very unbecomeing & abusive answer, and was thereby provoked, and compelled for peace sake, & to prevent the breaking out of unruely waters (my inheritance being at stake (though then in lease to a tennant) to demand his answer upon oath, & was put to a great deale of troble & charge in obteining his first peevish & impertinent answer ('twas soe adjudged by the Lord Chancellor, upon Mr White's appeale to him) & then a second answer, wherein hee confesed great part of what I had suggested in my bill to bee [?just], & therein set forth my letters to him, and admitted his tenure to bee as I had [?alleged]. I intended to proceed and like a faire and friendly adversary. I shewed to him some bold strokes in his answer, with the opinion of a very learned lawyer (now [?judge] & Lord Chief Justice) thereon, shortly after which [*illegible*] that I had then a commission to examine my witnesses, and had given notice to execute it. Mr White, by the advice of his wife signified to mee by their first Mr Smith, he requested a friendly accommodation, and made some seeming friendly proposals to that purpose, declareing that by ill advice hee had been misguided, & kindly offered & made many protestations of a firme future friendship, whereto giving credit I was soone prevailed on & cherefuly submitted to his own propositions, but was therein deceived, as I think I have formerly told you, & would not have now repeated, had not you tempted mee thereto by affirming & tempting others to believe, that I was the aggressor, and making your selfe soe merry therewith as to set it to a [*illegible*] tune, with a noteable artful banter of restitution, and of takeing Mr White's answer off the fyle, as the [?epperest] method or expedient you as his physitian could find out or propose to sweeten his sower & singularly rough temper, & restore his blith & pleasant humor, as you are pleased to phrase it.

Mr Brinsden, I would not have Mr White forget his answers upon oath, and doe tell you & him, that it cannot, must not, be taken off the fyle, but remaines a record, and this I hope may ease, if not, as you say, sweeten & smooth his sower & rough humor as you propose. But Sir, what troubled mee, and invited mee to troble you, was the complaint of my tennant in my late purchase at Backhampton, that[1] that Mr White insisted to have & actually sued him for a great deale more for his tythes than was his due, or was ever paid or taken for that farme. Therefore to prevent strife, I renewed my friendly application to Mr White as well by word of mouth, as by letter now in his hands whereto I received much the same unkind returnes, which invited mee further like [?promody] as formerly, but I forebore to troble him dureing his illness, & knoweing you to bee his true friend, I prayed your neighborly interposition therein to preserve peace and prevent strife, & you doe know the fruites I have received thereby.

Sir, I canot think you doe Mr White any great kindness in urgeing that my bill you [*illegible*] his answer to it parte of any of his due, nor in reviveing the matter, as to the verdict you mention ~~against John Rose~~, for that as I have (and I believe you have been) told by men of integrity that was obtained by the wilfull perjury of those who swore as instructed, that Rose would have had the Vicar take his tyth ridge out of that piece of wheate lyeing next the highway yearely, to which the learned & judicious judge, giving credit, might declare as you mencon to bee hard on the Vicars part, because of the casualties. But I have heard that Mr White was soe sensible of the wrong thereby done that hee openly confest it, & I think agreed to wave it, of which hee can better informe you, if you think it worth your troble.

Sir, I doe pretend to know Mr White [?*intus et incut*][2] (as the poet), haveing had 15 yeares experience both of his divine & moral precepts & practices & example, and alwaies pittied him, but never aimed, consented, nor indeavoured, to defraud or oppress him, as you [?unkindly charge], but have ever been and shall ever bee willing that hee shall receive his full due, & duely paid without troble. And for that very end I have insisted & requested to have, & if I can, will have, a faire and true terrier, and a true coppie thereof to remaine in the parish or church chest for the information of all concerned, & to prevent strife. But if I cannot obteine it dureing his life, hee being as you say dangerously ill, if it shall please God you shall survive him and become his successor there[3] ~~it is hoped~~

1 Page break.
2 Inside and out.
3 In fact, John White's successor as vicar of Avebury, in November 1712, was John Mayo.

~~you may~~, I am sure you will not make it difficult, but bee willing to [?receive] & to doe right, & will performe the Christian duties enjoyned by the Church, especially baptizeing, catechizeing, visiteing the sick, burying the dead, &c., too much neglected there for severall yeares past, & will encourage all your neighbors duely to frequent Gods house, & to pay you all your dues, & to shew you all due respects, and to live as becomes Christians under a Godly minister, in the best church government in the world.

In truth Sir, I did think (as I told you) that the wise and prudent ~~persons~~ to whom you say, you shewed my letters, in order to obteine their opinion thereon, had been only Mr White and his wife, because you seemed to speak their angry words, but you now tell mee, it was to not soe few as twenty juditious clergie & gentry, some as farr as Bristoll, Winchester and Sarum, who all agreed with you that I was the wrong doer, yet in the same letter you honestly say, you did not shew to nor acquaint any one of them with my letters to Mr White nor his to mee, before my bill, nor his answers to it, upon oath, to all which my letters, on which you say you took such learned advice, I did particularly referr, as you are pleased to acknowledge, and I cannot but think your friendly indeavor therein would have been more satisfactory, had you shewed them the whole.

Upon my word, Sir, my letters to Mr White were honestly intended, and not, as you scandelously reflect, like the subtile & malicious questions of the Pharises & Herodians to ensnare our Blessed Saviour, and if you meant as you say I am pretty sure you woud not have have [sic] made such an comparison, had you remembered the advise of St Paul to the Corinthians, & the charity hee preacht & explained to them. 1 Cor 13, 1.[1]

Sir, you doe seeme to have taken a good deale of paines to informe yourselfe about the quantity & vallue of the ell ridges, couching the sheep, &c., for which you [*illegible*].

Yet beleiveing it well intended I doe thank you for your kindness therein, if any, nor doe I think it fit for mee to inquire what private wayes and bye paths you frequented 45 yeares agoe as you menton, knowing that that many young men make use of some without enquiring whether lawfull if they find them pleasant or convenient.[2]

You may if you please, tell mee in which of my letters & in what words I expressed such terrible threats of suites & Chancery law as you delight to often charge mee with culling [*illegible*] distressed enough Abbingdon law.[3]

There are severall fictions & surmises in your last, [?perticularly] that husbandmen may sowe smutty[4] smutty or trash wheate, barley, & pease in that piece of wheate lyeing next the church yearly on purpose to defraud the viccar

1 'Though I speak with the tongues of men and of angels, and have not charity, I am become as sounding brass, or a tinkling cymbal'.

2 This is probably a reference to the fact that, in the early 1670s, Brinsden had been accused in the Consistory Court of having been the father of Anne Plummer's illegitimate child; CF. WSHC D1/42/61, f.46-55.

3 Legal slang for summary execution without trial.

4 Page break.

(your own words) which I think not worth my thanks or further notice. The rather for that I have already trespast upon your patience, & made this too lyeable to your just censure of being long winded & too full of goodmorrowes, as you are pleased to express. Upon the whole matter, Master Brinsden, I think your strained compliments & whole contents of your letters, have soe stronge a byass that I don't think fit to say more, to ad to or alter it, but will take this liberty to tell you, that I am & shall alwaies bee as greate a lover of peace as the most peaceable of your good neighbors, and I should have been glad if the viccar had been named in your lyst with those you named.

Sir, I doe heartily joyne with you in the Godly prayer & exhortation wherewith you conclude yours, & doe beg leave to ad the advice of our Saviour, that wee may all heartily indeavour that our righteousness may exceed that of the Pharases, Jews, & doe think I have herein taken panes to show that I am, with great respect & integrity

Sir

Your true friend & servant to my power

R.H.

My wife thanks you for your prayers & good wishes & returns you the like, you may if you think fit present my true respects to Mr White, with whome I am in perfect charity, but noe lover of his rough humor.

Verso Note: Draught of a letter to Mr Brinsden, 21 May 1712, being an answer to his of the 22 of April 1712

Proverbs 24, 29.[1]

Proverbs Cap 17.[2] The beginning of strife is unto breakeing out of waters.

79. John Mayo to Sir Richard Holford WSHC 184/1, pt.2.

Avebury

16 June 1715

Sir Richard,

Mr Norris was so very kind as to call at my house lately & brought me the good news of your honor's health, which he soon deeply alloyed by saying that your good lady was but in a weak condition. I hope it hath pleased God by this time to bless her Ladyship with a better state of health. We did ourselves the honor of drinking your health, though Mr Norris's visit was a morning one. I take this opportunity to thank your Honour for all your favors, particularly for the paper of tobaco I lately received by Dame Rose. The Farmer Rose continues a very honest kind neighbour & my Dame is no changling.

The Farmer has offered to pay me 20 or 30 shillings, but I rather choose

1 The text is 'Do not say, I shall do to him as he has done to me. I am paying off an old score'. The citation is followed by Holford's indecipherable short-hand – perhaps of the text?

2 Actually Proverbs 17, v.14. Followed by short-hand as in previous note.

to wait your return into the countrey. If you please to cast your eye on the next page you will see how & how much money I have disposed of to the children, on your account, to encourage them to learn & say their catechism publickly in the church last year.[1] My wife joyns with me in good wishes for your own, your good lady, & all your family's health. We pray you & her Ladyship to accept of our most humble duty, & good Mr Holford to accept of our humble service, whose civilities to us when he was in the countrey we shall not easily forget. I am, honoured Sir,
Your Honours most obedient & most humble servant
J. Mayo[2]
1714

Verso Note: Mr Mayo 16 Junii 1715. I writ fully to him the 7th of July.
Address: To Sir Richard Holford in Lincoln's Inn Fields, London.

80. Thomas Alexander to Lady Holford WSHC 184/1, pt.2.

Backhampton
12 December 1720

Good Lady,
I understands by [?Farmer] Caswell's letter that your Ladyship is desirous to have a true account or description of the land which Joseph Griffin held of late by the life of one Goody Wyers. Now this Goody Wyers lived below Caln betwixt that and Chipnam, and, as I am informed, she has been dead this two years,[3] whereby it does appear that this land hath belonged to your Ladyship two year. As for the valuation of the said land, it measures but seventy three perches, and it wants about seven perches of half an acre, it being arable ground. And as for its situation, it lyeth plain south from your Ladyship's farme house that [?Farmer] Caswell lives in, about half a mile from thence, in the ascent near the top of the hill in Backhampton Field, and tis sowd but once in two yeares. Wherefore John Griffin (that sowd it last) says it is worth but half a crown a year, and [?Farmer] Caswell saith it is worth but two shillings, but methink it may be worth five shillings a year. Tis true the land is poor and out of heart for want of soiling. This is the best account I can give about the land, and I fancies no one can give a better.

Good Lady, I sent you a letter the last week, wherein I did indeavour and desire to acquaint your Ladyship that I have received the rent from Cleeve Pipard, wherein I did and do here again make bold to desire your Ladyship for to lend mee the money untill Michaelmas next. In so doing your ladyship will or would do mee a very great kindness, and I should be over and above obliged to your Ladyship for so doing, but if your Ladyship do not think it proper to lend it mee,

1 This account is not transcribed here, but shows expenditure of 8*s.* 5*d.* between Easter Day 1714 and the following spring.

2 Page break.

3 Perhaps Elizabeth Wier of Mannings Hill, Bowood, a nonconformist, buried 12th May 1717 according to **www.familysearch. org**.

I desires your Ladyship to send mee an answer by the next post, for Joseph Rose is very importunate to have it ever since I told him that I had it. Altho himself would not go one quarter of a mile after it, or as they told mee, he never said a word to them about it besides he carried your letter, that was for Mr Spackman, fortnight or three weeks in his pocket before he delivered it. So wishing your Ladyship all health and happiness in this world, and in the world to come joy to all eternity. And so I assume the boldness to subscribe myself,
Your Ladyships most humble servant
Tho Alexander[1]

Good lady, Farmer Rose dyd and left so much wealth or something that his family can scarce sleep in their beds for fear of being robbed or for some noise. Wherefore thay have borrowd almost all ye guns in the village to keep guard, ha ha ha.

And Farmer Caswell gets money so fast on your Ladyship's farme that a poor man can scarce live by his wife and some of the family. The world so much mended with them since they came to Backhampton that the young men has their broad cloath sutes, & the women has silk and sattin, and when they came to Backhampton first some of the children had scarce cloathes to put on. Tis sign they have a good bargain, they have a brave parcell of land for their money. Tis pitty but that it were all measured.

Now if your Ladyship will so pleased to send mee a letter I desires it may be directed to mee only & not to any of them.

Verso Note: 12 December 1720. From Alexander, to borrow the rent he hath received.
Verso Address: To Lady Holford att Lyncoln Inn Field, London.

81. Humfry Wall to Mr Hall WSHC 184/1, pt.2.

[11 January 1721/2]

Sir,
My Lady received yours and in answer thereto orders me to let you know that as to the £500 you mention you may assure yourselfe that the late tenant farmer John Rose paid interest for it yearly at £5 per cent, and before & during his living there, Sir Richard expended great sumes of money for the benefit of the tenant, & my Lady is very unwilling to comply with anyone that will not make reasonable allowance for it. You mention a tenant's proposal, att the old rent & allowances, but doe not mention his name or place of abode, & therefore I suppose you intend to treate noe farther with him about it, but if you doe, her Ladyship would have you insist on £370 with the usuall allowances, except lop shrouds & windfalls, & the old orchard to the double hedge, which her Ladyship particularly reserves to herselfe, & unlesse a tenant will come up pretty near it, I

1 Page break.

believe my Lady will not be willing to let it, & I doubt not but that her Ladyship will soon hear of a tenant for it. Many proposals has been made to her Ladyship since she came to town, but her Ladyship has referred them to you to treate with them, & I doubt not but you will espouse her Ladyship's interest herein as far as the thing wil beare, there being just grounds for the present advancement of the old rent. Mr Holford is now in Oxfordshire, & therefore shall refer all other matters til his returne, which we expect very soon, & in the meanetime hope we shall heare that you have soe farr advanced in the treaty as that nothing will be left but their approbation, her Ladyship being interrupted from writeing herselfe desires her service to you by, Sir
Your most humble servant
H.W.[1]

Note at foot:[2] 1721 Jan 11. Copy of letter to Mr Hall.

82. T.H.,[3] to Samuel Holford WSHC 184/1, pt.2.

26 August 1723

Sir,
I am very much concerned that your Worship make delays in coming down into the countrey as you were wont to do, but hoping all things are well, and that your Worship will be so pleased as to come amongst us very speedily, for Farmer Peter[4] have company of unruly servants about him, that has and will confound every thing which they come near. In the wheat harvest they lodged the reapers in your blankets, and some in your beds, as I am informed, and he has a kind of a Welch housekeeper. I hope you do know what quantity of small beer you have in your house, for I am afraid you were dismissed of some of it. I have sent you (by ye flying coaches) a baskett full of apples and peaches, and it were all ye peaches that I could have, for the farmer and his housekeeper and their friends have cleared as twere imagined 3 or 4 bushells of plumbs and ½ a bushell or 3 pecks of peaches, besides raspberries, strawberries &c., and all would not satisfie them. So wishing your Worship all health & happinesss and a good journey down into our countrey, and am,
Your Worship's humble servant
T.H.

Note at side: I should have write much more, but we have sickness in our family; besides, I hope very speedily to see your Worship in the countrey, which att present makes me forbear.

Verso Address: To Samuell Holford, esq., att Lincoln-Inn Fields, London, these.

1 Humfry Wall.
2 Written upside down.
3 Perhaps Mr Hall, as in letter 11 January 1721 from Humfry Wall. (no. **81**).
4 Peter Griffin.

83. John Caswell[1] to Samuel Holford WSHC 184/1, pt.2.
29 October 1725

Sir,
These are to let you know that we have long since expected your Worship would been at Avebury, hoping that your absence has not been caused through any sickness or illness of body. Wherefore we are desirous to hear from you, and also to know whether your Worship do design to come down into the country speedily or where I must return your money up to London. If it must be returned, we desires your Worship would send us word.

So I and my wife gives our service to your Worship, wishing you all health & happiness in this world, and in the world to come joy to all eternity. And so I assume the boldness to subscribe myself
Your Worship's humble servant
John Caswell
Backhampton
Oct ye 29th 1725

Verso Address: To Samuell Holford, esq., att Mr Benyon's, over against Jefferson's Coffee House in Red Lyon Street, near Holborn, these.

84. John Caswell to Samuel Holford WSHC 184/1, pt.2.
[16 November 1725]

Sir,
These are to acquaint your Worship that we received your letter and that we are much obliged to your Worship for your permit. As for the ballance of our account we will send it next week, and this week if we can procure it by any mean send you return. But if we cannot procure it my son Timothy shall bring it up next week with a copy of our last reckoning. So I and my wife, and Thomas Alexander, gives our duty and service to you, wishing your Worship all health and happiness now and for ever. And so I assume the boldness to subscribe myself
Your Worship's humble servant
John Caswell
Beckhampton November ye 16th 1725

Thomas Alexander designs to make bold to write unto your Worship next week.

Verso Address: To Samuel Holford esq., att Mr Benyon's over against Jefferson's Coffee House, Red Lyon Street, near Holborn, these.

1 He had been a tenant of the Holford family property at Beckhampton since at least 1713; see *AWS*, p.61-2.

85. Peter Griffin to Samuel Holford WSHC 184/1, pt.2.

[22 November 1725]

Sir,

These are to acquaint you that I have received your letter of the 18 of this instant month wherein is mentioned that Mr Smith of Alton[1] is at London, and for his use I am orderd to pay unto Mr Buckeridge at the Tuns in Marlborough one hundred & twenty pounds, of which, on sight whereof, I have to Mr Buckeridge answered according to your and his satisfaction I hope.

Sir, we had such a great flood at Avebury, 'tis fortnight alias fourteen nights since that the water rusht and came into every room of your Worship's house that has its flour[2] on the ground. It came so suddenly that we were put hard to it, or had scarce time to get your beer out of the cellars, where the water was afterward as deep as a man's middle. We set your beer on wooden horses in the great hall till the water were sunk, and since that have carried it into the cellars again, hoping that it is not diminished, for we have taken all the care imaginable, and also to cleanse and dry these rooms.

Sir, these are to inform your Worship that Farmer Caswell have promised Thomas Alexander, that his son Timothy designs to or shall set out for London the next Wednesday hoping to be in town the Friday night to Saturday morn of this week. He says he would have returned your money if with conveniency, but could not, some time sooner. So I and Farmer John Caswell and Thomas Alexander gives our duties and services to your Worship, wishing all health and happiness to attend you now and for ever. And so I assume the boldness to subscribe myself,

Your Worship's humble servant

Peter Griffin

Avebury, November 22d 1725.

Verso Address: To Samuell Holford, esq., att Mr Benyon's over against Jefferson's Coffee House, in Red Lyon Street, near Holborn, these. Pray direct it with care and speed.

86. Robert Holford to Richard Holford WSHC 184/1, pt.2.

24 September 1737

Dear Dick,

I thank you for your letters. Tis true I have a young stranger come into the world, who stares about him, & thinks it an odd place. I intend to name him Stainer. His mother & he are as well as can be expected. Your Cambridge friend is gone to Cambridge, an honest fellow he is, & I hope will be a creditt as well as a comfort to his relations. There are so many of them now, that they must shift for themselves, & endeavour to help one another. I can easily imagine your time

1 Alton Priors.

2 Floor.

does not pass very pleasantly, but however I think it passes usefully, for although reading law, be not the most entertaining study, yett where property is to bee preserved, it is necessary if it were only not to be imposed upon by every country jackanapes, that upon the foot of being bred a hackney writer, setts up for a governor & person of understanding. I think you are perfectly right in what you have done about the schoolmaster. It will give you that authority in the parish which you ought to have. When they see you do insist upon it & will maintain it they will be quiett, & they must, for they are a parcell of sorry rascalls, who say one thing today, & another tomorrow,[1] & the next day swear they never said either, I am glad to see that you are coming to have that contempt of them which they deserve. What you do I would advise you to do with temper, & am sure more you keep your temper, the more you will despise them. I am glad you are pretty well, & hope to see you shortly in towne. In the mean time I shall be glad to hear from you, & do assure you that I very sincerely am,
Your affectionate friend & uncle
Robert Holford

Here is sad work between ye King & ye Prince.[2]

Verso Address: For Richard Holford esq., att his house at Avebury, near Marlborough in Wiltshire.

87. John Cures[3] to Richard Holford WSHC 184/1, pt.2.
[5 May 1739]

Sir,
I was favoured with yours of the 26th April Tuesday last. Yesterday I saw the hatches in disputte. I find about 9 yeares since the hatches for watering South Mead stood below on the left hand of Bath Road. But when the tennant of your estate had occasion to penn the water for watering the mead, it often threw the water soe high in the road that made itt almost impassable, and to cure this evel itt was thought proper to remove the hatches to where they now stand, and make a bridge in the road to convey the water under itt to water the meadows. I presume that Mr Smith would take advantage of you by saying that you diverted the river out of its ancient course, by which his estate suffers, though in my oppinion itt is much the same, since South Mead has allways & must still be watered whether the hatches stand as they doe or just below the road. Mr Smith would have your estate subject to him. You may water your mead when he does not want to water his. Your tennant since has putt down the hatches & noe notice taken, by reason as I apprehend Mr Smith has putt his ewes & lambs into his own meads. You may bring an accord or indite him for a trespass, and if you forbid him first recover

1 From here, the text is written at right angles in the left-hand margin.
2 A reference to the estrangement between George II and Frederick, Prince of Wales.
3 He has not been identified, but may perhaps have been acting as Holford's agent.

costs on the accord that you will please to consider how your family & he stand, whether he can return the same compliment or not to your disadvantage. Your tenant apprehends that if hee goes on with his farme long, he will not be inclined for law, however, I conceive for this yeare you will heare noe more of him, unless a good flood happens. Shall we not have the pleasure of seeing you this [?somer].[1]
Sir, your most obedient humble service to command
John Cures
5th May 1739

Verso Note: To be carried to Avebury, about watering South Mead.
Verso Address: Richard Holford esq., at his lodgeing in Grange Court, neere Clare Market, London, present.

88. Stayner Holford to Peter Griffin WSHC 184/1, pt.2.
[3 February 1742/3]

Farmer Griffin,
Yours of the 29th of the last month came to my hands yesterday, when I expected to have received a bill for the one hundred pounds which I hope a post or two will bring. I am sorry you meet with difficulty in raising it, but in my last I convinced you of the necessity of my having it. I am not much surprized at Mrs Holford's manner of writing to you, for it is like the rest of her ill treatment to me.[2] You may make yourself easy, & need be under no apprehensions from receiving hurt on account of her demand on the estate you rent of me, for if she arrests you, or takes on your stock on account of any demand she has on me, I will protect & defend you. It is true she has a legacy left her by my brother of three hundred pounds, but that is not payable till a year after his death, and then it is to be paid by me, and not to be demanded of you, which your own reason will tell you. That part of the house, stable, & gardens, with the goods made use of by my brother, I imagine she is to have the benefit of during her life, but she has no power to carry away or destroy anything, which I desire you'l take notice of. As to her writing letters to you about sending fowl, or giving directions to Nurdin,[3] or any thing else, you are under no obligation to pay any sort of regard to them. I must repeat what I said in my former letter, that I am greatly sollicited to discharge my brother's debts, and I have no other way to do it but out of the arrears of rent due from you, therefore must insist on your exerting yourself to enable me to do it by paying the arrears that you owe as soon as possible. And when that is done you may depend upon all the indulgence in my power. Remember me kindly to your wife, & Cousin Bailey,[4] and be assured that I am
Your Friend &c

1 The mss is torn at this point, and a word appears to be missing.
2 See *AWS*, p. 93-4.
3 Probably Holford's gardener.
4 Richard Baily, a leading Avebury dissenter; see *AWS*, p.57-8. The precise relationship to Griffin has not been traced.

S.H.
Portsea, 3d.

The letter Mr Kentish wrote to you was by my desire.
Portsea 3d February 1742
To Farmer Peter Griffin

Verso Note: 3rd February 1742. To Peter Griffin.

89. Stayner Holford to Peter Griffin WSHC 184/1, pt.2.

[21 January 1742/3]

Farmer Griffin,
When I was in Wiltshire you promised about this time to pay me one hundred pounds. I therefore desire you'l not fail forthwith of sending me a bill for that sum drawn on some person in London, which you must be accountable for. And I also must insist, that you do not upon any account fail of letting me have another hundred pounds at Lady Day next. I would not be so pressing upon you for money, but that my late brother's creditors are pressing on me, which cannot be paid but out of the arrears of rent due from you, as particularly directed by my brother. When the creditors are satisfyed you may depend on having all the favour and indulgence that is in my power to give you. I shall expect your answer soon, and desire to be kindly remembered to your wife & cousin Baily, and am,
Your Friend &c
S.H.
Portsea near Portsmouth, 21st January 1742.

To Farmer Peter Griffin.

Verso Note: 21st January 1742. To Peter Griffin.

90. Peter Griffin to Stayner Holford WSHC 184/1, pt.2.

Avebury
29 January 1742/3

Honoured Sir,
I receved your leter of the 21st of this instant and as you require me to pay you one hundred pounds shall endeavour to do it soon as can get safe return, but corn sells very low and a £100 is a great while araisseing, and must desire you not to be so pressing on me for money at a time when corn is so very cheap. In some time it may double prise. I receved a letter from Mrs Holford who informes me that I should pay no more money to you, that your receipt without her hand is not good. She likewise requires me to pay her £300, and the first money that

I make it being left her as a legacy.[1] But I receved another letter 27th of this instant which saith nothing of any money, but only to send her some fowles, and to acquaint Nurdin[2] to get the garden in good order against she comes into the country, which will be early in the spring. I likewise receved a letter from one Mr Kentish, who informes my by your order not to pay aney money to aney person but you only and that you will indemnifie me from all harm, and as you require me not to pay any regard to Mrs Holford nor her letters must desire that you will protect and stand by me. When you write pleas to let me know whether it be in her power to arest me or to make any seasure on my stock. My wife and cousin Baily joyns with me in service to you, which is from your most obedient tenant to command,
Peter Griffin

Verso Note: 29th January 1742. Peter Griffin
Verso Address: To Stayner Holford esq., att Portsea, near Portsmouth, Hants., by the way of London.[3]

91. Robert Holford to Stayner Holford WSHC 184/1, pt.2.
10 February 1742/3

Dear Nephew,
There is a bill brought into Parliament for mending the road to Bath, which now goes through Abury. It is now printed & I have read it & do verily think if it passes as it now is, it will do your estate a great deal of prejudice, for it turns the road quite from Abury, which must be a great disadvantage to the village, & consequently I think to you, besides that what of your land may bee gone over in the new road, by the power the Commissioners have, & may be worth considering, & looking after. Your tenant can best inform you, but really by what I can att present judge you will be greatly injured & therefore you should give Mr Coppinger[4] directions if you think fitt, to look a little into it, & prevent any injury being done you. I did not gett sight of the bill till last night, or else you should sooner have known it. As to your affair with Mrs Holford, I have delivered a paper [?screed] from Mr Coppinger. I have no answer, but that she is too much out of order to look upon it. It was att their earnest desire that I spoke to Mr Coppinger, to end it if he could, without filing the bill, but he hath convinced me by a letter he shewed me from you about her writing to your tenant, that I was very idly imployed , & therefore will no more concern myself about it.

1 Amongst other bequests, she received £300 in the will of her husband, Richard Holford, which was to be paid out of arrears of rent – but by the manorial lord, Staynor Holford, not by the tenant; see TNA PROB/11/721/329 and C11/818/16.
2 Probably Holford's gardener.
3 There was no direct mail route between Avebury and Portsea; mail had to go via London. See the map of mail coach routes in Vale, Edmund. *The Mail-Coach Men of the Late Eighteenth Century.* Cassell, 1960, p.xvi-xvii.
4 Presumably a London lawyer acting on behalf of Robert Holford.

I am your affectionate friend & uncle
R.Holford

Verso Note: 10th February 1742. Uncle Holford[1]
Verso Address: For Stayner Holford esq., att his house att Portsea near Portsmouth in Hamshire.

92. Peter Griffin to Stayner Holford WSHC 184/1, pt.2.
[20 February 1742/3]

Honored Sir,
I have sent you this bill for one hundred pounds which I hope will be paid according as drawn. I should have sent sooner but could not get return. Therefore hope you will excuse me. Pleas to send a line or two to let me know if it be excepted and before it is become dew if can be known, because the man requires the money before the bill is dew. I received your letter of the 3d of this instant and am glad to hear in it that I am under no obligation to any person but you, whome shall endeavour to obey as much as in my lyeth. My wife & Cousin Baily [?joyn] with me in service to you, which is, Sir, from your most obedient tennant to command,
Peter Griffin
Avebury 20th February 1742

Verso Note: 20th February 1742. Peter Griffin
Verso Address: To Staynor Holford esq., att Portsea, near Portsmouth, Hants., by the way of London.

93. Stayner Holford to Peter Griffin WSHC 184/1, pt.2.
[21 February 1742/3]

Farmer Griffin,
I did on the 3d instant write to you, and gave you a full answer to every thing you desired, & imagined before this you would have sent me a bill for £100 as you promised. I am sorry you should give me the trouble of writing to you again on the same occasion, when I have so often in former letters assured you of the necessity I am under of insisting on having it forthwith. Therefore for your own sake hope you'l not oblige me to act very contrary to my inclination, by using such measures as the law has put in my power for the recovery of my rent, which would distress you. I desire you'l not trifle with me, and injure yourself, but send me a satisfactory answer very soon, and at the same time send me word what steps are taken in relation to having a turnpike for repairing the Bath Road, and whether there are any thoughts of turning the road out of Avebury, and if so inform me, whether it will be any advantage or disadvantage to the lands that the carriages now go over,

1 Robert.

and if the road should be turned lett me know whether the carriages will not then go over part of my land, and if it will be so much as it now is. Remember me kindly to your wife & Cousin Bailey, and believe me to be
Your Sincere Friend
S.H.
Portsea 21st February 1742.

Address: To Farmer Peter Griffin.

Verso Note: 21st February 1742. To Peter Griffin.

94. Stayner Holford to Peter Griffin WSHC 184/1, pt.2.
[24 February 1742/3]

Farmer Griffin,
I yesterday received yours of the 20th instant with a bill dated the 17th instant drawn by Jacob Wilkins on Edward Halsey, and indorsed by you for one hundred pounds, and have this day sent it to London, and when I know that it is accepted & paid will send you word, not hearing from you sooner occasioned my writing again on Monday last. The former part of my letter is answered by the receipt of the bill, and I desire your answer the latter part, and am with kind remembrance to your wife & Cousin Bailey.
Your Sincere Friend &c
S.H.
Portsea, 24th February 1742

Verso Note: 24th February 1742. To Peter Griffin.

95. Robert Holford to Stayner Holford WSHC 184/1, pt.2.
2 March 1742/3

Dear Nephew,
My son Bob & Mr Howard sett out tomorrow for Portsmouth in order to go on board the Warwick, Captain Misenor, to the East Indies, with a convoy that is to sail from thence with them. As they are fearfull of being robbed by the way, they don't think it proper to carry much money with them. Mr Howard, who is a gentleman I am much obliged to, hath desired me to write to you to help them in this matter. I therefore beg the favour of you to pay to Mr Howard for me forty pounds, & I will pay it here att an hour's warning as you shall direct. If this be inconvenient to you let me know, that I may think of some other method, or in that case if you can assist them to gett it from anybody else, it will be a kindness to me, because I would not have them disappointed, & I will punctually comply with such directions as you shall give about it & acknowledge myself
Your obliged friend & Uncle
Robt Holford

I believe Mr Howard will bring this letter himself, who is a person deserves all ye civility you can shew him.

Verso Note:
£ 26-05-00 belongs to Mr Howard
13-15-00 is Bob's own to bee kept for him by Mr Howard
40-00-00

Verso Note: 2d March 1742. Uncle Holford.
Verso Address: For Staynor Holford, esq., at his house in Portsea, near Portsmouth in Hamshire.

96. Robert Holford to Stayner Holford WSHC 184/1, pt.2.

3 March 1742/3

Dear Nephew,
This morning my son Bob sett out for Portsmouth with Mr Howard, a very honest gentleman that goes of the Council to Bombay, to meet the ship there in which they are to go to the East Indies. He will make you a visitt to take leave of you. Mr Howard desired me to write to you to assist them in a matter of money, which he thought not advisable to carry with him in the coach, & therefore if you will pay him for me forty pounds, I will pay it here as you shall direct, or if it be not convenient for you pray help them to gett it & I will punctually pay it here to your directions. I pray God bless them & send them a good voyage. Bob hath got an ugly cold, but I hope a change of air & exercise will do him good. As to your affairs with Mrs Holford, I can tell you nothing. I told Mr Jones all that I knew, & what I thought of it, which I suppose he hath told you since, that I have not seen or heard from her. It cannot be long before you will be able to judge what is proper to be done, & while she continues ill, I would not advise you to too much hast to them, indeed I would advise a little more.

I hope, however, they will agree to what is reasonable, & to your satisfaction. She hath sent me a copper plate which was made for a print of your grandfather, which is mentioned in ye paper of particulars, which you shall have when you please. I shall be glad to hear from you & am,
Your affectionate friend & uncle
Robt Holford

I sent a letter by Mr Howard who will I believe bring it to you, it is much of the same purport with the first part of this, & he is a very good sort of man, & worth your acquaintance

Verso Note: 3rd March 1742. Uncle Holford
Verso Address: For Stayner Holford esq., att his house in Portsea, near Portsmouth, Hamshire.
Whinarton

97. Peter Griffin to Stayner Holford WSHC 184/1, pt.2.
6 March 1742/3]

Honoured Sir,
I received your letter of the 24th February, and desire as you have receved the bill I sent you to inform me as soon as possible where it be excepted, being something doubtfull of the goodness of him. I hope you will not require me to return any more at [?our] Ladi-day, for cannot possibly do it. There is an Act of Parliament granted and sent down in order for the erecting of a turnpike in the parish of Avebury at the Craws Ways near Backhamton and elsewhere, if the trustees think propper, for the repairing the road from Sheppard Shord to Marlborough the lower way, form Sherrel[1] Hill to the Craws Ways, it being the Bristoll Road, & likewise from the house of George Stretche's[2] to the Craws Ways, & you have the honor of being amongst the number of trustees with your unckle and cousin at London. I cannot find but it will be both to your advantage and mine too, the act expresses it is to be set up the third day of May, and it is appointed for the trustees to meet at Avebury sometime in Aprill, at which time it will be propper for you & all gentlemen haveing estates in the parish to be present, & you in particular having so considerable an estate. You being a trustee will have the act sent you which gives a particular account when the meeting is. My wife & Cousin Baily joyn with me in service to you, which is from your most obedient tennant to command,
Peter Griffin
Avebury 6th March 1742/3

Verso Note: 6th March 1742. Peter Griffin.
Verso Address: To Stayner Holford esq., at Port Sea, near Portsmouth, Hants., by the way of London.

98. Stayner Holford to Robert Holford WSHC 184/1, pt.2.
[9 March 1742/3]

Honoured Sir,
I had the favour of both your letters on Saturday last, one by the post, & the other by Mr Howard in his way to Portsmouth. But he & my cousin Bob thought it necessary to proceed immediately there to inquire after the ship and prepare things to be in a readiness if the ship should sail on a sudden. And therefore did not choose to stay with me then. However, the next day they & the two other gentlemen that came with them in the coach to go to the East Indies were so kind as to dine with me, when my cousin had a slight fit of his ague, and as they did not expect to sail very soon, they deferred taking the money, and I gave my cousin & Mr Howard a general invitation to my house, and desired they would spend all the time they possibly could with me, but the next morning a message

1 Cherhill.
2 Presumably the Catherine Wheel, which was then in the village.

was sent to me to lett me know that the ship was then unmooring in order to sail. I went immediately with the forty pounds, which I delivered to Mr Howard, as you directed, for which he gave me two bills for twenty pounds each, and I went with them to the waterside and saw them take boat. My cousin Bob went away with great chearfulness & good spirits. He carried with him a quart bottle of the decoction of camomile flowers & Roman wormwood, which has often cured me, & many others in this country of the ague, and does not require [?repearing] as the Jesuit bark does. One bill is sent to the Commissioners of the Salt Duties, and the other I have sent to Mr Coppenger to enable him to pay Mrs Holford her quarter's annuity due the 25th December last, before Lady Day next.[1]

Mr Coppenger has for a long time, at your request, with my approbation, put a stop to the proceedings against Mrs Holford & Mrs Metcalfe[2] on account of their illness, but I suppose they are both well enough to take money, and I dare say if the annuity due to Mrs Holford is not paid within the time limited, her illness will not prevent her taking proper measures for the recovery of it, and therefore I see no reason why their illness should prevent their doing me justice. And you certainly must be convinced by their long ill treatment to me, that unless severities are used they will not do mee justice, for which reason I have by this post wrote to Mr Coppenger to proceed against them without any further delay, and am

Honoured Sir

Your most dutiful nephew and obedient humble servant

S.H.

My cousin Bob desired me to send his duty & love, and Mr Howard his service.

Portsea, 9th March 1742

Address: To my Uncle Holford

Verso Note: 9th March 1742. To Uncle Holford

99. Stayner Holford to Peter Griffin[3] WSHC 184/1, pt.2.

[11 March 1742/3]

Farmer Griffin,

I presume your bill dated the 17th of the last month is paid, otherwise should have

1 This annuity was due under Richard Holford's will; TNA PROB/11/721/329.

2 Ann Holford was the widow of Richard Holford, and the daughter of Mrs Metcalfe. Staynor Holford, who was named as joint executor (with Ann) of his brother Richard's will (PROB/11/721/329) brought a case against them in Chancery regarding that will; see TNA C11/818/16.

3 There are two copies of this letter, with minor differences in wording, but none of any significance. The copy transcribed is probably the one that was actually sent, as it is more carefully written; the other copy (not transcribed) appears to be a rough draft with a number of deletions.

heard before this, and must now desire you'l not fail sending me a bill for one hundred pounds at Lady Day next, which you may remember I told you, I should expect, and as the demands run high upon me, must insist upon your sending it to me. I can admit of no disappointment, and after Lady Day next, and when that is over I hope it will be in my power to indulge you with more time, and am with kind remembrance to your wife & cousin.
Your Friend &c
S.Holford
Portsea, 11th March 1742.

Verso Address: To Mr Peter Griffin at Avebury near Marlborough, Wilts.

100. Stayner Holford to Robert Holford WSHC 184/1, pt.2.
[15 March 1742/3]

Honoured Sir,
Inclosed are the letters directed for Mr Howard which you desired me to send. I have sent Mr Coppinger my thoughts on Mrs Holford's answers to my demands, and have taken the liberty of desiring him to confer with you upon them, and if she does not immediately comply with what I have therein required, I have desired Mr Coppinger to make no further delay, but to proceed in the bill filed against Mrs Holford & Mrs Mettcalf. ~~Be pleased to give my duty to my aunt, & love to my cousins, and am~~
Honoured Sir
Your most dutifull nephew and obedient humble servant
Staynor Holford

My mother is in Kent, my brother Arthur Jones send his best respects.
Portsea, 15th March 1742.

Verso Note: 15th March 1742. To Uncle Holford.

101. Robert Holford to Stayner Holford WSHC 184/1, pt.2.
22 March 1742/3

Dear Nephew,
I have received yours with the letters inclosed which I have delivered to a person who had authority from Mr Howard to receive them, but if you paid any thing there for the postage lett me know it, & I will pay it. I have paid one bill of £20 to Mr Coppinger, but the other, which you say you sent to the Salt Office, I have heard nothing of, which I wonder att, having expected it every day; should I send for it? I have seen your answers you returned to Mr Coppinger to the paper he sent you. I think them very reasonable & fair, as would make an end of anything that people have a mind there should be an end of, but indeed what they are doing or intend to do I do not know, or enquire; tis such sort of proceeding as I

have not been used for. I believe our friends are gott into a warmer climate than our own by this time. Wee complain of colds generally here, which I have not escaped, but am otherwise pretty well. I hope you are so, & am
Your Affectionate friend & uncle
Robt Holford.

Verso Note: 22d March 1742. Uncle Holford.
Verso Address: For Stayner Holford esq., att his house in Portsea near Portsmouth in Hamshire.
Whinarton.

102. Peter Griffin to Stayner Holford WSHC 184/1, pt.2.
23 March 1742/3

Honoured Sir,
I receved your letter of the 11th of this instant, and am glad to hear in the former part of it that the bill I sent you is excepted, but sorry to hear in the latter part that you require a bill for a hundred pounds more, which I cannot raise without some considerable disadvantage, corn being so cheap, but as you insist upon it shall endeaver to do it soon as possible. I receved your last, wherein you mention the great arrears I owe you. I own they are very considerable, but as you are a gentleman of good sence, I hope you will take it in consideration that such arrears cannot be discharged on a suden, and was they to stand as they are, you cannot be any looser my heaving a good stock on the premises. The trustees[1] are to meet on Munday the 18th day of April, when I hope to see you. My wife & Cousin Baily joyn with me in service to you, which is, Sir, from your most obedient tenant to command,
Peter Griffin
Avebury. 23d of March 1742/3.

Verso Note: 23d March 1742/3. Peter Griffin.
Verso Address: To: Staynor Holford esq., att Portsea near Portsmouth, Hants., by the way of London.

103. Robert Holford to Stayner Holford WSHC 184/1, pt.2.
9 April 1743

Nephew Stainer,
I heard yesterday by accident that your sister Holford[2] was dead. When I came to town from Hamstead[3] I sent to enquire, & find that she died on Thursday morning. As Mrs Metcalf hath not thought fitt to take any notice of it to me,

1 Of the turnpike.
2 Ann Holford.
3 Hampstead, Middlesex.

perhaps no more civility may be shewed to you, & therefore I think it proper you should be informed of her death, which makes a good deal of alteration in your affairs, that you may act accordingly. I have paid both the bills, but you forgot to endorse one of them.
I am
Your affectionate friend & uncle
Robt Holford

Verso Note: 9th April 1743. Uncle Holford
Verso Address: For Stayner Holford esq., att his house att Portsea, near Portsmouth in Hamshire.

104. Peter Griffin to Stayner Holford WSHC 184/1, pt.2.
[23 April 1743]

Honoured Sir,
I received your two letters deated the 10th of this instant, & likewise your last of the 18th. I should have sent you an answer to the two former ones sooner, but I sent you a letter deated the 6th of this instant with a bill inclosed in it for £50, and expected to hear in your last letter that you receved it, but as you said nothing of it, I fear it is fawlen into bad hands through the neglect of some postmaster, and desire you will give me some time to look into it. Mrs Holford is buryed at Avebury[1] and as you require me to take care of your goods, shal obey it, but as to keeping them that came with her out of the house, I had no trouble a tawl for they were orderd not to come near the house. We have brewed two hogsheads of ale for Mrs Holford's use, which is as good as we can make it, and hope that will do for you. If you pleas to have a hogshead of steal beer brewed mention it in your next. We will make a reserve of some pidgeons for you. The trustees[2] met, about fifty of them, on Munday last, but did but little business, onely chose a number that should act. They meet again next Munday and the Munday following, when they are to fix the pleaces for the gates. I have acquainted Nurdin[3] what was in your letter, and he will endeaver to have every thing in good order against your comeing to Avebury. My wife & Cousin Baily joyn with me in service to you which is, Sir, from your most obedient servant to command,
Peter Griffin
Avebury 23d April 1743

Verso Note: 22d April 1743.[4] Peter Griffin.
Verso Address: To Staynor Holford esq., at Portsea nere Portsmouth, Hants., by the way of London.

1 Ann Holford was buried 17th April 1743, according to the Parish Register. Her husband Richard's will (TNA PROB/11/721/329) had given her the occupancy of the manor house at Avebury for life.
2 For the Turnpike.
3 Probably Holford's gardener.
4 This date is a scribal error, since the letter is dated 23rd April.

105. Richard Bailey to Stayner Holford WSHC 184/1, pt.2.

[30 April 1743]

Honoured Sir,

I received your letter deated the 25th of April, and as you desired we have informed my cousin Griffin consarning the bill he was to send you for £100, and likewise to answer your letters. He sent you a letter deated the 6th of this instant with a bill inclosed in it by my own hands for £50. The bill was drawn by Thos Neate of Caln and dew in two days after the deat of the letter, and by a letter we have had from the person it was drawn on, it was paid when dew, to one Buckhanna, the time being so short that the bill could not be mis-carried, and therefore it must be some great villeaney in the persons whose hands it went thorough, which I hartily wish may be proved. It was some considerable disadvantage to the farmer to raise this £100 before this misfortune hapned, which makes it more so, but he will endeaver to do it soon as possible. If I can be of any servie to you in any kind shall be very ready to do it, which is, Sir, from your most obedient and humble servant to command,

Richard Baily

Avebury 30th April 1743

Verso Note: 30th April 1743. Richard Baily.

Verso Address: To Staynor Holford esq., at Portsea near Portsmouth, Hants., by the way of London.

106. Peter Griffin to Stayner Holford WSHC 184/1, pt.2.

[1st May 1743]

Honoured Sir,

I receved your two letters one of the 24th and the other of the 27th April, and am sorry to hear that you give me no more comfort in my misfortune than to think so lightly of me as that I should onely pretend to send you a bill for £50. I am not so wake as to think the shaming of such a thing would be of any service to me. I sent it as I mentioned in my last letter and fear it will be all the money lost to me unless the villeaney can be found out. It was likewise mentioned in the letter that the bill was sent in how nessary it was for all gentlemen having estates in the parish to be presant at the meeting of the trustees consarning the turnpike, and you in particular, when you was at Avebury said you would advize with your unckle consarning your estate being excepted from diging or picking of flints. Your takeing that affair on your self made me not mention it sooner than the 6th of April. There are severall estates excepted but none in the parish besides your unckels. Not withstanding this misfortune shall send you a bill for one hundred pounds soon as possible, which is, Sir, from your most obedient tennant and hope so to continue

Peter Griffin

Avebury 1st May 1743

Verso Note: 1st May 1743. Peter Griffin.
Verso Address: To Staynor Holford esq., at Portsea near Portsmouth, Hants., by the way of London.

107. Thomas Smith to Stayner Holford WSHC 184/1, pt.2.

Kennet
29 May 1743

Sir,
There is a way that goes cross Backhampton Feild for near a mile through your your [sic] Uncle Holford, the Dutchess of Marlborough, and Mr Beake's corn feild, which each of the tennants are willing to have stopt up, and the rather because when the Dutchess is dead the master believes the Duke will consent to the exchange of lands, and then each estate wil be much more valuable in lyeing in several instead of being intermixt and in common. Mr Norris of Chipenham, Mr Neale of Cosum,[1] and Mr Talbot of Lacock, I yesterday dined with and as they were Commissioners of the turnpike I mentioned to them Master Holford's desire of having the French Way stopt up, it haveing allways been a disputable way, and I believe they will desire that it may be no longer kept open. I apprehend that the Commissioners have a power by a clause in the act, fol. 242, to turn and alter the way, and for that purpose to purchase lands, which you and I can accommodate them with, for the turning of the French Way, which is what I am willing to comply with for the good of the publick and the service of my neighbors. Mr Norris[2] desired me to acquaint you that several proposals had been made to your relations that were last possest of your estate in order to exchange such lands as lay in Avebury, that each estate might be in several by which meanes both his and your estate would be the more valuable by a great many hundred pounds. On this affair, Mr Norris desired me to acquaint you that he should be glad to see you next Tuesday at Mr Stretche's, where ye Commisioners of the Turnpike are to meet. I beg the favour of you not to mislay the inclosed letter because I will show it to Mr Norris and some other Commissioners of my acquaintance. I have not been at home one day since you came into the country. If I had had any time before I should have communicated the substance of this scrole to you. If it is convenient I will wait on you for half an hour after evening service. If you should have any thoughts of exchangeing lands I suppose you will have the usual covenant in your tennant's lease for that purpose. I am, with compliments to your good family,
Sir, your most humble servant[3]
Thomas Smith

1 Corsham.
2 Probably John Norris of Bromham, who owned Pophams (or Little Avebury Farm) in Avebury; see *VCH Wilts* 12, p.93.
3 This signature clause is written on the side at right angles on the recto of the folio; the previous page was on the verso.

Verso Note: 29th May 1743. Mr Thomas Smith of Kennett.
Verso Address: To Staynor Holford esq., these.

108. Peter Griffin to Stayner Holford WSHC 184/1, pt.2.
[26 June 1743]

Honoured Sir,
The letter which is inclosed was carried to some of your friends at Avebury. They paying no regard to it, was brought to me, who put it forward. It's a custom, and what is allowed for the going off tenant, to carry off the wheaten crop. Now it being so cheap, it may be a great advantage to me to keep it over year, but shall not do it unless you think proper of it. It's allowed to sell the straw and chaff, so that it cannot be any disadvantage to your estate. I should not have been troubled for leaving your estate had I hold this year, as I was entred upon, but when I consider how many years I have lieved in it, what care and pains I have taken, and to be turned out so suddenly it grieves me very much, and for to take one in which is no better than my self. I wish may prove as good a tennant as I have been. If do, it's more than any of our neighbours who are well acquainted with us both do think, excepting those who ware consarned in it. It's an old saying that a new broom sweepes clean. If not when new it cannot be suposed will when old. I may venture to say that him nor no other person will manage your estate in a better husbandlike manner than what I have done, not onely your lands, but all reparations which was my agreement to do, not spearing any cost or charge for the same, for want of which your estate in a few years may be thirty or forty pounds a year wors than now is. I have suffered very much by dry summers, for severall years past it have cost me scores of pounds a year for hay. Now this year there is a plentifull crop, not onely of English grass, but upwards of sixty acres of very good clover, which now I cannot have any benefit of. I am not onely sorry for myself, but you allso, to think how you are deceved in your suposed friends att Avebury. My wife and cousin joyn with me in service to you and all the good family, which is, Sir, from your most obedient tennant to command,
Peter Griffin
Avebury 26th June 1747.

The bill that have been so long acomeing to light will will [sic] be paid soon. In my next may informe you better, as to the wheat, which is mentioned above, don't desire to carry off no more than about 40 acres which is nere Backhamton.

Verso Note: 26th June 1743, Peter Griffin.
Verso Address: To Staynor Holford esq., att Portsea, near Portsmouth, Hants., by the way of London.

109. Stayner Holford to Peter Griffin WSHC 184/1, pt.2.

[18 October 1743]

Farmer Griffin,

By bonds from you & your Cousin Griffins to me for eight hundred & fifty one pounds six shillings & seven pence half penny.

Farmer John Rose, having received of you sheep & other stock upon Avebury Farm valued at seven hundred & ten pounds eight shillings & two pence, he has paid the same to me towards discharging part of the bond given to me by you for eight hundred and fifty one pounds, six shillings and seven pence half penny, so that the ballance due from you on the said bond is one hundred & forty pounds, eighteen shillings & five pence halfpenny, which sum should have been paid some time since. This is therefore to desire that you will forthwith pay me the same, otherwise I shall be obliged to write to your cousin Griffins, who were so kind, as to be securities for you. If you think proper to entrust your cousin Richard Bailey, who is acquainted with the road hither, or any other person to bring me the money, I shall deliver yours & your cousin Griffin's bonds to him upon your sending me a letter of advice for my so doing, by the person that brings the money to me. Your cousin Griffins must also send me a letter to deliver up their bond to the person that pays me the money. When the day is fixed for the persons being here it is proper you should send me a letter of advice by the post to prevent my being from home. I am

Your humble Servant

~~Your Friend &c~~

S.H.

Portsea 18th October 1743.

Verso Note: 18th October 1743. To Peter Griffin.

110. Peter Griffin to Stayner Holford WSHC 184/1, pt.2.

[28 October 1743]

Honoured Sir,

I receved your letter of the 18th of this instant, and I own the money which is dEw to you from me, two ballance of accounts is one hundred and forty pounds eighteen shillings and five pence half penny, barring about twenty pounds you had of me after the accounts was settled, and that it should have been paid before this time, but expected to have seen you at Avebury before now. But as you require me to send to you, must desire you to stay till the latter end of December, by which time shall not fail of sending. I shall informe my cousins of sending a letter to you in order to deliver the bond up to the person I shall send, which is, Sir, from your most obedient and humble servant to command.

Peter Griffin

Avebury 28th of October 1743

Verso Note: 28th October 1743, Peter Griffin

Verso Address: To Staynor Holford esq., at Portsea near Portsmouth, Hants., by the way of London.

111. James Mayo to Stayner Holford WSHC 184/1, pt.2.

31 March 1744

Sir,

I am desired by Farmer Rose to let you know that he had the favour of yours of the 11th instant. The cheese, he says, shall be made according to your orders as good as possible in the month of May. Mr Overton has given direction to a mason in this parish to make your oven. Peter Griffin has not left the house neither does he intend so to do till midsummer, before which time the Farmer says he can by no means take up his residence there. The walls of the pond & the yard are very much out of repair; the Farmer therefore desires you would give orders to Peter Griffin to put them into such repair as they ought to be at the expiration of his time.

The Farmer is very desirous of having the feed of the old orchard & is willing to allow you one tun of the best hay in lieu thereof, which is more than the produce of the orchard will be.

The Farmer desires his humble service. I desire my service may be made acceptable to Mr Jones, Mr Watkins &c.

I am, Sir

Your very humble servant

James Mayo

Verso Address: To Staynor Holford, esq., at Portsea near Portsmouth.

112. James Mayo to Stayner Holford WSHC 184/1, pt.2.

[19 September 1745]

Sir,

I beg leave to give you this trouble at the request of Farmer Rose, to inform you of the death of your tenant John Fowler of Beckhampton.[1] The master in Chancery[2] came last night to Abury, and I suppose sets out again this morning. Upon his stopping yesterday at Beckhampton. William Fowler, son of John Fowler, thought proper, as the Farmer informs me, to say something to him about renewing, but upon the master's telling him that the new stating of the house was not his business, but yours, he said he would write to you upon this subject in a few days. William Fowler, or rather the late deceased John Fowler, has lately erected a large stable on the common or wast ground on the east side of the turnpike, which stable, it is imagined, is, upon any emergency to be converted

1 Innkeeper at the Hare and Hounds since 1724; see Raymond, S.A. 'The Inns of Avebury 1600-1800', *WAM* 117, p.162. The parish register records his burial on 14 September 1745.

2 Robert Holford, Stayner's uncle.

into a dwelling house, viz, in case you should not think proper to come to such terms about new stating as shall be approved of by the said William Fowler, who I find is the only surviving life. It is generally thought that the house which Mr Stretch is building at Beckhampton[1] will not be in the least prejudicial to yours. The farmer has secured the greatest part of his barley, & joyns in humble service with
Sir
Your most obliged & most humble servant
James Mayo
Abury
September 19, 1745

Verso Note: 19th September 1745. Revd. Mr James Mayo. To inform me of the death of John Fowler and of several particulars relating to his son William Fowler
Verso Address: To Staynor Holford, esq., at Portsea, near Portsmouth.

113. James Mayo to Stayner Holford WSHC 184/1, pt.2.
[27 April 1746]

Sir,
I realy thought that I had lost Farmer Rose's custom because I was in hopes that he himself had acknowledged the receipt of your last letter long before this time. But he now tells me that I am always to have the honour of being his scribe in writing to you, & therefore I am this moment awaked & surprised by him out of a very sound sleep, & ordered immediately to acquaint you that he is now upon sending two bills, one of forty pounds, & the other of thirtysix pounds eight shillings, which are both payable upon sight, & which are to be inclosed in a letter & sent to the Post House at Marlborough on Sunday morning next the 7th of May.

The charge & expence of repairing the house & orchard walls has been estimated by experienced workmen which upon a moderate computation will amount to the sum of twenty pounds & upwards. The Farmer joyns in humble service with
Sir
Your most obliged & humble servant
James Mayo
Abury 27 April 5 o'clock morning 1746

Verso Note: 29th April 1746.[2] Mr James Mayo. Advice of two bills sent to me for £76.8.0. An estimate of the charge in repairing the house & orchard walls.
Verso Address: To Stayner Holford, esq., at Portsea, near Portsmouth.

1 The Catherine Wheel.
2 Probably the date of receipt.

114. James Mayo to Stayner Holford WSHC 184/1, pt.2.

[2 July 1746]

Sir,

Farmer Robert Rose has lately received two letters from you wherein you desire to know what rents he always gave for that part of Mr Phelps's estate which lies at Abury, and what rent a tenant can now afford to give for it. In answer to which the Farmer has desired me to inform you that the rent which he gave for it was four score pounds a year, but that several sacks of seed wheat & other considerable privileges were yearly allowed to him by Mr. Phelps.

The rent which the farmer gave for that part of the estate which lies at Beckhampton was twenty pounds a year, which he thinks is now well worth the money, but that if a tenant was to rent both as he did there must be twenty pounds a year based upon this estate at Abury, otherwise no tenant could live upon it.

The estate at Abury has this great inconvenience attending it, viz., that it is far from being compact, that some of the lands lie near three miles distant from the other, & not above seven acres of pasture ground belonging to it.

The largest piece of ground belonging to this estate contains about eight acres, which is just without the Wall Ditch. The other pieces lie scattered all over the fields in single acres & halfs at a mile & a half distance on each side of the village.

The Farmer thinks, however that if you could purchase this estate at the rate of three score pounds a year, and could purchase at the same time two other small estates of about thirty pounds a year each, the lands of which estates lie intermixed and in several parts contiguous to the lands of the estate which we have been speaking of, they might all be made convenient enough for a tenant.

Had it not been to have obliged you, the Farmer says that he should have been very unwilling to have given you this information, indeed, he says the reason why he has delayed it so long was fearing lest, if the contents of this should ever reach the ears of the widow of Mr Phelps, who is now living here at Abury, it might be the cause of an ill neighbourhood between them.

He has, however, now delivered his real sentiments of the affair, which he hopes you will only make a private use of and shall always be glad (without prejudice to himself) to do his best service for you in this or any other affair. The farmer & his family joyn in humble service with,

Sir,

Your most obliged & humble servant

James Mayo

Abury July 2d 1746.

Verso Note: 2d July 1746. Mr James Mayo. Relating to Mr Phelps's estate at Avebury.

Verso Address: To Stayner Holford, esq., at Portsea, near Portsmouth.

115. John Norris to Stayner Holford WSHC 184/1, pt.2.

Chippinham
24 May 1749

Sir,
I have now before me a letter from Mr Kentish to Mr Smith, & this intimated to be done by your directions. There seems now to be a general spirit amongst the landholders of the tithing of Avebury to throw their estates into severalty by making mutual exchanges, & to this they are very much encouraged by seeing the advantages their neighbours hope from an agreement of the same nature. Jointures, entails, & infancy will make an Act of P absolutely necessary for carrying this scheme into execution, but when tis once completed, I can't see it will be attended with any other expence, since inclosing the lands so exchanged will be no ways necessary. It is impossible for me to make any estimate of the advantage you will gain, but as your share of property is far the greatest, your improvement in proportion must be so. Mr Smith has taken so much pains in bringing this matter to maturity, that when things are ripe for execution, I should willingly with your consent and approbation, indeed, out of gratitude to Mr Smith, who is on this occasion a common benefactor to all the landholders, employ Mr Martyn[1] an attorney of this town, & Mr Smith's son in law, to be our sollicitor. Mr Smith I believe has by this time communicated to you the articles & agreement made by our neighbours att Badbury previous to their Act of P. This session of P draws so near a conclusion, that an attempt of this nature will att present be impracticable. In the interim before another session is opened, I hope all things may be so digested & consented to, that we may lose no time in bringing it on the next winter. Our owners of lands in the tithing of Avebury are so very fickle & inconstant, that when they are agreed I hope in justice to your own interest as well as my own that no time will be lost. The referrers on my part are Mr Neate of Barton & Farmer Nalder [2]of Kinnitt.
I am, Sir, your most humble servant
Jo Norris

My share of property is so little intermixed with yours that I can't be supposd to act but for the general advantage of all that are concerned.

Verso Note: 1749 May 24th from Mr Norris to Mr Holford
Verso Address: To Stayner Holford esq., att Portsea near Portsouth, Hamps.

116. Stayner Holford to unknown addressee[3] WSHC 184/1, pt.1.

1 Samuel Martyn.
2 John Nalder; see *AWS,* p.104-6.
3 Staynor Holford's name is written on the verso in pencil in a modern hand, and his authorship may be deduced from the content of the letter. We do know from other letters that Staynor frequently consulted his uncle Peter Holford on matters such as this. The name of John Rose is written in pencil on the letter, but the

[29 May 1750][1]

Dear Sir,

About a fortnight since Farmer Rose, and Richard Bayley of Avebury came here to propose to me my accepting a consideration in lieu of a right of feeding sheep on lands lately agreed to be exchanged by Mr Norris, Farmer John Rose, & several other proprietors of lands at Avebury, which exchange has been negociated by referree chosen by the several landlords, without having the benefit of an Act of Parliament to direct and give sanction to such procedure. This application of Bailey's was only verbal. I therefore gave him for answer, I was not properly informed who were the proprietors, nor what was desired of me to be complyed with, and also said, that I was very well satisfyed with my property at Avebury, and the conditions of it, and that I should act with the greatest caution and best advice, before I should consent to make any alteration or reduction in it. I had some discouse separately with Farmer Rose, whose account of it to me was near the valuation of what is sett forth by the referrees in the inclosed paper, but I must consider him as a party interested in the affair, therefore it will be imprudent to rely on his report. On the 11th instant, I received a letter from Mr Norris with the referree's account inclosed, which I am desirous you should peruse, and therefore have sent you the copy of them.

I am satisfyed with the nature & conditions of my property of Avebury, but if my neighbours are restless, & scheming with a view to increase their own properties, I apprehend that I shall be frequently troubled with applications on such heads. Therefore as I would willingly act, and give such answers as may preserve my peace & fortune without appearing obstinate, ~~ill natured~~, unneighbourly and negligent, I shall be much obliged to you for your free thoughts, & advice how I may behave myself [?to] support such medium.

I apprehend the exchange of lands, disposing, compromising, and adjusting of customs & privileges appertaining to estates may lay a foundation for much litigation, expecially as the present proceeding is without having the benefit of an Act of Parliament to confirm it. I am determined not to consent to a general exchange, as was proposed some time since, and which seems to be hinted again by Mr Norris in his letter, and shall be thankfull for your sentiments how I may answer his letter in regard to the proposal depending. And if upon an inquisition when I am at Avebury the particulars should appear to be truly stated, and you should not disapprove of my parting with such privilege, what sum do you think will be a valuable consideration for it? It is to be considered that though the annual value to me as sett forth by the referrees is but small, my parting with it will make the field be of great value to the purchaser, especially as it is bounded on the side of the new road, which goes through Beckhampton, and he thereby becomes absolute owner of it, which will enable him to build houses, much to the prejudice to the Hare & Hounds

---

letter's contents make it clear he was not the addressee.

1 This date is uncertain. It is written with other notes (not transcribed) which seem to be irrelevant to the letter.

Verso Note: Copy of letters about exchange of lands.

117. James Mayo to William Fowler WSHC 184/1, pt.1.

[10 July 1753]

Wm Fowler

I do not pretend to say positively that you are in a state of damnation, but I very much fear that you are not far from it, it being expressly declared by Saint John that no murtherer hath eternal life abiding in him, and by St Paul that whoremongers and adulterers God will judge, and again in another place that neither fornicators nor adulterers shall inherit the Kingdom of Heaven. I do not say that I can bring you to the gallows for any particular crime you may have been guilty of, but I verily believe that I can go near to do if I attempt it, and I really think it would be a charitable action to spend ten guineas in endeavouring to bring you to repentance (which is now absolutely prevented by a continual hurry of worldly & sinfull business) by punishing your body in this world that so your soul may be saved in the day of the Lord Jesus.

I do not say that I will indict your house, but if you don't keep better orders for the future my best endeavour shall not be wanting.

I do not say that I will cause the turnpike gate to be removed from your house to the cross road where it ought, by the Act of Parliament, to stand, and where I myself can build a house that shall be much more convenient than yours, but I do assure you that, if you do not mend your manners for the time to come, I will most certainly give you such a character to all the Commissioners as you most richly deserve. I do not say positively that I will cause the way called French Way over Beckinton Field to be opened, but I do say that I can & will open it by going with my own waggon & horses whenever I think proper, and if such a thing should happen, and the road at the same time should go (as in all likelihood it will) through the Devizes to Bath, nothing can save you from ruin & destruction. Therefore pray take care of yourself and let me hear no more of you. Keep within the bounds of your licence, which is to furnish travellers on the road with proper refreshment. Bring none of my parishioners to poverty by suffering them to continue sotting in your house by picking their pockets and sending them, upon a day or two's sickness, to the parish for relief. Consider that you stand upon a very ticklish bottom, for I solemnly declare that unless you turn over quite a new leaf, unless you keep yourself, and all who may be under a necessity of calling at your house, within the strictest bounds of sobriety & temperance, unless you endeavour to break off your fomer sins by a true & sincere repentance and lead a Godly, a righteous & a sober life[1] for the time to come, I will prove a worse thorn in your side than ever you felt before from the day you was born even unto this day.[2]

Wm Fowler

1 A quote from the general confession in the *Book of Common Prayer*.

2 Page break.

God is my witness that what I have here written has proceeded from a sincere & conscientious design of doing service to him and to all my fellow creatures, particularly to those whom God hath committed to my charge, and that what I have said may have its desired effect on your heart shall be the earnest & fervent prayer of your faithfull pastor,
James Mayo
Abury July 10th 1753

Verso Address: To Wm Fowler at Beckinton.

118. Henry Howson to Stayner Holford WSHC 184/1, pt.1.
[21 March 1754]

Sir,
I am exteamly obliged for your favour of the 17th instant, which I duly received, with the enclosed; and return you many thanks for your care &c.

I have not been well for near three weeks past, having had a very bad cold, attended with a fever, which has confined me; but I am now much mended. I have many times wished to be at home, but the affairs in which I am embarqued has detained me here contrary to my inclination.

The oysters were only a small acknowledgment for the many civilitys you and family have been pleased to shew Mrs Howson, for which I should be glad of all occasions to return in a gratefull manner. Till I received your favour, I did not know of Mrs Howson's going to Churton, nor of Mrs Amor's illness; therefore, if Mrs Howson is not returned home, if it is not giving you too much trouble, I should be very glad to have a line from you which will be very acceptable.

I wish I knew any news to write you, but I know little. The ministry are very much puzzled to settle the great affairs of state since the death of Mr Pelham. The following are talked of:

The Duke of Newcastle will continue at the head of the Treasury.
The Honourable Henry Legge will be Chancellor of Exchequer &c.
Sir Geo Littleton, treasurer of the Navy.
Sir Tho Robinson Secretary of State.
Hen Fox will continue Secretary of War.

I hope Mrs Holford and Mrs Jones are well, to whom I beg my compliments, as does also Mr Clark & his family, and I am with much esteem,
Sir,
Your most obedient & very humble servant
Hen Howson

Mr Clark's servant is just now returned from London without a line for me, so that I presume Mrs Howson is not got home
Stratford 21st March 1754

If you please my compliments to Mr [?Harris].

Verso Address: To Staynor Holford Esq., at Avebury near Marlborough, Wiltshire

119. Stayner Holford to Peter Holford GA D1956/L1.

[5 February 1756]

Dear Sir,

My late tenant John Rose is now declared a bankrupt, which appears very strange and unexpected to every person that has heard the particulars. The acting Commissioners were Mr Roger Holland, a Welsh judge, Mr Edward Montagu, a barrister, & Mr. John Ball an attorney at Caln. The circumstances on which they thought proper to ground his being a bankrupt were, his servant girl's swearing that she had by her master's order denyed him to some persons some time in the last summer, his shepherds swore that he had within thirteen years past once bought about 50 or 60 sheep and drove them to a fair without bringing them on this estate, but joined them on the road with a much greater number of sheep from this estate & drove them together to the said fair, the shepherds also swore that he had several times bought small parcels of sheep, brought them to this farm, kept some & disposed of the others with sheep bred on this estate. These men with his carter also swore that he had bought & sold bacon, cheese, & coals, which things were sold to his servants, labourers, and tradesmen, and brought by him as back carriage from the markett towns where he had carried corn from the farms he occupied, and this was the immediate consequences of his being a farmer, and in some degree or other practised by almost every farmer in England. These are very trifling circumstances, and bear no proportion to the business of a man who occupied farms to upwards of £500 a year. This is an occurrence much taken notice of by farmers, & probably may spread, and therefore worthy the attention of landed gentlemen. I am accidentally informed that the day the Commissioners thought proper to declare him a bankrupt, they had much discourse about what directions they were to give relating to the judgments and distresses, and ordered the attorney attending on the affair to call in the judgement creditors for the money they had received for effects taken in execution of the judgments on Rose's own farm. And the attorney at the same time added that, as I was in possession of the stock on this estate, which I am, not only by the power of the distresses, but by having the lease delivered to me soon after old Michaelmas last, and the rent ceasing from that time, he would not then give any directions about it, and said it was deferred for a further consideration, and notice was sent to me that the Commissioners' first meeting is to be on 25th [?July], for the creditors to attend to prove their debts. I do not consider myself as a common creditor, shall pay no regard to it, and shall be obliged to you for your thoughts on this affair, & what you think of the validity of my distresses. Mr. Young executed the distress, & I believe was legally & properly done. I have been told by sensible people that the stock on every estate is deemed a security for rent in arrear, & that nothing but a judgment can sett it aside. The best compliments of this family wait on you

& Mrs, Holford[1] and am,
Dear sir,
your very affectionate cousin and humble servant ,
Staynor Holford
Avebury 5th February 1756

I am sorry that I have no frank.

Verso Address: To Peter Holford, esq., in Hatton Garden, Holbourn, London.

120. James Mayo to John Scane WSHC 184/1, pt.1.
[11 February 1756][2]

Sir,
I hope you will not think me impertinent in taking this method of informing you that there is no road or drove for any sort of cattle to or from Abury Farm through the church yard, and if you will use your influence with the labourers in restraining them from the commission of any trespass of this kind, it will be esteemed a very great favour by
Your humble servant
J. Mayo
To Mr Holford's Bailiff

121. John Scane to James Mayo WSHC 184/1, pt.1.
[12 February 1756]

Sir,
In answer to the note you sent me last night, I must inform you, it is my master's directions & my own inclination so to behave towards the neighbours' property, as I would be done by in the strictest sense with good manners & good nature in every circumstance. I am, Sir, your humble servant.[3]
Avebury 12th February 1756
To the Revd James Mayo.

Note on separate sheet of paper, relating to this and the previous letter: '12th February 1756. Note without a date sent by Mr Mayo to my bailiff, John Scane, on the 11th Febry 1756, and his answer this day.

1 Ann, wife of Peter Holford, nee Nutt.
2 No date given, but the next letter states it was written the day before this one.
3 Unsigned, but by John Scane, Holford's bailiff.

122. Stayner Holford to Peter Holford GA D1956/L1

[10 June 1756]

Dear Sir,

On the 28th of last month I had the copy of a petition delivered to me, the original of which had been before my Lord Chancellor. It was signed by the two assignees acting under Rose's bankruptcy. The greatest part of the content are notorious falsities, & the other part deceptive and false representations. Mr Solomon Hughes, an attorney at Devizes, & undersheriff of this county, is severely attacked in regard to his behaviour in my late tenant's affairs, and my property is the object aimed at. My acquaintance with Mr Arthur Jones of Lincoln's Inn[1] made me advise with him in the begining of these affairs. The petition (that is the copy of it) is now before him, and Mr. Hughes was with him a few days since to receive his directions preparatory to a reply. The Attorney General is retained for me, & Mr. Jones is also engaged. I have great reason to believe him to be a good natured sensible man and that he will do everything in his power to preserve my property. If you will be so kind as to call on him, he will inform you of the particulars, and if you should think of any thing that may be of service, I shall be much obliged to you to mention it to him. What Mr. Hughes will prepare by way of answer I believe will be sent away by Sunday's post, and you may on Monday evening or Tuesday morning see the whole. As to my proceedings & conduct in this affair, I have related them in my own method to Mr. Jones. If all things can be gott ready, & Mr. Jones approves of it, the petition & answer will be heard on Wednesday next. I have only to say on this occasion that this case may happen to every landed gentleman in England. Two instances of the same kind have very lately happened in this neighbourhood on large farms, the property of gentlemen of great fortune. I had but one road to pursue, which I did with the greatest equity, and hope it will appear so to the Chancellor, and am sure if you can contribute to my success you will readily do it. The affectionate and respectful compliments of all here wait on all where due, and am in hast,
your affectionate cousin & humble servant
Staynor Holford
Avebury 10th June 1756

Verso Address: To Peter Holford, esq., in Hatton Garden, Holbourn, London.

123. Stayner Holford to Peter Holford GA D1956/L1

[20 June 1756]

Dear Sir,

I have the pleasure of your very obliging letter from Brockenhurst, and assure you, that we here are very glad to hear that you, my cousin Holford, & little girl are well. The sanguine concern & hearty disposition shewn through the whole of

1 The reference is not to Arthur Jones, Staynor Holford's half-brother, but rather to the latter's cousin, also Arthur Jones; cf letter below, 20th June 1756.

your letter for the preservation of my property I take very kind, and am glad you think I could have acted no otherwise than I have done on the affair depending. Indeed it is the cause of every landed gentleman in England, and presume to hope that my Lord Chancellor will in his equitable character consider it. It was from the beginning a calculated attack on my property, for it is apparent that John Rose, my late tenant, in conjunction with one Jones and Smith his near relations & judgment creditors, had in their scheme valued the stock on this estate at about £1200. The debts on the judgments are about £840, and the remainder was supposed to pay me my year's rent of £380. Affairs were so finely calculated that the stock was reduced to that shape in a clandestine manner some few hours before the executing the writts on the judgments, for sheep to the amount of £88-15-0 were drove away, & sold in an irregular manner on a road by John Rose at the time he knew I was in pursuit of them. The sheriff by his writts had the same power to distrain the stock on John Rose's own farm as well as on mine, and therefore with great equity thought he would dispose of the stock there at the same time he did part of the stock on my farm, in order to pay the money he was impowered by law to raise. This was his own intention of proceeding entirely free from any partiality to my interest, because he was a person I had never seen, nor heard of till many days after the execution of the writts.

Rose, with Jones & Smith his near relations, perceiving by the sheriff's intended manner of proceeding that sufficient effects would remain on my farm not only to pay me my year's rent, but also my arrears, were thrown into the greatest consternation. The consequences of this lead them into the scheme of a bankruptcy entirely to plunder me, as originally intended. The first attorney the judgement creditors employed did not behave to the satisfaction of his clients, because they discovered he was disposed to act like a man of credit & some reputation towards me. Accordingly, they discarded him and have employed one more to their liking.

Mr. Jones is my old acquaintance, first cousin to my brother here, and I have always found him a very good natured, sensible man. I advised with him in the begining of the affair, and he was so kind as to take things from me in my own way, and as you are disposed to give me all the assistance in your power, be pleased to call on Mr. Jones to see the copy of the petition, and enclosed are my rough thoughts & reply to it, wrote in a very hasty manner, which I hope you will excuse, and be able to find out sufficient for your information & my defence. Mr. Jones has something of this kind but I thought it right for you to have them to peruse at some leisure hour before the petition shall come on to be heard.

Mr. Hughes is preparing affidavits & everything proper to a reply to be laid before Mr. Jones in the business like way, and when the whole is sent to Mr. Jones I will lett you know, that you may then see it and consider it in the proper dress.

The affidavits to support the petition, which I have seen, are artfull, obscure, and false representations made by John Rose the bankrupt, Robert Rose his father, well known to your father for his bad character, which he mentioned to me the last time I was so happy as to see him here, the two judgment creditors, and four other fellows of the meanest rank &c. The reply is to be supported by my own affidavit, Mr Solomon Hughes the present sheriff & his brother, who was the sheriff last year,[1] and three farmers of large property of their own, & good reputation.

The attorney for the bankrupt & judgement creditors took much paines to gett better evidence. If the Attorney General should be Chief Justice before the petition is heard, I should be very glad if you & Mr. Jones would fix on another person to be retained in his room, and take care it is accordingly done. I am sensible it is Mr. Hughes province to direct his agent in town to do it. Mr. Jones knows who he is and I wish he would send for him & order accordingly. You judge very right in saying this is an affair of great consequence, not as to the sum of money depending, which indeed I do not choose to loose, but to guard against the spreading of this contagion, which it most certainly will if the Chancellor does not nip it in the bud. The farmers are a numerous body of people, many of them very bad, strongly attached to each other, and spare no pains to spread their success in cheating their landlords. Mr. Jones has a copy of Rose's note for the delivery of the lease, which I would have you see. Be so kind as to own the receipt of this letter, with your thoughts on the affair. I have no frank, & paying the postage is not a safe way, therefore hope you'l excuse it. Our joint & affectionate compliments wait on you & whole family, and am,
Dear sir, your much obliged cousin and most obedient servant
Staynor Holford
Avebury 20th June 1756

124. Stayner Holford to Peter Holford GA D1956/L1

[22 June 1756]

Dear Sir,
Since my pacquet sent to you on Sunday last, I have fresh perused & considered the several parts of the copies of the affidavits on the part of the petitioners. I hope & believe what Mr. Hughes will prepare in a proper manner, & what I have already troubled you with, will in your opinion be sufficient for my defence & reply to every part sett forth by complainers relating to my own property & conduct, but, as I conceive, what they have falsely sett forth in a manner designed to perplex, relating to the privilege of the going off crop, is not so much known as I desire it may be, is the motive for my now attempting to do it in such manner as by your assistance, the council, & by them the Court, will clearly perceive the iniquitous representation in the petition & affidavits.

The farms in this neighbourhood are usually lett to commence at Lady Day, when the rent of the going off tenant ceases, and the rent of the new tenant takes place, and he (the new tenant) directly has possession given him on this farm of all the Downs for the feed of his sheep & cows, all the meadow, pasture, and grass for the feeding his cattle, and the crop of hay with all the arable land to plough

1 Holford is actually referring to the under-sheriff; cf letter above, 10th June 1756. Sheriffs are listed in Jackson, J.E. 'Sheriffs of Wiltshire', *WAM* 3(8), 1857, p.229.

and sow preparatory to the next year's crop, with such yards, stables, buildings &c as are necessary to his occupation for the first year. The going off tenant is only allowed to continue the possession of such part of the arable lands to reap such corn &c as he had sowed before the expiration of his term. This was the situation when Rose came here and by his lease he was at the expiration of it to be allowed the usual privilege of the arable land as before mentioned, on condition of his leaving the said several lands in such order & course of husbandry as particularly mentioned in lease. The quantity of acres he would have been so entitled to, if he had performed the covenants of his lease & paid his rent to Lady Day, were about one hundred & seventy, which they have in their affidavits valued at ten shillings an acre by the year, & claimed half a year of such lands gratis, by which the sum can be only forty two pounds ten shillings in the shape the deponents have put it in to have paid for rent before the new tenant had possession of all the lands, and notwithstanding the tenant by a calculated scheme left my estate long before the expiration of his lease, & was unable to proceed on the occupation, & impracticable for his creditors or assignees, and otherwise most notoriously injured me. I did submit, at the tenant's desire, as by his note will appear, to accept his lease and to pay him under the valuation of two farmers, one of his own appointment, £68 2s 6d for such work as he pretended was done preparatory to the next year's crop, and as to all the corn sowed at the time he deserted the estate, which was only about twenty six acres of wheat, six acres of vetches, & fourteen acres of turnips, it was seized & sold by the judgment creditors for thirty nine pounds four shillings, and consequently for Rose the tenant's use, whether the debt was real or feigned, which he nor his creditors in equity, were not entitled to by way of a going off crop, unless the rent had been paid to Lady Day. It is clear to all the reputable people in this country that I am the injured & plundered person, and should have been the complainer in this cause. The valuation of £300, clear of every charge to be gott by bankrupt or his creditors, for the present crop on the ground, which I have at much pains & expence sowed on the farm is, & must be, so apparently false to you & every gentleman knowing the circumstances of this affair, that I shall not presume to offer any thing more on it, only to say, if the crop would produce so much as £300 clear of all charges, the tenant has for eleven years used & enjoyed my property greatly under the value of it, much to my injury and to his advantage. I am [?inclined] to think on this circumstance only, when properly represented to my Lord Chancellor, he will dismiss the petition with my costs. I have no reason to doubt of Mr Hughes's drawing up the brief &c like a man of business, but I consider the success of this cause depends upon the skill of the council, their full knowledge of the affair, and yours and Mr. Jones's friendly assistance.

I think Mr. John Edwards of Symond's Inn is Mr Hughes's agent. I have asserted nothing in my last or this, but what can be supported by affidavits, and if on yours & Mr. Jones's perusal of what Mr. Hughes shall send any thing shall appear wanting, be so good as to lett me know, and pray lett the cause have all the help you & Mr. Jones shall judge convenient. You will oblige me in giving my

compliments to Mr. Jones,[1] and be pleased to lett him know, as I was writing to you on this subject, I thought there was no occasion for my troubling him with a letter on purpose, with what I have here said. When Mr Hughes's papers are sent, I shall write to him, and am,
Dear sir, your affectionate cousin and obliged humble servant
Staynor Holford
Avebury 22d June 1756

What day is the petition to be heard?

Verso Address: To Peter Holford, esq., at his house in Hatton Garden, Holborn, London.

125. Stayner Holford to Peter Holford GA D1956/L1

[22 July 1756]

Dear Sir,
The several affidavits with the papers thereto belonging were finished on Saturday last, and Mr. Hughes said he would send them on Sunday evening by the machine[2] of his agent. I hope you & Mr. Jones will think the matter therein contained sufficient to preserve my property. You was very kind in going through the draughts &c., with Mr. Hughes when he was in town, and think some of your remarks very essential, particularly the question relating to Rose's bankruptcy. He was only found a bankrupt in the usual way, and the Commission sued out about the 12th January last, and all my accounts &c with him were settled some months before that time, for which reason Trevanion, the bankrupt's attorney, found it absolutely necessary for his scheme to gett some act of bankruptcy sworn to about the midle of August last, which was by ordering his servant[3] to deny him to a person who accidentally called upon him for about thirty or forty shillings. Upon the foundation of this act the whole fabrick subsists, because the petitioners depend on having every act of mine since that time accounted for & settled under the Commission, and that I should be on the footing of a common creditor, but notwithstanding his being denyed in August, which was only known to him & his servant, he continued to go about his business as usual to the publick fairs & marketts to the day the writts were executed. On gathering these circumstances together, it fully appears, that Rose, & the judgment creditors, calculated for the writts to be carried into execution on the stock of my farm only, which upon the strictest valluation appeared to be between 12 & 13 hundred pounds. I mean in the shape they had dressed it for their intended purpose, because many things actually belonging to the occupation here were removed a few days before. The said sum was to be disposed of in the following manner – about £840 to the judgement

1 Arthur Jones, Stayner's half-brother's cousin.
2 Stage coach.
3 i.e. John Rose's servant.

creditors, £380 to me for one year's rent, and £50 for the sheriff's poundage & all expences, and so my good tenant was to sett down quiet on his own farm, and I was to have treated him with the stocking of it. There is one circumstance I must desire you to particularly observe in the affidavit of John Nalder,[1] who is a farmer of as good a character as any in this county, and occupys lands contiguous to mine between 5 & 6 hundred pounds a year, is well acquainted with my farm, and has deposed that John Rose by his ill treatment of my property has injured me to the value of £200, that is, the lands will require £50 a year for four years to put them in the same course & order as they were in when Rose took to them. I hope this circumstance will be observed by the Court, and as the affair depending is to be determined by equity, I hope the Chancellor will think restitution ought to be made me. If you can think of any thing more that is necessary to be [?done for] for the support of this cause, pray let me know. Have the petitioners (that is their attorney) on seeing the affidavits sent up on my behalf a right to make any additional affidavits before the cause is heard? I believe the brief is not yett sent up. When it is shall be glad if you will peruse it, and see that a proper abstract is made of the several & essential parts in all the affidavits. The people in the country are not so clear & exact as you great ones in Chancery, therefore be so kind as to supervise the whole and lett it appear in a proper dress.

I suppose you & Mrs Holford will think of going into Gloucestershire[2] some time in the next month as usual. We here shall be glad if you will take this place in your way, and desire our best compliments. I am
dear sir,
your most affectionate cousin, & obliged humble servant
Staynor Holford
Avebury 22d July 1756

Verso Address: To Peter Holford, esq., at his house in Hatton Garden, Holborn, London.

126. Staynor Holford to Peter Holford GA D1956/L1
Dear Sir,

[1 August 1756]

By yesterdays post I received a letter from Mr. Jones,[3] acquainting me that he had not seen any papers relating to the affair depending since Mr. Hughes left the town. I am much surprized at it because all the affidavits & other papers were finished yesterday fortnight, & Mr. Hughes said he would send them away directly. I suppose they are in the hands of his agent, Mr. Edwards, but was in hopes before this to have heard that they were in Mr Jones's hands, and that you & he had been so kind as to have perused them, and as some addition has been

1 See *AWS,* p.104-6..
2 That is, to Westonbirt.
3 Stayner's half-brother's cousin.

made to them since the rough draught, sufficient matter will in your opinions appear for my defence. I apprehend the day of hearing draws near; therefore shall be glad to hear soon from you. I have wrote by this post to Mr. Jones to begg the favour of him to send to Mr. Edwards for the papers. My mother & brother join with me in best compliments to you & Mrs Holford, and am,
Dear Sir, your most affectionate cousin and obliged humble servant
Staynor Holford
Avebury, 1st August 1756.

127. James Mayo to Stayner Holford WSHC 184/2

[19 August 1756]

Sir,
I have the privilege of choosing & cutting & carrying away two ell ridges of wheat as soon as it is ripe from some one or other of the pieces that shall be sown on your farm every year, & need not inform you that I have likewise a right to all the small tythes of your yard, barton or backside.

Please to let me know whether you are willing to contract for these tythes or whether you intend that I shall take them in kind as they become due, & you will oblige
Sir
Your humble servant
James Mayo
August 19 1756

Verso Note: 19th August 1756. Letter from the Reverend Mr James Mayo
Verso Address: To Staynor Holford, esq.

128. Staynor Holford to James Mayo WSHC 184/2

[19 August 1756]

Sir,
In answer to your letter this day, I must inform you, that what has customarily been paid for my estate to the Vicar of Avebury, I shall be ready to pay at your usual and appointed time, and am Sir,
Your humble servant
S.H.
19th August 1756

Verso Note: 19th August 1756. Letter to the Reverend Mr James Mayo.

129. James Mayo to Stayner Holford WSHC 184/2

20 August 1756

Sir,
I know not that any particular sum has customarily being paid for your estate to the vicar of Avebury since my institution.

If you are ready to pay what shall be agreed on, I shall be satisfied, but unless you think proper to come to such an agreement I shall proceed to take what is due to me in kind, immediately, and without further notice
I am Sir,
your humble servant ,
James Mayo
Aug 20th 1756

Verso Note: 20th Aug 1756. 1st letter this day from the Reverend Mr. James Mayo.
Verso Address: To Staynor Holford, esq.,

130. Staynor Holford to James Mayo WSHC 184/2

[20 August 1756]

Sir,
You have omitted to say what you require for my estate. You know what you have received since your institution, and also what was paid during your father's long incumbency, which I shall readily pay, as I said last night.

If you will with violence, as threatened in your letter, enter on my property, and possess yourself of it, I must apply to the laws of my country for my defence. I would recommend gentle methods in adjusting every dispute with my neighbours, and believe a court of Justice & gentlemen of a jury would be amazed to hear, that a clergyman should reject such methods. I am sure angry & resenting men disturb themselves most, as well as injure their own interest. Therefore give me leave to advise you not to be too hasty. I have heard your brother[1] is a clergyman of sense, & good character. Mr Preston,[2] another clergyman I know to be such. Suppose you advised with them? I, & this family, always meant you & your family better than you conceive, and it is far from our inclinations to lessen the income of a clergyman of the Church of England, who behaves as such. It is too often the misfortune of gentlemen residing in recluse country villages to suffer themselves to be sett at variance with their neighbours by false stories, and representations from mean people, which should be particularly guarded against. I am
Sir
Your humble servant
S.H.
20th August 1756

1 John Mayo, rector of Beechingstoke.
2 Nicholas Preston, rector of Alton Barnes.

Verso Note: 20th August 1756. Letter to the Reverend Mr James Mayo.

131. James Mayo to Staynor Holford WSHC 184/2

[20 August 1756]

In consideration of what is due to me from your estate I require what it may be really worth, & can you blame me. What I have hitherto received since my institution or what was paid during my father's long incumbency is nothing to the purpose. A man can be guilty of no violence I apprehend in possessing himself legally of what justly belongs to him, & is as much his own property as the cloaths he wears. In such cases the law must be his defence & protection.

I am altogether for gentle methods, but you know that there is a tameness which very nearly resembles gentleness, & can hardly be distinguished from it, & whatever you may think of it I had rather make my appearance before half a dozen courts of justice than be unjustly deprived of one single wheat corn.

How can a man be too hasty if the corn is ripe & the weather fine? You have certainly received a true character of Mr Preston & my brother, & as you have thought proper to mention their names, suppose that instead of my advising with them, the matter in dispute was to be referred to them? A clergyman of the Church of England who suffers his income by any means to be lessened ought no longer to be looked upon under that character, but should immediately be sent to the conventicle & fed with the crumbs which fall from the rich man's table. [1] I am glad to find that you are sensible of the misfortune which attends the residing of gentlemen in country villages. When a person's eyes are open tis more likely that his law should be shut against all false stories, & that instead of keeping company with mean people he should be contented to dine alone every day with Duke Humphry.[2]

I am, Sir,
Your humble servant
James Mayo
August 20th 1756

Verso Note: 20 August 1756. 2d letter this day from the Reverend Mr James Mayo.
Verso Address: To Staynor Holford esq.

132. James Mayo to Staynor Holford WSHC 184/2

[20 August 1756]

Sir,

What? Send me for advice to gentlemen whose judgement & advice you yourself reject! Hah! Hah! hah!

1 A reference to dissenting ministers, who were entirely dependent on support from the wealthier members of their congregations.

2 A reference to Duke Humfrey's Library in Oxford. Reading is recommended rather than conversing with the lower classes.

You can neither produce witness nor receipt for any particular sum that was ever paid for your estate during my father's incumbency or mine. But was that in your power, yet would it avail you nothing, since I have living witnesses to prove that they have known the tythes taken in kind, & I myself can prove that contracts between vicar & tenant have often varied in my father's time. When I find you are inclined to contract it will be then soon enough to inform you what I require. Is a person by a due course of law to possess himself of what he has an undoubted right to every year? Ridiculous. I have already applied to a person knowing in the law who I have the greatest reason to think will support me under my claim whenever called upon.

What do you mean by saying that you are sorry that I do not choose to set this affair in a clear light in a neighbourly way, after you have rejected the proposals which I have made? Your own letter shall expose you. I am, Sir,
Your humble servant
James Mayo
August 20th 1756

Verso Note: 20th August 1756. 3d letter this day from the Reverend Mr James Mayo.
Verso Address: To Staynor Holford, esq.

133. Stayner Holford to James Mayo WSHC 184/2

[20 August 1756]

Sir,
Though you & I happen to dissent in opinion in the affair depending, I have reason to believe, what you have received since your institution, and what was paid during your father's long incumbency, and long before, will by a court of justice be thought to be all I can be compelled to pay, and if you will force me there I cannot help it. You have desired to know if I would contract, or agree for it, but have not informed me what you require.

I do not allow that you have a right to enter on my estate to take any part of my property, and your apprehending that a man may possess himself without a due course of law of what he shall be pleased to call his just right, I believe you will not find to be a legal proceeding, if you should apply to a person knowing in the law.

I am sorry you do not choose to settle this affair in a clear light in a neighbourly way, and am
Sir
Your humble servant
S.H.
20th August 1756

Verso Note: 20th August 1756. 2d letter this day to the Reverend Mr James Mayo.

134. James Mayo to Stayner Holford WSHC 184/2
Abury

7 October 1756

Sir,
I do hereby give you notice that your present composition for two ell ridges of wheat and other tythes due from your estate in the parish of Abury shall cease on the 10th day of this present instant October being old Michaelmas Day, from which time I do intend to take the said ell ridges & tythes in kind, agreeable to law & the custom of this Parish.
I am, Sir
Your humble servant
James Mayo
Vicar of Abury

Verso Address: To Staynor Holford esq., at Abury.

135. Stayner Holford to Peter Holford WSHC 184/1, pt.1.

2 December 1756

Dear Sir,
I hope you & family had a good journey to town, and that this will find you all well. It was my intention before this to have wrote to you on the subject I mentioned to you when here, but was willing to gather every information I could before I gave you any trouble about it.

My grandfather purchased this estate about the year 1695, before which he was informed that the premises were tythe free paying only a small modus, vizt., two ell ridges of wheat nearest the parish church, valued at £3 per annum one year with the other, the privy tythes of the backside valued at most at £1 per annum. These words are taken from the particulars given to him before he purchased, which he shewed to the vicar of Avebury, who had been the incumbent twenty years, and he confirmed it by saying that he & all former vicars had received & taken the said £4 per annum in full satisfaction for all manner of tythes for this farm. About one year after the purchase was made the vicar & tenant then on the farm had some disputes, for which the vicar refused to accept the £4 per annum. The tenant therefore applied to his landlord to support & defend him in the usual & customary payment. Upon this my Grandfather in a friendly manner desired to know of the vicar why he would not accept the customary payment or else shew to him his authority for making a new demand, which was by saying that he would enter on any part of the estate sowed with wheat, and take such ell ridges as he thought proper. The vicar refused producing such authority, but persevered in his demand, upon which Sir Richard exhibited a bill in Chancery to compel vicar to sett forth his demand about the year 1696, whereto the defendant put in a very insufficient answer. The plaintiff took exceptions to the answer, the answer reported insufficient, the defendant took exceptions to the master's report, the

5th August 1698 the exceptions came to be argued and the defendant ordered to answer, the defendant put in a second answer and it being very irregular, several papers being annexed to his answer which ought to have been ingrossed on parchment, the plaintiff's clerk having copied the same, acquainted the defendant's clerk thereof the 9th November 1698. The defendant obtained an order on petition at the Rolls for a commission to take his answer *de novo*, and all proceedings to stay in the mean time. The defendant returned another answer and put the plaintiff to take a copy of it, and did by his clerk often promise to pay the plaintiff's costs but delayed so to do, therefore moved for plaintiff's costs or that it might be examined by a master, and reported. All these law proceedings I collected from a brief for a motion the 14th November 1699 at the Rolls. It was not moved, because the defendant prayed it might not, & compounded with the plaintiff. By memorandum dated the 2d October 1701 written by John White the vicar's own hand, it is sett forth that Sir Richard was prevailed on to accept the sum of forty pounds as a composition for the costs in the suit against him. I have also of the same date on stamp paper a general release written and signed by John White setting forth that all contests and controversies between Sir Richard & the said White were in a friendly manner accommodated & ended. I have likewise a terrier copied from one in the Bishop of Salisbury's court dated 5th May 1682,[1] which I found among other papers, made out by John White, vicar. As to my farm it says "that the vicar has the privilege of choosing, cutting, & carrying away of two ell ridges of wheat as soon as it is ripe, containing three yards or thereabout in any of the pieces following" and so names such pieces of ground as are usually sowed with wheat. The terrier in one general article also says "the vicar has a right to all small tythes, and offerings, excepting wooll & lambs," which does not allude to my farm in particular. In another general article it is said ["] there[2] is a composition for the cows, & all the circumstances about them". Now by his answer he swears on the 17th April 1697 that there hath been paid, and is due to the vicar, two ridges of wheat yearly out of that piece or parcel of wheat which lyeth nearest the church, which is directly contrary to the terrier of his own making, and which on oath he also says he knew nothing of. Upon a search lately made I am informed that there is no other terrier before or since entered in the bishops' court. The contradictory & false behaviour of this vicar as to his terrier and answer was in the opinion of Sir Thomas Trevor the then Attorney General thought to be willful perjury. It is imagined the vicar has some old person to prove the tythes were taken up in kind some one year only, but that must be between 40 & 50 years since, because it has not been done since the present vicar or his father, the immediate predecessor, have been incumbents,[3] and, if so, it was suffered by the tenant without the knowledge of Sir Richard, who has sayd no act of the tenant should hurt his inheritance.

1 Printed in Hobbs, op cit, p.17-18.
2 Quote mark not in mss, but inserted to balance quote mark at the end of the sentence.
3 This sentence interlined between the previous deletion.

I believe I have here sett forth the whole of the affair so farr as related to my grandfather. I could not tell how to make it shorter though great part of it may appear unnecessary to you, which I hope you'l excuse.

I may here observe that for upwards of 40 years past a regular and uninterrupted payment of four pounds per annum has been made as a full composition for the tythes of this estate. This I am persuaded can be supported by the oaths of several persons, particularly Peter Griffin, who is eighty two years of age, always lived in the parish, was many years a servant on the farm, & afterwards a tenant 21 years, and says he never knew any instance of the tythes on this farm being taken in kind. Therefore I rather think it was only threatened & not done. The receipts for such payments are the property of the occupier and not easily to be come at. I have one that was given to Peter Griffin by the present vicar for the use of his father, acknowledging four pounds to be in full for one year's tythes, as no tythes in kind have been paid or demanded within 40 years past. I have heard there are acts now in force in favour of so long a composition, therefore imagine this prescription will be an additional strength to me which Sir Richard had not.

I am assured the like attack is designed to be made on your brother's property at Beckhampton as the like notice has been given to the occupier there. I shall therefore here send you the words of the terrier relating to that farm vizt "the vicar hath the privilege of choosing, cutting & carrying away of an ell ridge of wheat, when ripe, upon each of the four farms at Beckampton, out of any of the pieces thereunto belonging!"[1] I believe your brother's farm was made up of two small farms, & consequently I suppose two ell ridges are demanded from it. I have heard that a composition has been paid for the said farm, upwards of 40 years, in lieu of the ell ridges & small tythes. I have no papers to give me a more clear light relating to that estate. If I had would have sent them to you. However trifling our suffering these ancient compositions to be defeated may at first sight appear to you, I am sure our grandfather & your father, if living, would strongly have opposed it, well knowing that it is opening a gate to further incroachments & contentions, which the tenants will always magnify.

I shall be glad to be favoured with your thoughts on the validity of the terrier, so ~~essentially~~ contradicted by the oath of the person who made it.

If the compositions cannot be supported, it is very essential to confine the vicar to take the ell ridges out of that piece of wheat lying nearest the church, which the vicar swore to in his answer to the bill relating to this farm, and Sir Richard was of opinion that the two ell ridges for Beckhampton Farm were those also lying nearest the church. Your advice in this affair I shall thankfully receive, but your station in the law is such that I think it will be proper to acquaint Mr. Jones of Lincoln's Inn with it, that he may appear to act for me if occasion should require. The compliments of this family wait on you, Mrs Holford, the family in

1 See Hobbs, Steven, ed. *Wiltshire glebe terriers 1588-1827.* Wiltshire Record Society 56. 2003, p.17-18.

Bedford Row, & cousin Richard, and am,
dear Sir,
your most affectionate cousin and most humble servant
S.H.
Avebury 2d December 1756

Verso Note: 2d December 1756. Letter to my cousin Peter Holford about the composition paid in full for tythes.

136. Peter Holford to Stayner Holford WSHC 184/2

Hatton Gardens
11 December 1756

Dear Sir,
I have yours of the 2d instant with an account of your evidence relating to the tythes of Abury and Beckhampton. You mistake me very much if you think I should be willing to let in the parson to make any encroachments upon the estate of my brother or your own, or that I imagine it to be a very trifling matter. I am far from thinking so in any case whatsoever, and especially in a case where I see the temper and disposition of the parsons to be so intolerably troublesome as it appears to be in the present case. By the letters you shewd me I saw enough of the man to convince me it was necessary to keep him at arms length if possible, and indeed I find the universal character of him is such that I would advise you never to write to him, for I am sure you will find no good can come of corresponding with a man of that sort. By the proceedings you have given me an account of I can learn no more than that there was a dispute between my grandfather and the parson in the year 1696 & the succeeding years, and in 1701 the matter was ended & the parson agreed to pay the costs. This determines nothing, for the same proceeded no further than the bill and answers, and it is not impossible that the parson found himself in a scrape by being detected in haveing sworn so contrarry to the terrier, and was glad to compound and get off upon paying the costs. But be that as it may, I owne I have great doubt with myself relating to the composition you seem to think is establishd, perhaps as to the question whether the right to two ell ridges is general or confined only to those nearest the church. The matter of Parson White may be very strong evidence against the present incumbent, for that answer (by order which may be [?obteind] of course if askd for) may be received in evidence in any other suit between the parson and his parishoners, but with regard to the general question whether a modus is established in this parish, I own I think both the terrier and White's answer are rather evidence against it, and I don't see any evidence that seems to me strong enough to support it; as to any Acts of Parliament in favour of the complainant, from the length of time, I know of none such, & I believe there are none, for I have known them broke thro' after a much longer time; indeed it can't be, for if there were any such it might be in the power of one parson to bind all his successors and establish a modus. For if the parson shoud happen to continue to

fifty or sixty years, & take a certain composition all that time, by this rule all future incumbents would be bound to take the same; but [?it] is certainly otherwise by the law. However, there is nothing more intricate [diffic]ult[1] to advise about than these questions concerning tythes, and if the parson does become troublesome and disturb you by breaking into the custom [ ][2] you should take the best opinions in the law; if I [?was] to recommend I should rather choose Mr Wilbraham than any other upon a question of this kind as he has had great experience in the Exchequer upon these matters which were formerly almost allways there. Of late they have come more into Chancery, but we have not had very many of them. I have seen Mr Young in town since I have been here, but he mentiond nothing to me of any notice to my brother's tenant. I desird him to enquire about it, and I dare say shall hear from him if he hears any thing material. I find he has not a better opinion of the parson than other folks, and not a very good one of the person who is manager of my brother's farm, so that he will look pretty sharply after him. I thank God we are all well here, but shall be greet sufferers in our Court by the loss of Mr Chancellor, for th[ere][3] can't be much business while the seal is in commission. [?That] will soon grow very burdensome to the suitors. I have a piece of domestick news to tell you, but would not wish you to publish it because though it has been talked of, it is not yet settled, My sister is in treaty with a gentleman upon the subject of matrimony.[4] His name is Askew, & his profession physick. His father is a very eminent physician at Newcastle, and there is a very considerable fortune in the family. I think the match is much to her advantage in point of fortune, and the gentleman of very fair character. Some little objections arise in the matter of settlement at present; but I believe will very soon be removed. Perhaps the matter may be a little delayd by his father liveing at so great a distance, and its being necessary to write to him upon every minute matter in the settlement. I have nothing to add but our compliments to the family with you, and that I am
Your affectionate cousin and obedient humble servant
P. Holford

Verso Address: To Staynor Holford esq., att his house att Abury, near Marlborough, in Wiltshire.

1 Torn.
2 Torn.
3 Torn.
4 Elizabeth Holford married Anthony Askew at Holborn, Middlesex, 7th March 1757.

137. Stayner Holford to Peter Holford[1] WSHC 184/2

Avebury
21 December 1756

Dear Sir,

I am obliged with yours of the 11th instant, and think more could not be said on the affair as related by me to you. I purpose soon to send by carrier to Mr. Jones the several papers I have mett with about it, which he will be able to digest and put things into a proper form to have Mr Wilbraham's opinion, as you have recommended if occasion should require.

I am informed by a clergyman who is acquainted with the church law, that by an act now in force of the 2d and 3d of Edward the 6th there are the following words "that every subject shall without fraud yield & pay all predial tythes in kind as hath of right been yielded & paid within forty years before the making of this act, or of right & custom ought to have been paid". I am told the following explanation has been made on these words in a like case with mine. As hath of right been yielded relates to tythes in kind yielded within forty years, and furthermore of right & custom ought to have been paid are understood to relate to a rightful custom *de modo decimandi* which ought only to be paid. Now this *modus decimandi* of £4 has been paid many years, above forty, by mine & ancestors' tenants. I offered it to pay it for the last year, & am still ready to pay it. I conceive this prescription arose at first from a real composition in lieu of the two ell ridges & small tythes, and made beyond the memory of man, which I suppose is now lost. Therefore the prescription, which has so long subsisted, I apprehend to be in my favour. Now I must here observe that John White the vicar did in his answer swear that he knew of no ancient terrier, record, or writing, setting forth the vicar's dues. Therefore can the terrier made by him a few years preceding his litigation with my grandfather, which he swore that he knew nothing of, and also on oath essentially contradicted, be admitted in evidence against my modus? The 8th of this month was appointed by the vicar to receive his customary payment for tythes. I directed my bailiff to go to him, and offer to pay him the £4 for one year to Michaelmas last, which was the year of my occupation. He refused to accept it, and said that, as a dispute was like to arise between him & me, whether there was a modus established on my farm or not, he would not then take the money for the last year, and added, that if it was a modus he ought to be paid by me for the preceding year to Michaelmas 1755, which the late tenant had not done, but if I would admit that there was no modus, he would take the £4 for the last year and for the future the tythes in kind. I would not have troubled you with so long a reply to your letter if I did not consider your brother's property & situation to be similar to mine. I was lately to see Mr. Young who has been much out of order, and acquainted him with what I had wrote to you. He seemed to imagine that you would write to him about it.

1 The letter does not name the addressee, but it obviously follows up the letter of 2nd December 1756 above. On its verso is written 'An Account of some Discourse that passed between my Brother Arthur Jones & Mr James Mayo on the 14th June 1757 relating to the Modus &c., 1757'; see below, p.309–10.

Your sister has the most sincere wishes of this family for her happiness in the affair depending. She does in our joint opinions merit a gentleman of fortune, character, & understanding, and we hope such will be her lott. Be pleased to present our best compliments, with the salutations of the approaching season to your mother & sister, which we desire you & Mrs Holford will accept, and am, dear Sir &c
S.H.
Turn over[1]

This 2d
As a limited quantity of wheat the produce of two ell ridges is allowed by the vicar to be in lieu of all tythes of corn & grass for my farm, it is admitting a modus which is in this 4th. Therefore the dispute is whether the long prescriptive payment of £4 is not to be defended, for by the management of John White, a former vicar, there is no ancient or original record to be found how such modus was first established, and the money long paid taking one year with the other, is the real value of the thing required.

Sir, this 3d which is either land, a sum of money, or yearly pension, is given to the parson £4 by composition as satisfaction of all tithes in kind.

This [?5th].

By looking over your letter again I find you do with me believe that the vicar may be obliged to take the two ell ridges out of that piece nearest the church, and have reason to believe that by my Grandfather's fixing it to that piece, and having his costs paid him he thought his conquest compleat, for by the casualties of bad seasons, ordinary husbandry, &c., which wheat is very liable to, such particular piece may be of small value to the vicar, and therefore the certain payment, which has been made during the incumbency of three successive vicars, is in favour of the vicar, & I am perswaded your brother's estate at Beckhampton has the like advantage.

138. James Mayo to Mr Jones[2] WSHC 184/2

[5th January 1757]

Sir,
If a good understanding between Mr Holford's family & mine is to subsist no longer than whilst the same be promoted, setled, and maintained, between me & any other person or persons in this parish (with whom I have at present no sort of intercourse) then I might beg leave to say that though a seeming intimacy may revive between us, yet will it again soon languish and decline. If a real friendship can be established between your family & mine I desire to go no farther. I am determined to climb no higher for fear.

This intimation is designed to prevent you from repenting of the favour this

1 Page break.
2 Probably Arthur Jones. Staynor Holford's half brother.

day intended.
Sir
Your most humble servant
James Mayo
Abury January 5th, 1757

Verso Address: To Mr Jones.

139. Stayner Holford to Peter Holford GA D1956/L1

[3 March 1757]

Dear Sir,
Soon after I was favoured with yours of the 26th of last month, Mr. Hughes came here and brought with him copies of the charges against us. I see nothing new in that relating to me, but what had been before sett forth in the petition, which was answered by the affidavit sent on that occasion, except the article about the rise of the value of corn, and that I sold the same for more than it was valued at to me. To this I must observe that the corn was only a part of other things taken in distress for my arrears of rent, which fell short in quantity, &, reckoning one article with another, the effects were not worth what they were valued at to me, and the whole valuation was a small sum short of the money due to me. I am perswaded this charge appears to you ridiculous & absurd, and presume it will to the Master who is to pass the account, because after the goods were legally valued to me, & in my possession, I undoubtedly was to stand to all casualties. I should be glad to know from you if this will be allowed a sufficient answer to that charge, or if there is a necessity of replying to it, as no sum is sett against it.

Mr. Hughes is fully enabled to reply to every other charge by the papers he had to answer the petition, which are in Mr. Edwards's hands. As to his abilities & character as a sollicitor, I can only know through Mr. Hughes, who is ready to attend the Master directly if there is an absolute necessity, but he has wrote to Mr. Edwards to have it put off till after Easter because he is engaged at this time at the Assizes & other business. Be so obliging as to send for Mr. Edwards, & direct what shall appear to you proper to be done. The advantages I receive from your friendly assistance in this affair are to me so apparent, that I must repeat my particular thanks, and am with the best compliments of all here to you & family,
Dear Sir, your affectionate cousin and obliged humble servant
Staynor Holford
Avebury 3d March 1757

Verso Address: To Peter Holford esq., at his house in Hatton Garden, Holborn, London.
Verso Note: Saturday March 26th [*illegible*].

140. Stayner Holford to Peter Holford GA D1956/L1

[30 April 1758]

Dear Sir,

Mr. Hughes[1] of Devizes sent a purpose messenger yesterday, to inform me, that he had by the last post received a letter from Mr. Edwards to acquaint him that the Master had disallowed £26 odd money paid to the sheriff's officers &c, and the Master did in the margin of his report make this item: 'it is included in the sheriff's poundage'. I am sensible this only affects Mr. Hughes. He seems disturbed at it, and signifyed a desire of my mentioning it to you. As he was in the begining of this affair, though an entire stranger to me, obliging & civil in his office of sheriff, allow me to desire the favour of you on the receipt of this to send for Mr. Edwards to know the particulars from him, because the affair is to be finally determined before the Master on tomorrow night, and I shall be glad if it should end more in favour of Mr. Hughes. Within these few days I have heard that the stock on your brother's farm[2] is soon to be valued, in order to pay the fortune due to the son of the late tenant, who is now of age, and that the farm is to be continued under the management of William Woollridge, who has been there for some years. As I have heard you have a security for the rent from Farmer Griffin of Ogbourn, I apprehend you run no risque while that subsists. I thought it right to mention the circumstance, and also to acquaint you that Mr. Young is still at Bath. We shall be glad to hear that you, Mrs Holford, and my little cousin are well, and also my aunt & the rest of the family, and am with our compliments,

Dear Sir, your affectionate cousin and humble servant

Staynor Holford

Avebury, 30th April 1758.

141. Stayner Holford to Peter Holford GA D1956/L1

[19 December 1758]

Dear Sir,

I have been informed by accident that the three gentlemen named for one to be fixed on for sheriff for this county for the ensuing year have by application to their friends obtained the promise of being excused serving that office, which was the case, I think, in the year 1756, when one Mr Jacobs[3] of Tottenham was without his knowledge appointed, which was done about the begining of January, and so calculated that he had not time to endeavour to avoid that troublesome & expensive office. The sheriff so named is, according to a cant word, called a pockett sheriff, and as I have reason to apprehend I may meet with such treatment as Mr Jacobs did, I must beg the favour of your advice & aid to keep clear of it. One Mr Maddox, Clerk of the Assize, has the list of the gentlemen of this county proper to serve, and from his list am told the judges fix

1 Solomon Hughes; see letter 10th June 1756 above.

2 At Westonbirt.

3 John Jacob, per Jackson, op cit, p.229.

on three names. As I suppose you know Mr Maddox, imagine you may easily obtain a sight of the list, and if my name is not there the reason for your looking over the list may remain with yourself, as I am desirous of keeping off it. You may also, I conceive, of him learn who is to serve, and if I should be the person fixed on, begg you will use your endeavours to gett me excused, which in justice may be urged in my behalf, as there are a great number of gentlemen in this county who have long resided here, and never served that office, and some who would be pleased with it, therefore no difficulty can arise on fixing on a proper person without fixing on me, who have resided here but a short time, and indeed my deafness renders me an improper person. To you also, my great dislike of the office, & expence attending it, make me very desirous to avoid it. I am told that, by application to any of the judges, gentlemen get clear of it, but this I leave to you. If you have the least doubt of not getting me clear, be so obliging as to lett me know by return of the post, for I am determined to use every effort in my power to avoid it, and should be glad to know when the person must be fixed on. I am assured that the gentlemen nominated, when they make interest to be excused, take the liberty of naming some person in their room, and so the appointment is accordingly made. The persons named for the ensuing year are James Harden of Mere, William Norris of Nonesuch,[1] & William Liddyard of Ogborn St. Andrew.[2] I am perswaded you will be so kind as to do what you can in this affair, and excuse this trouble given you by,

Dear Sir,
your affectionate cousin and obliged humble servant
Staynor Holford
Avebury 19th December 1758

My mother & brother join with me in the salutations of the approaching season to you, Mrs Holford, your mother and family.

If I have not an answer by first post shall depend on your interest to keep out of this troublesome office I am assured the nomination will be in a few days.

142. Samuel Martyn to Stayner Holford WSHC 184/2

31 December 1758

Sir,

I have frequently talked over the affair of your tythe with Mr Mayo, and find him still unwilling to accept of the annual payment of four pounds. He says that he can prove the taking the tythe in kind in some articles or other for many years and in particular the cutting the elridges of wheat, and that this ought to convince you that there is no modus. I find him disposed to have this matter setled amicably, and I shall be very glad to contribute every thing in my power towards effecting it, & if you are inclinable to let me see any papers &c likely to convince him

1 He actually served in 1759; cf. Jackson, op cit, p.230.

2 Ogbourne St Andrew.

that the modus is established, I will wait on you any time tomorrow you shall be pleased to appoint, or next Tuesday morning, or any other time after next week as shall be most agreeable to you for that purpose.

Mrs Martyn joyns me in the compliments of the season to yourself, Mrs,[1] and Mr. Jones[2] and we are extremely sorry it has not been in our power to have waited on you before now, but that we intend ourselves that pleasure the first light nights

I am Sir, your most obedient servant
Sam Martyn
Kennett, 31st December 1758.

Verso Address: To Stainer Holford esq^{r}., these.
Verso Note: 31st December 1758. Letter from Mr Martyn.

143. Stayner Holford to Mr Martyn WSHC 184/2

[31 December 1758]

Sir,

I cannot at present fix on any day for the business you mentioned, but, as you said some day after next week will be suitable to you, I will then appoint some day when I shall be very glad to see you to finish the affair in an amicable way, as it is my desire so to do. My mother & brother join with me in the compliments all the season, and we shall be very glad to have the favour of yours and Mrs Martin's company whenever it is agreeable to you, and am,

Sir
your most humble servant
S.H.
Avebury 31st December 1758
Sunday evening 9 o'clock

Verso Note: 31st December 1758. Letter to Mr Martyn about the affair with Mr Mayo.

144. Staynor Holford to William Norris WSHC 184/1, pt.1.

Avebury
14 June 1761

Sir,

I was favoured with your letter of the 3d instant relating to the sheep [?feed] I have on your farm here, and am equally desirous with you to have it adjusted in an amicable manner, & soon. ~~Therefore as Mr Martyn is now at Kennett~~

1 Anna Jones, who married Evan Jones after Stayner's father died.
2 Arthur Jones, Staynor's brother.

My bailiff has acquainted me that John Clements,[1] one of the assessors of the land tax for a division of this parish, read to him part of a letter which he said he had received from you, wherein you said, you had been informed I was disposed to have your farm here taxed at five pounds ~~a year~~ more than the real rent is, and that my farm is taxed at twenty pounds less than it should be. I am sorry any person should take the liberty to tell you such an notorious falsity, which I am inclined to sett you right in, notwithstanding I have not the pleasure of knowing you. It is an established rule with me to be very cautious in attending to, or believing reports raised, & artfully represented, by the generality of inhabitants of country villages, too often the cause, and most commonly designed to create misunderstanding and variance between Gentlemen, whose landed properties are contiguous, and their motives for so doing are easily seen through.

Your tenant's brother Mr John Nalder, as he has a considerable property in this parish and particularly in this tithing is in that as well in other respects a very proper person for me to consult with relating to the several rates to be raised here. He told me that you did, in his presence, insist on having an increase of rent of fifteen pounds a year to commence at Lady Day 1760. In consequence of this it was thought reasonable to desire the assessment might be made accordingly, but in being afterwards told, it was not to take place till Lady Day 1761, no additional tax was laid on your farm. Since the assessment has been preparing this year, I have been told that you have agreed with your tenant for an advance of ten pounds a year only, therefore I am sorry you should imagine I should be so weak, uncivil, & unneighbourly to desire that you should pay a tax for more rent than you have agreed for. I must furthermore observe that I am informed there is a ground rent of five pounds a year payable to you on a lease for the land where the Catharine Wheel House at Backhampton now stands. This I am sure you well know is chargeable with the land tax. Now to put it beyond all doubt in your opinion that I am disposed your property here should have every advantage, as farr as my assent will give it, have suffered the assessors to make out the rate for this present year without any additional tax for the advanced rent of ten pounds a year, & also on the five pounds a year for the ground rent.

I will now inform you how my farm stands assessed, and the reasons I imagine why you have been falsely told it is undercharged twenty pounds a year. This farm with the premises appertaining to it were used, occupied, & lett for three hundred and sixty pounds a year. My grandfather, & others my predecessors, finding great difficulty to get good tenants with a property sufficient to stock it, were compelled to lend five hundred pounds at £4 rent which occasioned the tenants to say they gave three hundred & eighty pounds a year, which sum I agreed for with my last tenant, but he failing with a large arrear of rent the neighbouring farmer said it was owing to the farm being over rented, upon which I consented to lett it for three hundred & sixty pounds a year, and treated with three different persons about it, but they refusing it on those conditions, I

1 John Clements was the Avebury schoolmaster and vestry clerk, who subsequently became a surveyor; see *AWS*, p.64–5.

was most unwillingly forced into the occupation of it. This being the true case, I am sure neither you, or any Gentleman acting as a Commissioner of the Taxes would think it reasonable for me to pay a proportion more than after the rate of £360 a year ~~and if this should not give content, and I be forced to an appeal, I then as the law directs shall apper upon oath, that the person, who seemed most [*illegible*] desirous, & in real earnest to take the estate offered only three hundred & twenty pounds a year.~~[1] And I assure you I can make it appear on oath that the sum offered me was considerably less. The house I live in has wrongfully been represented to be separated from the farm, for till very lately the tenants lived in it, and I have now only a small unfinished house, which my servant must dispense with, but not such as a person of suitable circumstances to occupy the farm would be satisfyed with. And if such separations & distinctions of landed property are to be made by mistaken people, it will be productive of many disputes in this neighbourhood & other places. Therefore I am inclined to think you will take a proper opportunity to signify me your thoughts on what I have here said. A long harmony & friendship subsisted between your Grandfather & mine, which was not to be disturbed by misrepresentation.
I am Sir, your most obedient Servant
S.H.
Avebury, 14th June 1761.

Turnover[2]
P.S.
Upon my coming to reside here, I found that I was overcharged in the land tax.

On my inquiry into the cause of it, was told that it was usual to lay more in proportion on the great farms than on the others. This grievance I had remedied, and your farm received the proportional benefit.

Verso Note: Mr Holford's answer to the [blank]. The underwritten is what Mr Holford has to offer for his being relieved in the land tax.
14th June 1761. Letter to Wm Norris, esq., at Bath.

145. William Norris to Stayner Holford WSHC 184/1, pt.1.
[2 March 1762]

Sir
I am now to acknowledge the receipt of your letter of the 24th of last month touching the affaire now in treaty between us. The inclosed one of Mr Mayo relative to his motives for not relinquishing his right of feed for a few poultry sheep on the piece of land at Beckhampton. as it impeaches, or at least seems to impeach, my character, so it justly merits my Indignation.

Had the Vicar sett before you in a fair light the dispute between himself,

1 Deleted in mss.
2 Page break.

Glasier the landlord,[1] & Hiscock the tenant of the Catherine Wheel, & my overtures on Glasier's behalfe in consequence thereof, it would not have answered his purpose, as his reasons, assigned in the letter, to every candid & impartial person would appear altogether frivolous & insufficient.

For this cause the cunning Priest (for Priests to their own emolument were ever so) has thought proper to throw a veil over the naked transaction, & thereby conceal its deformity, well knowing that in its undress it could not but disgust the unprejudiced observer. Tis now my business to strip it naked, if I may be allowed the expression, & divest if of its mask, in which view the cunning, the insincerity of the Vicar, that pretended defender of the antient glebe of Avebury, will manifestly appear.

About three years ago Glasier, the landlord of the Catherine Wheel, attended by his attorney, came to inform me that an action was brought against Hiscocks his tenant by Mr Mayo the Vicar of Avebury, in quality of Vicar, for pulling down & removing a wall erecting by the said Vicar in front of the said Catherine Wheel Inn, &, as they apprehended, on part of the land granted on lease to the late George Stretch. As at that time I was entirely unacquainted with the situation of my property at Avebury, with the nature of the exchange of lands that had lately taken place there (which exchange by the bye I have many reasons to wish had never been effected), I promised Glasier my countenance on that occasion, not knowing that the piece of land in question had, by the late award, been allotted to the Vicar. After Glasier had been at much trouble & expense in this affair, & that notice of tryal had been given him, it was discovered that the Vicar's right was too well grounded to admit of a dispute, and which the vicar (had he, in his composition, less of the flesh & more of the Spirit) might have imparted to his opponent at the beginning, but that would not have answered his purposes. No! The flesh prevailed, the Vicar had another purpose to serve, to which his pretended zeal for, & defence of, the ancient glebe of Abury was only a cloak, as will appear by the sequel. Such being the situation of things, Glasier applied to me, some little time before the Assizes, to use my endeavours to prevail on the Vicar to putt off the tryal, if possible, to accommodate matters some other way. In this view I wrote to Mr Martyn, his attorney in the cause, I believe aright, as the vicar observes in his letter, offer him an equivalent, or even a piece of land of greater value than that in dispute (which offer I am yet ready to make good when properly called upon) but as to any other kind of compensation, as intimated in his letter, I defy the priest or any of his agents to make it appear

That the tryal was putt off is certain; & that the priest still has it in his power to bring it on again is no less certain; but that a verdict, as he seems to suggest, would have been given in his favour, is not quite so certain; as Glasier's council were too well apprised of the iniquity & indirect tendency of the action to lett it pass unnoticed by the court & jury. They would have been informed

1 One wonders if he was a partner in Glasier & Co., the Bristol coachmasters, who in 1768 were running no fewer than twelve services per week to London (presumably passing through Beckhampton); see *AWS*, p.39.

that the design of it was to compel Hiscocks, or Glasier, one or both of them, to reimburse to the Vicar a sum of money which he had inadvertently obligated himself to pay on Stretch's account, then, at the same time, a long, & as I am told, unadjusted account between him & Stretch for lodging, board &c is yet depending, not to mention some private anecdotes that might have appeared, on that occasion, relative to the Vicar, & perhaps, not in the least advantagious to his character. From what has been presented, I will leave you to judge whether the Vicar's reasons for not signing the article are not, as I have said before, equally frivolous & insufficient. After having been allready so prolix, into which I have been led by the suggestions of Mr Mayo , so greatly to my prejudice, I cannot well think of detaining you much longer.

In regard to the many advantages resulting from the late exchange, which not only yourself, but many of your neighbours, are pleased to bestow, in such profusion upon my farms at Avebury, give me leave to observe to you that, at present, &, I fear in future, they will be found to exist only in nubilus, for I dare affirm, & have by me authentick vouchers to prove it, that, notwithstanding the large expence of many hundred pounds, allready incurred by this exchange, my estates there are now lett, at a less rent than they have been for fourscore years past. Now wherein the reality of these advantages consists I must own I am much at a loss to find out.

I cannot well conclude, Sir, without assuring you that I am equally desirous with yourselfe of finally adjusting matters between us if it can be done upon reasonable termes, & have given Mr Martyn full power to treat on that head, but to comply precipitately with the demands of all parties concerned, however unreasonable & exorbitant they are, is, I am persuaded, what neither Mr Holford nor any Gentleman of character would expect.

I am, Sir,
Your most obedient Servant,
Wm Norris

Mr Martyn has promised to call upon me, the middle of this week, to confer farther about this affair.
The Circus, Bath, March 2d 1762

Verso Note: A Letter of Mr Norris to be preserved, 1761.[1]

146. Peter Holford to Staynor Holford[2] WSHC 184/1, pt.1.
[15 December 1763]
Verso Address: To Staynor Holford, esq., att Avebury, near Marlborough, Wilts.

Verso Note:

1 This date seems to be in error; should be 1762.
2 The text of this letter is missing.

15th December 1763
Letter from my Cousin Peter Holford about the Death of his Brother Robert & the disposition of his fortune.

147. William Fowler to Staynor Holford WSHC 184/1, pt.1.

Backhampton
6 April 1765

Sir,
I am informed Mr Popham will not grant me a licence on the next licencing day because I am the turnpike man. To remove that objection I think it right to acquaint you that I am very ready to resign that employment into the hands of the Trustees at their next meeting, or whenever they shall think proper, and to shew my respect to the Commissioners, & also to prevent any inconvenience, or injury arising to the toll, I will consent that the person who shall be appointed my successor may attend at my house to receive the toll at the gate till a convenient house is erected for that purpose. I humbly hope you will gett this represented to Mr Popham, and that he then will be so good as to sign a licence for me as usual
I am, Sir
Your Most Humble Servant
William Fowler

Verso Address: To Staynor Holford, esqr.

148. Staynor Holford to Edward Popham, J.P. WSHC 184/1, pt.1.

Avebury
4 January 1766

Sir,
By the death of William Fowler on the 26th September last, who kept the Hare & Hounds at Beckhampton, the house, & lands thereto belonging are become my property, which house was erected in the Year 1669 being then thought absolutely necessary for a publick house for the entertainment of travellers of the inferiour sort, and a parcel of lands granted at the same time for the resting of fatt cattle for the markets in London. On this establishment it has continued ever since without any interruption till the 29th September last. I have lett the house & lands to one John Coombs, whom I have reason to believe will behave in a decent, sober, & proper manner suitable to his station. He waits on you with a certificate[1] from the principal inhabitants of this parish setting forth their sentiments of him, and that it is necessary to continue this house as a Publick House.

I shall therefore esteem it a great favour if you will order a licence to be made out for him. I purposed waiting on you this day, but am out of order with a cold, therefore hope you will pardon this interruption, and am,

1 The certificate is printed below, p.313

Sir,
Your most Obedient humble Servant
S.H.
To Edward Popham Esq

Verso Note: 4th January 1766. Letter to Mr Popham to desire a licence for John Coombs to keep a publick house.

149. Peter Holford to Stayner Holford WSHC 271/14

Westonbirt near Tetbury
15th October 1766

Dear Sir
I have intended for some time past to have come over for one day to Beckhampton and Avebury to enquire a little how things went on at my farm,[1] & pay a visit to you, but we have had so much disturbance in this part of the country that our time has been sufficiently engaged, and we have not been without some apprehensions of danger to our houses and even our persons in this neighbourhood, but besides this I am now attacked with a little complaint that has made me lay aside all thought of any excursions, & think only of going directly home to London. I have had a violent pain in my back that made it very difficult for me to rise out of a chair. I could scarce turn in bed nor possibly walk cross a room without assistance. I am now better, but not well enough to ride, but I suppose I coud do well enough in a coach or chaise, and propose going to London sometime next week. I believe I shall humbly have the pleasure of seeing you this season as I propose to go the Cirencester road home but should be obliged to you for a little intelligence, as it is long since I heard from Mr. Young, and do not know where he is or whether he has been at Fyfield for a twelve month past. I hope you have not in any respect found any inconvenience from the rioters. I find your neighbourhood has not been quite free from them. I have promised to meet some great neighbours tomorrow at Tetbury, and the high sheriff by their desire to consent on some method for preventing future disturbances here. I never acted as a Justice of Peace in the county, nor do I know that I am in the Commission. But Lord Botetourt[2] assures me I am. However I never qualified.[3] I have indeed a commission as one of the Deputy Lieutenants of the county, which I accepted at the desire of Lord Ducy when he was Lord Lieutenant,[4] but have scarce thought of it since. However, I think the duty of every gentleman in the country who has strength and health enough to be active at this time and give the best assistance

1 At Beckhampton.

2 Norborne Berkeley, 4th Baron Botetourt, MP for Gloucestershire 1741-63, and colonel of the Gloucestershire Militia from 1758, who became governor of Virginia in 1768. See *Oxford Dictionary of National Biography*.

3 That is, he had never taken his *dedimus potestatem* – his oath – or paid his fees. Hence he could not legally act.

4 Matthew Ducie Moreton, 2nd Baron Ducie, of Tortworth, held the office 1755-8.

in his power. This I have determined to do, and flatter myself I have been of some little use in helping to quell some insurrections, and am assisting to supply the poor with bread, which they had made very difficult by the very means they took to prevent a scarcity. A letter proves too too short to explain this to you, only in general I can say we do not grow corn enough in this country to supply our cloth manufacturers, and by their rioting they had stopd all carriage and communication with those countries from whence the supply comes. This is now in some degree opened, and I hope we shall be at peace, but I am not clear in that. If the little military force we have was absent, I would not answer for the consequences till some further regulations have taken place. But Sir I beg the favor to hear from you as soon as convenient, directed here, to let me know if Mr. Young is in the country, and if you think my comeing will be attended with any particular conveniences I will endeavour if I am well to come that way home and stay with your leave a few hours at your house. If I do it will be only my wife & self and Sally in a postchaize, and I shall send my servants in the coach home by Cirencester. I shall be allways glad to see you and hear of your health. By the papers I fear Mr Jones has lost his brother.[1] I am sorry for it if it be so, the rather as he must be a considerable loss to his family. My wife & Sally desire their respects, I beg mine to Mr & Mrs Jones and am Sir,
Your affectionate cousin and obedient humble servant
P. Holford
Verso Address:
To: Staynor Holford esq., Att Avebury near Marlborough, Wilts.

150. Mr Jones to Lord Bruce WSHC 9/35/178

Avebury
[12 August 1773]

Mr. Jones returns his most respectful compliments and thanks to Lord Bruce for his present of fine venison.

Avebury Saturday 12th August 1773.

Whenever Lord Bruce crosses this part of the country Mr Jones. would be glad of the honour of showing him every civility in his power.

151. Arthur Jones to Mrs Williamson WSHC 271/2

[23 April 1784]

Dear Niece,
The reasons for my replying so soon to your last is to answer your question about the plan of this farm. I delivered it to you to get it refresht or new tracet to preserve it as it was then done. But if you know of any man who will not only do that but will give you a fresh copy of it for about 14s or 15s I have no objection

1 This was probably Thomas Jones, who was buried at St Stephens, Coleman Street, London on 12th October 1766 – three days before this letter was written.

to such expence. The antiquity of the old one should be preserved, because time gives sanction & authority to the possession, custom & usage of landed property. If a new copy is to be made from it, it is proper for my name and the date of the year should be inserted with these additional words, that is, the Royalty & Manor of Avebury with the Manor of Truslows Avebury. This is necessary because I have lately purchased the last and am vested with two distinct manors, & appoint two game keepers for the same. I think you must be tired with what I have already said about the paper. The defect of my sight is to be out of the question, the Colenel[1] & you are to please yourselves. If fashionable, handsome, & proper you are to have the credit of it. If not so, you are to have the blame. So look to it. You are not limitted as to price. Sorry to hear you had the headache by your last note. The weather at this instant promises to change for the better. Indeed I wish much for it, for I am still suffering. With love & good wishes, I am yours & Colonel's affectionate unkle
Arthur Jones
Avebury
23d April 1784

PS what is become of Mr. Charles Garth's widow & family

Verso Note: Mr Jones, 23d April 1784.
Verso Address: [Mrs] Williamson, [ ] Gardens, London.

152. Arthur Jones to Mrs Williamson WSHC 271/16

[8 December 1786]

Dear Neice,
I am with you much surprised at your not hearing from France at the time you mentiond. It is as natural to believe he is getting better, and that your sister's attention is taken up with nursing, as to think he is no more.[2] However, according to your promise, I shall depend on hearing from you on the next report from your sister. I am daily getting better, but my legs will not suffer me to walk much, and am not yet fixt about my going to Bath. Am glad their Majesties were so gracious to you when at Court, and I will insist on it it [sic] our duty, right, and sensable to be pleased with it. I have for some time past felt an unpleasant sensation in my bowels, and am forct to be very attentive to what I eat and drink. Your advice joined with Mr Devans on this head may be of help. I have been thinking tincture of rhubarb may be of use. If so the essential is to have the best rhubarb properly prepared from the best brandy, a pint of which send me packt in a strong bottle to the care of Mr Higgins. I have received the cloths. Thank the Colonel for his care about it, but shall not attempt to fitt it on till I am stronger. Let the ring remain in your hands till I direct the conveyance of it. I wish the Colonel at his leisure to

1 Adam Williamson.
2 The reference is probably to William Belford, the husband of Ann's sister Mary.

say how the mony matters stand between us. You never said how the Bristol wine turned out. George Cuthbert is here. He told me he was lately in town, when he askt you to stand godmother to his child. I am glad Lord Ailesbury is polite and civil to the Colonel and you. If I was the original cause it's the more pleaseing to me. I need not say the repitition of report of your & Colonel's health afford me pleasure. I am your very affectionate uncle
A. Jones
Avebury
8th December 1786

Verso Address: Colenel Williamson, Spring Gardens, London.

153. John Ward to Adam Williamson WSHC 184/6

[undated, early 1791]

If all the landowners in Avebury are competent to enter into, and will enter into … reasonable articles of agreement properly drawn up, referring it to Commissioners to divide and allot the common fields &c of Avebury in severalty, I see no great reason why that method should not be preferred to the more authentic one of applying to Parliament. But it is probable that all the proprietors will not come into reasonable terms, and some of them may not be competent on account of their being minors, tenants for life only, or from other disabilities, and therefore it is most probable you will find it necessary to apply to Parliament. I think there can be no difficulty in ascertaining your property as it now lies, nor in allotting you an aquivalent in severalty, whether are you are absent or present, if your people know your sentiments as to the situation you would wish your land to[1] to lie in. It generally happens, however, on these occasions that the little freeholders have their allotments laid nearest home, and the great landowners are obliged to take part only of their lands near home, and be content to have the remainder made up by the distant lands, in which case they have a greater quantity in proportion to the inferior quality and relative situation of their allotments, which are capable also of improvement by building a barn [?or] stable upon them. One of your greatest difficulties with or without an act may probably be the fixing on Commissioners. Three are as many as are necessary, but the freeholders will have a jealousy of your choosing two of them, and on the other hand you would not like for them to choose two. There may be also objections to your choosing one, the rest of the freeholders another, & for these two to fix on a third - or for the person who has the second estate in the place choosing the third.

When you have fully made up your mind to the business, it would perhaps be the most advisable measure for you to call a meeting of all the freeholders at Avebury to take the matter into consideration, when I shall be readily able to form an opinion whether an agreement without an act will do. And at the same time it would be vastly desirable if three commissioners could be agreed upon

1 Page break.

by a general consent, without any particular choice. Suppose, for instance, the 3 gentlemen now employed in a similar business for 5 tithings in which Lord Ailesbury is principal ownerr[1].

Verso Note: Mr Ward's letter to me. I keep the original.

154. John Ward to Adam Williamson WSHC 184/6

Marlborough
3rd May 1791

Dear Sir,
Mrs. Williamson desires me to send you the enclosed sketch of a letter,[2] which it may be convenient (if you please to write it to me) to produce when the bill is in Parliament as my authority to signify your consent. The business wears a very favourable aspect, & I think there can be little doubt of the act being obtained the next session of Parliament.

I hope this will find you in perfect health & spirits. Mrs Ward & my brother join me in respectful compliments & the most sincere good wishes for your health & happiness. Your very amiable lady appears very well, but I have long perceived that she will not be at ease till she is with you at Jamaica.
I am Sir (with great esteem), your obliged & most obedient humble servant
John Ward

Note written at right angles across the top of the letter: Answered 4th July 1791. Dated 3[d] May. Ward.

Verso Address: Major General Williamson &c, Jamaica.

155. Adam Williamson to John Ward WSHC 184/6

Jamaica
[3 May 1791][3]

Sir,
Though you are already acquainted with my wishes respecting the Avebury enclosure, it may be proper for you to have express directions under my hand, & therefore I hereby desire you will apply to Parliament the next session for a bill for dividing and allotting the common fields, downs, &c., of Avebury, and to give the proper notices, draw up a petition in my name, and pursue the other usual measures for that purpose, and you will signify before the Committees of Parliament my consent and wish that the bill may pass into a law
I am &c

1 Conjectural reading.
2 See next letter.
3 This letter is undated, but was drafted by John Ward, and sent to Adam Williamson for approval with his letter 3rd May 1791.

A W
To Mr. John Ward, Marlborough, Wilts.

Verso Note: Sketch of a letter proposed to be written by General Williamson to J. Ward.

156. Richard Hickley to Mrs Williamson WSHC 184/6

Avebury
28th June 1791

Honoured Madam,
I shall have the sheep shorn this day week, that is the 5th July. Will if possible get the man to weigh it in the course of the same week, but if so twill be near a fortnight before I can pay the money to Mr Ward. You say Scanes money is £60, is that right.[1] As to others, must play them of as well as I can. Don't know what to say about butter, the cows gives but very little milk indeed. Wee could make a small matter more, but if so must throw all the scumed milk to the pigs, which would be a great waste as now wee can make a very small chees every day.
I am Madam your very humble servant
Richd Hickley

Quite dryed up for want of rain.

Verso Address: Mrs Williamson
Verso Note: 28th June 1791 letter.

157. Richard Hickley to Mrs Williamson WSHC 184/6

[29 July 1791]

Honoured Madam,
I was much pleased to receive yours of the 24th, and very glad to hear you are so well. Have been anxious to hear from you for some time. Should have wrote long since but waited to hear from you first. Am sorry to find wee are not to see you once more before you go. May the great preserver of all things send you a safe voige and a happy meeting with the best of men. Many thanks for your kind letter, likewise for a very nice pare of spectacles. Have sealed your letter and sent it to Mr Ward. Will in two or three days carry him the money to pay Bet Scane. She is now in the country, as I suppose waiting for the money. Indeed, one day I met her by chance, told her she should have the money before she left Avebury. As to Phillips, he must wait till Michaelmas for his. Have sold the wool, and received £1 5s 0d per tod, the same as I did the last year, and at same time

1 Elizabeth Scane, servant, received a legacy of £80 in Arthur Jones's will; see TNA PROB11/1181/174

received the remainder for last year which came to four pounds. Next week I will send you the stated account from the 22d June to the 31 July. Am sorry to say the wheat in our neighbourhood, particularly at Avebury has suffered very much by the frost we had in June. The barley & oats are good. I observe what you say about cuting the corn, but in general wee are condemned for cuting it too soon. Shall not begin this fortnight, let the weather be ever so fine. The hay, though but a small crop, has been made very well. Shall finish in about a week more, & hope wee shall bring about the exchange of lands, as I am hartily sick of cows. Will take care to have the dogs fed as well as possible. Old Joe[1] is quite stout, eats & drinks all day long. Believe has taken a fresh lease of his life.

Thank God the rioting is over. You are certainly right as to Dr Priestly[2] being a very bad man. I have known him many years since when he lived at Calne, & told Mr Robert Nalder[3] when first heard of it that Priestly was at the bottom of the mischief. But he is a great favourite of the Nalders.

My wife joins with me in duty to you and hartily wishes you a safe arrival at Jamaica.

I am, Madam, with great respect, your very humble servant
Richd Hickley
Avebury
29th July 1791.

Verso Note: July 29th 1791. Letter
Verso Address: Mrs Williamson, Dover

158. Richard Hickley to Mrs Williamson WSHC 184/6
Avebury

3 August 1791

Honoured Madam,

I received your note yesterday. Am very glad to hear my master is quite well. My wife desires her duty & many thanks for your kind intended present. Inclosed is the stated account from the 22d June to 30th July by which there is a balance of £38 10s 5½d due to you. Think Col. Jones is right with respect to feeding cows with potatoes. Will try them in the winter. The garden I think has turned out tollerable well considering what this season has been. As to fruit, little or none. The frost took care to send all that going. But the young trees grow very well. I cald on Mr Ward yesterday as Scane is not going from Avebury this week. Shall carry the money to Marlbro next Monday, which will suit me better than this week. Will pay Phillips as soon as I can, perhaps about Michaelmas. Forgot in my last to mention the plan of the Downs which J. Clements drawed. Twil be proper for me to have it, likewise the plan of the estate, but that of the Downs in

1 Joseph Brown.
2 One of the founders of English Unitarianism, who lived at Calne between 1773 and 1780. He worked as librarian at Bowood House; cf. *VCH Wilts* 17, p.109.
3 A prominent Avebury dissenter; see *AWS*, p.108.

particular. Suppose Mr Holford don't intend exchanging his lands, as he has gave Mr Ward[1] no answer, or Mr Symkins either, but as it can be done without them it don't signify. Thank God all is well at Avebury
I am, Madam, your most obedient humble servant
Richd Hickley

Verso Note: August 3d 1791; letter.
Verso Address: Mrs Williamson, Dover

159. Richard Hickley to Mrs Williamson WSHC 184/6

Avebury
22 August 1791

I am very glad to hear by Mrs Belford that my master & your self are quite well. Am very busie with the harvest. Thank God the weather is remarkable fine. Wee began reaping Wednesday last, hope shall finish this week. The wheat has suffered by the frost, but not so much as I expected. If the weather continues fine wee shall have a quick harvest. Mr Ward came over yesterday with the notice for the inclosure. Fixed it on the church door, and stayed the service of the church. He will attend two more Sundays. Thank God the cattle of all kinds are very well.
I am, Madam, with great respect, your most obedient humble servant
Richd Hickley

Verso Note: 22nd August 1791
Verso Address: Mrs Williamson.

160. Richard Hickley to Adam Williamson WSHC 184/6

Avebury
4 October 1791

I hope in God my mistress and Mr Belford is safe arrived and in good health.[2] Think by the uncommon fine weather we have had for some time, they must have had an exceeding good voyage. Don't remember such weather at this season of the year. Am hartily glad to hear you are quite well. Inclosed is the farm account from the 30th July to to the 24th September, which when compared with the last account sent my mistress believe you will find right. Have had an exceeding fine harvest, the crops on the whole pretty good. Hope now the expensive time is over to raise money to pay the bills &c. Thank God the cattle of all kinds are very well. Am sorry the wheat markets are coming down so fast, best wheat £12 per load, but don't think it will be so cheap long. Barley sells for

1 'Mr W' in mss.
2 Mrs Williamson actually arrived in Jamaica 31st October 1791; Jamaican Family Search **www.jamaicanfamilysearch.com/Members/Barche03.htm**

a good price, from 26 to 30 shillings per quarter. Am busie planting the crop for the next harvest, but want rain very much, the ground is a great deal to dry. I fear sheep will be rather cheap this fall; shall know more about it after Weyhill fair.[1] My self and wife desire our duty to you & my mistress, and I am, with great respect,
Sir, your most obedient humble servant,
Richd Hickley

Verso Note: Letter, Hickley, 4th October 1791.

161. John Ward to Mary Belford WSHC 184/6

Marlborough
5 October 1791

Madam,
I have received the enclosed letter from Richard Durnell, & have underwritten a copy of my answer to him. If you have no directions about the legacy, I will request favor of you to forward the letter to General Williamson in your next packet for directions, with Mrs Ward's & my respectful compliments. As soon as you have any advice of Mrs Williamson I shall esteem it a particular obligation if you will favour me with the accomt of hers and your sons safety.

I have seen Mr. Hughes[2] the attorney concerned for the Ogbourne inclosure. He does not appear desirous of joining with Avebury which he thinks will save very little money, as there would be double fees if they were joined, & the Ogbourne act will have very many particular clauses in it relating to the property belonging to King's College, Cambridge, & that college will expect to choose a Commissioner, so that on the whole it is probable that Avebury must have a seperate act & have no concern with Ogbourn.

Lord Ailesbury has had a fall from his horse, by which he has hurt his right hand, but is in no pain, & is getting well fast. Lord Sydney is at Tottenham Park.[3]

Mrs Ward joins me in respectful compliments to yourself, the Miss Belfords & Reynolds.[4]

I am, Madam, your most obedient humble servant
John Ward

Note written at right angles across the top of the letter: Answered by the Sandwich, 15th January 1792. Dated 5th October 1791.

1 A century earlier, Defoe wrote that Weyhill was 'the greatest fair for sheep … that this nation can shew'. That had not changed; see Bettey, J.H. *Rural Life in Wessex 1500-1900.* Alan Sutton, 1987, p.82.
2 He has not been identified.
3 'T.P.' in mss.
4 Elizabeth Rennald was buried 2nd August 1803; Mary Rennald on 14th March 1804; they were aged 67 and 69 respectively. They resided in the manor house, and were presumably sisters, probably related to General Williamson.

Verso Note: Mrs Belford[1] to be sent to my sister next packet Avebury

162. John Ward to Richard Durnell[2] WSHC 184/6

5 October 1791

Sir,

I have received yours, in answer to which I write to inform you that General and Mrs Williamson are gone to Jamaica, and have left no papers or orders with me respecting your son's legacy.[3] I will send your letter to the General by the first packett, & make no doubt but I shall have orders to pay you the legacy if the case is as you state it, in the course of 4 or 5 months, with interest from the time of its becoming payable. If on inquiry I find anyone at Avebury has authority to pay you, you shall hear from me in a few days.

I am
your humble servant
J. Ward

163. Richard Hickley to Adam Williamson WSHC 184/6

Avebury
31 October 1791

Honoured Sir,

Have sent the account from ye 24th September to ye 28th October by which there is a ballance to you of £7 8s 10d. Hope before this time my mistress is safe with you and in good health. Thank God we are all well at Avebury. In my next shall make myself debtor for the sheep, have sold them, but they are not taken away yet. The sheep fairs have been rather better than was expected. Barley sells well, but wheat is very low. Have just got the seed into the ground; a very fine season for sowing. The winter seems seting in betime. Mrs Tanner, your tenant at Hungerford, is dead about a fortnight since. I went to her son immediately about the rent as I found he was clearing the house, for fear he should pay the rent to Mr Munday. He has promised to pay me three quarters, which will be due ye 5th February next, provided you give me a line in your next authorising me to receive it, as I am a stranger to him. He don't chuse to pay the money without it. Brown[4] has let the other house adjoining to a Mr Manning,[5] a clergyman, who is coming to serve the church at Hungerford for one year certain at twelve guineas,

1 Ann Williamson's sister Mary married Captain Belford; cf. Boddington, Reginald Stewart. 'Jones', *Pedigree register*, 1, 1908, p.200.

2 Durnell is not named in the letter, but his name is inferred from the contents of Ward's letter to Mrs Belford, as above.

3 It has not been possible to identify this legacy; the name Durnell is not mentioned in any Avebury will.

4 He was described as a gardener in the letter below dated 30th March 1794, and appears to have been employed to look after Williamson's Hungerford property.

5 He has not been identified.

& the two paddocks belonging to the mansion at two guineas per year making together 14 guineas per year, to commence from Michaelmas. I intend going to Bath next week to settle with Mrs Jenny,[1] then on to Bristol and pay Eames[2] & Hale,[3] wine merchants.
I am Sir, with great respect, your most obedient humble servant
Richd Hickley

Verso Note: Hickley letter October 31st 1791.

164. Richard Hickley to Adam Williamson WSHC 184/6

[5 December 1791]

Honoured Sir,
Inclosed is the farm account from the 28th October to the 5th December, by which there is a ballance due to you of £140 6s 8d, which with the last ballance believe you will find right. Hope my mistress & yourself are in good health, & that the country agrees with her. Hope poor Tom is better. I have paid old Joe one year's annuity due to him Michaelmas 1790.[4] Though my mistress said nothing to me about it, I thought it right to pay him as he was quite pennyless. Paid the Miss Renald fifty pounds due this day, for which have taken their joint receipt. Likewise paid my self one year's waigers due last Michaelmas, & four pound ten shillings for one year's intrest on the hundred pounds left by my master.[5] Have bought a good strong cart horse of Mr Nalder.[6] Thinks as soon as I can spare the money to have another of him, then shall make shift for some time. Should be glad to buy a good mare to breed colts if I can meet with one. Wee have one mare in fold. The old gray horse is dead, but that is no loss at all, as he was quite worn out with old age. I have not been to Bath yet, as I could not make it convenient, purpose going in a few days. The gentleman that took the house at Hungerford insisted on haveing that as Mrs Tanner lived in. I thought it better to let him have it then to shut them both up. So there is half a year due from Tanner 5th November last, and Mr Manning takes it up from Michaelmas. The gardener has enlarged the clumps of firs going to the Down. Made one on the wall ditch behind Crook's house,[7] one by the reck barton gate, likewise a good one in Hatchet's Field. I have fenced them with odd stuff as cheap as possible.

1 Her house was in Miles Court, Bath, according to Sir Adam Williamson's will; cf. TNA PROB 11/1315/334.
2 John Eames was a wine merchant at 9 Queen Square, Bristol, c.1783-1794; see **http://westcountrybottles.co.uk/mike4/P17.html**
3 Henry Hale was a wine merchant at Redcross Street, Bristol, c.1793-1794; see **http://westcountrybottles.co.uk/mike4/P17.html**
4 Joseph Brown, servant, received an annuity of £10 in the codicil to the will of Arthur Jones, 21st January 1786; cf. TNA PROB11/1181/174.
5 See Arthur Jones's will, TNA PROB11/1181/174. Hickley also received a life interest in the tenement he occupied, and his daughters received £10 each.
6 Robert Nalder.
7 This might be either Stephen or William Crook; see *AWS,* p.71-2.

Hope now wee have done with painting & carpenters.

Had on Saturday night last a deep snow, since that very hard frost. That is no good for the hay. Thank God all is well at present.

My wife & self desire our duty to you & my mistress, & I am, Sir, your very humble servant
Richd Hickley
Avebury 5th December 1791

Verso Note: Hickley letter December 5th 1791. Answered February pacquet 1792, & wrote also to Gardiner.
Verso Address: Major General Williamson, Jamaica.

165. Richard Hickley to Adam Williamson[1] WSHC 184/6
[2 January 1792]

Honoured Sir,
I hope my mistress and you are in good health. Wee are in expectation every day of hearing from you. By the inclosed account there is a ballance due to you of £39 10[s] 4[d], which hope you will find right when compared with the last. I have been to Bath and Bristol, paid Mr Wiltshire and the wine merchants. Wiltshire's bill was more than I expected, but believe it to be right [£]32 0[s] 6[d]. Mr Eames & Hale [£]47 18[s] 6[d]. Have been twice to Bath to settle with Mrs Jenny. The first time she was not at home the second met with her just arrived. She raised many difficultys, but has promised to give me a letter in a fortnight's time to come and settle. Hope in my next to give you a full account; she is a very odd lady. Thank God the cattle and all things are well on the farm. Wheat £12 per load, barley 32s per quarter.
I am, Sir, your most obedient humble servant,
Richd Hickley
Avebury 2d January 1792

May God send you a happy new year and many of them.

Verso Note: January 2d 1792

166. Richard Hickley to Mrs Williamson WSHC 184/6
[30 January 1792]

Honoured Madam,
Your letter gave us all great pleasure to hear of your safe arrival and finding my master in good health. Am sorry you had such a narrow escape. Since that have had a letter from Mrs Belford, which if possible gave us more pleasure then the former. Hope in God things will turn out as one could wish. By the account sent

1 An arithmetical calculation on one of the folios of this letter is not transcribed here.

there is a ballance due to my master of £10 1s 10d, which I believe is right. Have heard nothing of Miss Jenny since I was at Bath. By the advice of Mrs Renalds and sent her a hare and a brace of snipes as by your order, to keep her in good humour. Fear I shall have a hard matter to get the rent of her. If don't hear from her soon will go down again. There has been a gentleman to take Stoney Hall. He likes the place and is to let one know when to meet him there. Miss Renalds agree with me and thinks twill be much the best to let it as it will soon tumble to pieces if not inhabited. Suppose we may get about forty pounds per year for it. He comes from Maidenhead, I don't know his name. Hope the exchange of lands will go on soon after the Parliament meets. The Beckhamton people are like to come into it. Mr Ward has wrote to Mr Holford. He says if the Duke of Marlbrough and Mr Sutton are agreeable he shall have no objection, and I find they are agreeable. If so wee shall have it don compleate, but fear twill not be forward enough to stop the cows from going another summer. I will follow Mr Ward to drive it as fast as possible. Thank God the cattle of all kinds are well, but, haveing such a short cut of hay last summer, fear I must buy a great deal, which is the worst thing a farmer has to do. But a great deal depends on the spring. Have bought a mare of Farmer Packer, which intends for breeding. Have had bad luck with the mare that was in fold. About three weeks since she cast her colt. Cannot account for it, as she had don but very little work for some time, but those things often happen. I have taken the bond of Packer. Miss Rennald saw it canceled. Would have sent it to you, but thought it not worth while. Poor Shipway[1] has lost his wife; she has left him five small children. What is become of poor Tom. I saw his father and mother the other day. They seems very uneasy at not hearing from him, and says they are sure he is dead. Hope [?Tins] is well

My self, wife and children, Mitchel,[2] gardener, Ruth,[3] Joe, and every one begs yours and my master's acceptance of our duty and I am, with great respect, Madam, your very humble servant
Richd Hickley
Avebury
30th January 1792

Verso Note: 30th January 1792. Letter.
Verso Address: Mrs Williamson.

167. Richard Hickley to Mrs Williamson WSHC 184/6

[6 March 1792]

Honoured Madam,
I am very glad to hear by your letter that you, my master, and Mrs Belford are

1 John Shipway was a mason who did some work for the Williamsons; see *AWS*, p.306-7.
2 The housekeeper in the manor house.
3 The maid at the farm; see below, Hickley's letter 2nd February 1794. She left her position to be married, but no marriage (or subsequent baptism) appears in the parish register.

all well. By the account sent there is a ballance due to me of £4 5[s] 6[d], which believe is right. I observe what you say about oxen. To be sure, where people has conveniance to keep them they pay very well, but Avebury at best is not a good place on account of hay, and when the Downs are exchanged will not do so well as at present. But when that takes place the course of the husbandry will be so altered there won't be near the work to be don as at present. Therefore think twelve or thirteen horses will do the work as well as that number and four oxen do at this time. Have four at present. Shall keep them till the barly season is over, and then dispose of them. Buying hay is a dreadful thing for a farmer. If the spring should be backward I must buy a great deal. Have bought a small reek by the lump, think about 8 tons and a half, cost 23 guineas. Shall not buy any more so cheap. Our lambs are coming in, have got about a hundred. Have hitherto had tollerable good luck, what with buying hay and some sheep to make up the summa stock. Fear cash will run very short with me this summer, but will be as frugal as possible. Have not settled with Mrs Jenny; about a month since she sent me a letter saying she had received the hare and snipes, very good and acceptable, and should send for me as soon as she had got it in her bills, but have heard nothing of her since. If I don't hear very soon will make her another visit. I have not received any money of Mrs Belford. Her bill is £41 2[s] 5[d]. You say you think there must be a mistake about the calves. £11 4[s] 8[d] was the money they sold for, I have many times sold 8 calves for half that sum. If they could have been made fat they certainly would have sold for more money, as the last of them fetched £3 3[s] 9[d]. If the cows had milk the fore part of the summer, could have made them all near as good. Have talked to Mrs Renald about the butchers bill. Think on the whole not very extravagant. The gentleman I mentioned about taking Stoney Hall has taken a house at Reding,[1] so that is over. Mr Manning is not got into the other house, suppose he intends keeping it the year and then give it up. Mr Ward is gone to London to get the bill past for the inclosure . There is no doubt but it will be don, as all the partys have signed it except Crook.[2] Clements[3] is measuring and planing the downs and fields. The cows certainly must go one more summa, as it won't be laid out by the time. I intend selling such of the cows as will sell, and buy young ones in their room to go on the Downs this summa, as I think that will answer best. Have planted some willows in Bar Close. Intend to plant more if I can get them. The trees in general grows very well.

I am, with great respect, Madam,
your most obedient humble servant
Richd Hickley
Avebury
6th March 1792

1 Reading, Berkshire.
2 William Crook.
3 John Clements.

Verso Note: Letter, Hickley, March 6th 1792.
Verso Address: Mrs Williamson.

168. John Ward to Adam Williamson WSHC 184/6

London
22 March 1792

Dear Sir,
It has afforded myself and family the most sincere pleasure and satisfaction to be informed that Mrs Williamson arrived safe in the West Indies, and that you are both well, and you have our very fervent wishes for a long continuance of that inestimable blessing, as well as of every other you enjoy. Lord and Lady Ailesbury frequently enquire for you both, and are, (with the ladies), very glad to hear so good accounts and desired when I wrote to you I would present their compliments & good wishes to you.

I have the pleasure to send you herewith an Avebury act, which has passed both Houses of Parliament, and will receive the Royal assent the first time the King goes to the House. You will, I am sure, both of you, be not less surprised than pleased to find that Beckhampton is included in it, especially when I inform you that it is not only with the consent of Mr Holford, but that in several letters and conversations he has expressed himself with great liberality & handsomeness with regard to the present [?persons][1] of Avebury, however poignant his feelings appear to have been upon former transactions, and on my leaving him this morning he desired his respects to you.

I wrote to him first on the subject last autumn, but, not receiving an answer, I got Lord Ailesbury to assist me with an application to him through Mr Montagu (another master[2]), which had the desired effect. The very mixed state of your property and common rights in Beckhampton rendered it a very desirable thing to you to include that tithing. I do not know that it is at all eligible to you to have Silbury Hill & lands lying that way allotted to you in point of convenience, but I should be glad to know how far you wish for it (supposing the master[3] who has now the principal part of the land about it should not make a point of having it allotted to him) as a monument of antiquity. I do not think any sort of timber, except perhaps Scotch firs, and those of a very ragged appearance, would grow on so barren and exposed a spot.[4]

I have received your favor with Durnell's money, £30, & will settle with him on Saturday fornight, & will deliver the receipts to Mrs Reynolds. Lord A[5] desired I would mention to you Lieutenant Bentham of the Artillery at Jamaica,

1 Or perhaps 'possessors'.
2 In Chancery.
3 That is, Peter Holford, master in Chancery.
4 There had been previous attempts to grow trees there earlier in the century, evidently unsuccessful; see *AWS*, p.11. Letters below indicate that Mrs Williamson encouraged Richard Hickley to plant some more.
5 Lord Ailesbury. A major Wiltshire landowner, based at Tottenham Park.

as the 2d son of the adjutant of one of the Devonshire Battalions of Militia, & who is one of the worthiest men he ever knew. I also beg leave to recommend to your and Mrs Williamson's notice, when you return (please God) to Avebury, & to your friends here the new curate of Avebury, Mr Chester[1] & his wife, who will I hope be found very pleasant agreeable people & Mr C., a very modest , well behaved young man. Mrs Chester is daughter to Mr Hope of Marlborough. Lord A was so kind to make interest with the Bishop of Salisbury for his ordination 4 months before the usual time at my request.

I hope you will pardon the haste with which I write, being much engaged & preparing for my return to Marlboro with my wife & brother, who write with me in respectful compliments & very best wishes to yourself & Mrs Williamson. I am, dear Sir, (with the highest esteem & respect), your obliged and most obedient servant
John Ward

Lord Bruce remains in Italy yet – very well.

Note written at top of letter, at right angles: Answered by the [?Queen][2] Charlotte, 18th June.

169. Richard Hickley to Mrs Williamson WSHC 184/6

Avebury
3 April 1792

Honoured Madam,
I received yours of the 9th February. Wee are all glad glad[sic] to hear that you and my master are quite well. By the account there is a ballance to you of [£]24 13[s] 0½[d] . In my last I wrote my opinnion about oxen when the Downs are exchanged, which will certainly take place, as the act has passed both Houses[3] waiting only for the King's sanction. I saw Mr Ward the other day he told me he had wrote to you by this paquet the particulars. Last week in my road to Bristol cald on Mrs Jenny; she has promised to settle with me next Saturday. I find there is a year and half's rent due this Lady Day. The last setling was Michaelmas 1789. Since that you received £40 which brought it to Michaelmas 1790, so there is the taxes to be allowed for the whole time which is two years & half. When I go to Bath will call on Mrs Wroughton & Mr Milmoth with your compliments, likewise Mrs Goddard if there. What I did at Bristol with regard to wine, suggar, &c., Mrs Renald has wrote fully about. There is only one cask of strong beer, which is very good. We intend sending it with the wine &c. As to finishing the farm house chamber, think with Mrs Renald it will be the best way to let it alone till you are nearly coming home, as, if you please to recollect, was agreed on

1 William Chester; see *AWS*, p.406-7.
2 Or perhaps Lady. Presumably a ship rather than the Queen herself!
3 Houses of Parliament.

before you left Avebury. At present it is a useless room; shall not do anything to it till I hear from you again. The kind of cart you mention if on springs pay the same tax as a one horse chaise.[1] Have heard nothing from Hungerford for some time. Shall go there tomorrow to buy some bacon to send with the wine &c. Perhaps may hear what is done. The gardener has consulted with me about the men employed by him. He says if there is no family in the summer the garden may be cropt in a very different manner, by which one man's labour may be saved. The garden at present is certainly a great expence. Am sorry to say wee have had but indifferent luck lately with the lambs, but as it is no more than neighbours fare must not grumble. Have had a very cold wet season hitherto. Hope we shall now have fine weather, as are beginning to sow barley. Wheat sells very low which, is greatly against the farmer

Wee all desire our duty to you and my master
and I am, with great respect, Madam, your most obedient humble servant
Richd Hickley

Verso Note: Hickley letter, 3d April 1792
Verso Address: Mrs Williamson, Jamaica.

170. Richard Hickley to Mrs Williamson WSHC 184/6

[30 April 1792]

Honoured Madam,
Inclosed is a letter from Mrs Jenny, likewise a copy of the account settled with her. We had some dispute about the new grate & altering the chimney, but she has a letter from my master authorizeing her to do it, which have sent a copy of. The rent is paid up to Lady Day last. The cash received by me as by the account sent is £34 19s 7d, the ballance of my account is £33 15[s] 4½[d]. Have had a dreadful blow by buying so much hay, which has robed me of every bit of cash I could get. Hope now that expence is over, as the weather is very fine. Shall soon have some grass added to that. Have had bad luck with the lambs, which will make me buy more sheep than otherwise should have don. Have been endeavouring to sell of some of the worst old cows as I shall not milk above five or six this summer. Tomorrow is the day fixed for the Commissioners' first meeting in order to survey the lands. Hope they will do things to the best advantage. I shall give them close attendance. Have sent the cask of beer, 2 sides of bacon, & a small box of garden seeds, to Bristol to the care of the wine merchant. Believe they sailed about the 19th instant. Should have sent your shoes at same time if the man had not neglected to make them. If I can get them will send them by Mr. [?Eavans].[2] I cald on him last Saturday. As he was not at home could not learn when he intends seting off.
I am, with great respect, Madam, your very humble servant

1 A small closed carriage for two passengers.
2 Or perhaps Ewens.

Richd Hickley
Avebury, 30th April 1792

Verso Note: Hickley's letter 30th April 1792
Verso Address: Mrs Williamson, Jamaica.

171. Richard Hickley to Mrs Williamson WSHC 184/6

[5 June 1792]

Honoured Madam,
I have yours of the 22d March. Am glad to hear you and my master are so well. Please to accept mine and my wife's duty & thanks for yours & my master's kindness to my daughter Ann for the £10, but as money is so very short cannot think of paying it before next winter, when hope it will be more plenty. The ballance is [£]57 9[s] 7[d]. What with buying hay, sheep, &c., cannot tell how to get on. It will be impossible for me to supply Mrs Renalds with money to go to town, as I cannot pay them their fifty pounds till the wool is cut & sold, but will let her have what I possibly can. You mention Crook's farm bills.[1] Those I have charged are two years' farm bills, that is, in the husbandry only, which has nothing to do with repairs. The money due to him on the former stateing was £171 14s 7d. Then his bill ending the 29th November last was £41 7s 10d, which together makes £213 2s 5d, out of which he has had £80 0[s] 0[d], so the money due to him at this time is [£]133 2[s] 5[d]. Must endeavour to let him some of it as soon as I can, then Stroud's bill.[2] The ballance of the bill is [£]14 4[s] 7½[d], after I had paid him £10, as you will see in the account of June 1791 was [£]4 4[s] 7½[d]. What he has done since is [£]4 13[s] 10½[d], making together [£]8 18[s] 6[d]. The bill I charged in the account of 28th January last. What I mean by cash advanced, the gardener is to pay the men which he accounts to me for. Then I claim the money he realy pays them. The £12 16s 0d you mentioned was for sixteen weeks labour which you may see by tracing back the accounts. I don't charge to you cash advanced to him, & their labour also. Horse farriers bill [£]6 3[s] 6[d] for cureing the mange. Hope wee are got quite clear of it now. In the winter will try the pond in Bar Close by treading it with the cattle, but I think it impossible to make it hold water, unless it was to be properly clayed, and even then think the springs wold break through in the bottom. I mentioned in my last my thoughts about oxen. Tis impossible for us to keep them when the Downs are exchanged. I talked of seling the four we have, but find I must keep them this summer. Have bought another young horse, I think very cheap as they are now sold, as some of the old ones are quite worn out. Must replace them as fast as I can spare the money. Hope wee shall make something of poultry this summer. I sell pidgeons at 3s per dozen fowl's eggs, &c., at the times price. Have 8 cows left,

1 Probably Stephen Crook.
2 Stroud was a glazier who was also a sheep shearer, but he was not from Avebury; see *AWS*, p.290.

milks five of them. Shall make what cheese I can, that wee may have some to sell, but unless wee have more grass on the Downs than at present shan't make much. Mr Richd Jones[1] has been enquiring of me by Mrs Renald about sheep, but I shal guard against that. I sent him word as the lands were going to be exchanged should keep a greater stock, therefore not sell any this year. Have broke up the ground at Beckhamton, as I could not bring it to a good turf. Am like to have a fine crop of barley in it. The barley in general is like to be good this year, the wheat but indifferent. Wheat at this time sells so low that there is but little money to be got from that, and at this season of the year having nothing else to sell is very much against the farmer.

I don't know what to do with Beaven the shoemaker.[2] Can't get no money of him, nor believe ever shall. He owes three years rent last Lady day which is £10 10s 0[d]. I think it is of no use to try him any longer, but I shall let him bide till I have your answer. Yesterday I was attending the Commissioners of the exchange of lands. Am going again today. A very troublesome business, so many customs & rights to set forth, require great <u>care</u>. Suppose they must have two or three more meetings before it will be finally settled. Thank God the cattle of all kinds are well.

Wee all beg your acceptance of our duty
and I, with great respect Madam, your most obedient humble servant
Richd Hickley
Avebury
5th June 1792

Verso Note: Hickley's letter 5th June 1792.
Verso Address: Mrs Williamson, Jamaica.

172. Richard Hickley to Mrs Williamson WSHC 184/6

Avebury
9 July 1792

Honoured Madam,
As the sheep are not yet shorn have not been able to let Mrs Renalds have any money. Wee shall shear them on Friday next. Suppose it may fetch about £90 or something more, as wool is like to be sold well this year. Shall pay them the fifty pounds due to them, and let her have the remainder on your account to go to London. By the account there is a ballance to me of £43 19s 02d. which I want very much, but must do as well as I can. Very little money to be made at this season of the year. The Commissioners for divideing the lands are to meet on the 17th of this month. Hope then partly to know what lands we are to have. Suppose they will have two or three more meetings before it is finally settled.

1 He inherited the manor on Williamson's death.
2 Nothing more is known of the Beaven family. The surname is rare in Avebury.

Mr Symkins,[1] Amor's[2] landlord, is dead. Don't know who is to succeed him, tis thought his brother in law, the present Lord Mayor of London.[3] Wee are very busy at haymaking . Have thank God a tollerable good crop. Hope next winter to guard against buying any.
I am, Madam, with my duty you and my master, your very humble servant
Richd Hickley

Verso Note: Hickley letter 3d July 1792
Verso Address: Mrs Williamson, Jamaica.

173. Richard Hickley to Mrs Williamson WSHC 184/6

[31 July 1792]

Honoured Madam,
I have yours of the 8th May. Have answered many things in my last letters as you mention such as Crook's, Stroud's, Shipway's and other accounts. The money due to Crook[4] at this time is £133 5s 0d besids what may be due for work don in the husbandry only, as that account is always kept by itself. There is nothing of any consequence due to either Shipway or Stroud, as they were paid in full not long since. The banking & planting the hedge you mention is from the Bar going to Kennet. I have thrown down that high bank & planted a frith hedge, by which have got a considerable piece of ground into the inclosure. Nobody found fault with me but Mr Crook.[5] He and I had a very high quarrel about it. Everyone else says tis a good job. The reason was he thought I had got too much ground by it. Have inclosed the taylor's bill as you ordered. If any more tradesmens' bills will send coppys of them, but hope I shan't have many more to pay. The gardener accounts to me for the things he sels out of the garden. I makes my self debtor for the money in the account, then I claim the expences for the labour as he has the money of me to pay them. Bailey, the fellow that used to work in the garden, is under sentence of death for a highway robbery committed on Beckhamton Downs on an old man of Calne that gathers eggs & poultry. I took him up & was on his trial at Salisbury. He is a most desperate villain. As to Mrs Belford's replacing the beer, tis a great mistake. When she came to Avebury there was the beer of at least 46 bushels of malt, when she went away there was not a drop in the cellar, except 2 casks of strong beer, one of which was sent out to Jamaica. The other is now in the cellar, but not very good. When she went away ordered me to brew 16 bushels on her account, so there was 30 bushels short, and the first brewing she had was 17 bushels of your malt, which was made the other

1 William Simpkins, who owned a portion of Avebury Truslow manor; see *VCH Wilts*12, p.93. He was succeeded by Charles Simpkins.
2 John Amor; see *AWS,* p.56.
3 Sir John Hopkins. He purchased the property from his brother in law, Charles Simpkins, c.1795; see *AWS,* p.239.
4 Probably Stephen Crook.
5 Probably William Crook, who also objected to the enclosure.

year. I expected I should have been paid for it among other things had from the farm, otherwise should not have let her had it. So at least there is 47 bushels short of what should have been. Believe Mrs Renald explained this matter to you sometime since. Mrs Renald agrees with me not to brew any more beer to send out till wee hear if that sent turns out good. I am afraid it will not. I think the direction you sent for brewing a very strange one, both as to management, & quantity of malt. 6 bushels of malt can never make beer of a body fit to send into such a hot climate. I have paid to Mrs Renald on your account £72 8s 0d, and thirty pound in part of the fifty due to them the 5th June last. Will pay them the other twenty as soon as possible. The wool sells well this year. I have taken a shilling per pound in part, think the price will be thirteen or fourteen pence per pound. Had it not been for buying so much hay it would have don very well. Hope next winter shall not want to buy any. You say the turkeys were sold cheap. Mrs Renald says they were not worth the money in London. Wee shall have but a few this year. Have only two young hen fowls, had no more hatched. Pretty well of for ducks & chickens. The worst season for hay making I have known this many years; it rains almost every day, but what with cuting a little, and then stoping, have made none very bad, yet when wee are to have a harvest cannot tell. The weather is very cold and wet, the corn don't ripen, think twil be three weeks at least before wee begin. Don't know what to say about keeping the lambs for stock the next year; have not made up my mind about it yet. The Commissioners of the inclosure are met this day. Am going directly to attend them. Hope to know this meeting how it is to be. I did not like their discourse at any rate the last meeting, but found afterwards they had altered their minds, I mean as to laying out the lands. Old John Clements is ill and not able to attend this meeting. The Commissioners complain and says he is too old for the business, which is realy the truth. They have cald in a young man, which is very clever at such business, as an assistant to Clements, which is quite right, otherwise there may be mistakes by [?which] some one or other may be injured. Our corn markets have rose very considerable within this two or three weeks, believe owing to the backwardness of the harvest. Hope they will hold so. Inclosed is a letter from Mr. Eavens and one from Mr Tucker. Mr. Eavens certainly has behaved very strange in this affair. I think the old mansion should have been white washed this summer as the wet is apt to get into those old walls if not don once a year. The roof of the green house must have something done to it, otherwise the gardener says the plants will all be lost next winter. Will have it patched up for the present so as to keep dry. I hear nothing about Hungerford whither sold or not.
My self & wife desire our duty to you & my master,
and I am, with great respect, Madam, your very humble servant
Richd Hickley
Avebury
31st July 1792

Verso Note: Hickley's letter, 31st July 1792.
Verso Address: Mrs Williamson, Jamaica.

174. Richard Hickley to Mrs Williamson WSHC 184/6

[4 September 1792]

Honoured Madam,

Wee now nearly know the allotment of land each person is to have. Cannot say it is done quite to my mind, though at the same time don't blame the Commissioners, for as the parish is circumstanced, I don't think they could have laid it out otherwise. The haveing so much land at Thornhill that is over the London Road makes it not convenient, being at such a distance from home. Before the exchange you had only 44 acres in that field; now will have, I suppose, near 80, which, as I before observed is not so handy as one could wish, it being so far from home and a great way to drive the sheep from the Downs to fold, but as the Beckhamton people had not land to give in lieu of it, you was obliged to have it. You to keep the 20 acres next to Bar Close, and I believe about six or seven acres adioining to it towards Monkton. That is all you have in that field, then to have all that field between the road going to Kennet and South Meadow cald Weeden field, to keep the meadow, and to have South Meadow furlon, that is the land next the meadow towards Beckhamton, suppose about 40 acres, but at present cannot ascertain the number of acres of the whole. I don't think wee shall have so many acres of plowed land as before. The haveing so much Down, suppose near 400 acres, makes the plowed land come short. The haveing plenty of Down is a good thing, but then should have plowed land in proportion to take the dung, as there must be a great number of sheep kept on the farm, otherwise I don't know what is to pay the expence of inclosing. Think next summa to keep at least fifteen hundred or more if I can raise money to buy them. The inclosure at Beckhamton you are to keep. I wished Mr. Dyke[1] to take it, but his tenant found fault with it, so he gave it up. Indeed tis of no consequence whether you keep it or give it up. Silbury Hill is allotted to you. Tis of no great value, neither is it valued at much only twenty five shillings per year. Cheap enough. Since the allotments the Duke of Marlbro's steward and Mr Sutton wanted to have it. Mr Ward was inclined to let Mr Sutton have it. I insisted, as it was allotted to you, it should not be gave up. To be sure Mr Ward attends the meetings in order to make his bill, but of no more use with regard to the exchange of your property. Then you are at such a distance. I fear twil be an expensive piece of business, though certainly a good job when done. When the whole is finished will as you desire get Clements or some person to draw a rough plan of the estate and send out. Clements is in a poor way, don't think he will hold it long. Has been of no sort of use in this business. Had not the Commissioners cald in a young man as they recommended, it would never have been don. Have inclosed Dixon the taylor's bill. Thought I had done it in my last, suppose I enclosed something instead of it. About a month since wee had the most dreadful storm of rain ever remembered. The water course at this season of the year being full of weeds, and large quantitys

1 Thomas Webb Dyke owned 147 acres in Avebury in 1795; see Sandell, R.E., ed. *Abstracts of Wiltshire inclosure Awards and Agreements.* Wiltshire Record Society, 25. 1971, p.18.

of hay being swept away throwed the water out of the natural course in the morning, when wee got Bar Close, the new garden, pleasure ground and every part was under water. All the lower rooms in the house up to my knees. It has don no great dammage in the house except three or four books which were in the little parlour in the bottom of the book case. But the garden has suffered severely. Though the water remained only four days, almost everything is destroyed. But what is worse than all, it sanded a fine crop of grass in South Meadow. Luckely it was not cut, if it had would have been washed away. Wee happened to have a few fine days afterward to make it, but tis so full of grist I fear the sheep won't eat it. Every person that has land near the river has suffered by it. In your last letter you desired to have a light cart made, which would be very handy. But we have lately had with us the window inspector. He makes a point of chargeing those sort of carts with three pound ten shillings duty, the same as a one horse chaise. Therefore I think when you know this you won't have it made. The most backward and wetest harvest we have had for many years past. Have not housed a handfull of wheat or any grain whatever. Have not half don reaping. Continual rain every day. If it don't take up dry very soon the corn will all be spoilt. It makes me very unhappy, but must be borne with. About three weeks since there came a gentlemen to Hungerford that wishes very much to take Stoney Hall from one to five years certain. His name is De Montalt, believe he is a single person. Appears to be a man of property. I rather think him a gentleman that has left France. Think fifty pounds per year may be had for it. He told me he would continue Brown, and give him twenty pound a year, if you would give him the other ten. By the advice of Mrs Rennald I wrote to Mr Hickey[1] about it. He gave me a short letter of three lines saying if Mr De Montalt would make his proposals to him he would consider of it, and give him an answer. The gentleman will return to Hungerford in a few days, when I will recommend him to Mr Hickey.
My wife with me beg yours and my master's acceptance of our duty, and I am, with great respect, Madam,
your most obedient servant
Richd Hickley
Avebury
4th September 1792

Note at foot, written at right angles: Hickley letter 4th September 1792.

175. John Ward to Adam Williamson WSHC 184/6

Marlboro
1 October 1792

Dear Sir,
I was much honoured & obliged by your kind letter of the 16th of June. I was in Yorkshire at the time it arrived, with Lord & Lady Ailesbury, who were happy to

1 He appears to have been the Williamson's land agent at Hungerford.

hear so good an account of you and Mrs Williamson, and his Lordship is much obliged to you for your friendly wishes to him & his family.

I have been obliged to attend his Lordship in Yorkshire this summer, which has prevented my being present during all the Avebury inclosure business, but it has been attended to by my brother, & we procured an able assistant to Mr Clements for the surveying & calculating branches of the business, & I have reason to think the business has been very well done & much to your advantage, at least Hickley appears very well pleased with your allotments. The value of Silbury Hill was a mere trifle, & it would have been a bad thing if such a monument of antiquity in the front of your house had not been allotted to you. Since my return from Yorkshire, I have been at Weymouth with Mrs Ward & a little party, where we had as many opportunys as we could wish for of seeing & hearing their majestyes,[1] the 6 princesses, the Prince of Wales, Duke & Duchess of York, Mr Pitt, Lord Chatham, Lord Salisbury, & many more of the courtiers, & of sailing with the fleet of frigates, which was very pleasant, but the weather was exceedingly bad, & so it has been all this harvest, as I am afraid you will learn from your bailiff's reports, for a worse time can scarcely be remembered.

I can give you no Avebury news, nor any other that will be interesting. Our friend Garlick,[2] who you honour by inquiring for, has been to Leyden & taken a doctor's degree, & is at present with his relations at Farley[3] in much better health than he has been, but where he will settle is at present undetermined. Mr & Mrs Gar<u>lick,</u> or Gar<u>like,</u> as they have changed it, are well, as are my dear wife & 5 children, which I hope will soon be increased to 6, <u>who</u> (that is my wife), with my brother, join me in respectful compliments & sincere good wishes to yourself & Mrs Williamson. It is just now a busy time with me. I have entered on the office of mayor, & Lord Ailesbury's courts, the Quarter Sessions, & other business hurries on all at once, which I hope will plead my excuse for writing in this slovenly hasty manner, to get it ready for sending to Tottenham Park, my good Lord having sent me word that he expects Col. Whitelocke there, & that he would carry any letters, which I have sent word to Avebury.

I can recollect nothing else worth notice, & so will conclude with fervent wishes for yours & Mrs Williamson's good health & speedy & prosperous return to old England

Dear Sir, your obliged & obedient servant,
John Ward

Note written at right-angles across the top of the letter: Answered by the Westmorland, 14 January 1793. Dated 1st October.

1 George III visited Weymouth annually; cf. Vale, Edmund. *The Mail Coach Men of the Late Eighteenth Century*. Cassell, 1960, p.82.

2 He has not been identified.

3 Perhaps either Farleigh Hungerford or Monkton Farleigh.

176. Richard Hickley to Mrs Williamson WSHC 184/6

[2 October 1792]

Honoured Madam,

Three days since wee received yours of the first of August. Are glad to hear you and my master are in good health. Am freted almost to death about the harvest, believe we never shall get it in. I never can remember such a summer. Cannot have two dry days together. There is a great deal of wheat out in this neighbourhood. Wee have got ours in tollerable well, though I don't know how wee did it. The barley & oats are almost all out. I have housed only about sixteen acres of barley, the greater part of our neighbours not a handfull. If the weather don't alter soon it will all rot in the ground. Can give you no further information about the exchange of lands at present than I did in my last. Cannot say I am quite in good humour about it. As I said before, haveing so much land over the London Road twil be expensive to make roads & drove ways over the water course & meadow, but I will if possible make the Commissioners do part of it at the publick expence. Yesterday received a letter from Mr Cuthbert saying the card tables you mentioned would be sent to Salisbury, & from thence by the Marlbro carrier. Will take care to fetch them as soon as they arive. Shall not think any thing about white washing the house now, but in the spring it certainly must be don. Otherwise the walls will tumble to pieces. I realy think three shillings a dozen a very good price for our pidgeons. You say my late master used to sell them for four, but I don't remember his ever selling one in all the years I liveed with him. Miss Rennald thinks them very dear at three shillings. The old sort of weather coming on this morning, rain every day. I heartily wish wee could exchange weather with you for a fortnight. By the account there is a ballance to me of £77 4[s] 6[d]. Hope now to raise some money, otherwise I must run away very soon. The person I mentioned in my last about taking Hungerford house has not been heard of since; suppose gone to the Deavil. Has taken in the people at the Bear.[1] I am this day going to Hungerford as one of the tenants is going out of the house, and has not a farthing to pay the rent, so suppose must destrain on his goods. Tis for half year six guineas. That place is a perpetual plague. I don't think the great house will ever be either let or sold. The quarter's rent due from Mr Tanner will be lost unless you send me an order to receive the money. He told me he would not pay it unless I had an order from my master. The paleing before the farm house looks very well. If you recollect, you gave orders for [?one] porch to be made at the door before you left home. Have not put down a pump yet at the farm, The springs keep so high there is no doing it. Shall go to Bristol next week to see about the cyder, & enquire when any ship goes out. The brown paper charged in the accounts to repair the top of the green house, otherwise the plants will all be destroyed in the winter by the frost. The garden begins to recover it self again from the injury it received by the water, only there will be very little winter crops.

Wheat sells for a good price, and tis thought will be dear all the winter

1 Presumably refers to an inn in Hungerford, rather than the one at Beckhampton.

owing to the vast number of French people there is in this Kingdom. Many people think it will kick up a dust among us. Provisions tis said are vastly dear in London.
I am, with great respect Madam, your very humble servant
Richd Hickley
Avebury
2d October 1792

Verso Note: Hickley letter October 2d 1792.
Verso Address: Mrs Williamson, Jamaica.

177. Richard Hickley to Mrs Williamson WSHC 184/6
[6 November 1792]

Honoured Madam,
I went to Bristol about three weeks since to enquire when any ship was to sail for Jamaica. Found there was one going in about a fortnight. Went to the cider merchant and ordered 20 dozen, but he will not send it under ten shillings per dozen unless a large quantity was to be sent to have the draw back allowed, which would bring it much cheaper. Desired the favour of Mr Eames to get it shiped. I sent the other things the 24th of last month, so suppose by this time they are gone, but have heard nothing from Mr Eames since. Was in hopes I should have had your determination about beer before this time. Tis certainly a very great price you give for small beer. It may be sent from hence much cheaper, but the buying casks, caseing and carriage to Bristol, and the freight afterward, will make it come dear. Suppose it may be delivered to Bristol for four pounds per hogshead, or somewhere there about, which will be a saving of more than half. I think if any is sent it will be best to send three or four hogsheads at one time, some ale and some small. If I find by your next that sent turns out good will at all events as soon as I can get some malt made, brew two hogsheads of ale and two of small, and send in the spring or the first opportunity. Have sent a cask of harness oil. The other things are packed in seven boxes. Hope and believe they will come safe. Don't know the name of the ship as Mr Eames could not tell. Should have sent the mops as you desired but had sold the wool before I knew you wished to have them. Will keep the wool next spring, and have a quantity made. The inclosure business is not over yet. The Commissioners are to meet on Monday next. There are several things which I want to have altered. Crook[1] and Amor canot agree with my self and Mr Nalder[2] as they are two scoundrels. The Commissioners see them as such; therefore wee have them on our side. After twelve weeks miserable wet weather, that is since wee began harvest, hope to finish in a day or two if the weather don't alter again. Have about 8 acres now out, which is almost rotten. Wee had the home harvest supper last night as our

1 William Crook.
2 Robert Nalder.

meat would not keep any longer. Many people has the greater part of their barley out at this time. In my next account shall give you the account of the sheep sold and bought. I think it much the best to buy this autumn for the summer stock, as they will certainly be very dear in the spring of the year owing, to the wetness of the summer. One half of the people in the country cannot keep any this winter, therefore those that can keep them sound will have a great price for them in the spring, besides great danger in buying for fear they should be rotten
I am, with great respect, Madam, your most obedient humble servant
Richd Hickley

Note at foot: supposed to be wrote 6th November 1792

Verso Note: Hickley's letter, 6th November 1792
Verso Address: Mrs Williamson, Jamaica

178. Mary Powdich to Adam Williamson [with reply] WSHC 184/6
[3 December 1792]

Dear and honoured Sir,
From the proofs I have received of your Excellency's friendship and goodness to me, I have every reason to believe & hope that you still continue my friend, therefore flatter myself you will not be offended at my addressing you on a subject that makes me very uneasy, which is from having some hints given me as if the note for ten pounds advanced me by your Excellency was to be shortly demanded of me, and being at this time as totally unable to repay it as I was at the hour it was lent me, I thought it best to acquaint your Excellency with my distress on the occasion, & to beg you will have the goodness to write to your bailiff that he may not call it in or put me to any trouble about it, for I really, my good Sir, am greatly disturbed, and must beg your patience till better times may enable me to pay the money. I am very sorry to be obligd from the necessitious state of my affairs to be so intruding on your Excellency's goodness, but I trust the assurance that nothing but want of means prevents me paying the ten pounds will prevail on you to give orders by the first ship to your bailiff that no steps may be taken in it without your express command, which I shall be happy to have confirmed by a line from your Excellency's hand to put my heart at ease from the anxiety that I at present experience from this and other causes of the like nature, which disappointments in life & fortune has made me but too subject to, for these, many many years. Your Excellency's kind compliance with this request will add to the great obligations already conferred upon me for which I shall be truly grateful.

I sincerely hope the country agrees with you & my kind friend Mrs Williamson, to whom I beg my most respectful compliments & best wishes, & that health, the great blessing of life, attends you both is my earnest hope, & I pray that your Excellency may soon return to your native country, laden with honors & riches, and long live with Mrs Williamson in health & happiness to enjoy them. This is the sincere wish of her, who has the honor to remain with

the greatest respect & gratitude
Your Excellency's most devoted & most truly obliged though distresed humble & obedient servant,
Mary Powdich
Hungerford
December the 3d 1792.

Verso Address: Post paid to London [*illegible*]. To His Excellency General Williamson, Governor of Jamaica, Spanish Town, Jamaica.

[On same sheet, in different hand]

Madam,
My gentleman having so much publick business, I undertake to reply to all private letters from England. We are entire strangers to anything having been said to you on the subject of the £10 0[s] 0[d], excepting at the time of the auction of Stoney Hall, &c, when you was rather cautioned not to be speaking sentiments regarding that property, without any foundation, & that you had better employ your thoughts another way, alluding I believe to the above. This was repeated to me. Whenever it is convenient which for your sake sincerely wish may be soon. Imagine you will repay it till when has [*illegible*].
Your humble servant
A.W.

Answer to the letter received March 10th 1793.

179. William Richardson to Mrs Williamson WSHC 184/6
[4 December 1792]

Honoured Madam,
I have procured 15 bushell of has for to [?raise] qwick[1] from. I paid 10d per bushel for gatheren amounted to twelve & sixpence which I received from Hickleay. I shall plant the most of the garden with potatos this year. I have saved all the peas & beens that I shall want. [?Kidneay] beens & other seeds do not ripen at all. I have tryed diferant sorts for tow years but it will not dow to sow aneay seed except peas & beans. But it is a general complent every wheare ther is a greate maneay sorts of seeds never was nare so dear in England. Last week I planted oute 3 dozen of gosburis & cwrants. I have got great plentie of young ones to plant out I have in the nursery at present. The oaks that I bought have don vere well, 2000 [?sedlen], bech, 200 younge ashes. I have soed a deall of ashes seed last year but that seed don't com oup for ten years after its soed the [?12 ripen] [*illegible*]. My sedlen[2] firs suffered verey much with the water, theaye come oup well. I shall saye

1 Quick thorn?
2 Seedling.

[?nothing] what number, for I am not sartan till spring, thos that is alive is verey white in the leaf. A great mouneay[1] died after the water went up. The hous was not white washed last year. Ther is a deal of the plaster spoled of which is a great short sason stones walls is [?neatrealy][2] damp, &, when not where white washed, the weet[3] penitrates into the walles mor & mor every year. If not white washed next summer the hous will be in a woful state befor the third winter is over. I have had more fiers burnt this last month but a hard mater to have it done. The paper in the drawing rowm and dames rowm is verey much damaged. I have had the top of the greenhouse covered. It rained in all over so bad that I could not preserve the plants without it was done in a verey untimeleay season owing to the wetness of the weather. I have propigated 5 dozen of mistles.[4] I have got mor plants in the house [?awy]. On half there I have [?reserv] for Mitchel & Ruth.[5] I myself joines our duti to you wishing you a hapi new year and maneay returnes of the season, my duti to the General. I am your humble servant
Wm Richardson
Evebury December 4 1792.

N.B. The month of November have been the finest weather we have had since the month of June.

180. Richard Hickley to Mrs Williamson WSHC 184/6

[4 December 1792]

Honoured Madam,
We are all happy to hear my master and you continue so well. By the account sent the disbursments runs very high, but as I had an opportunity of buying sheep for the summer stock of a neighbour, which I know to be perfectly sound and of a good sort, thought it best to take the chance and not to run the risque of buying several different sorts in the spring and perhaps half of them rotten, as after such a wet summer they certainly will be. Last week I had a letter from Mr Eames the wine merchant, saying he had shipped the wine with the other things sent from Avebury on board the [?Hero], Capt. Powel, which sailed on the 23d November, and this morning I sent to Bristol 2 sides of bacon with a box of shoes, to be shipped on board the Stephen, Capt. Bendy, which is to sail in a few days. Some time since a person asked me if Mrs Jenny's house was to be sold; if so he should like to buy it. His name is Saunders, resides now at the Devizes. Has been in this country[6] for some time. As a window inspector has made a number of surcharges in this parish as well as others I told him I would mention it to you. Mrs Jenny's first 7 years are expired on the 21st of this month, and as she has gave no notice

1 Many?
2 Naturally.
3 Wet.
4 Mistletoe?
5 The housekeeper and maid.
6 Presumably county is meant.

to quit she certainly intends holding it for seven years longer. As to Hungerford, nothing I believe is to be don with it but a continual expence. The inclosure business is nearly over, except the wast part, I mean the payment of the money. How am I to meet that. They are to meet in February next when I find a rate is to be made for payment. Whether the whole or a part is to be collected cannot tell. Find the expense will at least be one year's rent. Have began making making an inclosure in the best part of the Down. Shall inclose about 25 acres, which I hope will prevent our buying hay in future. Am making a bridge over the river in South Meadow by Silbury Hill for the sheep to pass over to Thornhill. The Commissioners talked of allowing me £20 to make it. After teasing them for some time got £30 then £35.[1] So it stands at present, but when they meet again I will try for more, as I am satisfied that sum will not nearly pay for it. Wee had a great debate about the Vicar's tithes, that is the two ell ridges of wheat he has a right to take from your estate. The Commissioners over perswaded me to give land in lieu of it. According to their valuation it would take nine acres of land to compensate for it, which I thought a great deal too much, even supposeing he should raise the composition money, which suppose he will as I find he intends to raise the whole parish.[2] They desired me to write to you on the subject but I would not advise you to submit to it on any account. I know old Clements [3]put them on it as he is a great advocate for the parson. By the next paquet I will send you a plan of the estate as it is to stand. The cash received as mentioned in the account for plowing, bringing grass seeds, &c., is what I received of the different people who took part of your land into their allotments, which I plowed, dunged, and sowed with grass seeds before wee knew where the allotments would fall. As that was the case with everyone more or less, have paid Mrs R[4] the £20 due to them, that is the remaining part of the £50 due to them in June last. Tomorrow there is £50 more due to them, but don't know when I shall pay them, but they are very good not to push for the money as soon as due. As Mrs Jenny is not at Bath shall not receive her rent till Lady Day. She has not been there this summer. When I went to Bristol last cald and looked over the house, found it very clean & dry, and in tolerable good repair, very little wanting to be don to it. Could not find when she is to return. Cannot receive Hatchet's rent till Lady Day; [5] indeed that may suit me as well as at present. Have sown about 100 acres of wheat this season so far. The exchange was luckey, Mr Nalder[6] has not a bit to sow in his allotment. I find the estates concerned in the inclosure are to be rated. Then of course the parish rates will follow. If they don't set yours at more than 450 think I

1 The accounts for August 1793 (below) show that he actually received £49.

2 That is, the land which was still tithable by the vicar (many tithes in the parish were in the hands of lay rectors). See Hobbs, Steven, ed. *Wiltshire Glebe Terriers, 1588-1827*. Wiltshire Record Society 56. 2003, p.17-18.

3 John Clements.

4 Mrs Rennald.

5 Thomas Hatchett was the tenant of the Flying Waggon (now the Waggon and Horses). For the previous names of this inn, see *AWS*, p.320.

6 Robert Nalder.

must comply. If that will not satisfy them I will force them to a valuation through the parish. But this won't take place till Lady Day.

Barly sells for good price, but yields [?uncommonly]. Malt seven shillings per bushel, and good for but [?little] when made. I hear there has been a riot in London.[1] Have just heard they are quieted for the present. Believe owing to the high price of provisions.

Thank God we are all well and beg your acceptance of our duty.

I am, with great respect Madam your most obedient humble servant
Richard Hickley
Avebury
December 4th 1792

Should have said at present the estate is rated at £380.

Verso Note: Hickley letter 4th December 1792
Verso Address: Mrs Williamson, Jamaica.

181. Richard Hickley to Mrs Williamson WSHC 184/6

[31 December 1792]

Honoured Madam,
Inclosed is the plan of the estate as it now realy stands, which is not so compact as one could wish, it being so great a distance from the Thornhill land to the further part of the Down, in length more than 3 miles. All the land is very handy to the Down, except the 75 acres in Thornhill Feild. You will see by the plan where wee are to cross over with the sheep from the Down to Thornhill, that is, at the bottom of South Meadow by Beckhamton Meadow, over the London Road straight into the field. The bridge is made but shall have a great job of work to raise the road to keep the [?sheep] above the water. The whole of the plowed land [?on] the estate is about 340 acres. I think about 20 [?acres] less than it was before the exchange. The value [?will] be swallowed up in the Down. The haveing 421 [?acres] of Down is certainly a great quantity, and [?when] the summers prove kind wee shall be able to [?raise] a large stock of sheep. But the worst part is [?that] yesterday received a letter from Mr Ward saying he [?has] received a rate from the Commissioners of the Avebury inclosure wherein the amount of your part of the expence is £266 12[s] 4[d], a fine sum of money though not so much as I expected. Whither the whole or a part of the money is to be paid the next meeting, which is in February, cannot tell, but I must see him before the time. But be that as it will, I shall have none for them. The unavoidable extra expence attending it makes it impossible for one to get on. Inclosed is Hitchcock's the malster's[2] two year's bills, £35 6s 6d, likewise Lavington[3] the nursery man's bill

1 See Emsley, Clive. 'The London 'Insurrection' of December 1792: Fact, Fiction, or Fantasy?', *Journal of British Studies,* 17(2), 1978, p.66-86.

2 James Hitchcock. See *AWS,* p.88-90.

3 Perhaps Thomas Lavington of East Kennet; see the will of John Clements, WSHC

£10 0s 0d. Have paid Stephen Crook[1] £50 more towards his former account. There now remains due to him £83 2[s] 5[d] on the last stateing the last year's farm bill, and what little has been don for repairs I have not yet got the account of. Am now brewing beer to send out in the spring, beer, ale, and small, a large cask of each sort. Have made some malt for the home consumption, but must buy the malt for yours. The barley in this neighbourhood is such miserable stuff, it will not make malt, at least not good for any thing. Don't know what any of us shall do with it, owing to its laying so long on the ground in the harvest. If the frosty weather don't mend it, wee never shall sell it. [?Have] had very bad luck at breeding colts. Had the [?mortification] to find this morning that the mare that [?cast] her colt last winter had don the same again. [?Cannot] account for it, as she has done very little work [?for] some time. In your last desired to know who [?Miss] Goddard[2] was married to, but I have not had [?the] opportunity to enquire, but will the first time I go into that part of the country. Wee are making broth for the poor people, and poor they will be as the cloathers manufacture almost all their wool with machines, which deprive the poor people of their bread. Indeed, tis not the poor that suffers, but the land holders, as it makes the poor rates run very high.[3] It's more than time some stop was put to it. Shall now and then kill a porker to keep down the butcher's bill. The large quantity of beef charged in the account is some that I bought for the workmen on the farm. The other farmers in the parish bought some bull beef to give their men. I thought it right by consulting Mrs Rennald to give mine some which believe you will approve of. The small quantity was for my self and the servants at the house. Some of it Mrs Rennald had to dispose of as she thought proper. My self & wife desire our duty and thanks for a nice piece. The winter hitherto has been very mild, which is much in favour of the farmer in regard to hay. The sheep, thank God, are well. I find a great number of them about the country are rotten. Suppose Mrs Rennald has informed you that old Mrs Neate is dead[4] about a week before the annuity was due.[5] I fear Hatchet's wife won't hold it long, as she is in a very poor state of health.[6]

That you and my master may live to see many happy returns of the season is the prayer of
your most obedient humble servant
Richd Hickley
Avebury
31st December 1792

Note at foot (in a different hand): To desire Mr Ward not to prevent, if possible,

P3/C/1138.

1 A carpenter; see *AWS*, p.303.
2 She has not been identified.
3 For the effect on the poor of industrialisation, see *AWS*, p.178.
4 Sarah Neate, aged 90, was buried 16th December 1792.
5 Details of her annuity have not been traced.
6 Hannah Hatchett was buried 23rd March 1795.

a [?lane] being made in our grounds near the house – to take great care of banks &c.[1]

Verso Note: Hickley's letter, 31st December 1792.
Verso Address: Mrs Williamson, Jamaica.

182. John Ward to Adam Williamson WSHC 184/6

Marlborough
1 January 1793

Dear Sir,
I beg leave to return you and Mrs Williamson my most grateful thanks for your very flattering attention to my recommendation of my friend Mr Chester, of which I am truly sensible, and flatter myself he will prove worthy of the honour and confidence you are so good to place in him.

Lord Ailesbury desires me to add that he shares in the obligation to you for the preferment you have the goodness to give Mr Chester in Jamaica, for whose welfare he interests himself on account of Mrs Chester's family (with which he has long had connexions) as well as from the good accounts he has had of Mr Chester. I am sorry to find Mr Chester cannot get into priests' orders,[2] and wish that circumstance may not be the occasion of inconvenience to him and disappointment to you. He appears a very worthy good young man and I am confident Mrs Williamson will be greatly pleased with Mrs Chester.

The Commissioners have made a rate dividing the expenses of the Avebury act, the surveyors, commissioners, & other expences which are computed to amount in the whole to £891 6[s] 2[d]. Your share is set down at £266 12[s] 4[d], which if you please you may direct Hickley to pay to me when it is convenient. I wish it could have been done for a smaller expence, but I have no doubt the improvement will greatly exceed the expences.

The western canal scheme from Newbury to Bristol has been lately revived with great spirit by the Bristol merchants, who have subscribed £1,200,000, which is £900,000 more than wanted. A [?reserve] however is made for a landowner, and should it come by Beckhampton I will make a claim of what shares I can for you, as it may turn out a beneficial concern, & the shares may sell at an advanced price. I think you had better, if you do not approve of having any shares, write me two letters, one accepting what shares I may have secured, & the other declining them, that I may make use of which of them the circumstances of the time I receive them may render most advantageous to you . And I hope also that if I should not be able to receive any shares for you on account of your not being present to answer for yourself, you will take the will for the deed. If you write two official letters you will of course inform me by a seperate note which of the two you prefer. If you absolutely decline any shares, I may still perhaps accept

1 This presumably relates to the construction of the canal at Hungerford.
2 Presumably because there was no bishop in the West Indies.

them in your name or for some other friend, if you have no objection to that. £500 or £1000 at the most, is what I hope to secure for you, but in the present rage for canals I cannot be answerable for that.

Lord & Lady Ailesbury, & the young ladies, are well, as was Lord Bruce[1] when the last advice from Italy came away. Doctor and Mrs Garlike are in Staffordshire. He wishes to settle in Wiltshire as a physician, but has not yet heard of a house but what is either too big, too little, too dear, with half a dozen other toos. His health is much improved. My wife (who promises me a 6th child in a few weeks) & family are well, who with my brother unite with me in respectful compliments and every good wish to yourself & Mrs Williamson, & I am, with sincere attachment & respect,
Dear Sir, your obliged & most obedient servant
John Ward

Note written at right angles across the top of the letter: Answered by the Prince William Henry packet, 11th March 1793. Mr Ward.

183. Richard Hickley to Mrs Williamson WSHC 184/6

Avebury
4 February 1793

Honoured Madam,
I shall say nothing about the inclosure business at present, as the Commissioners are to meet in a few days, when the whole of the business will be setled. In my next will send a full account. The casks charged in the account are some that I bought at a sale at Marlborough, which will answer as well as new ones, and not cost a quarter part so much. The leveling on the Down is the new inclosure I have made, that is, pareing of the mole hills, and making the ground smooth, fit for mowing. The banking is the bounds. Shall plant it with barberry plants, what we call cross thorn, which will come cheaper than white thorn, and I think grow much better on that light land. Have inclosed 26 acres, which hope, after a year or two, when properly manured, will grow a good crop of hay. The weather has hitherto proved very mild, which is much in favour of the hay, but yet fear I shall be forced to buy a little at the last. Have sold the four oxen, as wee shall have no opportunity of keeping them another summer, for a good price. The haveing so many beggar old horses makes it very expensive to replace them. Must buy one or two more this summer if possible, then wee shall be pretty stout. Have not had time to go to Hungerford yet. Intend going in a few days. Have had another person offering to purchase the house, a young man going into the clotheing business. All I could do was to refer him to Mr Hickey. Have heard nothing of him since. The inclosure at Beckhamton has nothing to do with the common lands. What I meant by exchanging it was to have land for it in a more convenient place. But as they did not think proper to take it, tis of no consequence. I find

1 The son of Lord Ailesbury of Tottenham park.

the canal from Newbury to Bristol is certainly to take place, the people are all mad to become subscribers to it. A fourth part of the subscription is reserved for the land holders whose land it passes through. Tis to go by Beckhamton. I don't find it will touch any part of your estate, which will be so much the beter. Great preparations are going on for war. The helish doings in France[1] makes one's heart bleed to think of it. Hope the devil will be up sides with them. Notwithstanding the show of loyalty in burning the effigy of Tom Paine in almost every part of this Kingdom, there certainly are thousands ripe for rebellion at this time.
I am, with great respect, Madam, your very humble servant,
Richd Hickley

Verso Note: Hickley's letter, 4th February 1793.
Verso Address: Mrs Williamson, Kings House, Jamaica.

184. Richard Hickley to Mrs Williamson WSHC 184/6

Avebury
[2 March 1793][2]

Honoured Madam,
I received yours of the 18th December last with the order for receiveing Mr Tanner's rent, but as I find he is at Bath have not been to his house. Have been to Hungerford to settle with Brown. Fear wee shall have trouble to get the year & half rent of Mr Manning, which will be due at Lady Day next, eighteen guineas for the house, & three guineas for the paddocks belonging to the great house. He has never lived in the house since he took it, nor has he any thing in the house or on the premises, except two old cows & an old horse, all not worth three pounds. Brown says he is in London. Has wrote to him, but have had no answer. The other person has paid her rent, nine guineas for three quarters due at Xmas. Since that, have remained in the house by the week, but are expected to leave it in a few days. There is a person from Bedwin, an apothecary, that wishes to take both the small houses as soon as they are void. If Manning quits it at Lady Day will let him have it. If Brown receives the year & half of Manning, with what he has already received, he will be nearly paid his two year's waigers, which when don will send you the full account. The person I mentioned in my last that wanted to take or purchase Stoney Hall has wrote to Mr Hickey, but has had a very trifling answer. The other day Mr Garlick of Marlborough cald on me & Mrs Rennald, said he had applied to Mr Hickey about it and that his first answer was his commisson was only to sell it. Since that he signified to him he[3] he thought the gent would be satisfied for him to do as he pleased. I perswaded him to purchase it. His answer was he did not know if it might agree with his health. He asked what the

1 Louis XVI was executed on 21st January 1793, a few days before this letter was written.
2 The date actually written at the head of the letter is 4th February 1793. According to the recipient, this was incorrect it was actually written 2nd March 1793; see verso note below.
3 Page break.

rent might be. I told him I could not tell what Mr Hickey asked for it. I advised him to go to London and speak to Mr H himself. He said Mr Ward was going this week and he would get him to call on him. I sometime since mentioned to you that a person was desirous of purchasing Mrs Jenny's house at Bath. He is still very desirous of haveing it. I hear she is now at Bath. Shall see her at Lady Day and hear what she says about it. In a former letter you mentioned the great price of small beer, and wished to have some sent out. As I said in my last, have brewed of each sort beer, ale, and small, the beginning of January. Think it will be very good, which may be sent in April or May, which may best offer. Cannot at [?present] tell the cost as I don't know what sized casks it will go in. Don't find the ship is sailed from Bristol that took on board the last hogs of wine and two sides of bacon about three weeks since. Received a letter from Mr Eames, the wine merchant, saying the ship was detained on account of the [?rumour] of a war, & wished to know if it would not be right to insure the wine & bacon. By consulting Mrs Rennald gave him an order to have it don. Find the ship Mr and Mrs Chester are going in is detained on the same account. They have been at Bristol for some time. You mention keeping a large stock of pigs. The keeping more than the farm yard will maintain is throwing money away intirely, except buying a few grains & bran, but even buying much of that will not answer. Our lambs are beginning to come in, hope wee shall have good luck with them, but the hay being but very midling last year makes the ewes very poor. Find half the sheep in the low country are rotten. The business of the exchange of lands is now over. Had many debates, and some small alterations the last meeting. There is to be one more meeting, I think in June next, to sign the award. Believe Mr Ward has collected all the money except yours and Mr Nalder's. Wee have agreed for him to lay down the money and to be paid intrest for the same, but don't think he should charge the intrest till he has paid the money, which won't be till the next meeting. I don't think the pond in Bar Close will ever hold water, as the springs break up in the bottom when they are high, which has been the case this winter. Otherwise should have penned the cows in it as you desired. By the account there is a ballance to me of [£]72 16[s] 8[d]. Expences comes faster than I can raise money. Tis out of my power to keep them lower. You [?would] think by the account the thatcher's bills are very high, but the thatching on the farm buildings should have been paid last spring, as the work was don then. Old Farmer Brown is dead.[1] I have with the advice of Mrs Rennald let Beavens & the other house where David lives to Mrs. Brown,[2] as she is very desirous of living at Avebury, for six guineas per year. David is to have the house where Ball the taylor lives in the churchyard, which will be much better for him as the rent is less, & the house quite as handy to his [?work]. Shall do only the necessary repairs such as belongs to the landlord. If she chuses to make any cornannmention[3] in the inside to do it at her own expence, and whenever she leaves it to leave it in the same state it

1 There is no burial entry in the parish register.

2 Perhaps the widow of George Brown of Winterbourne Monkton, who was buried there 18th February 1793.

3 Ornamentation?

now is. If required to take it from Lady Day next, fear I shall have some trouble to get Beaven out of the house, though think he shortly will be starved out. He has a wife and two small children, & he not able to work. Of course he must go to his own parish
I am, with great respect, Madam, your very humble servant
Richd Hickley

Verso Note: Hickley's leter 4th February 1793 dated wrong as it should have been 2d March.

Address at foot: Mrs Williamson, Kings House, Jamaica.

185. Richard Hickley to Mrs Williamson WSHC 184/6

Avebury
31 March 1793

Honoured Madam,
I received yours on the 25th January & that of the 1st February. As to the parson's tythes you so often mention, I don't think it of any consequence. What I meant by altering it was, the Commissioners thought it would be best to give land in lieu of the modes so as the estate might not be incumbered with any sort of tythe or payment whatever. That I strongly objected to the moment they first mentioned it, so there the matter rested, and stands just the same as it did before, that is, to pay the £4 0[s] 0[d]. To be sure all he could do if not satisfied with the money would be to take up the corn in kind. If he could do that, the two ell ridges I find is about three quarters of an acre. I think the many civility's Mr Mayo has received from my late master considered, he would not think of making any alteration in <u>your</u> property if in his power. In short I don't think he will, as I hear nothing about it. Have paid J Clements for the last year, and taken his receipt for the same, as he collects all the Parson's tythes. In my last mentioned having spoke to Mr Ward to pay when wanted the £266 12[s]-4[d] for the expence of the inclosure, but as you say my master will order the payment of it. Think it will be in time as it won't be paid till the next meeting in June. Don't think any alteration will be made in the parish taxes this year till wee know better how things will be. Find Mr Garlick is of from purchasing or taking Hungerford. The other day I was with Mr Whitelock,[1] the person I mentioned that wanted to take it, he says if he can take it reasonable he will have it if not will take the small house. Said he has a brother in Jamaica: probably you must know him. A few days since received a letter from Mrs Jenny, which have enclosed, but it will be a great disappointment to me, as I intended going to Bath this week to receive her rent, which I stand in very great need of. The stoppage of those country banks is very hurtful to people in business, but tis thought after some time they will get on again.[2] Have received

1 Nothing is known of him.
2 There was a run on the banks in 1793.

the draft of Mrs Rennald for £50 to help on a little. A very expensive time coming on, the paying for wintering sheep & buying hay more than I expected. Will break me down. Wee had not half a crop of barley and that wee have cannot sell. To be sure a little of the best sold for a good price, but the ordinary black stuff will not sell for any money at present. You ask when I began selling new wheat. Have been selling it ever since harvest, old and new together. The old has been gone for some time, indeed wee had not much old, and that very indifferent, and the new is worse. How should it be good, and such a dreadful harvest as we had. Instead of having fine weather at this season the winter seems to be just siting[1] in which is very much against the cattle. Have not so good luck with the lambs as I could wish, owing to the badness of the hay. The ewes are very poor, and of course has but little milk. I observe what you say about the [?pine][2] tea and laudenum. It certainly is very good in the flux, but of no use when they are short of milk. Have got some by me in case it should be wanted. I received your paper for the account of cattle. A very good method when the flock vareys often, but our stock is the same still, except at lambing time and Michaelmas, when we sell of. Think that the only time to give you the account. Have inclosed the two last butcher's bills for you to see what is had. It's the cats' and dogs' meat that makes them much more than they otherwise would be. Have paid old Joe for one years annuity to Michaelmas.[3] He is a miserable obiect, eat out with dirt & filth but as hart whole as ever. Have paid Shipway his bill for what jobs he has done to the 8th January last, that is about the house & farm. Likewise a bill of Mrs Clements[4] for small articles. The cash received for the wool is £23 18s 0d, which with what I received before makes the price £1 15s 0d per tod, the highest price I ever remember it to have sold for. A few days since a person cald on me with the bill sent for wine in my late master's time. I told him him I should not pay it tell sent to you for your inspection. I remmember my master used to have wine of him, but whither any thing is unpaid know nothing about. Have not received the quarter's rent of Mr Tanner yet. Wee hear Mr and Mrs Chester went from Bristol about a fortnight since. Am just going to the Easter vestry to settle the the parish accounts.[5] Am sure the poor rates next year will break the farmers unless some alteration is made. They have no spinning work at all. The greater part of them rely on the parish intirely for their support.
I am, with great respect Madam, your most obedient humble servant
Richd Hickley
Avebury
2d April 1793

A very deep snow last night.

1 Setting.
2 Or perhaps rue.
3 See p.xxx, n.xxx.
4 She was the wife of John Clements, and was probably helping to run his grocery business; see *AWS*, p.66 & 68.
5 Hickley was churchwarden; see WSHC D3/15/20.

Verso Note: Hickley's letter, 30th March 1793.
Verso Address: Mrs Williamson, Jamaica. By May packett.[1]

186. John Ward[2] to Adam Williamson WSHC 184/6

Dear Sir,

Marlborough
April 1793

Though I have little to say I cannot omit writing to thank you for your very obliging favor of the 12th of January by which I was happy to receive so good an account of your and Mrs Williamsons health, & sincerely hope you will long continue to enjoy that blessing both in the West Indies and afterwards at Avebury. You will have heard before you receive this of an intended marriage between Lord Bruce and Miss Hill, daughter of the late Lord & present Lady Barwick of Shropshire, & sister of the present Lord Barwick. Lord Bruce became acquainted with her by accidentally seeing her & Lady Barwick in distress in Rome about 6 or 8 months ago enquiring for lodgings. He offered his services, & succeeded in getting lodgings for them, & afterwards renewed his acquaintance. Lord Ailesbury has been acquainted with the progress of their connexion & applied to for consent, which he has given with much pleasure, having heard Miss Hill is spoken of by everybody as a young lady highly accomplished, & of a very excellent disposition, & being desirous his son should marry early in life, & that his happiness should be consulted in the choice he should make. He is in his 21st year & Miss Hill about the same age.

Doctor Garlicke has been here and took the liberty of looking at your house at Hungerford but did not altogether approve of the situation, & his friends in the north are very earnest with him to settle at Derby, & he is gone to look at that situation. He desired when I wrote I would present his respectful compliments & thanks for the kind remembrance of him in your letter.

187. Richard Hickley to Mrs Williamson WSHC 184/6

Avebury
30 April 1793

Honoured Madam,

I yesterday received your paquet, but as the Miss Rennalds are gone to town put it under cover & sent it to Mr Lewis last night. Shall not receive mine in time to answer any thing that may be nessacery. Think wee are not like to have any summer this year, very cold and wet weather going on, I think much like the last spring. Am sowing oats and barley. Am doubtful whether we shall have a crop or not. Am forced to sow near a dubble quantity, the seed is so very bad. Think all things combine together this year for bad luck. Had the misfortune yesterday to

1 This clause written at right angles.
2 He does not sign the letter, but it is in his handwriting.

loose a good horse owing to a stoppage of urine. I tried several powerful things, but all to no purpose. Wee stood in need of two before, and now must buy three, but unless I can have some method to draw for money must give out farmeing. The expences are so great, and little or no corn to sell makes it impossible to get on. The estate may and certainly will be better in time, but it will be a work of time to bring it about. On the whole I like it tollerable well, was it not for the expence. Should now be glad to send out the beer if any ship was going. Wrote to the wine merchant last week to let me know of the first opportunity. Have paid Miss Rennald the fifty pounds due to them the fifth December last. Have heard nothing about Hungerford since my last.
I am, with respect, Madam, your most obedient humble servant,
Richd Hickley

Verso Note: Hickley letter to the 30th April 1793
Verso Address: Mrs Williamson, Kings House, Jamaica.

188. Richard Hickley to Mrs Williamson WSHC 184/6

Avebury
4 June 1793

Honoured Madam,
Inclosed is a very exact plan of the estate, which believe you will be able to understand very clearly, every piece of land being marked that belongs to you, with the name of the piece and the measurement, and, at the bottom of the plan is the name of every piece belonging to you and no one's else. The Down is all yours with the new inclosure or penning as he calls it, which is what I meant before by the new inclosure. This I intend for pasture, that is for mowing for hay, as it's the best part of the Down, and, when the summer is not too dry, may cut a tollerable good crop. The new inclosure at Beckhamton, as the man calls it, is the small field you often mention, the same as my late master had inclosed many years ago. That has undergone no alteration, but stands the same as before the exchange. You see it marked by the side of the road with Hatchet's House, and land on the other side cald Folly Hill Inclosures.[1] The Wal Ditches those two marked GW belong to you, the others one to Nalder,[2] the other to Thring[3] as marked. The old inclosure as cald is the Hundred Acres, the same as it ever was. Crofts, as you observe, is the piece before my house. I hope and believe there is no part of it but you and my master will very clearly understand. Wish it could have been sent without being folded, as it's certainly don very well. From the south west part of Thornhill field to the north east part of the Down is more than three miles. Should have liked it better if it had laid more compact together, but as it could not be don it must be borne with. You wished to have one of the old

1 Hatchet's house is now the Waggon and Horses, once known as the Folly.
2 Robert Nalder.
3 Richard Thring, a prominent dissenter; see *AWS*, p.228-9.

plans sent, but believe they are not at at [sic] Avebury. Mrs Rennald and myself have searched for them in every place wee could think of. She says she thinks they are in London. Indeed, tis of no great consequence, for the greater part of the land you have now you had before. Please to accept mine and my wife's duty and thanks for a present of three guineas, likewise for some pork and veal that Mrs Rennalds gave us. The children desire their duty and thanks for a present from London by Mrs R.[1] Have received the three quarters rent of Mr Tanner for one of the small house at Hungerford due at Xmas 1791. Mr Whitelock has got one of them, Mr Manning the other. Find Mr Hickey offered Whitelock the mansion for £30 a year. I think very cheap, but he thought it too dear. In short, believe on the whole he could not afford to give the money. Last week I went to Bath to settle with Mrs Jenny. Received £28 in part. She is a very odd lady. Pretended she had not collected the tax bills together. Promised to get them and send them to me next week. I sounded her about purchasing the house. She said she had no objection to have it but that it was too dear. I gave her to understand there was a person I thought would be glad to have it at all the money if not more. She gave her answer that could not be, as she has a lease of it, but that some person had cald on her about it which believe was the same I meant, Saunders the person I mentioned to you some time since. I know he would be glad to buy it, but as she has entered on the second seven years how can that be don, as I'm sure she won't give it up. Said she should like to purchase it for a relation, but that she would not let her come to Bath to reside while she lives. So the matter rested. Said she intended writing to the General, as she had received an exceeding civil letter from him. I have not received Hatchet's rent yet, as he says at present cannot raise the money. Hope to receive it in a few weeks. His wife is in a very poor way, rather inclined to be dropsycal. The Commissioners of the exchange of lands are to meet on the 17th of this month. I hope to put a final end to the business. Hear nothing at all more about the tythes, fancy that matter is all over with respect to your property. I rather wonder at Mr Ward writing to you about bringing the cannal as one may say through your house. I never understood if it was to be done that it would come through Avebury, but by Beckhamton. Most people I believe think it never will go either way. It seems to be come a dead letter. They say the money subscribed was put in one of the Bristol banks and all lost.[2] If so, so much the better, as wee country farmers want no cannals near us. You enquire about the new rick staddles and their not wanting repairing. They are things that always want repairing. Wee have not one good one on the farm, except those two new ones. Staddles for the wheat must be had, but as for the barley, shan't trouble about, as that may be put on the ground with plenty of straw under it. Am now brushing up the Mansion House a little, that is, mending the craks in the walls, and whitewashing to keep the wet out. Have been stoping up some of the windows, as many as will save four pounds per year, and in your absence the house will be just as well as before. It's abominable to pay so much tax and no

1 Rennald.
2 Presumably during the 1793 run on the banks.

family in the house. Have just don sowing barley. Are very much in want of rain to fetch it up. If wee don't have some soon shall be as bad of as last year, when wee had altogether so much. The wheat looks exceeding well in the ground, the grass wants rain very much. I agree with you about suckling calves as tis my intention to suckkell this summer. Have three calves at present, and five cows, but only four that gives milk. Shall make no chees, at least but very little, as I think wee have near enough to serve the family the year out. Your desire to have one or two sent out, have none that will do for that, but if wee send the beer will buy a cupple of good ones. Fear there will be no possibility of sending the beer this summer. The war is so hot no one will stir without a convoy. What with the war, taxes, and the stagnation of trade, half the country will be ruined. Will take care to get some rabits if wanted, likewise the corks and harness oil. About a fortnight since had the misfortune to loose Harper,[1] one of my shepherds; the poor fellow died with a mortification in his bowels. But I have the satisfaction to know he was properly attended, and all the care taken of him that lay in my power. Am rather at loss at present, but think I shall soon get a proper person that will answer my purpose as well. At present are like to have tollerable stock of poultry, but no great quantity of pidgeons yet. Have got Beaven out of the house at last, but not a farthing of money, nor ever shall. Mrs. Brown and her two daughters are in the house, that is, in the two tenaments. David is in the house in the churchyard very handy to his work. I have done only the nessacery repairs, that is to keep it wind and weather bound. What alteration she chused to make is at her own expence, which has been very considerable. The rent to be six guineas. You mention making bounds on the Wal Ditch from the rickyard to the road if any odd stuff, but there is not a bit about the premises, but if there was tis intirely throwing money away, as that put up before you left home will be all rotten before next winter is over, and oak timber is got to such a price and so scarce in the country there is no quantity to be got, at least without giving a very extravagant price.
I am, with great respect, Madam, your most obedient humble servant
Richard Hickley

Note at foot (at right angles): Hickley's letter, 4th June 1793.

189. Richard Hickley to Mrs Williamson WSHC 184/6

Avebury
2 July 1793

Honoured Madam,
I received yours of the 1st April. Am sorry you should have any cause to complain of my conduct, as I flatter myself I have always endeavoured to give you the best information with respect to the business committed to my charge as lay in my power. In the first place you mention about the exchange of the lands. If you will please to examine my former letters you will find I have given you the account

1 William Harper buried 26th May 1793.

of what past at the different meetings of the Commissioners. In my letter of the 1st of February I said I shall say nothing about the inclosure business, as the Commissioners are to meet in a few days. Indeed I could not till after the meeting. Then in that of the 4th March, I gave you the account of what passed, which was very trifleing. By that of the 2d April mentioned my thoughts with respect to the parson's tythes. Since that could say nothing till after the 17th June, which was the last meeting, when all the business was setled, and the Commissioners, surveyors and others received their money. I spoke to Mr Ward about your money. He said he had a letter from my master signifying I was to pay the money as the profits came in. I told him it would be some time before I could pay any part of it. He gave for answer that he must wait till I could. I wished to know what intrest he would require, but could get no answer to that. After beging very hard at the meeting I got £14 more toward making the bridge and road, which was more than I expected. I did not expect to have got a farthing more than what was allowed before. The whole of the money now to be allowed is £49, which on the whole is tollerable well. Shall not receive it if I can get on without it. Twil be deducted from the £266 12s 4d. I certainly have mentioned more than once where the new inclosure is made on the Down. Mrs Rennald will I believe attest that I do consult her in all your business, except the management of the husbandry, which tis not to be thought she should know any thing about. Am sorry you should think any thing about my being <u>lifted up</u> as I flatter my self I have none of that nonsensical pride about me, perhaps not so much as I ought to have. If you look in my letter of the 4th December you will see I gave the reason for buying sheep in the autumn. Have found the mistake of the 16s and allowed it in the account. As to the produce from the farm with respect to poultry last year, or indeed any thing else, cannot brag about. Believe every farmer in this country has found it so. I endeavour to make the most of every thing as far as lay in my power. Was the estate my own could not do more. Certainly but little money was made of butter & chees for <u>sale</u>. The produce of four or five cows from the Downs after the family has had a little cannot be great. Shall make but very little this summer, that is butter and chees, as I keep calves enough to suck all the milk. The keeping more cows cannot answer by any means, for to eat up the grass in the summer and buy hay in winter will not do. If wee have a little more pasture for hay, shall have more sheep to consume it in the winter. Indeed shall cut but very little this summer. Have had no rain worth noticing for this three months. The wheat is like to be good, but the barley in general is but very midling. You have the account of the horses bought at different times since my late master's death. Have bought two lately; have 12 in the whole at this time, all pretty good except one. The expence of buying horses has been very great since you have had the estate. To be sure when you came to it the horses were all old and worn out. You say Gale the woodman's bill,

[£]4 2[s] 10[d], its for hedging. The smiths bill you say is large. The fixed price for shoeing the horses, keeping the ploughs, harrows, drags, harness, &c., in repair is sixteen pounds per year, then there is waggons, carts, gates, doors, and many things besides to be don, which sometimes makes the bills come to a considerable deal more. Inclosed is a bill of Lavington's the nurseryman. The barberry plants charged is what I have planted round the new inclosure on the Down, which is much cheaper and I think will answer better than white thorn. The seeds &c the gardener had, which he says is right, as it has not been in my power to pay Lee the nursery man at Hammersmith[1] the bill you left with me. Added to that things the gardener has had since of him, he thought it best to have what few seeds he wanted this year of Lavington, and not to send to Lee any more till he is paid, which shall be don as soon as lay in my power. Likewise a bill from Mr Eames the wine merchant for twelve dozen of bottles, 11 gallons of brandy, four stone jars, 18 dozen of corks, this by Mrs Rennald's order. The other bill for the carriage of the above things from Bristol. The bacon and box of shoes were put on board the Stephen, Capt Bendy, then the Capt altered his mind and said he would go to some other part of the island, which gave Mr Eames a great deal of trouble to get some other ship to take it. After all find he altered again and went to Kingston. Dare say you have it long before this time. The beer has been ready for some time but there is no prospect of any ship going from Bristol at present. Since the last meeting of the Commissioners for the exchange, Mr Mayo[2] has been at Avebury. Indeed he was at the meeting, but nothing was mentioned. Since that one of the Commissioners has been to look over the vicar's tythes, that is, the land liable to pay to him. By chance I happened to meet him. Among other things had some talk with him about your payment. Said he thought he might venture to set an acre of your best wheat at eight sacks to the acre and at one pound seven shillings per sack. Now the two ell ridges as they call it is three quarters of an acre, so of course that must be six sacks for the vicar, which at one pound seven shillings per sack is eight pounds two shillings. I told him I could venture to affirm that wee never had more than six sacks to the acre, that is one with the other, and not often that. He said he could not think that to be right. I gave for answer whither you believe it or not I know it to be true. But pray Sir, how do you prove the measure. The terrier expresses three quarters of an acre or <u>there about</u>. Now I think if Mr Mayo was to go to reaping the he might find himself in the wrong, because it says he is to <u>cut</u> and carry away. He said any court would confirm and settle it at three quarters of an acre. I said how far that might be law. I thought it would be difficult for him to <u>prove</u>. Besides there has been a certain sum of money paid for time immemorial. No one can remmember or ever heard of it being taken in kind. He said at last it was the most intricate piece of business he ever met with, take it altogether. Since that I met with Mr Mayo, had some talk with him about it. He talked very coolly about the matter. Said he did not wish to press hard on any person, but as the value of things was much more than it was a centry back, he thought some little alteration in justice might be made without hurting anyone. I mentioned to him, as I had to the Commissioner, about ascertaining the quantity of the land, and the fixed

1 James Lee, of the Vineyard Nursery in Hammersmith, was a leading nurserymen in the late 18th century; see **https://en.wikipedia.org/wiki/Lee_and_Kennedy**.

2 The Vicar resided in Wimborne Minster, Dorset, where he was master of the grammar school.

sum that was paid. Said he thought his predecessor could fix any thing of that sort only for his own life. I told him I thought if any alteration was made the General would dispute the affair, and if he was not satisfied he should write to him on the subject, as I would not suffer any alteration without it. So the matter rested; have heard nothing of it since.

I have received Hatchet's rent which was due last Lady Day, but have heard nothing about the remainder of Mrs Jenny's. She promised to write to me in a few days, though there is very little more money coming by the time the taxes are paid. Am going to shear the sheep this week. The war has hurt the trade of this country so much that the wool I suppose won't be worth so much at least by four if not five pence per pound as it was the last year. The stock of sheep at this time is nine hundred and fifty sheep and three hundred and sixty lambs. Have just began haymaking; the crop is very short owing to the dry weather. Hope what wee have shall make good, and not to starve the sheep as they were the last winter owing to the badness of the hay. Since stating the account find the ballance is so great, and I am so much in debt. Believe I must draw the forty nine pound allowed for the bridge of Mr Ward, as it's impossible for me to stand my ground without it. I have not setled Brown account at Hungerford, neither can I till he has received the rents of Mr Manning. The two small houses are now inhabited, but no hopes at present of leting the other

I am, Madam, your most obedient humble servant
Richd Hickley

Verso Note: Hickley's letter, 3rd July 1793.

190. A. Jenny to Richard Hickley WSHC 184/6

At Tompkins Dewe, Esq.,
No 23, Portland Place
London
18 July 1793[1]

Mr Hickley,

Since my arrival here received a letter from Mrs Williamson from Jamaica to say that they determined to sell no.4, Miles Court, offering me the refusal. But I am puzzled to whom to write my answer, because the address I don't know. Therefore beg you to inform me. Also if the deed for the sale is come over. I understand some person at Bath hav offered for it. I wish to know whom, but subject to my lease as [?since] new; [?an] query if 400 offered, as my lease to anyone but myself is an objectin, & was I to buy it £500 is beyond the price to any one. Allow me some days for my answer, because my time is devoted to two sick friends. [?Meantime] tis very likely I may return in 6 weeks, when weather is cooler. I am your well wisher,

1 The year is not stated in the letter, but it was sent to Mrs Williamson with Hickley's letter 5 August 1793.

A Jenny.

No chicken ever came, though I was to pay for them.

Verso Address: Mr Hickley, steward at Averbury House, near Marlborough, Wilts.

191. Richard Hickley to Mrs Williamson WSHC 184/6

Avebury
5 August 1793

Wee yesterday received yours of the 30th March, with Mr Ashe's bill inclosed. The first time I go to Bristol will call and have it explained. For my part I know nothing about it. I remember my master's haveing wine from him at different times, but cannot tell what money he received. Inclosed is a letter received from Mrs Jenny.[1] Intend writing to her in a few days with directions where to find Mr. Hickey. Don't think the old lady in reality wishes for any one else to have the house. Have not seen Saunders for some time, that is, the other person that wished to purchase it. Will see him the first opportunity. I know he is desirous of haveing it, but whether he would like to purchase it as tis circumstanced cannot tell. Suppose I shall not be able to settle the whole of her rent till she returns to Bath. Find Mr. Whitelocke is likely to have the large house at Hungerford, as Mr Hickey has wrote to know what land is to go with it. He is at present in one of the small houses. No signs at present of Mr Manning's returning, so how that rent is to be got cannot tell. If I knew where he was would go to him. Have weighed the wool and taken [£]1 2[s] 0[d] per tod in part. No one can tell you what the price will be at present. Have paid Mrs Rennald the fifty pounds due to them on the fifth July. You mention her leting me have fifty pounds. This she says she cannot do as she has no money at all. As to the £50 I had of her, will pay as soon as lay in my power. The haymaking is just over. Never had a finear time to be sure for making it, not a drop of rain till within these few days. On the whole the crops of hay are tollerable good, considering what a dry season we have had. Have no doubt but wee shall have enough for the next winter without buying. The hay charged in the account is what I bought in the spring. The harvest is at hand; shall begin reaping in two or three days. The wheat is very good, but the barley is but very indifferent owing to the dryness of the weather. Whoever might mention about the farmers spoiling the partridges' eggs or Adam Wiltshire's secreting the game, I do not believe one word of it, as I never heard any thing of the kind. I saw your plan for planting Silbury Hill by taking of the top. I conceive you do not know the size of the top of that hill as it now is. Don't think it much less than half an acre of ground. Twil cost a deal of money to make a fence round it, that is, I mean the top of it. To be sure a plantation on the top of that hill in a few years would look beautiful. As to a hedge round the rick yard, think will not answer, as it never will make bounds to keep the cattle out, especially the pigs, without

1 The letter dated 18 July 1793 above.

a paleing on the outside. The present one has been up for many years, and is got very feeble indeed. Have heard nothing about Mr Mayo and his tythes since my last. Inclosed is a bill of Mrs Mitchel's for churwomen which I have paid
I am, Madam, your most obedient humble servant
Richd Hickley

Verso Note: Hickley's letter 5th August 1793
Verso Address: Mrs Williamson, Kings House, Jamaica

192. Richard Hickley to Mrs Williamson WSHC 184/6

Avebury
9 September 1793

Honoured Madam,
I said in my last I had received yours of the 30th March but made a mistake as it was the 7th June. Wee are happy to hear you are well and quiet those miserable times, to be sure the accounts wee have in the papers[1] makes one shudder. Thank God we have none of these calamitys at Avebury. Have just don the wheat harvest, which has been the finest I have known for these many years. The wheat in general is very good and housed exceeding dry; as to the barley and oats, cannot say much about, that is but very indifferent indeed owing to the dryness of the summer. Have got in all the oats and began cuting a little of the barley, but must give out again, as some of it won't be ripe this month or five weeks. Indeed it never will be all ripe, as it did not come up regular. Have not very good luck with the turnips. I sowed a great many, but the weather continuing dry so long they never came up. Have got about nine or ten acres, which believe will be tollerable good. Are like to have a good crop of after grass, which will help us very much. Thank God the sheep and all the cattle are in good health. Have received the £49 of Mr Ward allowed for the bridge and road. Have paid for the materials and building the bridge. The other part of the work, that is the carting and filing the earth &c comes into the common weekly labour of the farm, and charged as such. Have a great deal more to do to it yet, but that must remain to be don at odd times in the winter, in frosty weather when nothing else can be don. Have another considerable job to do, that is to cleanse the river all down by South Meadow, as was ordered by the Commissoners, that is, for every one whose land it past through to do his own part. It certainly is a very proper thing to be don, as it will prevent the water from overflowing the lands on each side. Shall begin my part as soon as possible to get it done before the rain sets in to bring the water down. The cannal business is settled. It is fixed to go by Great Bedwin & Pewsey, so we shan't have them near us, which think will be much the better. The expence is estimated at three hundred thousand pounds. The people at Marlbro are very much out of humour about it. They say their town will be ruined. How will the house at Hungerford come of by it. I mean Stoney Hall. I understand by

1 Newspapers were evidently available in late 18th century Avebury.

the survey it is to go through the shrubery in the front of the house and where the barn stands. Will not that make the premises of more value if sold. I think it a pity it should go so near the house. Have not heard if Mr. Whitelock has taken it or not, but rather think he has. Intend going up in a few days. I hear Mr Manning is gone abroad. If so that money will be lost, or at least be some time before it will be got. Tis two years at Michaelmas, twenty eight guineas. I think if he is not heard of by that time, I must take possession of the house and let it to some other person. There is nothing on the premises but two old trumpery cows and three or four dogs, all which Mr. Whitelocke has taken into his possession to keep, and stand the chance of Manning's paying him for the keep when he returns. If there had been property enough to have paid the rent, I would have seized. Have wrote to Mrs Jenny, but as she is not returned to Bath have heard nothing from her since. No account of any ship going from Bristol for Jamaica; how wee are to send the beer and other things cannot tell. Believe the preserved things are very fine; wish we could send them away directly. The Beckhamton club of shooters met yesterday. Don't think there will be much game for them, as I have seen but very few partridges this season. Adam Wiltshire[1] had tollerable luck for the first day: six brace of birds and one hare, which Mrs Rennald sent of last night. There is a mistake of ten shillings in the account, that is, in the money received of Mrs Rennald for her goods received from the farm, which I will make my self debtor for in the next month's account. Believe she has mentioned it in her letter.
My wife and self desire our duty to you and my master, and I am,
with great respect, your most obedient humble servant
Richd Hickley

Verso Note: Hickley letter, 9th September 1793
Verso Address: Mrs Williamson, Kings House, Jamaica.

193. John Ward to Adam Williamson WSHC 184/6

Marlborough
20 September 1793

Dear Sir,
I am greatly ashamed to think how long I have neglected to thank you for your obliging letters of January and March last. That I intended to have behaved better, I send you the inclosed unfinished letter to prove. The fact is I did not think it worth sending, & I have lately had so much business on hand that I could not get time to look over my papers & letters.

Our canal proprietors have determined on taking the Bedwin & Pewsey & Devizes line, which will of course miss Marlbro & Avebury, which is a great disappointment to us, but could not be avoided. The engineer has planned to go through Hungerford, across your court on the south of your house, & so under your barn and through your garden &c., but you need not be alarmed at such

1 Williamson's gamekeeper, *AWS*, p.300.

an invasion of your property, as I will take care to insert a clause in the act for the purpose of securing you against any loss by such a measure. In the first place, I think it will make your property sell better than it would do otherwise for the purposes of trade. But the clause I shall propose is that the proprietors shall either pay you for the injury to your property by cutting through in such sum as a jury shall assess, or shall purchase the house, yard, outbuildings, garden, &c., at a price to be fixed by a jury, either plan to be at your option, which I think will make you pretty safe, as juries in deciding between public bodies and a private individual generally lean in favour of the individual. I hope there may be time, however, for me to hear from you before the act passes, & as no man can answer for the success of a clause, I can only say that I will do my best to get what I have mentioned allowed of.

Dr Garlicke is at present settled at Ashborn,[1] but continues to say he would come to Marlbro if he could get a good house. Mrs G is in a family way, which has not been the case for several years before. We have paid them a visit this summer and found them well.

Lord Bruce is most happily married to Miss Hill. They are not to come home till next summer & are to live in a house of Lord Ailesbury's adjoining the Park,[2] which will be a very comfortable situation for them, & nothing can be more grateful & pleasing than their letters to Lord Ailesbury are.[3]

I hope this will find my good friend Mrs Williamson and yourself in good health & spirits, & in no danger of being disturbed by the French or any other trouble. We seem to be in very hot water in the Netherlands,[4] but I sincerely hope our successes at Toulon[5] will bring about a peace.

I hope my friends Mr and Mrs Chester are by this time comfortably settled in Jamaica & in good health, & that Mrs Williamson and you have found no reason to disapprove of my recommendation of them, & shall be obliged to you if you will present our kind remembrance to them when you see them. Mr and Mrs Hope[6] are much better than they have been, & Ellen is very well, & I can assure them she is surprisingly improved since she has been at Hungerford School, & is as fine sensible a child as one would wish to see.

I have taken the liberty of inclosing my little account, & our bill of charges upon you since the death of your late worthy friend, & if there is no error you will find a balance of £53 3[s] 9[d] which if you please to order Hickley to pay to me, with the inclosure rate, at his convenience you will oblige me. But I do not wish to put you or him to any inconvenience about it. He has had a bad year last year & I know he has no money at present. I have made free to put down the

1 Ashbourne, Derbyshire.
2 Tottenham Park.
3 Ward was an agent for Lord Ailesbury, and evidently had access to his correspondence; see WSHC 9/1/459-471.
4 The Allies, after enjoying several early successes, had been forced to withdraw.
5 The Anglo-Spanish forces were in fact forced to withdraw by Napoleon.
6 They have not been identified.

legacy Mr Jones gave me.[1]

Lord and Lady Ailesbury, & the Lady Bruce, are very well. The latter have spent this summer in Seamour Place. Lord & Lady A are at Tottenham Park, & told me of Ensign Lippeatt's being called to Jamaica, by whom I believe this packet will be sent, & desired their compliments & best wishes to Mrs Williamson & yourself & thanks for your kind remembrance of them.

Mrs Ward and my brother join me in most respectful compliments to Mrs Williamson & yourself, & the sincerest & best wishes for your health & happiness. I am, dear Sir, most truly & sincerely, your obliged & obedient servant,
John Ward

P.S. Mr. Hope and Mr. Mayber were taken into our Corporation in August last. I recollect no other news of this place or neighbourhood.

Verso Note: General Williamson

Additional Page[2]
Pray say whether you approve of the canal coming through your estate which I hope you will as I trust it will be a great improvement to it. In both your official letters, only in that letter by which you accept the shares, you had better make it a condition of your consenting to the canal coming through your property that you have some shares in the canal.

Verso Note: General Williamson.

194. John Ward to Adam Williamson WSHC 184/6

Marlbro
27th September 1793

My dear Sir,
I received with the greatest pleasure your very obliging letter of the 11th of July. Since writing the inclosed, which was to have gone by Ensign Lippeatt, but he does not go, I find, to Jamaica. Mrs Hope had a letter from her daughter at the same time, & I never saw a person so much affected with the sensation of gratitude as she was, & Mr Hope is also truly sensible of & obliged to Mrs Williamson and you for your great kindness to their son & daughter, & Mrs Ward & myself join with them in best thanks to you, & pray make our best regards acceptable to them.

Mr Whitelocke, a surgeon, has taken Stoney Hall, & has desired me to say he should be glad to purchase it, that is, the house, buildings belonging to it, paddock, garden & pleasure ground adjoining, & I suppose he expects to give at

1 Arthur Jones bequeathed him 'five guineas for a ring'; TNA PROB11/1181/174.
2 This is a separate page, and appears to be part of the letter not sent referred to above. The original letter is not signed.

least as much as was bid by Pearce for it at the auction.

Mr Mundy is also a candidate for this property, as I have heard, so you see there is nothing to be apprehended from the alteration of our canal line. Our best compliments & most sincere good wishes ever attend Mrs Williamson & yourself, and I remain,

Dear Sir, your obliged and most obedient servant,
John Ward

Lord Ailesbury has undertaken to get a friend to forward Mrs Hope's letter to her daughter, but I do not think it will arrive so soon as this. Mrs Hope is much better than when Mr Chester was here, & now her anxiety is so much relieved I have no doubt she will recover her spirits & strength. Mr Hope is very well.

Verso Note:
I should have said that Lord & Lady Ailesbury desired me to make their best acknowledgements & compliments, & are much obliged to you for so kindly offering any services, & particularly for your attention to the daughter & son in law of a very old friend whose family have always been his Lordship's most steady friends at Marlborough .

I am almost ashamed to send so large a packet.

Note at top of letter: 'Answered by the Antelop to send him balance Mr Ward the [?Princess Royal [£]53 3[s] 9[d]'

Verso Address: General Williamson, Lt Governor of Jamaica.

195. Richard Hickley to Mrs Williamson WSHC 184/6

[1 October 1793][1]

Honoured Madam,

I received yours on the 13th July with the draft for £100 to buy the horses, but as I have bought two since the receipt of your letter shall buy only one more at present. The money will be very acceptable. Last week received a letter from Mr Eames, the wine merchant, saying the West India fleet would sail the end of next month or the beginning of December. Shall get the things ready and send them to Bristol as soon as possible. Shall not have it insured, as you think it not necssary. Shall be happy to see Mr Belford at Avebury, but should be much more so to see you all. Think the gentlemen of the Beckhamton Club has behaved in a very strange unaccountable manner, particularly Mr Northey. He one day sent for Adam Wiltshire and told him he was not to shoot while they were there, and that he had a letter in his pocket from the General, in which he gave orders that

1 Note written across the top of the letter: 'Supposed to be wrote the latter end of September or 1st October'. In fact, although the letter is undated, it must have been written in October, as Hickley refers to November as 'next month'.

his game keeper was not to kill any game till after the gentlemen of the Club were gone. This Wiltshire came and told to me. Cannot say but it made me rather warm, as I knew it must be a falsehood. I had some inclination to go to him. However, after teling the story to Mrs Rennald I ordered him to shoot as before, and if they forbid him any more I would give them a meeting, but to be careful to keep within bounds, for if they had an opportunity they were base enough to lay an information against him. However, heard no more about it afterward. Very dirty work for a gentleman indeed. About a fortnight since I went to Hungerford. Mr. Whitelocke has taken Stoney Hall of Mr Hickey at £30 and is got into it. The other small house he went out of I have let to a person of Hungerford of the name of Foot,[1] a grocer, for one year at the usual rent of twelve guineas. Find there is no truth in the report of Mr Manning's being gone abroad, as he was expected at Hungerford in a few days, and that he realy had paid some of his debts there. Intend going up next week to see how matters stand. The weather is fine, but not like to finish harvest for some time. Very bad barly. Indeed, there is not a bit of good barley in this parish, nor, in short, in the neighbourhood, but as wee cannot help it must be content. The cattle of all sorts thank God are well. I am, with great respect, Madam, your very humble servant
Richd Hickley

Verso Note: Hickley, supposed to be wrote the end of September, or first of October 1793[2]
Verso Address: Mrs Williamson, Kings House, Jamaica.

196. Richard Hickley to Mrs Williamson WSHC 184/6

Avebury
8 November 1793

Honoured Madam,
We received yours of the 10th of August, & likewise that of the 31st within two days of each other. Wonder how they hapened to be so near together. Last week I carried the beer & other things to Bristol, which have inclosed a sort of list that is the number of articles sent. If I had received your letter in time would have sent a cask of harness oil as you desired, but I was gone with the things when the pakuet came. I thought it much the best way to carry the things to Bristol with our own waggon, which certainly was a very great saving. To have hired the carriage would have cost 8 or 9 pounds, which by taking the advantage of bringing back a load of coales did not cost above one pound eleven shillings, exclusive of the horses' labour. The things were put under the care of Mr Eames and to be shiped the next day. Find the fleet is to sail in a few days. Hope the beer will turn out good, but tis not so rich as I could wish, owing to the badness of the malt this year, though I allowed a much greater quantity of malt than usual for the

1 He has not been identified.
2 A similar note is written across the top of the letter.

same quantity of beer. Think as near as I can calculate the cost of the three casks delivered at Bristol, exclusive of the small beer made after, it is about £16 10s. Have forwarded Mr Eames' letter. He told me he expected the certificates by the next paquet. He is a very civil man, & willing to render any services that lay in his power. If I had received the bill of his which you inclosed would have paid him, but must take some other opportunity. Mr Ward seems not pleased at not being paid the money for the inclosure. I thought when the sheep were sold to have paid him a £100 or so in part, but Mrs Rennald seems to have such a demand for money it will be impossible for me to pay him any. Besides there is a great ballance due to Crook the carpenter.[1] Cannot possibly put him of any longer any longer. Lee the nursery man, the malster &c., which must be paid. Have not sold the sheep yet, & when I do fear shall have but a bad market, as they sells at a very low price this year owing to the failure of the turnips. Bad sale of sheep, not half a crop of barley, and a very very burthensome poor, all seems to combine against the farmer. Hope another year to see better times, otherwise believe you must give out farmering. Must thrash out the wheat as fast as possible, and do the best I can. Am determined when I have got the estate in some form another year, if possible, to raise hay and turnips, & keep the sheep at home, as I cannot bear the thoughts of paying so much money for wintering them abroad. Have finised the barley harvest, such as it was, about a fortnight since. The weather was very fine, which was very much in favour of the fodder, which is very good though but little of it. You mention my buying Welch oxen to eat the straw, but that will not pay so well as taking in of cows at eighteen pence or two shillings per week each, which intend doing to eat what straw we have to spare. I observe what you say about the South Down sheep. Must own I like them very much. Have had a great deal of talk with Mr Mighell[2] about them at different times. Many people are geting into the sort of them, but it is the general opinion, after they becomes plenty in this country, they will not be approved of, that is, they will not sell. Therefore I wish to waite a year or two to see the event, as it would be a sad piece of business to have them to change again if they should not answer. Since my last a gentleman of the name of Escott[3] of the Beckhamton club of shooters cald on me, making very heavy complaints against Wiltshire the gamekeeper, charging him with destroying the game &c., and that he could bring a person to prove that Wiltshire said the first year he was gamekeeper he kild a 100 brace of birds, and that he kild the birds in the winter, which prevented the breed in the spring, and a great deal of such talk. I told him I could not take upon me to swear it was not true, but my being about the manor continually, if it realy was so, I certainly must see something of it, and that I did not believe a word of the matter. Have talked to Wiltshire about it. He says he will make oath he never said any such thing. He produced part of a letter wrote by the General, wherein I think he says he wishes the gentlemen of the club to sport on his property, but not as they told Wiltshire

1 Probably Stephen Crook.
2 Joseph Mighell purchased East Kennett manor in 1789; see *VCH Wilts.*, 12, p..121.
3 He has not been identified.

at Beckhamton that he was not to shoot till after they were gone. He said if the corn was not cut by the first of September the gentlemen would wish to keep back a week or two, provided I would keep others back, and not let Wiltshire kill before they came, and a great deal of such talk not worth mentioning. I told him on the whole that I could say nothing about the matter, but that I should write to my master on the subject, and there was plenty of time before the next season to have his directions how to act. He cald afterward on Mrs Rennald, and she, as she is very capable of, played him of very well, and sent him of in very good humour as suppose she will inform you of. So the matter ended. I never knew game so scarce since I have been at Avebury as within these two years past, but don't believe one word of what they say about Wiltshire's destroying or secreting it. Here is in this parish a scoundrel, one Joseph Robbins,[1] which I know is a very great enemy to the game. He is employed by the hunters and coursers to find hares for them, and if there is a hare in the parish he knows where to find it. I have given him a good repremand and told him I would acquaint the General of it. Wish my master would give him a line or two by way of cheaque. Wee are like to have the worst winter with respect to the poor that ever was known, owing to their want of employ. No doubt but they will rebel in a short time, I mean in the great clothing towns, and destroy those spinning machines, which think will be so much the better. Suppose not less than 250 women and children in this small parish without employ all this winter. A work house can be of no sort of service unless there was something for them to do. Wee must send them out on the Downs to dig flints to mend the roads, or something of that sort, to keep them out of idleness.

The Commissioners of the turnpike roads are going to to [sic] take of a piece of your land at Thornhill by Silbury Hill, by way of making the road more straight. Tis but a small corner. They have promised to meet me on the spot in a few days to settle the value of the land. Will take care to have the full value, otherwise will not agree with them. Thank God we are all well. Sorry we had not an opportunity of seeing Mr Belford before he left England
I am, with great respect, Madam, your most obedient humble servant
Richd Hickley

Inclosed is a bill received from the fish monger at Bath.

Note at foot (at right angles): Hickley, 5th November 1793.

197. Richard Hickley to Mrs Williamson WSHC 184/6

Avebury
30 November 1793

Honoured Madam,
I have at last sold the sheep, the ewes for a tollerable good price, more indeed

1 He has not been identified in the parish, and was probably not a parishioner.

then I expected, the lambs at a very low one owing to the failure of the turnips. Have paid to Mrs Rennald [£]108 14[s] 6[d], which was rather more than I could spare, the demands are so great. The home stock of sheep for the winter is 930. Hope next summer we shall have a good handsome stock of fourteen hundred or more. Have bought two more horses. Did not intend buying but one, but found I could not get on without hurting the rest, as the exchange of lands makes a great deal of extra work till such time as the lands are brought into regular place, after which the work will be considerable less than it used to be, and I hope the produce more. Shall be forced to make another inclosure on the Down to raise hay, if possible to keep the sheep at home another year. The expense of puting them out to winter is so great that nothing will stand before it. The gardener is going to make a plantation on the Down, which in time may look very handsome, but I don't know what to fence it with; must look out and buy something as cheap as I can.

Have settled with the Commissioners of the roads for the piece of land as I mentioned by Silbury Hill. The quantity they have taken is only ¼ of an acre and 25 pole. You are to have the old road in lieu of it, which will be considerable more than what they take, they to make it fit for the plough, so on the whole I think there is no harm done. Have heard nothing from Hungerford since my last. Thought to have went up before now, but realy have not had time. I hear Mrs Jenny is at Bath. Intendgoing very shortly to settle the last year's account. I hear nothing about that prateing Saunders that pretended to purchase it, so suppose he has given it up. Least you should wonder why 20 sacks of wheat sells for no more than [£]16, the reason is the whole country is come to 8 gallon measure, that is 8 gallons to the bushel, which before was nine and a half, so that in 16 sacks there is 96 gallons differance, which when compared together makes it much the same. I don't know that it's either good or hurt to the farmer.[1] Wheat at this time sells better than was expected. Barley is very dear, but that is no great advantage to us, as wee have had but little to sell. Have not thrashed any yet on account of the fodder. The wheat sowing is don, and have had a very fine season for it, so wee live in hopes of a crop if please God another year.

We are all glad [?to] you and my master are in good health, and beg your acceptance of our duty,
and I am, with great respect,
your most obedient
humble servant
Richd Hickley

Verso Note: Hickley 30th November 1793.

1 For local reactions to this change, see Waylen, James. *A History, Military and Municipal, of the Ancient Borough of Devizes*. Longman Brown & Co., 1859, p.470-71.

198. Richard Hickley to Mrs Williamson WSHC 184/6

Avebury
31 December 1793

Honoured Madam,

Wee received your very melancholy letter of the 7th October, which indeed was a great shock to everyone that had the least regard for two such pleasant & promising young people. Yours and my master's tender and affectionate regard for them am satisfied is felt and clearly understood by all their friends, and indeed by every one else, but the will of that great God who knoweth what is best for all his creatures must be submited to. Thanks be to him that you and my master did not receive any injury by visiting them in their illness. Wee have had a short visit by a great stranger, Mr Belford,[1] who is grown a very stout fine young gentleman, and looks exceeding well. He and Isaac undertook to walk from Southampton to Avebury in one day. Did reach this place till one clock in the morning almost tired to deat, covered with water and dirt as it rained nearly all the way. I don't think he will willingly undertake such another journey. When they returned I took two saddle horses and carried them to Salisbury, where they took coach and went home the same evening. I took him round the estate and showed him every part of the lands, which believe he will be able to explain to you when he comes to see the plan which I sent out last. Have bought some rough oak stuff for the fence round the plantation on the Down, which the gardener is making. If Silbury Hill is planted must buy some more, if I can get it, as it won't do to go to the carpenter for timber if it can be avoided. Have just began thrashing out some barly, which sells for a great price, at least such of it as is fit to make malt. Have thrashed only one load, which sold for 36 shillings per quarter, eight gallon measure, but the great misfortune is wee have but very little of that sort. You mentioned my buying oxen to eat the straw, but I have taken in cows at two shillings per week each, which am satisfied will answer much better. The winter hitherto has been remarkable fine and mild, which is very much in favour of the hay and cattle. Likewise, the wheat on the ground looks exceeding well. Last week I went to Hungerford, where I found things much the same as ever, that Mr Manning that rents one of the small houses has not been there, so the rent is not to be come at yet. Old Brown is full of grumbling about his money. He thinks he is used very ill. I told him I could not pay him without the General's order, and that he must waite till the rent can be got. The rent of the land he has always received in part of his waigers. I wish Manning would come and pay the money, that Brown's account might be setled, as tis not so well to have in arrears. I think when Mr Hickey let the house to Mr Whitelocke, he should have made an agreement for a certain sum to have been paid by him for looking after the garden as part of Brown's waigers, whereas as things now stand, he has the garden looked after at your expence. Tis thought he will not remain long in the house as I hear he has but very little or no practise in the town, believe he is very poor. The beef charged in the account is what I bought for the people in the farm,

1 Presumably a son of Mary Belford, Ann Williamson's sister.

which believe Mrs Rennald will give you the full account. I am to return you mine, my wife and children's duty and thanks for a fine piece of beef, and a turkey on which we feasted this Christmas, not forgeting the [?dona]. That you and my master may live to see many more happy returns of the season is the sincere wish of your most respectful and obedient
humble servant
Richd Hickley

Verso Note: Hickley, 31st December 1793
Verso Address: Mrs Williamson, Kings House, Jamaica.

199. Richard Hickley to Mrs Williamson WSHC 184/6

[1 February 1794][1]

Honoured Madam,
Wee received yours of the 24th November. Am very glad to hear you and my master continue so well. Wee have had death as a visitor at the farm house, but at the same time must confess tis no great loss. Poor old Joe died on Friday last, after being worse than usual about a week with his old disorder, a stoppage of urine.[2] By the advice of Mrs Rennald I sent for Mr Pinkney[3] of Marlbro, as she thought it would be wrong to let him die without any assistance. Mr P. thought he had greatly injured himself by taking a whole bottle of daffy at one draft the day before he died. He certainly suffered a great deal, so think tis a very happy deliverance for himself and others. Wee buried him on Sunday last in a very decent manner, my self & wife, John Clements & his wife, the gardener & Mrs. Mitchel, Stephen Crook & Ruth were the mourners. This was not don without consulting Mrs Rennald. You often say I don't consult her, but that is a mistake, as don't move in anything without her approbation. I cannot at present give you the particulars of his affairs but will in my next. His annuity is paid up to Michaelmas 1792, so if he had lived till Lady Day there would have been a year & half due to him. Had in his pocket when died three pound six shillings & six pence, but believe he owes the greater part of that. As to his cloaths, they are worth but a very trifle. He has a brother living somewhere, believe at Chichester in Sussex, but I don't know where to write to him so think what trifle may be due to him when the funeral expence is paid will and ought to be yours. Will keep a particular account of what the expence is. You say I did not send you the cost of the beer, but that I certainly did as near as I could calculate, which you must have received long before this time. You say only four calves sold, whereas I have sold 12, which together made twenty eight pound four shillings. That and supporting the two houses with butter & chees, added to that the milk which Mrs Rennald has, though but a trifle, yet tis a something, all this put together I realy think on

1 The letter is undated, but there is a note in a different hand at the top of the letter 'suppose it 1st February 1794'
2 Joseph Brown, buried 2nd March 1794, aged 74.
3 He has not been identified.

the whole the five cows are not to be found fault with. As to my having plenty of cash, believes that is never to be the case, as there is a great deal of money now to be paid, or at least as soon as it can be raised. The ballance of Crook's old account, land, window, & other taxes, wintering sheep, the gardener's year's waigers, & many other things. Indeed there is always something to take away the cash as fast or faster than I can get it. To be sure, there will be Mrs Jenny's & Hatchet's rent at Lady Day to help out, if I can get it. Fear Hatchet will lay back in his rent, as he is at a great expence, what with sickness and other things. His wife is under the physician's hands at the Devizes. Has been there for some time. Is rather better than she was, but don't think she will ever be stout again. Have paid Mrs R[1] the fifty pounds due to them the 5th December last. The leveling on the Down as charged in the account is where I am making a new inclosure adioining to that made last year, in order to raise hay if possible to keep the sheep at home next winter. Our lambs are just beginning to come in, hope we shall have good luck. Have got a very good shepherd, which is a great article where there are so many sheep. Believe we shall have plenty of hay without buying this spring, as the winter has hitherto been remarkably mild. Have paid the singers 2 crowns as you ordered, that is one for this year and one for the last, which I forgot to charge. Mrs Rennald says I had better stay till Easter before I give Fowler the clark[2] his half crown. The post and rails round the new orchard in Bar Close that is behind the new garden is quite rotten, and something must be don to it. I think to turn that fence that goes along by the cow house as far as it will reach, & make out the rest with such stuf as I can get, so to inclose the whole together. Then the gardener may dig it up and plant it with what he thinks proper. It is now said the cannal is to come by Avebury, but many people say it will never go anywhere. At least I hope they won't bring it <u>here</u>, as it certainly will cut the lands all to pieces. You may wonder how Shipway the mason's bill comes to so much. The puting in some new hatches in South Meadow, and brushing up the old mansion, is the greatest part, otherwise it would have been but at trifle. Mr. John Nalder of Barwick[3] has lost his wife. About three weeks since she died in childbed. Has left four children behind. Wee hear the French have made all the blacks free.[4] Will not that be attended with bad consequences.
Wee all desire our duty to you and my master, and I am, with great respect, Madam, your most obedient servant
Richd Hickley

Verso Note: Hickley, suppose 1 February 1794
Verso Address: Mrs Williamson, Kings House, Jamaica.

1 Rennald.
2 Samuel Fowler, the parish clerk; see *AWS*, p.415.
3 Lord of the manor of Berwick Bassett. For his relationship to the other Nalders mentioned in these letters, see *AWS*, p.106-7.
4 In St Domingo (now Haiti).

200. Richard Hickley to Mrs Williamson WSHC 184/6

Avebury
2 February 1794

Honoured Madam,
Inclosed is a letter from Brown of Hungerford, which believe is full of complaints about his money, but I realy think he ought to wait till the rent can be got of Mr Manning. I have often told him that I cannot settle with him till that is paid. Indeed I have not money to spare, and if I had think he should stay. He has the rent of the land and one of the small houses regularly paid to him. Therefore he is not kept out of all his money. He pretends to be quite pennyless, which I will not believe a word about. He is a covetous old fellow, and his wife is worse. Wish wee could find where Manning is, that I might write or go to him. As Mrs Rennalds says, to go to take the house out of his possession, would be forfeiting all the rent, and tis the opinion of most people that he will come some day or other and pay the money he owes. At Lady Day next he will owe two years and a half rent for the house, which is £31 10s 0d, and two years for the padocks to last Michaelmas, which was the time Mr Whitelocke took to them, so the whole money due from him at Lady Day will be £35 14s 0d, more than enough to pay Brown if it could be got. If not he must wait till it can. Have paid old Joe for one year's annuity, which was due at Michaelmas 1792,[1] likewise one years waigers paid to my self, and two years intrest on the £100 left by my late master. Should have been glad with some of the children's money, but must stay till it is more plenty. Have paid Hitchcock the malster, though wee have had but little malt in the year. Yet the price being great makes the bill run high. Ruth at the farm has given warning to leave her place at Lady Day next. She is going to be married, as she says. I recollect what you said with respect to keeping her at the farm in case she should marry, but Mrs Rennald and myself perfectly agree that plan will not do on any account. Whither there is any particular reason for her being married I cannot pretend to say. Fear the match will be but an indifferent one, as I hear the man has two or three bastards already. Shall look out for a proper person between this and Lady Day. I should have went to Bath last week to settle with Mrs Jenny, but having a very deep fall of snow, Mrs Rennald advised me not to go, and as the other year will soon be expired, think it as well to stay and settle the whole together. Mr Robert Nalder and my self have agreed to exchange that piece of land cald Crofts opposite my house by the Wall Ditch for a little meadow of his that lies, if you recollect, on the left hand just without Bar Close, by the side of Bar Piece, joining to that meadow belonging to Mr. Mighell. Tis about 2 acres. I know you will be pleased with it, very handy to put a few ewes and lambs in the spring of the year, and always bears a good crop of hay. I was very glad to catch hold of it. Had I been in his place should not have chused to have parted with it. As the award was not signed, the Commissioners could value and alter it without any trouble. Have fenced in a large piece of ground with post and rails for a plantation on the Down as you ordered. As to Silbury Hill, the gardener

1 See p. 342, note 10.

says there will not be time to plant it this year, neither have we stuff to fence it at present. Will endeavour to get some the first opportunity to be in readiness when it may be wanted. A plantation on that hill would look very handsome. Hope long before this you have received the beer &c safe. Very strange the paquet is not come in yet. Wee have expected it for these three weeks past. Believe this country will be ruined by a long expensive war. Fear the alied powers will not be able to conqur those French devils after all. Thank God all is well at Avebury.
I am, with great respect,
your most obedient humble servant
Richd Hickley

Verso Note: Hickley 2d February 1794.
Verso Address: Mrs Williamson, Kings House, Jamaica.

201. Richard Hickley to Mrs Williamson WSHC 184/6

Avebury
20 March 1794

Honoured Madam
I have with the assistance of Crook[1] the carpenter and the gardener made a calculation of the expence of inclosing Bar Piece with a park paleing & sunk fence at the end next to Monkton, the fence next the turnpike road to be the height you mention, four feet & five, which in my opinion is too low, but the calculation is made as such. A very different sum from what you thought, but I am fully satisfied it cannot be done for very little if any less.

250 oak posts	[£]37-10-00
4450 feet of rails	40-00-00
6000 feet of paleing	46-10-00
Labour & nails	35-00-00
	159-00-00

This is only one fence, that is, the outside one. You say there is no need of a fence in the inside, but that hurdles will do to protect the trees. But as the gardener says, & I agree with him, that to plant trees without properly securing them is throwing money away. For instance a hurdle thrown down or a whole broke in a hedge for three or four hours, without any one's discovering it, may be a means perhaps of spoiling the whole. Indeed the gardener says he never will plant any more trees unless they are properly fenced. Now if the outside fence is to cost £159 wee allow a low paleing in the inside, & the posts and rails not so stout as the other, will at the least cost £120. Then another article is the loss of land it will occasion. When the Commissioners of the exchange of the lands set out the roads & drove ways, they were all ordered to be forty feet wide. For

1 Stephen Crook.

instance, the turnpike road going to Monkton is only 22 feet, then there is 18 feet to be taken out of Bar Piece to make up the 40. This is an advantage to you while it remains in the present state, because while it lays open wee can plough quite up to the road without any one taking any notice, though wee have no right to do it. But was you to inclose it must be left the full width of 40 feet. What I mean by being an advantage is what land was wanted by the side of any road to make it 40 feet was not valued at anything to the person who has it. For instance the road going from Avebury to Kennett suppose is not more than 20 feet. Then as you have the land on each side you gain the width of 20 feet for nothing. Likewise the same on the Downs. Whoever allotment any road passes through, let it be ever so long, is allowed the 40 feet for nothing, though perhaps the iniury done by it's being at road, particularly on the Downs, is little or nothing. As I said before, while it lays open wee can plough to the usual place as no one will trouble their heads about it. But was it to be inclosed the act of parliament would compel you & others whose land any road might pass through to leave it the full width. So what you would loose there by inclosing, I mean Bar Piece, would be about ¾ of an acre of land worth about £24 15s at 30 years purchase. The whole expence as under

Outside Fence	[£]159-00-00
Do Inside	120-00-00
Trees	12-00-00
Value of the land	24-15-00
	[£]315-15-00

I think when you see this account you will not wish to have it done.

Verso Note: Hickley, 20th March 1794
Verso Address: Mrs Williamson, Kings House, Jamaica

202. Richard Hickley to Mrs Williamson WSHC 184/6

Avebury
30 March 1794

Honoured Madam,
I have received your two letters one of the 10th January, & the other of ye 5th February. Am very glad to hear you & my master continue so well, which wonder at considering the fatigue you both must have. Am very much obliged to you for your attention to my health, which thank God is now quite good. I eate a great quantity of watercress as you recommend, which certainly is a very fine thing. Have taken 10 or 12 bottles of Norton's drops[1] this winter, 2 of which am to thank you for, as Mrs Rennald has paid me for them. They have been of infinite service

1 A popular remedy for a variety of illnesses. It is reviewed in Smythson, Hugh. *The compleat family physician.* 1791, f.680-1.

to me. The dreadful accounts of so many of the fleet being wrecked is realy very shocking. The William & Elizabeth, I think, is the name of the ship that poor Lady Amelia Cook was on board[1]. Don't find any of the crew or passengers are saved. The other day I cald on Mrs Hope[2] with the letter you returned. As Mrs Rennald says, it went from her who was in a great deal of trouble, but exprest great satisfaction at yours & my master's great attention & kindness to the unfortunate young people & their little property, which is all lost. Wee hear there is nine or ten ships lost, & very few of the people saved. I have received the £100 of Mrs Rennald for the legacy, & given her a proper discharge for the same, drawn by Mr Ward, of which she will give you the account.[3] Likewise have paid my self the ¾ of a year's intrest due on the same, that is, from last summer to Lady Day. Also have given her, John Phillips,[4] & Bet Scanes discharges for theirs. Have heard nothing of that lady for this twelve month or more, perhaps dead. If so hope she has repented of her guilt while alive; otherwise fear she will fare badly in the next world. Have paid all old Joe's debts & funeral expences. As I said in my last, he had in his pocket when dyed three pounds six shillings & sixpence. The whole of the expence came to three pounds eighteen shillings & four pence, so there remains eleven shillings & ten pence, which I have charged to you in my account. His annuity was paid to Michaelmas 1792, & as he died on the 28th February 1794 there was due to him just seven pounds. Then take out eleven shillings & ten pence as I have charged, there will remain due to him six pound eight shillings & four pence, but as there is no person to make any claim, believe it's all yours. He has a brother somewhere but don't know where to write to him. As to the trifle of cloaths left, will put it away in case the brother should ever come to claim it. In your first letter you mention what quantity of wheat on an acre is a good crop. I have known 46 bushels to the acre, at 8 gallons to the bushel, on a particular piece of ground or so, but not at Avebury. Wee reckon it a good crop if we get 28 bushels to the acre, that is one with another, throughout the crop, & 38 bushels to the acre of barley is a very good crop. The quantity of acres of wheat cut the last harvest was 98 acres, which I gave you the account of when the inclosure first took place; indeed you have it in the reaping account. Have sowed this year about 86 acres, that is what is growing on the ground to be cut next harvest. Shall sow about 95 acres of barley & oats this spring when the lands are brought into regular order. Shall sow about 100 acres of each sort every year, I mean 100 of wheat & 100 of barley. You say no mention is made of the number of sheep for the summer stock. That I cannot tell, as don't yet know

1 This was one of the ships involved in the 'Wreck of the Ten Sail' on Grand Cayman, 8th February 1794; see **https://en.wikipedia.org/wiki/Wreck_of_the_Ten_Sail**. Despite Hickley's comment, many survived the disaster, including Lady Amelia Cooke (who was the daughter of the Duke of Atholl).

2 She has not been identified.

3 A codicil to the will of Arthur Jones bequeathed Hickley £100; see TNA PROB11/1181/174.

4 John Phillips, Arthur Jones's butler, received £100 in his will; see TNA PROB11/1181/174.

what number of lambs wee shall raise, but hope near five hundred. Have hitherto had very good luck with them, & no cows charged at straw. That will come in the next account, as they are not yet gone. You say 18 cart horses a very wrong calculation, whereas we have but 13. Had not the old ones dyed wee should have that number & more, but while they were alive had no occasion to buy more. So on the whole we never should have had that number, as I think 13 or 14 at the farthest will do the work. Now the lands are laid several, believe I said in my last that the plantation on the Down was finished & fenced in with posts & rails. As to hedging it round, that would not have done. The willows in Bar Close grows very well, but as they were but small when planted will be some time before they get up to be large. Indeed, large ones will not do as they generally dy if planted too large. Have planted a great many in different places where I thought they would grow. Will take care to get the nets from Hungerford the first opportunity. Your new tenant, Mr. Whitelocke, is set of after being there only half a year, without paying the rent, unless Mr Hickey has got it within these few days. Mr H wrote to him to pay the half year's rent to Brown the gardener, but believe he was gone before the letter came to Hungerford. He is gone to Chatam[1] Barricks, believe as an apothecary. Mrs Rennalds has wrote to Mr H to inform him where to find him. Mr H says he was to give him a quarter's notice whenever he left the house so suppose he will make him pay the rent till Midsummer. No hopes as yet of Mr Manning's returning to pay that money. Mrs Rennald has made a search in the bundle of bills to find a bill of Penny Hancock the fishmonger,[2] but no such thing is to be found, so suppose tis not paid. When I go to Bath will call & pay it, as must go soon. The other day received a letter from Mrs Jenny saying the moment the bank dividends were paid I was to come & settle the two year's rent. She is a quear old quist as ever I met with. Suppose she never will purchase the house. As to that Saunders I mentioned sometime since, don't know what is become of him.

Have just begun sowing barley & oats. The weather is very fine for the season. Shall sow about 95 acres this spring. Are like to have the forwardest spring we have had for some years. Fear wee shall have some difficultys in setling the parish rates this Easter. They have not been altered yet. Wee have two or three new farmers coming into the parish this Lady Day. Rider[3] at Beckhamton [?Farm] has taken an estate cald Higdens belonging to one Dyke, formerly Mr Howson's.[4] Some other person has taken a part of what Crook rents of one Griffin,[5] & Mr Tanner[6] is coming to the estate which he purchased at Kennet

1 Chatham, Kent.

2 Of High Street, Bath, in 1791; see **https://bathhistoricaldirectories.org.uk/**.

3 John Rider tenanted Chestermans, and was also the innkeeper at Beckhampton House until 1795; see *AWS,* p.240-41.

4 Henry Howson, gent., was buried at Avebury, 9th May 1779. For his will, see WSHC P3/H/1466.

5 John Griffin; see Sandell, op cit, p.18.

6 William Tanner purchased an estate in West Kennett c.1784; see *VCH Wilts* 12, p.97.

where Mr Thos Nalder [1]lives. New lords, new laws, so don't know how wee shall get on.

Have hired a servant in Ruth's place, one from Compton,[2] a very decent looking girl. Her late mrs gives her a very good character. The waigers to be four pounds ten shillings. Have now got a little work for the poor at spinning of cotton. Tis but little for doing it, but something is better than nothing.

Please to accept my thanks for some pork, as Mrs Rennald always gives me a piece when a pig is kild. You talk of selling some, but a small pig may be dispenced with without as when the two legs are cut for hams that breaks deep into the pig.

I am, with due respect, Madam, your most obedient humble servant
Richd Hickley

Note at foot (at right angles): Hickley, 30th March 1794.

203. Richard Hickley to Mrs Williamson WSHC 184/6

Avebury
2 May 1794

Honoured Madam,

I think you will not much like the account this time but realy tis not in my power at present to keep it lower. But as I have often said, if I live till another year will get rid of that cursed affair of puting the sheep out to wintering. Am sure no farm will bear such expence. I am determined at all events if possible to raise turnips enough to keep them all at home, or at least the greater part of them, for though wee give such an extravagant price, they don't keep them a bit the better. Indeed, I have known them kept better for four shillings & four & six pence than they now are for seven & eight. All they trouble about is to get the money wee have. A very good breed of lambs this year, have liveing at present 470 lambs and 896 sheep, which together makes 1366. I think as many as wee shall manage to keep them well. Had thoughts of keeping more, but over stocking is no profit, especially as I intend wintering the lambs at home. However, at furthest shall not keep above 20 cupples more. Have paid Crook the carpenter £40 more towards the old balance of [£]83 2[s] 5[d], so there now remains due to him on that account [£]43 2[s] 5[d], which intended to have paid long ago, but twas not in my power. Such accumulation of expence & but little to sell makes things very unpleasant. Have sold this year only about 108 quarter of barley, whereas ought to have sold at least 250. But still, bad seasons wee cannot help. Have not setled with that old lady at Bath. She keeps playing me of as though she had not money to pay. Have now fixed to settle in about a fortnight. Neither have received Hatchet's rent. He talks of paying very soon. Mrs Rennald wished to have had more money before she

1 Thomas Nalder was the owner or lessee of properties in both East and West Kennett, and was related to the other members of the Nalder family mentioned in these letters. See *AWS*, p.107.

2 Presumably Compton Bassett.

went to London, but twas no more in my power to supply her than it was to raise the dead. Think the house may do without whitewashing this year, as it was don last summer. The look don't signify so as the wet is kept out. Have got a servant in Ruth's place. I think there is no harm in the exchange; believe she will do very well. Think wee shall have a good stock of poultry this summer. Believe Ruth rather repents going away, as I don't find there is like to be any husband in the case.[1] Have had only 2 calves yet. Have five cows in the whole, the other three will not calve for some time, and one of them is old & good for but little. Intend buying one tomorrow at Calne fair, as we must make some chees this summer & suckkle what calves we can. Have very fine weather for the barley season, but begin to want a shower. If the rain hapens to come soon shall have a good crop of hay, if not shall be badly of. I hear the Parson has been making some fresh stir about the tythes, & that he has wrote to you on the subject. This I had from J Clements, who is at the bottom of all the mischief. If he has wrote to you, I shall know your determination before you receive this. The regulation of the parish rates has not taken place as yet, but will be brought forward in a few days, which suppose will be a very disagreeable business. You will wonder the cows at straw are charged at different prices, but I was willing to take them at the best bargain I could make, sooner than go without them. Indeed, there was a great difference in their size, which made a considerable odds in the keep. The money received of Bailey[2] the wool man was what was left in arears last summer when he had it, as wee could not tell what the current price would be at that time. The price is more than was expected. Fear it will be low this year if the war continue. Am happy to hear the Duke of York has gained a complete victory over those hell hounds the French.[3] Fear the beer & other things are lost, otherwise you certainly must have had it before your last letter came away. Thank God wee are all well, & beg your acceptance of our duty
and I am, with great respect, Madam, your most obedient servant ,
Richd Hickley
6th May 1794

Verso Note: Hickley, 6th May 1794
Verso Address: Mrs Williamson, Kings House, Jamaica

204. Richard Hickley to Mrs Williamson WSHC 184/6

Avebury
2 June 1794

Honoured Madam,
Wee are rather surprised at not receiving the packet before now, as wee ought to have had it a month ago. Hope it has not fallen into the hands of the French,

1 No marriage is recorded in Avebury parish register or in other local registers that have been checked.
2 This is a common Avebury surname, but this individual has not been identified.
3 A reference to the Duke's victory at the Battle of Beaumont in April 1794.

who are a set of the worst villains under the heavens. But thank God they have given them a good floging lately. Have sent a statement of Mrs Jenny's account. I was with her about a fortnight since. Not a word said about purchasing the house, so suppose she has given it up. Have heard nothing of that Saunders for a long time. Suppose he thinks no more about it. Have received the year's rent for the cottages of Mrs. Brown due at Lady Day. Have not received Hatchet's yet. Believe he has been paying doctor's bills for his wife, which fancy have been pretty considerable. She is much better than she was some time since, but don't think ever will be stout any more. Have paid Godwin the shoemaker at Bath,[1] and the fishmonger Hancock as it certainly was not paid before. Paid the gardener one year's waigers, which was due the 11th December last. In short, what with one thing or the other, as soon as a shilling comes in tis gone again. Have finished sowing barley, and had fine rain to fetch it up, so hope we shall have some to sell next year. Am now sowing turnips, but want a little more rain for that business. The wheat is tollerable, but not so good as the last year. Am like to have a fine crop of hay, which will be a great treasure. Have not been at Hungerford for a long time, so know nothing what is going on there. Find by Mrs Rennald that Mr Hickey desired Whitelocke to pay the three quarters' rent to Brown, which believe is not don.
I am, Madam, your most obedient & very humble servant
Richd Hickley

Verso Note: Hickley 2nd June 1794.
Verso Address: Mrs Williamson, Kings House, Jamaica.

205. Richard Hickley to Mrs Williamson WSHC 184/6

[June 1794][2]

Honoured Madam,
It realy is very astonishing that wee have not received any packet since the 19th March. Surely there must be one if not two lost, as they never laid back like this before. Wee are very anxious to know how you are. Suppose you have heard that Lord Howe has given the French a handsome drubbing at last.[3] Pray God they had such a one every week till they were conquered. I forgot to charge in the account six shillings, which I took the liberty to give the ringers on the occasion, as was sure you would much approve of it. The Miss Rennalds were very loyal & much pleased at the event. In short great reioicing all over the country, that is by the well disposed people. Here is a great number of villains in this Kingdom I

1 Probably Daniel Godwin, shoemaker of Cheap Street, mentioned in a 1791 directory; see **https://bathhistoricaldirectories.org.uk/**. The payment was probably for the box of shoes sent to Jamaica in late 1792; see letter above, 4th December 1792.
2 The precise date is not stated, but it is probably several weeks later than the previous letter.
3 A reference to the naval 'Battle of the Glorious 1st June', which took place off of Ushant.

think wee want half a hundred guillotines fixed in different parts of the Kingdom, and some considerable use to be made of them. There is a little bill from one Page of Newbury[1] for coales had at Hungerford in the year 90. Mr Ward of Marlbro gave it me, & I paid him the money. Sometime since I mentioned to you that the Commissioners of the turnpike roads had taken a piece of land at Thornhill to make the road straight, & that I had agreed to take the old road in lieu of it, they to break it up & make it fit for the plough, which would have answered very well, but when the matter was rightly considered, the old road could not be taken away, as it must be left for a road into the Duke of Marlbro's meadow. Have now agreed for the Commissioners that exchanged the lands at Avebury to put a value on the whole corner they have taken, which believe is about one acre and 26 pole, but will have it measured exactly, & you to be paid for it in money, which I think will much the best. As all the Thornhill land is sown with wheat this year wee could not come at Silbury Hill to feed it with the sheep; therefore have let the Hill to one of the Beckhamton farmers for one year at three guineas & half. As I think it was valued to you at only 25 shillings per year that will answer very well. Very lucky it was not planted this summer, as the weather turns out so dry. I fear the greater part of those trees planted on the Downs will dy. Have had no rain for some time. The weather is very hot. We are in the midst of haymaking so want fine weather and rain at the same time. The clover grass is very good, but the natural grass is very short. Dry weather is very much against the turnips, but still hope we shall raise some. Have got ten acres up which believe will stand. Shall sow twenty more as soon as rain comes. The barley will be good if not dry too long. The wheat is not bad, but not so good as one could wish. Have now got two large inclosures on the Down. Dry summers will not suit them, but as to that wee must take chances, wet or dry. Am going to shear the sheep this week. The cut of wool will be good, but fear the price will be but indifferent, the clothing business is so very dul. How the poor will be maintained next winter cannot tell. We have got a little work for them at present at spinning of cotton. Tis but a trifle for doing it, but still something is better than nothing. No regulation about the poor's rates as yet, but think there must be before any more money is collected. Have neither seen or heard from Hungerford for a great while, so know nothing what is going on there. I hear the cannal is going on; cannot tell if they go near the house or not. Have just heard that the Duke of York and his army is surrounded by the enemy.[2] Hope in God this is a false report. The inhabitants of this county as well as others have been very liberal in their subscriptions towards raising a cavelry of horse in each hundred for the home defence of this Kingdom. It consist of the yeomanry and tradesmen, in short such people as chuse to go, to be cald together once in each week to be disciplined, to find their own horses, the arms and dress to be found out of the subscription money. Believe the intention of it is to keep those Jacobin scoundrels

1 He has not been identified.

2 He had been defeated at the Battle of Tourcoing in mid-May, and narrowly escaped capture.

in order. For my part, if cald on am determined to go, as one may spare three or four hours once in the week without much inconvenience.
I am, Madam, Your most obedient and humble servant,
Richd Hickley

Verso Note: Hickley letter, certainly the end of June 1794.
Verso Address: Mrs Williamson, Kings House, Jamaica.

206. Richard Hickley to Mrs Williamson WSHC 184/6

Avebury
30 July 1794[1]

Honoured Madam,
We were much pleased to receive yours of the 14th March, likewise to hear of the safe arival of Mr Belford. Am very glad he gave you a pleasing account of Avebury. You mentioned planting trees in the hedges on the Down, but think that will not do, as I have known many planted since I have been at Avebury, but none of them came to anything. However one may plant a few by way of trial. That meadow you speak of by Bar Close has been sold some time since to a Mr Tanner, the person that bought the Kennet estate where Mr Thomas Nalder did live. Fancy it was a very dear purchase. Have had a consultation about the hot house but believe the expence will amaze you. The old cherry tree by the porch door in the pleasure ground has been dead for some time. The others are grown very old, but notwithstanding that they bore a fine crop this year. The trees in the farm garden grows very fine, better than those in the new orchard in Bar Close. Think the copper on the church will now do very well, as I don't find little or no rain come through since the man has altered it. I observe you make mention of that piece of ground cald Crofts opposite my house, but believe before this time you know I have exchanged it with Mr Nalder for a little meadow of his by Bar Close adioining to that meadow of Mr Tanner's you have been mentioning, which think much for the best. Wish you could have had the other, then they might have been thrown together, but as it cannot be had must be content without it. Wee have just done haymaking, & began reaping the wheat. The hay is very good, though not so much as one could wish owing to the dry season. Have lately had some very fine rains, which will make the after grass very good. Am very sorry to say the wheat has received a great iniury by the blight within this fortnight or three weeks. Some of it is struck very hard indeed, which will be very hurtful to the yield; it will be so very thin and light. I don't find it to be a general thing all over the country, only in some places. Have got two old stacks left, which hope will in some measure make out for the new, that is, to sell some of the new with it. The harvest is forwarder than it has been for some years past. The barley & oats are like to be good, and will soon be fit for the sythe if the weather continue fine. Have sold the wool and fixed the price at one

1 Completed 5 August 1794; see foot of letter.

pound seven shillings per tod, a better price than I expected, though some people won't sell for that. But I think they are wrong. Should the war soon be over the price certainly will be lower. Am just returned from Bristol with the waggon. Have carried down 16 quarters of oats, two small sides of bacon, one dozen and half of shoes, one dozen and half of mops, and two jars of cherry brandy to be shipped on board the Ocean, suppose the same ship that brought your last letter. Have got a cupple of fine hounds for Mr Belford, but they are not to be sent to Bristol before the ship is ready to sail. As to the oats, was obliged to buy them as wee have none of our own. The crop was so bad the last harvest had not enough for the horses. Have been forced to buy what they have eate for some time. And as to buying those trumpery stinking things at Bristol, would not have answered. At any rate have left the oats and other things to the care of Mr Eames. He says the ship will sail in about a fortnight but he has promised to give me timely notice that I may send the dogs and what other things may have to send. Have paid him twelve pounds seven shillings and six pence for goods had of him lately, which Mrs Rennald sent for brandy and jars for the liquor. Sent out 30 dozen of bottles, corks, hampers, &c for the current wine made last year. Should have paid him the bill you returned to me, but found you had paid it; likewise paid that ballance due to Ash the distiller,[1] which have sent you the particulars of. The gleaser's bill is only for such nessacery things as could not be avoided, such as mending windows, garden lights, the gutters on the house, &c; that to Lavington the nursery man the greater part is for barberry plants for the new inclosure on the Down, the rest for seeds for the garden. Was rather surprised the other day to find that Mr Whitelocke had not left the house at Hungerford. Hear he is gone abroad, and that his wife & family are in the house. Still, the half year's rent is paid to Brown by Mr Hickey's order. No news yet of Mr Manning.

4th August.

Have just received yours of the 7th June, with the two Mr Mayo's letters to you which think are very strange ones. Should have thought they might have had more sense than to have said anything about the matter. Wee all know he never would have had the living had it not been for my late master, and not only that, but in many other respects he was a great friend to Mr Mayo's family. Shall take care not to pay him any more than the four pound as usual. I don't understand what he means by the pidgeon house, as it was always acknowledged that three pounds were paid for the wheat and twenty shillings for the farmyard. Old Mayo always gave the receipt as such. Am sorry for the loss of the beer, cannot concieve how the cask could leak. Am very certain that a piece of tin was nailed over each bung, and should have thought it impossible. Hope it was not the best that was lost. One Viner at Hungerford[2] has applied to Mr Hickey for the house that Mr Manning rents. Whither he can take it out of his possession without forfeiting the rent due, he is the best judge. At Michaelmas next will be due three years rent

1 He has not been identified.

2 Perhaps Thomas Viner, hop merchant and seedsman, recorded in the *Universal British Directory* at Hungerford in 1790; see **www.hungerfordvirtualmuseum.co.uk**.

for the house and two years for the two padocks, in the whole forty two pounds. Hope the money won't be lost.
I am, with great respect Madam, your very humble servant
Richd Hickley
Avebury 5th August 1794

Verso Note: Hickley's letter, 5th August.
Verso Address: Mrs Williamson, Kings House, Jamaica.

207. William Richardson[1] **to Mrs Williamson**WSHC 271/16
[5 August 1794]

Honoured Madam,
I have received yours dated March 27 in which you mention the plantation at the [?Rempel]. It grows well. Have had the wall of the [?sharaubes][2] on each side the gate in the court, dos well, have covered the wall. I have planted a vine against the oven at the farm twise, it have ben destroyed twice, buye the cattle. The pear tree dos well against the fence, also the trees in the farm garden have had good fruit upon them this year. The trees [?grawes] in the church yeard, but theay will not hide the end of the farm house for two or three years. The trees round the pigon house doe not do at all. Theay ar tou much shaded buy the large trees that theay will com to nothing. The ivy at the back of the stables does well. The Spanish chesenut dos nott so well as I should wish them. As for [?backing] of pears & mushell plums, there is no roum for aneay more except you alow mor ground. Your garden is as full as it can bee of fruite trees. I have sent you a plan of the hot house. Of which I should wish to build the length & bredth. Will be expleaned in the explanation of the [?plane]. The old wall most be puld down. It is not stronge enouf for the back wall. The bricks will do again for builden the shackes at the back of the [*illegible*] house.

The sashes is decayed very much, but theay will do for the pine [?adit] ther, for I think it proper not to take the old glass for the house. I have sent you a skech of the ground plan & [?nearleay] report it will coost in buildinge. I have seant to London 7 dozen of apricots buy Mrs Renald's orders. Have made ten gallons of chery brandy [*illegible*] to Bristoll. I have [?this] season 221 lb cheris. Have made them all into chery brandi. I am now making [*illegible*]. I have sent the leist of what I have sold for ten months. Will join in our deuti to you, glad you ar well. My deuti to the governor.
Evbury
August 5th

Verso Note: letter from the gardner, August [*illegible*] 1794.

1 He is not actually named in the letter, but is referred to as 'the gardener' on the verso. He does sign other letters; see for example the letter dated 1st December 1794
2 Shrubs?

Verso Address: Mrs Williamson.

208. Richard Hickley to Mrs Williamson WSHC 184/6

[31 August 1794]

Honoured Madam,

The ship from Bristol is not yet sailed. Have sent this morning to be shipped with the other things six hams, 2 dozen bottles of goosberrys, and one jar of raspberry brandy. The hounds are to remain till the last thing. Tomorrow is the day for partridge shooting to commence. Wee have had some fuss about Adam Wiltshire's shooting, which Mrs Rennald will explain to you. The gentlemen of the Beckhamton Club are not to meet till the 8th instant, as there is more birds this year than for two or three years past, and as Wiltshire is not to shoot, hope the gentlemen will send in a good quantity, as they have promised to send as many as you may want. Last week wee had a dinner at Beckhamton Inn,[1] that is the Avebury farmers, by order of the gentlemen of the Club, the intention of which is to encourage them to preserve the game, as they have taken it into their heads that the farmers destroys it, which I don't believe one word of. However, wee are to have a dinner annually, and to fix the time when we would wish them to come, as they say they don't wish to come till the corn is out of the way, provided the farmers will preserve the game as much as lies in their power. At the dinner were myself, Robert Nalder, Lavington, Jefferys, Philpot,[2] Hatchett, Tanner, Rider &c.; everyone was there except Crook[3] and Amor.[4] What was their reason for not coming cannot tell, nor indeed don't care. Wee are to thank you and my master for a sumptuous dinner last Sunday three weeks, when wee drank your healths in a noble bowl of punch, and the Sunday night all joined in chorus of God save the King. The wheat harvest has been don for some time, but very little to the barley. I have housed about 14 acres, which is all that is carried in the parish. Have had very fine rain, which is very acceptable if it takes up dry again, as wee wanted rain to begin sowing wheat.

The parish rates are not yet regulated; suppose a regular valuation must take place through the parish. I don't care much about it so that everyone pays his proportionate part. The cattle of all kinds, thank God, are well, except an old horse which died this morning. That is but a small loss, as he has been a very good servant, and quite worn out. Don't yet know how sheep will sell this fall, but the lambs were sold tollerable well at Tan Hill fair.[5] As [sic] sorry to say the grub worm is got among the turnips, which if continues will hurt the sale of

1 Alternative name for the Catherine Wheel.

2 William Philpot tenanted property in Avebury from both James Sutton and the Duke of Marlborough in 1789; see WSHC 473/352, land tax assessment. He and his eponymous grandfather served as Beckhampton's tithingmen for most of the second half of the eighteenth century, WSHC 9/23/1.

3 William Crook.

4 Probably John Amor.

5 For Tan Hill fair, see *AWS*, p.16-17.

sheep. Wee all beg your acceptance of our duty and thanks and
I am, with great respect Madam, your most obedient humble servant
Richd Hickley
Avebury 31st August 1794

Verso Note: Hickley's letter & account, 31st August 1794. Answered in Miss Rennalds, 4th November 1794.
Verso Address: Mrs Williamson, Kings House, Jamaica.

209. Richard Hickley to Mrs Williamson[1] WSHC 184/6

Avebury
27 September 1794

Honoured Madam,
Wee received yours of the 17th July, wherein you desired to have some more strong beer sent out, but as the malt was not very good this year, and I did not know if you would wish to any more sent, have not brewed any. I don't think it will do to brew any till the new malt comes in, which will not be till the end of November, and of course not fit to send till the spring, & by that time shall hope to see you at home to drink it at Avebury. However will brew some as soon as possible. Did not receive yours in time to send the harness oil, as I believe the ship has sailed these three weeks from Bristol. Hope the dogs will arrive safe, as the captain has promised to take great care of them. Am sorry the oats could not be sent. I find by Mr Eames they must be sent by convoy. Fear it may be some time before they may be sent, & at the same time lie about & get stale, though I saw them shut up in a very dry place at Bristol. Don't think the gentlemen of the Beckhamton Club of shooters has behaved very handsome as to the game, to send in only 10 brace of birds and not one hare, such a plentiful season as this has been, as there certainly has been more birds this season then for three or four years past. As Mrs Rennald says, I think it very strange for them to give Adam Wiltshire five guineas. Should have thought if they had given him two it would have been sufficient, but think their scheme for that was for him not to kill many after they were gone. Indeed I asked him if he had not such a charge, which he could not deny. But I will make him kill as many as possible as there is a great plenty left. I cannot settle with the trustees of the turnpike road for the piece of land at Thornhill. I agreed with them for one of the commissioners of the exchange of the lands at Avebury to put a value on it, which he did, though I must confess he set it pretty high. His value for the acre and twenty six pole came to fifty eight pounds, which at 30 years purchase is 32 shillings per acre or more. Now they will not pay more than 25 shillings at 30 years, which comes to only £40 or there about, which they have offered to pay me, but I refused to take

1 This and the succeeding letters were written after Mrs Williamson's death on 27th September 1794. Jamaican Family Search **www.jamaicanfamilysearch.com/Members/Barche03.htm**

it. I told them if they would make it fifty pounds I would [?venture] to take the money. Mr Henage[1] said if the General was at home he would not wish to take more than the customary price. I gave for answer if the General was at home he might do as he pleased, but as they had partly cald in a person to put a value on it, I could not think of taking so much less than the sum he set it at. Suppose the affair must be left till the next turnpike meeting, unless they should agree among themselves to give the £50. To be sure 25 shillings per acre is more than the value in the occupation of the farm, but then it is to considered tis more than a twelve month since they took possession of the land, by which there is a crop of wheat lost this year at not less than eight pound, and a year's intrest of the money, besides the expences in the husbandry, and the taxes will not be lessened by selling it, therefore if the matter is rightly considered the tenants profit will be lost every year as the intrest of the money will not make that good. All this I mentioned to them, but they did not chuse to see it in that light. Wee finished the harvest last Friday & had the supper the same evening. The barley on the whole is as good as was expected, & suppose will sell pretty well. The wheat turns out but very indifferent owing to the blight. Good old wheat sells at a good price. The sale of sheep at present is but dull. Have not sold any yet. Shall make them up in as good order as I can before they are sold. Shall sell 200 ewes and about 160 lambs. Have very fine weather at present for sowing the wheat; have about half done. Shall sow about 100 acres this [?year].

I am, with great respect, Madam, your most obedient humble servant
Richd Hickley

Verso Note: Hickley 27th September 1794. Answered in Mrs Rennold's letter, that is, to say that I approve.
Verso Address: Mrs Williamson, Kings House, Jamaica.

210. Richard Hickley to Mrs Williamson[2] WSHC 184/6

Avebury
2 November 1794

Honoured Madam,
On Thursday last we received the very disagreeable news of poor Mr Belford's death, which really grieved us all very much. The loss of such a fine, good natured, amiable young gentleman is very shocking to any one that knew him, much more so to you & my master, who had so great a love for him. Hope in God you will bear up under it, as it is the will of the Almighty who knoweth what is best for us. Since hearing of the above melancholly event, have heard of something that gives us much pleasure, my master being made governor of St

1 Presumably one of the Turnpike Commissioners; perhaps Walker Heneage, lord of the manors of Compton Bassett and Compton Cumberwell; see *VCH Wilts.*, 17, **www.british-history.ac.uk/vch/wilts/vol17/pp146-159**

2 Anne Williamson died 19th September 1794, before this letter was written. See *AWS*, p.165.

Domingo.[1] Hope in God we shall now soon see you in England. I realy am very sorry that I made such a blunder in my account of the 31st May, & to fall into the same error in that of the 2d & 30th of August, which you will see long before you receive this. I have been so bewildered for a very long time to find my self so much in debt, & yet could not find out the cause till since my last account went out. Am very much vexed about it, but hope you will excuse it. Have inclosed a statement of the whole from the 29th March to this time, which hope & believe you will find to be right. Mrs Jenny sent for me to take the half year's rent, & to inform me that she was going to quit the house, that she had been offered £60 for the unexpired term of the lease, but that if the General would take it he should have it for £40. I refered her to Mr Hickey, as I told her he was the only person that had any power to act in that case. Since that I received a letter from that Mr. Saunders who wished to buy it sometime since, wherein he says he still continues in the same mind, & that he will give £500 for it, but that he will not allow any thing for the lease. I wrote imediately to Mr Hickey to inform him of it, but have heard nothing of the affair since. I saw through the old lady's craft, & realy think if she could get clear of it would give it up without any premium at all. Have sold the sheep for a tollerable good price, rather better than I expected. Shall keep the greater part, if not all, the lambs at home this winter, as we have a tollerable good crop of turnips. You mention in your letter of my buying turnips, but this is the wrong country for that, as every one has work enough to raise them for himself, & more than can be don. The poor rates are not setled yet, but seems to be come to a determination for a valuation through the parish. They wanted to raise your estate & no one's else, which I will not submit to on any account. Let every one pay his proportioned part, let it be little or much. Have now don wheat sowing, & had a good season for it. It comes up very fine. Hope if we live till another harvest shall have a better crop than the last. I found my self under the necssity of buying four oxen to help get in the wheat in time, as early sowing is of the greates consequence in this country. Had thoughts of selling them again, but as we have two large inclosures on the Down think wee may keep them constant, & will be cheaper than horses. Four oxen and 12 horses, which is the number we have at present, will do the work, & it cannot be don with less. I thought at one time 12 or 13 horses would be sufficient, but find now to the contrary. The Trumpery field, as you call it, at Beckhamton, for my part don't call it such, for last summer I cut as good a crop of clover in it as ever I wish to have. It's now sown with wheat & looks very fine. As to keeping a little flock of sheep for your return, cannot answer at any rate, for they certainly would cost dubble the value of them, & on the other hand wee keep no weather sheep at all. As to raising calves, to keep them three years before they comes to the bucket, considering the price of hay & the value of grass, will make them come very dear. The afair of making a dung mixon is often don in the winter, but in general tis carried out in the summer, & fallowed in that depends on the use it is for.

Have begun fating some porkers, but I think fating hogs for bacon will not

1 St Dominque, now Haiti.

pay considering the price of barley, as am sure it may be bought much cheaper than wee can fat it. Have heard nothing about the cannal at Hungerford for some time. Find Mr Manning will not give up the house he rents of you, therefore should think he means some day or other to come & pay the rent.
With mine and my wife's duty to you & my master, I am, Madam, your most obedient humble servant
Richd Hickley

Verso Address: Mrs Williamson, Kings House, Jamaica.

211. Richard Hickley to Mrs Williamson WSHC 184/6

Avebury
30 November 1794

Honoured Madam,
Wee were sorry to find to by your letter that you have been so very ill; hope in God you are now quite well. I have paid Mrs Rennald the fifty pounds that I had of her in March 1793, as may be seen by the account. Likewise, according to your order, have paid my five girls the £10 each.[1] Am very much obliged to you for the £10 to Nancy as I had that before. Suppose a receipt not necssary as the account will prove that I have received it. Have paid Hitchcock the malster, which is more than it ought to be. To be sure, the price of malt is great, but yet think the gardener is rather extravagant with the beer, as I have told him, as the greatest part of the malt was brewed at the house. Am sure I cannot make less do at the farm; so many people to drink small beer all the summer, and in short winter too, as all the farmers finds the carters in beer winter & summer. Will have some more made this year and try if less won't do. If the expence is the same it will not be felt so much. The seven shillings charged on account of waigers to Mrs Mitchell was a mistake, as I charged only eight pounds for the whole, whereas according to your order her waigers for the last year was seven guineas & 20 shillings for the intrest, as usual, together making eight pounds seven shillings. The glass bottles are some that I bought at a sale, there being some wanting to bottle of the current wine. Thought it cheaper than to buy new ones. Last week I received a letter from Saunders saying he had a letter from Mr Hickey offering the house at Bath for 500 guineas, but that he had no power to sell without the deeds being sent out for the Governor to execute them. I saw Mr Ward the other day. He wished to know how he is to have the money for the inclosure. Shall I pay him some at a time, as I can raise it, or will you send him a draft for the whole. Hope now to raise a little money, but there are realy so many things to be done after an inclosure takes place, tis astonishing. I heard last week that Mr Manning was seen in London. If so should hope he would come to Hungerford and pay the rent for the house. Shall go to Hungerford next week, perhaps may

1 Presumably the bequest made to them in the will of Arthur Jones, TNA PROB11/1181/174. He died in 1789.

hear something of him. I hear the cannal is not to go through Stoney Hall, but the house above, but don't know the truth of it. Have just received a letter from Mr Eames of Bristol to say he is going to ship the oats with other thing for the Governor. Shall send down a box with the damsons &c. Will desire him to send 10 gallons of harness oil, as I have not time to get it unless had known it sooner.
I am Madam, your very humble servant,
Richd Hickley

Verso Note: Hickley &c; 30th November 1794. With his account from 31st October to 29th November 1794. Answered in Miss Rennald 23d February 1795.
Verso Address: Mrs Williamson, Kingston, Jamaica.

212. William Richardson to Mrs Williamson WSHC 184/6

[1 December 1794]

Honoured Madam,
I have sent the list of what I have sold. The grapes in the hote house ripened well, those on the open walles do not ripen at all. Have had a good crop of Bath [?aupuares] of forty pownd weight that did not ripen. I was sorry to se such a quantity of fruite & not com for preservtion. That is a [?certain] prof that grapes will not do aneay good in the open grownd in this country. Have juste packed the damsones, nine jars of them, one jar of [?mornyeas], one jare of onions, 3 botles of cantilup, one bottle of mushromes, to be sent from Avebury next Thursday. Have sent the bill of the damsons and the bill of my expences to Malborough with straberis, &c. Have given awaye good maneay cabbage & greens to the por people that I coud not sell. We all joine our deuti to you in hope that the General & you are both well. My deutye to the General. I am your most obedient & humble servant
Wm Richardson
Avebury
December 1st 1794.

213. Richard Hickley to Adam Williamson WSHC 184/6

Avebury
2 February 1795

Honoured Sir,
Wee are rather uneasy that no packet is arrived, as it certainly should before this time. As you did not wish to have the oats sent out which were carried to Bristol a great while since, & I could not sell them there to my liking, brought them back again. Thought it would pay better to keep them for sowing, as I must have bought for seed. The box of preserves charged in the account is same that was to have been sent with the oats Mrs Rennald thought it best to sell them for what they would fetch rather than bring them back. Wee have the severest winter that has been for many years past, the country covered with snow, which makes

the cattle consume a vast deal if hay. The other day came on a sudden thaw, the ground being frozen very hard, & a large quantity of snow on the ground, caused the largest flood ever remembered, the house & garden entirley [?flooded], but did not stay for long to do much damage. Think I must lay out 10 or 15 pound to raise the banks in Bar Close to prevent it in future.
I am, Sir
your very humble servant
Richd Hickley

Verso Note: Hickley letter 2d February 1795.

214. Adam Williamson[1] to Richard Hickley WSHC 184/6

[c.1798][2]

Dear Hickley,
Have so much business on my hands at this time that shall only reply to your questions respecting the sale of the mansion house at Hungerford. Shall be glad to sell it, as it has been more a source of trouble than anything else since in my possession. Therefore shall enclose you the very lowest price I will take. I would wish you to consult Mr Mundy[3] on the best mode of disposing of it, as I believe he will readily oblige & serve me. At the same time must observe that I will not let any sum whatever remain unpaid by the purchaser, as a reserve in case of any attack from the Lears, as I'm perfectly clear myself that they have not the least shadow of right, and that Mr Mundy knows. And less than the sums I shall here enclose to you, either separately or together, will not take, let the consequences be what it may. As at all events this navigation to be carried on immediately from Newberry to Bristol (& on which occasion have been wrote to for my consent for carrying of it thro my lands at Avebury) will enhance the value of every property in or near Hungerford.★[4] ~~Therefore if Mr Mundy wants his £600 will pay it. The grounds are let, the house can let no doubt, & if not it may stand till it drops. The small houses will always let. Probably by the time I return the navigation will be open, & I may take it into my head to pull down the mansion entirely & build several small ones, or, in short, I know not what scheme, any rather than throw it away. This is all I shall say on or think on the subject, as I will see it all go to the devil rather than give myself further concern regarding of it. I recollect that I have by chance heard that Mr Mundy~~[5] has a mind to the estate himself, I have not the least objection.

1 He does not sign, but it is his handwriting.
2 This letter is undated, and may well be earlier than this.
3 Probably Seymour Mundy, a Hungerford attorney, who was frequently consulted on poor law matters in late eighteenth century Hungerford; cf. Durrant, Peter, ed. *Hungerford Overseer's papers, 1655-1834*. Berkshire Record Society, 27. 2021, passim.
4 Appears to be a sign for a footnote. See below.
5 Deleted in mss.

*I propose to pay off the mortgage the first of August and have written to Mr Mundy to that effect. I do not exactly know the usual mode, but suppose it proper to give three months notice before a mortgage is paid off, that the mortgagee may have time for the disposing of his money in such manner as he may judge proper. I shall take care to have the money remitted in time. or to give you an order for that may be necessary. The sum secured was six hundred pounds. As soon as the mortgage is paid off the two small houses being personals may be disposed of, & from the certainty as I said before of the canal going through Hungerford these houses would sell well. When the mortgage is paid off Mundy will of course give you up all the papers relative to the whole of the premises, & I should be very glad to have his bill that I may get rid of the whole. The grounds are let, as I shall always be sure of Stoney Hall[1] as tenants for them doubt could also let, and after the mortgage is paid off and Mundy's bill also paid.

I shall give myself very little trouble about Stoney Hall. [2]It may crumble to ruin for ought I care. I recollect that by chance I heard Mr Mundy had a mind for the estate himself. I cannot have the least objection, & he knows very well that the title is good.[3]

215. Richard Hickley to Adam Williamson WSHC 184/6

Avebury
28 February 1798

Honoured Sir,
I have sent you the inclosed charge of the new assessed taxes for your inspection. This added to that in town will make a fine sum. It will be proper for you to know if the additional three quarters tax on servants and horses are charged in London. If so it must be taken of, as you stands charged for it here. If you are over rateed and intend to make your appeal, you will be pleased to let me know soon as the appeal will be at Marlbro on Monday the 12th March.
I am Sir your most obedient servant
Richd Hickley

1 In Hungerford.
2 The house was in fact demolished soon after to make way for the Kennet and Avon Canal; cf. **www.hungerfordvirtualmuseum.co.uk**
3 This appears to duplicate Williamson's comment above.

3
THE MEMORANDA

	Reference	Date	Description
1	WSHC 184/2/2	1701-10-02	Settlement of Chancery Case, Sir Richard Holford v.John White
2	GA D1956/E2/8	1717-1723	Lady Holford's Accounts
3	WSHC 184/1, pt.2	1721-01-09	Peter Griffin's Proposal for taking Avebury Great Farm
4	WSHC 184/3	1753-10-12	Opinion on Stayner Holford's Land Tax Assessment
5	WSHC 184/4/1	1755-10-14	Rose's Servants: their Particulars about the Stock
6	WSHC 184/2	c.1756	Stayner Holford's Remarks on the Tithe Dispute
7	WSHC 184/2	1756-09-04	Nicholas Jones's Opinion on Avebury Tithe Dispute
8	WSHC 184/2	1756-10-19	Peter Griffin's Statement relating to the Modus
9	WSHC 184/2	1757-06-14	Discourse between Arthur Jones & James Mayo re Modus
10	WSHC 184/2	1758-01-09	John Scane's Attempt to Pay Tithes
11	WSHC 184/2	1758	Remarks on the Dispute with Mr Mayo
12	WSHC 184/2	1760-01-03	Samuel Martyn's Opinion
13	WSHC 184/2	1760?	Statement by Stayner Holford
14	WSHC 184/3	1761	Appeal against Land Tax Assessment 1761
15	WSHC 184/1, pt.1	1765-12-04	Certificate for John Coombs
16	WSHC 271/2	1772-12-11	Arthur Jones's Advice to his Successors

17	WSHC 271/2	1780-09-10	Peter Holford's Title to the Beckhampton Estate
18	WSHC 271/2	1780-09-18	Valuation of Avebury Estate
19	WSHC 271/2	1783-09-24	Directions if Arthur Jones Becomes Ill
20	WSHC 271/2	Undated	Arthur Jones's Title
21	WSHC 271/3	1783-1787	Arthur Jones's Memorandum
22	WSHC 271/2	c.1788	Note re Avebury Estate

1. Settlement of the Chancery Case between Sir Richard Holford and John White WSHC 184/4/2

2 October 1701

Memorandum

That by mediation of Mr William Smith of Calston & others, I Sir Richard Holford, Knt., have been prevailed on to accept & receive of Mr John White, vicar of Avebury, for my costs in the suite against him the sume of forty pounds, and for that he seemes to be sorry for what is past & that he was ill advised, & promised for the future to live more neighbourly & peaceably, & on his part to avoid all kind of misunderstandings, I have as a demonstration of my friendship submitted to give, & do now give to his seven younger children forty shillings a piece, and to Mrs Mary White his eldest daughter fifty three shillings & three pence which do make up fifteen guyneas & halfe a guynea, being £16 13s 3d, and I do desire & direct that the said Mr John White do permit his eldest daughter to enjoy & dispose of her £2 13s 3d to her own use as she shall thinke fit, & that he do put forth the other £14 for the benefit of his younger children. Witnesse my hand

Rich Holford

I the said John White do agree & promise that I will put forth & dispose of the £14 above mentioned that Sir Richard Holford gave to my younger children, to the best benefit & advantage of my said children, when I have an oportunity, & will pay the same accordingly, witnesse my hand

John White

The said parties put their hands hereto & the £14 paid in our presence

Wil Skeate

Emanuell Skeate

Verso:

A Memorandum of Mr John White, Viccar of Avebury, for £14 for his 7 younger children. 2 October 1701. Hee hath a copy of it, whereto I put my hand.

2. Lady Holford's Accounts, 1717-23[1]

GA D1956/E2/8. [p.26].

1718 October

Small rents received at Beckhampton

Mr Spackman of Cleeves paid for Thomas Alexander one year's rent to Lady Day	£1-10-00
Received of Kathi Pope one year's rent due at Michaelmas	4-00
Received of William Philpot, Edy Pontin's rent for one year due at Michaelmas	10-00
Received of Widdow Rose one year's rent to Michaelmas	2-06
Received of Richard Fowler one year's rent to Michaelmas	4-00
Received of Martha Bradfield one year's rent to Michaelmas	3-04

[p.27].

29 September 1718

Accounted with John Caswell for his rent due at Our Lady Day 1718

His yeare's rent due at Lady Day 1718	£210-00-00
Mrs Truslow's for part of Goddards	1-10-00
	£211-10-00
His disbursements for year ended at Our Lady Day 1718	
Paid land tax 1 year to Lady Day 1718 for the Parsonage	£10-00-06¾
Ditto for Goddards	6-02-07½
Ditto for Truslow's	5-08-05¼
Lord Ailesbury's rent	10-06
Paid his share of vagrant money	12-06
Paid the thatcher for ½ a day's work for thatching & straw & pikes for mending Goddards house	5-00
Paid 4 quarter's annuity to Mr Thomas Goddard due Lady Day 1718	20-00-00
Paid ditto to Mrs Truslowe	20-00-00
	62-19-07½
Which £62 19s 7½ d being deducted out of the said £211 10s there remaind due at Our Lady Day 1718	£148-10-4½

1 These accounts are written at the end of Sir Richard Holford's bound journal. In contrast to that journal, there is no pagination. However, the pagination of the journal has been continued here.

Received in part of rent as per letter from Sir R.H. to J Caswell, 23 January 1717	£25-00-00
Received more as by a [?letter] from Sir R.H. to J Caswell 12 March 1717	5-19-06
	30-19-06
13 October	34-19-04½
Received more in cash	17-11-06
Received more in cash	65-00-00
	£113-11-00
Which said £113 11s being deducted out of the said £148 10s 4½d there remains due at Lady Day 1718	£113-11-00
1719 March 30th	34-19-04½
Received by the hands of [ ] Brabant a grazier of Calne on accompt	
September 4th 1719	34-00-00
Received then of John Caswell the ballance of this account	
For all which John Caswell has my Lady's receipt	19-04½

[p.28].

~~Farmer Rose pray pay the limeburner's bill and take his receipt~~.

September 1719

Backhampton small rents

Received of Widdow Rose 1 years rent dew at Micklmas 1719	2-06
Received of Kathrine Pope 1 years rent due at Micklmas 1719	4-00
Received Edee Pontin's rent for one yeare dew at Micklmas 1719 by William Philpott	10-00
Received of Martha Bradfield one years rent due at Micklmas 1719	3-00
Received of Richard Fowler one years rent dew at Micklmas 1719	4-00
Thomas Alixandrs rent not yet payd	
Frances Heller's rent not yet payd	

[p.29].

September 5th 1719

Accounted with John Caswell for his rent due at Lady Day 1719

His years rent due at Lady Day 1719	210-00-00
Mrs Trusloe's for part of Goddards	1-10-00
	211-10-00
His disbursements for ye year ended at Lady Day 1719	
Paid four quarter's annuity to Thomas Goddard	20-00-00
Paid four quarter's annuity to Bridget Trusloe, widdow	20-00-00
Paid the land tax for the Parsonage one year	10-00-06¾
Paid the land tax for Goddards	6-02-07½
Paid the land tax for Trusloe's	5-08-05¼
Paid the Lord Ailesbury's rent	10-06
Paid the vagrant money	12-06
	62-14-07½
Which £62 14s 7½d being deducted out of the said	211-10-00
There remains due at Lady Day 1719	148-15-04½
16 September 1719	
Paid for two audits at 8s per piece in 1715: 1716	16-00
Paid for one audit 8s [?acquittance] 1s messengers fee 16s 8d by reason of non-payment	1-05-08
	2-01-08
Which sum of £2 1s 8d deducted out of £148 15s 4½d the remaines will be	145-13-8½

16 September 1719[1]

Then received of John Caswell the sume of forty six pound & thirteen shillings & eight pence half penny in parte of his year's rent due at Lady Day 1719, which sume with the bill of disbursements above cited amounts to one hundred & eleven pounds which sume I say received and allowed by me, Susan Holford	46-13-08½
And there remaines due of his year's rent at Lady Day 1719	100-00-00

This hundred pound was paid to Mr Web of Marlborough as part of Trusloe's annuitys

[p.30].

	Due 2 yeares rent att Lady Day 1721	420-00-00
	More one yeare's rent for Trusloe's to Lady Day 1720	1-10-00
		421-10-00
1720[2]		
March 31	Paid by Mr. Hunt	60-00-00
Nov 19	Paid by Mr Goddard	100-00-00
Feb 1	Paid by Mr Halsey	60-00-00
1721 Sept 18	Paid Lady att Avebury	10-00-00

1 Written in left margin.
2 Note dates given in old style.

Nov 6	Paid Lady at Avebury	20-00-00
13	Paid Lady at Avebury	38-00-00
	Land tax 3s per £, 1719 & 1720	43-02-03
	Lord of Aylesbury's quit rent 2 years to Lady Day 1721	1-01-00
	Vagrant and county bridge money 1719 & 1720	1-05-00
	Straw helming & thatching Goddards House	18-00
	1C[3] boards & nailes to mend Trusloe's stable	12-00
	Mending the carthouse: sprigs and nailes	10-00
	Rafters worke and nailes about the stable	10-00
	Thomas Goddard 2 yeare's annuity to Lady Day 1721	40-00-00
9 June	Bridget Trusloe's ½ year to Michaelmas 1719 £10-00-00; 1 yeare to Lady Day 1721 £15-00-00	25-00-00
	Peter Griffen paid per order	20-11-09
		421-10-00

[p.31].

Beckhampton quit rents

1721			Lives Michaelmas 1721
August 2	Received Elizabeth Holere 2 yeares rent for Martha Bradfield to Michaelmas 1721	6-08	Eliz & Frances
22	Received Nicholas Pope 2 yeares rent to Michaelmas 1721	8-00	Daniel & Nicholas Pope
22	Received Sicely Rose 2 yeares rent to Michaelmas 1721	5-00	Anne & Lucy
October 6	Received Mary Philpot 2 yeares rent for Pontin's to Michaelmas 1721	1-00-00	Mary Philpot
6	Richard Fowler 2 yeares rent to Michaelmas 1721	8-00	Richard Elizabeth & Samuel
24	Received Thomas Alexander 3 yeares & halfe rent to Michaelmas 1721	5-05-00	Rack rents
November	Received Frances Hellier by Farmer Caswel 1 year's rent to Lady Day 1720 £1-10-00		[Ditto]
	Received of herselfe 1 year to Lady Day 1721 £1-10-00	3-00-00	
		10-12-08	

3 100.
4 The mss brackets this and the previous entry as rack rents.

3. Peter Griffin's Proposal for taking Avebury Great Farm

WSHC 184/1, pt.2.

9 January 1721

Mr Peter Griffen's proposall for renting the Lady Holford's Farm att Avebury in the County of Wilts, the 9th Jan 1721.

To take a lease of all the land rented by Farmer John Rose from Lady Day next, except the old orchard to the double crabb hedge, att the yearly rent of £350 cleare of all taxes, parish payments, parish offices,[1] and all other taxes whatsoever except the land tax, and the tenant to keep all the mounds, fences, pales, gates, stiles, doores, racks, mangers and all such small repaires in tenantable repaire, and alsoe the thatching & glazeing of those windows used by the tenant, but not any other parte of the buildings whatsoever.

The landlady to reserve to herselfe yearly a dozen of pidgeons, 6 fatt capons or 3 turkeys, the depasturing of a saddle horse att grase 20 weekes, or in liew thereof one tunn of old hay, one quarter of good old oates, one hundred of the best new milk cheese made about the month of May, and 5 load of soyle from the yard to be drawn by the tenant to any parte of the orchards & near it, & the use of the tenant's wheate straw for litter when the family or any of them are in the county, & the landlady to have egresse & regresse to lop, cut, fell, shroud & carry away at seasonable times any parte of the timber, lop, shrouds, &c., on the premises, & alsoe to have the same liberty of planting more there.

The tenant to have the lop of one 4th parte of the withys on the premises yearly in liew of wood.

[f.2.]

The tenant to sow Rowleaze with grasseeds the 4 & last year of the the 7 yeares.

The rent to be made payable quarterly.

The tenant to supply the landlady with such kitchen goods and other goods & garden stuffe in the same maner as Farmer John Rose did whilst he lived there.

The tenant is alsoe to supply the landlady with good old hay and old oates & beanes at the market price for soe much as the landlady shall have occasion of when in the country.

The lease of seven yeares to be determinable at the end of 4 yeares either landlady or tenant giveing 12 months notice in writeing before.[2]

The tenant to take care of the landlady's goods in her absence as they shal be

1 In fact, Peter Griffin served continuously as churchwarden from 1723 until 1727; cf. WSHC D1/15/9, f.27v; D1/15/10, F.31 & 37V; D3/15/11.

2 He was required to vacate the farm in 1743; see his letter to Staynor Holford, 26 June 1743; above, p.173

desired, vizt to air & cleane them &c., in order to preserve them from damage.

Tenant will take care to preserve the fruit in the new orchard for the landlady's use, & alsoe to overlooke the new planted trees, & send word when any damage happens thereto, & get it rectified in the best manner or as shall be ordered.

~~Tenant to be allowed 30 pole of hedgewood yearly for and towards making good the fences but noe lops, shrouds, or windfalls~~.

Tenant to give bond of £1000 for performance of covenants.

If the landlady should dye before the expiration of this lease, then this lease to determine unlesse the succeeding landlord agrees to continue it on the same termes as before mentioned.

Tenant is not to plough up any pasture or meadow land, on forfeiture of 5s per acre per annum.

[f.3.]

Tenant is not to crosse crop any of the land, nor assigne the premises without landlady's consent.

Tenant is to spend all the soyle, hay, straw, &c., on the premises, & not elsewhere.

Landlady upon non payment of rent 40 dayes to re-enter. Tenant is not to alter any of the housing from what it now is without landlady's consent.

This proposal was made by me att London, the 9 January 1721, & I expect an answer in a fortnight.
Peter Griffin

Verso Note: 1721 Januеary 9. Peter Griffen's proposall for taking Avebury Farme.

4. Opinion on Stayner Holford's Land Tax Assessment, 12th October 1753 WSHC 184/3

Mr Holford's estate at Avebury has for several years past been assessed with a sum for the land tax greatly disproportioned to the sums assessed on the properties of several other persons in the same place, and this grievance has been complained of for twenty years past, but never obtained any relief till the present owner came to reside there, and on making a more strict inquisition on the assessments than he could to any purpose do, when he was a stranger to the place, he found that he stood disproportionably charged, as he had long apprehended, and receiv'd for answer by way of justification of such proceedings, that it had been customary to load the great estates with sums larger than in proportion on smaller properties. This uncustomary & unreasonable method of proceeding he endeavoured to represent to the assessors in the true light, the year he came there, and at the same time gave in an exact state of the rent paid to him, and desired to have neighbours fare. The assessors for that year thought it proper that the several houses should be assessed, and made some further alterations in the old assessment, which afforded him some small relief, but this was very artfully represented to the meanest of the people, as a great oppression. On this he desired to be particularly informed by the parish officers how the several individuals were oppressed, and that they would represent to him such persons as they thought objects of charity, and partly aggrievied by a tax on their habitations, for that he was willing to pay the tax assessed on such persons, and furthermore added that he desired they might not be assessed any other year, but charge such deficiencys on his estate. He imagined this method would with reasonable people have adjusted the whole affair, but has since reason to believe that it was not the owners of small houses or persons that merited the name of objects of charity were displeased, but persons whose duty it is to promote peace, & whose circumstances place them in another situation, and from this quarter he was informed that an appeal was made to the Acting Commissioners at Ramsbury unknown to him, though the assessors were acquainted with it. And the particular intentions of such appealers, which was to this effect, viz[t] That Mr Grant, who occupys his own estate there, had a rent charge on his estate payable yearly to the Exchequer for which he stopped the full tax, it was said, as assessed by Parliament, and also that he paid a certain yearly income to the Vicar, for which it was also said that Mr Grant & his ancestors there stopped the full sum charged by Parliament, and as these payments were reduced to a certainty, and was the nature & tenure of Mr Grant's having the estate, the assessors in their opinions, unthought of or unknown to Mr Holford, assessed them in the same manner as the Excise Officer was assessed, and which to his certain knowledge is in several places the practice to do in such cases, and then these appealers were pleased to point out to the Commissioners, that they might be relieved by charging such overplus on Mr Holford's house, as was charged on the above payments to the Exchequer & Vicar, more than on those lands in the parish that are liable to many casualties, which those payments are exempt from. Mr Holford is not displeased with having his house taxed separate from the estate, which was always before considered & included in the sum assessed on the estate in general, and what is the practice of the other part of this parish, meaning Kennett,[1] where the late Mr Smith[2] lived, and the present owners have a reserve of an habitation separate from the farm of the like nature with his, which he is also told is the case of Sir John Guy's estate & house at Kennett, and of a great number of houses exactly circumstanced with Mr Holford's in this county and neighbourhood, but notwithstanding these instances, he will not stand up for the equity of such proceedings, and only desires to have the like fare with his neighbours at Avebury, which upon an impartial & strict inquiry would appear he has not, and if a house which has from the original of the land tax been included in the assessment with the lands belonging to such mansion is now assessed separately, does not the like proceeding make the Vicarage House there, reserved to the Vicar separately from Glebe lands & tythe, liable to be assessed in the same manner? I mean after the rate that such Glebe & tyths have heretofore

1 West Kennett.
2 Thomas Smith, lord of West Kennett manor.

been let at together, which is evidently equitable, and what Mr Holford believes every gentleman acting as Commissioner of the Tax will think, and though he disapproves taxing of small mean cottages such as are inhabited by very poor tenants or owners, yet he does not think, that houses which are lett at a certain fixed rent, or inhabited by the owners, who are farr from being necessitous, should be allowed to escape such assessments, or only be charged with two shillings a year, when such house are or may be lett for three, four or five pounds a year. Mr Holford is likewise told by John Clemens,[1] one of the assessors, that the manner of laying this tax on his house was not so regular & civil as he is sure is the practice of most gentlemen acting in the Commission of the Taxes. And such as he has great reason to believe is the sensible and equitable practice of Mr Batson, who is the gentleman, John Clemens named to Mr Holford as called on him with great anger and passion to know why he had not assessed Mr Holford's house, which he would directly do without admitting Clemens to offer a reason why he had not done it, and Clemens also said Mr Batson added, that he would tax the house at twenty pounds a year, for to settle it at a less rent may affront Mr Holford, as a publick house in the parish, meaning the Catharine Wheel, was assessed at that rent, which till the last year, with other houses, escaped ever being taxed, though a certain rent of thirty pounds has been paid for it besides a ground rent of five pounds a year.[2]

Mr Holford desires Mr Charles Young will take some proper opportunity to represent this affair in a true light to Mr Batson, and to pray the favour that he will, when an occasion shall offer, direct & see that Mr Holford's property may not be heavier assessed with the land tax, than other persons' properties in the Division of Avebury, which is all he ever desired of the assessors, or does now desire.

12th October 1753.

5. Rose's Servants: their Particular about the Stock &c [3]

WSHC 184/4/1.

Avebury 14th October 1755. John Bridgeman says that four of the meanest horses, which he particularly knows were only the live stock kept on the farm belonging to John Rose, and that no other stock of cattle of any kind whatever was kept on the said farm, or has been kept there for many years past, and that there is not kept, nor has not been kept for several years, any ploughs, carts, waggons, or any other husbandry utensils at the said farm belonging to John Rose, but that they were only carried from the Great Farm at Avebury occasionally, and returned again as soon as such business was over, that they were carried there for, and it is

1 John Clements, the schoolmaster.

2 The author is here comparing the Catherine Wheel with the neighbouring Hare and Hounds, which was owned by Stayner Holford.

3 This heading is taken from the verso. The statement is written on three sides of a folded paper; the third side is blank.

also well known to all the servants, labourers & neighbours, and also to the most substantial and reputable farmers, who are well acquainted with this estate, that no part of the stock kept on this estate, either as to the numbers or quality of the cattle, or any husbandry utensils, were equal to what the occupation of such large property as this estate only required, nor equal to the stock always kept on this estate before it was occupied by John Rose. The truth of this I am ready to swear to
John X Bridgeman
Witness:
Ar Jones
Joseph Brown

The 14th October 1755. William Stevens says that what is written on the other side he knows to be true, and is ready to swear to the contents of it
William X Stevens
Witness:
Ar Jones
Joseph Brown

The 16th October 1755. William Reeves says, that what is written on the otherside he knows to be true, and is ready to swear to the contents of it
William X Reeves
Witness
Ar Jones
Joseph Brown

6. Staynor Holford's Evidence and Remarks Concerning the Tithe Dispute, c.1756 WSHC 184/2.

The underwritten papers are what I have mett with relating to the dispute between Sir Richard Holford & Mr White formerly vicar of Avebury.
Particulars by which Sir Richard purchased.
An abstract or brief account of the dispute & proceedings
Sir Thomas Trevor's opinion.
A notice that the Plaintiff did intend to move the Court to suppress the answer and to obtain costs.
An order to refers the answer to the master.
The Master's report
A petition for a commission to examine witnesses.
A list of witness to be examined on the part of the Plantiff on interrogatories
A copy of the notice of the intended execution of a commission.
An abstract or very short account of part of the proceedings.
A release from Mr White to Sir Richard
A memorandum of Sir Richard's agreeable to Mr White's release.

I never knew till the late notice for taking up tithes in kind, but that the annual payment of four pounds was the whole demand made on the farm for tithes, but as on such notice I imagined the present vicar had some terrier, or authority, which he conceived was sufficient for such demand, it became necessary for me to look over my papers relating to this farm, and there found, that my grandfather purchased it with a modus on it, and that on a like demand from a former vicar, a dispute in Chancery commenced, and the [f.2.] proceedings in that cause are filed in court, and may if a litigation was to arise be obtained in evidence, & notwithstanding the papers I have mett with do not contain the full proceedings entered in court, it is by them apparent, that the then vicar thought it most eligible to pray that the proceedings may stop, and that he would pay the plantiff's costs, and of course his own, and continued to receive the four pounds a year, by what I can find this affair was depending in Chancery about six years, which certainly was attended with great fatigue & expence. Since that time I have great reason to believe the payment of four pounds has been regularly made & accepted, but admiting that some instance has happened of a tenant's suffering an alteration without consent of the landlord, it can no ways effect the inheritance, and if such taking up the tithes in kind was thought more beneficial one year with another, then accepting the customary payments, it is very strange, it has been omitted so many years, and I am assured a short interruption will not destroy the prescription.

The decrease in the value of money has no relation to this affair, because it must be considered that the produce of the portion of land required from which the prescriptive payment arose is of no more value at this instant, taking one year with another, than it was on the original establishment, and thereby on a litigation it may clearly be made to appear that the several vicars have enjoyed an annual payment superior to the value of the produce, and so the prescriptive payment has always been in favour of the vicars, and it is apparent, it has been considered so by the several vicars by their continuing to receive it, and I am assured in this light the Court of Chancery would consider it.

[f.3.] If the two ell ridges in that piece of what nearest the church were, on the dissolution of monasterys, allotted for some provision for the vicars from this farm, & long by them enjoyed, & afterwards a certain portion of money in lieu of the same was established and accepted for a long continuance of years, I am well informed I may plead a prescription. It is almost apparent this was the case, because Mr White, the vicar, in his defence, only produced a terrier of his own writing made a few years before the said litigation, and concealed or destroyed the ancient records or terriers, which would have sett this affair in a clear light, and so it is charged in the bill.

The law implys that every tenant or occupier shall pay all tithes & customary payments for tithes, unless particularly agreed to the contrary, and this appears reasonable, because he that reaps & enjoys the crop should pay such demands as the crop only is liable to. Therefore the payment for the year 1753 is a personal debt on the late tenant.

By an act now in force of the 2d & 3d of Edward 6th are the following expressions. That every subject shall without fraud yield & pay all predial tithes in kind, as hath of right been yielded & paid within forty years before the making of this act, or of right & custom ought to have been paid. The determined sense of these words, as hath of right been yielded, relates to tithes in kind yielded within forty years. In the shape the present vicar makes his demand is allowing a modus in the plain words of the law as to predial tithes, and as to small tithes, which have not been taken in kind from this farm, they are liable to innumerable endless & very trifling disputes, unless the vicar can prove an uninterrupted [f.4.] custom to support it. And custom in parishes, though widely differing, and often carrying the face of inequality & seeming injustice respecting both clergy & laity, is of singular weight and importance, and if several instances of a weak or bad tenant suffering or allowing the whole or part of small tithes to be taken in kind unknown to landlord, it cannot be destructive of an ancient prescription, or any ways hurt the landlord's property. Common reason confirms this, for if the acts of bad tenants were to be entailed on the property, no landlord could be safe. The late tenant on this farm informed me that the vicar once sent to him for the key of the pigeon house to take some pigeons, and that he sent for answer, he would not lett him have the key or any pigeons & seemed much surprized at it. This particular I can swear to. It is somewhat strange to imagine that part of the small tithes were sometimes taken in kind, and the other part included in an annual payment.

On a late exchange of some lands in this parish, it is said that several small parcels of the ancient glebe lands were parted with & exchanged, and such pieces of the glebe are so ploughed & intermixed with other property that the terrier ceases to be of any use or information in that case, and it is also said, that the present vicar has established a certain annual payment, composition, or modus in lieu of vicarial tithes arising from such lands so exchanged, and that this conditional payment is agreed to be some writing drawn up at the time of such exchange. It is certain, that though the freehold of the glebe is in the parson or vicar after regular induction, yett it is with these limitations, first that he must [f.5.] not alienate, no, not even with the consent of patron and ordinary. Secondly, nor may he exchange, though with the like consent. Thirdly, may he commit waste, in either of these cases, he, or his representatives are liable to much trouble , and no authority less than an Act of Parliament can defend or support it. By several papers I find that a commission was actually obtained, & a list of witnesses prepared, who were to prove the prescriptive payment of four pounds, & all hostile proceedings going forward when Mr Tucker, Mr Richard Smith of Kennett, & Mr Archdeacon Yeates of Marlborough, at the request of Mr White, did apply to Sir Richard in the strongest manner to stop proceedings. I also by letters of Mr White find, that he was desirous the proceedings should be taken of the file in Chancery, but this Sir Richard would not consent to, well knowing it might be of use to his inheritance.

By several of Mr White's letters I find he never would have required any alteration in the prescription, if he had not been particularly ill treated, & irritated by William Skeate the then tenant on the farm, and I find that differences did run very high, because Skeate did tell Sir Richard that if he suffered the vicar to take up the ell ridges as he was confined to take them out of that piece nearest the church, he would sow some yearly on purpose for him, and the vicar finding himself so cramped by his answer on oath, he declined all further disputes.

7. The Opinion of Nicholas Jones[1] on Avebury Tithes, 4th September 1756

WSHC 184/2

Page First
The Avebury estate was an appendage to one of the greater abbeis, vizt the monastery of Cirencester. At the dissolution of these monasterys a provision, you say, was made for the vicar out of those estates, which were sold to lay persons, which provision or allowances were or ought to be set forth in a terrier.

N.Jones's advice and answer to this above paragraph.

I observe that you have a copy of the illegall [?and perverse] terrier (for t'is by no means an ancient record or any evidence) in your custody, made by the then vicar in 1680. The proceedings of the suit in Chancery between this dissembling vicar[2] and Sir Richard are I suppose on record, recourse to which might easily be had, which will prove one strong help, among others, in Stayner's favour. I call the vicar dissembling &c., because it appears to me that after he had reported & acknowledged to Sir Richard that he had for 20 years & his predecessors before him were only intituled to or had ever received but £4 per year as a modus or composition for all tythes due from this estate, I say after this report to Sir R.H., in 1680 he cooked up this spurious terrier. Now, though, you have a copy of this spurious terrier of 1680, I advize, 1st, that you apply to the Register at the Bishop's court at Sarum for a fresh copy of this spurious terrier of 1680, attested by the present living register, 2dly to get the register to search back even to or about the year the monasteries were dissolved in Henry the 8th's reign and see if there be any [?more] terriers or records relating to Avebury. Tis possible this provision of £4 might be found registered. I cannot tell the precise year the monasteries were dissolved but I think 'twas about the 26th year of Henry's reigne.[3] Admitting it so, it was about the year 1535. This to be fixed. I also advise further 3dly to get the register to search for a terrier (& give you copy if need thereafter be) every 40 year after the first [*illegible*] be fixed, till the year 1680, when the spurious terrier appeared.[4] To be particular, admit the original record

1 Nicholas Jones, one of Stayner Holford's half brothers. He appears to be advising his brother Arthur Jones. On the seventh page he refers to 'you and Stayner'.

2 John White.

3 The greater monasteries (which included Cirencester) were dissolved by an act of 1539; that was preceded by an act of 1535 which dissolved smaller institutions.

4 Search was presumably made, but no terrier other than that for 1680 was ever found.

or [?terrier] of this £4 modus be found and fixed at the year 1535. Let the register search for a repeated record or terrier (for they are and ought frequently to be made out afresh by each vicar & placed in the bishops court) in the year 1575, being forty years after, the same again in the year 1615, being 40 years more after, the same again in the year 1655, and least ancient records might have been lost or destroyed during the troubles & the usurpation of Oliver Cromwell, let the register search it on the [?last ocation] in the years 1660, 1661, or 1662, when on regulating things in church & state new terriers & records might be made & placed there. If such there be and what the nature of it is, by my advice of search, the precise distance of the time of 40 year between each search. I give you the following reasoning

[Page 2d.] Observe: by the 2 and 3 Edward 6th Chap 13 there are the following expressions: that every subject shall, without fraud, yield and pay all predial tythes in kind, as hath of right been yeilded and paid within forty years before the passing of this act, or of right and custom ought to have been paid. Regard the following explanation so essentially usefull & great to Stayner, the silver or gold I call, which does and must run through his whole defence or answer, viz: the sense of these words, as hath of right been yielded, relates to tythes in kind yielded within forty years, and observe especially, the words of right and custom ought to have been paid plainly and indisputably relate to a rightfull custom, *de modo decimandi*, which ought to be paid. Now, this *modus decimandi* of £4 Staynor (& ancestors who previously enjoyed this estate) always has paid, paid it this very last year past, and never did or does refuse paying the same. High, mighty & potent in Staynor's favour.

NB the Revd Mr Barford, rector of Wyley,[1] Wilts, who you know, may be usefull to Stayner in speaking to the Register.

In law – the proverb, the farthest way about is the nearest way home, is worth remembring. In searching the registry so far back & so often, you'll find twill be laying the axe to the root of the tree, and giving yn councell fundamental materials regularly to raise the superstructure. Item, tis my opinion, your scarlett vicar[2] will never, unless he be a real madman or fool, attack Stayner, nor do I indeed see, & notwithstanding the former advice of this letter, the occasion you will have to make such a far-fetched search, because I think, item, the follows argument, you may cut the matter short.

You say, in a year or two afer the purchase by Sir R.H. in 1680,[3] this former vicar brought his action or controverted about these 2 ell ridges. Now suppose this contest to have been in the year 1683 & deferred in 1684 – and that, ever since, this modus of £4 has been paid, and, which is very material to Stayner, accepted of ever since from time to time by the vicar. Why, the inference or

---

It is the only one recorded in Hobbs, Steven, ed. *Wiltshire glebe terriers 1588-1827*. Wiltshire Record Society 56. 2003.

1 Richard Barford, rector of Wylye since 1744.

2 James Mayo.

3 Actually, the purchase was made in 1692.

consequence to be drawn is this.

First, Stayner can easily truly prescribe time immemorial with respect to this modus, an established rule in [?that] Court & at comon law. Tis now 73 years since the suit determined, and if any Goody church[1] will find Herculean labour to pick up any old person in his parish to prove anything after this modus of £4 – or to make any notable report concerning any suit with Sir R.H., or his father's predecessors once [p.3d.] taking up the corn by force. 2ndly according to that part of the 2d & 3rd of Edward 6th chapt 13th vizt as hath of right been paid & yeilded within forty years. This accords to the sense put on it, which I can undoubtedly support, Staynor can easily make oute.

Sir R.H., you see, quickly demolished the quondam high priest under disadvantageous terms. How much more Staynor, who has apparently every valuable evidence, and advantages which Sir Richard had not, and as appears to me, could not easily (at least) obtain.

I wish I was as sure of recovering my lambs, as of Stayner's vanquishing this troublesome [?priest]. I verily believe his threats will evaporate in [?terms]. If he dares attack him, let him! And to his cost, let him perish in his folly.

The doctor's last letter to Stayner to acquaint him that the composition or modus should cease, from Michaelmas last, is as farcical and may be just as rationally injoyned and supported as if he had ordered Staynor to cease from turning a guinea ten times over before he parts with it (his wonted custom), or spitting five or six times before he drinks off a glass of wine, to cease from Michaelmas laste.

That general discharge you have under the former vicar's hands to Sir R on the determination of the suit in 1603 or 04 – will be extremely [?usefull] in the defendant Stayner's pleadings, and such a home thrust as your vicar cannot parry.

On revising your long letter critically again, I find the following paragraph, vizt., you say thus; the vicar imagines because he can prove that his father's predecessor[2] did once by force take up the corn (NB by the word corn I understand the two ell ridges he now demands) that will support him notwithstanding a suit was commenced on it and such a claim ever since dropped. To this I answer, from this paragraph by the emphatical words because he can prove. I infer the vicar can through some very aged person in your parish shall prove, the once taking up the corn (i.e.the said ell ridges) by his father's predecessor by force. Well! Be it so, allow he can prove such an act, such unlawfull, unjustifyable act, for such it is, unless immemorial custom would have supported their entering on another man's land, & taking this two ell ridges in any of the lands (NB any lands an absurdity to suppose!) belonging to Stayner's farm, I say, admit all this, what can such a proof avail? Nothing. I should rather say, worse than nothing. If, from so knavish, as well as foolish, examples and instances he [Page 4th.] attempts to take the two ell ridges (ie [?item] equal to an acre) of corn from any part of Stayner's estate, Stayner has an undoubted action against him as a trespasser and

1 Is Churchman meant?

2 James Mayo's father, John, preceded his son as vicar of Avebury.

intruder (to say no more of it) for even suppose he had a real right to the tythes of Stayner's corn, or to two ell ridges, yet unless custom could support him (and custom in parishes, though widely differing, and often carrying the face of inequality and seeming injustice respecting both clergy and laity, is of singular weight and importance). He dare not set forth or order his deputy or servant to go on any farmer's or occupier's lands, and set forth any tythes or his portion. If two ell ridges, though they may be conservedly and indisputably the vicar's real property, the common law enjoyns that the farmer or occupier shall fairly, and without fraud, set forth the minister's tythes (ie tythes indisputably due) and and [sic] the ecclesasticall office does direct that due and regular notice be given to the minister, that he, his deputy, or servant, may attend to be witness, see, and be satisfied, that the farmer sets forth his tythes, &c., fairly. More than this or less ought not, cannot be done, unless, I say, a custom is to the contrary. For instance, in my parish the farmers give me notice that their grain is properly shocked, fairly raked, & cocked &c, and I send my servants or tything man to tythe it & set it forth.

When a farmer does not give the proper notice, and set forth the tythes or (as custom directs) that the minister or his servants might do it – an action with treble damages lies against the farmer. I only relate what should be, and is done in general cases. Stayner's is widely different. He has no [?call] to set forth any tythes, &c., nor to regard the vicar's notice, gilded with that nonsensical humbug expression of the Doctor's – agreeable to the custom of the parish. Let him, trusting to that custom, bring his action, if he dares, against Stayner, for one single crown in hand paid to the learned clerk of councellor N.I.[1] I will [?ensure] Stayner's dignity, and though I'll not pounce, or, perhaps in charity, will not consign this black guard to outer darkness yet, for wailing and gnashing of teeth in this world, I'll be answerable for. I think I have said all that need be said, respecting Stayner's particular concern, & I shall conclude with the [?following] well worth remembering with regard to the pleading in the case. A *modus decimandi* is when land or some annual profit or pension, &c., hath been given time out of mind to a parson & his successors, in full satisfaction & discharge of all the tythes in kind for such a place. This prescription arose at first from a real composition, made beyond the memory of man, and suppose now lost prescription by custom immemorial. Stayner must plead. Thus end the 1st lesson!

[Page 5th.] I could greatly enlarge, and I will, what I have said, by various learned quotations, opinions, acts of Parliament, &c., but as I think, I have acted the Councellor beyond 7/8ths of my brethren, at any of the Inns of Court, by way of *forma pauperis*, I chuse to be further silent, till Stayner comes down a little handsomely, either by considering & paying me as a prime counsell ought to be, or, in return, assist me in obtaining of suits, whereof, as Sir John Falstaffe in the play of Henry the 4th says, you and Staynor, like the hangman, have no lean wardrobe.[2] To drop, if possible, my genius for humour, whether black, gray, blue,

1 Nicholas Jones; the writer of this memorandum.

2 Quoting Shakespeare's *Henry IV, part 1*, act 1, scene 2: 'Yea, for obtaining of suits,

or all the colours of the rainbow, pack up & send your cast off coats, waistcoats, & breeches, hats & perriwigs, &c', (or any thing fitts) for my son and I begin to be as tattered as the Prodigal in the parable lately come from swine keeping.[1]

Cousin Arthur[2] stands in my opinion as yours, a very sensible cool headed man. I advise you to send him all I have wrote on the subject. If there be any objection to the part where I have been merry with Stayner, scratch it out, or alter it. It's too long for you to transcribe, though really not longer than necessary (for one cannot be too nick nackety explicite where people cannot personally discourse) and tis such as will save Couzin Arthur devilish deal of trouble. I answer for it, he will with great facility extract the essence from my detail, to form a proper brief for his pleading hereafter.

Tom[3] will allow, I was his first fiddle at the opera of his dirty vicar, Egerton, and I was honoured with Dr Hays of the Commons & Arthur Jones[4] high commendations for the materials I furnished them with, and pointing out all the strickeinge places in that case, and I prophesy Arthur Jones's eulogiums in the present will be such as will incline me to expect he'll propose to me a partnership in all law cases. In this neighbourhood, I am the only Chamber Councill!

The parishioners at Abury must club their best sixpences to raise my fee to 2 guineas, & I will undertake, on telling me their case truly & undisguisedly (which country folkes for the most part to their hurt cunningly conceal) to advise and extricate them out of any ecclesiastical difficulties. I know nothing explicitly with respect to their lands the [*illegible*] can say nothing, but if their respective tenures be similar to Stayner's, you can easily judge in what I have said of Stayner's case, now the parishioners with theirs.

N.B. You should have sent me a copy of the terrier of 1680, which (you say) to you appears very obscure about the tythe having ever been taken in kind. Turn over

[Page 6th.] The following is the last paragraph of your letter I think to be answered, vizt: This parrish is in several tythings. In one of them the proprietors of lands about ten years since made an exchange of lands. Since the incumbency of the present vicar, he took on him to part with the glebe lands that lay in that tything for others, and established a modus in lieu of the tythes of such lands as were so altered or exchanged, and all this done without sanction of an act of Parliament necessary and honest in such cases.

I answer an act of Parliament can do almost anything in this world except making the rector of Paulspury[5] hop a horn pipe or alter the nature of spigots and

---

whereof the hangman hath no lean wardrobe. 'Sblood, I am as melancholy as a gib cat or a lugged bear.'

1 Luke, 15, v.11–32

2 He shared the same name as Nicholas's brother.

3 Thomas Jones, brother of both Nicholas and Arthur Jones, and half-brother of Stayner Holford.

4 This was probably the author's cousin, rather than his brother; see above.

5 This memoranda was written in Paulspury (see below), but this place has not been identified.

possetts. But I am in doubt as to its power in alienating or exchanging glebe lands. That the freehold of the glebe be in the parson, &c., after regular induction, yet tis with these following limitations, 1st, that he may not alienate, no, not even with consent of patron and ordinary, 2dly, nor may he exchange, though with the like consent, nor 3dly may he commit waste. The inferences from the forgoing you can easily make. If your vicar has parted with the Glebe lands or any part thereof, i.e. exchanged them, he is liable to be severely handled by the patron, Lord Chancellor, the Bishop of Salisbury, or Archdeacon of Wilts, and your churchwardens are very culpable and shamefully remiss in their duty in not presenting the matter at a visitation.

But after all, I cannot help thinking you quite out and wrong informed in this matter. The whole appears to me an impossibility! A high absurdity! If your vicar be a fool or a madman, can I suppose that the proprietor of lands, who with whom he exchanged the glebe or part, or the attorney concerned in drawing the reciprocal conveyances, fools or mad men also? For consider, the vicar cannot possibly make any title, as the ground plot for a conveyance of the glebe, or bind his heirs, executors, administrators or successors. Without a very discerning spirit, I divine the matter to be no more than barely this, vizt, I suppose that in this particular tything in your parish a considerable part of the glebe lies remote and inconvenient to your vicar or his tenant, which Glebe might be conveniently scituated for some proprietor or farmer who lives in this tything, which proprietor or farmer has lands equally circumstanced as to remoteness, I'll suppose, which prove convenient and near to the vicar or his tenant where they dwell, their house & barn are &c. Hence their exchange arose - exchange of lands - not an exchange, as you set it forth, by a regular deed and conveyance, a mutual investiture of these lands to their heirs &c &c. It's impracticable! But only a verbal or written agreement betwixt the vicar and proprietor for a temporary exchange, only and barely for the convenient and advantageous scituation between them respecting their mutual occupation, i.e. cultivating, ploughing, & sowing &c. If this be the case, the sort of exchange is, I apprehend allowable, & [Page 7.] and nobody has, I think, to do or interfere with it. Tis a reasonable indulgence, provided the vicar takes care, 1st that part of his glebe which is so exchanged for occupation sake only be fairly done by and managed that no waste be committed on it, that it be not unfairly plowed or pared away by degrees (which rascally farmers by an artfull management at the plough may [?from time to time] fraudulently do) and thereby the glebe hurt & lessened in point of value, lastly that the vicar on such exchange for occupation sake, sees and previously takes care, that the farmer or proprietor be not suffered to break up ancient greensword in the field, but only such land as always plowed &c.

Seeing to these points is incumbent on your vicar and a failure in any of them renders him obnoxious to some sort of punishment from the Archdeacon at a visitation either by himself or permitting any person to injure or alter the state of the Glebe as to break up ground &c., cutting timber down on the Glebe or hedges at an unseasonable time or unhusbandlike mannere. All this is committing or permitting waste, & for which, more or less, besides the archdeacon's cognisance, his successor has an action against his executor, &c., for the same as a certain species of dilapidation.

I think I am, upon the whole, right in my conjectures, but, if otherwise, be you more particular, and be sure to disregard the positive reports of any country farmer in this matter or indeed any, I mean fully believing it on hearing it. Country villages abound with gossips and tatlig people, lovers of contention, &c., even when the minister of a parish is in every respect a valuable irreproachable man. I make no doubt but your vicar is a dirty dog.[1] However, never entertain or give much credit to any thing said of him or what he does, vizt, particularly as to this reported exchange of Glebe &c., but what you are critically, demonstrably clear about, admitting not the least loophole for a doubt. Otherwise you and Stayner, if you intend a complaint against him &c., will most probably appear in a malicious as well as ridiculous light.

The vicar's conduct respecting his glebe, if such a real exchange as you assert be true, which I am morally certain is not, cannot, is only an incident in the play, without any sort of connection with Stayner's grand point concerning the modus of £4, &c., and can only be considered, at least by me, as a great gun to play upon the doctor, & put him to silence.

I have one observation more to make on part of this last paragraph relating to the glebe &c. The following are your words: and to establish a modus in lieu of the tythes of such lands as were so altered or exchanged &c. This part at first sight inclined me to suspect my conjectures with the exchange wrong, but I have considered it, and, I think, do so properly account for his establishing this modus on the lands altered &c., to myself that I still adhere to my own opinion about the nature of the exchange. I can, however, I fancy, extract a something which may prove very exaltedly serviceable to Stayner, & probably parishioners in general, and cause the doctor to fall by his own sword. Answer me very satisfactorily the following questions, vizt., how many years ago, and in what year, did your vicar part with or exchange (as you call exchange) the whole or part of the Glebe lands. 2dly particularly learn and [Page 8th.] and tell me what year the vicar established a modus in lieu of the tythes of such lands as were so altered or exchanged. 3dly tell me the precise value of the modus, what sum, & for how many acres of land, whether this modus is for all sort of tythes coming and arising from these exchanged lands, in gross, or did he establish a certain modus, so much from every acre.

You are both to blame in not having long ago rescued these great heaps of old family dusty papers by you from their confused state, methodized, sorted and tituled every useful paper with a brief hint on the backside of its contents, and rid yourselves of all such papers as Stayner & you considered as useless. It was lazyly deferred. What a plaguy deal of trouble shall I have when I come to the estate! Hem! Hem![2]

1 James Mayo.
2 He never did!

Collect together every usefull paper relating to this business, particularly the general discharge of the former litigating vicar to Sir Richard Holford on the determination of the old suit, and all other receipts of each vicar for the yearly modus of the £4 ever since, or as many as you can find, and let these receipts be regularly year by year methodized. The vicar every year should, and I suppose did, give Stayner's predecessors a proper receipt for this £4 modus, and I think Staynor has been carefull enough to have one duly and plainly wrote every year. He has, at least resided at Avebury, and one, he has, or will see to have, if he yet is to pay, or has paid, the modus for this present yeare.

But that it may not be quite so prudent and proper for Stayner else he might exhort his vicar to search these scriptures with the same frowning and looks and words which Henry the 8th did to Cardinal Woolsey, on giving him the papers which precipitated his ruin.[1]

Read over this!

And alter this – and then to breakfast, with what appetite you may. Vide the [*illegible*] play of Henry 8th.

You have reported the dissenting minister to be an honest sensible man, and the principal of that congregation a very valuable man and your very good neighbour. These I apprehend you may safely confide in, and it may not be improper for you to read this history to them, the better to obviate or correct what I may be out in, and also assist you in answering my questions.

In the multitude of [?Counsellor More's safety] I add only - Sally[2] was committed safe to the Tower last Wednesday morn, from whence Mr Bennett (who is extremely friendly) intended to escort her to his country house at East Ham. When she is wardrobed & settled I shall write to my brother Tom etc about her. Mary gives me a very pleasing report of Mrs [?Bent] in every respects Sally likes her much, & is quite well pleased, & I prophes will do. With duty & salutations I am your most affectionate brother

N.Jones.

Paulspury, 9ber 4th 1756

8. Peter Griffin's Statement relating to the Modus WSHC 184/2

The 19th October 1756

Peter Griffin, of the parish of Avebury in the county of Wilts., says he was born in the said parish about the year 1674, and has continued to live in the said parish the whole time, excepting about three years, and rented the Great Farm in the said parish twenty one years, which he entered on about the year 1722, and never paid more, or less than four pounds a year to the vicar for all tyths

1 The reference is probably to Henry VIII's words, 'If we did think, his contemplation were above the earth, and fixed on spiritual object, he should still dwell in his musings. But I am afraid his thinkings are below the moon, not worth his serious considering'.

2 Probably referring to the author's daughter Sarah.

for the said farm, and on his taking the said farm was informed that there was a customary modus or composition of four pounds a year to be paid in lieu of all tyths annually for the said farm, and that never any more was required of him, or in any other shape during his occupation. Peter Griffin furthermore says, that the present vicar, Mr James Mayo, about three weeks since, asked him whether he ever carryed any pigeons to his father's house at Caln without being paid for them. Peter Griffin says he replyed he never did to the best of his knowledge, or remembrance, and also says that he never heard, or believes, that any payment was ever made from the said farm but four pounds a year. Upon Peter Griffin's being asked what he knew of an old measure of land called an ell ridge, he said that he was unacquainted with such a measure, but has heard, that it contained sixty luggs, and that two of them is a tenanty acre.
Peter Griffin [1]

Verso Note: Peter Griffin's account.

9. An Account of some Discourse that passed between my Brother Arthur Jones & Mr James Mayo on the 14th June 1757 relating to the Modus &c., 1757[2] WSHC 184/2

On the 14th June 1757 I had some discourse with James Mayo[3] to the following effect.
In the first place he asked if I thought in early days £4 a year was established? To this I replied that was not an essential question, because a modus was or may be created at any time, & that as the present payment was near to the value of the thing required it added to the authority of it. To this he said, could I imagine that if £4 year was many years since paid things were now so altered that such payment bore no proportion to their present value. To this it must be observed that the vicars have time immemorial had the benefit & so considered that the modus was in their favour. He said that by his father's books he could prove a contract was entered into with some tenant on this estate, and that the pigeon house was exempted, & also that such books were in the opinion of the twelve judges to be admitted as evidence. This may be a mistake & it is only by a fresh determination or opinion that M.H.[4] can be satisfied by such reports. He said P Griffin could not or would not swear he never paid pigeons as tythe, or that they were not by proper persons demanded as tythe, or that they were not paid as such, but owned that Peter Griffin had told him he was paid for pigeons, & that he did not know he had paid any for tythe. Mr. Mayo's evidence in asserting [f.2.] circumstances, I conceive, are not to determine, but that he & all parties in case

1 In a different hand; presumably a signature.
2 Heading written on the verso of the letter (above) from Stayner Holford to Peter Holford, 21st December 1756.
3 'J.M' in mss.
4 Mr Holford.

of litigation are to be examined on interrogatories & the court will accordingly proceed. He also said that the annual payment had been omitted for fifteen years, & that the modus had thereby ceased. This was during the tenantcy of John Rose.[1] It is not to be imagined because the V sufered a running & unsettled account to remain in such state unknown to landlord, or complaining or taking any legal method to compel such payments, that it can hurt the inheritance & defeat the modus.

10. An account of John Scane's attendance on Mr Mayo to pay for Tyths, 9th January 1758.[2] WSHC 184/2.

January 9th 1758
I was to wait on Mr. James Mayo this day agreeable to a notice given to several of the farmers to pay the vicar's tythes or compositions for tythes. I accordingly made an offer or tender of eight pounds due from my master's Mr Holford's farm for a modus or composition due at Michaelmas last for two years, which Mr Mayo refused to receive, but he added that he would take a small sum less than has annually being paid, or a small sum more, and enter into an article to abide by the same during his incumbency, and that he believed the annual payment is at this present near to the value of what is required
John Scans

11. Remarks on the Dispute with Mr Mayo about the Modus for the Tyths of Avebury Great Farm belonging to me[3] WSHC 184/2

Mr Mayo's argument is the same as Mr Holford's, that is the preservation of the property for their successors. It is clear Mr Mayo does not act from a lucrative motive, because he offers to take less or a small sum more than has been paid for the tyths. It is also plain Mr Holford does not act from a lucrative motive, because he does not desire Mr Mayo to take less, or in any other shape to lessen what is his dues. So farr each stands on a mutual footing.

Mr. White was the only cause of this dispute, first by making a terrier without producing any ancient writings for the support of it, and in the next place swearing to that part of it relating to this farm, directly contrary to what is sett forth in the terrier, and, after a litigation of some years with Sir Richard Holford, dropped the suit, paid Sir Richard's costs, and continued to take the ancient prescription, and in this shape Mr Mayo's father came to it. Mr. James Mayo succeeded, and both of them are clear of any possibility of a charge of injuring the living as they have preserved it in the shape they found it. Mr Holford

1 'J.R.' in mss.
2 Heading From verso.
3 Note on the verso.

always has & still is disposed to adjust the matter in an amicable way, an instance of which he gave in rendering to Mr. Martyn,[1] on Mr Mayo's part, such information as he thought would have been definitive, and Mr Martyn thought Mr Holford's account was sufficient to satisfy Mr Mayo.

Mr Mayo may easily guard against his giving any additional strength to what Mr Holford conceives to be an ancient prescription, by expressing in his receipt three pounds for the ell ridges, and one pound for the small tyths. This method puts an end to the dispute with great safety to Mr Mayo's character, for it must be considered if Mr Mayo was to commence a suit in equity it must end on the explanation of the terrier, as Mr. White has by his oath in Chancery sett forth. Mr Holford believes Mr Mayo thinks the usual payments equal to the value of what Mr Mayo conceives he is entitled to by his terrier. If so there is no possibility of hurting the property of the vicarage, and therefore the payments have always been in favour of the vicars. I would gladly know what Mr Mayo would do in my situation. Would he not take the benefit of the laws of his country for the preservation of that property, which is by law established?

I desire Mr Mayo will come to my house and see what papers I have by me, which I am perswaded will convince him that what I have asserted is true, and consequently Mr Mayo cannot possibly be liable to the least censure for injuring the living by his successors, or in the least offend against his own conscience, because it will be very evident that he has made every inquisition in his power to be truly informed what claim the vicar had on this farm, and I am sure Mr Mayo will allow this offer is making every concession in my power to grant.

We both have been inclined to treat this affair in an amicable way, and hope it will end so.

Pray what did Mr. Martyn say to Mr Mayo on this affair?

An alteration in the usual payment may be injurious to the successors, because as Mr. White has confirmed by a record in Chancery, the ell ridges which lay nearest the church, he was glad to have the ancient payment continued, preferrable to an uncertain payment.

On the dissolution of monasterys, the farm was one of the lesser abbys. A portion of land to make some provision for a vicar was established, which is what the law calls a modus. For many years past, time immemorial, a certain yearly income has been paid in lieu of said land & tyths, which at this instant is the value of the said land and tyths, therefore has such long payments the right of prescription. The law positively says that a small interruption shall not destroy a prescription neither can the long repeated acts of a tenant without the consent of the owner effect the inheritance.

12. Samuel Martyn's Opinion

WSHC 184/2

1760 January 3rd

1 Samuel Martyn of West Kennet, attorney.

Mr Samuel Martyn an attorney of Kennett was here on the behalf of Mr. James Mayo, the vicar, to peruse & look over Mr. White's, a former vicar's answer in Chancery relating to the modus or ancient composition for tythes due from this farm. Mr Martyn on seeing the answer & having been informed that the sum of four pounds a year had been paid beyond the memory of man in lieu in full of all tithes from this farm, he said that he should advise Mr Mayo to accept of the said sum of four pounds a year without any further dispute or variation in the same.

Be it remembered that Mr Staynor Holford the owner of the great farm at Avebury did on Michaelmas 1755 begin to occupy the said farm, and some short time before the harvest 1756 Mr. James Mayo the vicar sent a letter to the said Mr Holford to give him notice that he would take up the ellridges of wheat & small tithes, agreable to a power sett forth in his terrier. Mr Holford said in answer he had no such power, and advised him not to proceed with violence on such an affair. The harvest passed over without any attempt, but when the day was appointed by the vicar to receive the several payments from his other parishioners, John Scane, Mr Holford's bailiff, attended & made an offer of the four pounds, which the vicar refused to accept, and continued to refuse to accept the same from the years 1757, 1758 & 1759, till which time Mr. Martyn had convinced him that as he was by the evidence of Mr White's answer confined to take the two ellridges of wheat laying annually nearest to the church, and that the payment of three pounds a year for the said ellridges, & twenty shillings for the small tythes had been the ancient payment, and the vicar believing that the said sum of four pounds a year was to the full value of the wheat which may happen to grow yearly on the said ellridges & small tythes, he consented to accept the said sum without any variation whatever, and accordingly on the 8th January 1760 the sum of twelve pounds were paid to him from for the two ellridges for four years after the rate of three pounds a year, and four pounds were at the same time paid for four years small tithes, which payment appears by a receipt here inclosed.

Whereas about Michaelmas 1755, John Rose, the tenant of this farm, did contrive to make himself a bankrupt in order to defraud the landlord of his arrears of rent, the vicar by the said circumstance was not paid the four pounds due from the occupier of this farm for the said year 1755, but went amongst other creditors of the said Rose to receive a dividend under the said bankruptcy, which only amounted to five shillings in the pound, by which circumstance the vicar only received 20 shillings. Mr Holford, taking the same into consideration, and not being in the least disposed to break or destroy the said annual payments of four pounds a year, or to deprive the present or future vicars of such ancient annual modus of four pounds, & to promote and encourage a good harmony between the said vicar & himself, did voluntary pay the said three pounds which were unpaid from the said John Rose for the year ending Michaelmas 1755, which also appears by a receipt here inclosed.

It should be remembered that during part of the four years that the arrears were growing due, the vicar & Mr Holford were in a state of great variance, and that every information and circumstance which the said vicar could gather, as well from his father's accounts, who was his immediate predecessor & had been incumbent here for near forty years, & from the old tenants of this farm & other ancient inhabitants of this parish, he the vicar could not prove any one instance that the wheat growing on the ellridges or small tithes had been taken in kind, or that there had been any variation of the sum of four pounds being paid annually in full of all tithes from this farm, and there is no doubt but that the very long and uninterrupted payment of four pounds has now the advantage & benefit of a prescription, and if in time to come the present or any other vicar should renew such claim as has been made on Mr Staynor Holford, or offers to take a less annual sum or a small matter more, the owner of the said farm must be a weak & unadvised man to suffer such alteration.

This memorandum was made 9th January 1760.

14. Appeal against Land Tax Assessment 1761[1] WSHC 184/3

The underwritten is what Mr Holford has to offer for his being relieved in the land tax.

Being informed by John Clements, one of the assessors of the land tax, that an appeal is to be made against the assessment for part of the parish of Avebury for this present year, particularly complaining that a farm belonging to Mr Norris in the occupation of Mr Robert Nalder, the other assessor, and my farm are not rated so high as they ought to be, I will therefore acquaint you with every circumstance relating to my farm, which I am inclined to believe will convince you, that I ought to be rated twenty pounds a year at least less than I now stand at, so farr am I from being the reasonable object of complaint.

My farm, with all the premises appertaining to it, were used, occupied, and lett for some years at £360 a year. My predecessors, finding great difficulty to gett good tenants with property sufficient to stock it, were compelled to lend £500 at £4 pounds per cent, which occasioned the tenants to say they gave £380 a year. This sum I agreed for with my last tenant, but he after a short occupation,[2] failing with a large arear of rent, the neighbouring farmers said it was owing to the farm's being over rented, which prevented any person treating

1 There are five copies of this document, which differ only in minor particulars. The original rough draft, which has many deletions and interlineations, bears the date 31st August 1761. It does not include the final three paragraphs below. However, another draft does, and dates these paragraphs 2nd September 1761. Both of these drafts were evidently used in order to compile the final three copies, which are identical, and printed here. These copies, however, give no dates. There are a few accompanying documents, not transcribed here. Notice of appeal (actually, notice that Holford intended to oppose the appeal) was given to John Clements, one of the assessors, on 5th September 1761. The appeal was heard 10th September 1761. It was not successful; the farm continued to be rated at £340.

2 In fact, John Rose tenanted the farm from c.1744 until 1755.

with me about renting it at that price, upon which I offered to lett it for £360 a year, and treated with three different persons about it, but they refused it on such conditions, and £340 a year was the largest sum offered me for it. This being the true case, I was obliged to stock it and unwillingly forced into the occupation of it. Therefore, as I have been thus wrongfully pointed at, hope you will direct I may be properly relieved, and only rated for £340 a year. The house I live in has falsly been represented to be separated from the farm, notwithstanding till very lately the tenants always lived in it, and I have now only a small unfinished house, that my servant must dispense with, but not such as is fitt for a tenant of suitable circumstances to occupy the farm, or would in reality be large enough to carry on the business as great part occasioned by the occupation is transacted in the house I dwell in. The appellants say, that farms in hand ought to be rated for the rent they last lett at. This is so unreasonable and productive of oppression that it scares merits a reply, for if men in bad circumstances & principles shall offer an advanced rent, and thereby gett possession of farms, and soon after fail, it cannot be equitable for the owners to be rated for such advanced rent longer than it can be supported, which is the case now before you. If the house I dwell in was lett for a certaine rent separate & apart from the farm, some reason might then be urged for taxing it, but at present my house & the house my bailiff lives in are both necessary & used in the occupation. Before I resided on this farm it had been rated in the land tax greatly disproportioned to the small farms, and many years to the advantage of the appellants. On my inquiring into the cause of such an unjust rate, was told that it had been customary to lay the tax more on the large farms without regarding the equality of the rate as the law directs.

This scheme to tax gentlemen's houses separate from the farms, notwithstanding such possessors may occupy their farms to which such habitations appertain, I am told has been concerted by several persons to make it general. Provided you admit of this unreasonable appeal, but to avoid giving any further trouble about the circumstances & merits of this case I am ready & willing to take the following oath, if required by the Commissioners, which is the final expedient the law directs in the like cases.

Stayner Holford maketh oath that as his farm at Avebury was unexpectedly deserted by his tenant long before the expiration of the lease, he directly applied to proper persons to gett him a new tenant. and in the space of several months two only offered. One proposed to give £320 a year and the other £340 a year, on condition that many expensive allowances were made to him. My not agreeing to these terms was forced unwillingly to stock & occupy it myself.

I am told the appellants conceive & assert that if any person offers money for lands & tenements in the owners hands, such sum is to ascertain the land tax, not allowing the owner the privilege of considering the character, circumstances, and many other essentials of the person so offering. If this unreasonable method was allowed persons of property would always be liable to be oppressed by bad men.

It is said a person who has some property adjoining to mine is to attend the appeal, and is to propose giving to me £400 a year for my dwelling house, farm & all the premises, and that it is said he has already offered that sum. My oath of the offer of £320 a year only, which was by this person, effectually stops more being said on that head, but if otherwise, sure every person has a right to except against any he shall not approve to lett his property to. This person in particular, I have clear & justifiable reasons to except against. One among them is, that the manure, stock, &c., proper to my farm may be introduced on his, much to the injury of my property, which was the usage I mett with from my last tenant, whose lands also laid contiguous to mine.

By this sort of treatment every person must be taxed at the will of persons residing near him who are interested in it, or be drove from his habitation & lands as they shall think proper.

I have heard some other alterations will be wanted in the assessments. It is therefore proper every person should be on his oath of what he has to say in relation to the rents.

15. Certificate for John Coombs[1] WSHC 184/1, pt.1.
Avebury 4th December 1765

We the principal inhabitants of the parish of Avebury in the County of Wilts have reason to certify to His Majesty's Justices of the Peace for this Division, that John Coombs is a man of good fame, and of sober life & conversation, and appears to be a proper person to be licenced to keep the Hare & Hounds at Beckhampton, lately occupied by William Fowler deceased, which has been a publick house without interruption very near one hundred years, and is necessary to be continued as such for the entertainment of travellers of the inferiour sort[2]
Staynor Holford
Ar Jones
Hen Howson
Js Godwin
Jno Griffin Grant
George Brown
John Nalder
Saml Martyn

Verso Note: 4th December 1765. Copy of a Certificate signed by the principal inhabitants of the parish of Avebury to obtain a licence for John Coombs to keep a publick house.

16. Arthur Jones's Advice to his Successors WSHC 271/2.
11th December 1772

1 See letter, Staynor Holford to Edward Popham, 4th January 1766. This document is a copy of the certificate sent to Popham.

2 It catered for the droving trade, rather than for coaches; see Raymond, Stuart A. 'The Inns of Avebury', *WAM,* 117, 2024, p.162.

I lately lett drop I entertained some thoughts of letting my farm. This brought on the application of many persons for tenants, and am satisfied I could lett for £420 a year, but think £400 the real value. But as it is probable my representatives may think it more eligible to sell the estate to answer the several demands on it, I think it right to leave to them every information in my power for their guide & safety. I will not answer for any of them to occupy without a constant residence & close attention & to be in a hurry to lett in a tenant to carry on the business immediately on my decease may be very injurious. Therefore would advise them to be cautions and lett the servants & business move on for some time with a seeming scheme to preserve it, & after all affairs are stated the several claimants & annuitants under mine & brother's wills paid, satisfied, & made easie, consult with some able person about selling it. If all the representatives agree so to do, to which end a safe & good opinion must be taken of some able council in the conveyancing branch in London, such nice matters never should be moved in the country, for by so doing a foundation has often been laid for litigation.

The paper here inclosed partly leads to establish the title, & will more so if I should survive a few years more. It is more than probable your council will call for further information, which you will on proper search find amongst my papers. Use your own senses in carefully looking them over, & thereby to avoid crowding your counsellor's hands with heaps of unnecessary papers which often are attended with inconveniences. My cousin Arthur has often told my representatives would be very able to make & support a good title, not only from the long & quiet possession, but from the repeated & natural devisers. This is the first & essential step to be taken before any declaration is to be made about sale, & you are to have from your counsellor the title fairly drawn out so signed & supported by him with full directions what papers are to be put into the hands of any person inclined to become the purchaser. The farm exclusive of mansion, gardens and the old orchard, £400 a year, thirty two years purchase 12,800, mansion &c., at £25 a year, 20 years purchase £500. The Flying Waggon[1] at Beckhampton £30 a year to be sold separately, 22 years purchase £660, the new built houses as well as you can as lives are settled on three of them.

No abatement should be made in the above price because the sum of them is £20 a year under what it may be lett for. And it can be made clear to any gentleman who will attend a little to an exchange of lands to make them separate & thereby render the whole more advantageous, the real worth would be increased one hundred a year and by the lowest valuation three score. To this it will be asked why did not Mr Jones make this exchange. First because the owners & occupiers of the several lands were not disposed to negotiate such exchange unless they could gain more than they were in equity intituled to. In the next place several owners dying, new tenants frequently introduced gave frequent

1 Referred to as the Hare and Hounds in Stayner Holford's 1766 will, TNA PROB11/932/345. On the other hand, it was still referred to as the Hare and Hounds in 1788; see the 'Note re Avebury estate' below.

hope to such negotiats, and at the period when the several parties seemed most inclined Mr Jones was advancing towards seventy, frequently disturbed with gout & other complaints, a single man, no relations, much distressed in point of fortune, his own circumstances nearly equal to his wishes at the above age, and his comfort [?sheweth] calling him to Bath for several months in the year, he declined engaging in the above exchange which would require some pains attention & expence.

Richard Holford was eldest son of Richard Holford, eldest son of Sir Richard Holford.

I would recommend to my representatives carefully to look over all papers they may find, & sort them to the best of their skill, before any strangers advice is asked on their affairs, & then only lay before them.

17. Peter Holford's title to the Beckhampton estate[1] WSHC 271/2

Avebury 10th September 1780

Peter Holford, the present owner of a farm at Beckhampton now lett to the Widow Jeffries holds the same by the following title:

About the 1729 Richard Holford, eldest grandson of Sir Richard Holford, succeeded as heir at law to this estate, as well as to the estate at Avebury, and had taken lawfull possession of the same. Soon after this Robert Holford, second son of Sir Richard Holford, sett up a claim of a morgage of about two thousand pounds, & also a further claim of debts due to him from the last owner of the Beckhampton estate to the amount of a £1000 added to these claims. He terrifyd, bullied his said nephew Richard Holford with variety of bugg bears of impeaching the title of this and the Avebury estate and by these means prevaild on his nephew Richard Holford the above grandson to Sir Richard Holford to sell & transfer this estate at Beckhampton to him, which at that period was worth six thousand pounds & more. Robert Holford, the father of the present Peter Holford, continued to hold this estate at Beckhampton as purchaser from his said nephew Richard Holford, & never by word or otherwise pretended to have any claim, right, or expectation of succeeding to the estate at Avebury, the property of his nephew Staynor Holford, at his discease. Therefore the present Peter Holford pretending to have any claim or right to the Avebury estate & behaving ill to my uncle Arthur Jones at the discease of his brother Staynor Holford was ignorant, impertinent, & foolish, for he was not content with this behaviour but went directly to the Commons[2] & did lodge a caveat against the will of his cousin Staynor Holford before the said will was enterd at the said office, but being in a few hours after better informd he returnd to the Commons & revoked the said caveat. Now, Robert Holford the father of this said Peter by his will left the

1 Written at the foot of the document in Arthur Jones's handwriting.
2 Doctors' Commons, the office of the Prerogative Court of Canterbury.

above mentiond estate at Beckhampton to his son Robert Holford, a minor, who went abroad in the East India Company's service about the age of fifteen, & there continued many years after his fathers discease till, 'tis belevd, about the age of twenty five[1] before which time he had remitted to his brother Peter Holford several considerable sums to be place in the publick securities for his the said Robert's use and benefit, & finding him self in a very declining state of health with a strong desire to return to his native country, he asked the advice of his brother Peter if the money remitted, together with the fortune his father left him would not support him as a gentleman on his return to this country, which he was assured was essential both to health & life. To this representation Peter Holford replyed it was not sufficient & that he would find himself under very awkward situation under such narrow circumstances, which was then believed to altogether about twenty five or six thousand pounds or more. On these repeated representations from Peter, his brother Robert sunk under them, & by his will made in India, after giving several legacies to Peter's children or others he then concludes by saying words to this effect as to all the rest and residue of my real & personal estate of every kind & nature what so & where so ever I give to my brothers & sister share & share alike.[2]

Under these directions, Peter Holford, Richard H., and Staynor H., with Elizabeth Askew, were intituld to equal share of the said property, & with this impression it was allowed by Peter Holford to take place as the true meaning of the testator Robert. But on the arrival of the will it appearing that there were only two whitnisses to it instead of three, as the statute directs for the devising real estates, Peter avails him self of this defect & setts up his claim & takes possession of the farm at Beckhampton as heir at law to his brother Robert.

Now Peter taking the advantage of this defect was in every sence shamefull, & so declared to be by his brothers & sister, for Robert leaving his country & continuing in India till his death it can not be supposed he was informed of what the statute required in such cases.

18. Valuation of Avebury Estate[3] WSHC 271/2

[f.1.]

Avebury September 18th 1780

1 Actually, he was probably about thirty-five when he died.

2 His will was proved in the Prerogative Court of Canterbury 19th December 1763. TNA PROB 11/894/337.

3 This statement was probably written by Anne Williamson at the dictation of Arthur Jones; there is a reference to 'my uncle Jones' on the final page. The verso notes 'Avebury 1786, 24 of September. A [illegible] memorandums necessary for my representatives to be partly his guide at my decease'.

The farm at this place which has been twenty five years in my own hands or occupation in very great order of husbandry, and all things thereunto belonging in the best repair, some of the lands improved, the road over the Downs being also removed,[1] the feed & herbage greatly increased, the statute labor for the highways, which was before a burthen to the occupation of the farm of twenty pounds a year, being now reduced almost to a trifle, and all the roads adjacent to the farm being made at the turnpike expence on the most improved plans, the parish expences regulated and much lower than heretofore, and the whole situation of this place from the innumerable advantages of it, it has been seeked & wished for by all persons of fortune & property to whom it is known. Therefore on the lowest calculation it must be valued at four hundred pounds per year and thirty years purchase	12,000
Cottages belonging to the said farm	130
Stock on the farm in which is included the lands that are manured & ploughed, all the corn & grass seeds growing & every advantage that the lands have out of the pure state of nature with the necessaries in the farm house	1,800
Furniture of the house, chariot, horse, &c	1,300
Carry over	15,250

[f.2.]

1 When the turnpike was opened at Beckhampton through West Kennett in 1745.

Brought Forward	15,250
The Flying Waggon[1] publick house at Beckhampton with lands thereunto belonging, now lett for twenty six pounds per year free of all taxes, and was lett to the last tenant for thirty, valued at twenty two years purchase which is under valued	572
The Catherine Wheel in Bishop Gate Street, London, lett on a lease for eighty guineas per year clear of all deductions & never to be sold by me or my representatives. Supposed to be under lett £20 per ann.	2,000
In the new South Sea annuitys fifteen hundred pounds with their chances but supped to be at seventy	1,050
In the three per cent Consols fifteen hundred pounds valued as the annuitys were	1,050
Total	19,922
Out of this my Uncle Holford[2] has disposed of by his will to be paid at the death of my uncle Arthur Jones	2080
Charged on the estate already by R.J.[3]	2000
Deduct this from the above sum	4080
remains	15,842

[f.3.]
By the stating on the other side my uncle Mr Jones has to dispose of £15,842

The under written is the particulars of annuitys & legacys charged on the estate by my brother Staynor Holford

Mrs Cuthbert	Annuity of	£40 per year
Mrs Walker	do of	20
Richard Jones	do of	10
		70

1 Originally the Bear; see above, p.xxxx
2 Stayner Holford is meant (see below, f.3), although the calculation (see below) seems to have nothing to do with his 1766 will (TNA PROB11/932/345).
3 Richard Jones, Arthur Jones's nephew. This sum was allocated 'towards purchasing a company in the Guards' for Richard, according to Jones's will (TNA PROB 11/1181/174).

These valued according to the different chances

Mrs Cuthbert's at five years purchase	£200
Mrs Walker's at seven years	140
Richard Jones at seven years	170
	410

Legacys to be paid[1]

Mrs Belford	500
Mrs Williamson	500
Mrs Warner	500
John Jones	50
Dorothy Cuthbert	50
George Cuthbert	50
Mrs Walker	20
	£1,670
Add the annuitys as valued above	410
	2,080

This accounts for the disposition on the other side by my brother Staynor Holford.[2]

19. Directions if Arthur Jones becomes ill WSHC 271/2

September 24th 1783

Read these directions, and as the disposition of my affairs are now altered, Mrs Williamson is to be sent for instead of Colenel Jones, and she is desired to attend to the within directions.

1784 September 10th

To send directly for Mrs Williamson whenever my master may be unusually ill & deliver to her this paper. Richard & John are to open this paper till Mrs W. arrives.

Avebury 27th of September 1780

It is my uncle's (Arthur Jones) particular directions, that when ever he may be

1 These appear to be the legacies Arthur Jones was intending to make in 1780. In the event, his 1786 will (TNA PROB11/1181/174) mentioned most of the names listed here, but the amounts differ, and a number of other legacies are added.

2 This is rather garbled; the sum of £2080 seems to combine legacies Arthur Jones intended to make with annuities Stayner Holford did make (although not by his will).

attackd by any severe illness, that I may be directly sent for, and that in such cases the medical help from Devizes & Marlborough may be immediately sent for, & that I would give a close & personal attendance on him, to take his keys, to order his servants, to promote order & quietness & every nurseing attention that servants are too often a stranger to, & if such illness shoud threatten to baffle all endeavours let every art be used to keep the heat warm, the bedding & all things about him in a warm state, & repeated applications of warm cloths to his stomach, & when life appears to be no more he is not to be striped, his bed cloths taken from him by ignorant people under the pretence of making a handsome corpse, but he is to remain in his bed till his person & all things about him are perfectly cold, to be put in to a double coffin of wood only, & the lid of it not to be put on or fastened down till his corpse shall change, which tis more probable the weather considerd may be about the seventh day.

20. Arthur Jones's Title[1] WSHC 271/2

Sir Richard Holford being on a treaty of marriage with Mrs Susanna Trotman his last wife did by deed dated the twentieth of August 1689 bind himself to lay out seven thousand pounds in land to be settled on himself for life, on his wife for life, and on the children of such marriage conditionally, and for lack of such children to Sir Richard's right heirs forever. In consequence of the settlement a marriage was solemnised and a son sometime after lawfully born whose name was Samuel. After his birth it appears by deed dated the twentieth of March 1698 that Sir Richard Holford had purchased a Avebury Farm, which cost him seven thousand five hundreds pounds, which was settled agreeable to the marriage articles. Sir Richard Holford made his will dated the 19th of July 1717, and therein bequeathed to his wife for her life, as an addition to her jointure, his Beckhampton estate, she paying there out to her son Samuel one hundred pounds per annum, and further devised the same by will in these words, viz, I do give and devise the same premises to my son Samuel and to the heirs males of his body as the farm & lands of Avebury are settled. This is the farm the late Robert Holford terrified Dick Holford to sell him, as by lease & release in Mr Jones's hands. The will proceeds no further as to the disposition of Avebury or Beckhampton.

Sir Richard Holford died the 11th of May 1718. His wife, whose maiden name was Suzanna Trotman, survived him. She took possession of Avebury estate as by her settlement, and Beckhampton purchased the 10th of December 1710 on the conditions of her husband's will, and enjoyed the same for about five years. She made her will dated the 19th of March 1722 and made her only child Samuel her executor. She died March the 20th 1722.

Samuel took possession of the farm at Avebury as the heir particularly named in his mother's settlement, such farm being purchased after he was born.

1 Verso: 'Avebury title to A.J., July 22d 1786. This paper may be of use to Mr Jones's representatives only'.

He took possession of the farm at Beckhampton as devised to him by his father's will. He continued in quiet possession of the said farms till the eleventh of June 1738 and then died intestate. Amongst his papers was found a deed dated the eleventh of April 1730 directing the uses of a recovery of the lands of Avebury and Beckhampton, which is his right heirs, but no other papers were found as evidence of such recovery being completed, except the attorney's bill for the making such recovery and all proceedings thereon, amongst which it appears that the recovery was entered at the proper offices.

Richard, the eldest son of Sir Richard Holford's eldest son, heir at law to his grand father and uncle Samuel Holford took possession on the death of his uncle Samuel Holford of Avebury and Beckhampton, and by deed dated the second of February 1731, it appears that he the said Richard Holford passed a fine according to the due form of law to cut off the entail of Avebury and Beckhampton. Richard continued quietly to enjoy the farm at Avebury without any claim whatever on it till his death, which happened on or about the third of November 1742, by which Richard held it upwards of eleven years, and by his will devised the same to his brother Staynor Holford and his heirs forever who enjoyed the same to the 30th of September 1767, and by his will dated the seventh of April 1766 he devised the same to his brother Arthur Jones and his heirs for ever.

21. Arthur Jones's Memorandum, as recorded by Ann Williamson[1]

WSHC 271/3

[p.1.]
Book of memorandums proper to be preserved for whoever may possess this property.
Ann Williamson
Perused by her at Avebury previous to her following her General to Jamaica, April 1791.

[p.2.]
June 8th 1783 Memorandum
Being at Avebury on a visit to my uncle, the underwritten is part of his discourses. That on his death the bailiff & his butler will have orders to seal up his desk & to dispatch a messenger to me or in case of extreme . On my arrival probably may find in the hands of his bailiff written directions for his funeral &c. He wishes to have his household & servants continued for three months after his decease provided they behave well & merit such favor in the estimation of his representative. As soon [p.3.] as convenient can be let my representatives signify

1 This is a small paper book of 64 un-numbered pages in Ann Williamson's hand. Pagination has been inserted here. A partial inventory of Arthur Jones's possessions, written on the final pages, has not been transcribed.

to my sister, nephews & nieces, sort of abstract of my will, & particularly so to their several interests in the same, & also the first convenient time that the several legacies in wills or codicils be informed of the notice I have taken of them. This is a decent & regular step & quiets clamors from wrong impressions.

As he has resided here many years, & has endeavourd to preserve & keep the property with all its priviledges, he wishes to devise [p.4.] the same to some one of his relations who may to him appear most properly qualified in mind & pocket to perpetuate & preserve the same, & to proceed in the discharge of the several duties becoming a sensible estate & well informed representative and under written is nearly the state of his property, which he is sensible is very liable to many essential alterations.

His estate at Avebury now in his occupation, & with the little field at Beckington[1] [?taken] from it, he values at £380 pound. [p.5.] per annum, which at thirty years purchase is

	£14,400
This is meant exclusive of the house, gardens, & a small part of the meadow ground adjoining, three cottages adjoining to his farm, as circumstanced by his will value	100
The close at Beckington let at per year £12	200
The Flying Weaggon ~~Hare & Hounds~~ publick house & Beckington & grounds adjoining £26 per annum (clear of all taxes)	500
House at Bath £35 per annum. Late lett to Mrs Jenny on a lease at £40 per annum.[1] Cost Mrs Ellison £600 & ought to be sold for not less than	500[2]
Catherine Wheel, Bishopsgate Street [?£4] per annum quite clear of all taxes, &c	2500
	£15600[3]

[p.5.]

1 Beckhampton.
1 This sentence is written in a different ink in the right-hand column.
2 700 deleted
3 Actually 18,200.

& may be lett for considerably more at the expiration of the lease.

In the South Sea new annuities	1500
In the 3 per cent consols	2300
Stock upon the farm if properly attended to	1800
His house & gardens exclusive of the farm set very low at	500
His plate, linnen, china & household goods of every kind, chariot & horses included	1800
Brought forward from the other side	15600
	23500

[p.6.]
It is to be observed that the publick stock on the other side ought not to be valued at more than £70 which is taking £300 out of every thousand which £900 in three thousand that is two hundred & forty pounds out of the eight hundred.

As to the several legacies charged by Mr Holford,[1] & several legacys which are or may be charged by my uncle Jones, & three hundred & thirty pounds charged by Mrs Ellison on condition which is paid with variety of debts, expences &c., which unavoidably will attend my Uncle Jones' affairs, there always must be very sufficient to make it the interest [p.7.] of any representative to struggle & strive to preserve the mansion, farm & landed property here, to make it a residence part of the year, but if such representative or representatives should not have that turn or cast of mind, they would act very wrong to let that transpire till some very considerable time till after the decease of the donor, and till all legacies, debts, annuities, and demands are fulfilled. And as the said estate is now in my uncle's occupation, he would advise continuing the same plan as long as the representative may approve. If to be sold, never encumber it with a lease or tennant on it, by its being [p.8.] [*illegible*] in that open state the farm the mansion &c may be of use in the sale of each other, & much depends on selling the farm stock, both as to the time of the year & great variety of seemingly small and triffling articles must be strictly, judiciously, & patiently attended to, for if once it is discovered you are negligent & ignorant of such matters such kind of purchasers will pick up shillings till they have picked away pounds. It is impossible to enumerate what is meant by the stock of a farm to persons unacquainted [p.9.] with such matters because the stock & condition of the lands anyways altered from the state of nature or amended by manure, cultivation, seeds or corn sown all fall under the articles of stock.

1 Stayner Holford.

My uncle after several year's experience says he has much reason to believe his present bailyff Richard Hickley is a sober, honest, sensible, diligent man, & well acquainted with the property & every circumstance of the country. Therefore if the representative should think of residing here four, five or six months of the year it would be much more pleasing & advantageous to continue the said baily & occupation of the property, [p.10.] it would be the more eligible plan & would be preserving a stable property which would afford comfort at the advanced age of sensible people.

Such representatives ought particularly to guard against being amused with good tennants, encreased rents, and being relieved from trouble & attention, because I am persuaded from the circumstances of the property & the landlord's residing part of the year he would be exposed to more disappointment, importuning, trouble & expensive repairs [p.11.] than if occupied by the present baily & under the present plan.

Such representative may also be amused about makeing an exchange of lands and altering the feed of the cattle & many such amusing stories of being beneficial to the estate. I would advise the owners of it to avoid such schemes & schemers, but to know & preserve every priviledge that may attend the property, & so to proceed, imitating the present posessor. It is probable a variety of persons may offer their advice and sentiments, but I [p.12] again repeat it may be injurious & very troublesome provided they owner shall not determine to sell it – which for part of the above reasons mentioned I say would be wrong.

Mr Hawkes of Marlbro is a wealthy, [*illegible*], sober very well informed man, & has for many years behaved with great friendly civillity to my uncle. He has a small legacy left in my uncle's <u>will</u> as a mark of his respect, & whereby his representatives may consult with him about any formalities or business which my representative in legal form may be unacquainted [p.13.] with. But a sensible sober man will not hurry, & will call in his own powers to be his guide, which is often times better than others, and it is usual on the change of landed property even from lawyers & attorneys if you intrust them with your affairs to create doubts & difficulties & magnify every possible event regarding the right & title of the testator to give. All this must be treated as very idle stuff & with the greatest silence. The succession of the property has been regularly possessed, devised, & descended to the present owner from the year 1728 without the least impeachment claim [p.14] or disturbance whatever, to go further back about title is a subject that need not be talked of, but it is said the law of the country wisely countenances long possession.

In a proper & reasonable time after the funeral, the house calm & quiet, & the family established as expressly wished by the testator, it is right for the representative, in the presence and with the help of the bailiff & John Phillipps his present butler, if then both in his service, to take an inventory, first of all the stock on the estate expressly & fully set forth, not only of the cattle & moveables [p.15.] but the quantity of land sowed with corn & grass seeds, & also the state of the lands ploughed or otherwise. This apparent attention creates an impression all around you, & is like putting locks & bolts for the preservation of it, & suffer not the smallest article to be omitted or spoken of as triffles or heaped together.

Next proceed with the above people to the house, gardens &c, & therein attend to the minutia of the whole. I need not say to a sensible kind how essential these steps are.

Administration is to be taken out by the representative, but I don't [p.16] conceive there need be any violent hurry for so doing to impower the executor to act, because the will speaks as soon as the testator is dead – but on this point Mr Hawkes or some such sedate person may advise.

Well consider & pay great attention about letting of the lands, for a bad tenant, or even a good one, will very soon become a great clog & burthen on the property, not only by repeating even a month's pleasing residence, but by encreasing useless & unnecessary repairs injuring all the property, converting & putting the land out of its proper tillage [p.17.] & husbandry and quarreling with all the neighbours, which ultimately tends to the hurt & disturbance of the owner, & the mansion house & gardens return to a state of ruin.

I think a manly well disposed mind with the cast of a good Englishman will see his interest in all this.

There is always a running account in Mr Elliott's hands, & by an application to him or his representative these matters are to be settled. He has a letter of attorney to receive dividends but not to transfer stock. My uncle [p.18] has not receits for all the stock at the South Sea House & bank. It is of small value, as it is the company's books are the record.

The Catherine Wheel rent is paid ½ yearly, Michaelmas & Lady Day. It is drawed for as soon as due & received by Mr Elliott.

There may appear some irregularity & disorder in my uncle's papers, but the infirmity of his sight must plead in that cause, & the last receits of the life tenant must be produced to be the guide. [p.19.]

My uncle possesses a royalty at Avebury which was purchased separately from the other part of the property, by which he has an undoubted right to appoint a game keepper,[1] which he has ever done.

Avebury 23d June 1786

Since the above Mr Hawkes of Marlbro is dead. Therefore recommends Mr Thomas Ward who married Mr Hawkes daughter,[2] is steward to Lord Ailesbury, be called in to transact all the legal forms of the law as may be necessary under my uncle's will. Then it is further more proper to observe that since the above my uncle has purchased a little manor[3] laying within the bounds of the greater manor & royalty, to which manor several annual quit rents are due and regularly to be paid, but the late owners [p.20.] of the said manor, being poor distressed people, they could not have the benefit of the law of their courts to compel the payment of the same which has occasioned many arrears to be now due, but the title to

1 See *AWS*, p.299–31

2 Thomas Ward married Hannah Hawkes 14th January 1784 at St Peter's, Marlborough.

3 This manor has not been identified; perhaps it was part of the dis-membered former manor of Avebury Truslow, although Jones's ownership has not been traced.

the same is so clear, that the above arrears cannot be disputed from the number of years there remains unpaid.

The above Mr Thomas Ward is appointed steward of the said manor, held a regular court directly on the purchase of it, and requisition was made on the several tenants to pay their arrears, which they declined doing (excepting one or two) unless compelled by the law of the country. Furthermore it is to be observed that a Mr Bill, uncle to the above Mr Ward, and steward to Lord Ailsbury, held a regular court about nine or ten years since, & required the payment of the arrears, which the tenants then declined, & the only [p.21.] remedy to be taken was by a bill in equity, but the owners being poor as before mentioned, they declined entering into such a cause, fearing the charges of it. But the title & claim to it may be clearly ascertained, as it particularly appears having recourse to the writings, letters, and other usefull notes on that subject.

Indeed, my uncle recommends that after a year or two quiet to employ the said Mr Ward to file a bill in equity, & take such other legal steps to compel such delinquents to the payment of the same, but let the representative keep all these matters in his own breast if his intention to take such steps on a future day.

The value of these matters may appear very trifling in the eyes of a stranger not accustomed to such affairs, because they are essential & add a usefull dignity to the property, particularly so if the estate was ever to be sold, [p.22.] because they empower you to appoint a gamekeeper to preserve & take the game all around you, which is so fine & open a country, is very usefull & the more so in the estimation of sportsmen in so rural an amusement, nay, it will add greatly to the value of the property & [*illegible*] for men of that turn, but indeed the law of the country usually expresses & decorates a property so circumstanced.

Here I again repeat that upon no consideration whatever attend to any person who may be pressing an exchange of lands or alienation or lessening the number of cows, the sheep feed, the boundaries, or the long established customs appertaining to the said property which have stood and been observed by my uncle and predecessors for more than an hundred & thirty years. [p.23.]

My uncle says that this estate was at the Reformation one of the lesser abbys, & as the church in general was exempted from tythes, small compositions or modus's were created & established to make some provision for vicars & parochial clergy, and that for much more than a century past four pounds a year have been regularly paid in lieu of all tythes without the least interruption or break of paying more or less than the said sum of four pounds, but as arguments have of late years been made use of that the general value of money has varied greatly since those days. [p.24]

The fixed sums are not a foundation for a modus, but where they have been created & established upon an unchangeable property, the Court of Exchequer in many instances has given them the sanction of an established modus.

It is well known that many terriers or registers of church property & revenues were sent to Rome on the Reformation, & there are instances of some being obtained from Rome & read and admitted as the evidence in Westminster Hall.

Again on a later date during the civil wars in this country, terriers, records, registers, & other evidences [p.25.] of church revenues were destroyed & lost, & it is also a fact that the parochial & other clergy have from their own invention, without authority or evidence, made terriers to answer their own profit and interest & so registered them in the Diocesan courts.

This being a lesser abbey and circumstanced as above recited is to be supported from the records office or the rolls in the Tower, but exclusive of these authorities the present terrier now in the Bishop of Sarum's court says that the vicar is entitled to two ell ridges of wheat out of that piece sown annually [p.26.] nearest the church & twenty shillings a year to be paid in lieu or composition for the lesser tythes. Now this description is very defective and obsolete, because we have no description of what this ell ridge is, but this is an undoubted foundation for giving the establishment and permanency to a modus.

If the present or any future incumbent should be so ill advised as to attempt to alter or litigate the validity of this ancient payment, you must be upon your guard, as then never to pay less, or ever to pay more, but adhere to the exact payments. It is well worth every gentleman [p.27.] being informed that if the clergy should attempt to be unreasonably disturbing, he is to be held to the strict letter of the statute law of this country, which is in many cases troublesome & affecting every parish, as for instance regarding residence, which is a penalty of ten pounds a month for being absent. Statute in full force & daily carried into execution.

24th June

Mr. Jones thinks it's proper to repeat that he thinks the bailiff Richard Hickley is an honest, sober, sensible, well disposed man, & merits my attention in all negotiations with him, but that he has a constitutional quietness which [p.28.] too often leads to relaxation, by which the business may be delayed and injured, & the labourer not at all times made the most of, & as he married a person unfit for the management of the farm business.[1] That necessary branch of it is committed to the care of common servants, young women, & strangers, and from this the farmer's duty ought to be doubled and daily & constantly enquired into by him.

[p.29.]

May 16th 1789

As my uncle has long been very ill, I thought it my duty to come to him to pay all the attention in my power in his intervals of pain he desired me to commit to paper the following notes. He wishes & recommends at all events for his immediate or future representative to occupy the farm, & to continue an occasional residence on the plan he & his brother have done for many years, much to their comfort & credit, & at the same time recommends in the strongest manner, for their interest, comfort, and safety, to continue & employ his present baily Richard Hickley on the establishment he is now on. My uncle says that in case he has not made legal

1 Hickley married Mary Mason at Pewsey, 2nd April 1777.

provision for giving to [f.30.] Richard Hickley's four younger children (the eldest having had it) ten pounds each to be paid to the father within one year after his decease, to enable him towards qualifying them to get their daily bread, which he here directs to be done.

My uncle also says that he has for fourteen years experience found his servant John Phillips an honest man, that he is ingenious and equal to being an useful servant in every branch of domestick life, a most excellent gardiner, & a very useful game keeper, whereby many advantages accrue, & preserves & adds a dignity to the property, therefore not hastily to be dismissed. Mr Jones wishes & recommends to his representative or representatives to [p.31.] entertain every esteem, affection, and respect for his good neighbour Lord Ailesbury, who has for many years past given every proof of a disposition to promote his happiness. A late one is very proper to remark. On the death of Mr Mayo, the late vicar of this parish, who dying in distressed circumstances, & leaving fifteen children, some very young, my uncle was applied to to use his interest to obtain the living vacant by his father's death for James Mayo, which, as intended residence could not be complied with, was very contrary to my uncle's inclinations. He waved them for the sake of mercy towards so numerous a family, & applied directly to his friend Lord Ailesbury to ask the Chancellor for it, which his lordship [p.32.] undertook to do in the most pleasing manner, & after many delays & difficulties raised by the present Chancellor, who is a character of that cast, his lordship obtained the nomination for my uncle. Now this is a circumstance that will give some little figure to the resident gentleman, & from decency & common gratitude put it out of his power of showing the least disposition to call in question the ancient modus.

[p.33.]

Avebury 24th June 1786

The nature of my little property is so circumstanced that it is absolutely necessary that I should appoint some person to be my representative. I am independent & unsettled property to the amount of six or seven thousand pounds, with which a part of my personals he may be enabled to pay off & discharge the legacies & other charges made by my will. If I wish to have all things properly done without compelling them to apply to an attorney to raise a sum of money to create a mortgage upon the landed property, and thereby defeat and destroy the very face of things which I wish to be continued some short time at least after my decease, & if he was not so qualified as above he will be plundered, imposed on [p.34.] and so distressed that the benefits arising to such a representative would be small indeed. All my nephews and nieces stand on the same ground of consanguinity, one with the other, & have not done anything particular to displease me, but as they are not circumstanced to answer the above description, they are not qualified for such an office, neither is any one of them my heir at law, for which they cannot have any proper cause of complaint, except it is against the very handsome legacies settled in my lifetime & increased & confirmed by my will to my nephew Richard Jones.

The above conditions were repeatedly told to my nephew Richard Jones many years since, & long before he had determined to marry, & when that affair was in treaty I told him that as the young [p.35.] woman had little or no fortune, it entirely defeated my intentions or wishes to make him my representative. No regard was paid to what I said on this occasion, but the consummation rather hastened.

These are facts with many more which may be added to support and defend me for acting in the manner I have done.

A.R.Jones[1]
24 June 1786

[p.36-8.]
[Blank]

[p.39.]

Avebury 24th June 1786

As it is possible some evil minded ill informed person or persons may be saying words tending to impeach Mr. Jones's right of disposal of every part of his fortune on his decease, it may not be unnecessary to make some few remarks on the same.

Richard Holford, the eldest son of Sir Richard Holford's eldest son, & heir at law, came into possession of the estates at Avebury & Beckhampton in the county of Wilts on or about the year 1728 or 1729 upon the decease of an uncle. He enjoyed [p.40.] and had quiet possession of Avebury for about twelve or thirteen years during his lifetime.

Passed a fine & suffered a recovery with the advice of Robert Holford, a master in Chancery, & uncle to the said Richard Holford, second son of Sir Richard. On this being done the said Robert Holford set up a claim of debt of upwards of three thousand pounds upon the property at Avebury & Beckhampton. On this claim & other circumstances which the said Robert urged, he prevailed on his nephew Richard to sell to him the farm at Beckhampton worth more than five thousand pounds, [p.41.] to discharge the above recited debt. On this title Robert became the purchaser from Richard, and of course barred himself and his representatives from every future claim on the property at Avebury.

Richard continued to enjoy it without any claim or pretence of claim for thirteen years till his death, during which period he was married three times, & made three different settlements on his wives under the sanction and affirmation of the most able counsel that he had a right in so doing but they all dying without issue he by will gave it to his own brother & heir at law, Stayner Holford, [p.42.] who possessed it enjoyed it and improved it for upwards of twenty six years, without any claim disturbance or pretence of claim from any person whatsoever, who by his will gave it to his brother Arthur Jones & his heirs for ever, who has been in the full possession of it for twenty years, & daily improving the same without any disturbance or claim whatsoever.

1 Jones signed this statement, although it was (presumably) written by Anne Williamson.

Now here is a regular, strong, and uninterrupted possession from the year 1728 to this present month of June 1786, a term of fifty eight years, which is a length of time the law of the country in any case admits is a [p.43.] legal title.

The Catherine Wheel in Bishopsgate Street, London, was also enjoyed by the said Richard & Steyner Holford for a much longer term than twenty years, & by the said Steyner given in fee to the said Arthur Jones and his heirs for ever. Every other part of Mr. Jones property nearly falling under the title of personals requires no remarks to be made.

If any impertinent claim of the C.W.[1] from Roger Stayner of Boston or Peter Holford or his heirs on the strength of any settlement of Richard Holford the elder brother (by the mother) of my uncle Arthur Jones, there is no occasion to be allarmed or terrified, but must, if compelled to it, be defended by the legal powers of the law of our country. A little & attentive search into the papers will [p.44.] furnish out great information necessary to such defence. Richard Holford was compelled to make such settlement, or not to receive £3000 under his grandfather Sir Richard Holford's will, & at the instant it was made the whole was in the possession of his mother Mrs Anna Jones, upon the authority of a settlement made by her first husband Richard Holford of his reversionary right of the said C.W. They held by his father Sir Richard by the [?courtesy], and again it must be observed that the legacy given by Sir Richard to his grandson Staynor was not so circumstanced, neither did he ever join in any writing to [*illegible*] the same to any more distant or un-named or unborn heir of Sir Richard Holford, for William Reeves, an eminent council, counselled in these matters said Steynor Holford was the heir to Sir Richard, & that the [p.45.] whole intent with him as an estate in fee, indeed there is great reason to believe Peter Holford is well convinced of this because on the death of Staynor Holford he made a faint & personal claim of this property, but my uncle Arthur Jones was directly admitted as the legal possessor under his brother Staynor Holford's will, and has enjoyed ever since near twenty years without the least pretence of claim or disturbance whatever. If Peter Holford had the least distant interest in it being on the spot of the above property, & a master in Chancery, he would from his professional knowledge long before this have set up his claim. If envious impertinent & nonsensical people should at any time pretend to talke of the tenure of the property of others, they should be rebuked with a proper contempt, by holding their [p.46.] ignorance up in a true light by saying legal right is the right all must submit to, and indeed it is the wisdom of every person to pay that respect to the laws of our country.

There may be little or no occasion to employ an attorney to proceed on the matters necessary as a representative to my uncle taking out administration at the Commons,[2] and afterwards to establish the title in the Chancery, as the property will benefit of real as well as personal estates; therefore a person of sober, regular character of the law may negotiate this matter in London, which will be less

1 Catherine Wheel.
2 Doctors' Commons, the office of the Prerogative Court of Canterbury.

expensive than employing a country attorney, but as it may be proper in some future day after the [p.47.] decease of my uncle to hold courts, recover quit rents, and other such lesser matters, he would recommend employing Mr. John Ward, an attorney of Marlbro, to transact everything that may be necessary to be done in the right at the Avebury estate.

He is very conversant in these matters, &, as steward to Lord Aylesbury, it is an increased security for his conduct.

In the 1st instance of Richard Holford settling the C.W. to come at the £3000, Mr.Lees, then an eminent concil, afterwards Lord Chief Justice,[1] was consulted; speaks to this effect, that Richard doing all in his power entitled him to the £3000 legacy, & that probably a further disputed inquest may not arise to it, which it is evident he doubted Richard's right to make such settlements. [p.48.]

In if any distant period any unforeseen event was to happen, as illness, age, infirmities, loss of bayliff, &c., the owner may be at a stark loss to go on, in such case he had better struggle a little while with the occupation & to no person let out that his future intentions are to sell, because that would be placing himself in a compulsive light, & a purchaser treating would take other advantage of it, as is always the case when necesitous persons are compelled to sell. The estate, house, garden, exclusive of the cottages & the property at Beckington must go together if things are continued in the state as at this instant. It is a pleasing object & ought to raise thirteen thousand five hundred pounds, for supposing thirty years purchase for the farm only at £400 per annum, [p.49.] is twelve thousand pounds, the house, garden, and conveniences added to it certainly must be worth fifteen hundred pounds. The advantages that have been received by this property within a few years last past are innumerable, as the roads over the Downs & the turnpike roads so multiplied[2] to the great convenience of the property & residence are of more real & intrinsic value than thirty pounds per annum, because the statute labor before such advantages cost the estate twenty pounds per annum.

Always remember to keep the house, buildings, &c., in repair, that nothing of that may operate by way of argument to any interested purchaser. Indeed there is no occasion to elucidate these matters.

[p.50.]

28th November 1788

The contents of this book were read to my uncle Arthur Jones, esq., by me Ann Williamson, when he said that he thought the greater part of it may be of use & information to any executor he may appoint by his will. But this instant he entertains thoughts of appointing his niece Ann Williamson separately & apart from every controul by her husband to be one of his executors, & Mr Thomas Ward of Marlbro steward to Lord Ailesbury to be the other of his [p.51.] executors.

May 21st 1787.

1 Sir William Lee, Lord Chief Justice 1737-54.

2 See *AWS*, p.35-8

If any future day my representatives should find the occupation so pleasing & advantageous to them as they could wish, & should think of letting it, it is my desire & request that they will first treat with Richard Hickley on that business, & give to him every evident & countenance to settle him for the tenement, before all other applications whatever let the their pretensions &c., be whatever they may think fit to set forth, for even a small triffling advanced rent they if can't get £400 a year [?next] rent, [p.52.] exclusive of the mansion & garden, & 4 per cent interest for the stock on a proper valuation they may prove prosperous & lasting conditions. Richard may give a bond & judgement to the amount of the stock, to guard against any possible injuries which may be done by any chicane of the law, & that will enable him to go with the occupation being an honest industrious good man.

22. c.1788. Note re Avebury Estate, c.1788[1] WSHC 271/2

As the estate at Avebury exclusive of the little property at Beckington[2] possesses the following advantages I shall after reciting them ascertain the reasonable value of the property.

In the first place, the value of it is a desirable & convenient purchase of innumerable people in easy circumstances situated in one of the most favored countys in the Kingdom for to have landed property in, & for residence within four score miles of London surrounded with turnpike roads which lead to every part of the Kingdom, a great essential, because you can convey all the property you will with great ease to three or four market towns at small distances. And this advantage also enables the resident to get every convenience & comfort to him, which can be wished for, the post every morning & easy convenience for traveling passing by every hour the face of the country [?dry] striking airy, the present owner after fifty years residence never sent for any of the faculty except for common drugs, the country abounding with plenty of farms of every kind vested with a royalty and two manors within that royalty. The property consists of arable, pasture, & downs, each rich in their quality, proportioned one with the other, so as to make as eligible as the size of it will admit, mostly laying near & round an old mansion & gardens in the best repaire, well planted & with every convenient office suitable to the sixe of the mansion, which is a very desirable respecatbl & comfortable being. There is a farm house situated in its proper place near the farm yard with barns, stables, & every other convenience, all in the best repair & adapted to the sixe of the estate. These are apparent facts not made up for a sale. Now half the advantages of it related & has been lett when it had not half the above advantages & when farming was at a much lower ebb, for four hundred pounds a year. Part of the mansion with garden, orchard & a small portion of meadow land not included in the above rent. The land &

1 Probably written by Arthur Jones.
2 Beckhampton is meant.

other taxes very moderate when compared with many neighbouring places, & the expences of highways near 3 pounds a year less than when the above rent was given at which time. The road to London, Bath, &c., was over the Downs, much to the injury & often times breaking out upon the lands.[1] The above is to be considered as an object of desire, and not to be treated for as a farm without any of the advantages here related. The whole is a free hold, tithe free, excepting a small & well established modus of four pounds a year to the Vicar, pays no sute services or quit rents to any lord paramount whatever, thus conditioned the value of it must be fixed at thirty two years purchase £12,800, the revenue as above mentioned of house gardens, &c.,£25 per year, twenty years purchase £500. The cottages belonging to the above, as there may be lives settled on them may be thrown into the above valuation, the Hare & Hounds with the grounds let with it at Beckington free of all kings taxes & parochial £26 per year, 20 years purchase £520 & may be sold & let for more on account of its situation. Here tis not improper to observe that the whole of the above property is in the best culture & not incumberd with leases, but may have imediate possession when terms are agreed to. It may not be improper to observe that the Hare & Hounds at Beckington is advantageously situated for all kinds of carriages from Bath & other great western towns to London & ought to be sold for seven or eight hundred pounds.[2]

The modus to the vicar may be supported & defended if any future vicar waso ill advised as to attempt to disturbe it, for the following reasons. There is no ancient terrier on record in the Bishop of Salisbury's court to ascertain the particular profits of this living, but about the year 1670 one White the then vicar was disposed to alter & defeat the customary payments to increase his own emoluments, & found the first step to be taken was to founded on an ancient terrier or written record. As such coud not be found he made a defective terrier as he thought woud answer his purpose and upon the strength of this he commenced a sute in the Chancery in the proceedings of which court he was examined on oath if he knew or had made any terrier with a tendency to support the cause then depending he said he had not nor did he know of any, by which it was proved he was guilty of perjury & was glad to get out of the scrape & submit of the payment of the modus of four pounds a year, which had been as galantly accepted by the incumbents from time immemorial & so has been continued from that period which is now 118 years without any attempt being made to defeat it, & here it may not be improper to observe that this modus has by

1 Coaches would go over the adjoining fields – and perhaps damage crops - if the road itself was too foundrous.

2 Originally known as the Bear, then as the Hare and Hounds, this pub had become the Flying Waggon by 1772 (see above, Arthur Jones's advice to his successors). Maybe Jones's memory was fading when he referred to it here as still being the Hare and Hounds. The change of name may have been occasioned by the fact that its clientele was changing. It had originally been intended for drovers, but here Jones was arguing that its situation gave it an opportunity to meet the upmarket needs of the carriage trade.

tradition the essential quality for the foundation of such, being a [?pring real] that is three ell ridges of which out of that piece of ground laying nearest the church, the ell ridges as so old and obsolete a measure it woud be difficult ascertain it & the accompt of the expression of the piece nearest the church may be defeated & lessend in its value, therefore the certain sum so long paid is the more preferable. As to the particulars of lands customs &c., there are two *[illegible]* for that information. The present owner has been in regular possession of it for more than sixty years, a title the laws prefer before all others.

4
RICHARD HICKLEY'S ACCOUNTS

May-June 1791

1791. Farm Account from 13th May to 22d June

[Income]		
May		
21st	To 16 sacks wheat	22-16-00
28th	To 16 sacks do	22-16-00
	To 5 quarter barley	6-15-00
	To a cow & calf	10-06-00
June		
4th	To 16 sacks wheat	22-16-00
10th	To16 sacks do	22-08-00
15th	To 10 quarter barley	13-15-00
21st	To 16 sacks wheat	22-08-00
	To chees & cold sundrys	8-09½
		144-08-09½
[Expenditure]		
May		
21st	Paid a cooper's bill	1-02-00
	Paid a bill to my wife	1-05-02
23	Turnpike & beer	1-10
	Turnpike for [?hundels]	7
	Paid for hundles	2-09-06
28	Turnpike, beer, & my expences	3-08
June		
2d	Paid land, window, & other taxes	44-18-04
	Paid for a bull	6-06-00
	4 sacks brans	14-06
	30 pound of turnip seed	15-00
4th	Turnpike, beer, & my expences	3-07
	Paid for 60 ewes & lambs	31-15-00
	5 sacks of grass seed	2-07-00
	2 oys of verdegreace	8
	Paid a bill for cleaning the terret & house clocks last year	17-00
10th	Turnpike & expenses	3-08
	Paid a highway rate	4-15-00
15th	Turnpike & beer	1-01-10
	Paid Dell[1] the turnpike man	15-06
21st	Turnpike, beer, & my expences	3-09
	To 8 weeks labour on the farm from the 28 April to 18th June	29-12-00
	Paid for weeding corn	7-18-01
	To thrashing 108 sacks of wheat	8-01-06
		144-11-02
Disbursed		144-11-02

[1] Stephen Dell; see *AWS*, p.319.

Goods sold	144-08-09½
Ballance to me	2-04½
To an old ballance as settled the 13th May	34-06-11
Real ballance due to me	34-09-03¼

July 1791

1791. Farm Account from the 22d June to the 30th July

[Income]		
June		
29th	To 15 sacks wheat	21-07-06
July		
8th	To cash received for 69 tods of wool at £1 5s 0d	86-05-00
	To do for 120 pound of lambs wool	3-15-00
	To cash received on account of wool last year	4-00-00
11th	To 16 sacks wheat	22-16-00
16th	To 16 sacks do	22-16-00
23d	To 15 sacks do	21-07-06
	For straw	3-02
		182-10-02
		108-16-09
To a ballance due to me		73-13-05
The 2d June of		35-02-11½
Ballance due from me		38-10-05½
[Expenditure]		
June		
27th	Paid for bricks & lime	4-01-00
	Paid thatcher's bill	6-14-01
	For washing sheep	17-06
29th	Turnpike & beer	1-10
	Cash paid Stroud2[2] towards his bill	10-00-00
	For shearing sheep	3-04-00
	Winding wool	5-00
July		
8th	My expences	1-10
	Gave the wool man's servant	2-00
	Paid for kiling rats one year	1-01-00
	For cow keeping	8-04
	For salt	14-09
	Paid for grinding corn	13-08
11th	Turnpike & beer	1-10
12th	Turnpike	1-06
	Paid for earthen-ware farm house	1-00
	Paid the postmaster for letters forwarded to London	1-09
16th	Turnpike & beer	1-10
18th	My expences	1-10
	Paid insurance for Avebury	4-17-00
19th	Paid Crook[3] the carpenter	30-00-00

[2] Probably a gang-master contracted for shearing, as well as being a glazier. See *AWS*, p.290.

[3] Stephen Crook. See *AWS*, p.71.

23d	Turnpike & beer	1-10
	My expences	1-10
	For a milk bucket & chees fats	11-00
	Paid the gardener his waigers up to the 7th December 1790	10-00-00
30th	My expences to market	1-10
	Paid horse farrier's bill	4-07-06
	For six weeks labour on the farm	20-10-06
	For haymaking	6-04-06
	For thrashing 44 sacks wheat	3-06-00
		108-16-09

August & September 1791[4]

1791 Farm Account from the 30th July to the 24th September

August		
[?1st]	To 40 lambs	14-00-00
4th	To 16 sacks wheat	22-16-00
6th	To 40 lambs	11-15-00
9th	To 16 sacks wheat	22-16-00
13th	To 16 sacks do	22-16-00
20th	To 16 sacks do	22-16-00
	To carriage of 3 load of lead to Swindon	1-13-00
	To carriage 2 load coales	1-00-00
24th	To 8 pigs	12-01-06
September		
15th	To 16 sacks wheat	21-12-00
	To straw &c	1-02-10
		154-08-04
[Expenditure]		
August		
3d	Turnpike & beer	3-04
	Paid for sheep pens	3-06
	Paid the farm maid one year's waigers to Lady Day last	5-05-00
8th	Paid E Scane her legacy[5]	60-00-00
9th	Turnpike & beer	1-10
13th	Turnpike, beer & my expences	3-08
20th	Turnpike, beer & my expences	3-07
	3 sacks bran	12-00
	Paid corn dealers for 8 load	8-00
	Paid for hoeing turnips	2-09-11
September 3rd		
	Paid for paint	1-16-00
	My expences	1-11
	For cuting 95 acres of wheat	31-09-07½
	Paid for 31 teg sheep bought last spring	32-11-00
	Paid the schoolmaster for work &c	1-17-04
15th	Turnpike & beer, my expences	4-10

[4] This was the first account sent after Mrs Williamson had sailed to Jamaica.
[5] She received £80 in the will of Arthur Jones, TNA PROB11/1181/174.

17th	My expences	1-10
24th	do	1-09
	Paid for keeping cows	1-13-09
	For cuting 91 acres of barley & oates	4-11-00
	For forking & raking do	4-11-00
	For raking after the waggon	1-12-10
	For 8 weeks labour on the farm	35-16-02
	For thrashing 76 sacks of wheat	6-03-03
	Cash advanced to the gardner for 16 weeks	12-16-00
		204-19-01½
Disbursments		204-19-01½
Received		154-08-04
		50-10-09½
To a ballance against me the 30th July		38-10-05½
To me		12-00-04

September & October 1791

1791. Farm Account from the 24th September to the 25th October

[Income]		
September		
27th	To 15 sacks wheat	20-00-00
October		
4th	To 16 sacks wheat	19-12-00
5th	To 10 quarter barley	14-10-00
14th	To 16 sacks wheat	20-00-00
	To 22 pigs	17-01-00
20th	To 16 sacks wheat	20-00-00
	To 8 calves to the butcher	11-04-08
	To goods, straw, &c	4-09
	To goods to Miss Rennald	2-01-05
		124-13-10
[Expenditure]		
September		
29th	Paid for paint	2-02-09
October		
1st	Turnpike, beer, & expences	3-06
4th	Turnpike, beer, & expenses	4-04
	Sack car	1-00
5th	Half a year's waigers to the farm boy	2-02-00
	Turnpike, beer, & my expences	7-04
14th	Turnpike, beer, & expences	4-04
	4 sacks of rye	5-04-00
20th	Turnpike & beer	1-10
	Turnpike for sheep	2-00
	20 pound figs for home harvest	8-04
	For pig keeping in the field	17-06
	Barrel of tar	1-00-00

27th 2 sacks of lime	6-00
By the butcher's bill from the 6th March to the 1st October	12-15-02
Paid Adam Wiltshire for kiling game the last year	5-08-03
Cash paid to William Phillips for the legacy[6]	50-00-00
For five weeks labour on the farm	23-04-04
For measuring harvest lands	12-00
	105-04-08
Received	124-13-10
Disbursed	105-04-08
Ballance to me	19-09-02
24th September	12-00-04
To master	7-08-10

November 1791

1791 The Farm Account from the 28th October to the 5th December

[Income]	
October	
29th To 10 quarter of barley	15-00-00
November	
3d To 16 sacks wheat	19-04-00
8th To 16 sacks do	19-12-00
To 7½ quarters barley	11-12-06
To cash received of Mr Bailey[7] to make up the current price of wool this year at £1 7s od per tod	7-06-00
15th To 10 quarter of barley	15-15-00
18th To 16 sacks wheat	20-00-00
To carriage of 4 load coales	2-00-00
To 100 lambs at 12s each	60-00-00
To 60 do at 10 each	30-00-00
To 100 ewes at 19s each	95-00-00
To 100 do at 15 each	75-00-00
30th To 10 quarter barley	16-00-00
To carriage 2 load coales	1-00-00
December	
3d To 16 sacks wheat	20-00-00
To straw &c [?paid] sundrys	1-11-01
	409-00-07[8]
[Expenditure]	
October	
29th Turnpike & beer	4-06
Sack, car, & my expences	2-10
30th Cuting pigs	1-10

[6] This was probably a portion of the legacy of £100 given to John Phillips, the butler, in the 1789 will of Arthur Jones; see TNA PROB11/1181/174.

[7]. Mr George Bailey.

[8] Actually £411-00-07.

November		
8	Turnpike & beer	1-10
9	Sack, car, & my expences	2-10
	By a dubble poor rate	19-00-00
	Chaff knife	4-06
	For pad locks	5-06
	Dozen rakes	3-06
	Long broom for farmhouse	1-08
	For 5 sacks horse beans	4-10-00
8th	Turnpike, sack, car, beer, & dealer	4-06
	Turnpike & beer do	1-10
	Paid Tayler the tin man	1-11-03
	For tinning a stew pan	1-00
	For one year's work to the sieveer[9]	11-00
12th	For 7 quarter of oats & 3 quarter of barley for seed last spring	11-11-06
	For patching sheep	10-08
	Paid Joseph Brown for one year's annuity to Michaelmas 1790[10]	5-00-00
13th	Turnpike & beer	1-10
18th	Turnpike, beer, & my expenses	3-09
	For grinding corn	9-00
	For one year's bill [?paid] Webb the smith	37-19-10
	For a cart horse bot of Mr Nalder [11]	31-00-00
	For half a year's land tax to Michaelmas	26-05-01
22d	For the hurdle man's bill	6-17-00
31st	Turnpike, sack, car, & beer	5-06
December		
3d	Turnpike, beer,& my expences	2-10
	To 5 weeks labour on the farm	20-08-00
	To one year's waigers to myself [?paid] the 10th October last	42-00-00
	To one year's interest on the hundred pounds left by my late master[12] due 2nd July last	4-10-00
	Paid to Miss Renalds for half a year [to 5th December 1791][13]	50-00-00
	Cash advanced to the gardner for 12 weeks to pay his men	9-05-06
	Paid the butcher's bill for sheep's heads and meat for the dogs to this day	2-03-08
		276-02-09
Received		409-00-07
Disbursed		276-02-09
		132-17-10
To a ballance 28 October		7-08-10
Ballance [?paid] Master		140-06-08

[9] Probably the person responsible for operating the water meadow hatches.
[10] Joseph Brown was given an annuity of £10 per annum in the 1789 will of Arthur Jones, TNA PROB11/1181/174. It is not clear why it was reduced to £5 when it was paid.
[11] Probably John Nalder, lord of the manor of Berwick Bassett, and lessee of a farm at West Kennett; see *AWS*, p.106-7.
[12] Arthur Jones.
[13] The bracketed words were added in a different ink on the left hand side of page.

December 1791

1791. The Farm Account from the 5th December to the 1st do.

[Income]		
December		
8th	To 1 calf & 3 odd sheep	3-19-06
10th	To 10 quarter barley	16-00-00
17th	To 10 quarter barley	16-00-00
21st	To 16 sacks wheat	19-16-00
24th	To 10 quarter barley	16-00-00
	To 6 pigs	4-07-00
29th	To 10 quarter barley	15-10-00
	To 1 pig	14-00
	To 48 dozen of glass bottles at 2s per dozen	4-16-00
	To straw	14-08
		97-17-02
[Expenditure]		
December		
8th	2 sacks brans	7-00
	Cow keeping	10-10
	Paid Taylor ironmonger for things the gardener had	13-04
10th	Turnpike & beer	1-10
	My expences	1-09
	Paid Day, upholder[14] at Marlbro	15-05-00
	Paid Lavington nursery man	12-12-06
	Betty Hacker[15] for her waigers	19-00
17th	Turnpike & beer	
	My expences to Bristol	
	Mr Wiltshire's waggoners bill	1-10
	Eames[16] & Hale[17] wine merchants bill at Bristol	7-06
20th	Turnpike & beer	32-00-06
	My expences	47-18-06
	Paid the gardner one year's waigers due the 7th December	2-08
	Paid thatcher's bill	1-08
	Butcher's bill to the 17th inst.	20-00-00
	3 sacks bran	3-12-05
24th	Turnpike & beer	1-03-02
	My expences	8-00
29th	Turnpike, beer, & my expences	1-10
	Load coal ashes	1-10
	My expences to Bath	6-00
	Paid the collarmaker's bill	9-03
	Cash paid Crook carpenter	6-06
	By 4 week's labour for farm	11-04-00

[14] Either an undertaker, or a dealer in small wares.
[15] She was probably Mrs Mitchell's maid at the manor house.
[16] John Eames; see note 2, p.220 above
[17] Henry Hale; see note 3, p. 220 above.

Cash to the gardener for 4 weeks	2-08-00
Load coals for the house	2-09-00
7 quarter on the 10th instant allowed dealers for 8 load of corn	8-00
	198-13-06
Received	97-17-02
Disbursed	198-13-06
	100-16-04
To an old ballance	140-06-08
Due from me	39-10-04

January 1792

1792. Farm Account from the 31st December[18] to the 28th January

[Income]		
4th	To 15 sacks wheat	18-15-00
6th	To 10 quarter barley	16-00-00
11th	To 10 quarter do	16-00-00
19th	To 10 quarter do	15-10-00
21st	To 14 sacks wheat	17-10-00
26th	To 10 quarter barley	15-15-00
28th	To 10 quarter do	15-10-00
	To straw [?paid] sundrys	1-12-08
		116-12-08
[Expenditure]		
January		
4th	Turnpike & beer	1-10
	Woodmans bill	4-10-00
6th	Turnpike, beer, & my expences	3-08
	Stroud glasier's bill	8-18-05
	20 new sacks	2-10-00
	Horse farrier's bill	6-03-06
11th	Turnpike & beer	1-10
	John Shipway's bill[19]	20-02-10
12th	for grains	9-00
	2 hundred fine bran	15-00
14th	My expences	1-09
	For clearing 9½ cord of wood	3-08-00
	For brest plowing six acres of land at 12s per acre	3-12-00
16	For half a year's rat catching	10-06

[18] In 1791.

[19] He was a mason; see *AWS*, p.306-7.

	Insurance for the house at Bath[20]	7-00
21st	Turnpike, beer, & my expences	3-09
26th	Turnpike & beer	4-06
28th	Turnpike, beer, & my expences	3-08
	2 load coal ashes	19-00
	4 corn dealers	4-00
	Butcher's bill from the 17th December to this day	3-13-06
	By a colt bought of Packer	19-19-00
	Butter for the servants at the house	12-03
28th	Stephen Crook's farm bills	20-02-08
	12 sacks of seed wheat	16-16-00
	Poor rate	9-10-00
	One year's composition to Mr Mayo [21]the Vicar	4-00-00
	For 4 weeks labour on the farm	15-05-06
	For 4 weeks do in the garden	2-12-00
		146-01-02
Received		116-12-08
Disbursed		146-01-02
		29-08-06
Old ballance		39-10-04
[?paid] master		10-01-10

February 1792

1792. Farm Account from the 28th January to the 3d March

[Income]		
January		
30th	To 10 pigs	6-12-00
February		
3rd	To 10 quarter barley	15-10-00
10th	To 10 quarter do	15-10-00
16th	To 10 quarter do	15-00-00
	To 8 cow leases las summer	4-16-00
	To 11 turkeys	2-04-00
18th	To 16 sacks of wheat	19-04-00
25th	To 10 quarter barley	15-00-00
March		
3	To 16 sacks wheat	19-04-00
	To straw &c	1-17-08
	To carriage of load coales	10-00
	To goods to Mrs Renald	2-12-00
		117-19-08
[Expenditure]		

[20] Tenanted by Mrs Jenny; see above, p.xxi.
[21] James Mayo.

3d	Turnpike, beer, and my expences	3-09
	Paid for tile for the farmhouse	6-15-09
10th	4 sacks of bran	16-00
11th	Turnpike, beer	1-10
	My expenses l	1-10
	For grinding corn	10-09
	Cash paid Stephen Crook towards the house bill	19-10-00
	Paid John Shipway the remainder of his bill	10-10-10
16th	Turnpike & beer	1-10
	9 load of coal ashes	1-05-00
	For Dixon[22] the taylor's bill	3-00-00
	Paid for laths for farm house	1-10-06
	For my part for repairing the common wells on the downs	19-10
	For making 12 mops	6-00
18th	Turnpike, beer, & my expences	3-08
22d	For 95 bundles of thorns & 24 do of drafts for hedging	1-13-06
	Turnpike & beer	5-00
	Butcher's bill	12-06
	For sweeping chimneys	9-00
25th	Turnpike, beer, and my expences	3-07
27th	Turnpike	3-00
March		
3d	Turnpike, beer, expences, 2 dealers	5-08
	20 quarters of oats for seed	20-00-00
	For banking & planting 74½ pole of hedge	5-12-01
	For a reek of hay about 8 tons and a half	24-03-00
	For my part of grass seeds sown in the common field last year	6-09-11
	Side of bacon for farm house 82 pound at 6¼ pound	2-02-08
	For five weeks labour on the farm	21-05-06
	For five weeks do in the garden	3-04-00
		132-07-00[23]

Received	117-19-08
Disbursements	132-07-00
	14-07-04
Old ballance	10-01-10
Ballance to me	4-05-06

March 1792

1792. Farm Account from the 3d March to the 31st do

[Income]		
March		
10th	To 10 quarter barley	14-10-00
16th	To 16 sacks	18-08-00
22d	To sack barley	15-00
24th	To 16 sacks wheat	18-08-00
26th	To 7 quarter barley	10-17-00

[22] Probably Thomas Dixon; see *AWS* 65 & 318.

[23] Actually £132-12-00.

	To carriage of load coales 29th	10-00
29th	To 6 pigs	4-10-00
	To a cow & calf	8-00-00
		76-02-06[24]

[Expenditure]		
March		
10th	10½ yards of sheeting for the farm house	11-4½
	2 hundred of bran	8-00
	Turnpike, beer, & my expences	6-11
14th	Turnpike & beer	2-06
16th	Turnpike & beer	1-10
17th	My expences	1-10
20th	Turnpike & beer for hay	5-06
21st	Turnpike & beer for do	5-06
	For 2 ricks of hay	26-00-00
	2 hundred of bran	8-00
24th	Turnpike, beer, & my expences	3-09
	For 4 quarts of turpentine	8-00
	My expences [?paid] Bristol	6-00
26th	Turnpike & beer	5-06
31st	Turnpike, beer, & my expences	4-03
	4 weeks labour on the farm	14-16-00
	4 weeks do in the garden	2-09-00
		47-3-11½

Received	76-02-06
Disbursed	47-03-11½
	28-18-6½
Ballance brot forward	4-05-06
[?paid] master	24-13-1½

April 1792

1792. Farm Account from the 31 March to the 23rd April

[Income]		
April		
4th	to 15 sacks of wheat	16-10-00
7th	to 7 quarter barley	7-10-00
	To carriage of load coales	10-00
	to cash received of Mrs Jenny[25] for rent to Lady Day last	34-19-07
14th	To 9 sacks of wheat	9-18-00
	To 5 quarter of barley	7-05-00
	To 8 quarter of barley	11-12-00
13th	To a cow & two calves	7-07-00

[24] Actually £75-18-00.
[25] See p.xxi above. She rented Williamson's house in Bath.

	To carriage of load coales	10-00
	To one calf	1-12-00
	To a cow & calf	5-10-00
	To 16 sacks wheat	17-04-00
	To carriage load coales	10-00
	To straw, eggs, &c	1-18-06
		121-16-01[26]
[Expenditure]		
April		
4th	Turnpike, beer, my expences	3-04
	2 sides of bacon for to send to Jamaica	3-05-06
	Gale Goodman's bill	1-07-08
5th	For wintering 31 sheep	9-06-00
	For wintering 40 do	11-10-00
	For wintering 40 do	11-10-00
	for wintering 60 do	15-00-00
	For wintering 20 do	5-00-00
7th	Turnpike, sack, car, & beer	5-06
	5 hundred of clover seed	9-00-00
13th	Turnpike & beer	5-00
	For a rick of hay	16-04-00
14th	Turnpike, beer & my expences	3-06
	8 corn dealers	8-00
	6 dozen of hurdle stakes	3-00
	sack of pollard	4-06
	for a cask for caseing a cask of beer to send [?to] Jamaica	18-06
	for a poor rate	19-00-00
	for a church do	6-06-08
	for 2 cow drinks	2-00
	8 tons & 17 hundred of hay	10-13-06
	For 24 quarter of barley for seed	34-04-00
	My expences [?paid] Bristol	6-06
	Butter, pig, meat, &c for the house	1-14-10
28th	Turnpike, beer, & my expences	3-07
	For 4 week's labour on the farm	16-14-00
	Threshing & winnowing 34 sacks wheat	2-13-10
	4 weeks labour in the garden	1-12-00
	Butcher's bill from the 3d March	1-19-01
		180-04-06
Received		121-16-01
Disbursed		180-04-06
		58-08-05
Old ballance		24-13-00½
To me		68-15-04½

[26] Actually £122-16-01

May 1792

1792. Farm Account from the 28th April to the 2d June

[Income]		
May		
1st	To 2 calves	1-11-06
4th	To 3 old cows	15-00-00
6th	To 2 calves	2-02-00
	To 2 cows and calves	11-04-00
10th	To 1 calf	1-00-00
15th	To 16 sacks wheat	17-12-00
18th	To 3 pigs	2-08-00
	To cash received of Thomas Hatchet[27] for one year's rent to Lady	26-00-00
26th	16 sacks wheat	17-12-00
June		
2d	To 16 sacks wheat	17-12-00
	To poultry, eggs, straw &c	2-09-11
3d	To cash received of the gardener for things sold from the garden	
[?paid] this day		16-09
		115-08-02
[Expenditure]		
May		
1st	For grinding corn	3-09
	For 35 cupples, ewes, & lambs	37-10-00
	My expences	1-11
	By a three year old horse	22-01-00
	3 dozen of waggon tacks	9-00
	Grains for pigs	16-06
15th	Turnpike, sack, car, & beer	3-06
	My expences	1-06
	2 sacks bran	8-00
	for making 270 pole of hedge	2-05-00
	Sulpher for the horses	6-03
17th	My expences	1-11
26th	Turnpike, beer, and my expences	3-09
	By half a year's land and a whole year's window & other taxes due	
last Lady Day		43-03-8½
	Adam Wiltshire[28] for kiling game	2-11-06
	Butcher's bill for the house	2-08-00
	For 5 week's labour on the farm	20-11-06
	Thrashing & winnowing 35 sacks wheat	2-19-07
June		
2d	5 weeks labour in the garden	1-12-00
	Paid the gardener for half a hundred of apple stocks	6-00
	For grains	4-00
	Turnpike, beer, & my expences	3-06
	Hundred of pollard	7-06
	3 corn dealers	3-00

[27] Publican at the Flying Waggon; see Raymond, Stuart A. 'The Inns of Avebury, c.1600-1800', *WAM* 117, 2024, p.159-67.

[28] The gamekeeper; see above, p.257; see also *AWS*, p.300 & 375-6.

	139-02-04½
Disbursements	139-02-04½
Received	115-08-02
Old ballance	23-14-2½
[?paid] me	33-15-04½
	57-09-07

June 1792

1792. Farm Account from the 2d June to the 30th

[Income]		
June		
9th	To 16 sacks wheat	17-12-00
	To carriage load coales	10-00
21st	To 16 sacks wheat	19-04-00
29th	To 16 sacks wheat	19-04-00
	To poultry, straw, &c	1-01-2½
	To cash received of the gardener	1-05-07
		58-16-09½
[Expenditure]		
June		
4th	My expences at Beckhamton to attend the Commissioners[29]	11-06
9th	Turnpike & beer	1-10
	Side of bacon 58 pound at 6¼d for the house	1-11-05
	4 dozen glass bottles	8-00
20th	22 cupples at £1 1s 6d each	23-13-00
	2½ hundred of pollard	2-08
21st	Turnpike, beer, & my expences	3-10
29th	Turnpike, beer, & my expences	3-07
	3 dealers	3-00
	Sack pollard	6-00
	4 weeks labour in the garden	1-08-00
	For corks & resin	1-10
	Thrashing & winnowing 43 sacks of wheat	3-00-11
	4 weeks labour on the farm	13-10-08
		45-06-03
Received		58-16-09½
Disbursed		45-06-03
		13-10-06½
Old ballance		57-09-07
		13-10-06½
[?paid] me		43-19-00½

[29] The Enclosure Commissioners.

July 1792

1792. Farm Accounts from the 30th June to the 28th July

[Income]		
July		
3d	To 43 pound of tailing wool	19-09
7th	To 10 sacks of wheat	12-10-00
	To 5 quarters barley	7-10-00
	To 74 tod & 8 pounds of sheep's wool at £1 8s od per tod	104-00-00
	To 115 pound of lambs' wool at 8½d per pound	4-01-00[30]
17th	To 15 sacks of wheat	20-05-00
28th	To 16 sacks wheat	24-00-00
	To goods sold from the garden	1-17-04
	To straw, poultry, eggs, &c	1-12-01
		176-15-02
[Expenditure]		
July		
5th	By washing sheep & lambs	17-00
	Shearing 8 hundred sheep & 410 lambs	3-03-00
	Winding wool	5-00
	8 pound suggar for vinegar	5-04
	A milk sieve	9
	My expences to market	1-06
	Cash paid Mrs Renald in part of the fifty pounds due to them 5th June	30-00-00
	Cash paid to Mrs Renald on my master's account	72-08-00
	Cash gave the wool man's servant	2-00
10th	By the smith's half year's bill	12-04-08
	Carriage of a cask of beer to Bristol	1-06-06
17th	Turnpike, beer, & my expences	4-00
	Paid the insurance for the house at Bath to Lady Day last	10-00
	Insurance for the farm to midsummer	4-17-00
	1 dozen of rakes	3-00
	For a grinding stone	8-00
	One year's waigers to Mrs. Mitchell[31] to 23d April	6-06-00
	For one year's interest [?paid] do on twenty pounds due 26 April	1-00-00
	For one year's waigers [?paid] the farm maid due Lady Day last	5-05-00
28th	Turnpike, beer, & my expences	3-04
	Bill to Mitchell for chur women	4-8½
	Butcher's bill to the 8th July	2-07-11
	Paid the several weeders of corn	6-13-11
	Barrel of tar	19-00
	Cow keeping six weeks	6-10
	12 quarter of grass seeds at £1 4s od	14-08-00
	For 4 weeks labour	15-12-06
	4 week's labour in the garden	1-08-00
		181-10-11½

[30] Actually £4 1s 5½d

[31] The housekeeper.

Disbursments	181-10-11½
Goods sold	176-15-02
	4-15-09½
Ballance brot forward	43-19-00½
[?paid] me	48-14-10

August 1792

1792. Farm Accounts from the 28th July to the 1st September

[Income]		
August		
11th	To 16 sacks wheat	24-00-00
	To carriage load coales	10-00
	To 40 lambs at 6s 6d	13-00-00
	To 10 do at 6s each	3-00-00
28th	To 16 sacks of wheat	24-00-00
	To poultry, eggs, straw &c	2-09-10
	To cash received of the gardener for goods sold	1-02-00
		68-01-10
[Expenditure]		
August		
11th	16 pound of tar thread	5-04
	Turnpike, beer, & my expenses	3-10
17th	My expenses attending the Commissioners[32] at Beckhamton	9-08
18th	10 pound of greace for waggons	3-04
	Soap & candles for the house	15-08
	Chees colouring	4-03
	11 sacks of horse beans	9-07-00
	For half a year's rat catching	10-06
28th	Turnpike, beer, & my expences	3-09
	Gallon of brandy	15-00
	My expenses at Beckhamton	9-06
	Load coales for the house	2-02-00
	Butcher's bill from 8th July to 1st September	3-05-11
29th	By the several people for hay making	12-14-9½
	For grass mowing	6-14-02
	For five weeks labour	19-18-06
	For five weeks labour in garden	1-18-00
	For 30 teg sheep bought last May at 17s each	25-10-00
	Paid the gardener for corks	4-07½
	28 pound of black cherrys	10-00
	For pepper	1-10
	For hoeing 17 acres of turnips at 7s per acre	5-19-00
		92-06-08
Disbursments		92-06-08
Goods sold		68-01-10
		24-4-10
Ballance brot forward		48-14-10
		72-19-08

[32] The Enclosure Commissioners.

September 1792

1792. Farm Account from the 1st September to the 29th

[Income]		
September		
29th	To 16 sacks wheat	24-00-00
	To carriage of coale	10-00
	To poultry, chees, &c	1-05-11
	To goods sold from the garden	6-10
		26-02-09
[Expenditure]		
September		
2d	By 122 pound of bacon for the reapers	3-06-00
12	Cow keeping 11 weeks	3-13-09
	Malt baskets for packing	3-08
	Carriage of two hampers from London	11-03
15th	My expences to market	1-09
29th	Turnpike & beer	1-11
	My expences	1-10
	For spice for Mitchell	1-05
	For 4 weeks labour	21-07-03
	4 weeks in the garden	2-00-00
	Paid the gardener for 30 pound of damsons	5-00
	Paid for jars & pots	7-00
	For 41 pound brown paper	6-09
		30-07-07
Disbursed		30-07-07
Received		26-02-09
		4-04-10
Brought forward		72-19-08
To me		77-04-06

October 1792

1792. Farm Account form the 29th September to the 4th November

[Income]		
October		
4th	To 16 sacks wheat	24-16-00
	To poultry	1-01-03
	To a fat calf	3-10-07
		29-07-10
[Expenditure]		
October		
4th	Turnpike, beer, my expenses	3-08
	4 sacks bran	12-00
	One year's work to the [?siveer]	10-06
15th	My expences to Bristol	7-06
	Sack of lime	2-00
20th	My expences to market	1-10
	A stone bottle	1-04
	Corn dealer for 6 load	6-00

	Carriage of 2 tables from Portsmouth	5-10
24th	Beer for loading goods at Beckhamton for Bristol	1-06
27th	My expences to market	1-11
	One year's measuring land	12-00
November		
4th	My expences to market	2-00
	Butcher's bill from the 1st of September to the 26th October	5-18-08
	Five weeks labour on the farm	23-18-05
	Five weeks do in the garden	1-18-00
		35-03-02[33]
Disbursed		33-03-02
Received		29-07-10
		5-15-04
old ballance		77-04-06
to me		82-19-10

November 1792

1792. The Farm Account from 4th November to the first December

November		
[Income]		
7th	To 16 sacks wheat	24-00-00
	To carriage of load coales	10-00
23d	To 16 sacks wheat	24-00-00
	To 7 pigs	5-05-00
27th	To 16 sacks wheat	23-00-00
	To 10 bushels barley	1-07-00
	To 16 cow leases at 12s each	10-04-00[34]
	To 3 heifers & a bull	17-10-00
	To 100 lambs at 13s each	60-00-00
	To 50 do at 10s	23-00-00
	To 36 do at 7s	12-12-00
	To 100 ewes at 18s each	90-00-00
	To 50 do at 14s	35-00-00
	To 80 do at 12s	48-00-00
	To 50 do at 10s	25-00-00
	To 10 quarter of barley	17-10-00
	To poultry & chees	1-13-00
	To cash received of sundry people for plowing, grass seeds, &c	19-05-00
		439-00-00
	Should be	439-16-00[35]
[Expenditure]		
November		
7th	By a poor rate	9-10-00
	Turnpike & beer	1-11

[33] Actually £35-04-02.
[34] Total is actually £9-12-00.
[35] Written in different ink. The accountant has attempted to correct his addition, but has still failed to give the correct amount, which is £437-16-00.

20th	Turnpike, beer, & my expences	4-02
27th	Turnpike, beer, & my expences	4-04
	My expences with the Commissioners [36]	18-00
	2 quarts of turpentine	4-00
	Corn dealers	3-00
	By a cask of harness oil	1-02-00
	The hurdle man's bill	5-17-06
28th	5 quarter of oats	7-10-00
	2 sacks beans	2-12-00
	150 bushels of peat ashes	5-00-00
	For reaping 79 acres of wheat	31-12-00
	For mowing 105 acres of barley	7-00-00
	Forking & raking of do	5-05-00
	Raking after the waggon	2-16-06
	By 120 lambs bought of Mr Blake at 16s each	96-00-00
	By 5 rams	17-17-00
	By 160 two teeth ewes bought of do at 18 each	144-00-00
	Cash paid Mrs Rennald	20-00-00
29th	Turnpike, beer, & my expences	3-10
	Load coales for the house	2-08-00
	Paid for grinding corn	11-06
	Carriage of goods to Bristol	1-13-06
	2 sides of bacon, 38 pound at 7d	2-11-04
	For brown paper for the green house & the alcove	6-01
	15 bushels of hass for the gardener	12-06
	Cow keeping	13-02
December		
1st	4 weeks labour on the farm	18-15-00
	4 weeks do in the garden	1-08-00
	My expences to market	1-10
	For 8 new scoops	10-06
	Butcher's bill from the 26th October to the 30th November	1-08-08
		389-01-04
	By right	389-01-04 [37]

To goods sold	439-00-0
Disbursments	389-01-04
	49-18-08
to the old ballance	82-19-10
to me	33-01-02

Verso: Hickley account from the 4th November to 1st December 1792. In this account Hickley has cast up sixteen shillings short in our favour.

[36] The Enclosure Commissioners.

[37] The accountant apparently attempted to correct this figure, but did not do so. Actually £379-02-04.

December 1792

1792. Farm Account from the 1st December to the 29th

[Income]		
December		
8	To 16 sacks wheat	21-12-00
	To carriage coale	10-00
15th	To 10 quarter barley	15-00-00
21	To 5 quarter barley	7-10-00
	Sack barley	18-00
24th	To 16 sacks wheat	22-08-00
28	To 14 sacks wheat	19-12-00
	To poultry	14-00
	To cash received of Mrs Rennald for goods from the farm	2-06-3¾
		90-10-03¾
[Expenditure]		
December		
4th	by Lavington's[38] bill	10-00-00
	By half year's land tax	26-01-01
8th	By turnpike & my expences	3-09
	Sack bran	4-06
15th	By turnpike, beer, my expences	3-09
21st	by turnpike & do	3-04
24th	By do & do	8-08
	By half year's rat catching	10-06
	By 2 year's malster's bills	35-06-06
	By cash paid for two reck staddles for corn	9-00-06
	By 68 bushels grains	17-00
	By cash paid Stephen Crook	50-00-00
	Gallon of gin to Mrs Rennald	6-00
29th	By my expences to market	1-11
	By 4 weeks labour	18-07-00
	By 4 weeks do in the garden	1-08-00
	By 74 pound of beef at 3½d	1-01-07
	By 11 score & half of beef at 3s per score	1-14-06
		155-13-07
Disbursments		155-13-07
Received		90-10-03¾
		65-03-03¼
Ballance brot forward		33-01-02
		98-04-05¼

[38] Probably Thomas Lavington.

January 1793

1793. Farm Accounts from the 29th December 1792 to the 2 February 1793

[Income]		
January		21-12-00
2nd	To 16 sacks wheat	18-00-00
5th	To 10 quarter barley	21-12-00
16th	To 16 sacks wheat	18-00-00
18th	To 10 quarter barley	10-00
	To carriage [?load] coales	16-00
	To sack barley	39-15-00
	To 4 oxen sold for	22-00-00
25th	To 16 sacks wheat	
February		
2d	To poultry eggs &c	1-12-02
	To 2 bushells barley	8-00
	To 10 quarter barley	18-00-00
		162-05-02
[Expenditure]		
January		
2d	Turnpike & beer	1-11
	2 sacks brans	9-00
	A horse bought of Isaace Joyce	27-06-00
5th	Turnpike, beer, my expences	4-00
	Gale[39] the woodman's bill	4-02-10
	Butcher's bill to 28th December	1-03-06
	Five sacks seed wheat	6-12-06
	Insurance for the house at Bath	7-00
16th	Turnpike & beer	2-00
	Eight second hand casks	4-08-00
18th	Turnpike, beer, my expences	4-00
	Load coales for the house	2-08-00
	8 sacks & 3 bushels of rye	10-10-00
	Sack of potatoes	3-06
22d	By leveling 25 acres & ¾ of turf on the down at 8s acre	10-06-00
	By making 267 pole of bank on the down for bounds	6-13-06
	By half a year's smith's bill to the 1st November last	12-02-04
25th	By one year's waigers to my self due 10th October last	42-00-00
February		
2d	Turnpike, beer, my expences	3-07
	By five weeks labour	23-03-00
	Five weeks do in the garden	1-15-00
	Paid Stroud the glazier for mending windows, &c	10-10
	Turnpike, beer, & my expences	4-00
	Butcher's bill to 2d February	1-11-04
	By 12 thatched hurdles for the gardener to cover the trees	12-00
		157-13-10[40]

[39] Probably Gale Goodman; see above, 4th December 1795.

[40] Actually £157-03-00.

Received	162-05-02
Disbursed	157-13-10
	4-11-04
Brought forward	98-04-05¼
	4-11-04
To me	93-13-01¼

February 1793

1793. The Farm Account from the 2d February to the 2d March

February		
6th	To 16 sacks wheat	20-16-00
9th	To 10 quarter barley	19-00-00
26th	To 7½ quarter barley	14-04-00
28th	To 16 sacks wheat	20-16-00
March		
2d	To 10 quarter barley	16-00-00
	To carriage coales	10-00
	To poultry & eggs	18-08
		92-04-08
[Expenditure]		
February		
6th	Turnpike & beer	1-10
9th	Turnpike & beer	4-00
	Poor rate	19-00-00
	Makeing & duty of five quarter of malt	3-04-04
	4 dealers	4-00
	Grubing 140 pole of bank	4-19-10
12th	My expences 3 days attending the Commissioners at Beckhamton	11-06
26	Turnpike & beer	2-00
28th	Turnpike & beer	2-00
March		
2d	Turnpike, beer, and my expences	6-06
	Salt	7-04
	Soap & candles for the house	1-18-06
	Paid Mitchell a bill for work & other articles	16-06
	6 sacks bran	1-10-00
	Turnpike for hurdles	2-03
	Cash paid corn dealers	7-00
	Chivers[41] bill for thatching the garden wall	5-11-00
	By do for thatching the farm buildings	6-09-00
	By do for thatching Hatchet's house[42]	1-04-06
	By do for thatching the hay, corn ricks and other work	5-07-02
	By 4 weeks labour on the farm	17-17-00
	By 4 weeks do in the garden	1-06-00
	By 18 pound of greace for the waggons	6-00
		71-08-03[43]

[41] Gabriel Chivers; see *AWS*, p.308.

[42] The Flying Waggon.

[43] Actually £71-18-03.

Received	92-04-08
Disbursed	71-08-03
	20-16-05
Brought forward	93-13-01
	20-16-05
To me	72-16-08

March 1793

1793. Farm Account from the 2d March to the 30th

[Income]		
March		
16th	To 16 sacks wheat	20-08-00
	To cash received of Mr George Bailey on account of wool for the last year	25-18-00
29th	To cash borrowed of Mrs Rennald by a draft	50-00-00
30th	To 16 sacks wheat	20-08-00
	To eggs,straw, &c	12-01½
	To cash received of the gardener	9-00
		117-15-01½
[Expenditure]		
March		
16th	Turnpike, beer, expences	4-00
	Butcher's bills from 2d February to the 30th March	2-14-04
	Shipway's[44] bill to 8th January	4-13-02
	To cow drinks	3-04
	3 sacks bran	13-06
	Cash paid to Joseph Brown for one year's annuity	5-00-00
	Paid Mr Mayo the vicar for one year's composition	4-00-00
23d	My expences to market	2-00
	Turnpike for hurdles	2-03
30th	Turnpike, beer, my expences	4-00
	Paid Mrs Clements[45] a bill for sundry articles	1-11-08
	Sack lime	2-11
	4 weeks labour on the farm	18-05-00
	4 weeks do in the garden	1-11-00
		39-07-02
Received		117-15-01½
Disbursed		39-07-02
		78-07-11½
Ballance brot forward		72-16-08
To Master		5-11-03½

April 1793

1793. Farm Account from the 30th March to the 30th April

[44] John Shipway.

[45] Ann Clements, wife of John Clements the former school-master; see *AWS*, p.68.

[Income]		
April		
6th	To 10 quarter barley	16-00-00
9th	to 16 sacks wheat	20-16-00
13th	To 10 quarter barley	16-05-00
23d	To 6 quarter barley	9-12-00
	To 6 sacks wheat	7-19-00
	To poultry & eggs	1-02-11
		71-14-11
April		
6th	Turnpike, beer, and my expences	4-00
7th	Turnpike for sheep	7-00
9th	Turnpike & beer	2-00
	Cuting pigs	4-04
	For a poor rate	19-00-00
	For a church do	3-03-04
	190 willow plants	1-11-08
13th	Turnpike, sack, car, beer, my expences	7-02
	To corn dealers	4-00
	Thomas Shewring[46] for wintering 130 sheep	42-05-00
	Isaac Lane for 62 do	16-05-06
	William Knight for 37 do	12-08-00
	Jermy Knight for 42 do	14-00-00
	John Woodard for 40 do	12-00-00
23d	For 6 hundred of clover seed	15-12-00
	Turnpike	2-00
	Cash paid to Miss Rennald due the 5th January last	50-00-00
	4 weeks labour in the garden	2-09-00
	4 weeks do on the farm	17-14-00
	Butcher's bill to 27th April	12-01½
		208-11-01½
Disbursed		208-11-01½
Received		71-14-11
		136-16-02½
Brought forward		5-11-03½
Balance		131-04-11

May 1793

1793. The Farm Account from the 30th April to the 1st June

[Income]		
May		
12	To 16 sacks wheat	23-12-00
	To carriage load coales	10-00
28	To cash received of Mr Tanner[47] for ¾ of a year's rent for one of the houses at Hungerford due at Xmas 1791	9-09-00
	To cash received of Mrs Jenny towards one year's rent due last Lady Day	28-00-00

[46] Shewring and the farmers named in the following entries presumably lived in the 'cheese country', where sheep could more easily be wintered than in Avebury.

[47] He is frequently mentioned in Richard Hickley's letters above.

	To cash received of the gardener for garden stuff	1-01-00
	To poultry, eggs &c	2-13-01
	To 9 sacks wheat	13-05-06
		78-10-07

[Expenditure]		
May		
4	by my expences to market	1-10
	By the collarmaker's[48] bill to the 1st October last	4-12-06
12th	My expences & turnpike	3-00
	By sack, car, & beer	1-08
	By half a year's land and one year's other taxes	43-13-00½
	to sacks bran	18-00
19th	My expences and 2 dealers	4-00
	By making 325 pole of hedge at 2d	2-14-02
	By insurance for Hatchet's house paid Lady Day last	10-00
25th	By my expences	1-08
	Barrel of tar	1-08-00
30th	By my expences to Bath	2-04
	By cash to my self as a present from my master	3-03-00
	By five weeks labour on the farm	19-13-02
	By five weeks do in the garden	2-06-00
	By a bill paid the gardener for shrubs and plants	3-04-00
	By butcher's bill to 2d June	1-13-06½
		84-10-00[49]

Disbursements	84-10-00
Received	78-10-07
	5-19-05
Brot forward	131-04-11
Balance	137-04-04

June 1793

1793. Farm Account from the 1st June to the [?1st] July

{Income]		
June		
5th	To 10 pigs sold	8-18-00
18th	To 16 sacks wheat	21-04-00
	To 3 fat calves	6-07-06
	To cash as by mistake in the account of the 1st December[50]	16-00
21st	To keeping nine cows 17 weeks at 1s per week	7-13-00
	To cash received of Thomas Hatchet for one year's rent due last Lady	26-00-00
Day		
July		
1st	To 16 sacks wheat	21-04-00
	To poultry eggs &c	2-01-04

[48] Collarmakers made harness for horses.
[49] Actually £84-08-22.
[50] Letter, Richard Hickley to Mrs Williamson, 2nd July 1793, above, p.291-4.

	To cash received of the gardener	1-08-11
		95-12-09
[Expenditure]		
June		
4th	By my expences to market	1-10
	By 40 bushels grains	11-08
15th	By my expences	2-00
18th	By turnpike & beer	4-06
	By my expences at Beckhamton with the Commissoners	5-00
	By James Porter the carrier's bill	12-06
27th	By Lavington the nursery man	6-07-09
	By 10 bushels grains	2-11
	By a poor rate	19-00-00
28th	By making 18 mops	7-06
	By five quarts of turpentine	7-06
	By a 4 year old horse	31-10-00
	By a 2 year old do	21-00-00
29th	By my expences	2-00
	By weeding corn & couching land	9-09-08
	By 4 weeks labour on the farm	12-17-03
	By 4 weeks do in the garden	1-12-00
July		
1st	By turnpike & beer	1-10
		104-15-11
Disbursed		104-15-11
Received		95-12-09
		9-03-02
Brought forward		137-04-04
		146-07-06

July 1793

1793. The Farm Account from the 2nd July to the 3d August

[Income]		
July		
20th	To 16 sacks wheat	21-12-00
	To cash received of George Bailey for 79 tod and 8 pound of wool at £1 2s od per tod	87-04-00
	To 78 pound of lamb's wool	2-02-00
	30th To 14 sacks of wheat	19-05-00
August		
2d	To 3 calves to the butcher	5-00-02
	To cash received of the gardener	1-01-02½
	To poultry, eggs & straw	1-15-04
	To 2 sacks barley	1-14-00
		139-13-08½
[Expenditure]		

July		
4th	By cleaning the terret clock	11-06
	By 3 door locks	11-06
	By washing 1310 sheep & lambs	18-06
	By shearing 1310 sheep & lambs	3-05-00
	Winding wool	5-00
5th	By insurance for the farm	4-17-00
13th	By my expences to market	1-08
15th	By turnpike	2-00
	By the coopers bill for mending tubs	2-00-08
	By spice for Mitchel for pickling	4-07½
20th	By 2 tubs for the orange trees	1-10-06
	By 24 pound greace for waggons	8-00
	By turnpike, beer, & my expences	3-08
	By six tons & eight hundred of hay	20-16-00
	By cash paid to Mrs Rennald due 5th July	50-00-00
30th	By half hundred salt	6-06
	By my expences to market	2-00
	By turnpike & beer	2-00
August		
3d	By my expences & 2 dealers	3-08
	By the butcher's bill from the 2d June to the 8d August	1-19-06
	By five weeks labour on the farm	15-17-00
	By five weeks do in the garden	2-08-00
	By grass mowing	7-17-11
	By the several haymakers	18-07-00
	By a bill paid the gardener	7-08
	By a bill to Mrs Mitchell	11-00
	By sack of pollards	4-06
		134-02-04½[51]
Received		139-13-08½
Disbursed		134-02-04½
		5-11-04
Brot forward		146-07-06
Ballance to me		140-16-02

August 1793

1793. The Account from the 3d August to the 31st

[Income]		
August		
10th	To 14 sacks wheat	18-18-00
	To 3 sacks barley	2-11-00

[51] Actually £134-07-04½

	To carriage of load coales	10-00
12th	To cash received of Mr Ward allowed for the bridge & road over the meadow[52]	49-00-00
	To poultry & eggs	1-01-05
	To cash received of Mrs Rennald	2-01-08
	To cash received of the gardener	14-11
		74-17-00
[Expenditure]		
August		
10th	By turnpike & beer	2-00
	By making 18 mops	7-06
	By my expences	2-00
	By Webb[53] the smith's bill to the first May last	9-02-09
17th	By my expences to market	1-10
	By 6 pare of harvest gloves	4-06
	By the butcher's bill from the 3d August to the 31st	1-04-07
31st	By my expenses	1-09
	By 4 weeks labour on the farm	18-13-02
	By 4 weeks do in the garden	1-18-06
	By cash paid for materials and building the bridge in South Meadow	20-04-03
	By bills paid the gardener	1-04-04½
		53-07-02½
Received		74-17-00
Disbursments		53-07-02½
		21-09-09½
Old balance		140-16-02
		119-06-04½

September 1793

1793 The Account from the 28th August to the 28th September

September	To cash received of Mrs Rennold omited in the last month	10-00
10th	To 16 sacks wheat	21-12-00
18th	To 16 sacks wheat	21-12-00
24th	To 12 sacks wheat	14-04-00
	To 1 quarter barley	1-14-00
	To carriage load coales	10-00
26th	To cash received by draft	100-00-00
	To poultry & eggs	3-07-03
	To cash received of the gardener	10-07
		163-19-10
[Expenditure]		
September		
2d	By dozen candels for the house	7-06
	By dozen do for farmhouse	7-06
	By one year's waigers to the farm servants due last Lady Day	5-05-00

[52] John Ward was a Marlborough attorney, and the Williamson's agent in the enclosure business. He received payment from the Enclosure Commissioners.

[53] George Webb; see *AWS*, p.311-12.

6th	By hoeing 9½ acres of turnips	2-06-06
	Cuting pigs	2-00
	By cuting 98 acres wheat	29-11-10½
	By 20 new sacks	2-10-00
7th	By my expences	2-10
10th	By grinding corn	1-02-01½
	By turnpike & beer	2-00
12th	By six sacks rye	6-09-00
15th	By my expencs	1-10
18th	By turnpike & beer	2-00
	By load coales	2-08-00
21st	By my expences	2-00
24th	By 24 bushels grains	6-00
	Turnpike & beer	2-00
	By 4 weeks labour	17-11-06
	By 4 weeks do in the garden	2-00-08
	By a bill to the gardener	6-00
		71-06-04
Received		163-19-10
Disbursed		71-06-04
		92-13-06
Brought forward		119-06-04½
Ballance		26-12-10½

October 1793

1793. The Farm Account from the 28th September to the 2d November

[Income]		
October		
19th	To 16 sacks wheat	21-04-00
24th	To 4 calves to the butcher	11-02-05
November		
2d	To 16 sacks wheat	21-04-00
	To 13 pigs	15-16-00
	To poultry & straw	1-10-08
	To cash received of the gardener	1-04-00
		72-01-01
[Expenditure]		
October		
5th	By a bill to Hancock	1-07-06
	By my expences to market	1-09
12th	By my expences to do	1-11
	By cash paid the gardener for one year's waigers due the 11th	20-00-00
December		
	By cash advanced to Mrs Rennold on my master's account	20-00-10
	By ¼ hundred soap for the house	17-10
19th	By cleansing 98 pole of the water course in South Meadow	9-16-00

	By turnpike, beer and my expences	4-00
	By the sieveer's bill for one year	15-06
	By half a year's land tax due at Michaelmas	26-05-01
	By one year's waigers to Mrs Mitchel due 23d April last	6-06-00
	By one year's intrest to her on £20 due 21st April last	1-00-00
November		
1st	By turnpike and expences to Bristol with goods	2-14-09
	By load coales taken up at the pit	16-00
	By the butcher's bill from the 31st August to the 25th October	3-08-11
2d	By turnpike & my expences	4-00
	By 2 bills to Mitchell	11-02
	By 2 do to the gardener	10-02½
	By five weeks labour in the garden	2-08-00
	By 5 weeks do on the farm	19-03-04
	By mowing 94½ acres barley & oats	4-14-06
	By forking & rakeing of do	4-14-06
	By rakeing after the waggon	3-18-03
	By sundry people for picking up couch on the land	2-00-05
		132-00-5½
Disbursed		132-00-05½
Received		72-01-01
		59-19-04½
Brought forward		26-12-10½
Ballance		86-12-03

November 1793

1793. The Account from the 2d to the 30th

[Income]		
November		
14th	To 16 sacks wheat	23-00-00
20th	To 150 ewes at 20s each	150-00-00
	To 47 do at 15s each	35-05-00
	To 120 lambs at 7/6 each	45-00-00
	To 41 do at 6s each	12-06-00
26th	To 4 pigs	3-03-00
29th	To 20 sacks wheat	24-10-00
	To a fat calf	2-19-00
	To straw	7-06
	To poultry	12-03
	To cash received of the gardener	12-00
		297-14-09
[Expenditure]		
November		
8	by 2 packing casks for beer	14-00
	By a new well bucket	8-00
	By side bacon for the harvest	3-06-05
	By side for the house	2-02-02

9th	By [?hessings] for patching sheep	9-08
14th	Turnpike, beer, & my expences	4-00
	By 2 two year old horse	20-00-00
	By a 5 year old horse	21-00-00
22d	Sheep pens at Marlbro	3-00
	By the hurdleman's bill	17-10-10
	By cash to Mrs Rennald	108-14-06
29th	By turnpike & beer	4-00
	By Wiltshire[54] the game keeper's bill for the last year	4-04-06
	By a poor's rate the 2d since last Easter	19-00-00
30th	By my expences to market	2-00
	By 64 pound turnip seed	1-12-00
	By 4 weeks labour	14-18-10
	By 4 weeks do in the garden	2-08-00
	Butcher's bill from the 25th October to 27th November	7-08
		217-09-07[55]

Received	297-14-09
Disbursed	217-09-07
	80-05-02
Balance	86-12-03
To me	6-07-01

December 1793 - February 1794
[Missing]

March 1794
1794. From the 1st March to the 29th do

[Income]		
March		
6th	To 20 sacks wheat	25-00-00
14th	To 12 quarter barley	17-10-00
20th	To 7 quarter barley	10-16-00
	To 10 sacks wheat	12-10-00
22d	To 20 sacks wheat	25-00-00
28th	To 10 pigs	8-15-00
	To cash received of Mrs Rennald for goods from the farm	2-01-10
	To cash received of the gardener	4-08
	To eggs	9-04-00
		102-06-10[56]

[Expenditure]		
March		
6th	By turnpike & beer	2-00
8th	By my expences	1-08
14th	By turnpike & beer	2-00
15th	My expences	2-00
20th	By turnpike & beer	2-00

[54] Adam Wiltshire; see note p.257 above.
[55] Actually £217-05-07.
[56] Actually £111-01-06. It is probable that the final two items in the account were added after the addition was calculated.

22d	By turnpike, beer, & my expences	4-00
	Insurance for Hatchet's house	10-00
	By 28 bushels grains	7-00
	By cash on Jas Brown's account[57]	11-10
	By cash to myself for ¾ of a year's interest on £100	3-07-06
29th	By my expences	1-11
	By 4 weeks labour	15-00-00
	By 4 weeks do in the garden	2-08-00
	By thrashing & winnowing 54 sacks wheat	3-03-04
	By 12 pound raisins for the wine	7-00
	By a bill to the gardener for spades, shott, paper &c	14-02
		27-04-05
Received		102-06-10
Disbursed		27-04-05
		75-02-05
Brot forward		18-19-11½
		56-02-05½

April 1794

1794. The Account from the 29th March to the 3d May

[Income]		
April		
1st	To 28 sacks wheat	28-15-00
22d	To 24 sacks wheat	27-12-00
	To cash received of George Bailey the wool man on account of the last year's wool to make the price £1 8s od per tod	28-14-00
	To keeping 10 cows 9 weeks at straw at 2s per week each	9-00-00
	To keeping 1 cow 11 weeks	1-02-00
	To 4 do, 4 weeks at 1/6 week	1-04-00
	To 6, 7 weeks at 1s each	2-02-00
29th	To 12, 3 weeks at 1/3 each	2-05-00
	To 20 sacks wheat	23-10-00
	To carriage load wood Mrs Rennald	5-00
	To a calf to the butcher	1-10-00
	To pidgeons, eggs, straw, &c	12-00
	To cash received of the gardener	7-09
	To 1 sack wheat	1-04-00
	To 2 bushels barley	7-06
		123-10-03[58]
[Expenditure]		
April		
1st	Turnpike, beer, & my expences	5-00
	By 1 dealer	2-00
	4 sacks of bran & 2 of pollard	1-07-06
	My expences on the 8th & 19th	3-09

[57] Actually, probably Joseph Brown; see note xxx above.

[58] Actually £128-09-03.

22d	Turnpike, beer, and my expences	4-04
	Sack pollard	7-06
	Dealer	2-00
	By wintering 97 lambs at 7s each	33-19-00
	By 49 do at 6s each	14-14-00
	By 49 do at 6/6 each	15-18-06
	By 20 do at 4s each	4-00-00
	By 65 do at 6/6 each	21-02-06
	By a poor rate which makes 3 in the year at 1s in the pound	19-00-00
	By a church do	3-05-04
	By a highway do	4-15-00
29th	Turnpike, beer, and my expences	6-06
	Dealer	2-00
	By making 672 pole of hedge at 2d	5-12-00
	By 24 quarter & half of grass seed	22-14-06
	By 17 quarter & half of oats for seed	23-00-00
	30 bushels grains	7-06
	by 4 hundred of clover seed	8-08-00
	2 new water & 4 well bucket	11-00
	By cash to Crook the carpenter	40-00-00
May		
2d	By my expences	1-08
	By five weeks labour on the farm	19-09-00
	By five weeks do in the garden	2-17-00
	By work don by the women on the downs weeding corn &c	9-09-10
	By thrashing & winnowing 43 sacks of wheat	2-13-09
	By cash to Fowler the clerk [59]for his Easter fees	2-06
	By the butcher's bill from the 28th February to the 1st May	1-17-02
		256-18-10
Disbursed		256-18-10
Received		123-10-03[60]
		33-08-07[61]
Brought forward		56-02-05½
		22-13-10½

May 1794

1794. Farm Account from the 3d May to the 31st do

[Income]		
May		
13th	To 20 sacks wheat	23-00-00
	To cash received of Mrs Jenny on account of rent from Lady Day 1792 to Lady Day 1793	3-19-02
	To cash received of do for rent from Lady Day 1793 to Lady Day 1794	30-07-09
	To cash received of Mrs. Brown for one year's rent to Lady Day last '94[62]	6-06-00

[59] Samuel Fowler, the parish clerk; see *AWS*, p.415.
[60] See previous note.
[61] Actually £133-08-07.
[62] See Richard Hickley's letter, 2nd March 1793.

22nd	To 20 sacks wheat	24-00-00
	To a calf to the butcher	1-08-00
	To cash received of the gardener	11-00
	To poultry, eggs, straw, &c	1-12-01
		91-04-00
[Expenditure]		
May		
6th	By 4 harrows & 1 roaler bought at second hand	2-07-00
	By one cow 3 year old	12-12-00
	By one year's waigers to the farm servant to Lady Day	5-05-00
10th	My expences to market	1-10
13th	By my expences to Bath	3-06
	By Godwin the shoe maker's bill	8-00-06
	By Hancock the fishmonger do	1-04-08
13th	Turnpike & beer	2-06
23d	By turnpike, beer, & my expences	3-11
	By a paper of starch & blue	3-08½
	By one year's waigers to the gardener due the 11th December last	20-00-00
	By land, window, & other taxes to Lady Day	39-17-06½
31st	By my expences	2-00
	By 4 weeks labour	15-05-00
	By the women for weeding	6-17-06
	By thrashing & winnowing 50 sacks wheat	3-11-01½
	By 4 weeks labour in the garden	2-07-00
	6 rubbers for the garden	2-00
	By the butcher's bill to the 30th May	1-09-05½
		119-16-03
Expences		119-16-03
Received		91-04-00
		28-12-03
Brot forward		22-13-10½
		51-06-01½

June 1794

1794. From the 31st May to the 28 June

[Income]		
June		
5th	To 20 sacks wheat	23-05-00
10th	To 20 sacks do	24-10-00
18th	To 20 sacks do	24-00-00
	To carriage load coales	10-00
20th	To six pigs at 12s each	3-12-00
	To cash received of Thomas Hatchett for one year's rent due Lady Day	26-00-00
	To a young calf	12-00
	To poultry, eggs, straw, &c	1-07-09

	To cash received of the gardener	1-04-08
		105-01-05
[Expenditure]		
June		
5th	by turnpike & beer	2-00
	By sack pollard	6-00
7th	My expences	2-00
	By 3 dealers	3-00
10th	By turnpike & beer	2-00
	By a poor rate	19-00-00
	By cuting lambs	11-00
18th	By turnpike & beer	2-00
	By my expences	1-10
	By a bill paid for coales had at Hungerford in 1790	1-07-03
	By tailing sheep	7-06
	By making 141 pole of hedge	1-03-06
28	By my expences & 1 dealer	2-09
	By 4 weeks labour	13-00-04
	By 4 weeks in the garden	2-08-00
	By haymaking 4 weeks	8-02-07½
		47-01-09½
Received		105-01-05
Expences		47-01-09½
		57-19-07½
Balance		51-06-1½
		6-13-06

July – August 1794
[Missing]

September 1794
1794. From the 30th August to the 27th September

[Income]		
September		
10th	To 20 sacks wheat	27-00-00
	To carriage load coales	10-00
20th	To carriage of load corn	15-06
	To carriage of load coales	10-00
	To a calf to the butcher	2-10-00
	To poultry, butter, & eggs	1-15-03½
	To cash received of the gardener	15-00
		33-15-09½
[Expenditure]		
September		
10th	By turnpike & beer	2-00
	By ¼ hundred soap	17-09
	By carriage of suggar from London	3-00
	By hoeing 28 acres of turnips	7-16-09

20th	By my expences	2-00
	By 100 bundles of thorns	1-09-00
27th	By my expenses & a dealer	2-10
	By the butcher's bill to the 27th	3-11-00
	By 4 weeks labour	18-09-08
	By 4 weeks do in the garden	1-16-00
	By 22 pound of paper for the green house	4-07
	By 6 baskets for game	2-00
	By a bill paid the gardener for pickling jars, skins, &c.	1-08-08
	By carriage of a portmanteau from London	5-06
		36-10-09
Expences		36-10-09
Received		33-15-09½
		2-14-11½
Brot forward		46-06-09
		49-01-08½

October 1794

1794. The Farm Account from the 27th September to the 31st October

[Income]		
October		
2d	To 20 sacks wheat	28-00-00
24th	To 19 sacks wheat	25-11-00
	To cash received of Mrs Jenny for half year's rent	16-14-08
31st	To 9 quarter barley	16-13-00
	To 11 pigs at 15s each	8-05-00
	To poultry, butter, & chees	3-01-00½
	To 100 lambs at 12s each	60-00-00
	To 30 do at 10s each	30-00-00
	To 150 ewes at 20s each	150-00-00
	To 48 do at 14 each	33-12-00
		371-16-08½
[Expenditure]		
October		
2d	by turnpike & beer	2-00
	By sack, needles, & thread	2-10
4th	By my expences	1-11
	By the year's work to the sieveman	10-06
11th	By my expences	1-10
25	By turnpike & beer	2-00
	By chees colouring	2-00
	By salt	13-10½
	By 2 dozen candles	14-09
	By six earthen dishes	2-06
	By linnen for puding cloths	2-03
	By figs for the home harvest	12-01½
	By half a year's land tax	26-05-01
	By making 135 pole of bank on the down for the new enclosure	3-07-06
31st	By turnpike, beer, and my expences	4-00

By 3 corn dealers	3-00
By 6 sacks rye	7-04-00
By the thatcher's bill	8-08-01½
By the butcher's bill	1-09-10
By mowing 103 acres barley & oats	6-00-02
By forking & raking do	4-05-10
By raking after the waggon	1-13-02
By five weeks labour	21-14-04
By five weeks do in the garden	3-00-00
By four oxen bought in	39-10-00
	126-13-07½[63]
Goods sold	371-16-08½
Disbursments	126-13-07½
	245-03-01
The real balance brot forward	103-13-11½
To my master	141-09-01½

November 1794

1794. From the 31st October to the 29th November

[Income]		
November		
7th	To 10½ quarter barley	19-08-06
14th	To 11 quarter barley	20-07-00
22nd	To 12 quarter barley	22-04-00
26th	To 20 sacks wheat	25-00-00
	To carriage [?load] coals	10-00
	To cash received of the gardener	1-14-00
	To poultry, butter, chees, &c	1-13-03
	To sack barley	18-00
		91-14-09
[Expenditure]		
November		
5th	By 14 dozen of bottles	1-16-00
	Bill paid Mrs Mitchel	8-09½
7th	By turnpike, beer, & my expences	4-00
14	By turnpike, beer & my expences	4-00
	By the cooper's bill for hoops	1-01-01
	Sack pollard	3-00
22d	By turnpike, beer, & my expences	4-00
	By Hitchcock[64] the malsters bill	27-09-06
	By one year's waigers to myself due Michaelmas last	42-00-00
	By cash paid to my five daughters[65]	50-00-00
	By cash paid to Mrs Rennald as borrowed of her in March 1793	50-00-00
29th	By my expences & 4 dealers	5-10
	By 4 weeks labour	16-12-00

[63] Actually £115-13-07½ .
[64] James Hitchcock; see *AWS*, p.89.
[65] Arthur Jones in 1789 bequeathed Hickley's five daughters £10 each; cf. TNA PROB 11/1181/174.

By 4 weeks in the garden	2-04-00
By Wells the hurdle man's bill	4-11-00
By 2 bills paid the gardener	16-07½
By cash paid Mrs Mitchell as part of her waigers last year	7-00
	198-06-10
Disbursments	198-06-10
Good sold	91-14-09
	106-12-01
Brought forward	141-09-01½
Due	34-17-00½

December 1794

1794. The Farm Account from the 29th November to the 3d January 1795

[Income]		
December		
9th	To 12 quarter barley	21-06-00
12th	To 12 quarter barley	22-04-00
16th	To 19 sacks wheat	24-04-00
	To 2 sacks barley	1-16-00
23d	To 12 quarter barley	21-10-06
27th	To 12 quarter barley	21-12-00
30th	To 20 sacks wheat	25-10-00
1795		
January		
3rd	To 12 quarter barley	21-06-00
	To poultry, chees &c	2-15-08
		162-04-08
[Expenditure]		
December		
4th	By cash paid Stephen Crook the carpenter	114-03-09
	By Webb the smith's half year's bill	14-02-06
	By Taylor the tin man's bill	13-04
	By Gale[66] the woodman's bill	16-16-05
9th	By turnpike & beer	2-00
	By my expences to market	2-00
12th	By turnpike & beer	2-00
16th	By turnpike, beer, & my expences	3-10
	By 190 pound beef	3-03-04
23rd	By turnpike & beer	2-00
27th	By turnpike, sack, car, & beer	5-06
	By my expences to market	2-00
30th	By turnpike & beer	2-00
	By 8 sacks of seed wheat	11-12-00
	By ½ a year's rat catching	10-06
	By cash paid for bread given to the poor people	10-00-00
		12-04-06

[66] Gale Goodman; see note XXX above

By two suits of men's mourning[67]	
1795 January	2-00
3 By turnpike & beer	2-00
By my expences	23-00-00
By five weeks labour	3-18-00
By five weeks do in the garden	211-09-08
Disbursments	211-09-08
Good sold	162-04-08
	49-05-00
Ballance brot forward	34-17-00½
Balance	14-07-11½

January 1795

1795. Farm Account from the 3d January to the 31st do

[Income]		
January		
10th	To 11½ quarter barley	20-08-06
14th	To 21 sacks wheat	28-00-00
17th	To 12 quarter barley	21-12-00
	To 2 pigs	1-12-00
24th	To 12 quarter barley	21-18-00
	To a box of preserves sold	2-08-00
29th	To 20 sacks wheat	28-00-00
31st	To 12 quarter barley	20-08-00
	To 3 quarter barley	5-02-06
	To poultry, chees, straw, &c	3-08-07
		152-17-07
[Expenditure]		
January		
10th	Turnpike, beer, & my expenses	3-11
14th	Turnpike & beer	2-00
	Bottle of [?stipptic]	2-09
	My expences to Bristol	8-00
	Carriage of 2 dogs to Bristol	7-06
17th	Turnpike, beer, & my expences	6-06
	Carriage of hamper from London	3-00
	do for bundle trees	3-00
	Bundle brooms	5-00
	Postage of letters	4-03
	Gave the coachman to forward a box to Falmouth	2-00
	Cash gave the singers	5-00
24th	Cash paid Mrs Rennald	50-00-00
	Turnpike and my expences	6-07
29th	Turnpike & beer	4-07

67 The parish register provides no clue as to who was being mourned.

	Shipway[68] the mason's bill	8-00-02
	One year's waigers to the gardener	20-00-00
31st	Turnpike, beer & my expences	4-00
	Load coales	2-08-00
	Corn dealers for 11 load	11-00
	Four weeks labour	18-06-00
	Four weeks do in the garden	2-00-00
	Powder & shot	1-00
	Two bills paid the gardener	7-06
	Butcher's bill from the 31st October	3-03-10
		108-05-07
Goods sold		152-17-07
Expences		108-05-07
		44-12-00
Brought forward		14-07-11½
Balance		30-04-0½

February 1795–March 1797
[Missing]

April & May 1797
1797. The Farm Account from 1st April to the 3d June

[Income]		
April		
7th	To 10 quarter barley	12-10-00
	To 11 quarter barley	17-00-00
	To 2 bushels wheat	10-00
	To sack wheat	1-07-00
17th	To 20 sacks wheat	26-10-00
18	To 12 quarter barley	14-08-00
	To cash received of Mrs. Brown for rent	6-06-00
May		
5th	To 20 sacks wheat	25-10-00
14th	To 2 sacks wheat	2-04-00
	To a barren cow	9-09-00
24th	To 20 sacks wheat	25-10-00
	To 2 pigs	1-12-00
26th	To 20 sacks wheat	26-10-00
31st	To 20 sacks wheat	25-00-00
	To eggs	6-06
	To a fat calf	2-10-00
		198-02-06[69]
To the ballance of the last account		77-10-07
		275-13-01
[Expenditure]		
April		
7th	Turnpike & beer	10-00
	18 young lambs	13-00

[68] John Shipway.
[69] Actually £197-02-06.

8th	Turnpike & my expences	6-00
	Turnpike for sheep	4-00
	Wintering 200 lambs	62-00-00
13th	Turnpike & beer	5-00
15th	Turnpike & my expences	4-03
17th	Turnpike & beer	10-00
	Poor rate	21-00-00
	Church do	8-10-00
18th	Land, window, and other taxes	47-17-05½
	Butter, chees, & bacon for the house	5-09-10
	Poultry	1-01-00
25	My expences	1-10
	Six quarter oats for seed	6-00-00
	My expences & corn dealers	16-00
May		
6th	41 quarter grass seeds	47-00-00
	Corks	18-00
	Cash to Fowler the clerk [70] & wife	5-00
8th	18 weeks pay to the girl at the house	1-16-00
	Bill to Mrs Mitchell	7-06
	2 sacks pollard	1-06-00
12th	Dressing corn ricks for the mice	11-00
	Cloathing for Miles[71] in the cavelry	2-09-06
	Cash advanced to him	1-04-00
17th	A cow & calf	16-16-00
	Turnpike, beer, & my expences	8-00
	Butcher's bill to 12 May	7-14-10
	28 tons and five hundred of hay	100-15-06
	Grinding corn	1-12-07½
24th	Turnpike, beer, and my expences	7-00
26th	Turnpike & beer	3-00
31st	Year's waigers to Mrs Mitchell	7-07-00
	One year's intrest on 20 pounds	1-00-00
	Year's waigers to the farm maid	5-05-00
June		
3d	Nine weeks labour	52-08-06
	Nine weeks do in the garden	7-07-02
	My expences & 2 dealers	4-00
		407-14-00[72]
		275-13-01
	Ballance	132-00-11

[70] Samuel Fowler, the parish clerk.
[71] One wonders if this was Miles Illingworth, one of Sir Adam Williamson's servants, who received an annuity of £5 in his 1798 will, TNA PROB 11/1315/187.
[72] Actually £412-13-00.

INDEX OF PLACE-NAMES

INDEX OF SUBJECTS

INDEX OF PERSONAL NAMES

WILTSHIRE RECORD SOCIETY
(AS AT DECEMBER 2025)

President: DR NEGLEY HARTE
Honorary Treasurer: IAN HICKS
Honorary Secretary: MISS HELEN TAYLOR
General Editor: DR TOM PLANT

Committee:
DR J. CHANDLER
DR J. HARE
S.D. HOBBS
MISS A. MCCONNELL
S. RAYMOND
MRS S. THOMSON

Honorary Independent Examiner: MS S. BROWN

PRIVATE MEMBERS

Honorary Members
OGBURN, SENR JUDGE R W
SHARMAN-CRAWFORD, MR T

ADAMS, MS S
BAINBRIDGE, DR V
BATHE, MR G,
BAYLIFFE, MR B G
BENNETT, DR N
BERRETT, MR A M
BERRY, MR C
BLAKE, MR P A
BOX, MR S D
BRAND, DR P A
BROCK, MRS C
BROWN, MR D A
BROWN, MR G R
BROWNING, MR E
BRYSON, DR A
CARTER, MR D
CAWTHORNE, MRS N
CHALMERS, MR D
CHANDLER, DR J H
CLARK, MR G A
COLCOMB, MR D M
COLLINS, MR A T
CORBIN, MR N
COUZENS, MR T
CRAVEN, DR A
CROOK, MR P H
CROPPER, MS C
CROUCH, MR J W
CROWLEY, DR D A
CUNNINGTON, MS J
DAKERS, PROF C
D'ARCY, MR J N
DODD, MR D
DYSON, MRS L
EDE, DR M E
ELLIOTT, DR J
ENGLISH, MS K
FORREST, DR M
GAISFORD, MR J
GALE, MRS J
GHEY, MR J G
GILES, MR D
GINGER, MR A
GODDARD, MR R G H
GRIFFIN, DR C
GRIST, MR M
HARE, DR J N
HARTE, DR N
HAWKINS, MR D
HEATON, MR R J
HELMHOLZ, PROF R W
HENLY, MR C
HERRON, MRS Pamela M
HICKMAN, MR M R
HICKS, MR I
HICKS, PROF M A
HILLMAN, MR R B
HOBBS, MR S
HOWELLS, DR Jane
INGRAM, DR M J
JOHNSTON, MRS J M
JONES, MS J
KITE, MR P J
KNOWLES, MRS V A
LANSDOWNE, MARQUIS OF
LAWES, MRS G
MARSH, REV R
MARSHMAN, MR M J
MARTIN, MS J
MOLES, MRS M I
NAPPER, MR L R
NEWBURY, MR C COLES
NEWMAN, MRS R
NICOLSON, MR A
NOKES, MR P M A
NOYCE, MISS S
OGBOURNE, MR J M V
OGBURN, MR D A
PARKER, DR P F,
PATIENCE, MR D C

Perry, Mr W A
Plant, Dr T
Powell, Mrs N
Price, Mr A J R
Railton, Ms A
Raymond, Mr S
Roberts, Ms M
Rogers, Mr K H
Rolfe, Mr R C
Rose, Mr A
Saunt, Mrs B A
Sheldrake, Mr B
Shewring, Mr P
Skinner, Ms C
Slocombe, Mr I
Smith, Ms M
Smith, Mr P J
Spaeth, Dr D A
Stone, Mr M J
Suter, Mrs C
Sutton, Mr A E
Tatton-Brown, Mr T
Taylor, Miss H
Thomson, Mrs S M
Wadsworth, Mrs S
Williamson, Mr B
Wiltshire, Mr J
Wiltshire, Mrs P E
Woodford, Mr A
Woodward, Mr A S,
Wright, Mr D P
Younger, Mr C

UNITED KINGDOM INSTITUTIONS

Aberystwyth
National Library of Wales
University College of Wales
Birmingham. University Library
Bristol
University of Bristol Library
Cambridge. University Library
Cheltenham. Bristol and Gloucestershire Archaeological Society
Chippenham
Museum & Heritage Centre
Wiltshire and Swindon History Centre
Coventry. University of Warwick Library
Devizes
Wiltshire Archaeological & Natural History Society
Wiltshire Family History Society
Durham. University Library
Edinburgh
University Library
Exeter. University Library
Glasgow. University Library

Liverpool. University Library
London
British Library
College of Arms
Guildhall Library
Inner Temple Library
Institute of Historical Research
London Library
The National Archives
Royal Historical Society
Society of Antiquaries
Society of Genealogists
Manchester. John Rylands Library
Marlborough
Memorial Library, Marlborough College
Savernake Estate Office
Norwich. University of East Anglia Library
Nottingham. University Library
Oxford
Bodleian Library
Exeter College Library
St Andrews. University Library
Salisbury
Bourne Valley Historical Society
Cathedral Library
Salisbury and South Wilts Museum
Swansea. University College Library
Swindon
Historic England
Swindon Borough Council
Taunton. Somerset Archaeological and Natural History Society
Wetherby. British Library Document Supply Centre
York. University Library

INSTITUTIONS OVERSEAS

AUSTRALIA

Adelaide. University Library

Crawley. Reid Library, University of Western Australia

CANADA

Halifax. Killam Library, Dalhousie University

Novia Scotia Provincial Library

Toronto, Ont

Pontifical Inst of Medieval Studies

University of Toronto Library

Victoria, B.C. McPherson Library, University of Victoria

NEW ZEALAND

Wellington. National Library of New Zealand

UNITED STATES OF AMERICA

Ann Arbor, Mich. Hatcher Library, University of Michigan

Athens, Ga. University of Georgia Libraries

Atlanta, Ga. The Robert W Woodruff Library, Emory University

Bloomington, Ind. Indiana University Library

Boston, Mass. New England Historic and Genealogical Society

Boulder, Colo. University of Colorado Library

Cambridge, Mass.

Harvard College Library

Harvard Law School Library

Charlottesville, Va. Alderman Library, University of Virginia

Chicago

Newberry Library

University of Chicago Library

Dallas, Texas. Public Library

Davis, Calif. University Library

East Lansing, Mich. Michigan State University Library

Evanston, Ill. United Libraries, Garrett/ Evangelical, Seabury

Fort Wayne, Ind. Allen County Public Library

Iowa City, Iowa. University of Iowa Libraries

Ithaca, NY. Cornell University Library

Los Angeles

Public Library

Young Research Library, University of California

Minneapolis, Minn. Wilson Library, University of Minnesota

New York

Columbia University of the City of New York

Salt Lake City, Utah. Family History Library

San Marino, Calif. Henry E. Huntington Library

Urbana, Ill. University of Illinois Library

Washington. The Folger Shakespeare Library

Winston-Salem, N.C. Z.Smith Reynolds Library, Wake Forest University

LIST OF PUBLICATIONS

The Wiltshire Record Society was founded in 1937, as the Records Branch of the Wiltshire Archaeological and Natural History Society, to promote the publication of the documentary sources for the history of Wiltshire. The annual subscription is £15 for private and institutional members. In return, a member receives a volume each year. Prospective members should apply to the Hon. Secretary, c/o Wiltshire and Swindon History Centre, Cocklebury Road, Chippenham SN15 3QN. Many more members are needed.

The following volumes have been published. Price to members £15, and to non-members £20, postage extra. Most volumes up to 72 are still available from the Wiltshire and Swindon History Centre, Cocklebury Road, Chippenham SN15 3QN. Volumes 73 onwards are available from Hobnob Press, 8 Lock Warehouse, Severn Road, Gloucester GL1 2GA. Volumes 1-69 are available online, at www.wiltshirerecordsociety.org.uk.

1. *Abstracts of feet of fines relating to Wiltshire for the reigns of Edward I and Edward II*, ed. R.B. Pugh, 1939
2. *Accounts of the parliamentary garrisons of Great Chalfield and Malmesbury, 1645–1646*, ed. J.H.P. Pafford, 1940
3. *Calendar of Antrobus deeds before 1625*, ed. R.B. Pugh, 1947
4. *Wiltshire county records: minutes of proceedings in sessions, 1563 and 1574 to 1592*, ed. H.C. Johnson, 1949
5. *List of Wiltshire boroughs records earlier in date than 1836*, ed. M.G. Rathbone, 1951
6. *The Trowbridge woollen industry as illustrated by the stock books of John and Thomas Clark, 1804–1824*, ed. R.P. Beckinsale, 1951
7. *Guild stewards' book of the borough of Calne, 1561–1688*, ed. A.W. Mabbs, 1953
8. *Andrews' and Dury's map of Wiltshire, 1773: a reduced facsimile*, ed. Elizabeth Crittall, 1952
9. *Surveys of the manors of Philip, earl of Pembroke and Montgomery, 1631–2*, ed. E. Kerridge, 1953
10. *Two sixteenth century taxations lists, 1545 and 1576*, ed. G.D. Ramsay, 1954
11. *Wiltshire quarter sessions and assizes, 1736*, ed. J.P.M. Fowle, 1955
12. *Collectanea*, ed. N.J. Williams, 1956
13. *Progress notes of Warden Woodward for the Wiltshire estates of New College, Oxford, 1659–1675*, ed. R.L. Rickard, 1957
14. *Accounts and surveys of the Wiltshire lands of Adam de Stratton*, ed. M.W. Farr, 1959
15. *Tradesmen in early-Stuart Wiltshire: a miscellany*, ed. N.J. Williams, 1960
16. *Crown pleas of the Wiltshire eyre, 1249*, ed. C.A.F. Meekings, 1961
17. *Wiltshire apprentices and their masters, 1710–1760*, ed. Christabel Dale, 1961
18. *Hemingby's register*, ed. Helena M. Chew, 1963
19. *Documents illustrating the Wiltshire textile trades in the eighteenth century*, ed. Julia de L. Mann, 1964
20. *The diary of Thomas Naish*, ed. Doreen Slatter, 1965

21–2. *The rolls of Highworth hundred, 1275–1287*, 2 parts, ed. Brenda Farr, 1966, 1968

23. *The earl of Hertford's lieutenancy papers, 1603–1612*, ed. W.P.D. Murphy, 1969
24. *Court rolls of the Wiltshire manors of Adam de Stratton*, ed. R.B. Pugh, 1970
25. *Abstracts of Wiltshire inclosure awards and agreements*, ed. R.E. Sandell, 1971
26. *Civil pleas of the Wiltshire eyre, 1249*, ed. M.T. Clanchy, 1971
27. *Wiltshire returns to the bishop's visitation queries, 1783*, ed. Mary Ransome, 1972
28. *Wiltshire extents for debts, Edward I – Elizabeth I*, ed. Angela Conyers, 1973
29. *Abstracts of feet of fines relating to Wiltshire for the reign of Edward III*, ed. C.R. Elrington, 1974

30. *Abstracts of Wiltshire tithe apportionments*, ed. R.E. Sandell, 1975
31. *Poverty in early-Stuart Salisbury*, ed. Paul Slack, 1975
32. *The subscription book of Bishops Tounson and Davenant, 1620–40*, ed. B. Williams, 1977
33. *Wiltshire gaol delivery and trailbaston trials, 1275–1306*, ed. R.B. Pugh, 1978
34. *Lacock abbey charters*, ed. K.H. Rogers, 1979
35. *The cartulary of Bradenstoke priory*, ed. Vera C.M. London, 1979
36. *Wiltshire coroners' bills, 1752–1796*, ed. R.F. Hunnisett, 1981
37. *The justicing notebook of William Hunt, 1744–1749*, ed. Elizabeth Crittall, 1982
38. *Two Elizabethan women: correspondence of Joan and Maria Thynne, 1575–1611*, ed. Alison D. Wall, 1983
39. *The register of John Chandler, dean of Salisbury, 1404–17*, ed. T.C.B. Timmins, 1984
40. *Wiltshire dissenters' meeting house certificates and registrations, 1689–1852*, ed. J.H. Chandler, 1985
41. *Abstracts of feet of fines relating to Wiltshire, 1377–1509*, ed. J.L. Kirby, 1986
42. *The Edington cartulary*, ed. Janet H. Stevenson, 1987
43. *The commonplace book of Sir Edward Bayntun of Bromham*, ed. Jane Freeman, 1988
44. *The diaries of Jeffery Whitaker, schoolmaster of Bratton, 1739–1741*, ed. Marjorie Reeves and Jean Morrison, 1989
45. *The Wiltshire tax list of 1332*, ed. D.A. Crowley, 1989
46. *Calendar of Bradford-on-Avon settlement examinations and removal orders, 1725–98*, ed. Phyllis Hembry, 1990
47. *Early trade directories of Wiltshire*, ed. K.H. Rogers and indexed by J.H. Chandler, 1992
48. *Star chamber suits of John and Thomas Warneford*, ed. F.E. Warneford, 1993
49. *The Hungerford Cartulary: a calendar of the earl of Radnor's cartulary of the Hungerford family*, ed. J.L. Kirby, 1994
50. *The Letters of John Peniston, Salisbury architect, Catholic, and Yeomanry Officer, 1823–1830*, ed. M. Cowan, 1996
51. *The Apprentice Registers of the Wiltshire Society, 1817– 1922*, ed. H. R. Henly, 1997
52. *Printed Maps of Wiltshire 1787–1844: a selection of topographical, road and canal maps in facsimile*, ed. John Chandler, 1998
53. *Monumental Inscriptions of Wiltshire: an edition, in facsimile, of Monumental Inscriptions in the County of Wilton, by Sir Thomas Phillipps*, ed. Peter Sherlock, 2000
54. *The First General Entry Book of the City of Salisbury, 1387–1452*, ed. David R. Carr, 2001
55. *Devizes Division income tax assessments, 1842–1860*, ed. Robert Colley, 2002
56. *Wiltshire Glebe Terriers, 1588–1827*, ed. Steven Hobbs, 2003
57. *Wiltshire Farming in the Seventeenth Century*, ed. Joseph Bettey, 2005
58. *Early Motor Vehicle Registration in Wiltshire, 1903–1914*, ed. Ian Hicks, 2006
59. *Marlborough Probate Inventories, 1591–1775*, ed. Lorelei Williams and Sally Thomson, 2007
60. *The Hungerford Cartulary, part 2: a calendar of the Hobhouse cartulary of the Hungerford family*, ed. J.L. Kirby, 2007
61. *The Court Records of Brinkworth and Charlton*, ed. Douglas Crowley, 2009
62. *The Diary of William Henry Tucker, 1825–1850*, ed. Helen Rogers, 2009
63. *Gleanings from Wiltshire Parish Registers*, ed. Steven Hobbs, 2010
64. *William Small's Cherished Memories and Associations*, ed. Jane Howells and Ruth Newman, 2011
65. *Crown Pleas of the Wiltshire Eyre, 1268*, ed. Brenda Farr and Christopher Elrington, rev. Henry Summerson, 2012
66. *The Minute Books of Froxfield Almshouse, 1714–1866*, ed. Douglas Crowley, 2013

67. *Wiltshire Quarter Sessions Order Book, 1642–1654,* ed. Ivor Slocombe, 2014
68. *The Register of John Blyth, Bishop of Salisbury, 1493–1499*, ed. David Wright, 2015
69 *The Churchwardens' Accounts of St Mary's, Devizes, 1633–1689*, ed. Alex Craven, 2016
70 *The Account Books and Papers of Everard and Ann Arundell of Ashcombe and Salisbury, 1745–1798*, ed. Barry Williamson, 2017
71 *Letters of Henry Hoare of Stourhead, 1760–81*, ed. Dudley Dodd, 2018
72 *Braydon Forest and the Forest Law*, ed. Douglas Crowley, 2019
73 *The Parish Registers of Thomas Crockford, 1561–1633* ed. John Chandler, 2020
74 *The Farming Diaries of Thomas Pinniger, 1813–1847*, ed. Alan Wadsworth, 2021
75 *Salisbury Domesday Books, 1317–1413*, ed. John Chandler and Douglas Crowley, 2022
76 *Returns to the Bishop of Salisbury's Visitation Enquiry, 1864*, ed. Helen Taylor, 2023
77 *Salisbury Domesday Books 1413–1478*, ed. John Chandler and Douglas Crowley, 2024

Further details about the Society, its activities and publications, will be found on its website, www.wiltshirerecordsociety.org.uk.

www.ingramcontent.com/pod-product-compliance
Ingram Content Group UK Ltd.
Pitfield, Milton Keynes, MK11 3LW, UK
UKHW022305250126
467344UK00002B/5

9 780901 333551